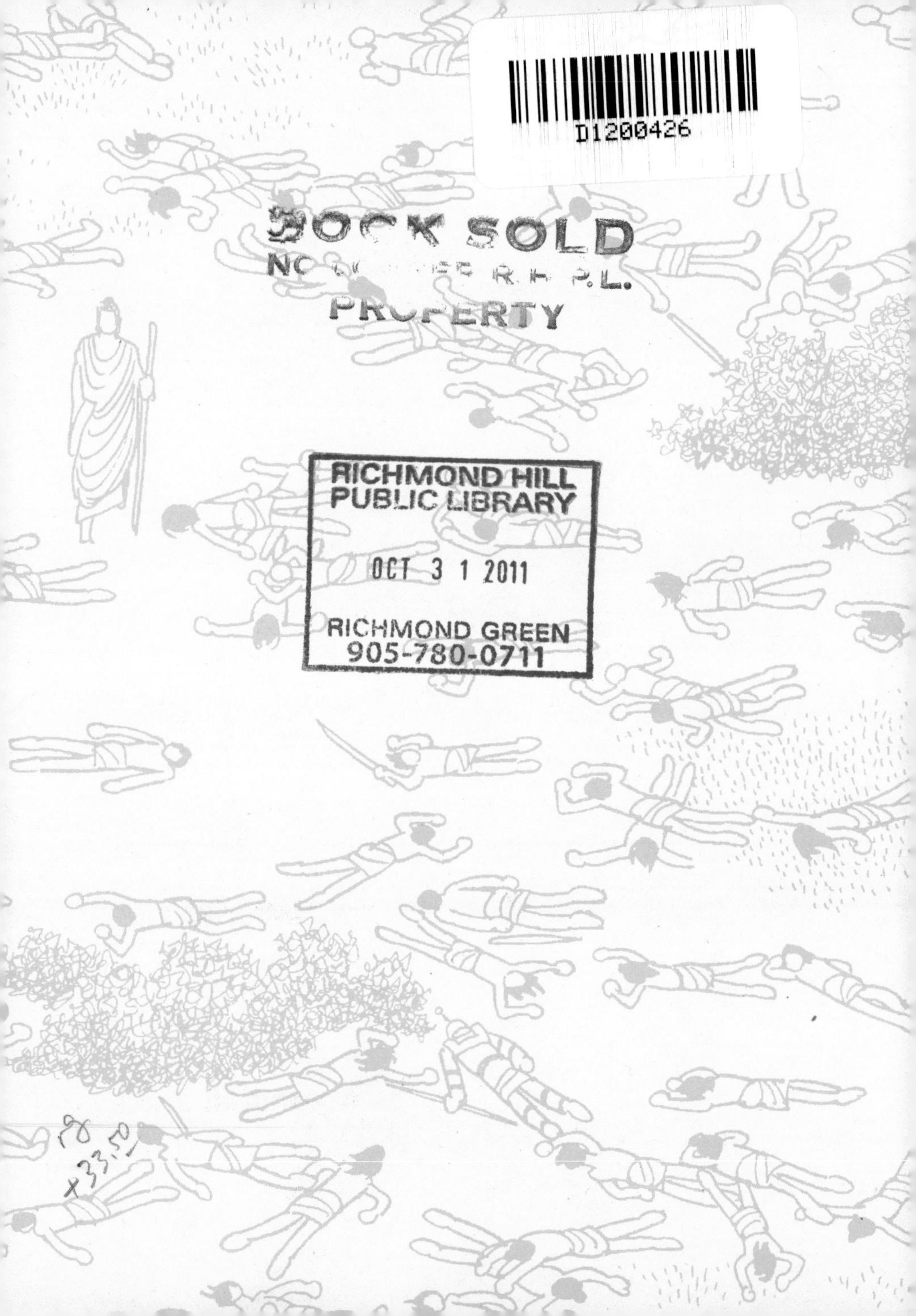

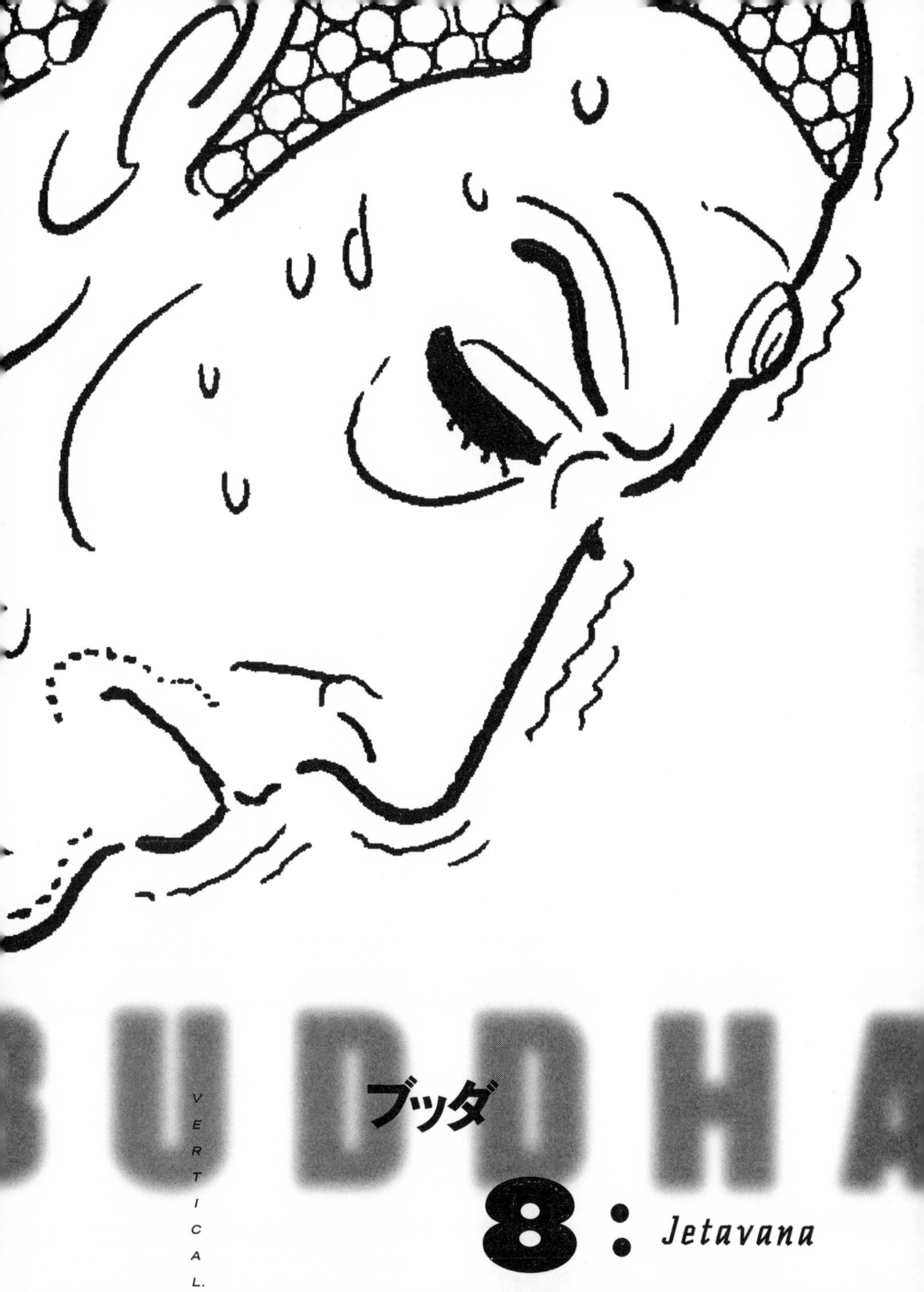

BUDDHA

ブッダ

8: Jetavana

VERTICAL.

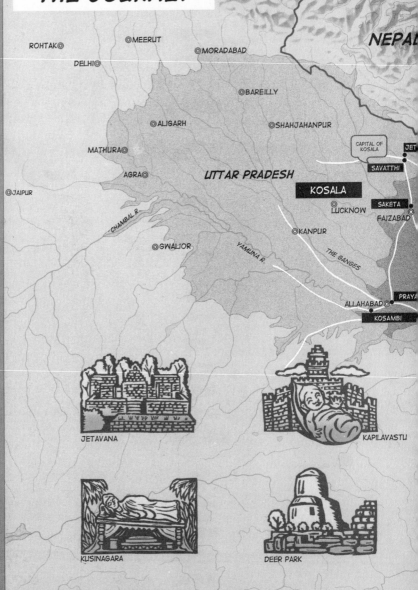

THE JOURNEY

ROHTAK○   ○MEERUT
                    ○MORADABAD
    DELHI○

                    ○BAREILLY

        ○ALIGARH
                        ○SHAHJAHANPUR
                                    CAPITAL OF
    MATHURA○   KOSALA   JET
                    UTTAR PRADESH   SAVATTHI
        AGRA○   KOSALA
○JAIPUR   ○   SAKETA
                                    LUCKNOW   FAIZABAD

                CHAMBAL R.   ○KANPUR
        ○GWALIOR   YAMUNA R.   THE GANGES

                                    ALLAHABAD○   PRAYA
                                              KOSAMBI

JETAVANA   KAPILAVASTU

KUSINAGARA   DEER PARK

NEPA

LUMBINI ANCIENT PLACE NAMES ——— MAJOR ROUTES ● PLACES VISITED BY THE BUDDHA

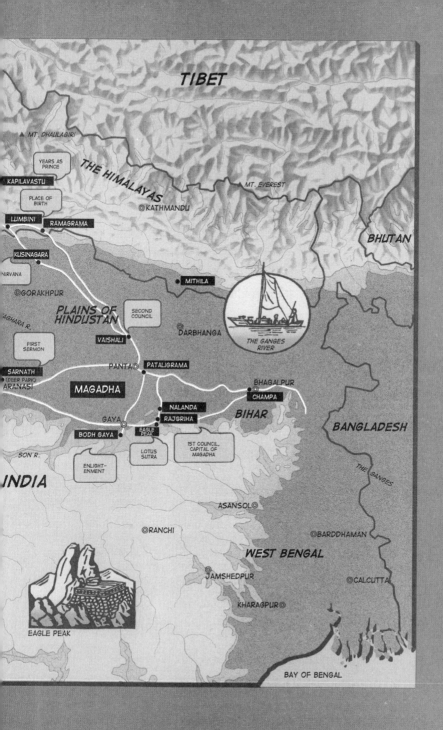

TIBET

▲ MT. DHAULAGIRI

YEARS AS
PRINCE

THE HIMALAYAS

MT. EVEREST

KAPILAVASTU

PLACE OF
BIRTH

⊙ KATHMANDU

BHUTAN

LUMBINI

RAMAGRAMA

KUSINAGARA

NIRVANA

⊙ MITHILA

⊙ GORAKHPUR

PLAINS OF
HINDUSTAN

SECOND
COUNCIL

⊙ DARBHANGA

THE GANGES
RIVER

AGHARA R.

FIRST
SERMON

VAISHALI

BHAGALPUR

SARNATH
(DEER PARK)

PANTA

PATALIGRAMA

CHAMPA

ARANASI

MAGADHA

NALANDA

BIHAR

BANGLADESH

GAYA

RAJGRIHA

EAGLE
PEAK

BODH GAYA

THE GANGES

LOTUS
SUTRA

1ST COUNCIL,
CAPITAL OF
MAGADHA

SON R.

ENLIGHT-
ENMENT

INDIA

ASANSOL ⊙

⊙ RANCHI

⊙ BARDDHAMAN

WEST BENGAL

⊙ JAMSHEDPUR

⊙ CALCUTTA

KHARAGPUR ⊙

EAGLE PEAK

BAY OF BENGAL

TRANSLATION- MAYA ROSEWOOD
PRODUCTION- HIROKO MIZUNO
SHINOBU SATO

PUBLISHED BY VERTICAL, INC., NEW YORK.

ORIGINALLY PUBLISHED IN JAPANESE AS *BUDDA DAI HACHIKAN
GION SHOJA* BY USHIO SHUPPANSHA, TOKYO, 1988.

ISBN 1-932234-50-0

MANUFACTURED IN CANADA

FIRST AMERICAN EDITION. THE ARTWORK OF THE ORIGINAL
HAS BEEN PRODUCED AS A MIRROR-IMAGE IN ORDER TO
CONFORM WITH THE ENGLISH LANGUAGE. THIS WORK OF
FICTION CONTAINS CHARACTERS AND EPISODES THAT ARE
NOT PART OF THE HISTORICAL RECORD.

VERTICAL, INC.
WWW.VERTICAL-INC.COM

PART SIX (CONTINUED)

PART SEVEN

PART SIX (CONTINUED)

CHAPTER EIGHT

DEVADATTA'S PLOT

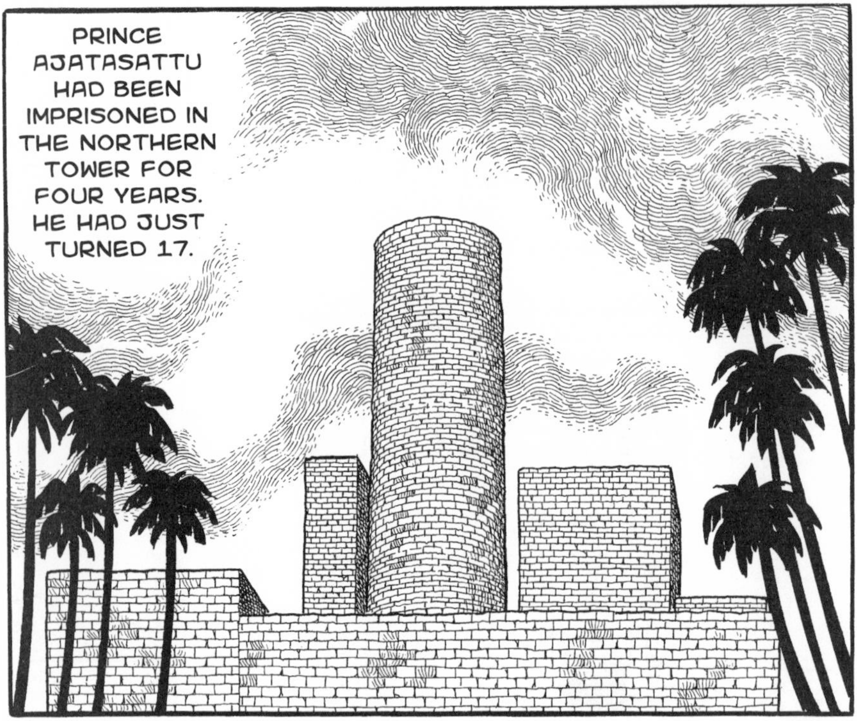
PRINCE AJATASATTU HAD BEEN IMPRISONED IN THE NORTHERN TOWER FOR FOUR YEARS. HE HAD JUST TURNED 17.

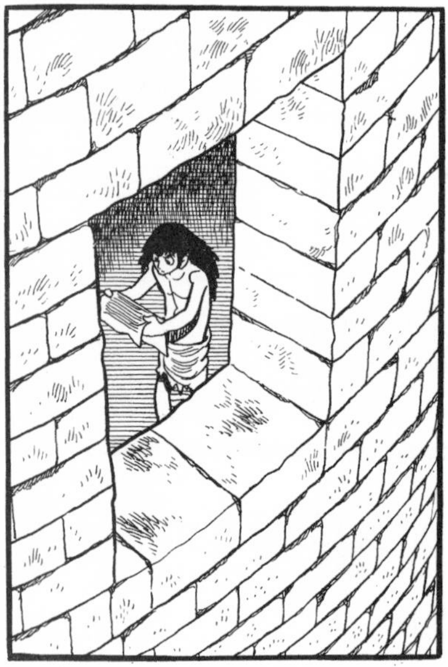

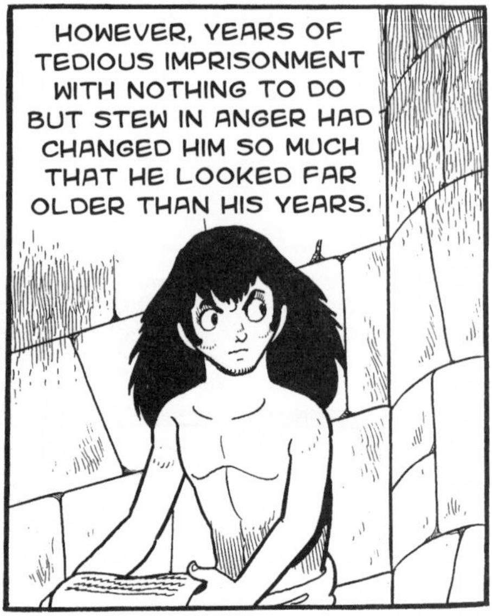
HOWEVER, YEARS OF TEDIOUS IMPRISONMENT WITH NOTHING TO DO BUT STEW IN ANGER HAD CHANGED HIM SO MUCH THAT HE LOOKED FAR OLDER THAN HIS YEARS.

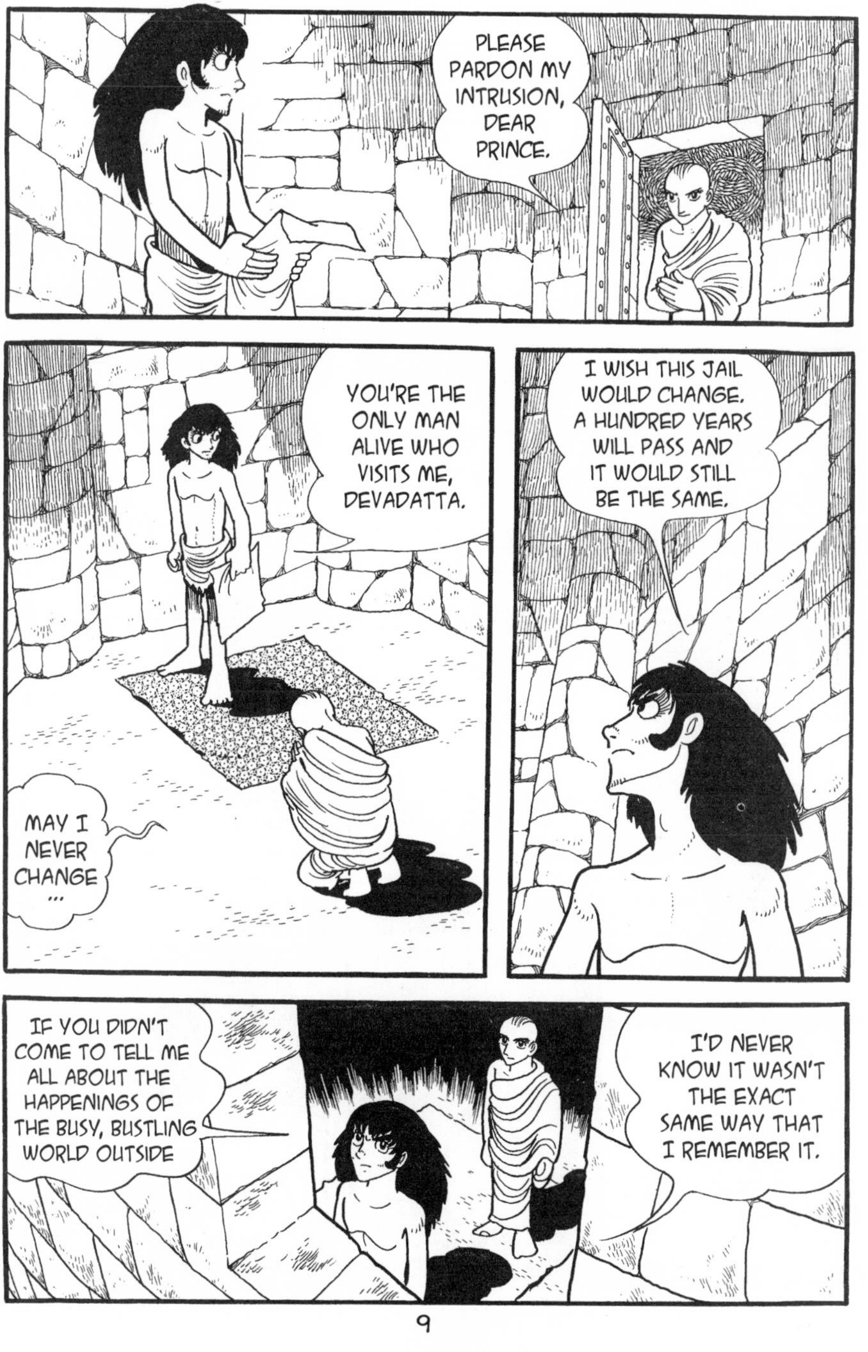
PLEASE PARDON MY INTRUSION, DEAR PRINCE.
YOU'RE THE ONLY MAN ALIVE WHO VISITS ME, DEVADATTA.
MAY I NEVER CHANGE ...
I WISH THIS JAIL WOULD CHANGE. A HUNDRED YEARS WILL PASS AND IT WOULD STILL BE THE SAME.
IF YOU DIDN'T COME TO TELL ME ALL ABOUT THE HAPPENINGS OF THE BUSY, BUSTLING WORLD OUTSIDE
I'D NEVER KNOW IT WASN'T THE EXACT SAME WAY THAT I REMEMBER IT.

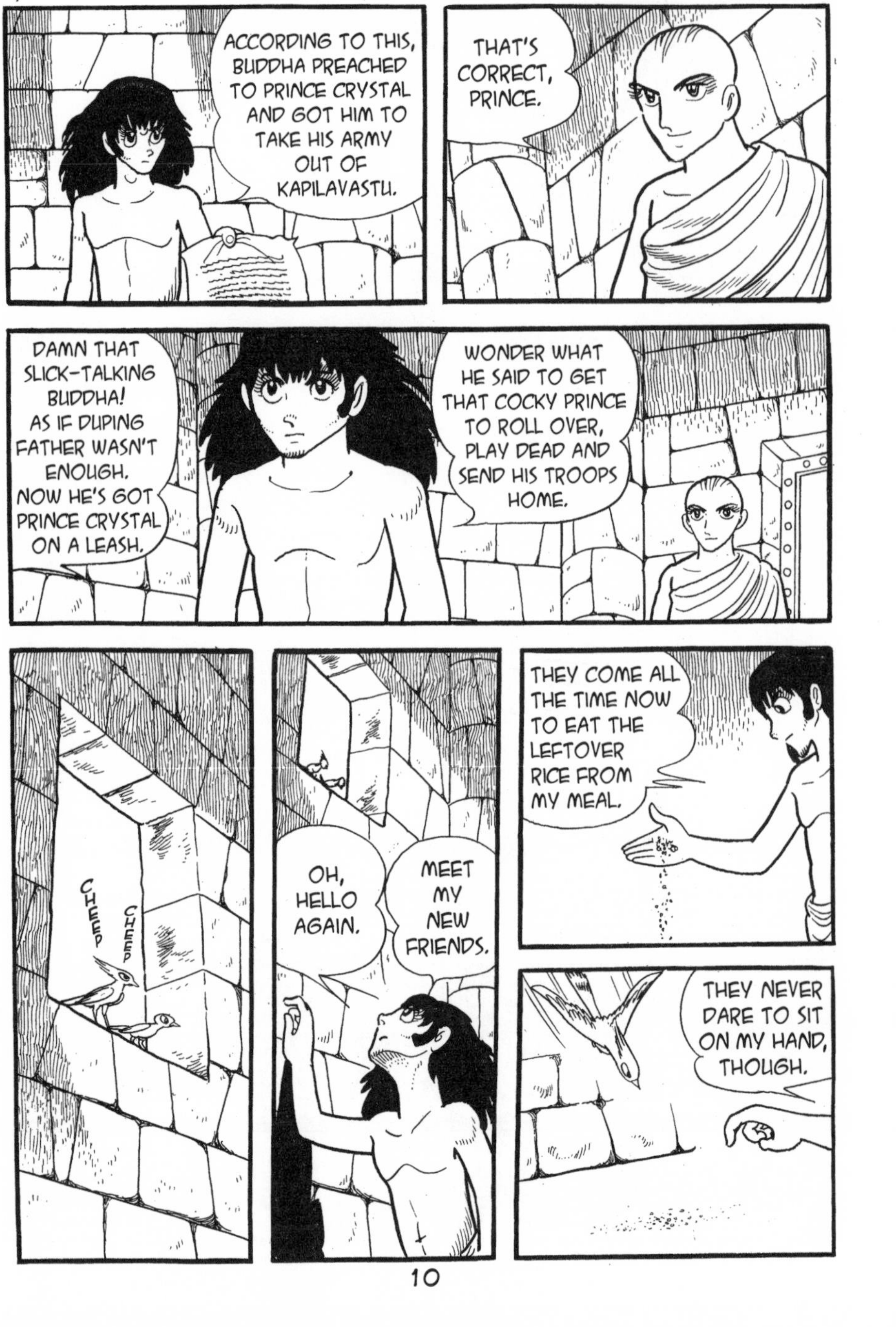
ACCORDING TO THIS, BUDDHA PREACHED TO PRINCE CRYSTAL AND GOT HIM TO TAKE HIS ARMY OUT OF KAPILAVASTU.
THAT'S CORRECT, PRINCE.
DAMN THAT SLICK-TALKING BUDDHA! AS IF DUPING FATHER WASN'T ENOUGH. NOW HE'S GOT PRINCE CRYSTAL ON A LEASH.
WONDER WHAT HE SAID TO GET THAT COCKY PRINCE TO ROLL OVER, PLAY DEAD AND SEND HIS TROOPS HOME.
CHEEP
CHEEP
OH, HELLO AGAIN.
MEET MY NEW FRIENDS.
THEY COME ALL THE TIME NOW TO EAT THE LEFTOVER RICE FROM MY MEAL.
THEY NEVER DARE TO SIT ON MY HAND, THOUGH.

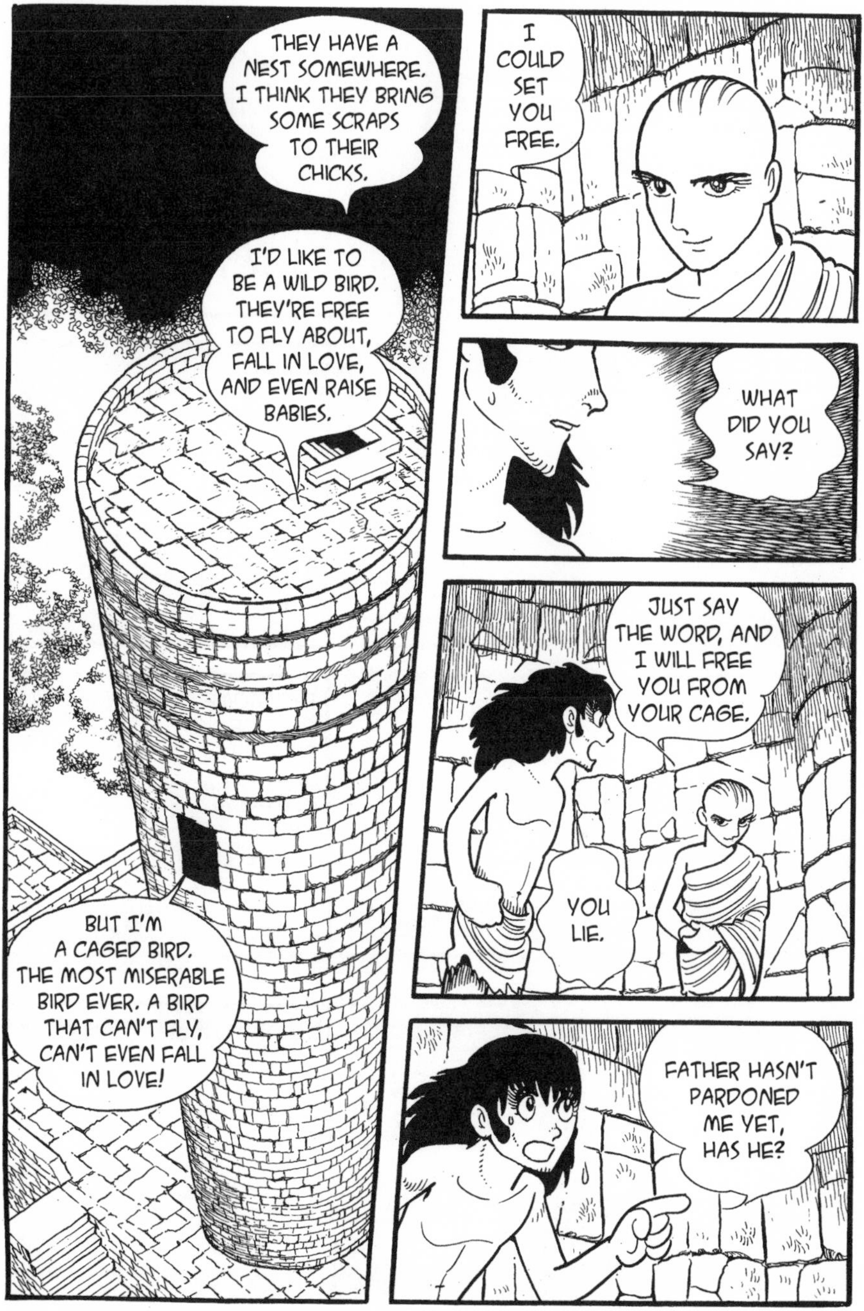

THEY HAVE A NEST SOMEWHERE. I THINK THEY BRING SOME SCRAPS TO THEIR CHICKS.
I'D LIKE TO BE A WILD BIRD. THEY'RE FREE TO FLY ABOUT, FALL IN LOVE, AND EVEN RAISE BABIES.
BUT I'M A CAGED BIRD. THE MOST MISERABLE BIRD EVER. A BIRD THAT CAN'T FLY, CAN'T EVEN FALL IN LOVE!
I COULD SET YOU FREE.
WHAT DID YOU SAY?
JUST SAY THE WORD, AND I WILL FREE YOU FROM YOUR CAGE.
YOU LIE.
FATHER HASN'T PARDONED ME YET, HAS HE?

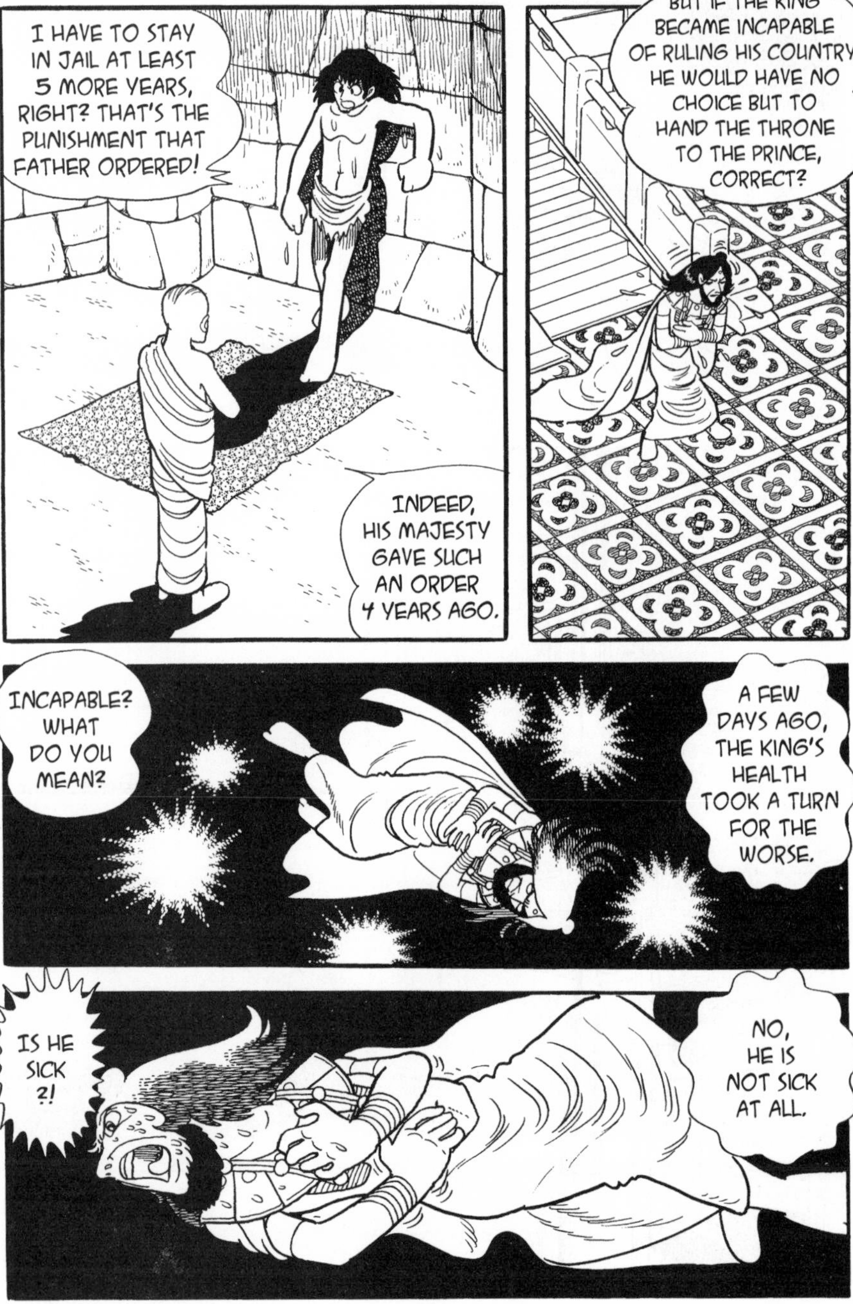
I HAVE TO STAY IN JAIL AT LEAST 5 MORE YEARS, RIGHT? THAT'S THE PUNISHMENT THAT FATHER ORDERED!
INDEED, HIS MAJESTY GAVE SUCH AN ORDER 4 YEARS AGO.
BUT IF THE KING BECAME INCAPABLE OF RULING HIS COUNTRY, HE WOULD HAVE NO CHOICE BUT TO HAND THE THRONE TO THE PRINCE, CORRECT?
INCAPABLE? WHAT DO YOU MEAN?
A FEW DAYS AGO, THE KING'S HEALTH TOOK A TURN FOR THE WORSE.
IS HE SICK ?!
NO, HE IS NOT SICK AT ALL.

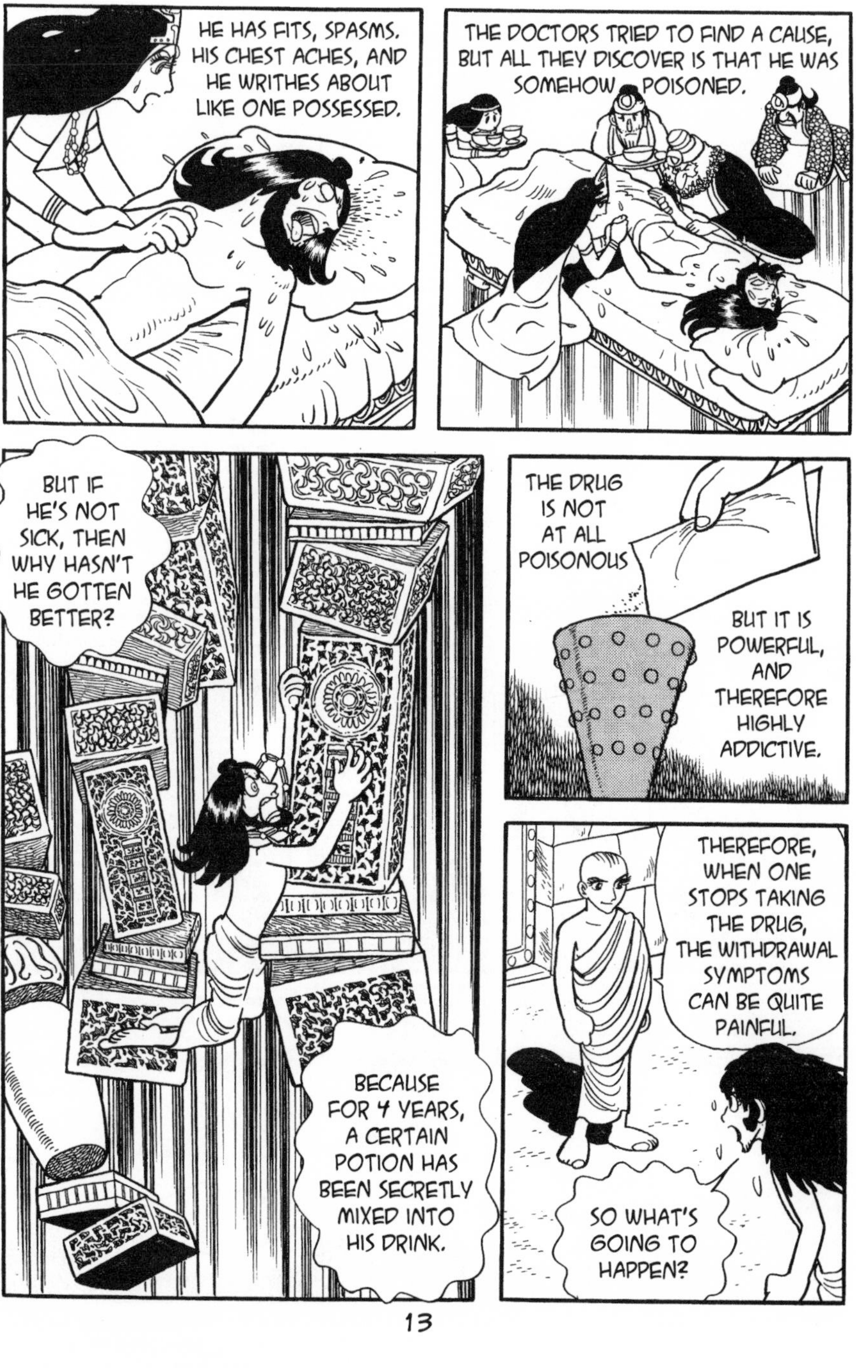
HE HAS FITS, SPASMS. HIS CHEST ACHES, AND HE WRITHES ABOUT LIKE ONE POSSESSED.
THE DOCTORS TRIED TO FIND A CAUSE, BUT ALL THEY DISCOVER IS THAT HE WAS SOMEHOW POISONED.
BUT IF HE'S NOT SICK, THEN WHY HASN'T HE GOTTEN BETTER?
BECAUSE FOR 4 YEARS, A CERTAIN POTION HAS BEEN SECRETLY MIXED INTO HIS DRINK.
THE DRUG IS NOT AT ALL POISONOUS
BUT IT IS POWERFUL, AND THEREFORE HIGHLY ADDICTIVE.
THEREFORE, WHEN ONE STOPS TAKING THE DRUG, THE WITHDRAWAL SYMPTOMS CAN BE QUITE PAINFUL.
SO WHAT'S GOING TO HAPPEN?

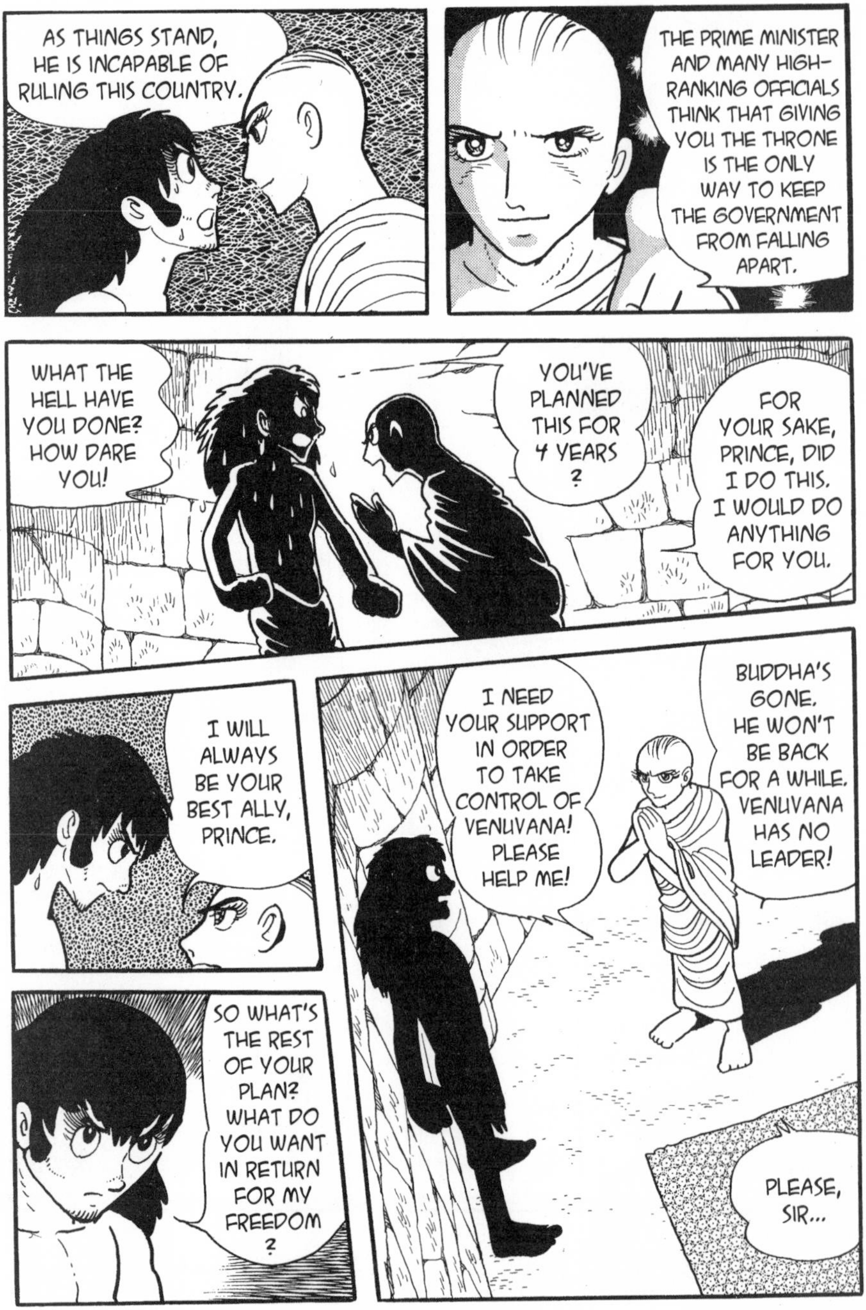
AS THINGS STAND, HE IS INCAPABLE OF RULING THIS COUNTRY.
THE PRIME MINISTER AND MANY HIGH-RANKING OFFICIALS THINK THAT GIVING YOU THE THRONE IS THE ONLY WAY TO KEEP THE GOVERNMENT FROM FALLING APART.
WHAT THE HELL HAVE YOU DONE? HOW DARE YOU!
YOU'VE PLANNED THIS FOR 4 YEARS?
FOR YOUR SAKE, PRINCE, DID I DO THIS. I WOULD DO ANYTHING FOR YOU.
I WILL ALWAYS BE YOUR BEST ALLY, PRINCE.
SO WHAT'S THE REST OF YOUR PLAN? WHAT DO YOU WANT IN RETURN FOR MY FREEDOM?
I NEED YOUR SUPPORT IN ORDER TO TAKE CONTROL OF VENUVANA! PLEASE HELP ME!
BUDDHA'S GONE. HE WON'T BE BACK FOR A WHILE. VENUVANA HAS NO LEADER!
PLEASE, SIR...

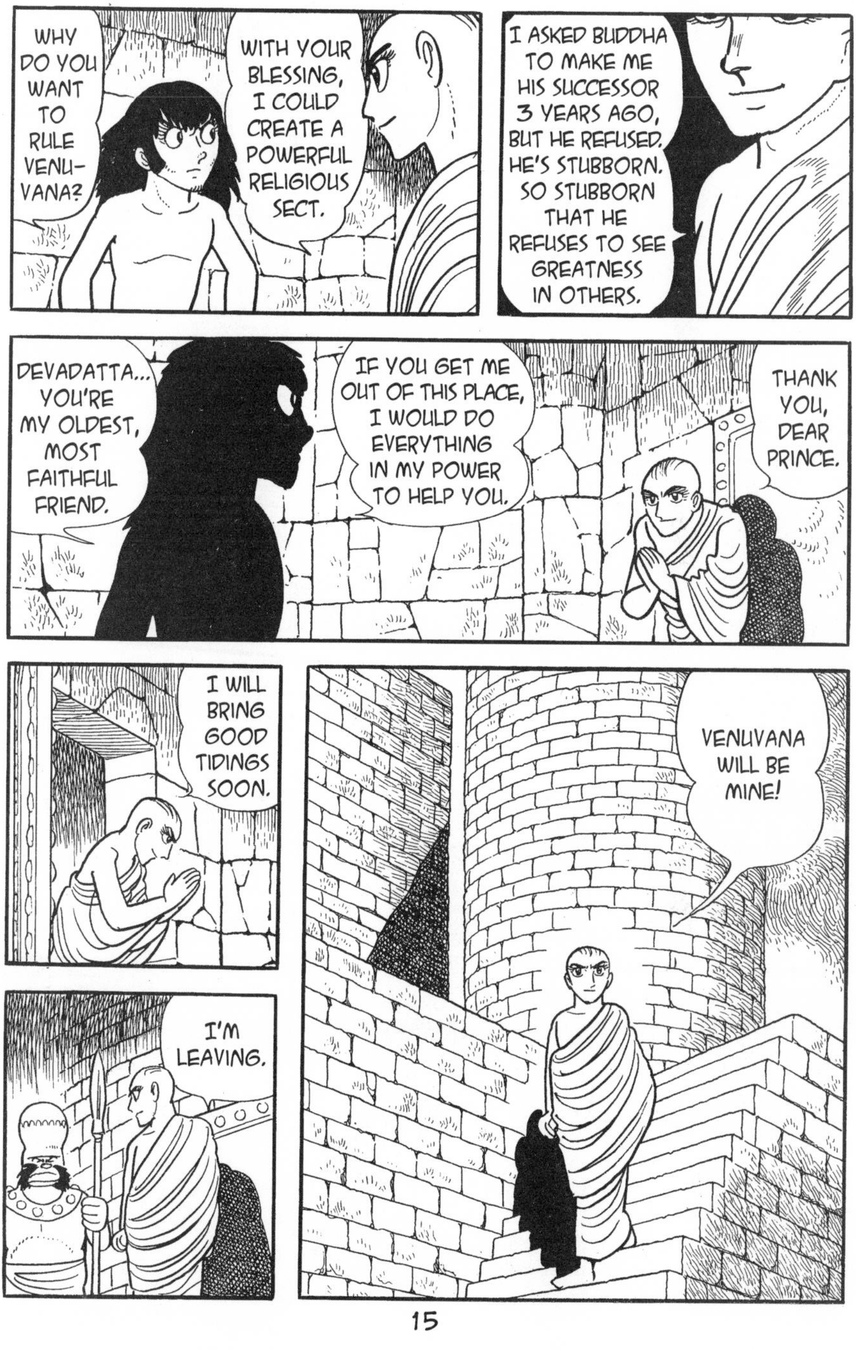
WHY DO YOU WANT TO RULE VENU-VANA?
WITH YOUR BLESSING, I COULD CREATE A POWERFUL RELIGIOUS SECT.
I ASKED BUDDHA TO MAKE ME HIS SUCCESSOR 3 YEARS AGO, BUT HE REFUSED. HE'S STUBBORN. SO STUBBORN THAT HE REFUSES TO SEE GREATNESS IN OTHERS.
DEVADATTA... YOU'RE MY OLDEST, MOST FAITHFUL FRIEND.
IF YOU GET ME OUT OF THIS PLACE, I WOULD DO EVERYTHING IN MY POWER TO HELP YOU.
THANK YOU, DEAR PRINCE.
I WILL BRING GOOD TIDINGS SOON.
I'M LEAVING.
VENUVANA WILL BE MINE!

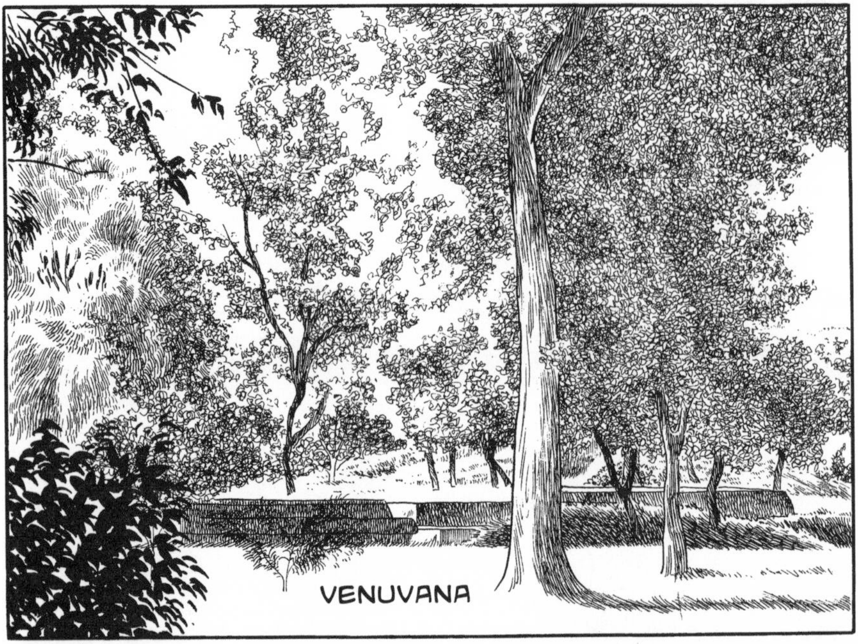
VENUVANA

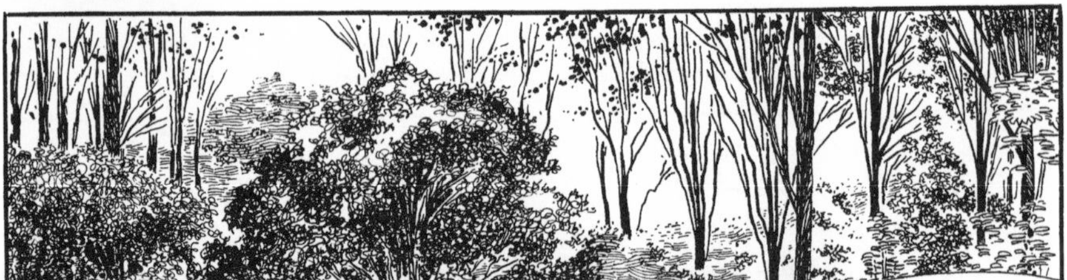
BAD NEWS!!

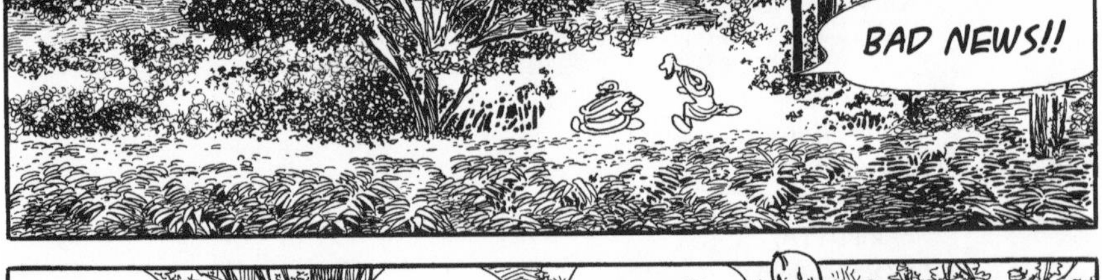
WHAT'S YOUR PROBLEM ?
IT'S NOT MY PROBLEM !
THERE'S TROUBLE BREWING IN THE CAPITAL!
THE KING HAS LOST HIS MIND!

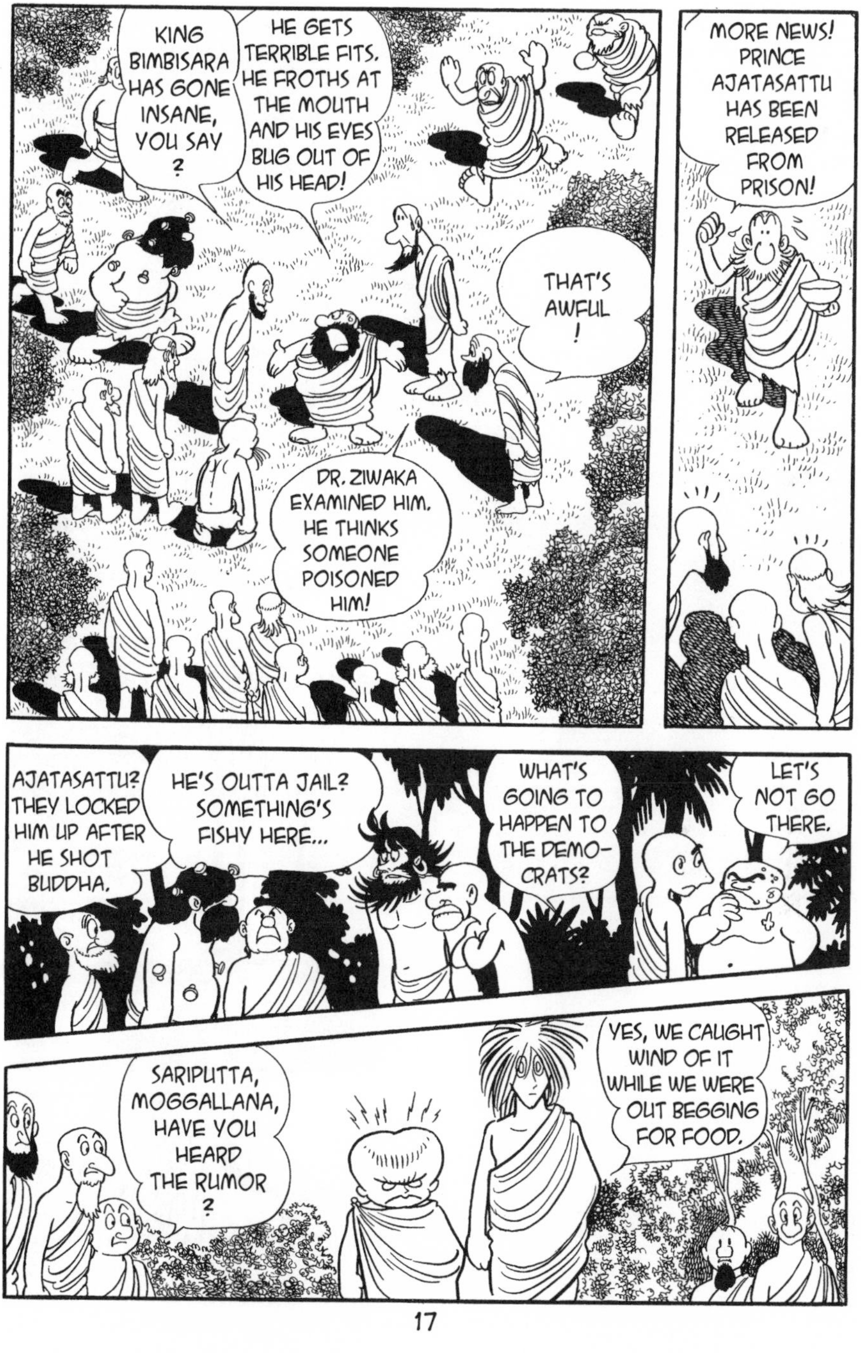
KING BIMBISARA HAS GONE INSANE, YOU SAY?
HE GETS TERRIBLE FITS. HE FROTHS AT THE MOUTH AND HIS EYES BUG OUT OF HIS HEAD!
THAT'S AWFUL!
DR. ZIWAKA EXAMINED HIM. HE THINKS SOMEONE POISONED HIM!
MORE NEWS! PRINCE AJATASATTU HAS BEEN RELEASED FROM PRISON!
AJATASATTU? THEY LOCKED HIM UP AFTER HE SHOT BUDDHA.
HE'S OUTTA JAIL? SOMETHING'S FISHY HERE...
WHAT'S GOING TO HAPPEN TO THE DEMO-CRATS?
LET'S NOT GO THERE.
SARIPUTTA, MOGGALLANA, HAVE YOU HEARD THE RUMOR?
YES, WE CAUGHT WIND OF IT WHILE WE WERE OUT BEGGING FOR FOOD.

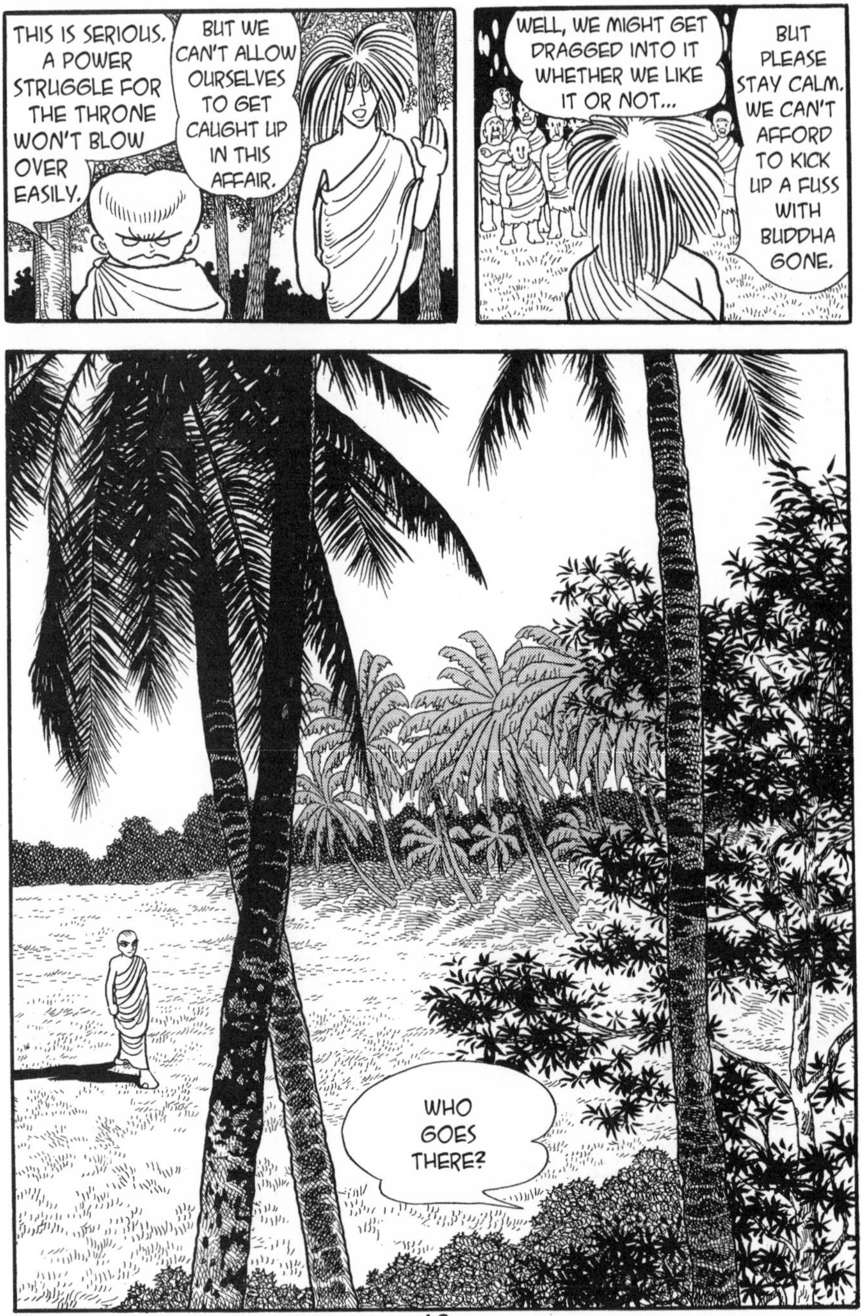
THIS IS SERIOUS. A POWER STRUGGLE FOR THE THRONE WON'T BLOW OVER EASILY.
BUT WE CAN'T ALLOW OURSELVES TO GET CAUGHT UP IN THIS AFFAIR.
WELL, WE MIGHT GET DRAGGED INTO IT WHETHER WE LIKE IT OR NOT...
BUT PLEASE STAY CALM. WE CAN'T AFFORD TO KICK UP A FUSS WITH BUDDHA GONE.
WHO GOES THERE?

HEY, IT'S DEVADATTA...

WE SHOULD ASK HIM FOR THE LATEST NEWS FROM THE CASTLE. HE'D KNOW.

HELLO SARIPUTTA, MOGGAL-LANA.

I MUST SPEAK WITH YOU AND THE SENIOR-RANKING MONKS IMME-DIATELY.

WHAT'S THE DEAL? WHY STAND ON CERE-MONY?

PLEASE JUST CALM DOWN AND LISTEN.

YOU MUST HAVE HEARD BY NOW THAT KING BIMBISARA HAS CEDED THE THRONE TO PRINCE AJATASATTU.

SO THE RUMORS WERE TRUE.

I HAVE A PROCLA-MATION FROM HIS MAJESTY, KING AJA-TASATTU.

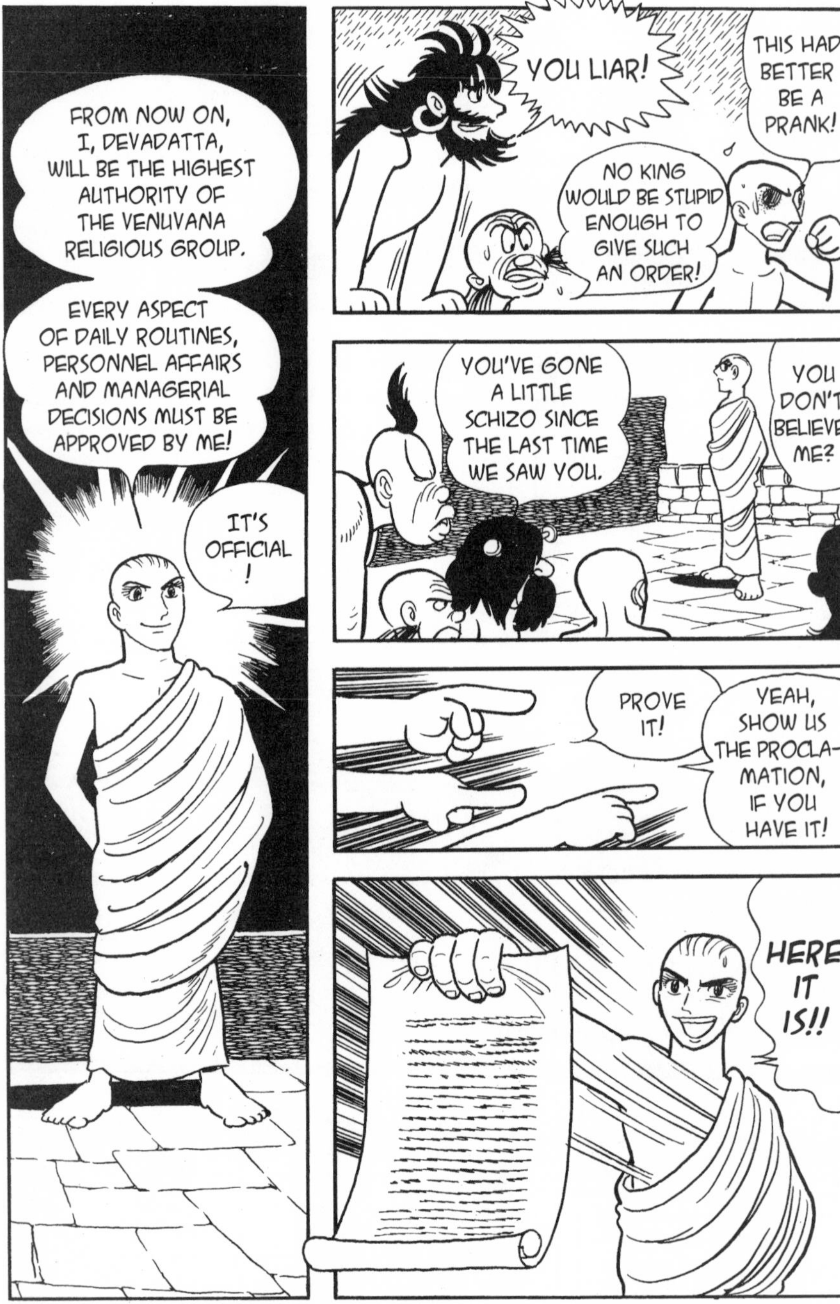
FROM NOW ON, I, DEVADATTA, WILL BE THE HIGHEST AUTHORITY OF THE VENUVANA RELIGIOUS GROUP.
EVERY ASPECT OF DAILY ROUTINES, PERSONNEL AFFAIRS AND MANAGERIAL DECISIONS MUST BE APPROVED BY ME!
IT'S OFFICIAL!
YOU LIAR!
THIS HAD BETTER BE A PRANK!
NO KING WOULD BE STUPID ENOUGH TO GIVE SUCH AN ORDER!
YOU'VE GONE A LITTLE SCHIZO SINCE THE LAST TIME WE SAW YOU.
YOU DON'T BELIEVE ME?
PROVE IT!
YEAH, SHOW US THE PROCLA-MATION, IF YOU HAVE IT!
HERE IT IS!!

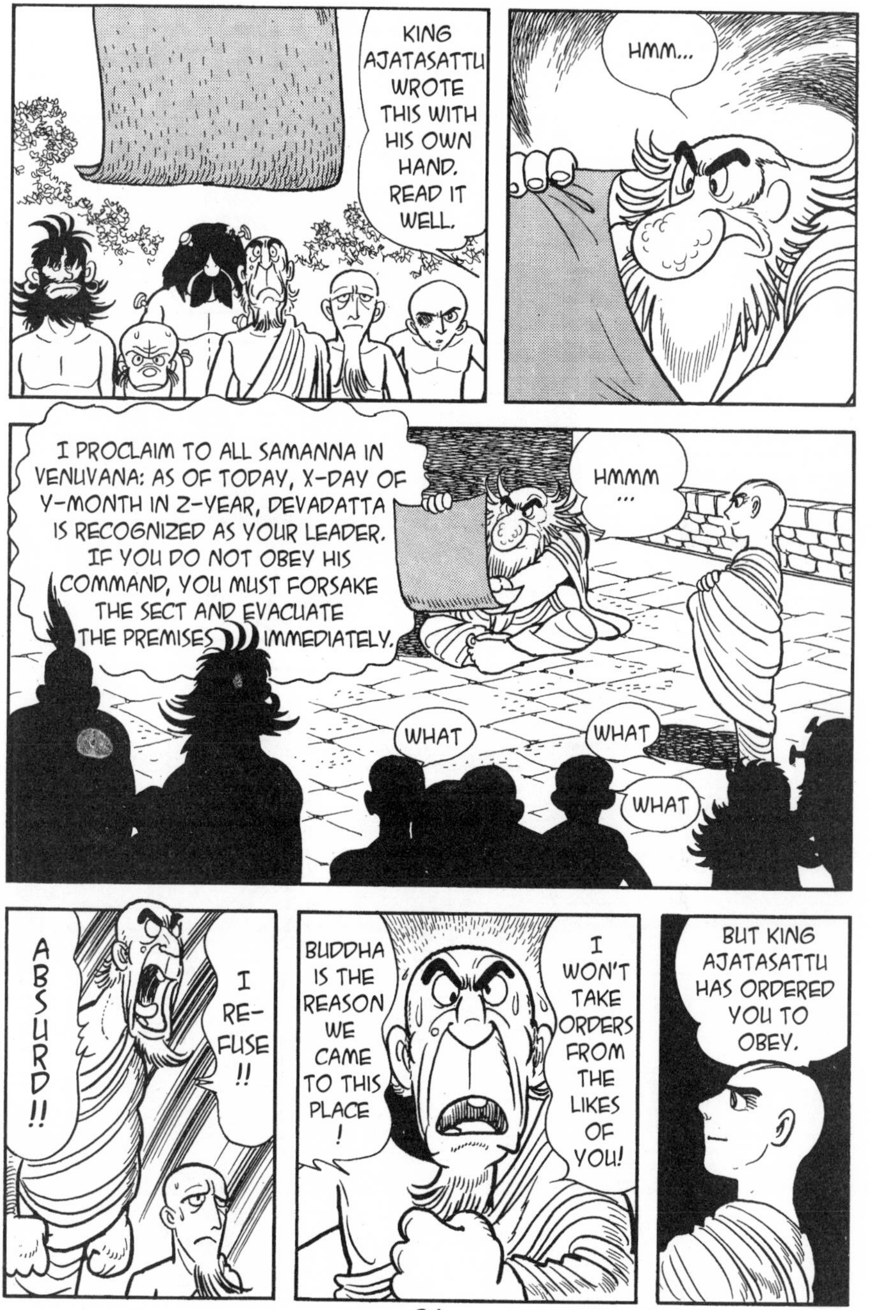
KING AJATASATTU WROTE THIS WITH HIS OWN HAND. READ IT WELL.
HMM...
I PROCLAIM TO ALL SAMANNA IN VENUVANA: AS OF TODAY, X-DAY OF Y-MONTH IN Z-YEAR, DEVADATTA IS RECOGNIZED AS YOUR LEADER. IF YOU DO NOT OBEY HIS COMMAND, YOU MUST FORSAKE THE SECT AND EVACUATE THE PREMISES IMMEDIATELY.
HMMM ...
WHAT
WHAT
WHAT
ABSURD!!
I RE-FUSE!!
BUDDHA IS THE REASON WE CAME TO THIS PLACE!
I WON'T TAKE ORDERS FROM THE LIKES OF YOU!
BUT KING AJATASATTU HAS ORDERED YOU TO OBEY.

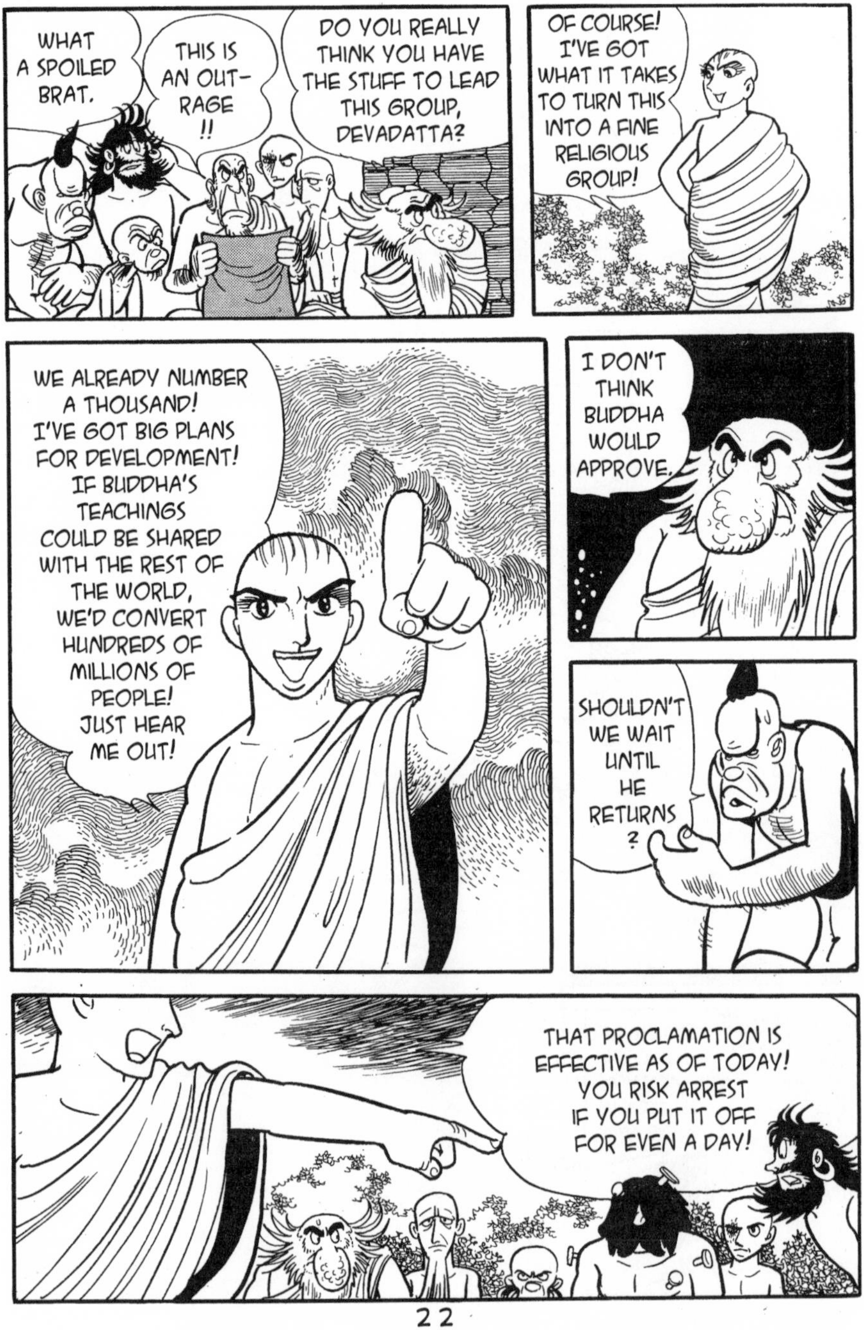
WHAT A SPOILED BRAT.
THIS IS AN OUT-RAGE !!
DO YOU REALLY THINK YOU HAVE THE STUFF TO LEAD THIS GROUP, DEVADATTA?
OF COURSE! I'VE GOT WHAT IT TAKES TO TURN THIS INTO A FINE RELIGIOUS GROUP!
WE ALREADY NUMBER A THOUSAND! I'VE GOT BIG PLANS FOR DEVELOPMENT! IF BUDDHA'S TEACHINGS COULD BE SHARED WITH THE REST OF THE WORLD, WE'D CONVERT HUNDREDS OF MILLIONS OF PEOPLE! JUST HEAR ME OUT!
I DON'T THINK BUDDHA WOULD APPROVE.
SHOULDN'T WE WAIT UNTIL HE RETURNS ?
THAT PROCLAMATION IS EFFECTIVE AS OF TODAY! YOU RISK ARREST IF YOU PUT IT OFF FOR EVEN A DAY!

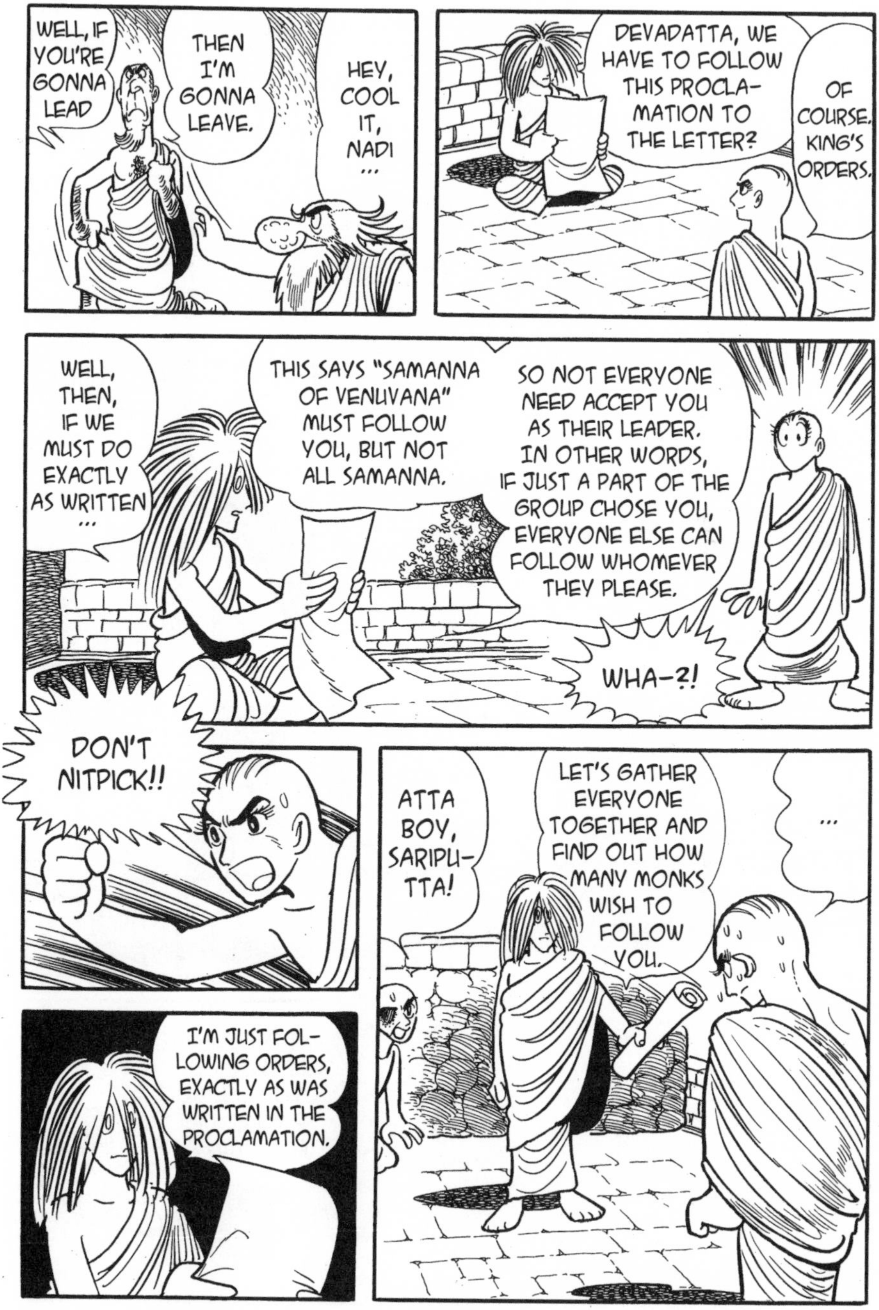
WELL, IF YOU'RE GONNA LEAD
THEN I'M GONNA LEAVE.
HEY, COOL IT, NADI ...
DEVADATTA, WE HAVE TO FOLLOW THIS PROCLA-MATION TO THE LETTER?
OF COURSE. KING'S ORDERS.
WELL, THEN, IF WE MUST DO EXACTLY AS WRITTEN ...
THIS SAYS "SAMANNA OF VENUVANA" MUST FOLLOW YOU, BUT NOT ALL SAMANNA.
SO NOT EVERYONE NEED ACCEPT YOU AS THEIR LEADER. IN OTHER WORDS, IF JUST A PART OF THE GROUP CHOSE YOU, EVERYONE ELSE CAN FOLLOW WHOMEVER THEY PLEASE.
WHA-?!
DON'T NITPICK!!
ATTA BOY, SARIPU-TTA!
LET'S GATHER EVERYONE TOGETHER AND FIND OUT HOW MANY MONKS WISH TO FOLLOW YOU.
...
I'M JUST FOL-LOWING ORDERS, EXACTLY AS WAS WRITTEN IN THE PROCLAMATION.

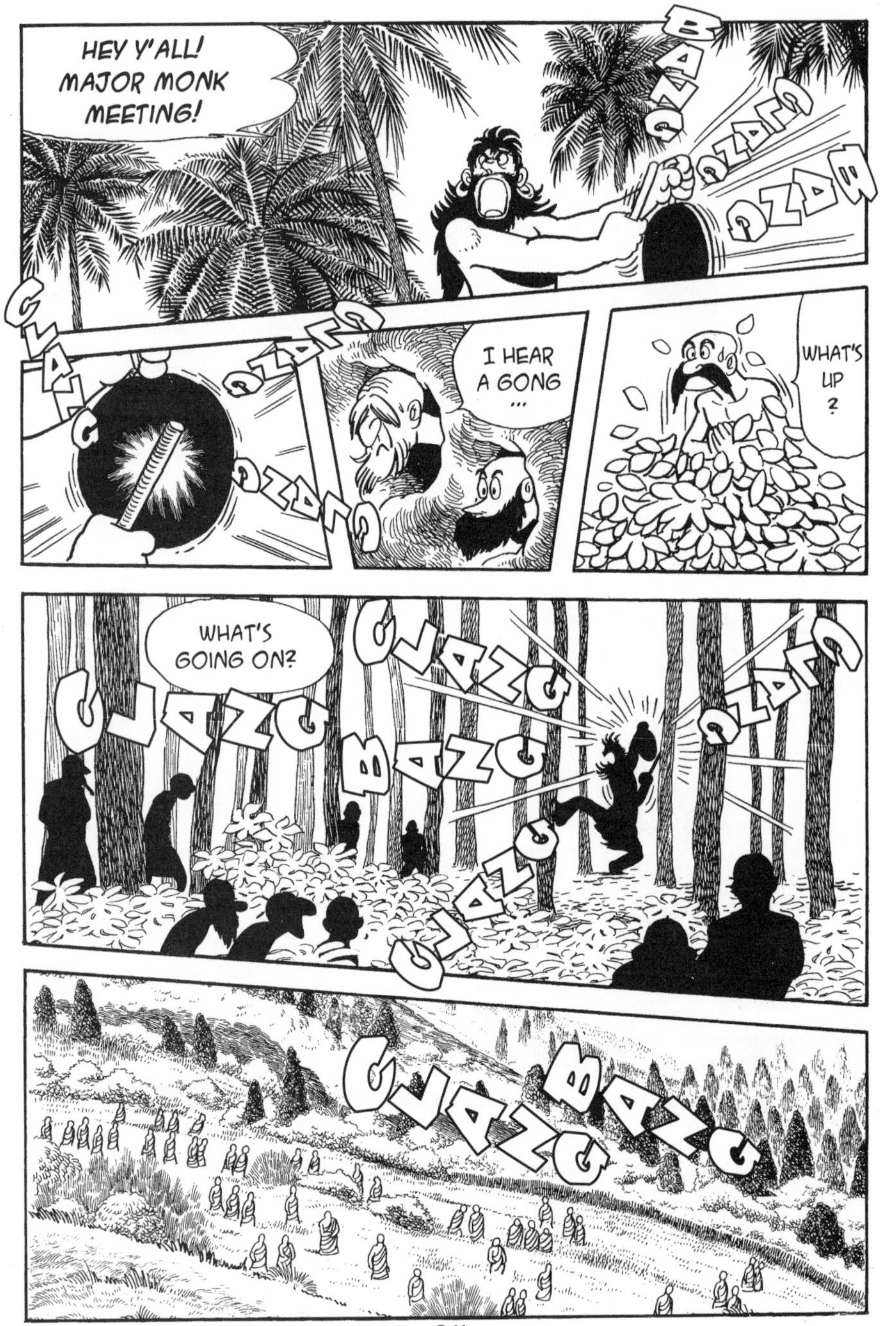
HEY Y'ALL! MAJOR MONK MEETING!
BANG
CLANG
BANG
CLANG
CLANG
I HEAR A GONG ...
WHAT'S UP ?
WHAT'S GOING ON?
CLANG
CLANG
BANG
CLANG
CLANG
CLANG
BANG

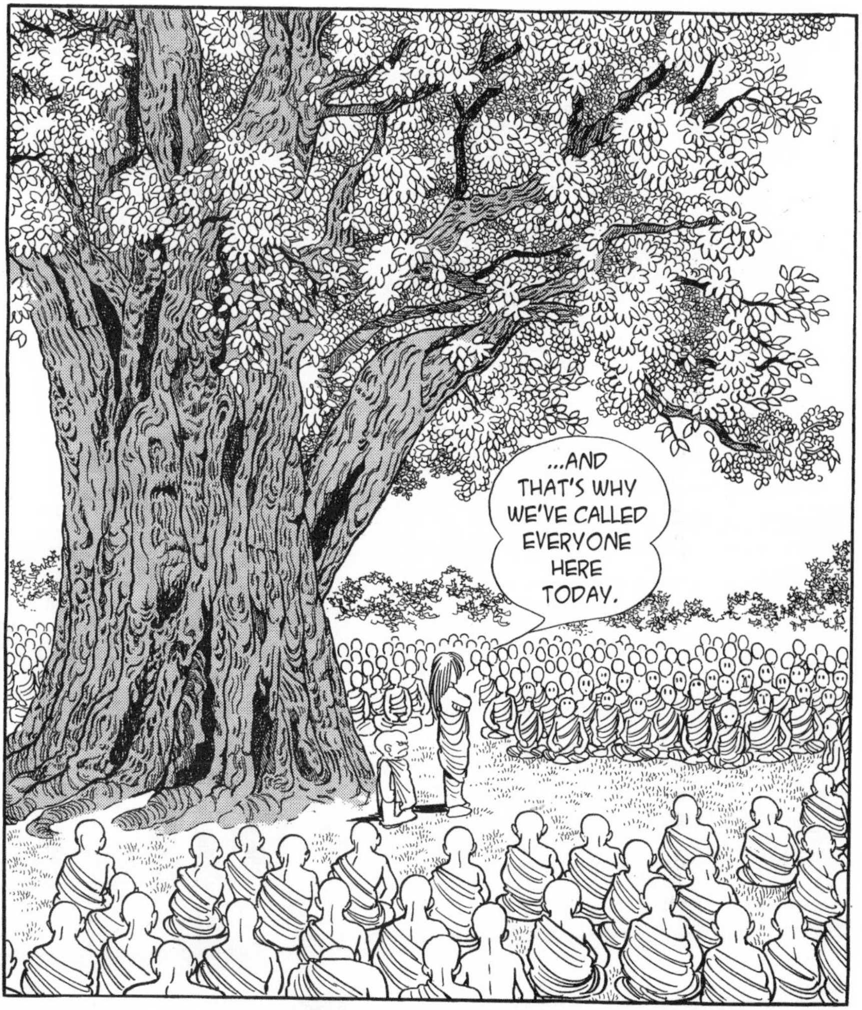
...AND THAT'S WHY WE'VE CALLED EVERYONE HERE TODAY.
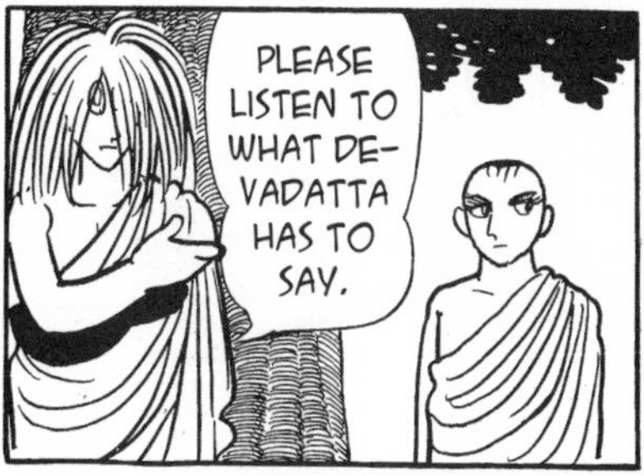
PLEASE LISTEN TO WHAT DE-VADATTA HAS TO SAY.
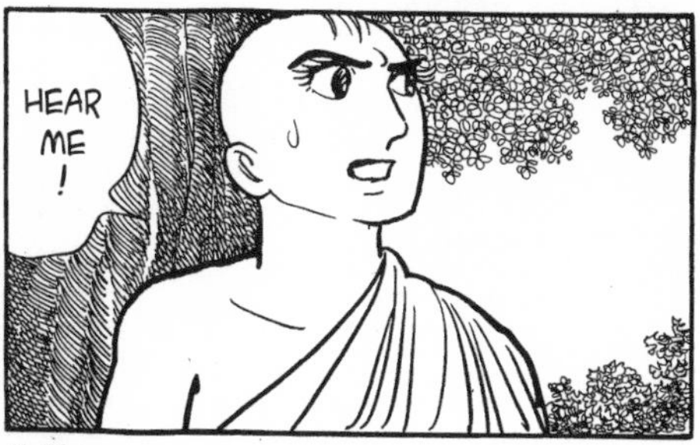
HEAR ME!

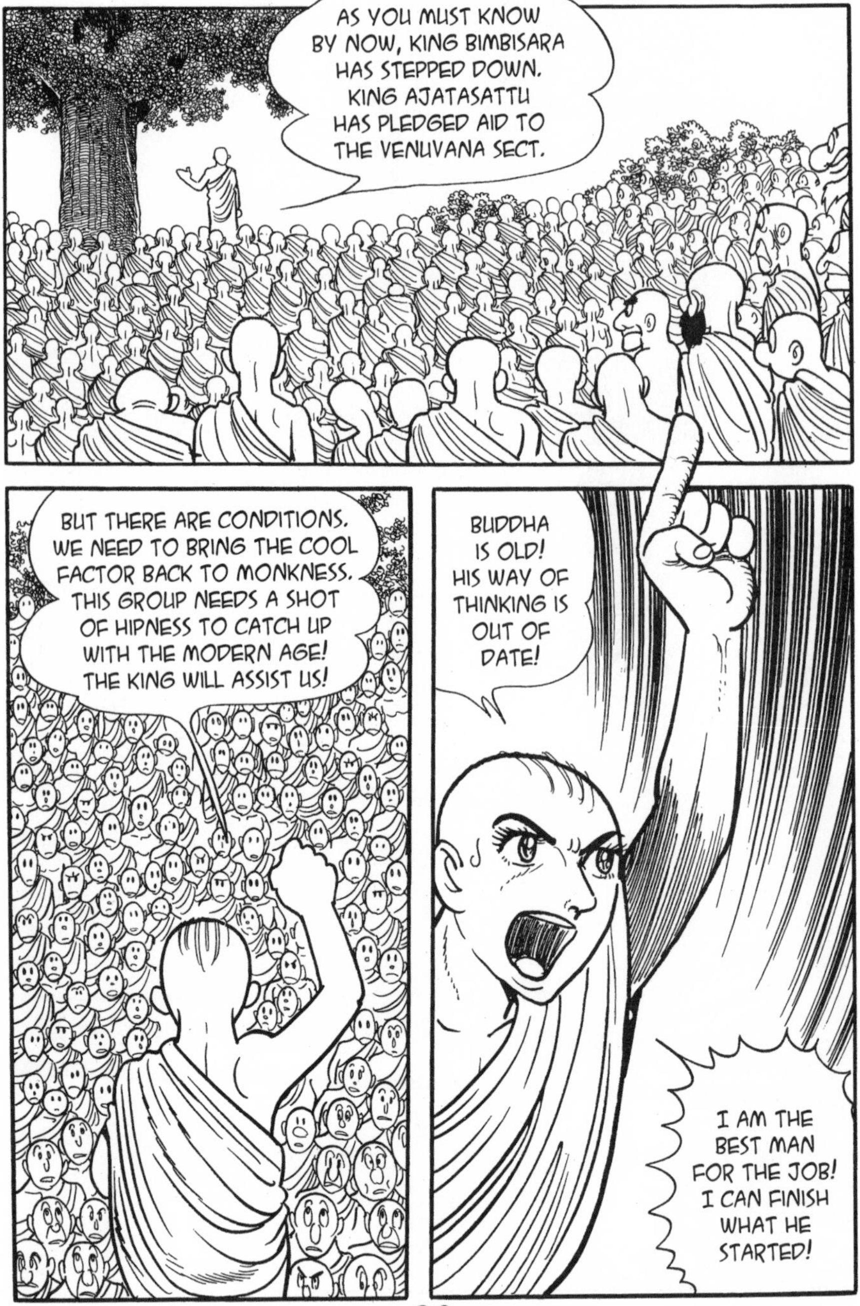
AS YOU MUST KNOW BY NOW, KING BIMBISARA HAS STEPPED DOWN. KING AJATASATTU HAS PLEDGED AID TO THE VENUVANA SECT.
BUT THERE ARE CONDITIONS. WE NEED TO BRING THE COOL FACTOR BACK TO MONKNESS. THIS GROUP NEEDS A SHOT OF HIPNESS TO CATCH UP WITH THE MODERN AGE! THE KING WILL ASSIST US!
BUDDHA IS OLD! HIS WAY OF THINKING IS OUT OF DATE!
I AM THE BEST MAN FOR THE JOB! I CAN FINISH WHAT HE STARTED!

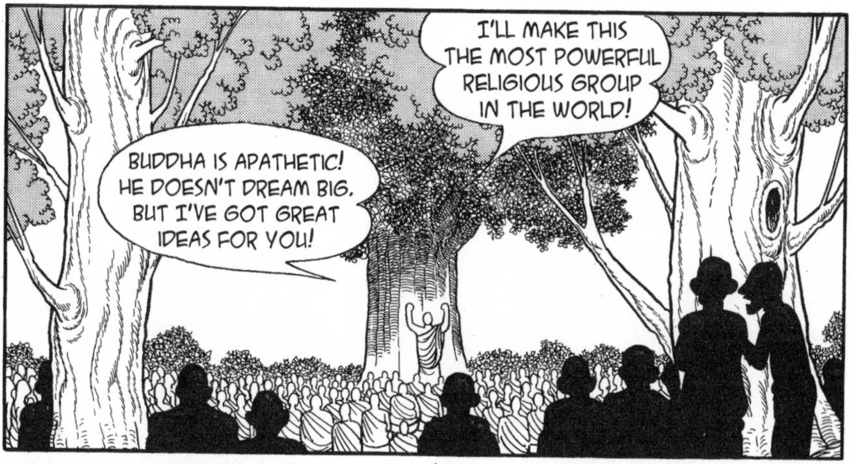
BUDDHA IS APATHETIC! HE DOESN'T DREAM BIG. BUT I'VE GOT GREAT IDEAS FOR YOU!
I'LL MAKE THIS THE MOST POWERFUL RELIGIOUS GROUP IN THE WORLD!

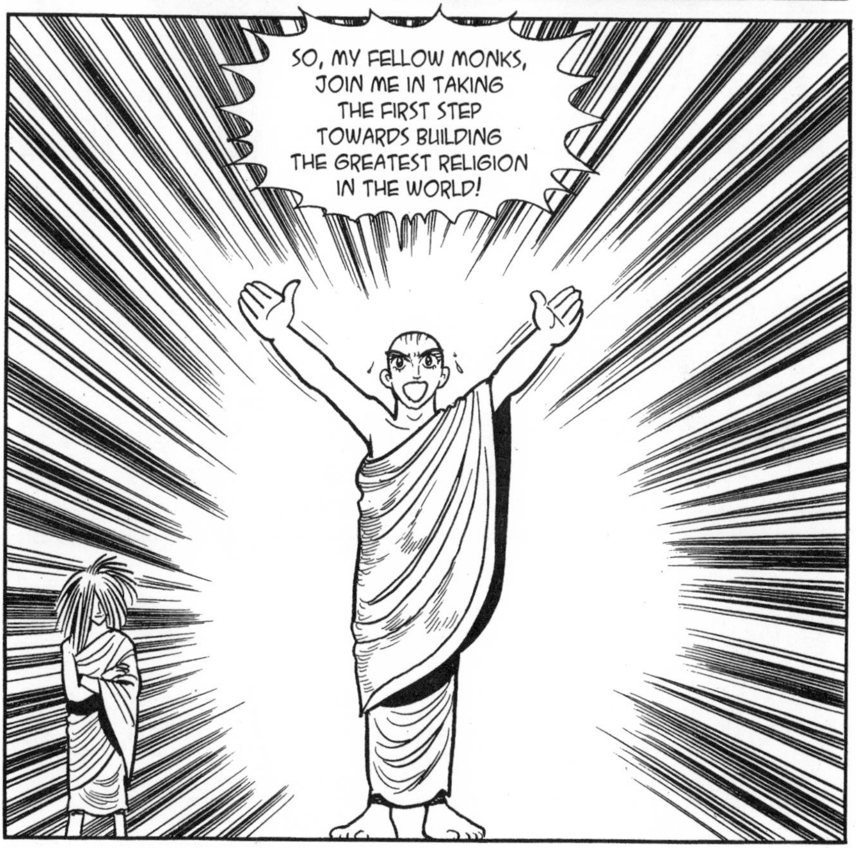
SO, MY FELLOW MONKS, JOIN ME IN TAKING THE FIRST STEP TOWARDS BUILDING THE GREATEST RELIGION IN THE WORLD!

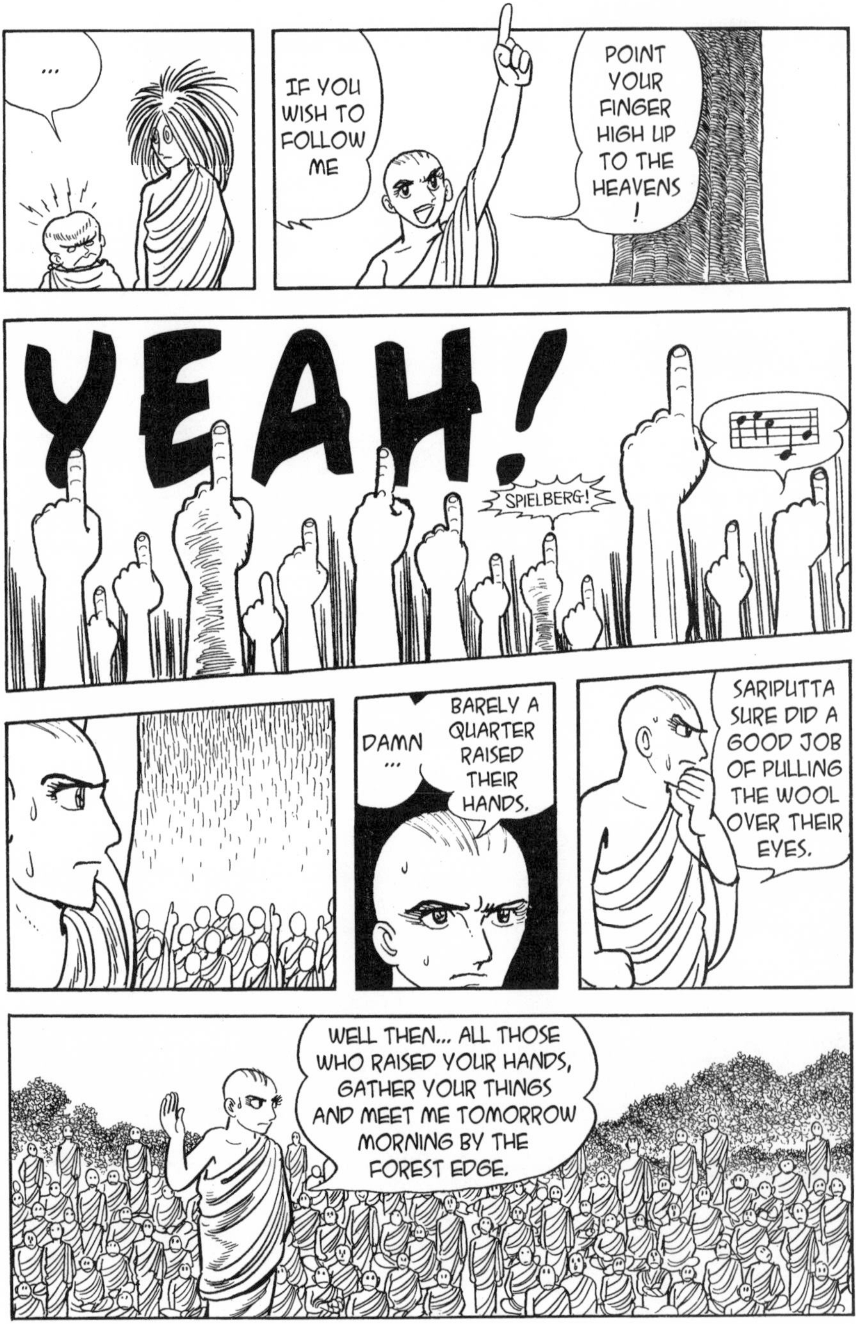
...
IF YOU WISH TO FOLLOW ME
POINT YOUR FINGER HIGH UP TO THE HEAVENS !
YEAH!
SPIELBERG!
DAMN ...
BARELY A QUARTER RAISED THEIR HANDS.
SARIPUTTA SURE DID A GOOD JOB OF PULLING THE WOOL OVER THEIR EYES.
WELL THEN... ALL THOSE WHO RAISED YOUR HANDS, GATHER YOUR THINGS AND MEET ME TOMORROW MORNING BY THE FOREST EDGE.

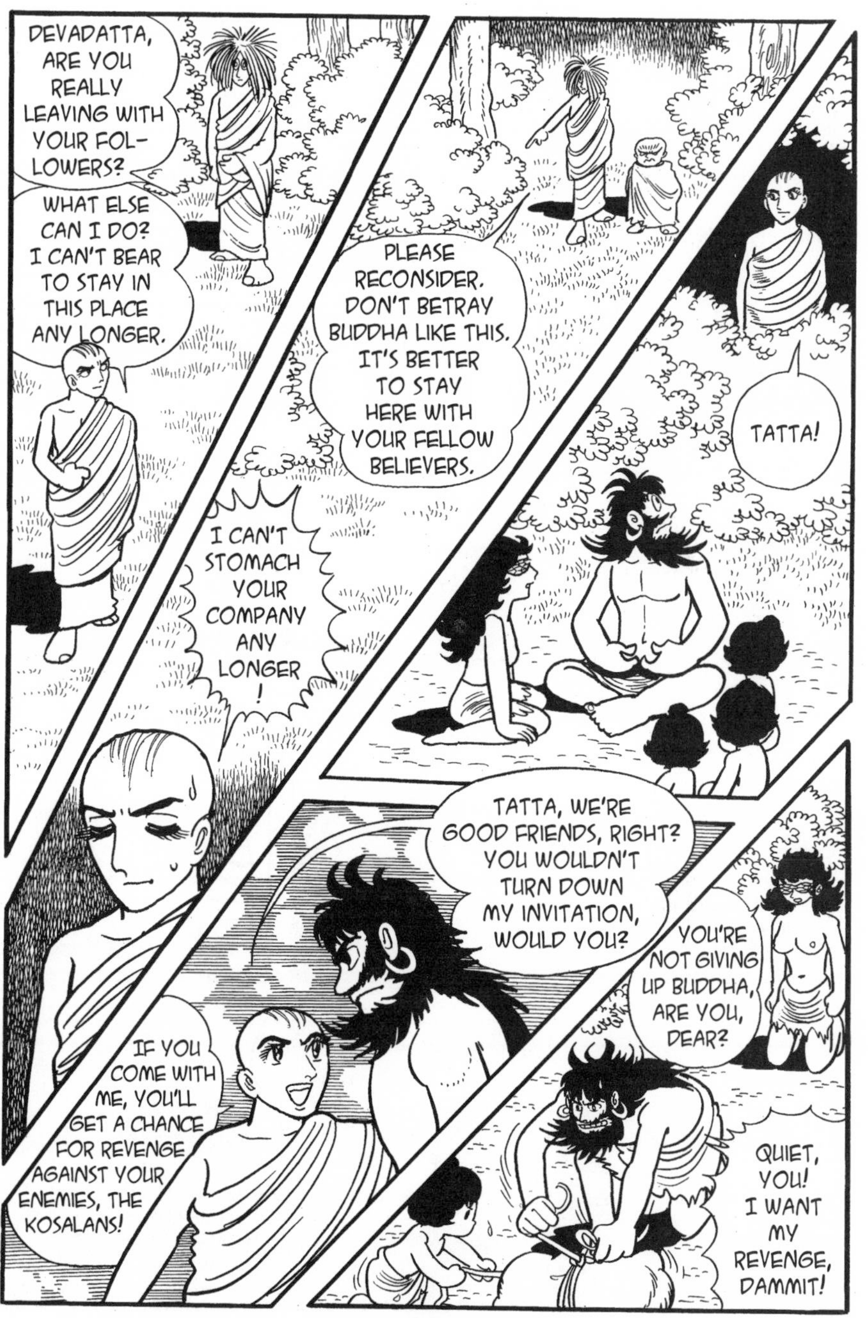
DEVADATTA, ARE YOU REALLY LEAVING WITH YOUR FOL-LOWERS?
WHAT ELSE CAN I DO? I CAN'T BEAR TO STAY IN THIS PLACE ANY LONGER.
PLEASE RECONSIDER. DON'T BETRAY BUDDHA LIKE THIS. IT'S BETTER TO STAY HERE WITH YOUR FELLOW BELIEVERS.
I CAN'T STOMACH YOUR COMPANY ANY LONGER!
TATTA!
TATTA, WE'RE GOOD FRIENDS, RIGHT? YOU WOULDN'T TURN DOWN MY INVITATION, WOULD YOU?
IF YOU COME WITH ME, YOU'LL GET A CHANCE FOR REVENGE AGAINST YOUR ENEMIES, THE KOSALANS!
YOU'RE NOT GIVING UP BUDDHA, ARE YOU, DEAR?
QUIET, YOU! I WANT MY REVENGE, DAMMIT!

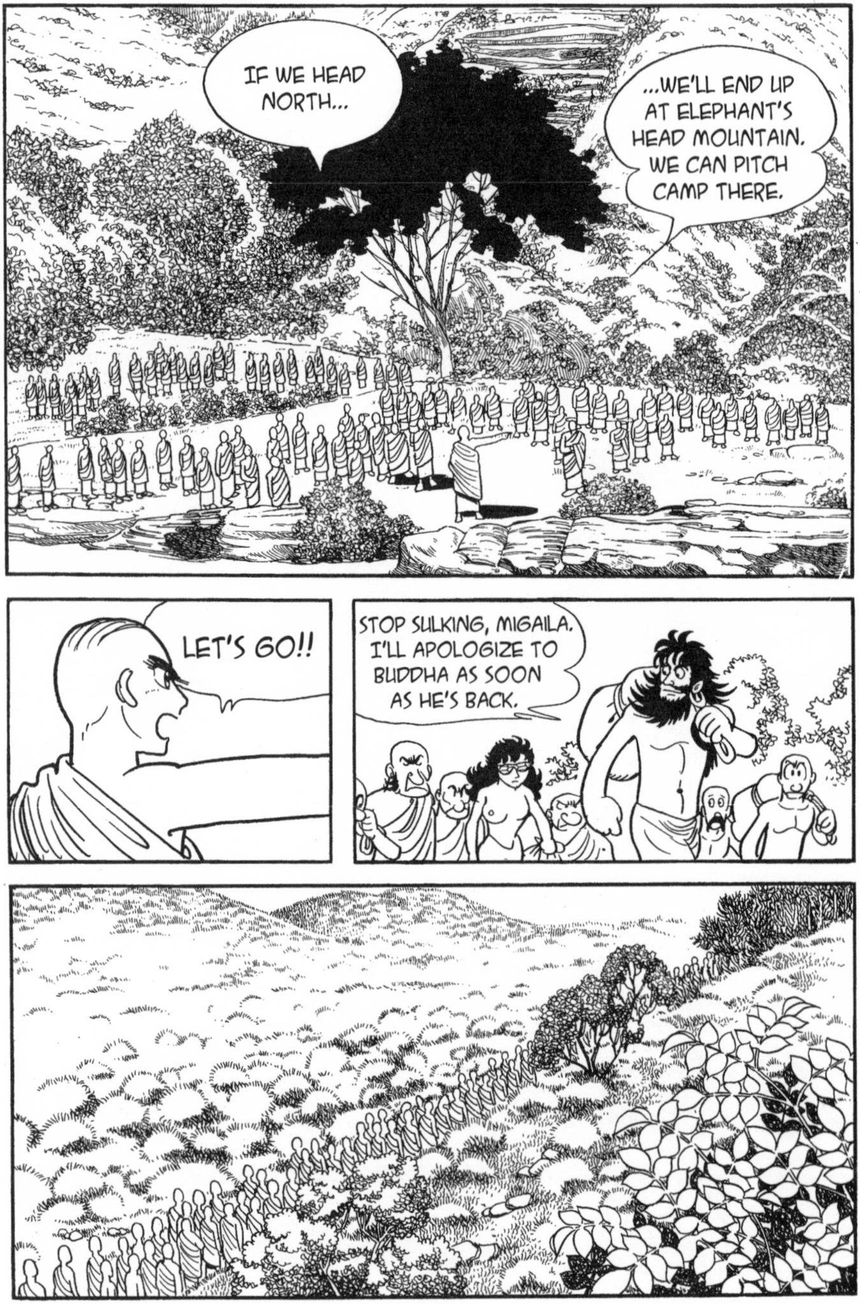
IF WE HEAD NORTH...
...WE'LL END UP AT ELEPHANT'S HEAD MOUNTAIN. WE CAN PITCH CAMP THERE.
LET'S GO!!
STOP SULKING, MIGAILA. I'LL APOLOGIZE TO BUDDHA AS SOON AS HE'S BACK.

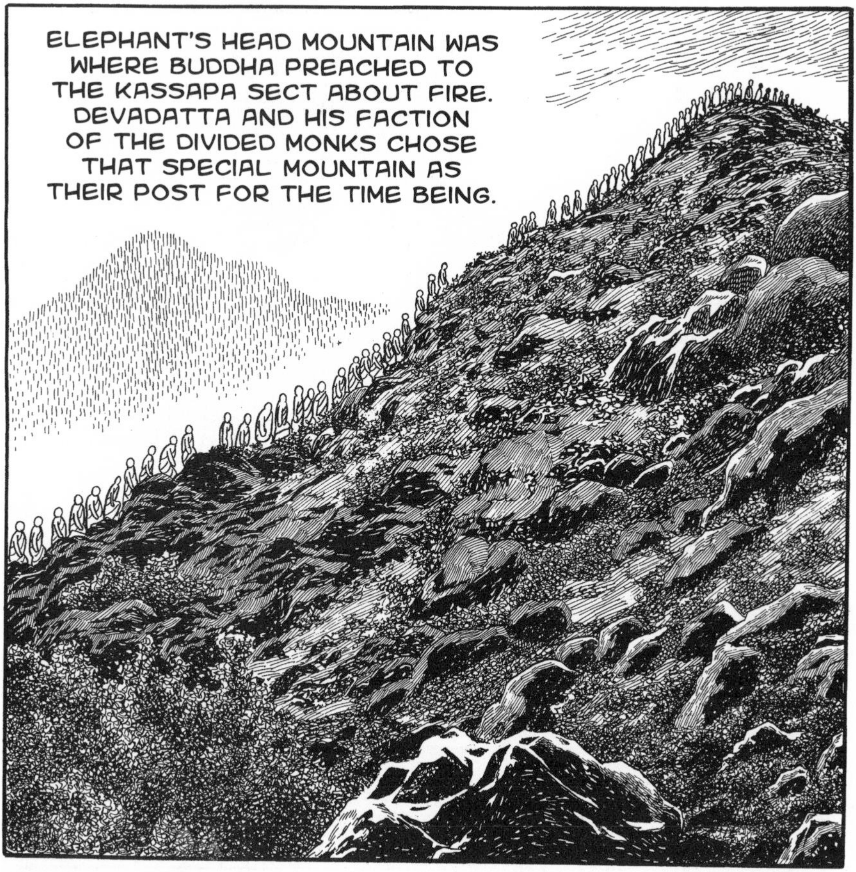
ELEPHANT'S HEAD MOUNTAIN WAS WHERE BUDDHA PREACHED TO THE KASSAPA SECT ABOUT FIRE. DEVADATTA AND HIS FACTION OF THE DIVIDED MONKS CHOSE THAT SPECIAL MOUNTAIN AS THEIR POST FOR THE TIME BEING.

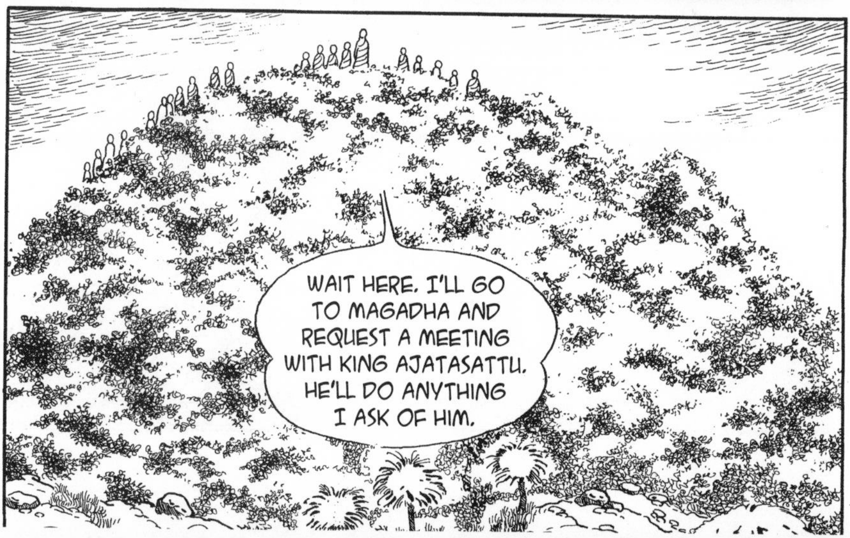
WAIT HERE. I'LL GO TO MAGADHA AND REQUEST A MEETING WITH KING AJATASATTU. HE'LL DO ANYTHING I ASK OF HIM.

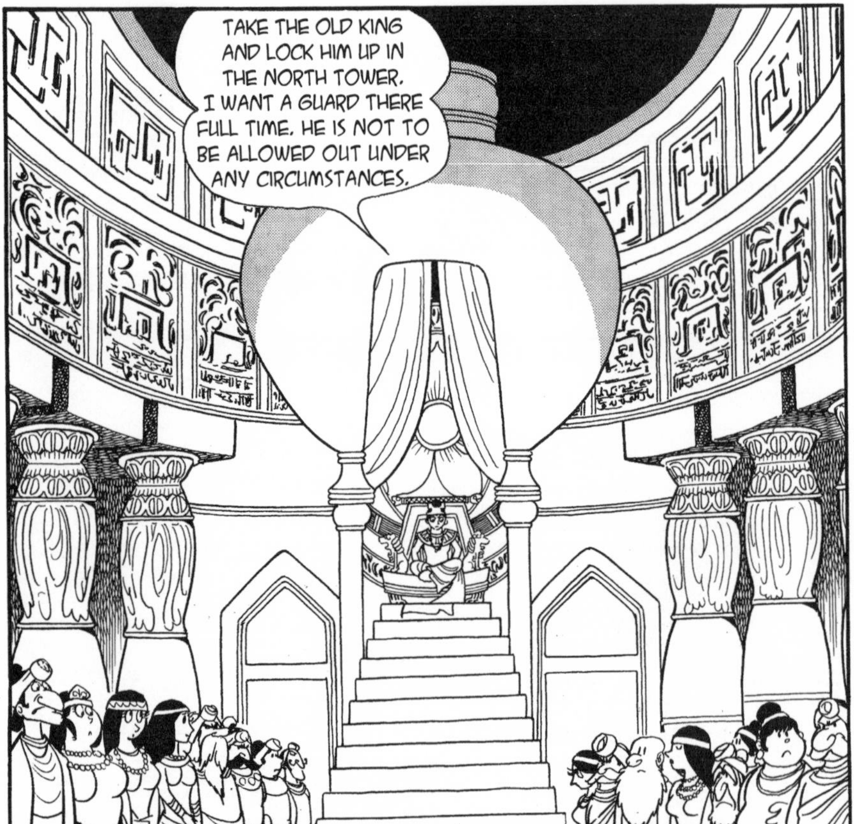
TAKE THE OLD KING AND LOCK HIM UP IN THE NORTH TOWER. I WANT A GUARD THERE FULL TIME. HE IS NOT TO BE ALLOWED OUT UNDER ANY CIRCUMSTANCES.

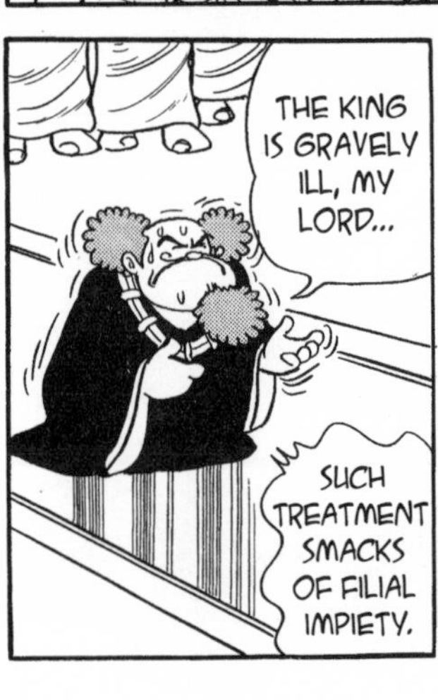
THE KING IS GRAVELY ILL, MY LORD...
SUCH TREATMENT SMACKS OF FILIAL IMPIETY.

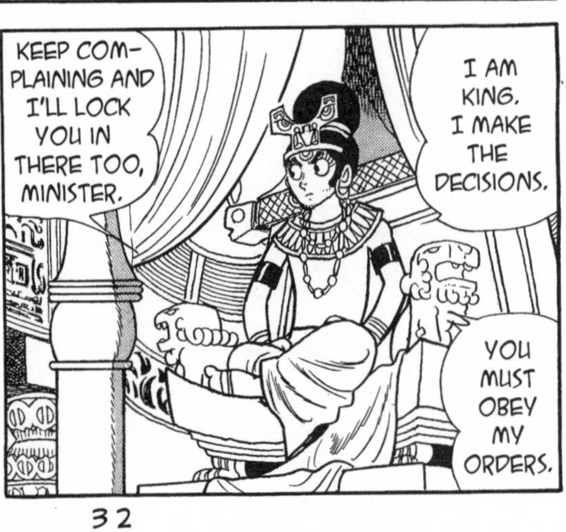
KEEP COMPLAINING AND I'LL LOCK YOU IN THERE TOO, MINISTER.
I AM KING. I MAKE THE DECISIONS.
YOU MUST OBEY MY ORDERS.

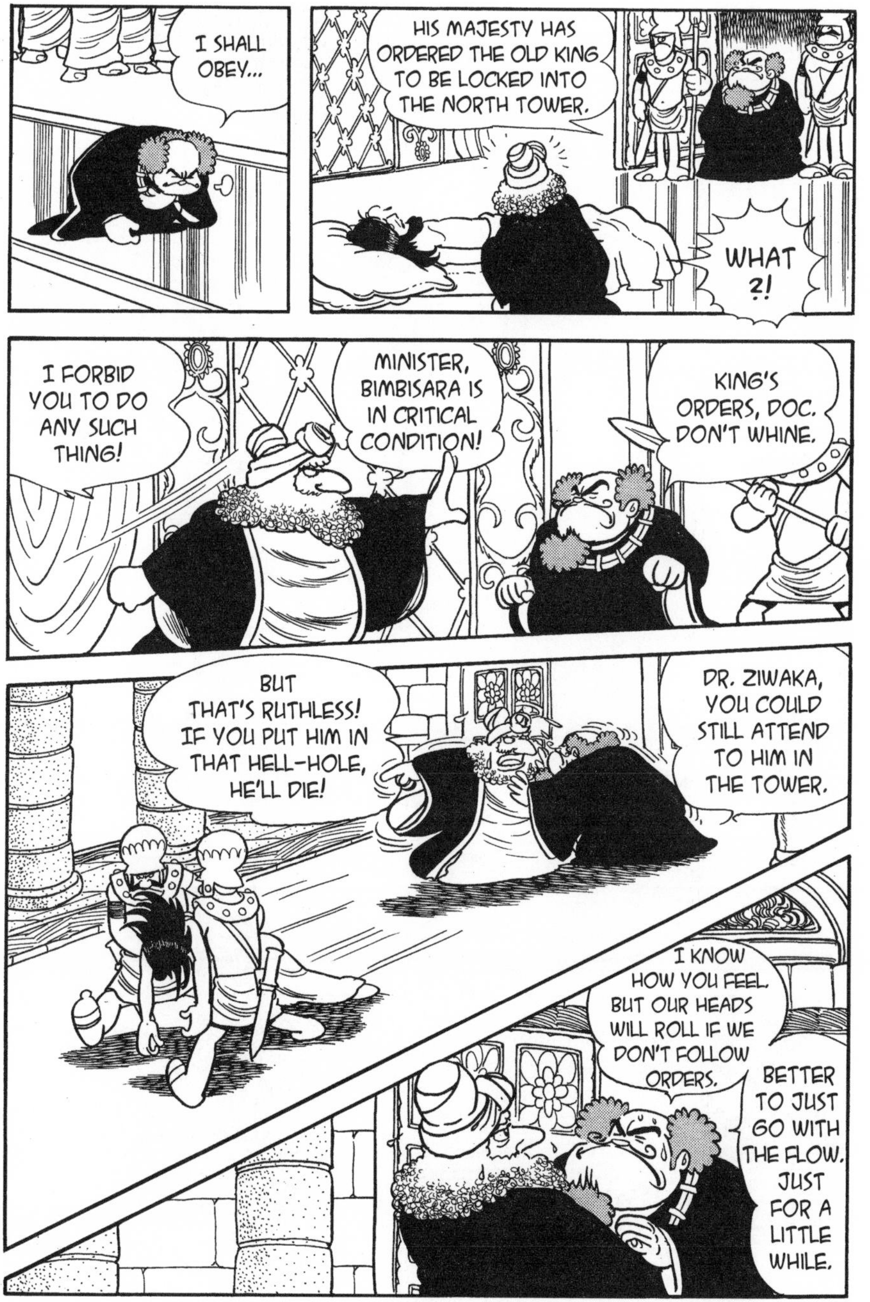
I SHALL OBEY...
HIS MAJESTY HAS ORDERED THE OLD KING TO BE LOCKED INTO THE NORTH TOWER.
WHAT ?!
I FORBID YOU TO DO ANY SUCH THING!
MINISTER, BIMBISARA IS IN CRITICAL CONDITION!
KING'S ORDERS, DOC. DON'T WHINE.
BUT THAT'S RUTHLESS! IF YOU PUT HIM IN THAT HELL-HOLE, HE'LL DIE!
DR. ZIWAKA, YOU COULD STILL ATTEND TO HIM IN THE TOWER.
I KNOW HOW YOU FEEL. BUT OUR HEADS WILL ROLL IF WE DON'T FOLLOW ORDERS.
BETTER TO JUST GO WITH THE FLOW. JUST FOR A LITTLE WHILE.

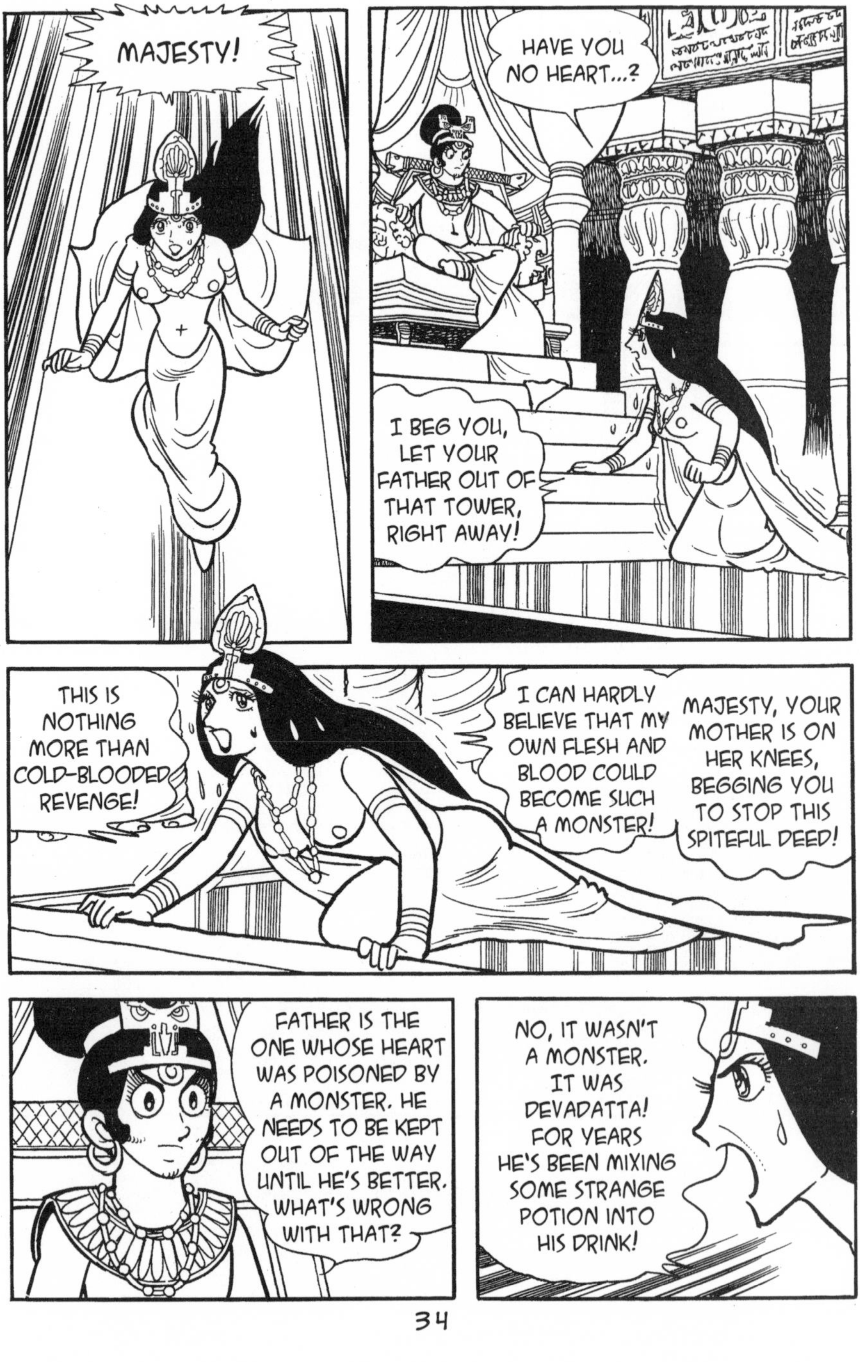
MAJESTY!
HAVE YOU NO HEART...?
I BEG YOU, LET YOUR FATHER OUT OF THAT TOWER, RIGHT AWAY!
THIS IS NOTHING MORE THAN COLD-BLOODED REVENGE!
I CAN HARDLY BELIEVE THAT MY OWN FLESH AND BLOOD COULD BECOME SUCH A MONSTER!
MAJESTY, YOUR MOTHER IS ON HER KNEES, BEGGING YOU TO STOP THIS SPITEFUL DEED!
FATHER IS THE ONE WHOSE HEART WAS POISONED BY A MONSTER. HE NEEDS TO BE KEPT OUT OF THE WAY UNTIL HE'S BETTER. WHAT'S WRONG WITH THAT?
NO, IT WASN'T A MONSTER. IT WAS DEVADATTA! FOR YEARS HE'S BEEN MIXING SOME STRANGE POTION INTO HIS DRINK!

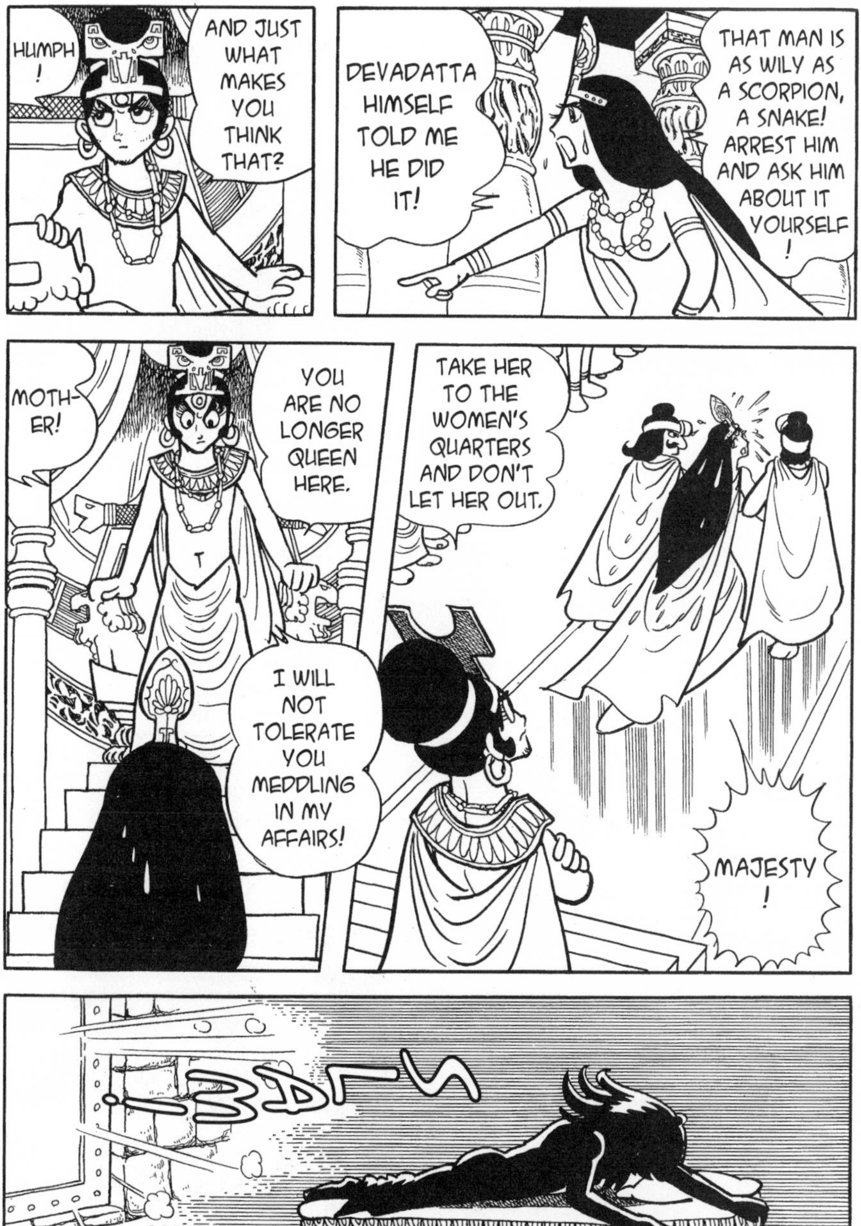
HUMPH!
AND JUST WHAT MAKES YOU THINK THAT?
DEVADATTA HIMSELF TOLD ME HE DID IT!
THAT MAN IS AS WILY AS A SCORPION, A SNAKE! ARREST HIM AND ASK HIM ABOUT IT YOURSELF!
MOTH-ER!
YOU ARE NO LONGER QUEEN HERE.
I WILL NOT TOLERATE YOU MEDDLING IN MY AFFAIRS!
TAKE HER TO THE WOMEN'S QUARTERS AND DON'T LET HER OUT.
MAJESTY!

 UHN...

 UHHH...

I—IT... IT HURTS! H—HURTS... SO MUCH...

W—WHY... WHY AM I...

UNH... UUHHH!

 AARGH! UHHN!

FIRST THE PRINCE WAS LOCKED IN HERE. NOW THE OLD KING HAS TAKEN HIS PLACE.

IS THIS WHAT THEY CALL KARMA? UNBELIEVABLE.

OH, IT HURTS!! S—SOMEBODY... HELP ME! AAAH!

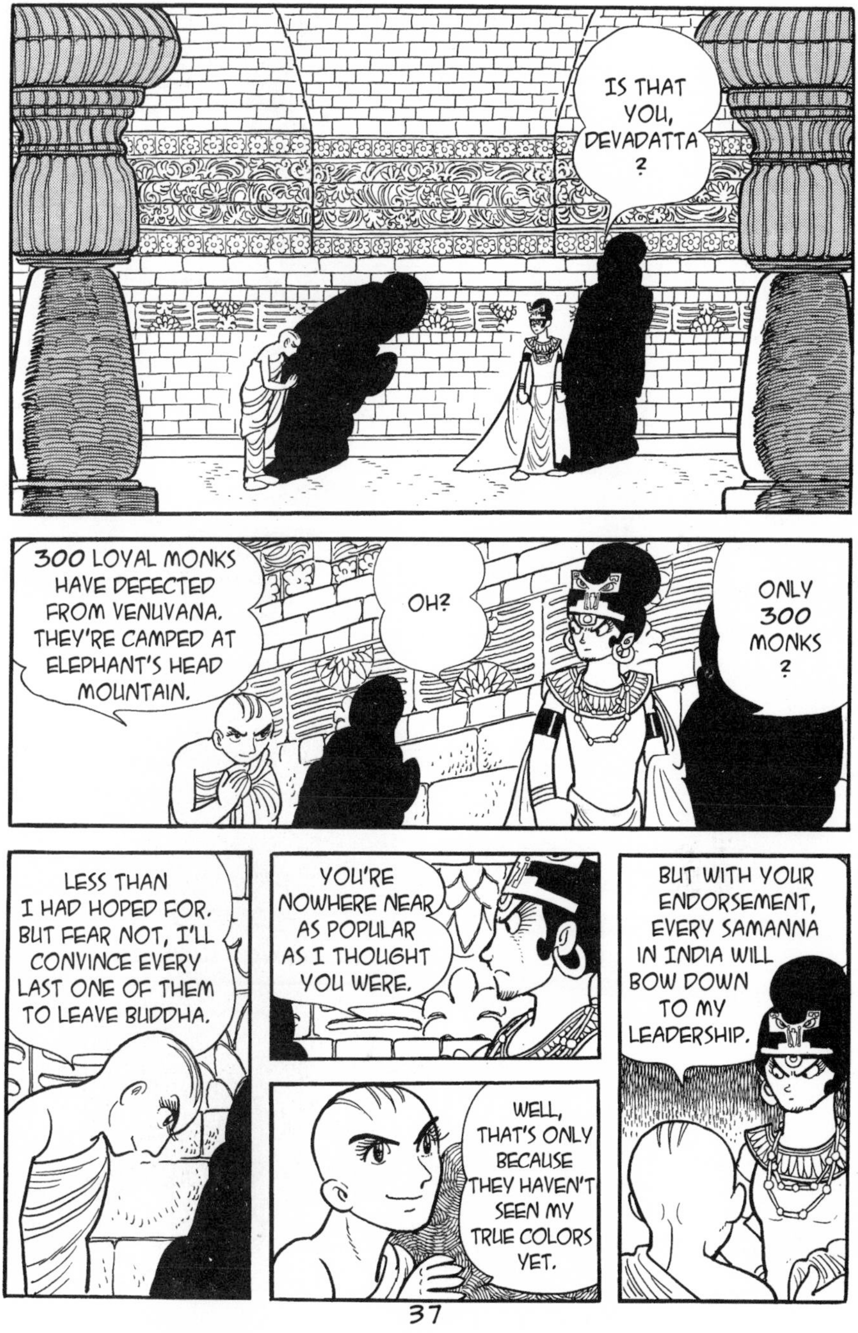
IS THAT YOU, DEVADATTA?
300 LOYAL MONKS HAVE DEFECTED FROM VENUVANA. THEY'RE CAMPED AT ELEPHANT'S HEAD MOUNTAIN.
OH?
ONLY 300 MONKS?
LESS THAN I HAD HOPED FOR. BUT FEAR NOT, I'LL CONVINCE EVERY LAST ONE OF THEM TO LEAVE BUDDHA.
YOU'RE NOWHERE NEAR AS POPULAR AS I THOUGHT YOU WERE.
WELL, THAT'S ONLY BECAUSE THEY HAVEN'T SEEN MY TRUE COLORS YET.
BUT WITH YOUR ENDORSEMENT, EVERY SAMANNA IN INDIA WILL BOW DOWN TO MY LEADERSHIP.

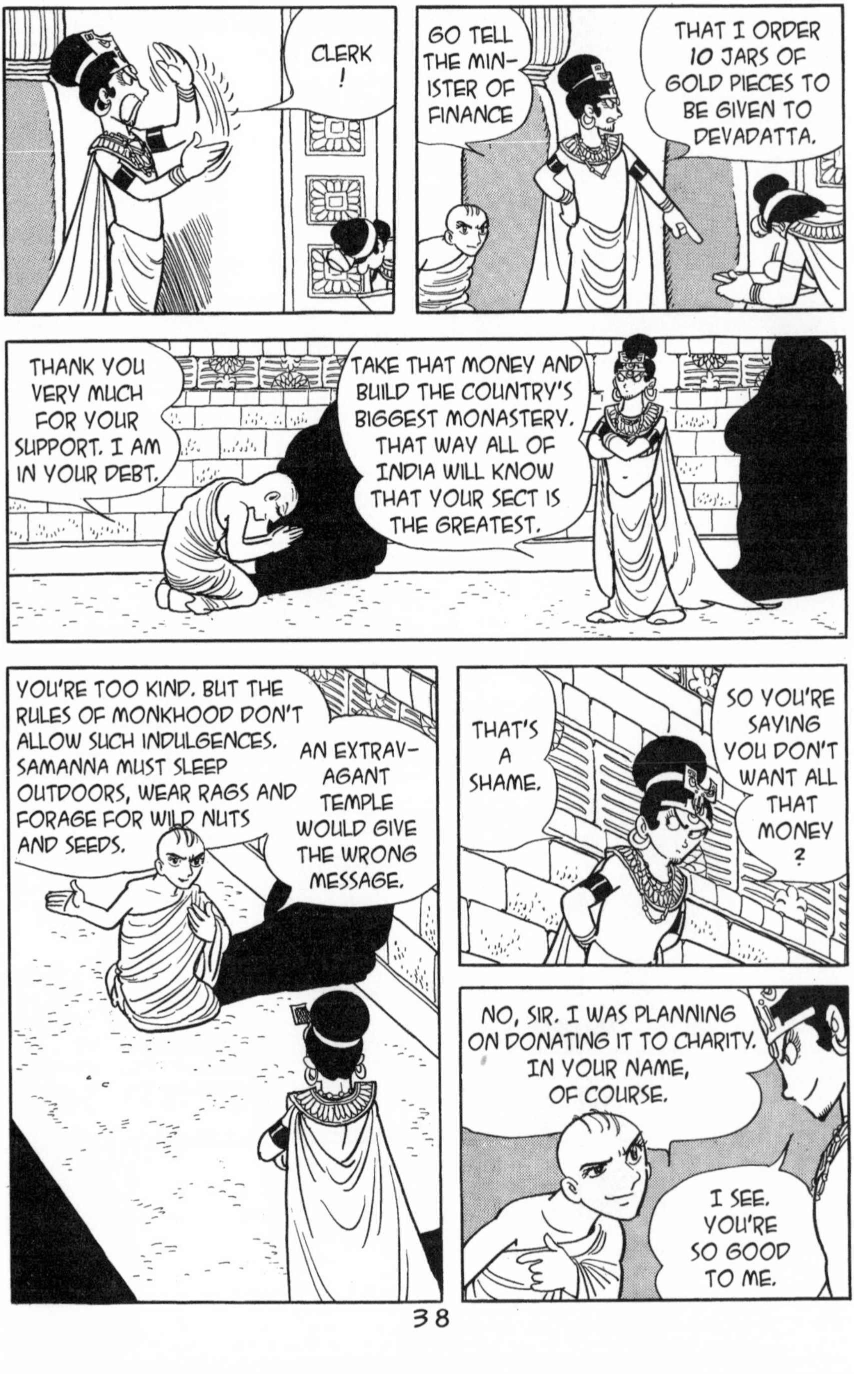
CLERK!
GO TELL THE MINISTER OF FINANCE
THAT I ORDER 10 JARS OF GOLD PIECES TO BE GIVEN TO DEVADATTA.
THANK YOU VERY MUCH FOR YOUR SUPPORT. I AM IN YOUR DEBT.
TAKE THAT MONEY AND BUILD THE COUNTRY'S BIGGEST MONASTERY. THAT WAY ALL OF INDIA WILL KNOW THAT YOUR SECT IS THE GREATEST.
YOU'RE TOO KIND. BUT THE RULES OF MONKHOOD DON'T ALLOW SUCH INDULGENCES. SAMANNA MUST SLEEP OUTDOORS, WEAR RAGS AND FORAGE FOR WILD NUTS AND SEEDS.
AN EXTRAVAGANT TEMPLE WOULD GIVE THE WRONG MESSAGE.
THAT'S A SHAME.
SO YOU'RE SAYING YOU DON'T WANT ALL THAT MONEY?
NO, SIR. I WAS PLANNING ON DONATING IT TO CHARITY. IN YOUR NAME, OF COURSE.
I SEE. YOU'RE SO GOOD TO ME.

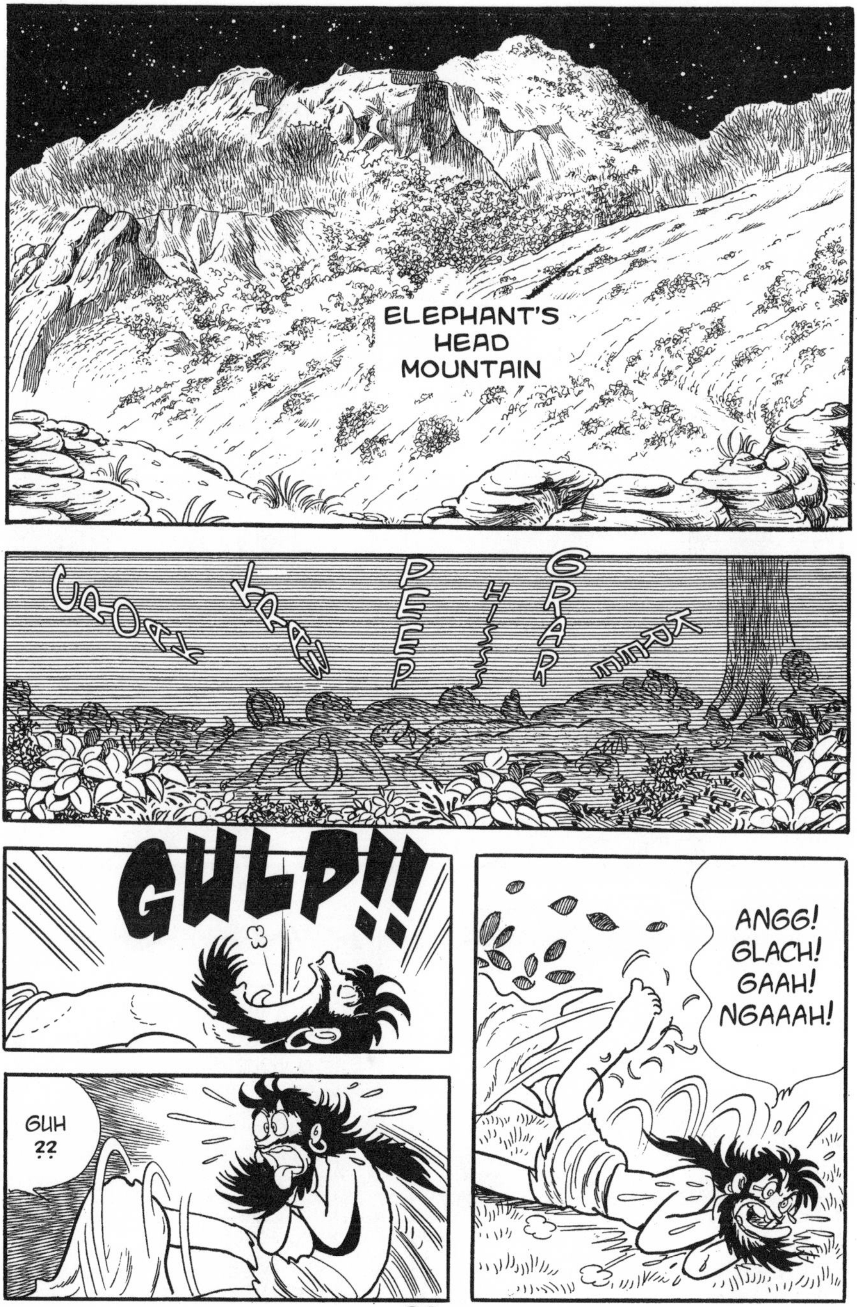
ELEPHANT'S HEAD MOUNTAIN
UROAK
KRAW
PEEP
HISSS
GRAR
KREE
GULP!!
ANGG! GLACH! GAAH! NGAAAH!
GUH ??

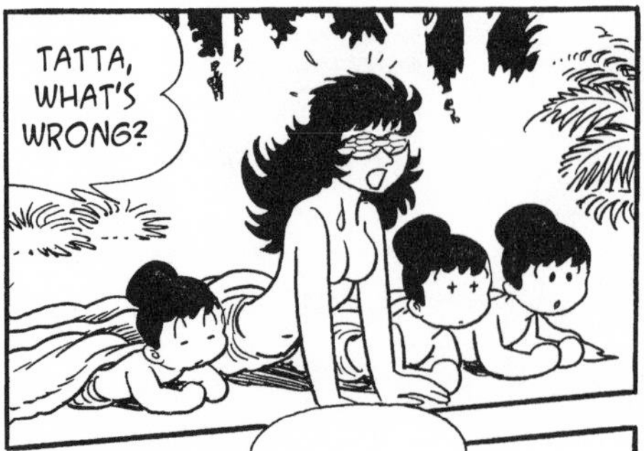
TATTA, WHAT'S WRONG?

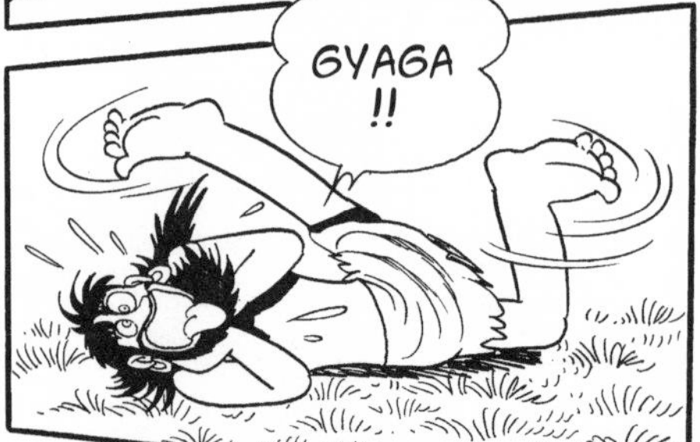
GYAGA !!

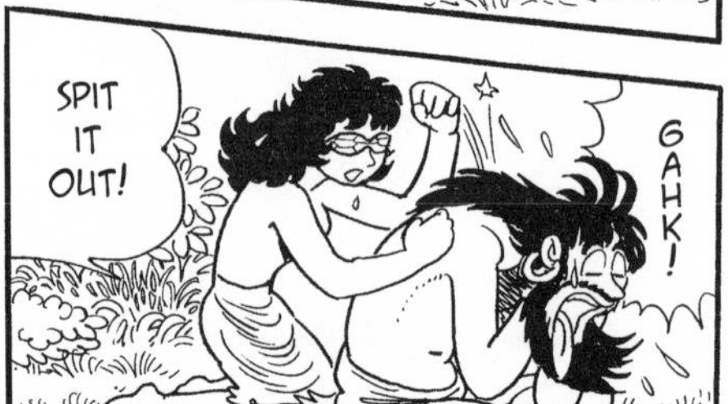
SPIT IT OUT!
GAHK!

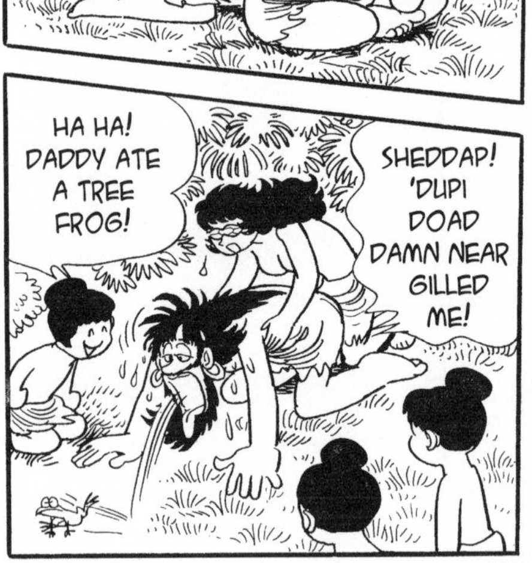
HA HA! DADDY ATE A TREE FROG!
SHEDDAP! 'DUPI DOAD DAMN NEAR GILLED ME!

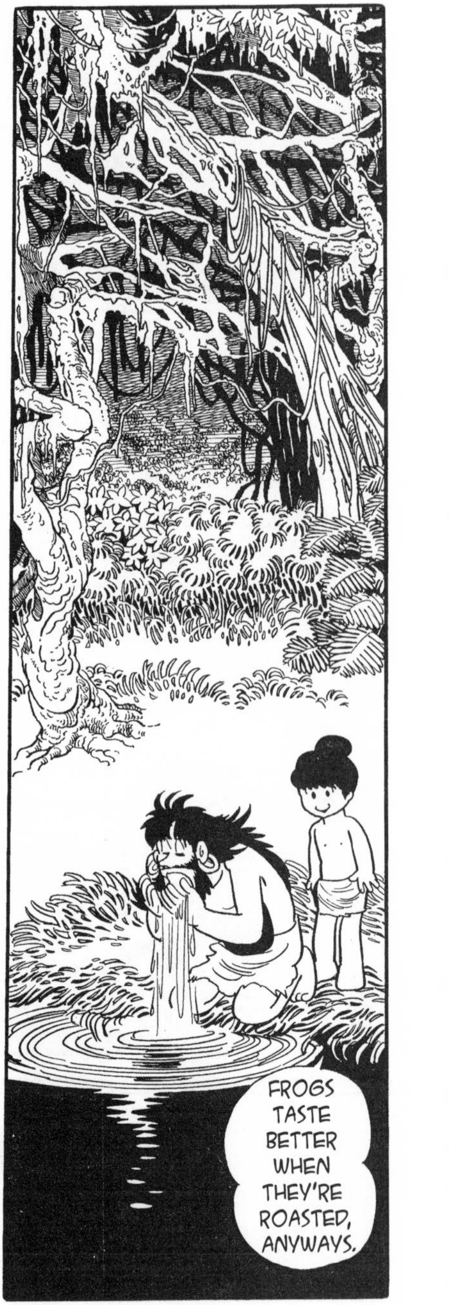
FROGS TASTE BETTER WHEN THEY'RE ROASTED, ANYWAYS.

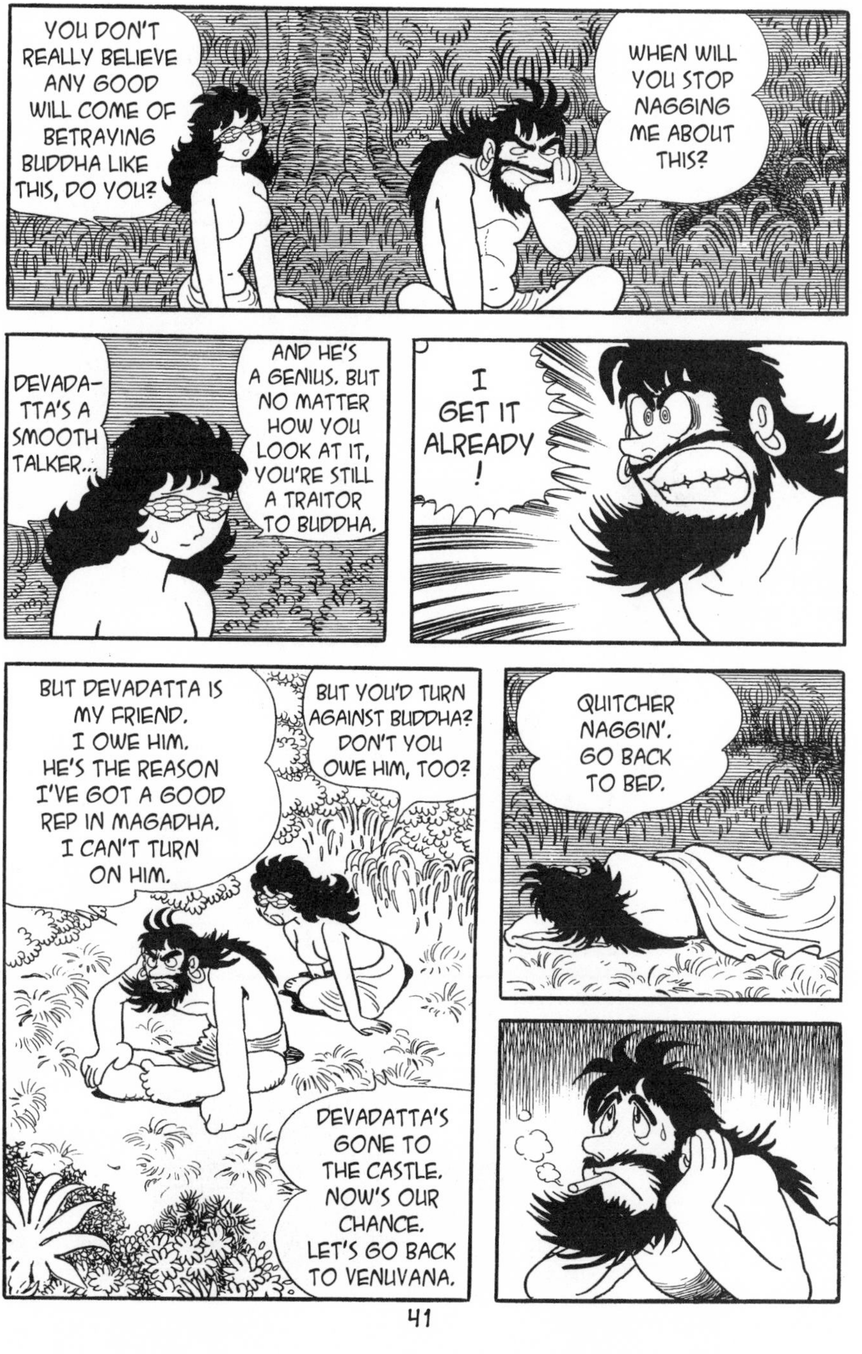
YOU DON'T REALLY BELIEVE ANY GOOD WILL COME OF BETRAYING BUDDHA LIKE THIS, DO YOU?
WHEN WILL YOU STOP NAGGING ME ABOUT THIS?
DEVADATTA'S A SMOOTH TALKER...
AND HE'S A GENIUS. BUT NO MATTER HOW YOU LOOK AT IT, YOU'RE STILL A TRAITOR TO BUDDHA.
I GET IT ALREADY!
BUT DEVADATTA IS MY FRIEND. I OWE HIM. HE'S THE REASON I'VE GOT A GOOD REP IN MAGADHA. I CAN'T TURN ON HIM.
BUT YOU'D TURN AGAINST BUDDHA? DON'T YOU OWE HIM, TOO?
DEVADATTA'S GONE TO THE CASTLE. NOW'S OUR CHANCE. LET'S GO BACK TO VENUVANA.
QUITCHER NAGGIN'. GO BACK TO BED.

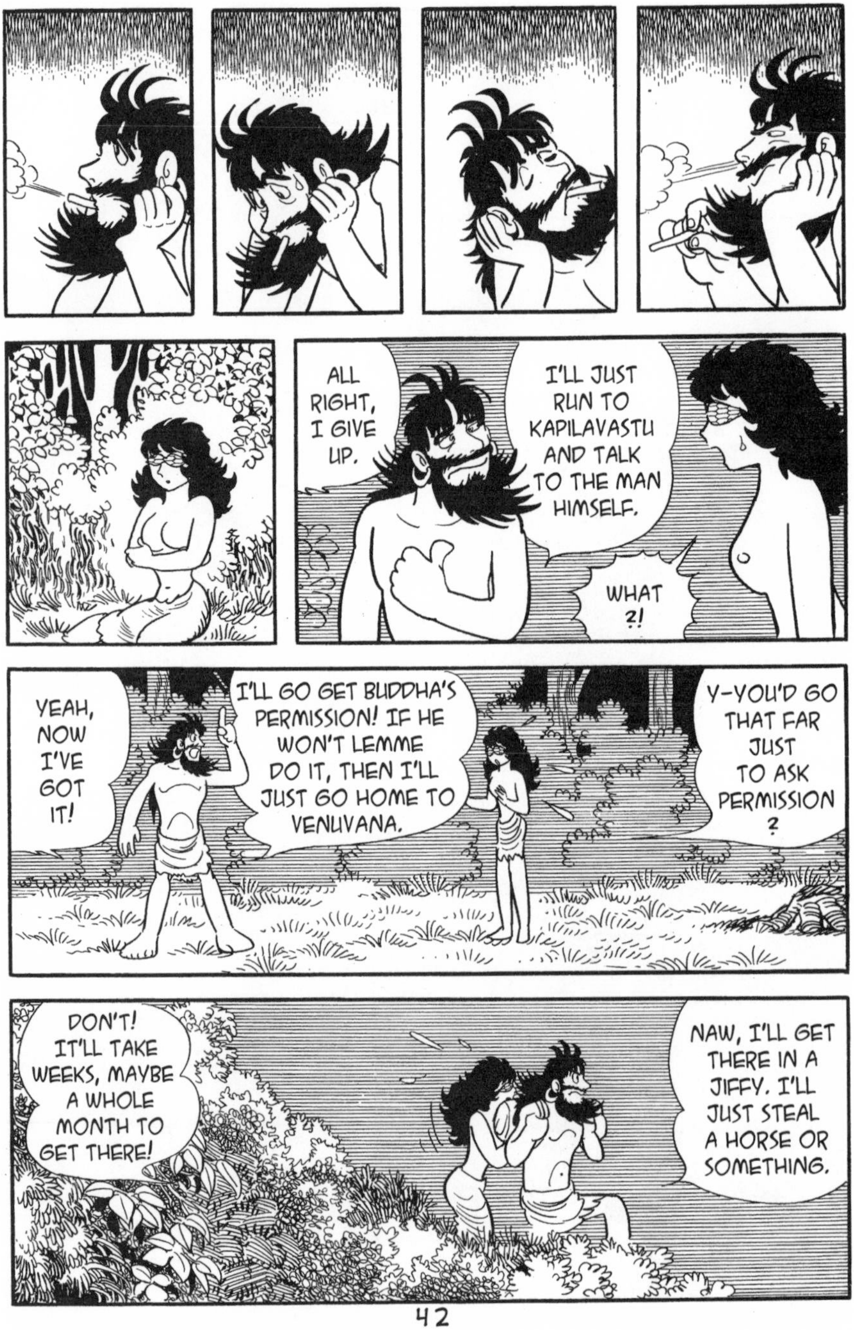
ALL RIGHT, I GIVE UP.
I'LL JUST RUN TO KAPILAVASTU AND TALK TO THE MAN HIMSELF.
WHAT ?!
YEAH, NOW I'VE GOT IT!
I'LL GO GET BUDDHA'S PERMISSION! IF HE WON'T LEMME DO IT, THEN I'LL JUST GO HOME TO VENUVANA.
Y-YOU'D GO THAT FAR JUST TO ASK PERMISSION ?
DON'T! IT'LL TAKE WEEKS, MAYBE A WHOLE MONTH TO GET THERE!
NAW, I'LL GET THERE IN A JIFFY. I'LL JUST STEAL A HORSE OR SOMETHING.

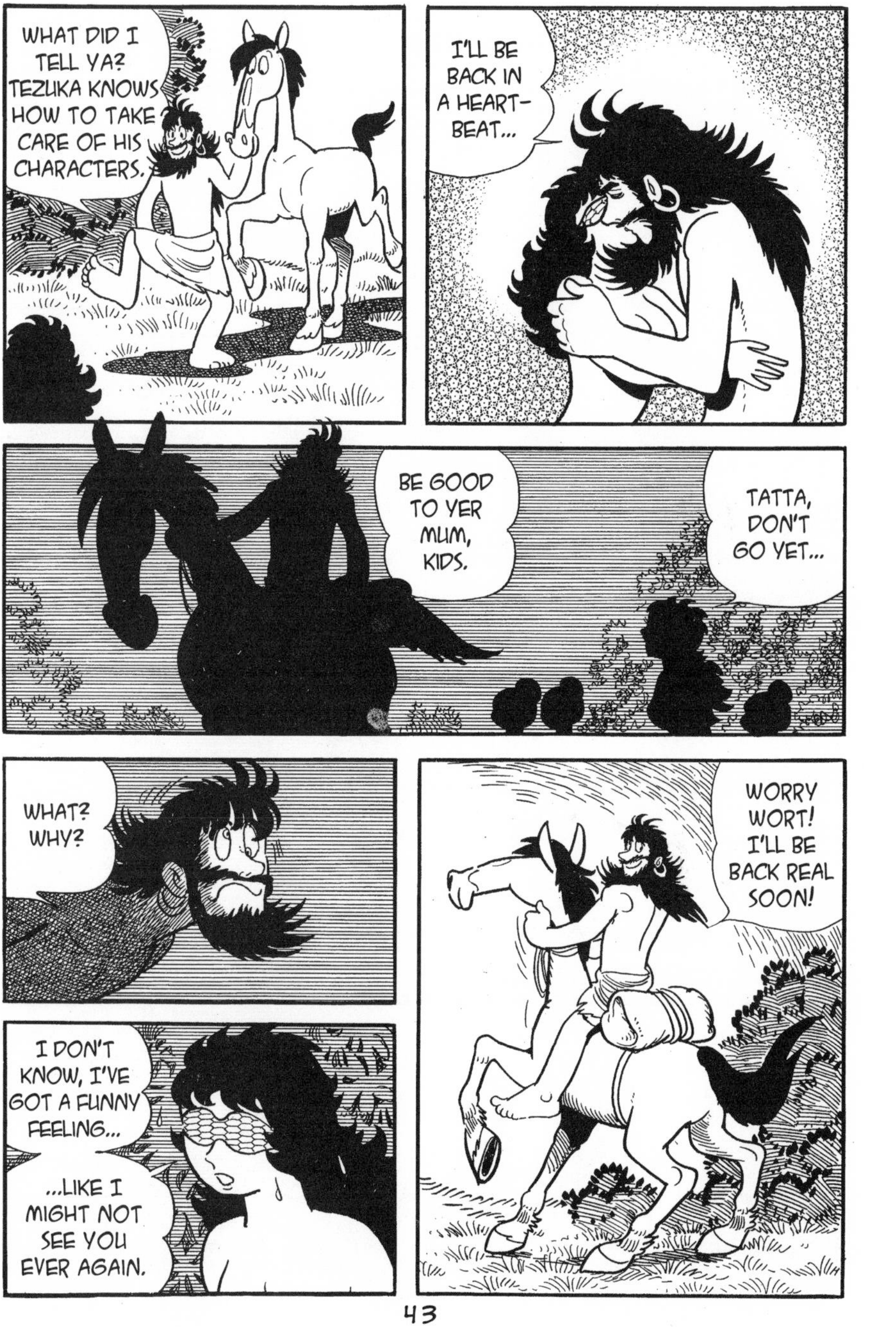
WHAT DID I TELL YA? TEZUKA KNOWS HOW TO TAKE CARE OF HIS CHARACTERS.
I'LL BE BACK IN A HEART-BEAT...
BE GOOD TO YER MUM, KIDS.
TATTA, DON'T GO YET...
WHAT? WHY?
I DON'T KNOW, I'VE GOT A FUNNY FEELING...
...LIKE I MIGHT NOT SEE YOU EVER AGAIN.
WORRY WORT! I'LL BE BACK REAL SOON!

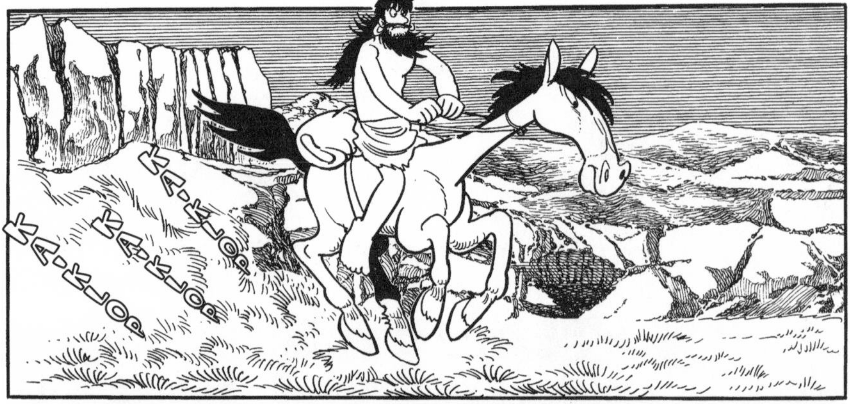
KA-KLOP
KA-KLOP
KA-KLOP

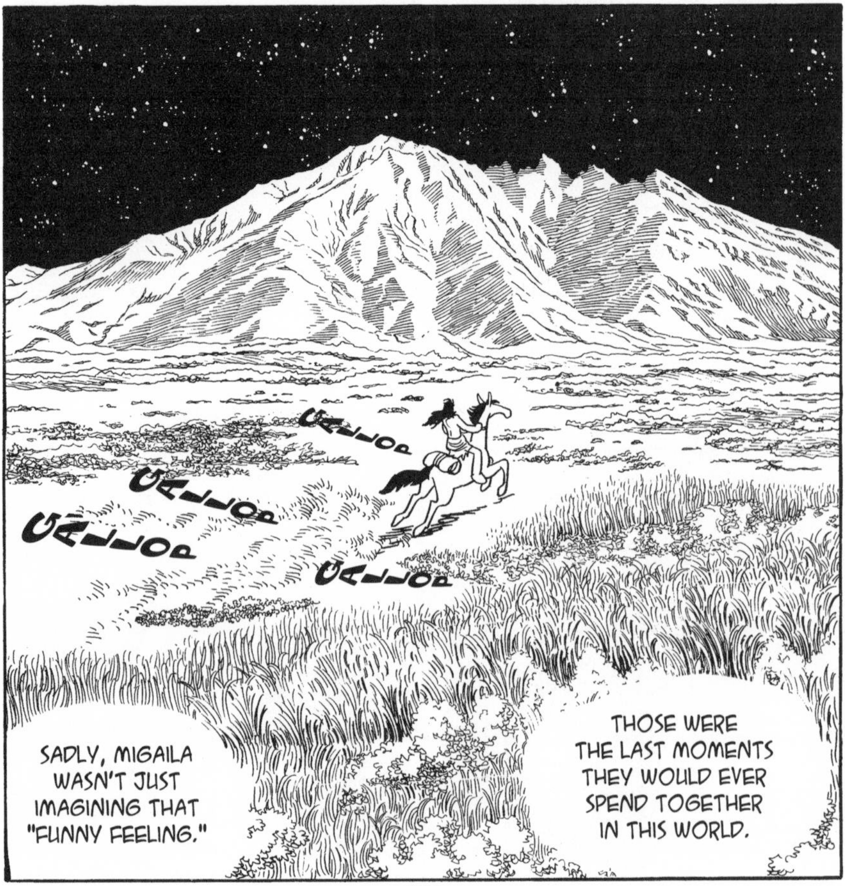
GALLOP
GALLOP
GALLOP
GALLOP
SADLY, MIGAILA WASN'T JUST IMAGINING THAT "FUNNY FEELING."
THOSE WERE THE LAST MOMENTS THEY WOULD EVER SPEND TOGETHER IN THIS WORLD.

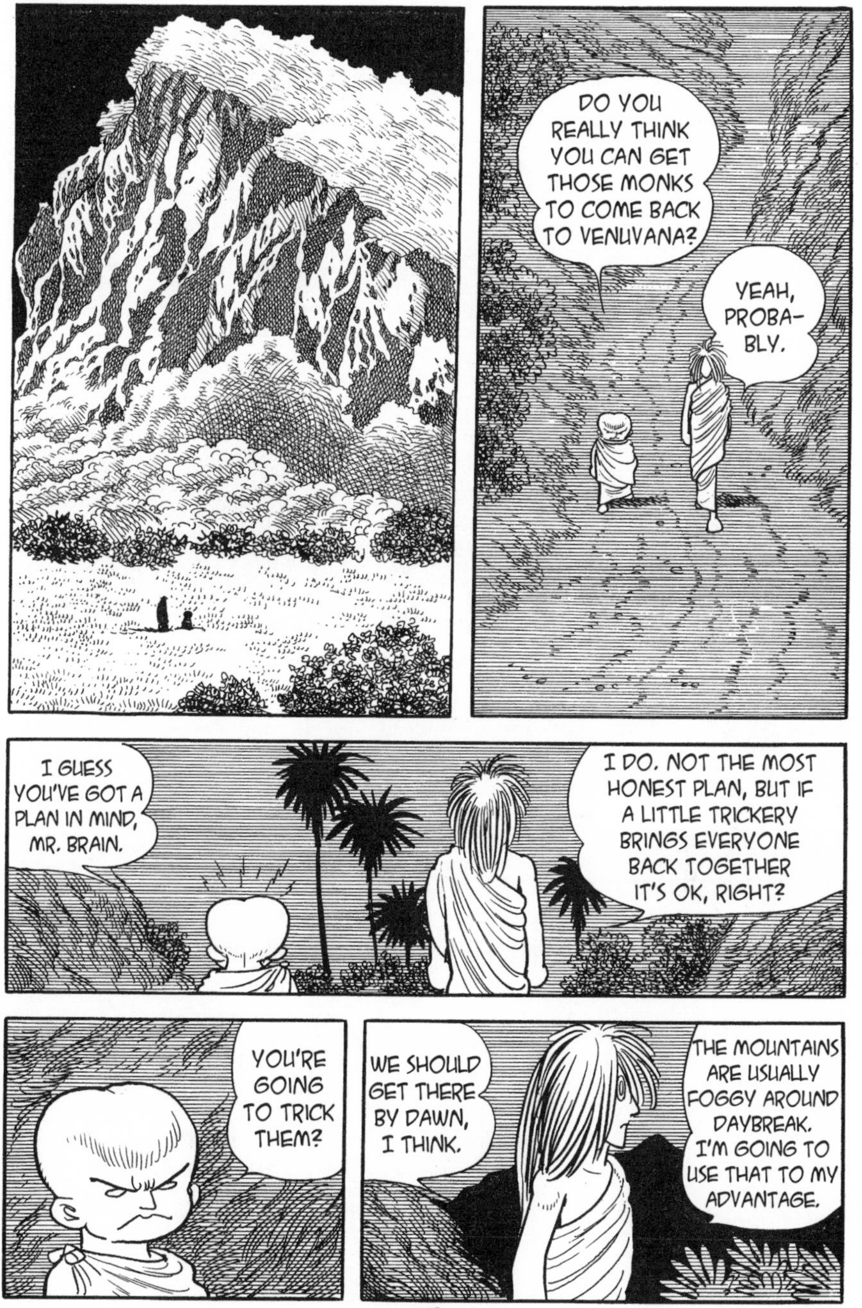
DO YOU REALLY THINK YOU CAN GET THOSE MONKS TO COME BACK TO VENUVANA?
YEAH, PROBA-BLY.
I GUESS YOU'VE GOT A PLAN IN MIND, MR. BRAIN.
I DO. NOT THE MOST HONEST PLAN, BUT IF A LITTLE TRICKERY BRINGS EVERYONE BACK TOGETHER IT'S OK, RIGHT?
YOU'RE GOING TO TRICK THEM?
WE SHOULD GET THERE BY DAWN, I THINK.
THE MOUNTAINS ARE USUALLY FOGGY AROUND DAYBREAK. I'M GOING TO USE THAT TO MY ADVANTAGE.

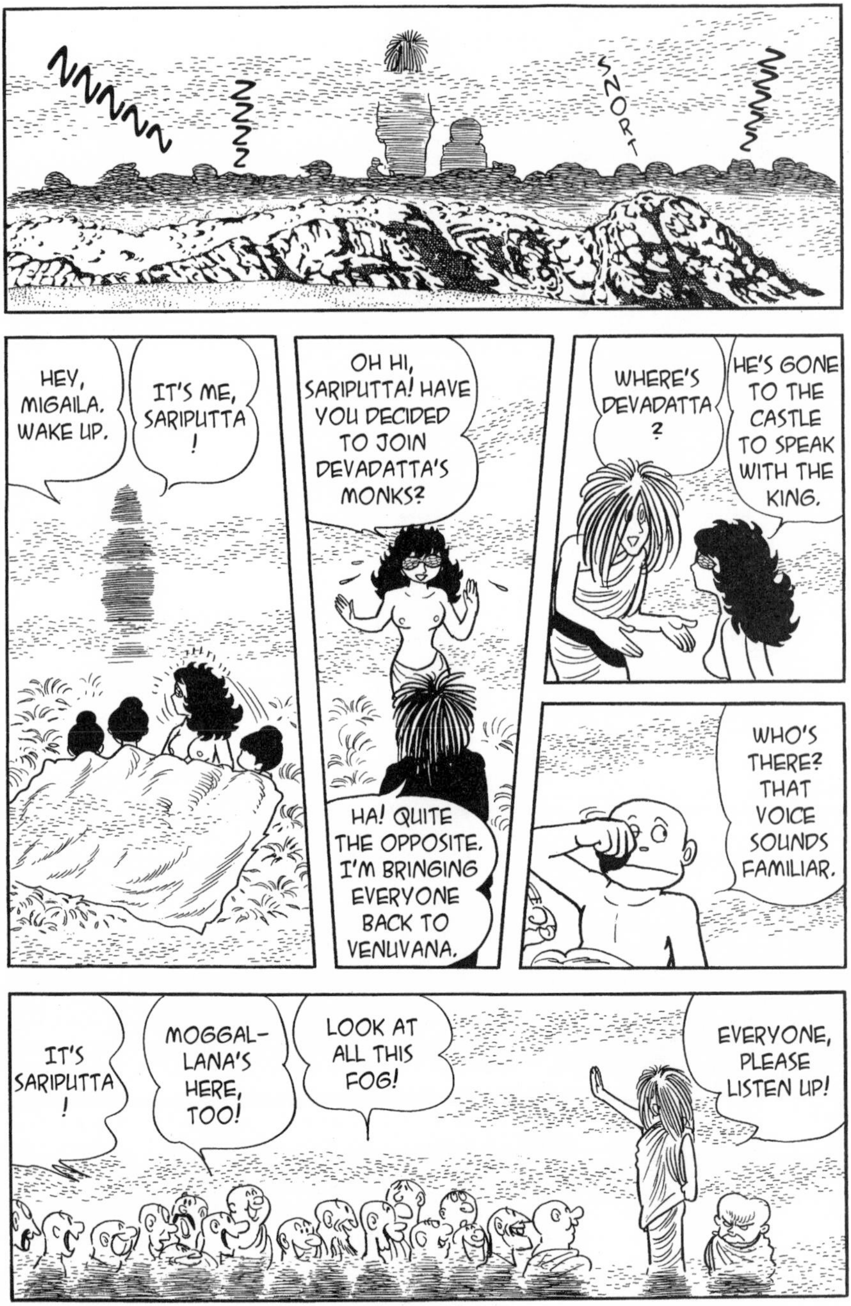
NNNNNN
ZZZZ
SNORT
ZZZZZ
HEY, MIGAILA. WAKE UP.
IT'S ME, SARIPUTTA!
OH HI, SARIPUTTA! HAVE YOU DECIDED TO JOIN DEVADATTA'S MONKS?
HA! QUITE THE OPPOSITE. I'M BRINGING EVERYONE BACK TO VENUVANA.
WHERE'S DEVADATTA?
HE'S GONE TO THE CASTLE TO SPEAK WITH THE KING.
WHO'S THERE? THAT VOICE SOUNDS FAMILIAR.
IT'S SARIPUTTA!
MOGGAL-LANA'S HERE, TOO!
LOOK AT ALL THIS FOG!
EVERYONE, PLEASE LISTEN UP!

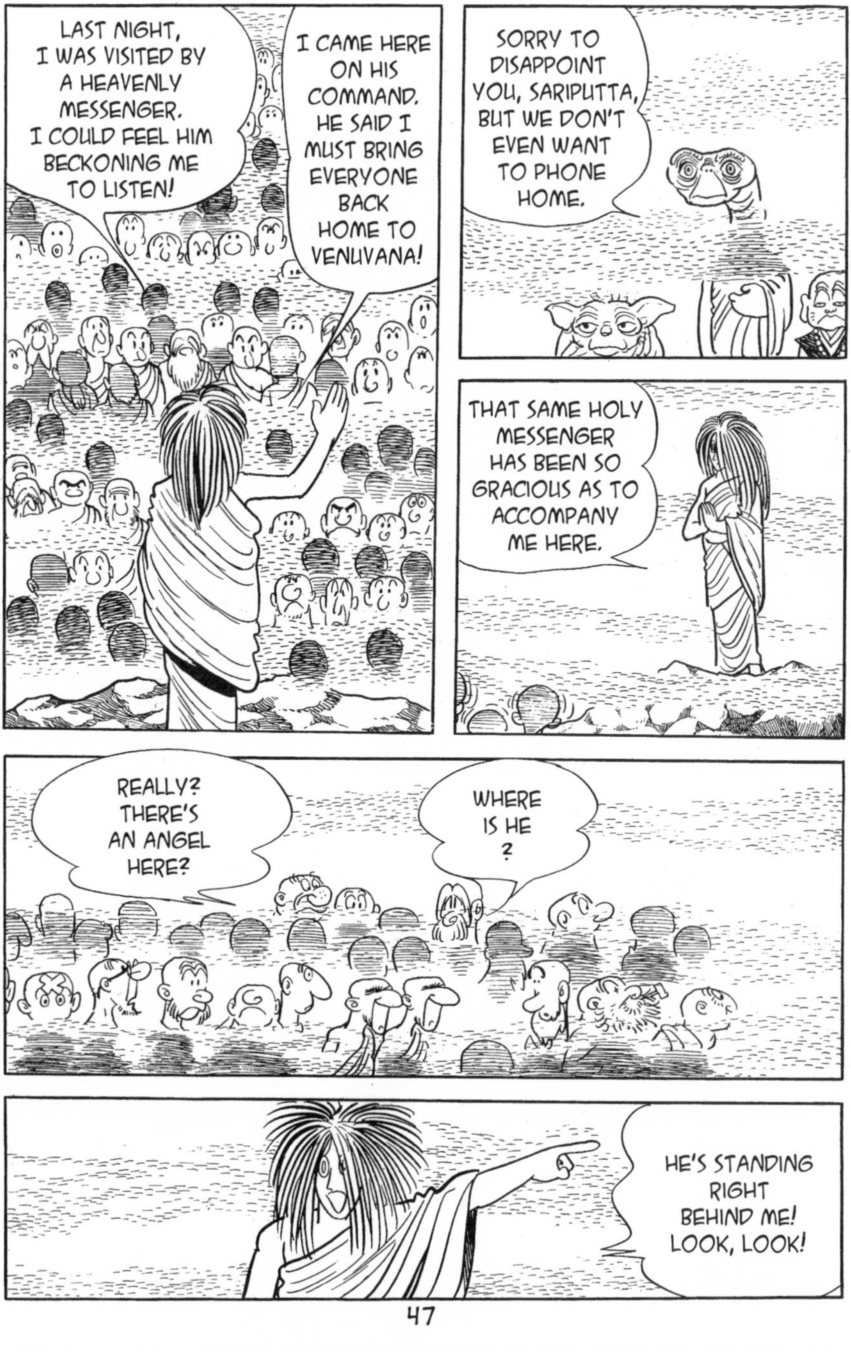
LAST NIGHT, I WAS VISITED BY A HEAVENLY MESSENGER. I COULD FEEL HIM BECKONING ME TO LISTEN!
I CAME HERE ON HIS COMMAND. HE SAID I MUST BRING EVERYONE BACK HOME TO VENUVANA!
SORRY TO DISAPPOINT YOU, SARIPUTTA, BUT WE DON'T EVEN WANT TO PHONE HOME.
THAT SAME HOLY MESSENGER HAS BEEN SO GRACIOUS AS TO ACCOMPANY ME HERE.
REALLY? THERE'S AN ANGEL HERE?
WHERE IS HE ?
HE'S STANDING RIGHT BEHIND ME! LOOK, LOOK!

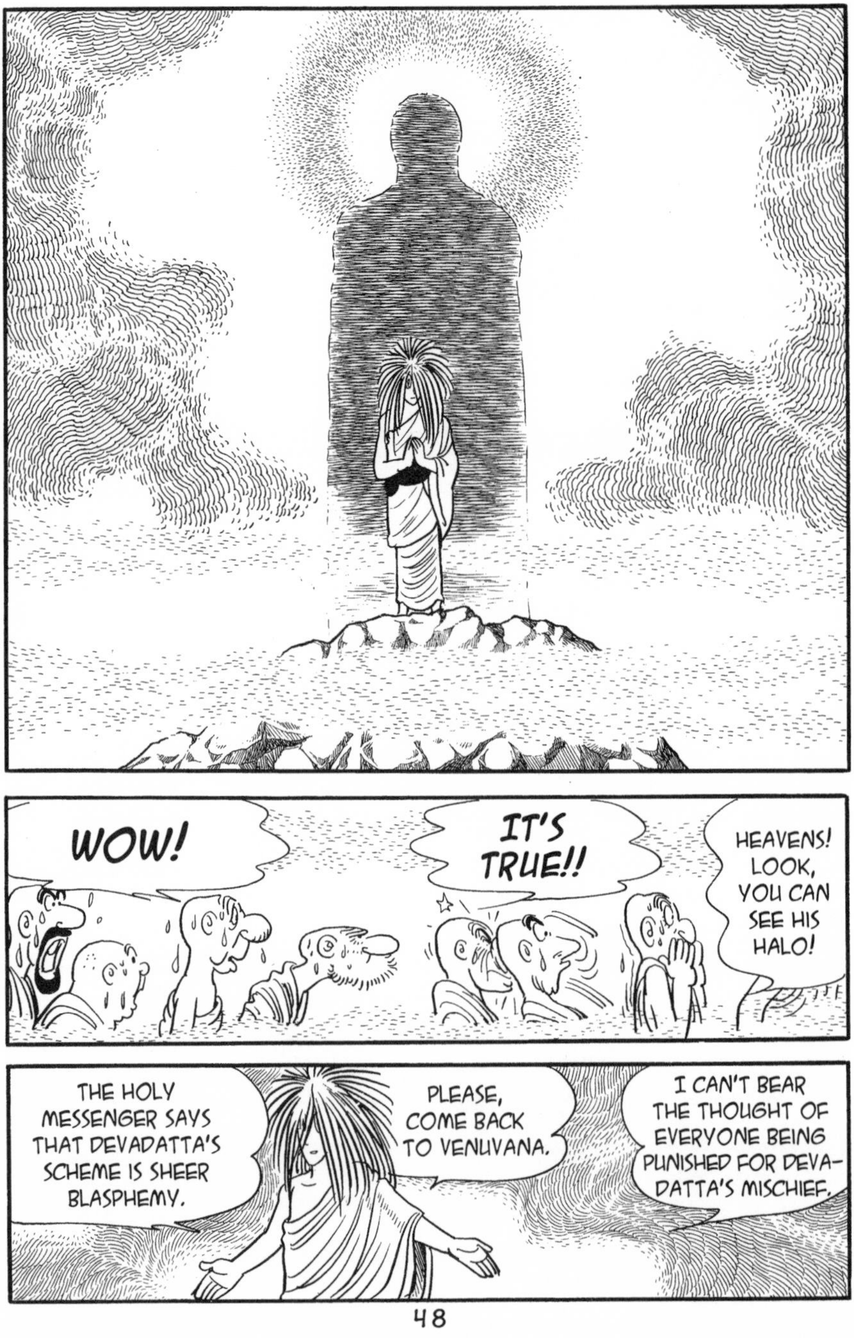
WOW!
IT'S TRUE!!
HEAVENS! LOOK, YOU CAN SEE HIS HALO!
THE HOLY MESSENGER SAYS THAT DEVADATTA'S SCHEME IS SHEER BLASPHEMY.
PLEASE, COME BACK TO VENUVANA.
I CAN'T BEAR THE THOUGHT OF EVERYONE BEING PUNISHED FOR DEVA-DATTA'S MISCHIEF.

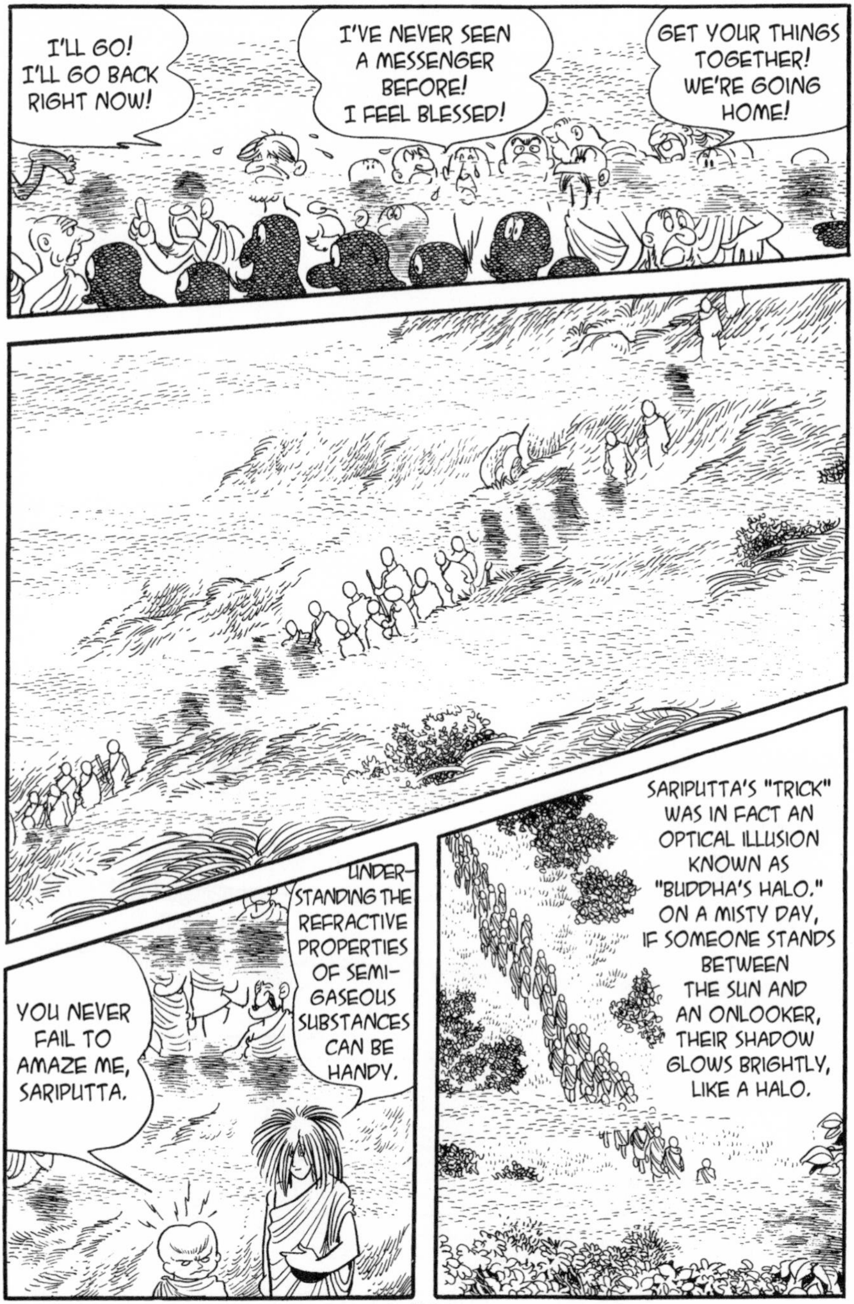
I'LL GO! I'LL GO BACK RIGHT NOW!
I'VE NEVER SEEN A MESSENGER BEFORE! I FEEL BLESSED!
GET YOUR THINGS TOGETHER! WE'RE GOING HOME!
YOU NEVER FAIL TO AMAZE ME, SARIPUTTA.
UNDER-STANDING THE REFRACTIVE PROPERTIES OF SEMI-GASEOUS SUBSTANCES CAN BE HANDY.
SARIPUTTA'S "TRICK" WAS IN FACT AN OPTICAL ILLUSION KNOWN AS "BUDDHA'S HALO." ON A MISTY DAY, IF SOMEONE STANDS BETWEEN THE SUN AND AN ONLOOKER, THEIR SHADOW GLOWS BRIGHTLY, LIKE A HALO.

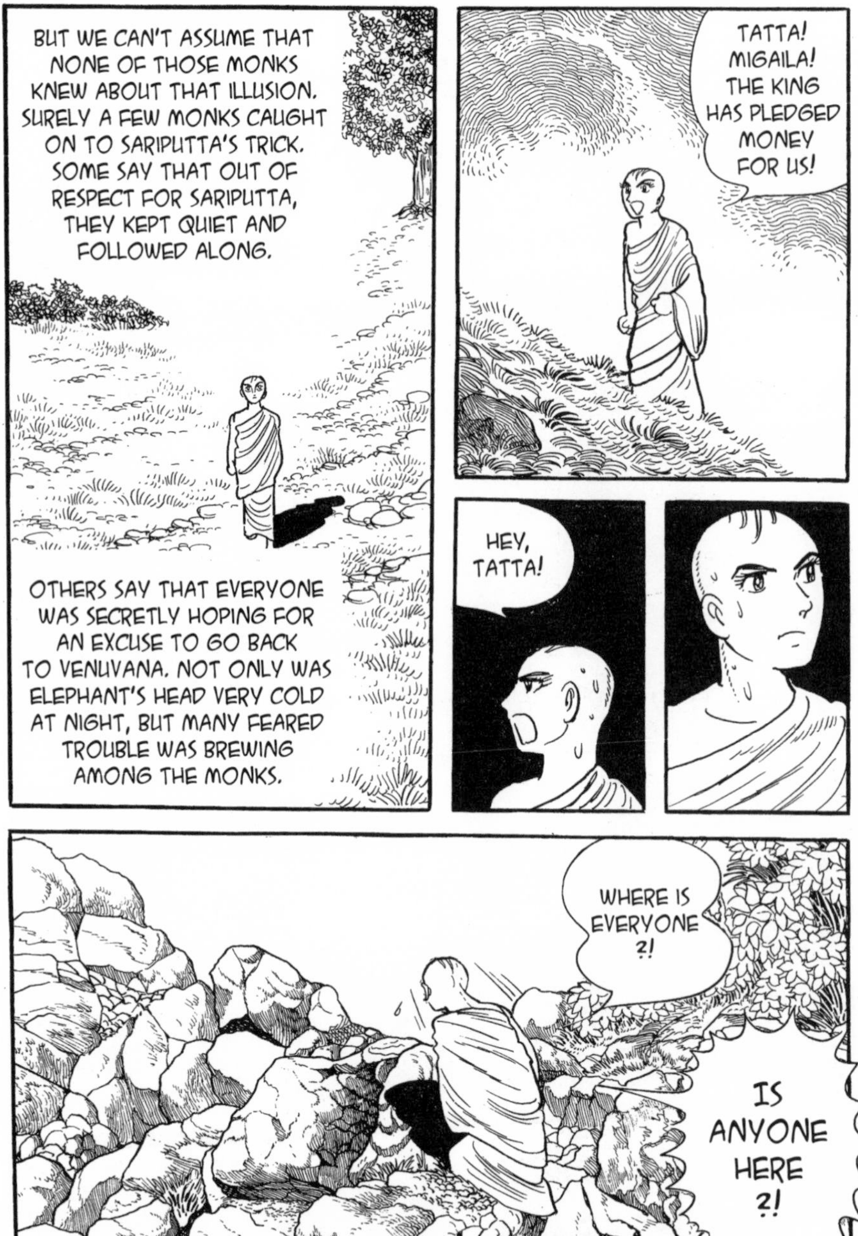
BUT WE CAN'T ASSUME THAT NONE OF THOSE MONKS KNEW ABOUT THAT ILLUSION. SURELY A FEW MONKS CAUGHT ON TO SARIPUTTA'S TRICK. SOME SAY THAT OUT OF RESPECT FOR SARIPUTTA, THEY KEPT QUIET AND FOLLOWED ALONG.
OTHERS SAY THAT EVERYONE WAS SECRETLY HOPING FOR AN EXCUSE TO GO BACK TO VENUVANA. NOT ONLY WAS ELEPHANT'S HEAD VERY COLD AT NIGHT, BUT MANY FEARED TROUBLE WAS BREWING AMONG THE MONKS.
TATTA! MIGAILA! THE KING HAS PLEDGED MONEY FOR US!
HEY, TATTA!
WHERE IS EVERYONE ?!
IS ANYONE HERE ?!

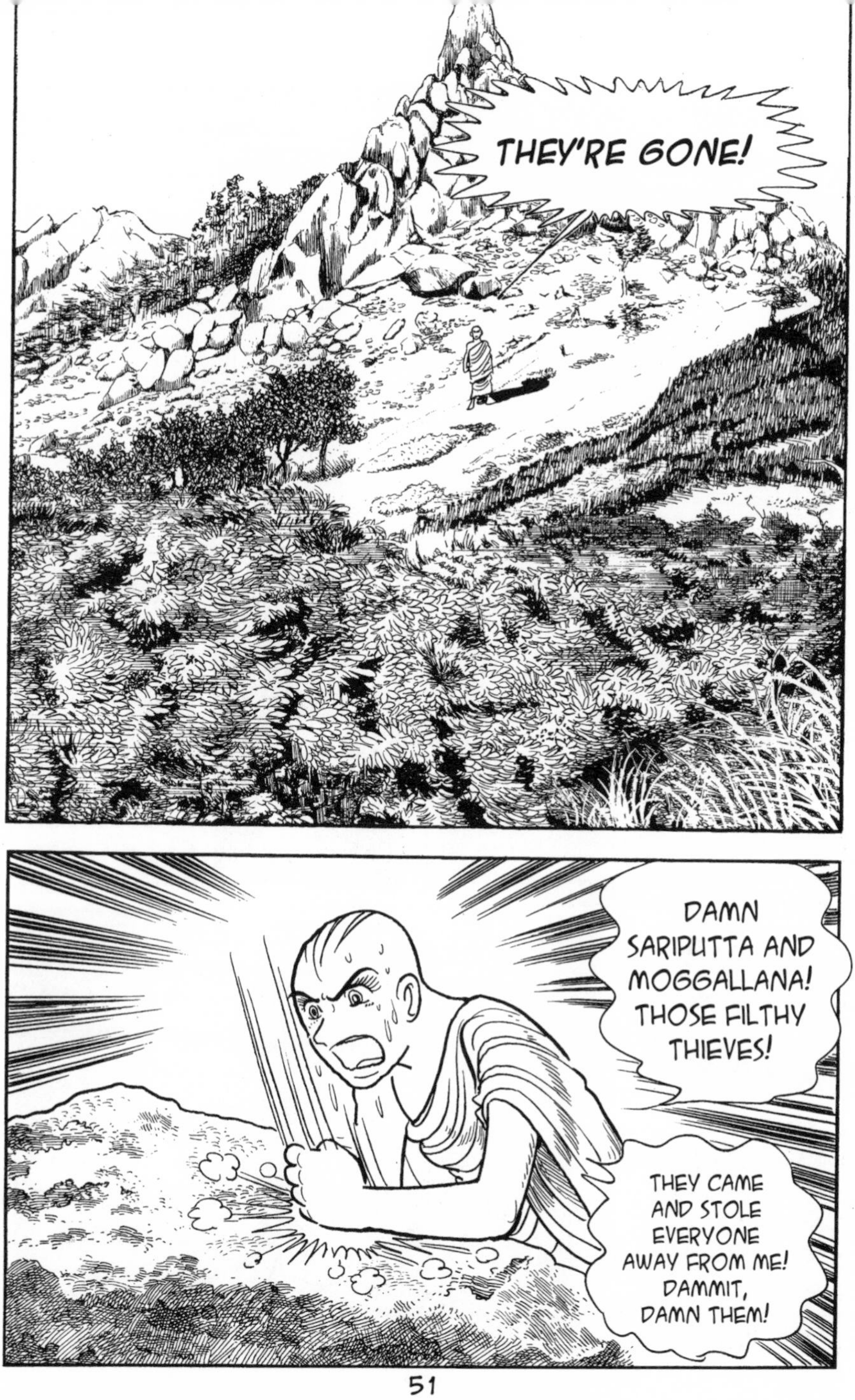
THEY'RE GONE!
DAMN SARIPUTTA AND MOGGALLANA! THOSE FILTHY THIEVES!
THEY CAME AND STOLE EVERYONE AWAY FROM ME! DAMMIT, DAMN THEM!

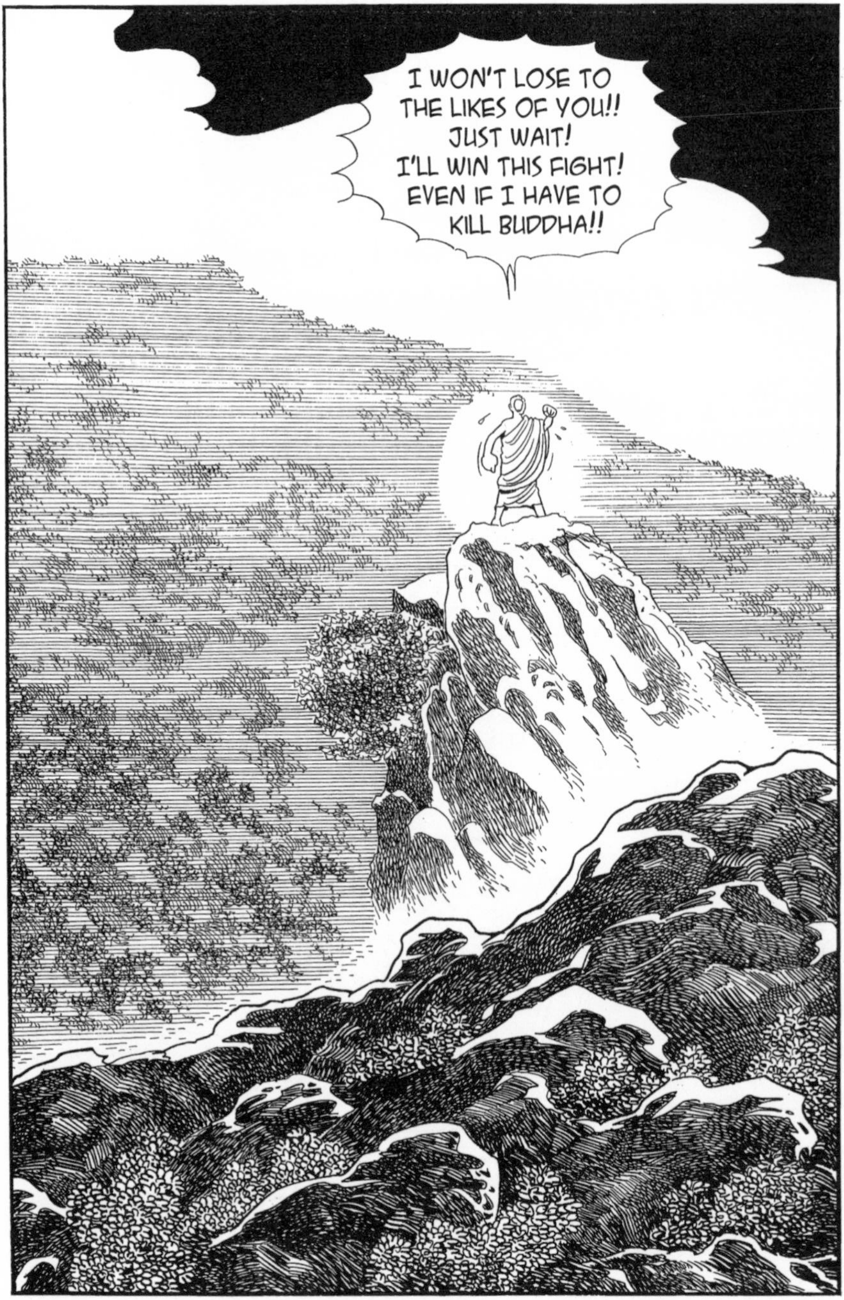
I WON'T LOSE TO THE LIKES OF YOU!! JUST WAIT! I'LL WIN THIS FIGHT! EVEN IF I HAVE TO KILL BUDDHA!!

CHAPTER NINE

NARADATTA

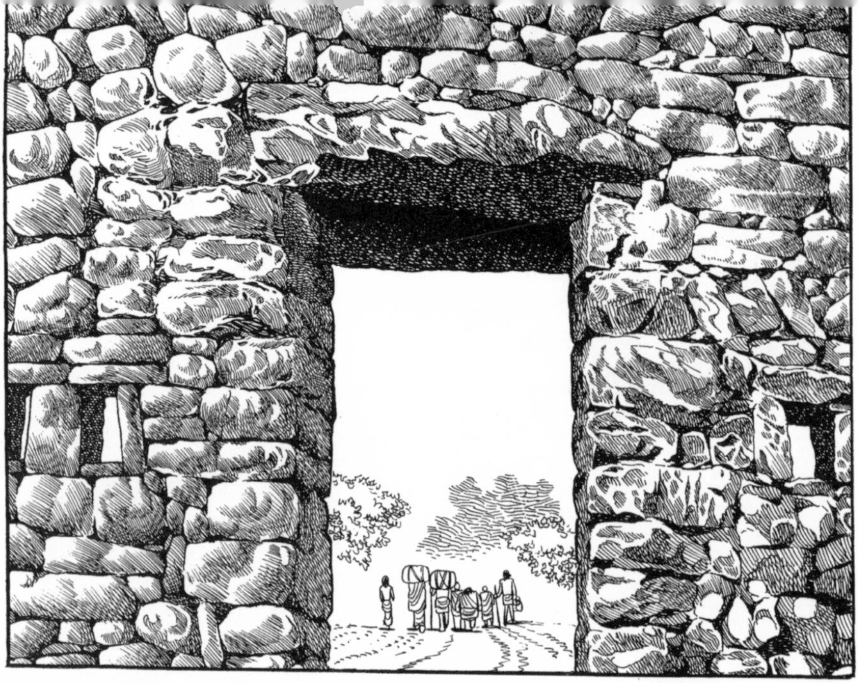

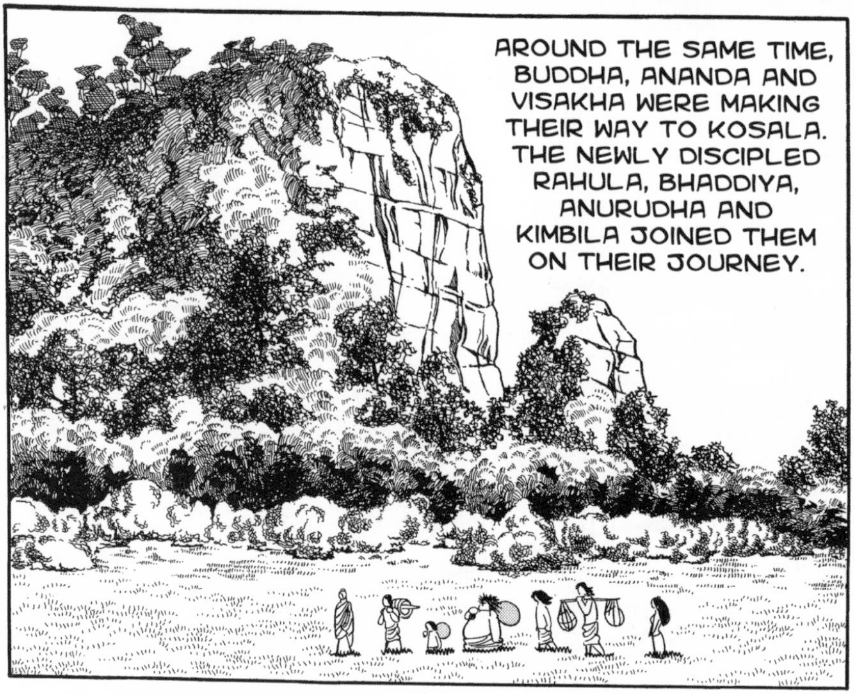
AROUND THE SAME TIME, BUDDHA, ANANDA AND VISAKHA WERE MAKING THEIR WAY TO KOSALA. THE NEWLY DISCIPLED RAHULA, BHADDIYA, ANURUDHA AND KIMBILA JOINED THEM ON THEIR JOURNEY.

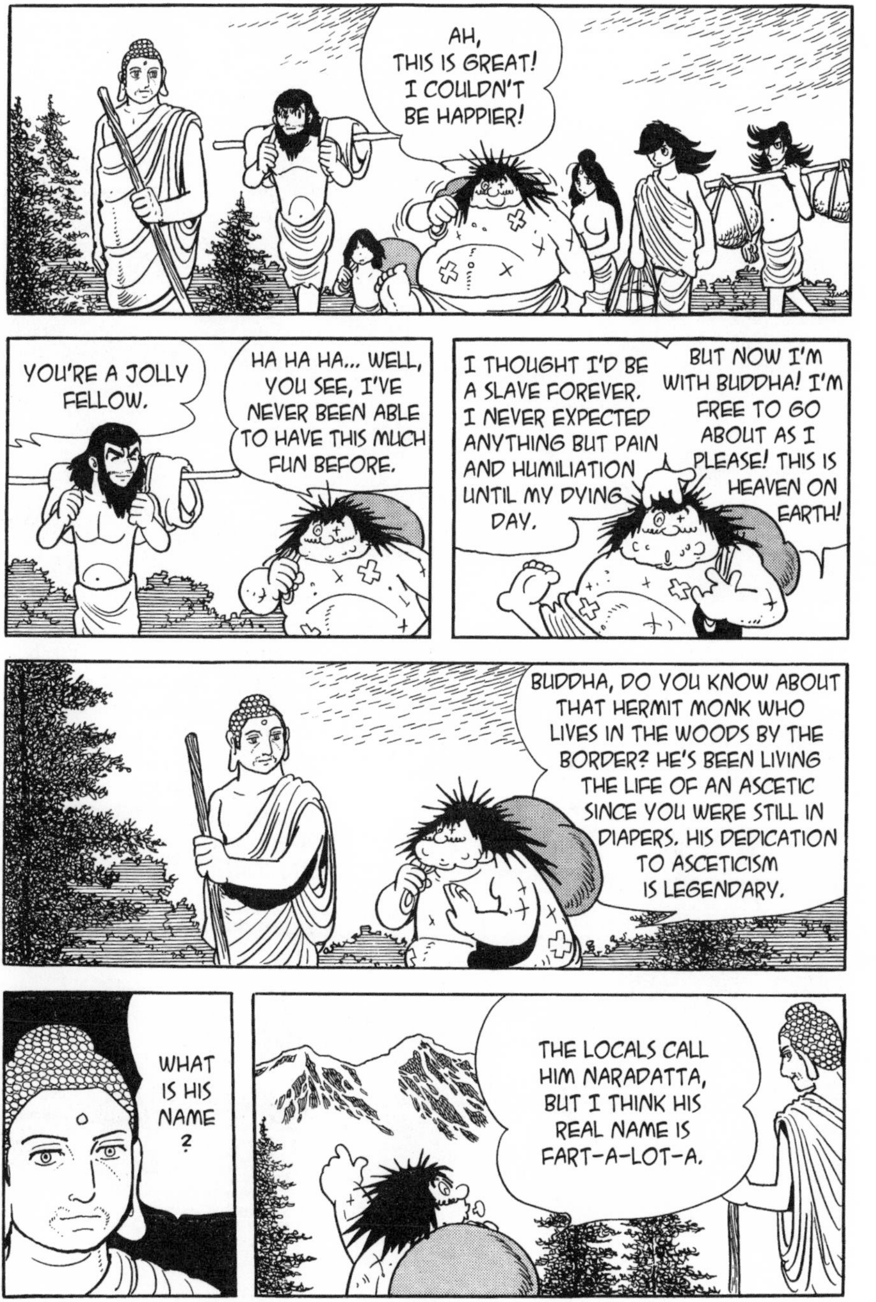
AH, THIS IS GREAT! I COULDN'T BE HAPPIER!
YOU'RE A JOLLY FELLOW.
HA HA HA... WELL, YOU SEE, I'VE NEVER BEEN ABLE TO HAVE THIS MUCH FUN BEFORE.
I THOUGHT I'D BE A SLAVE FOREVER. I NEVER EXPECTED ANYTHING BUT PAIN AND HUMILIATION UNTIL MY DYING DAY.
BUT NOW I'M WITH BUDDHA! I'M FREE TO GO ABOUT AS I PLEASE! THIS IS HEAVEN ON EARTH!
BUDDHA, DO YOU KNOW ABOUT THAT HERMIT MONK WHO LIVES IN THE WOODS BY THE BORDER? HE'S BEEN LIVING THE LIFE OF AN ASCETIC SINCE YOU WERE STILL IN DIAPERS. HIS DEDICATION TO ASCETICISM IS LEGENDARY.
WHAT IS HIS NAME?
THE LOCALS CALL HIM NARADATTA, BUT I THINK HIS REAL NAME IS FART-A-LOT-A.

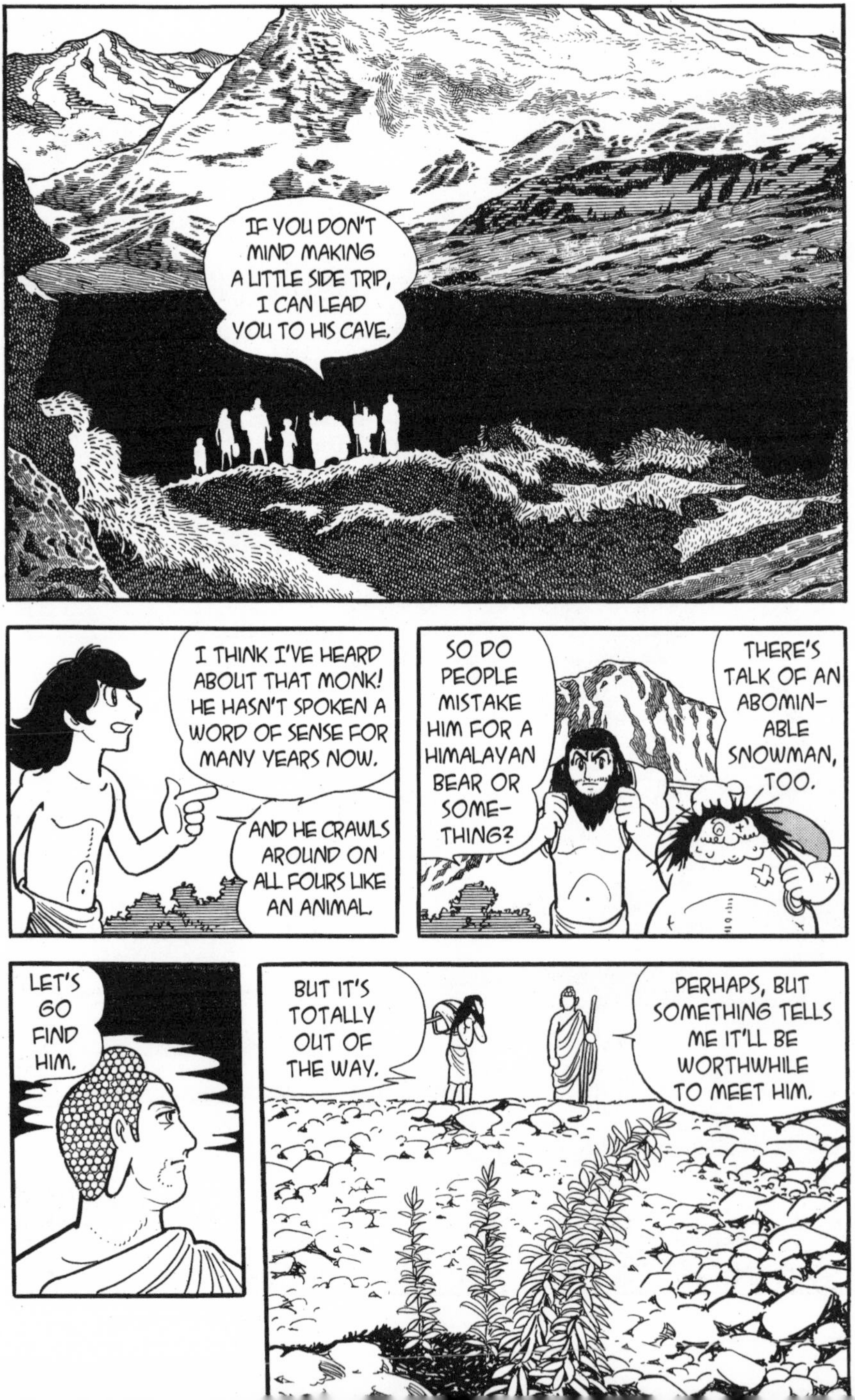
IF YOU DON'T MIND MAKING A LITTLE SIDE TRIP, I CAN LEAD YOU TO HIS CAVE.
I THINK I'VE HEARD ABOUT THAT MONK! HE HASN'T SPOKEN A WORD OF SENSE FOR MANY YEARS NOW.
AND HE CRAWLS AROUND ON ALL FOURS LIKE AN ANIMAL.
SO DO PEOPLE MISTAKE HIM FOR A HIMALAYAN BEAR OR SOME-THING?
THERE'S TALK OF AN ABOMIN-ABLE SNOWMAN, TOO.
LET'S GO FIND HIM.
BUT IT'S TOTALLY OUT OF THE WAY.
PERHAPS, BUT SOMETHING TELLS ME IT'LL BE WORTHWHILE TO MEET HIM.

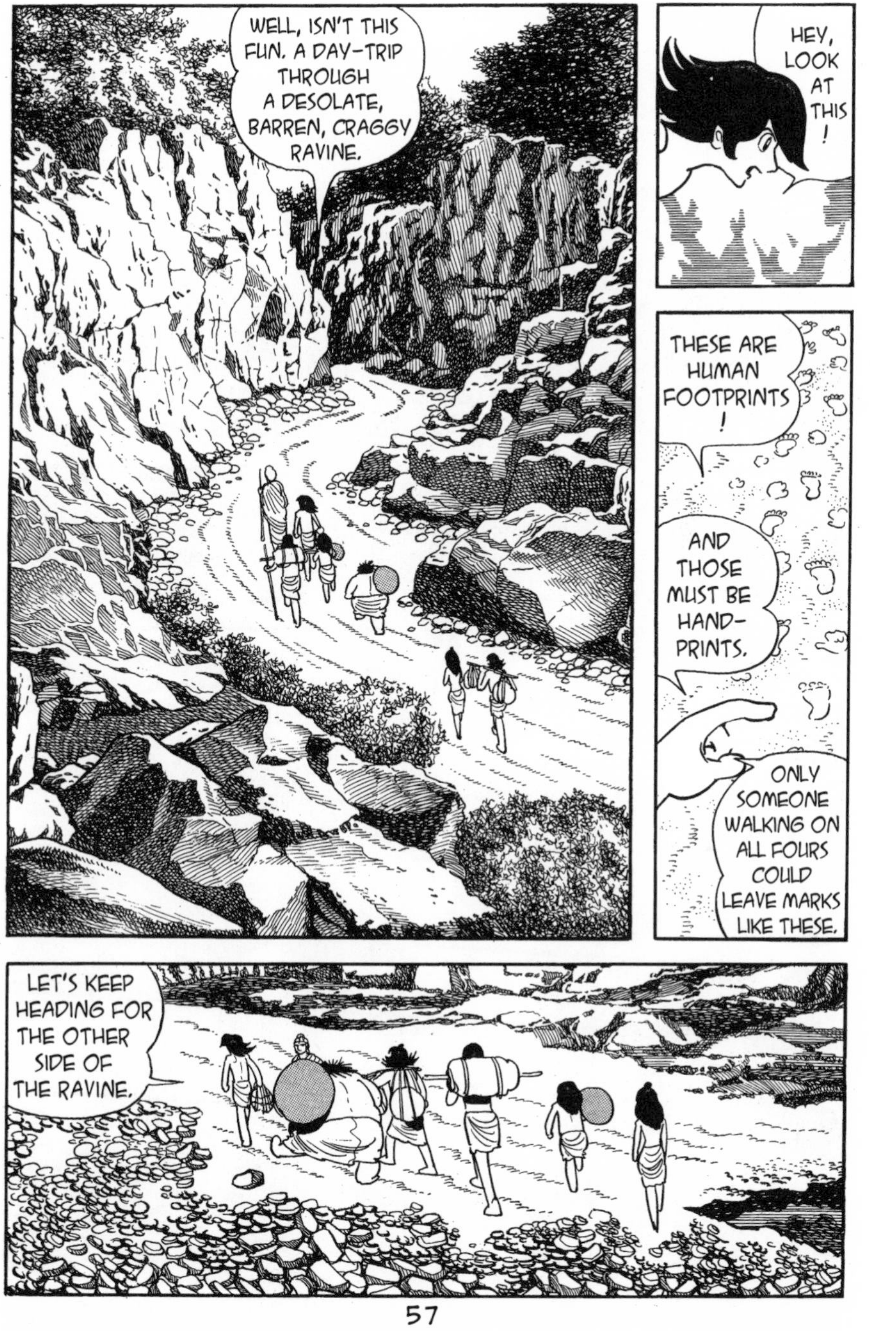
WELL, ISN'T THIS FUN. A DAY-TRIP THROUGH A DESOLATE, BARREN, CRAGGY RAVINE.
HEY, LOOK AT THIS!
THESE ARE HUMAN FOOTPRINTS!
AND THOSE MUST BE HAND-PRINTS.
ONLY SOMEONE WALKING ON ALL FOURS COULD LEAVE MARKS LIKE THESE.
LET'S KEEP HEADING FOR THE OTHER SIDE OF THE RAVINE.

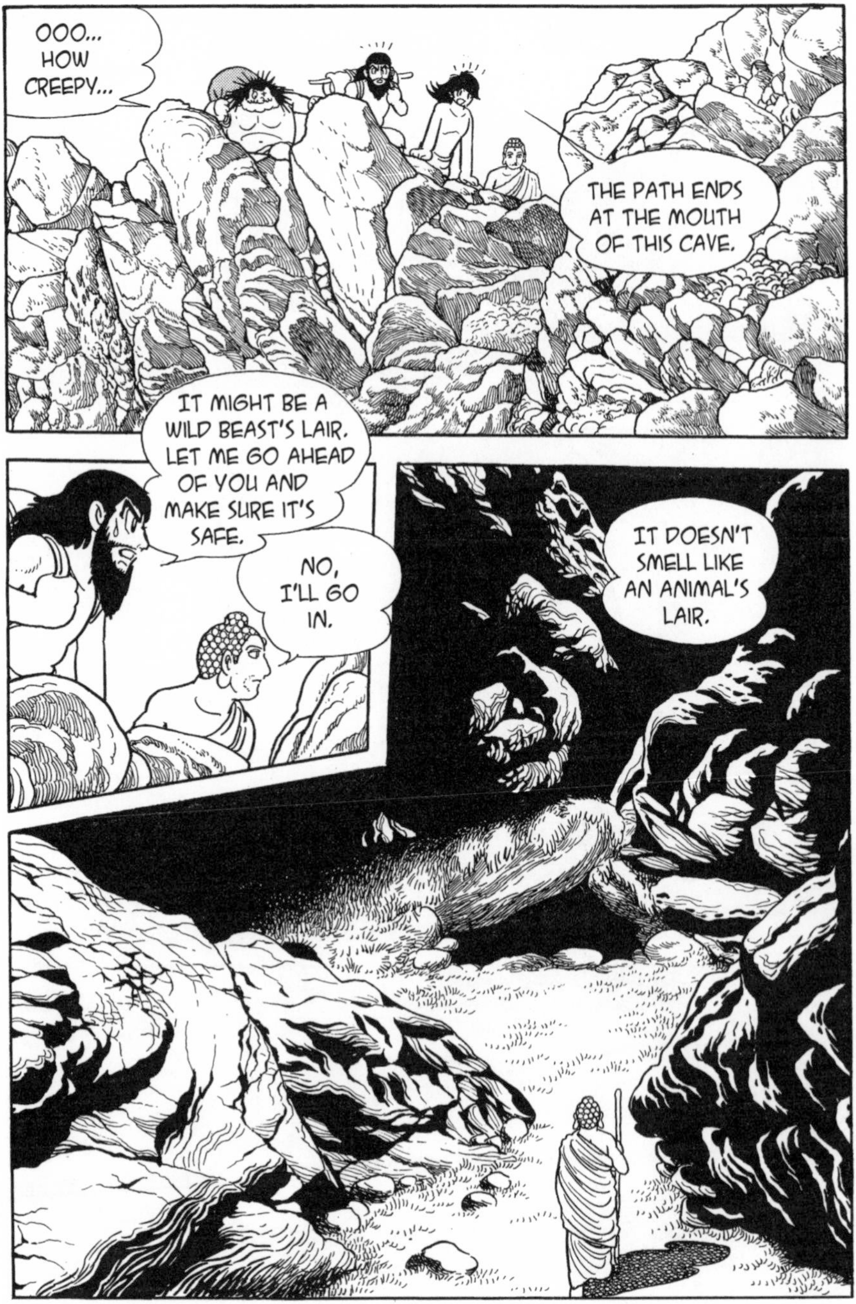
OOO... HOW CREEPY...
THE PATH ENDS AT THE MOUTH OF THIS CAVE.
IT MIGHT BE A WILD BEAST'S LAIR. LET ME GO AHEAD OF YOU AND MAKE SURE IT'S SAFE.
NO, I'LL GO IN.
IT DOESN'T SMELL LIKE AN ANIMAL'S LAIR.

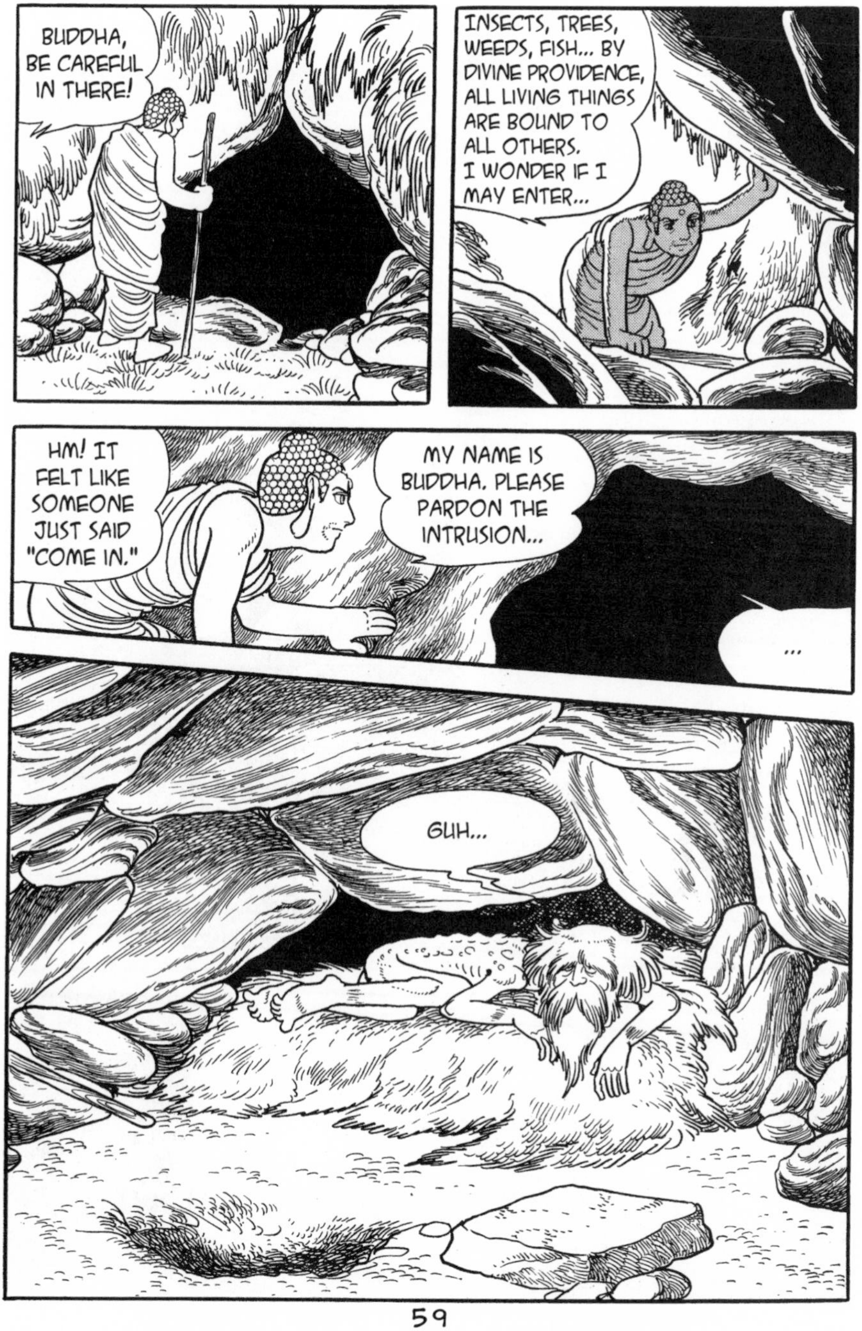
BUDDHA, BE CAREFUL IN THERE!
INSECTS, TREES, WEEDS, FISH... BY DIVINE PROVIDENCE, ALL LIVING THINGS ARE BOUND TO ALL OTHERS. I WONDER IF I MAY ENTER...
HM! IT FELT LIKE SOMEONE JUST SAID "COME IN."
MY NAME IS BUDDHA. PLEASE PARDON THE INTRUSION...
...
GUH...

UHN...
NUH...
G-GUH...

I WAS TOLD THAT YOUR NAME IS NARADATTA. IS THAT TRUE?

URG...
UNH...

?

YOU'RE TREM-BLING.

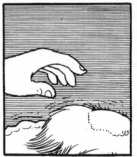

YOU'RE BURNING UP! WHAT A FEVER!

YOU'RE SO HOT THAT YOU'RE SHIVERING.

I ONLY WISH I HAD GOTTEN HERE SOONER.

60

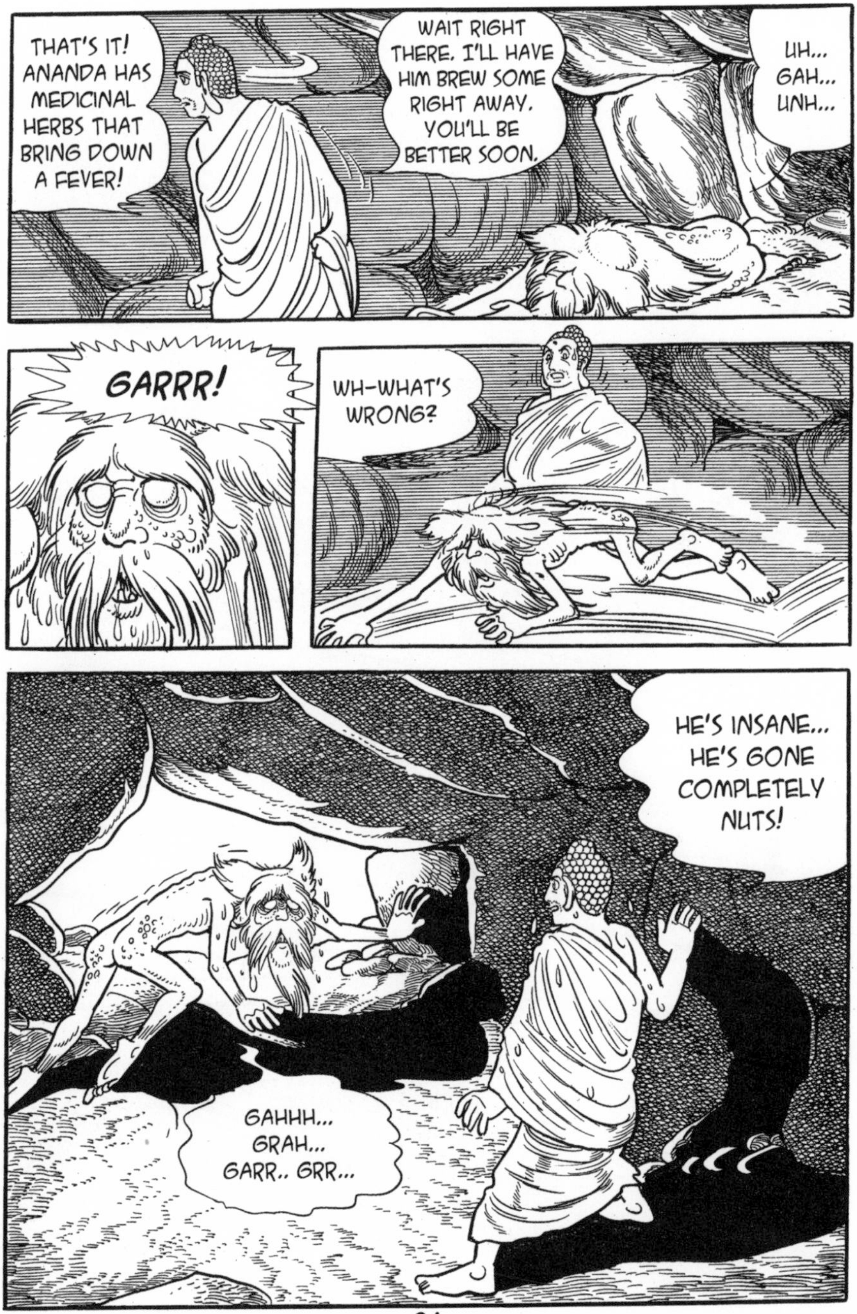
THAT'S IT! ANANDA HAS MEDICINAL HERBS THAT BRING DOWN A FEVER!
WAIT RIGHT THERE. I'LL HAVE HIM BREW SOME RIGHT AWAY. YOU'LL BE BETTER SOON.
UH... GAH... UNH...
GARRR!
WH-WHAT'S WRONG?
HE'S INSANE... HE'S GONE COMPLETELY NUTS!
GAHHH... GRAH... GARR.. GRR...

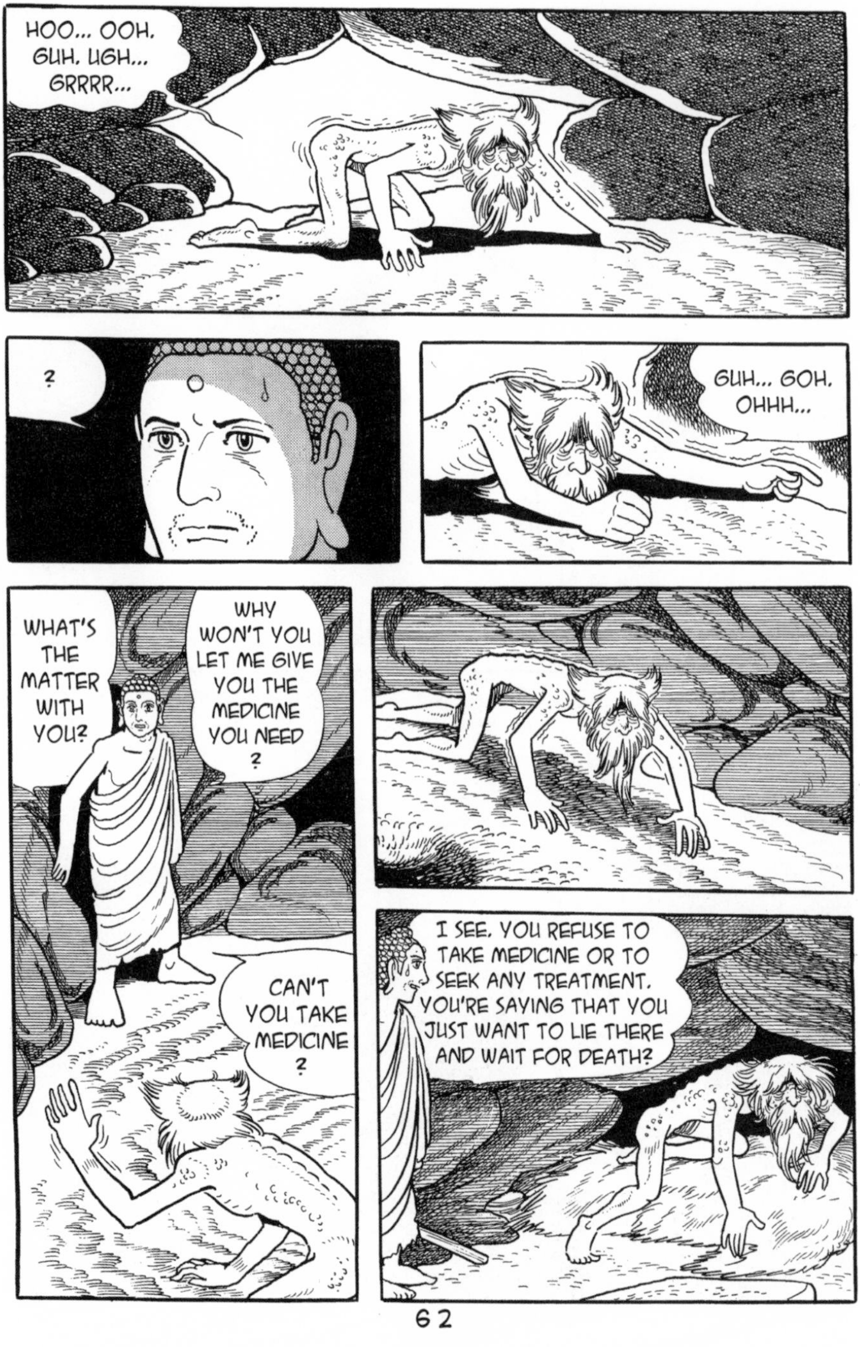
HOO... OOH. GUH. UGH... GRRRR...
?
GUH... GOH. OHHH...
WHAT'S THE MATTER WITH YOU?
WHY WON'T YOU LET ME GIVE YOU THE MEDICINE YOU NEED?
CAN'T YOU TAKE MEDICINE?
I SEE. YOU REFUSE TO TAKE MEDICINE OR TO SEEK ANY TREATMENT. YOU'RE SAYING THAT YOU JUST WANT TO LIE THERE AND WAIT FOR DEATH?

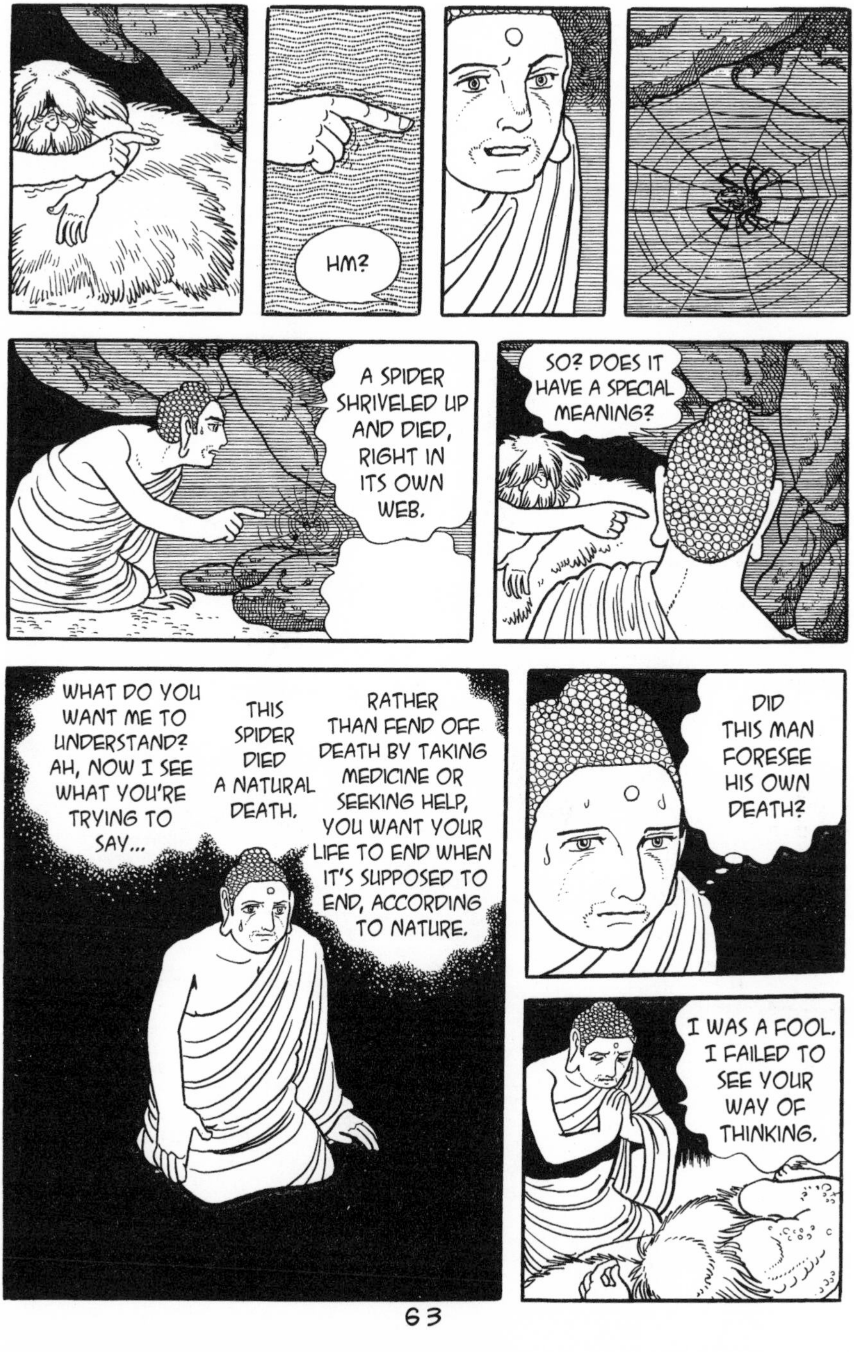
HM?
A SPIDER SHRIVELED UP AND DIED, RIGHT IN ITS OWN WEB.
SO? DOES IT HAVE A SPECIAL MEANING?
WHAT DO YOU WANT ME TO UNDERSTAND? AH, NOW I SEE WHAT YOU'RE TRYING TO SAY...
THIS SPIDER DIED A NATURAL DEATH.
RATHER THAN FEND OFF DEATH BY TAKING MEDICINE OR SEEKING HELP, YOU WANT YOUR LIFE TO END WHEN IT'S SUPPOSED TO END, ACCORDING TO NATURE.
DID THIS MAN FORESEE HIS OWN DEATH?
I WAS A FOOL. I FAILED TO SEE YOUR WAY OF THINKING.

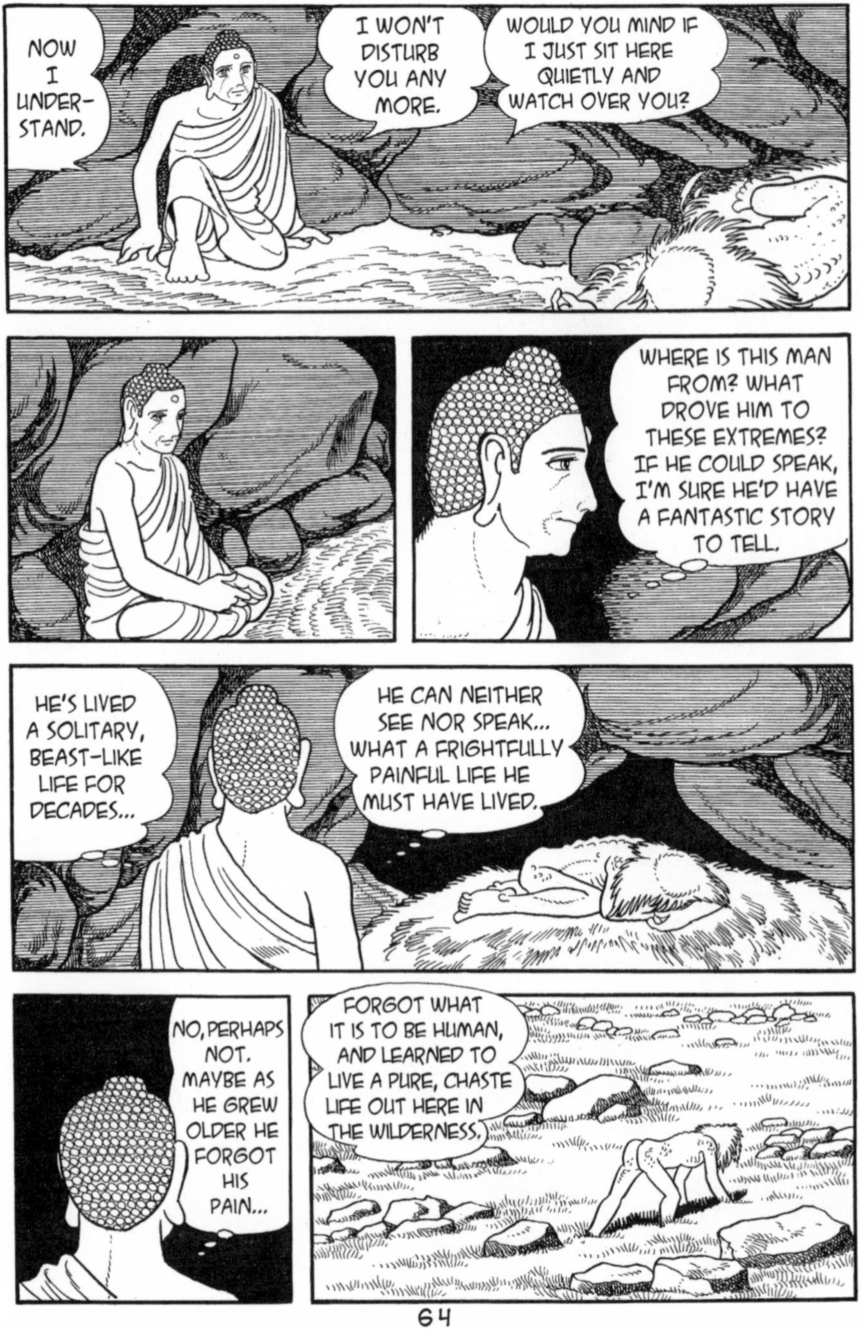
NOW I UNDER-STAND.
I WON'T DISTURB YOU ANY MORE.
WOULD YOU MIND IF I JUST SIT HERE QUIETLY AND WATCH OVER YOU?
WHERE IS THIS MAN FROM? WHAT DROVE HIM TO THESE EXTREMES? IF HE COULD SPEAK, I'M SURE HE'D HAVE A FANTASTIC STORY TO TELL.
HE'S LIVED A SOLITARY, BEAST-LIKE LIFE FOR DECADES...
HE CAN NEITHER SEE NOR SPEAK... WHAT A FRIGHTFULLY PAINFUL LIFE HE MUST HAVE LIVED.
NO, PERHAPS NOT. MAYBE AS HE GREW OLDER HE FORGOT HIS PAIN...
FORGOT WHAT IT IS TO BE HUMAN, AND LEARNED TO LIVE A PURE, CHASTE LIFE OUT HERE IN THE WILDERNESS.

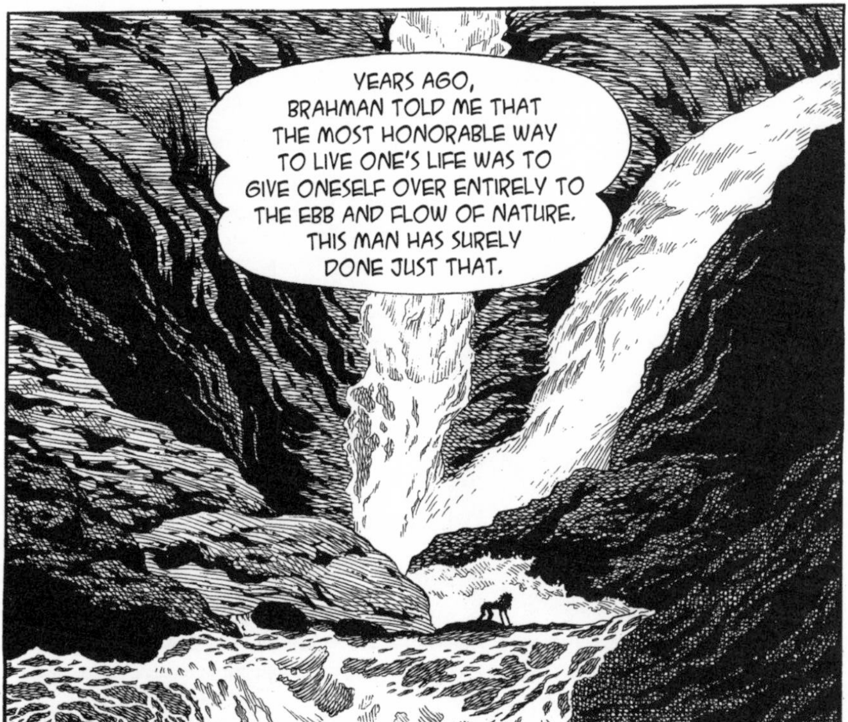
YEARS AGO, BRAHMAN TOLD ME THAT THE MOST HONORABLE WAY TO LIVE ONE'S LIFE WAS TO GIVE ONESELF OVER ENTIRELY TO THE EBB AND FLOW OF NATURE. THIS MAN HAS SURELY DONE JUST THAT.

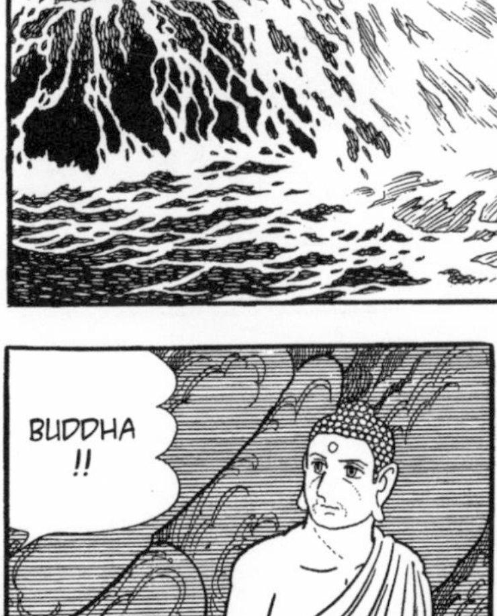
BUDDHA !!

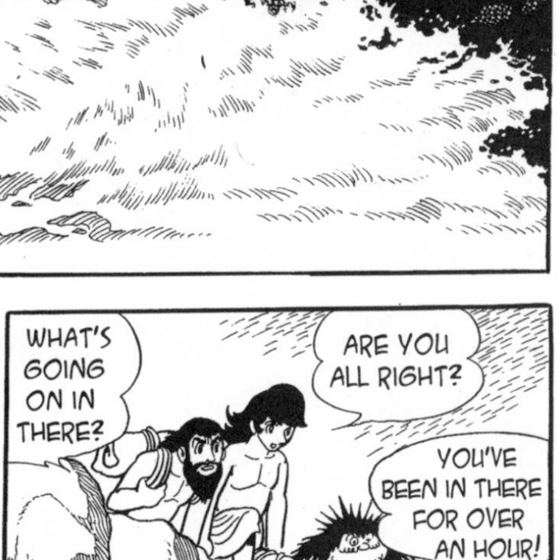
WHAT'S GOING ON IN THERE?
ARE YOU ALL RIGHT?
YOU'VE BEEN IN THERE FOR OVER AN HOUR!

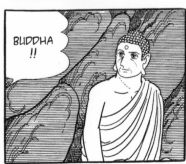

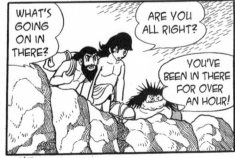

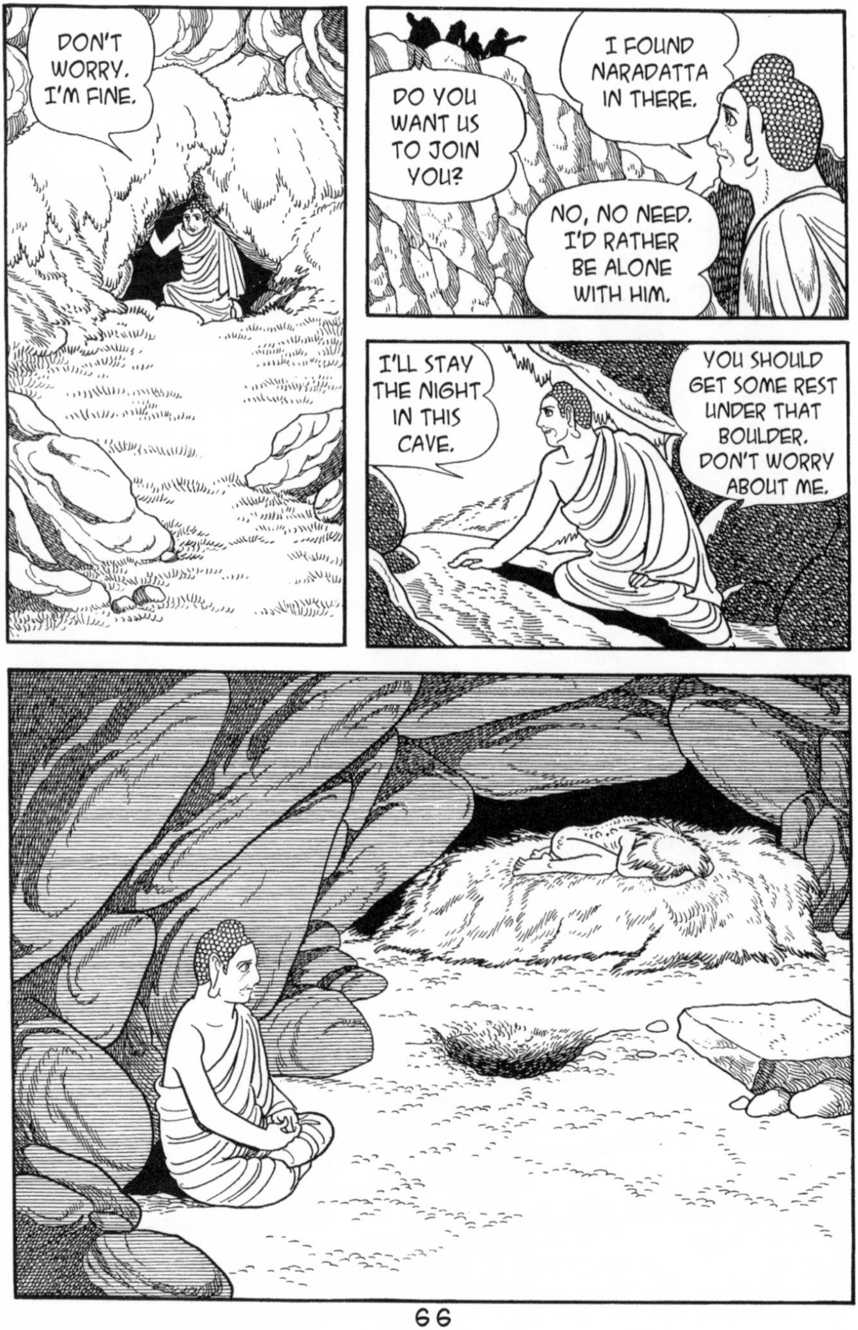
DON'T WORRY. I'M FINE.
I FOUND NARADATTA IN THERE.
DO YOU WANT US TO JOIN YOU?
NO, NO NEED. I'D RATHER BE ALONE WITH HIM.
I'LL STAY THE NIGHT IN THIS CAVE.
YOU SHOULD GET SOME REST UNDER THAT BOULDER. DON'T WORRY ABOUT ME.

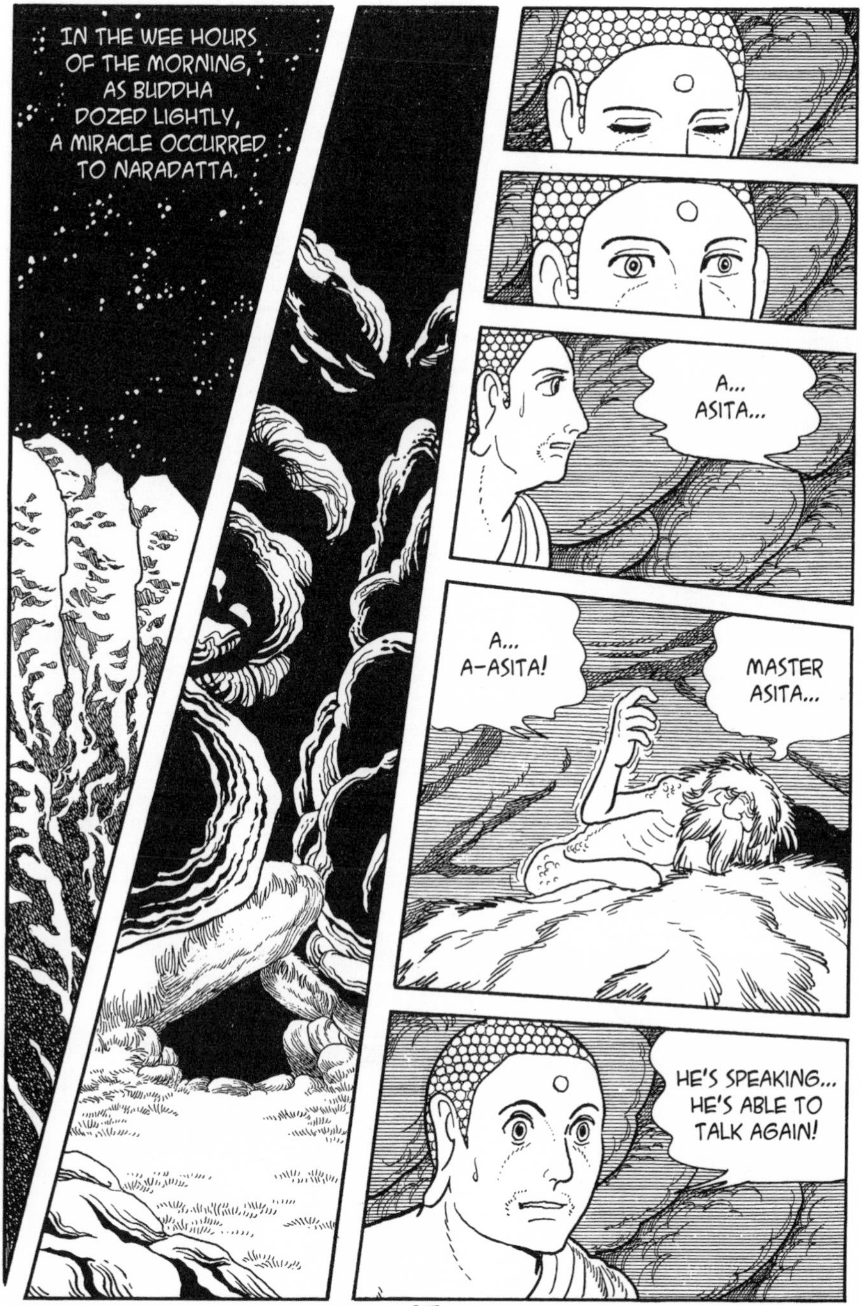
IN THE WEE HOURS OF THE MORNING, AS BUDDHA DOZED LIGHTLY, A MIRACLE OCCURRED TO NARADATTA.
A... ASITA...
A... A-ASITA!
MASTER ASITA...
HE'S SPEAKING... HE'S ABLE TO TALK AGAIN!

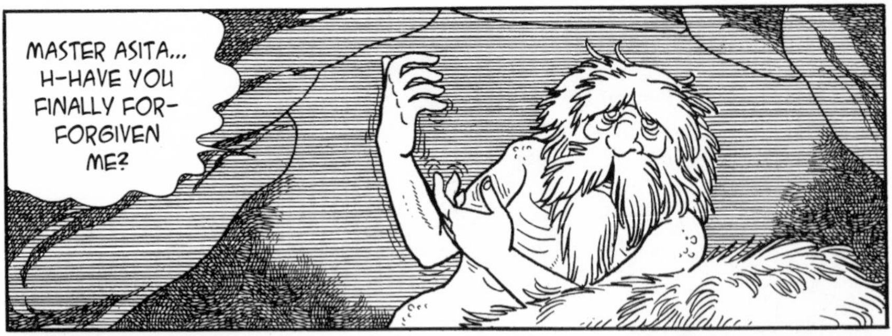
MASTER ASITA... H-HAVE YOU FINALLY FOR-FORGIVEN ME?

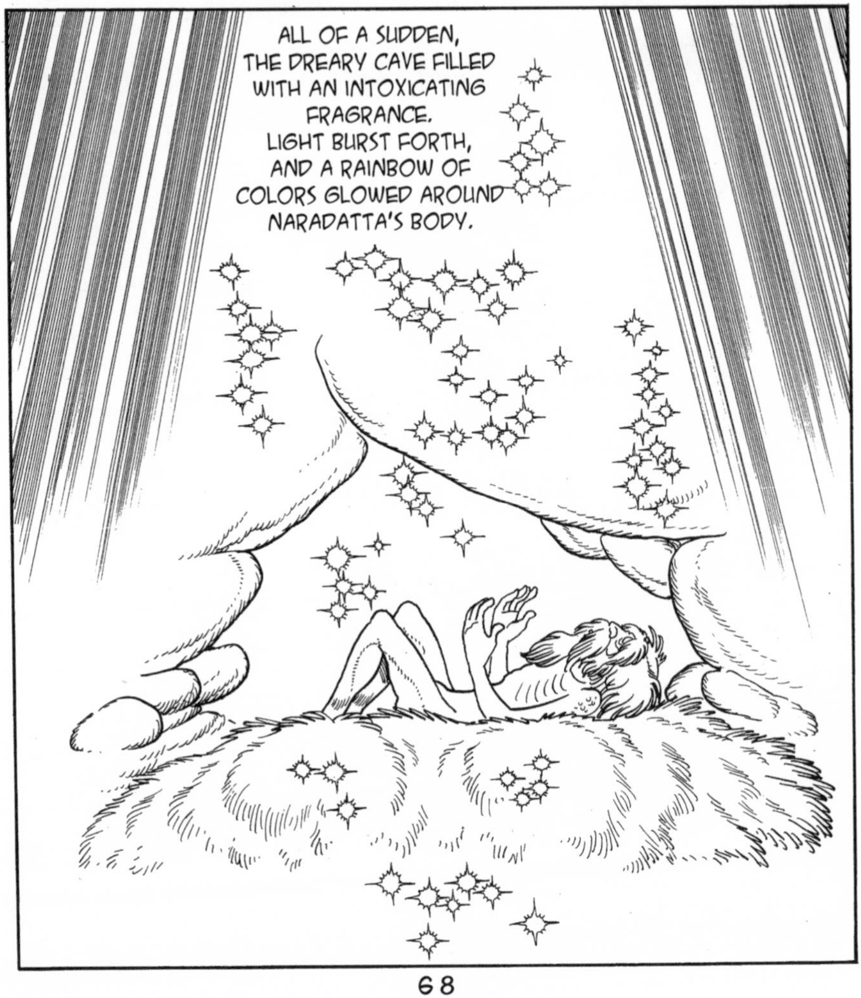
ALL OF A SUDDEN, THE DREARY CAVE FILLED WITH AN INTOXICATING FRAGRANCE. LIGHT BURST FORTH, AND A RAINBOW OF COLORS GLOWED AROUND NARADATTA'S BODY.

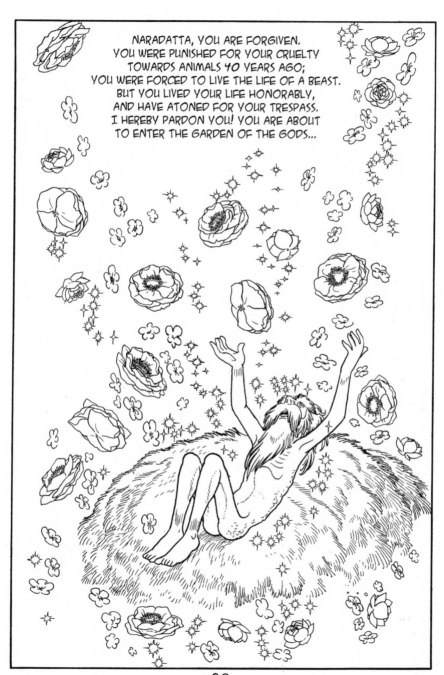

NARADATTA, YOU ARE FORGIVEN.
YOU WERE PUNISHED FOR YOUR CRUELTY
TOWARDS ANIMALS 40 YEARS AGO;
YOU WERE FORCED TO LIVE THE LIFE OF A BEAST.
BUT YOU LIVED YOUR LIFE HONORABLY,
AND HAVE ATONED FOR YOUR TRESPASS.
I HEREBY PARDON YOU! YOU ARE ABOUT
TO ENTER THE GARDEN OF THE GODS...

69

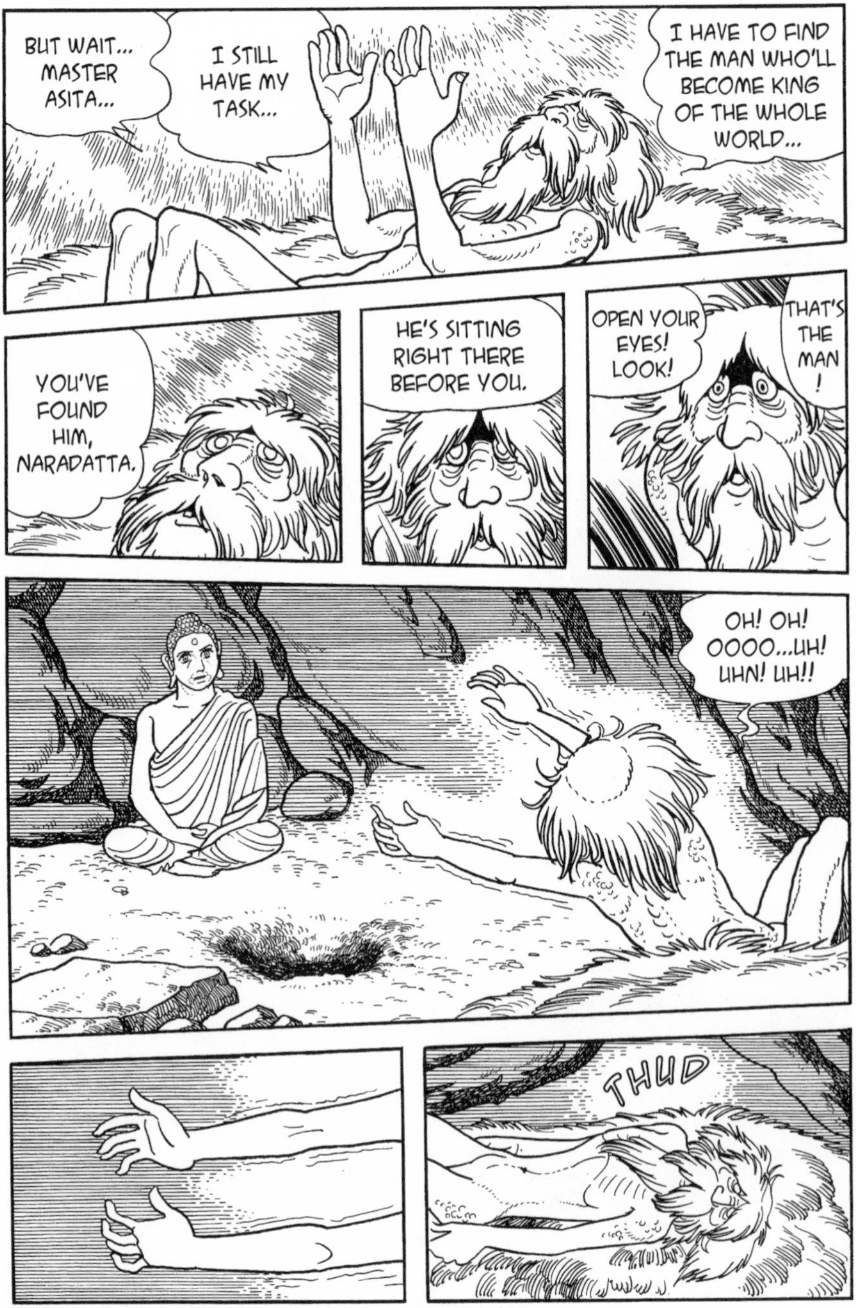
BUT WAIT... MASTER ASITA...
I STILL HAVE MY TASK...
I HAVE TO FIND THE MAN WHO'LL BECOME KING OF THE WHOLE WORLD...
YOU'VE FOUND HIM, NARADATTA.
HE'S SITTING RIGHT THERE BEFORE YOU.
OPEN YOUR EYES! LOOK!
THAT'S THE MAN!
OH! OH! OOOO...UH! UHN! UH!!
THUD

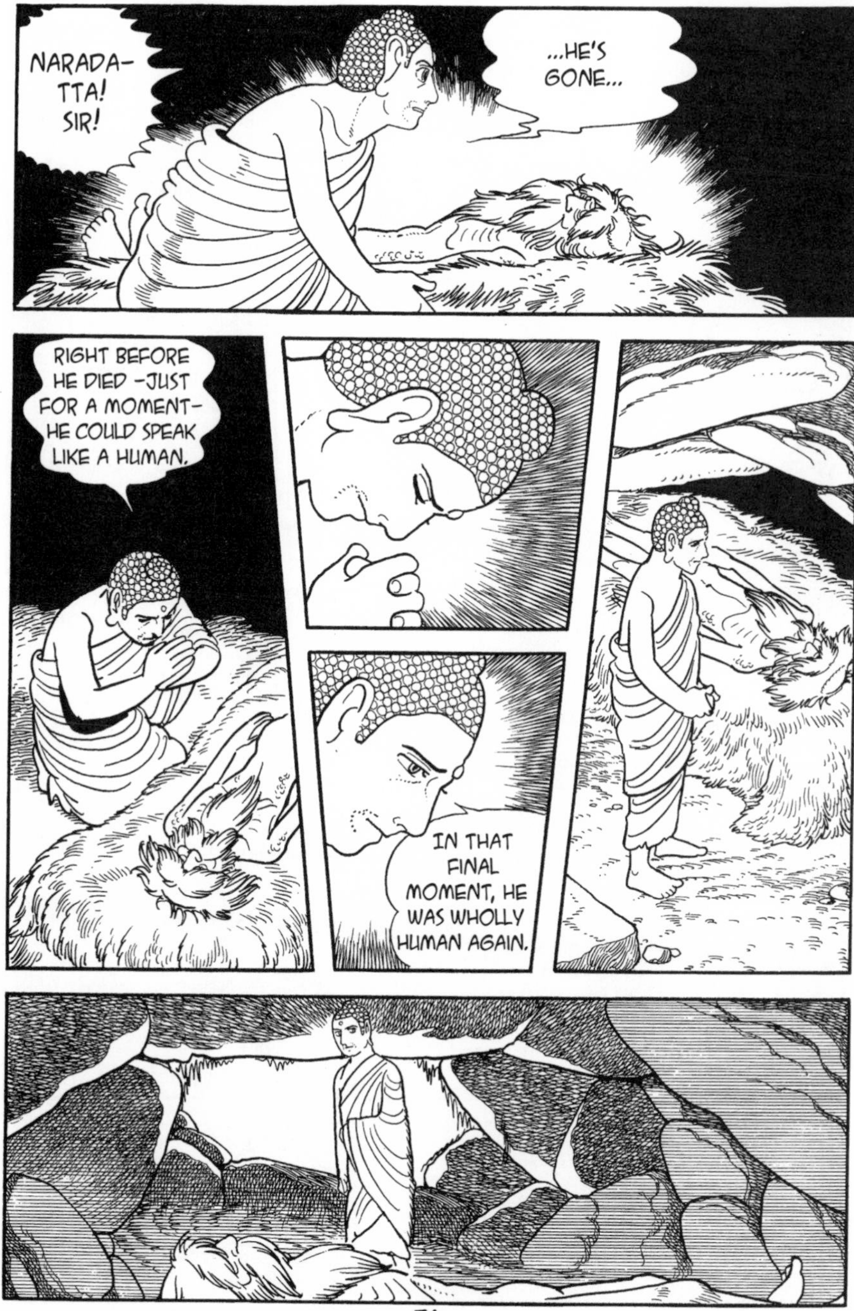
NARADA-TTA! SIR!
...HE'S GONE...
RIGHT BEFORE HE DIED -JUST FOR A MOMENT- HE COULD SPEAK LIKE A HUMAN.
IN THAT FINAL MOMENT, HE WAS WHOLLY HUMAN AGAIN.

HEY LOOK, BUDDHA'S BACK!

BUDDHA! WHAT HAPPENED?

NARADATTA PASSED AWAY A LITTLE WHILE AGO.

WHAT?

SHOULD WE BRING OUT HIS REMAINS?

NO, JUST LET HIM REST WHERE HE IS. LEAVE HIS BODY FOR NATURE TO TEND TO.

WHAT KIND OF PERSON WAS HE?

A FINE MAN. FINER THAN I COULD EVER HOPE TO BE.

HE WAS CLOSER TO GOD THAN ANYONE I HAVE EVER MET IN MY LIFE.

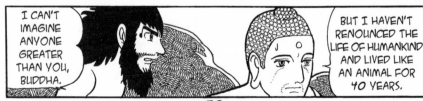

I CAN'T IMAGINE ANYONE GREATER THAN YOU, BUDDHA.

BUT I HAVEN'T RENOUNCED THE LIFE OF HUMANKIND AND LIVED LIKE AN ANIMAL FOR 40 YEARS.

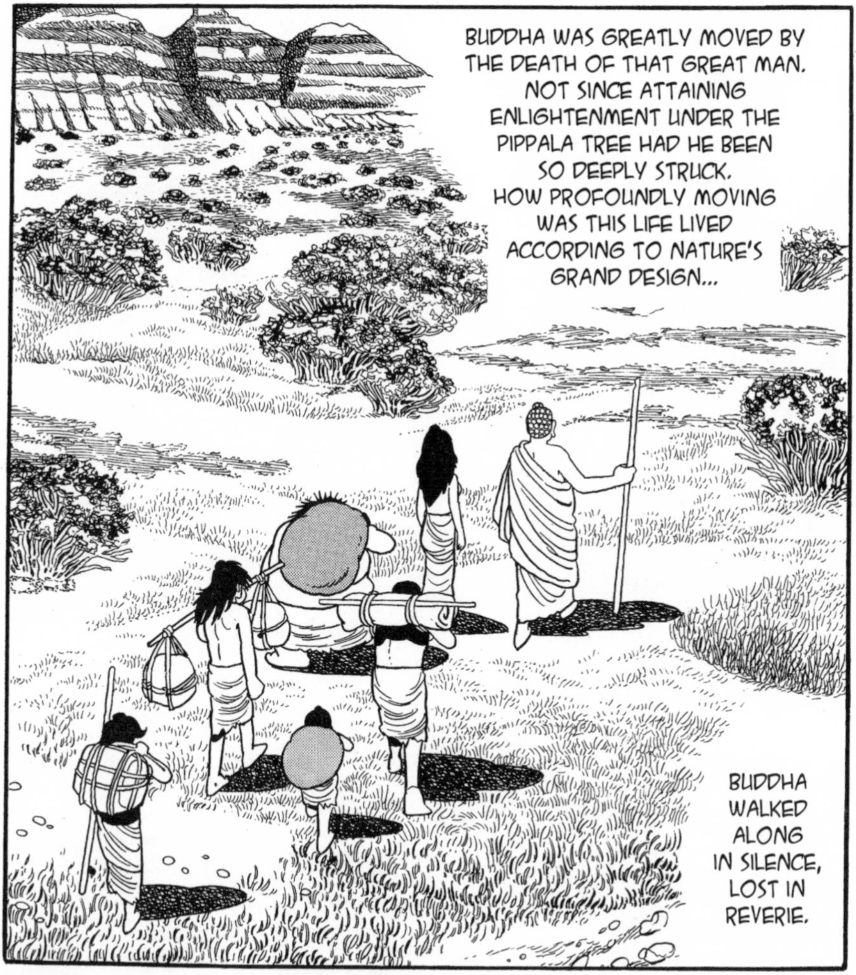
BUDDHA WAS GREATLY MOVED BY THE DEATH OF THAT GREAT MAN. NOT SINCE ATTAINING ENLIGHTENMENT UNDER THE PIPPALA TREE HAD HE BEEN SO DEEPLY STRUCK. HOW PROFOUNDLY MOVING WAS THIS LIFE LIVED ACCORDING TO NATURE'S GRAND DESIGN...
BUDDHA WALKED ALONG IN SILENCE, LOST IN REVERIE.

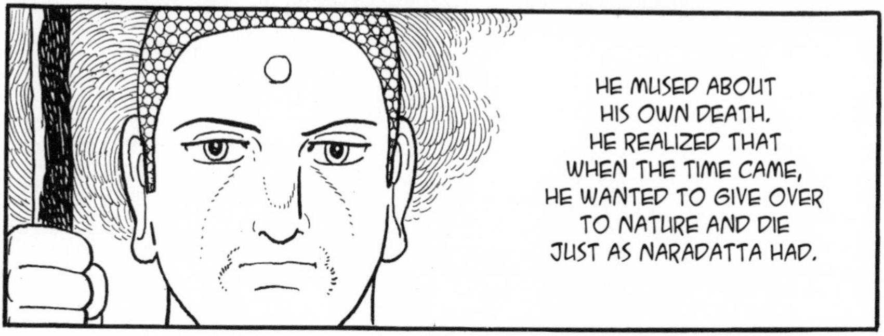
HE MUSED ABOUT HIS OWN DEATH. HE REALIZED THAT WHEN THE TIME CAME, HE WANTED TO GIVE OVER TO NATURE AND DIE JUST AS NARADATTA HAD.

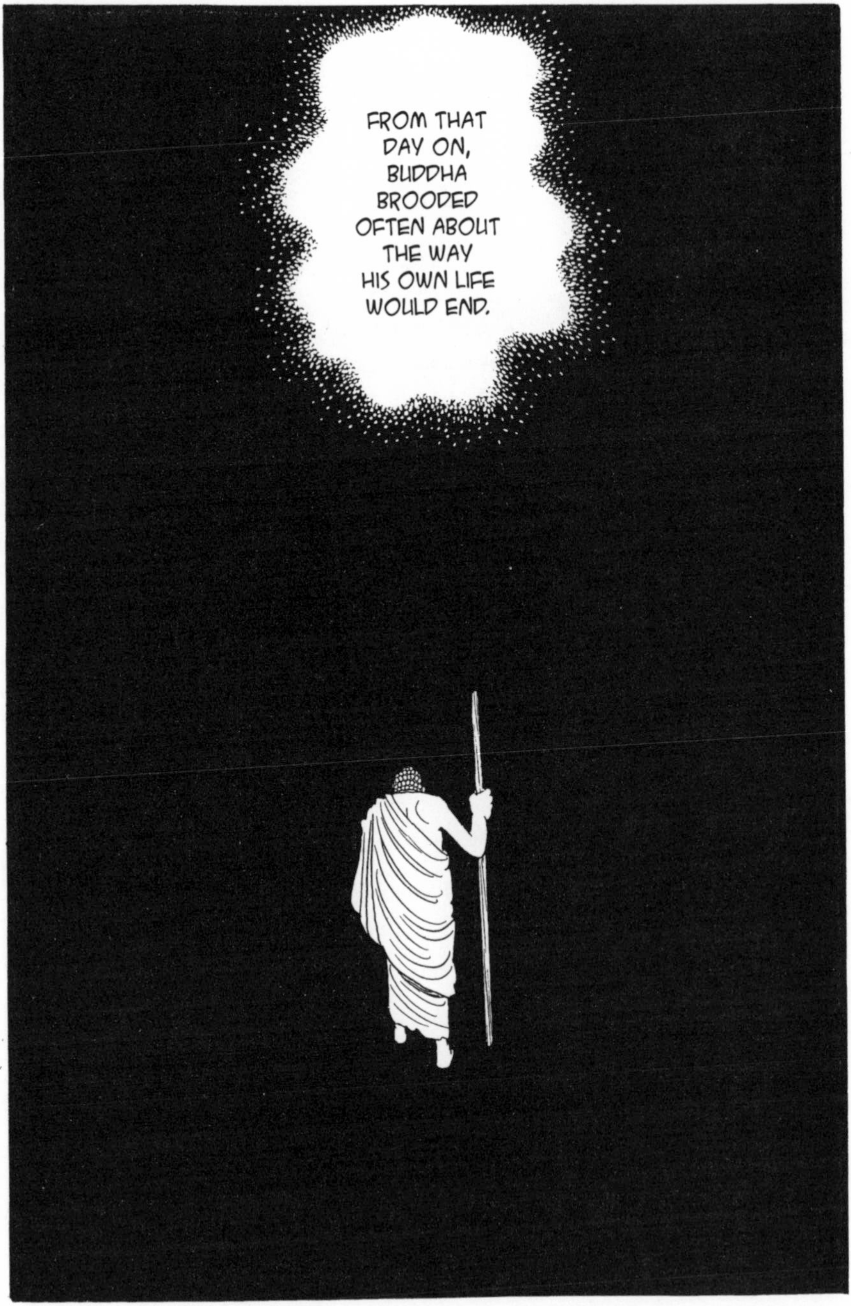
FROM THAT DAY ON, BUDDHA BROODED OFTEN ABOUT THE WAY HIS OWN LIFE WOULD END.

CHAPTER TEN

Jetavana

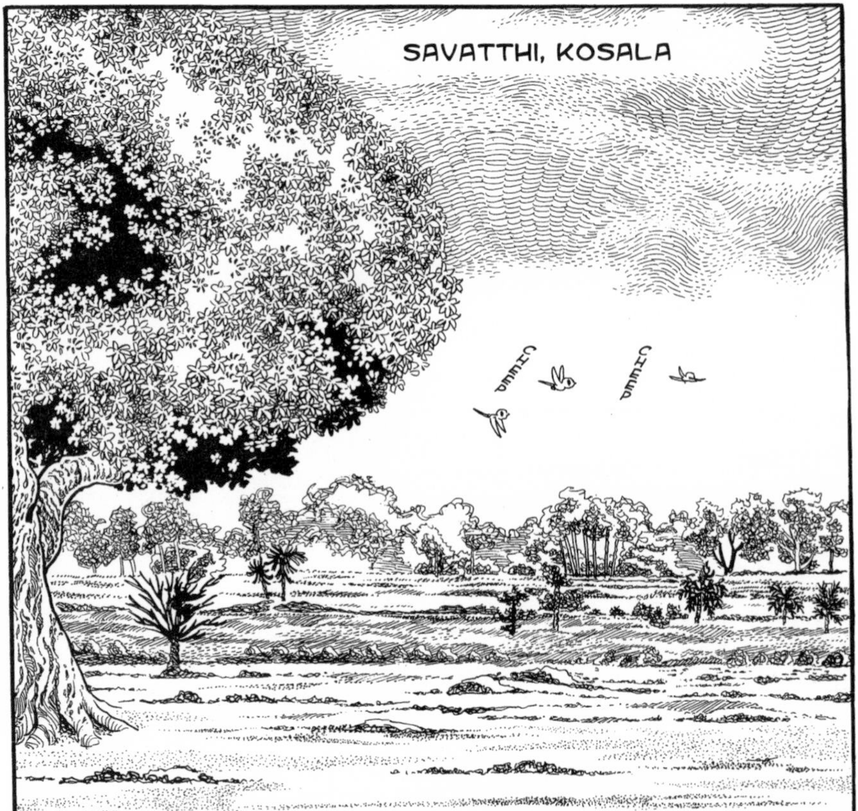
SAVATTHI, KOSALA
CHEEP
CHEEP
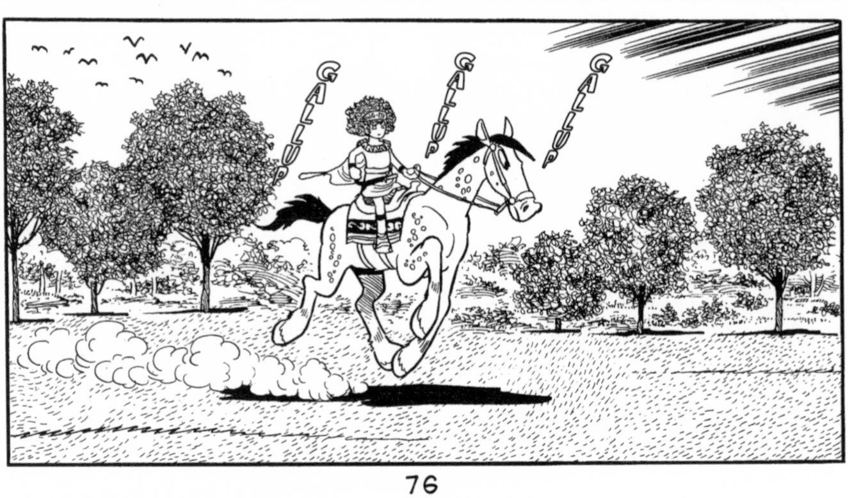
GALLUP
GALLUP
GALLUP

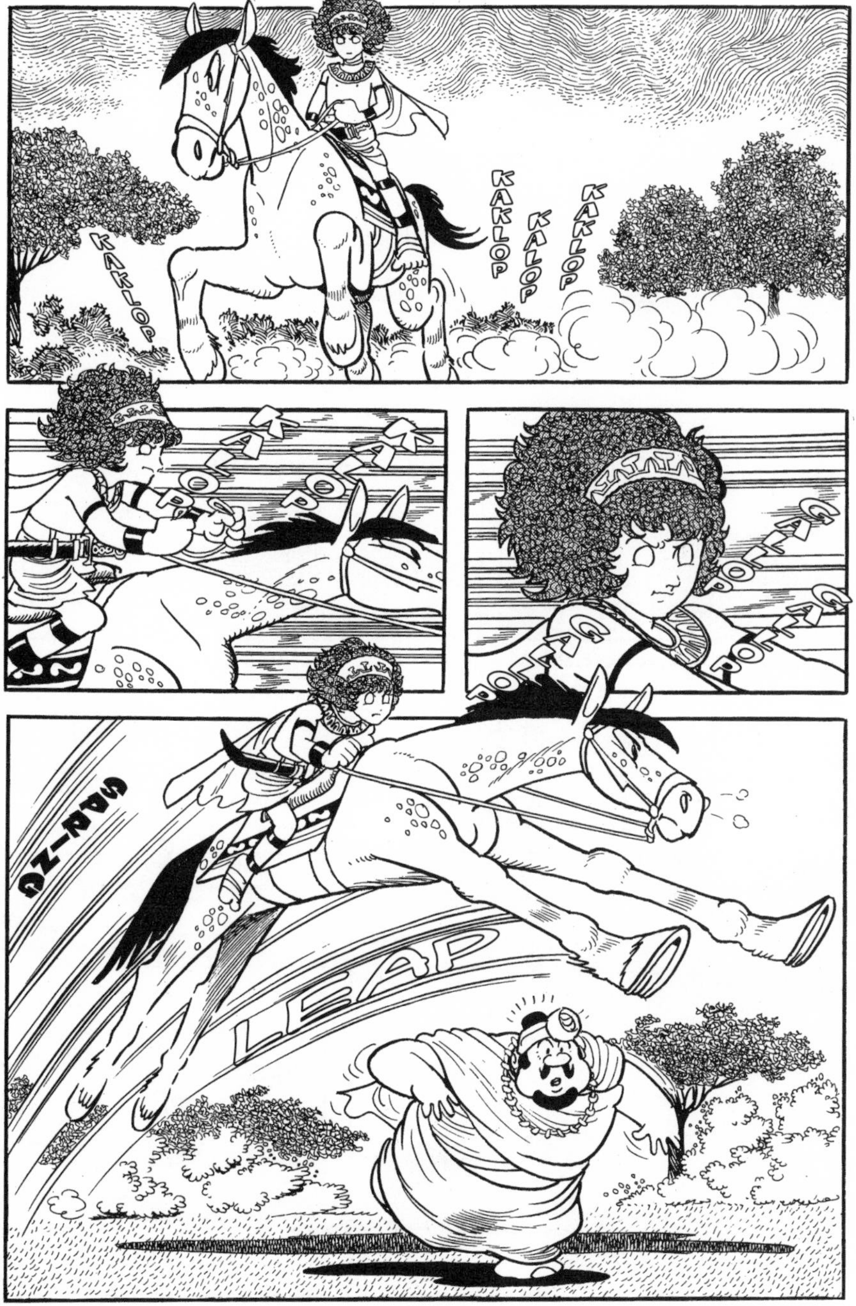
KAKLOP
KAKLOP
KALOP
KAKLOP
LEAP

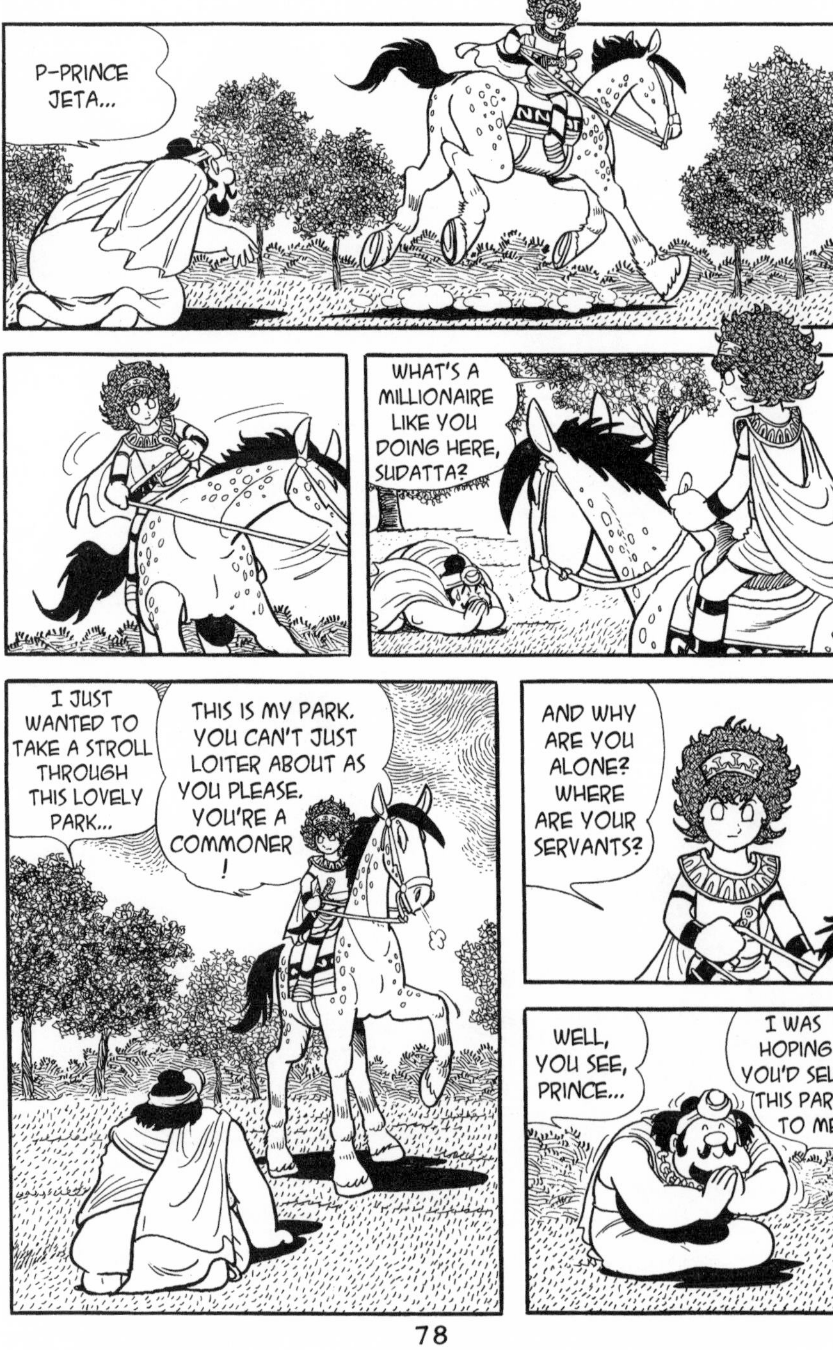
P-PRINCE JETA...
WHAT'S A MILLIONAIRE LIKE YOU DOING HERE, SUDATTA?
I JUST WANTED TO TAKE A STROLL THROUGH THIS LOVELY PARK...
THIS IS MY PARK. YOU CAN'T JUST LOITER ABOUT AS YOU PLEASE. YOU'RE A COMMONER!
AND WHY ARE YOU ALONE? WHERE ARE YOUR SERVANTS?
WELL, YOU SEE, PRINCE...
I WAS HOPING YOU'D SELL THIS PARK TO ME.

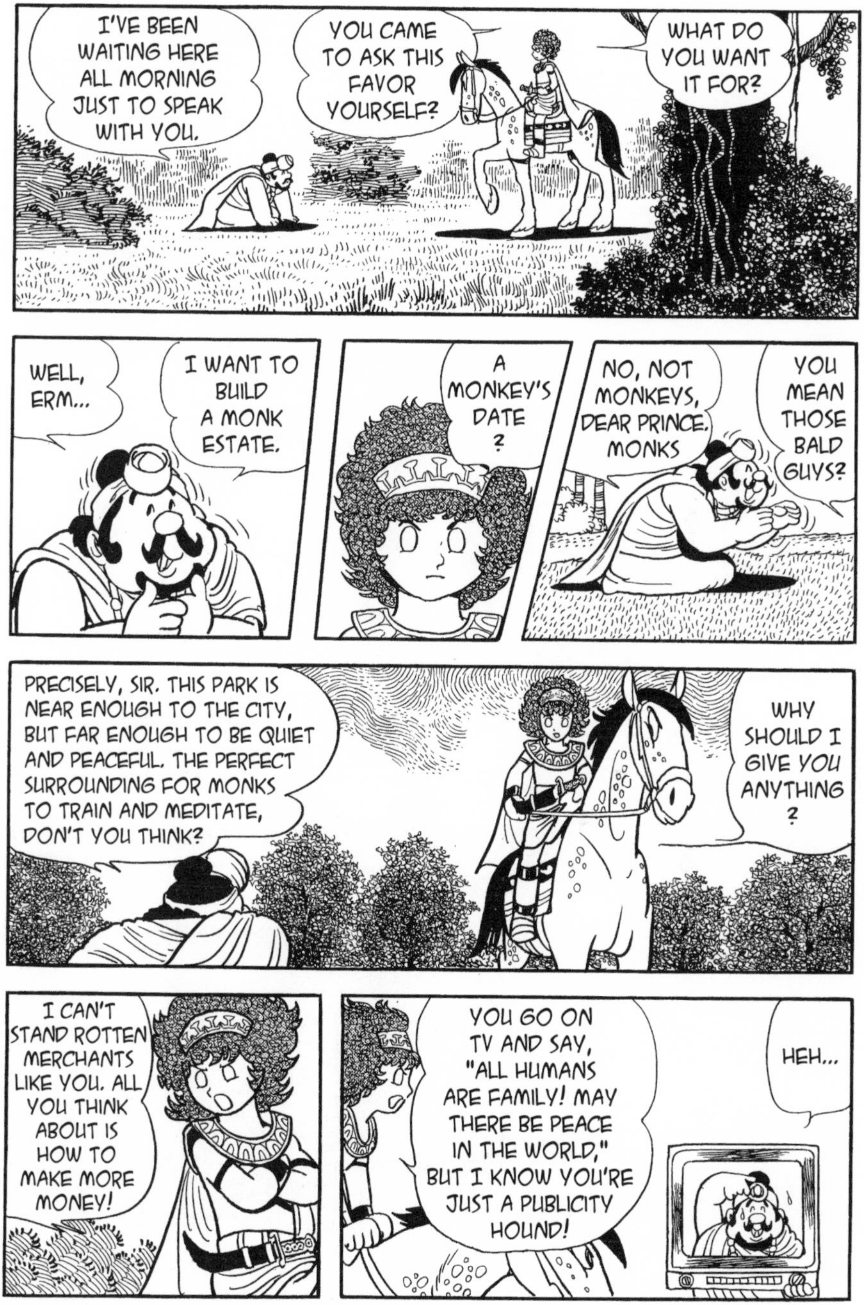
I'VE BEEN WAITING HERE ALL MORNING JUST TO SPEAK WITH YOU.
YOU CAME TO ASK THIS FAVOR YOURSELF?
WHAT DO YOU WANT IT FOR?
WELL, ERM...
I WANT TO BUILD A MONK ESTATE.
A MONKEY'S DATE ?
NO, NOT MONKEYS, DEAR PRINCE. MONKS
YOU MEAN THOSE BALD GUYS?
PRECISELY, SIR. THIS PARK IS NEAR ENOUGH TO THE CITY, BUT FAR ENOUGH TO BE QUIET AND PEACEFUL. THE PERFECT SURROUNDING FOR MONKS TO TRAIN AND MEDITATE, DON'T YOU THINK?
WHY SHOULD I GIVE YOU ANYTHING ?
I CAN'T STAND ROTTEN MERCHANTS LIKE YOU. ALL YOU THINK ABOUT IS HOW TO MAKE MORE MONEY!
YOU GO ON TV AND SAY, "ALL HUMANS ARE FAMILY! MAY THERE BE PEACE IN THE WORLD," BUT I KNOW YOU'RE JUST A PUBLICITY HOUND!
HEH...

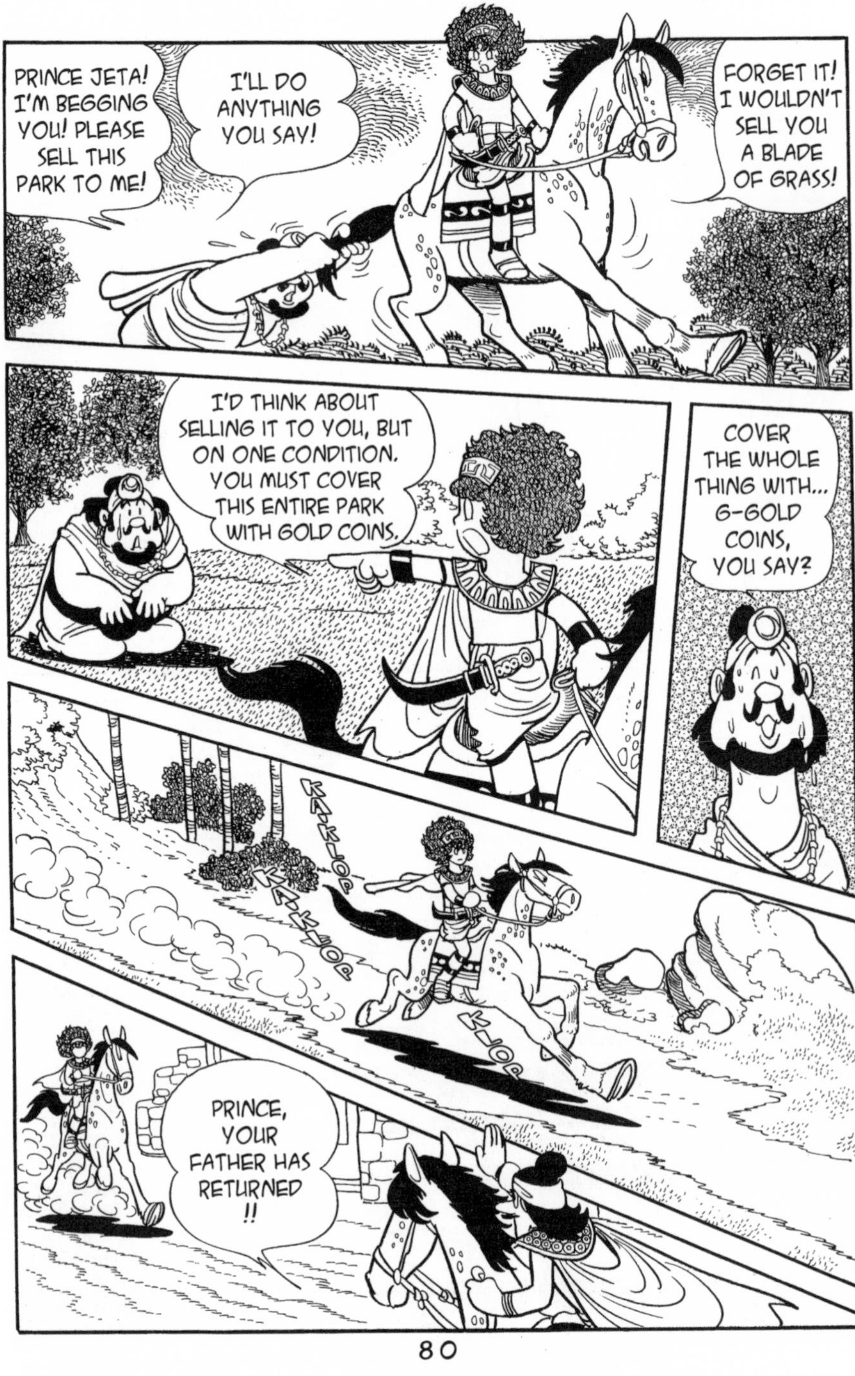
PRINCE JETA! I'M BEGGING YOU! PLEASE SELL THIS PARK TO ME!
I'LL DO ANYTHING YOU SAY!
FORGET IT! I WOULDN'T SELL YOU A BLADE OF GRASS!
I'D THINK ABOUT SELLING IT TO YOU, BUT ON ONE CONDITION. YOU MUST COVER THIS ENTIRE PARK WITH GOLD COINS.
COVER THE WHOLE THING WITH... G-GOLD COINS, YOU SAY?
KA-KLOP
KA-KLOP
KLOP
PRINCE, YOUR FATHER HAS RETURNED !!

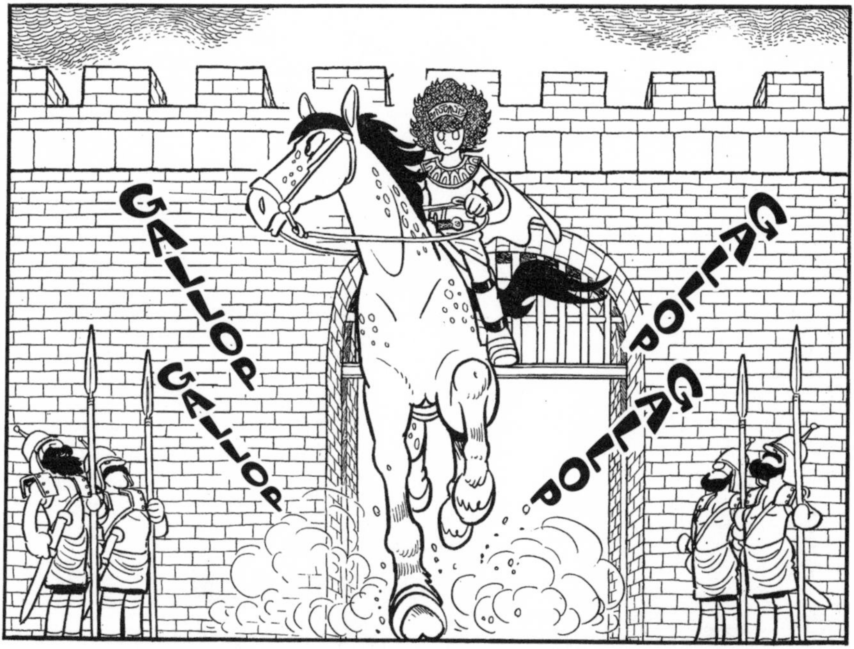
GALLOP GALLOP
GALLOP GALLOP

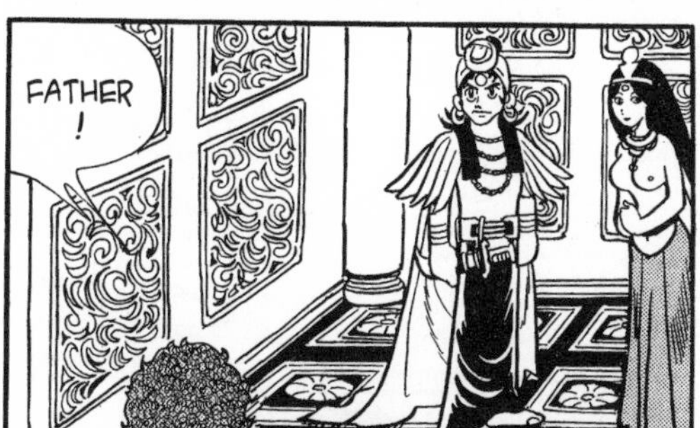
FATHER!

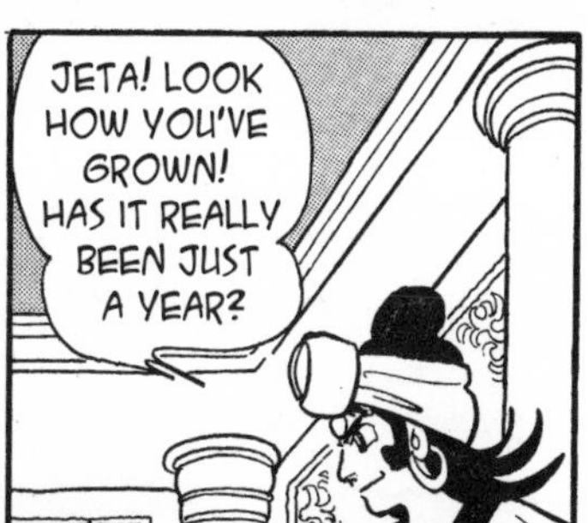
JETA! LOOK HOW YOU'VE GROWN! HAS IT REALLY BEEN JUST A YEAR?

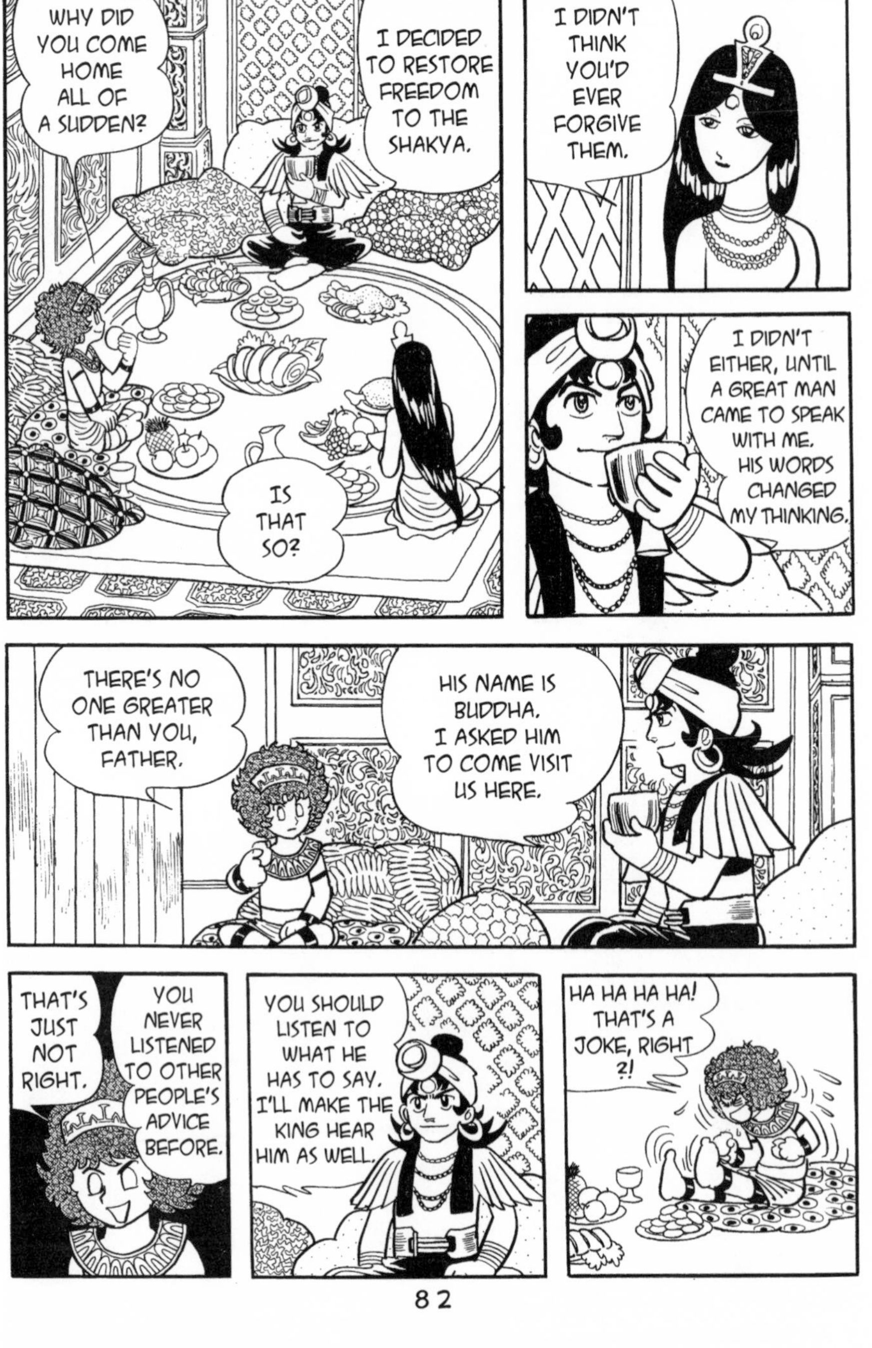
WHY DID YOU COME HOME ALL OF A SUDDEN?
I DECIDED TO RESTORE FREEDOM TO THE SHAKYA.
IS THAT SO?
I DIDN'T THINK YOU'D EVER FORGIVE THEM.
I DIDN'T EITHER, UNTIL A GREAT MAN CAME TO SPEAK WITH ME. HIS WORDS CHANGED MY THINKING.
THERE'S NO ONE GREATER THAN YOU, FATHER.
HIS NAME IS BUDDHA. I ASKED HIM TO COME VISIT US HERE.
THAT'S JUST NOT RIGHT.
YOU NEVER LISTENED TO OTHER PEOPLE'S ADVICE BEFORE.
YOU SHOULD LISTEN TO WHAT HE HAS TO SAY. I'LL MAKE THE KING HEAR HIM AS WELL.
HA HA HA HA! THAT'S A JOKE, RIGHT ?!

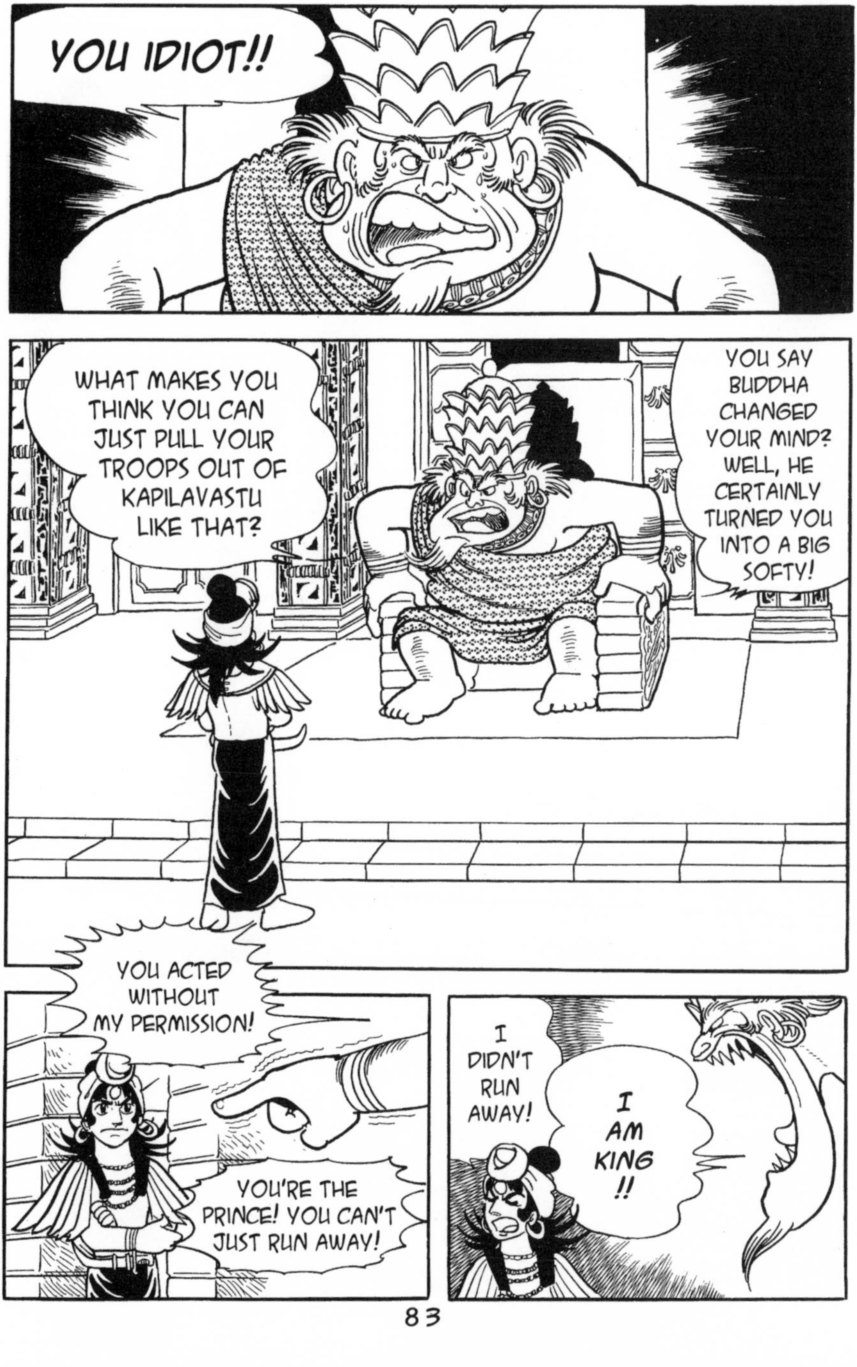
YOU IDIOT!!
WHAT MAKES YOU THINK YOU CAN JUST PULL YOUR TROOPS OUT OF KAPILAVASTU LIKE THAT?
YOU SAY BUDDHA CHANGED YOUR MIND? WELL, HE CERTAINLY TURNED YOU INTO A BIG SOFTY!
YOU ACTED WITHOUT MY PERMISSION!
YOU'RE THE PRINCE! YOU CAN'T JUST RUN AWAY!
I DIDN'T RUN AWAY!
I AM KING !!

I ORDERED YOU TO FORCE THE SHAKYA INTO SLAVERY AND KEEP CLOSE WATCH ON THEM.

YOU SHOULD HAVE BEEN HAPPY TO PUNISH THEM!

FATHER, I DID HAVE A GRUDGE AGAINST THE SHAKYAN PEOPLE.

BUT I FELT THAT THEY HAD SUFFERED ENOUGH. IT WAS TIME TO FORGIVE THEM.

SHUT UP

SHUT UP

SHUT UP!!!

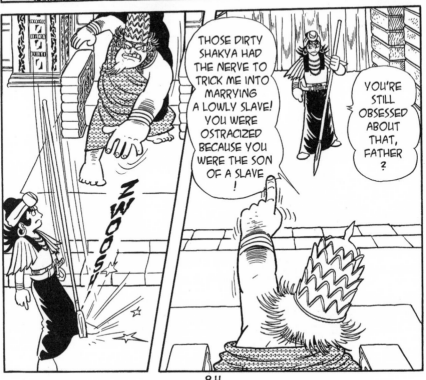

THOSE DIRTY SHAKYA HAD THE NERVE TO TRICK ME INTO MARRYING A LOWLY SLAVE! YOU WERE OSTRACIZED BECAUSE YOU WERE THE SON OF A SLAVE!

YOU'RE STILL OBSESSED ABOUT THAT, FATHER?

NWOOSH!

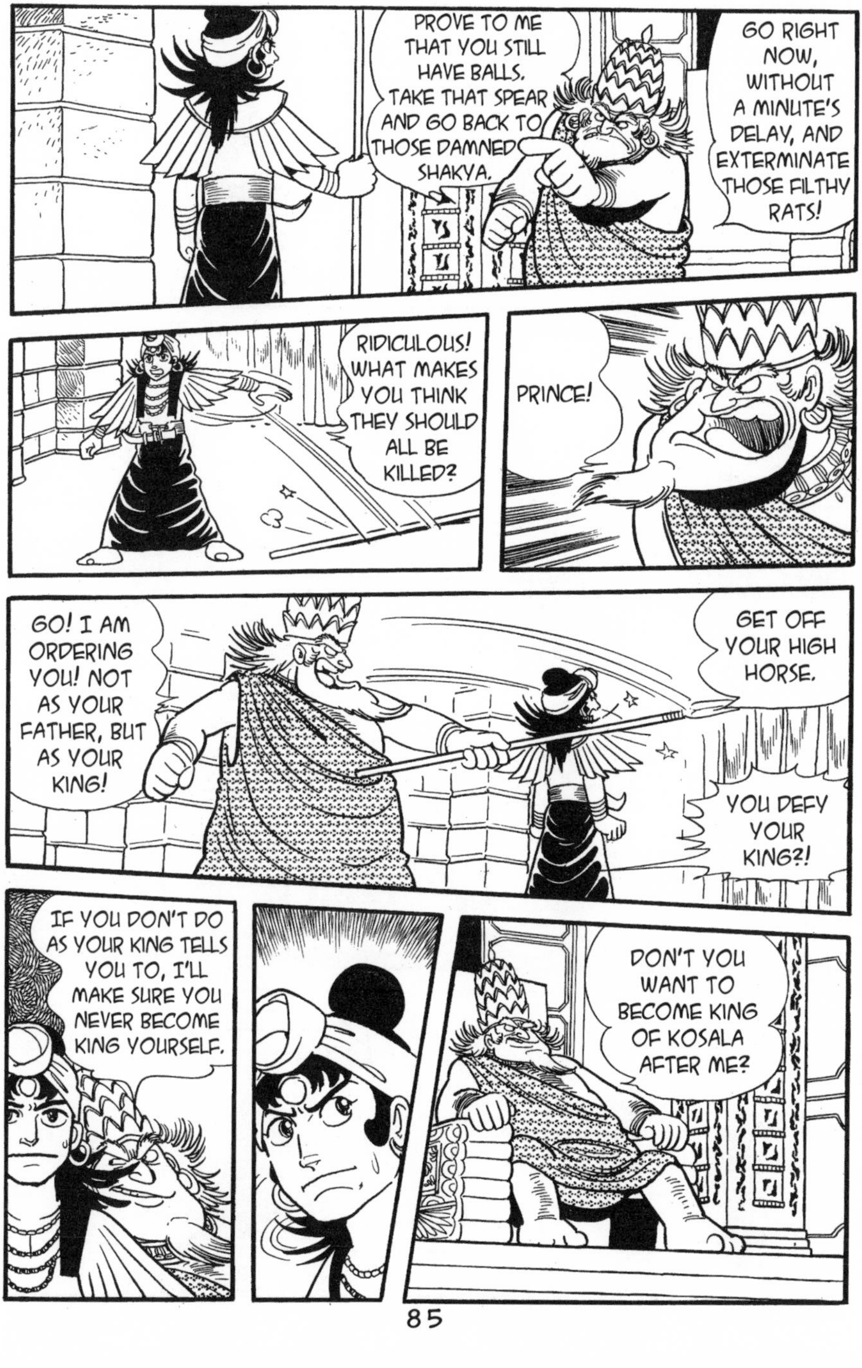
PROVE TO ME THAT YOU STILL HAVE BALLS. TAKE THAT SPEAR AND GO BACK TO THOSE DAMNED SHAKYA.
GO RIGHT NOW, WITHOUT A MINUTE'S DELAY, AND EXTERMINATE THOSE FILTHY RATS!
RIDICULOUS! WHAT MAKES YOU THINK THEY SHOULD ALL BE KILLED?
PRINCE!
GO! I AM ORDERING YOU! NOT AS YOUR FATHER, BUT AS YOUR KING!
GET OFF YOUR HIGH HORSE.
YOU DEFY YOUR KING?!
IF YOU DON'T DO AS YOUR KING TELLS YOU TO, I'LL MAKE SURE YOU NEVER BECOME KING YOURSELF.
DON'T YOU WANT TO BECOME KING OF KOSALA AFTER ME?

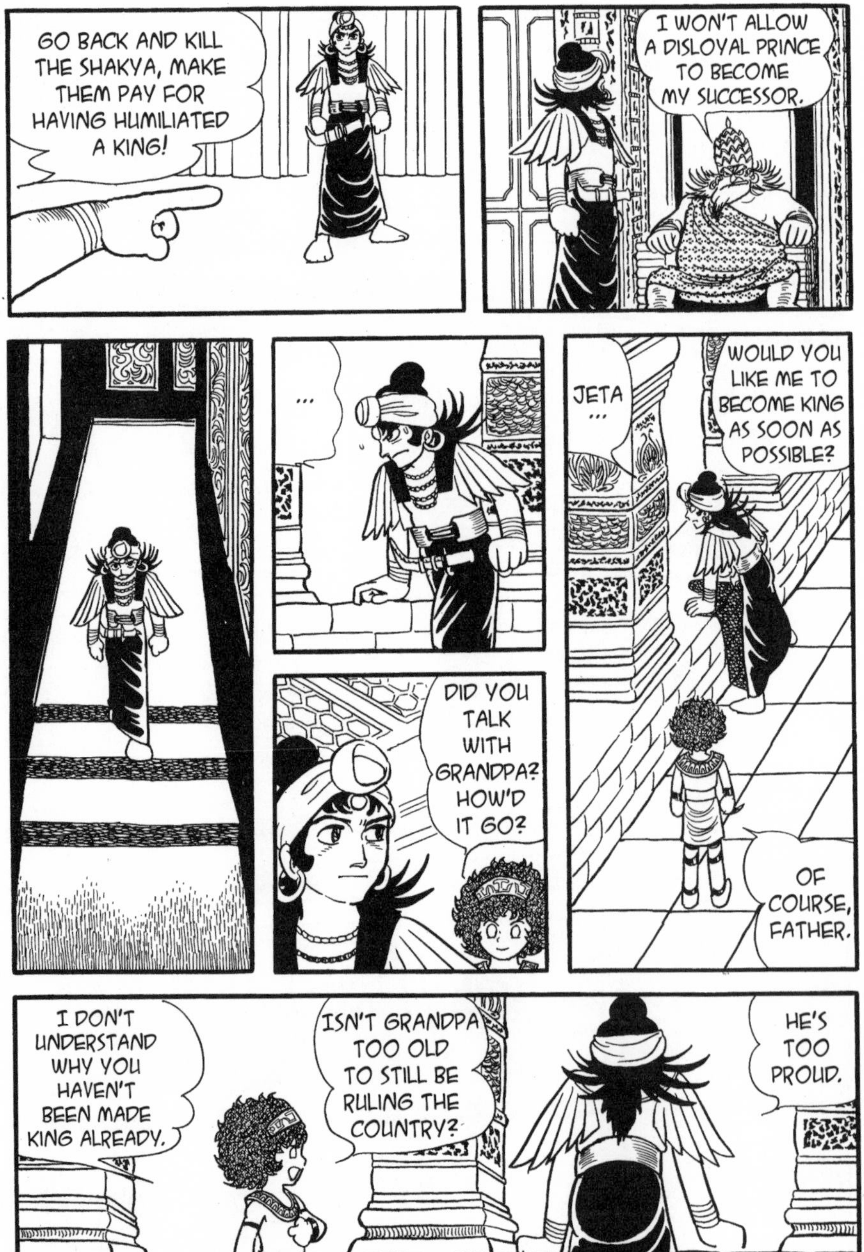
GO BACK AND KILL THE SHAKYA, MAKE THEM PAY FOR HAVING HUMILIATED A KING!
I WON'T ALLOW A DISLOYAL PRINCE TO BECOME MY SUCCESSOR.
...
DID YOU TALK WITH GRANDPA? HOW'D IT GO?
JETA ...
WOULD YOU LIKE ME TO BECOME KING AS SOON AS POSSIBLE?
OF COURSE, FATHER.
I DON'T UNDERSTAND WHY YOU HAVEN'T BEEN MADE KING ALREADY.
ISN'T GRANDPA TOO OLD TO STILL BE RULING THE COUNTRY?
HE'S TOO PROUD.

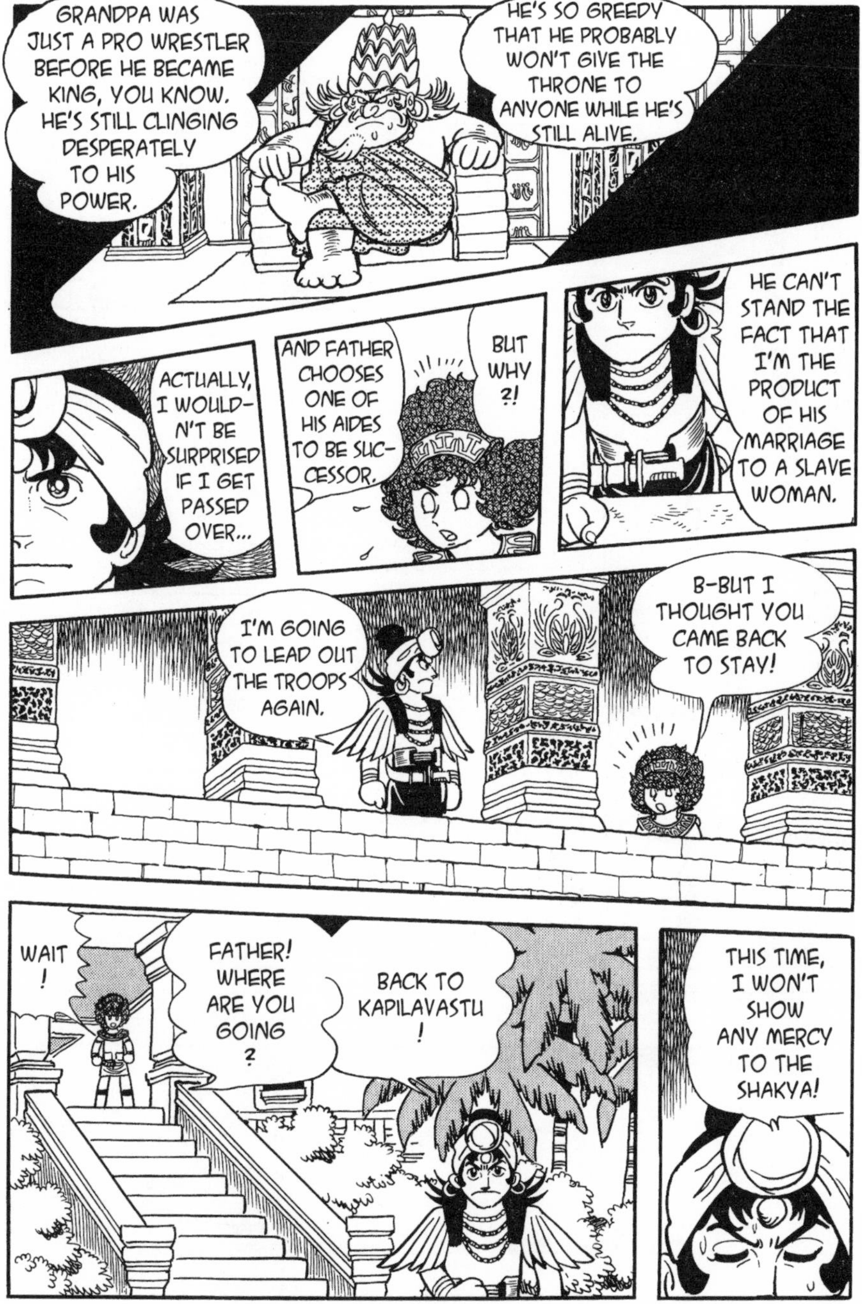
GRANDPA WAS JUST A PRO WRESTLER BEFORE HE BECAME KING, YOU KNOW. HE'S STILL CLINGING DESPERATELY TO HIS POWER.
HE'S SO GREEDY THAT HE PROBABLY WON'T GIVE THE THRONE TO ANYONE WHILE HE'S STILL ALIVE.
ACTUALLY, I WOULD-N'T BE SURPRISED IF I GET PASSED OVER...
AND FATHER CHOOSES ONE OF HIS AIDES TO BE SUC-CESSOR.
BUT WHY?!
HE CAN'T STAND THE FACT THAT I'M THE PRODUCT OF HIS MARRIAGE TO A SLAVE WOMAN.
I'M GOING TO LEAD OUT THE TROOPS AGAIN.
B-BUT I THOUGHT YOU CAME BACK TO STAY!
WAIT!
FATHER! WHERE ARE YOU GOING?
BACK TO KAPILAVASTU!
THIS TIME, I WON'T SHOW ANY MERCY TO THE SHAKYA!

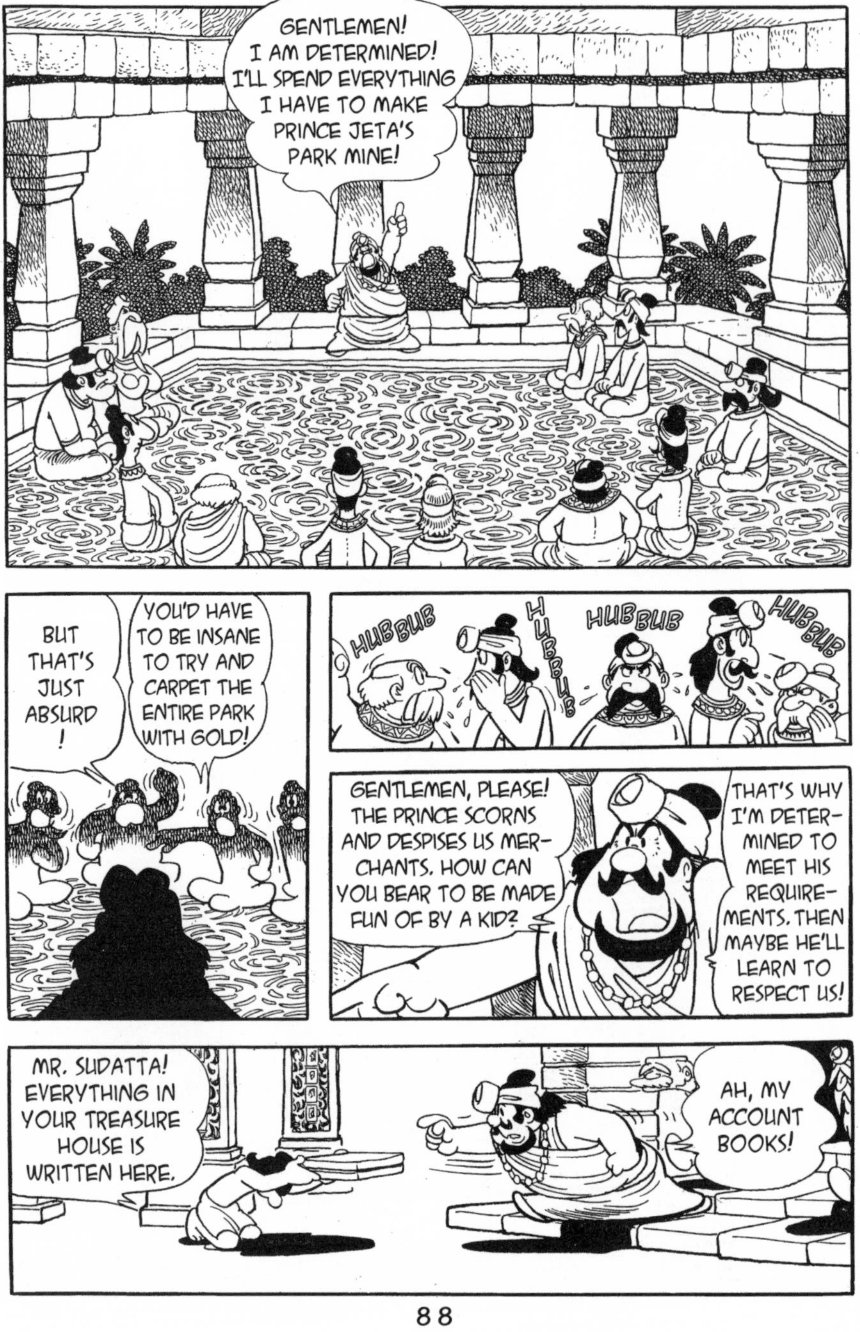
GENTLEMEN! I AM DETERMINED! I'LL SPEND EVERYTHING I HAVE TO MAKE PRINCE JETA'S PARK MINE!
BUT THAT'S JUST ABSURD !
YOU'D HAVE TO BE INSANE TO TRY AND CARPET THE ENTIRE PARK WITH GOLD!
HUBBUB
HUBBUB
HUBBUB
HUBBUB
GENTLEMEN, PLEASE! THE PRINCE SCORNS AND DESPISES US MERCHANTS. HOW CAN YOU BEAR TO BE MADE FUN OF BY A KID?
THAT'S WHY I'M DETERMINED TO MEET HIS REQUIREMENTS. THEN MAYBE HE'LL LEARN TO RESPECT US!
MR. SUDATTA! EVERYTHING IN YOUR TREASURE HOUSE IS WRITTEN HERE.
AH, MY ACCOUNT BOOKS!

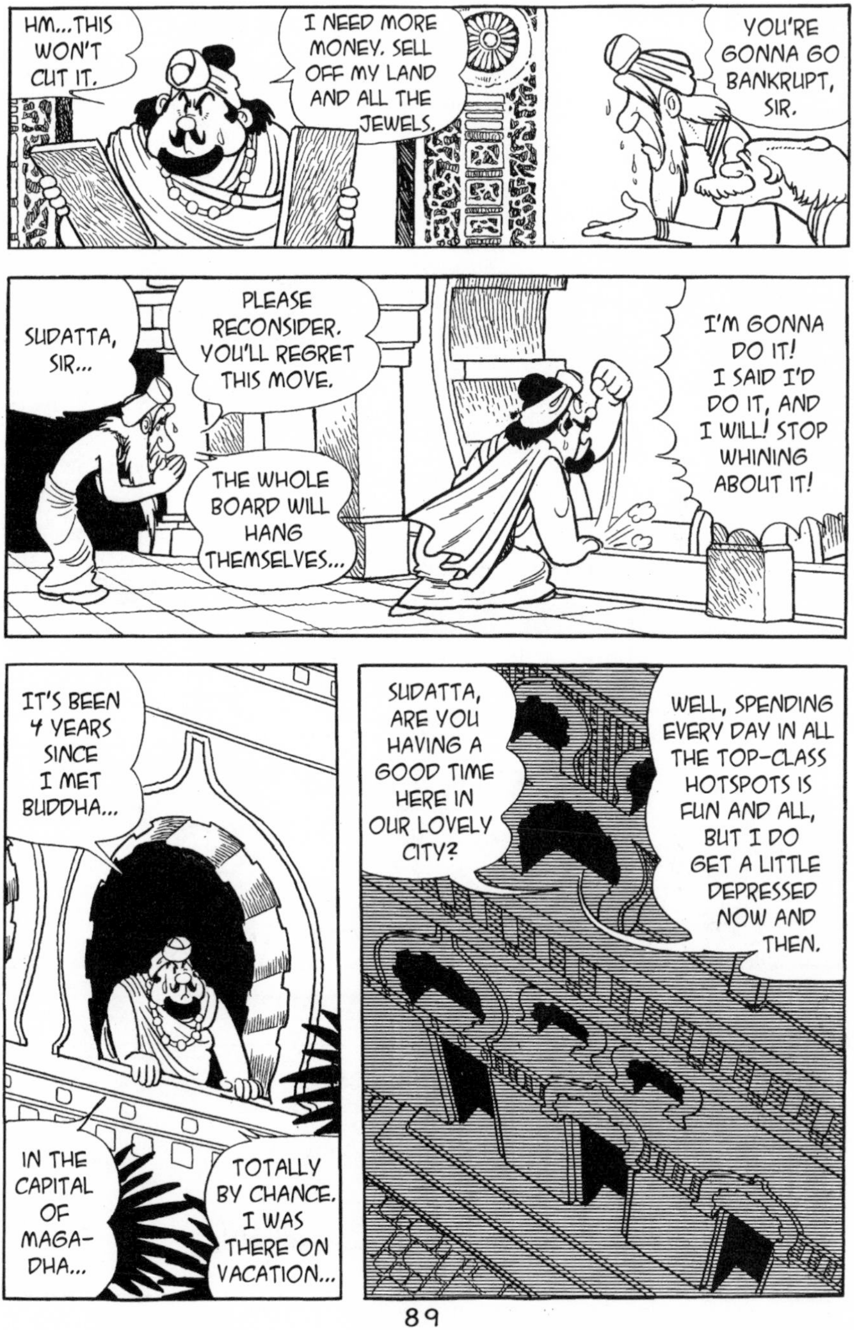

HM...THIS WON'T CUT IT.
I NEED MORE MONEY. SELL OFF MY LAND AND ALL THE JEWELS.
YOU'RE GONNA GO BANKRUPT, SIR.
SUDATTA, SIR...
PLEASE RECONSIDER. YOU'LL REGRET THIS MOVE.
THE WHOLE BOARD WILL HANG THEMSELVES...
I'M GONNA DO IT! I SAID I'D DO IT, AND I WILL! STOP WHINING ABOUT IT!
IT'S BEEN 4 YEARS SINCE I MET BUDDHA...
IN THE CAPITAL OF MAGA-DHA...
TOTALLY BY CHANCE. I WAS THERE ON VACATION...
SUDATTA, ARE YOU HAVING A GOOD TIME HERE IN OUR LOVELY CITY?
WELL, SPENDING EVERY DAY IN ALL THE TOP-CLASS HOTSPOTS IS FUN AND ALL, BUT I DO GET A LITTLE DEPRESSED NOW AND THEN.

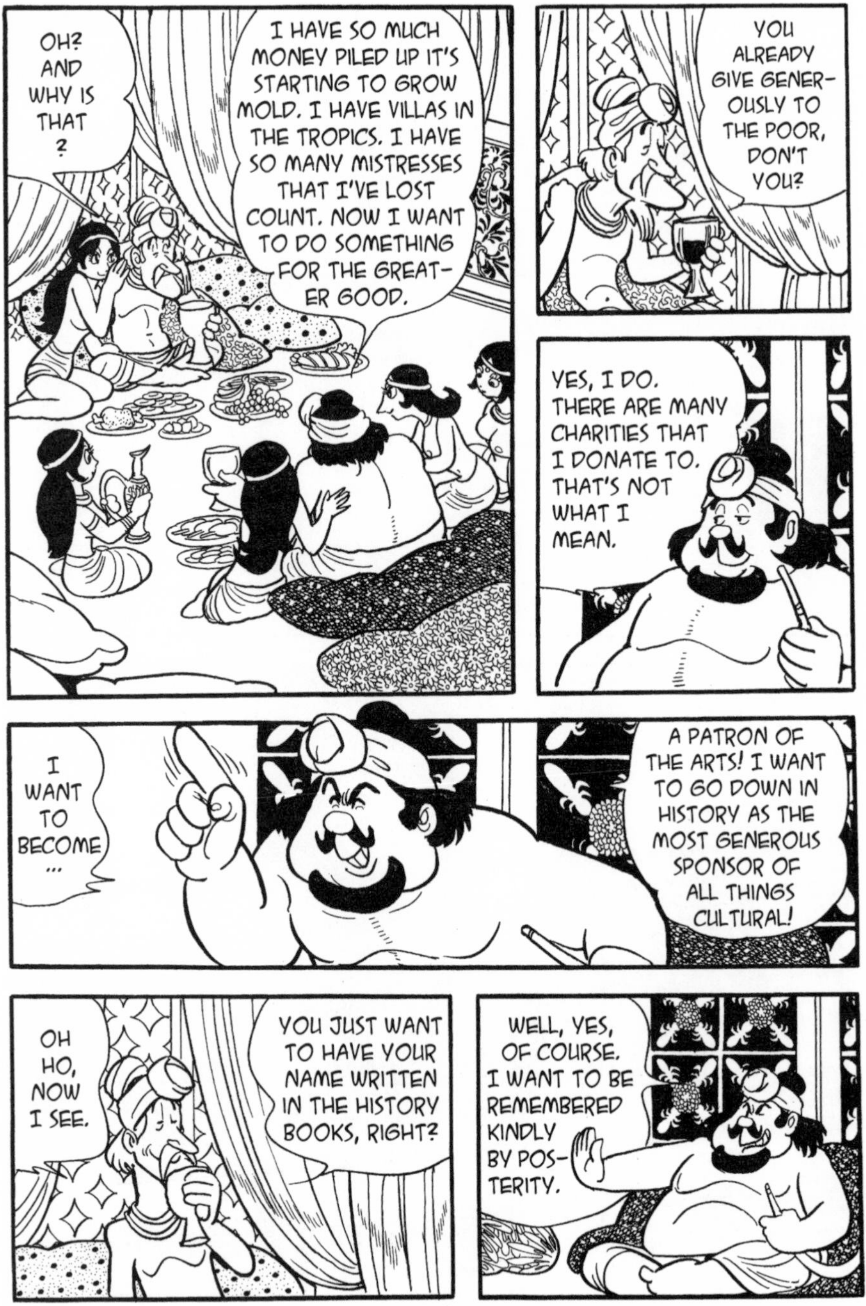
OH? AND WHY IS THAT ?
I HAVE SO MUCH MONEY PILED UP IT'S STARTING TO GROW MOLD. I HAVE VILLAS IN THE TROPICS. I HAVE SO MANY MISTRESSES THAT I'VE LOST COUNT. NOW I WANT TO DO SOMETHING FOR THE GREATER GOOD.
YOU ALREADY GIVE GENEROUSLY TO THE POOR, DON'T YOU?
YES, I DO. THERE ARE MANY CHARITIES THAT I DONATE TO. THAT'S NOT WHAT I MEAN.
I WANT TO BECOME ...
A PATRON OF THE ARTS! I WANT TO GO DOWN IN HISTORY AS THE MOST GENEROUS SPONSOR OF ALL THINGS CULTURAL!
OH HO, NOW I SEE.
YOU JUST WANT TO HAVE YOUR NAME WRITTEN IN THE HISTORY BOOKS, RIGHT?
WELL, YES, OF COURSE. I WANT TO BE REMEMBERED KINDLY BY POSTERITY.

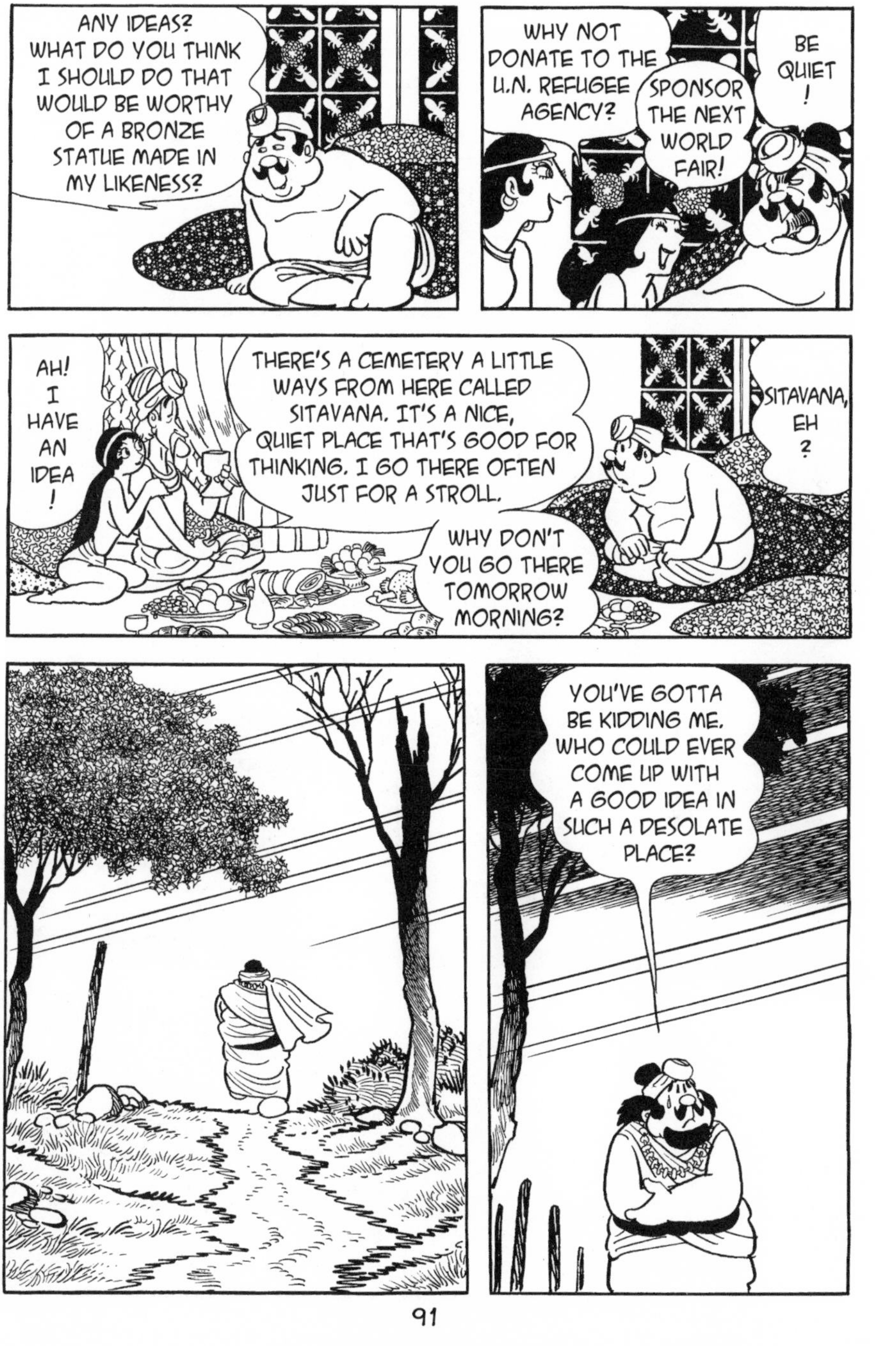
ANY IDEAS? WHAT DO YOU THINK I SHOULD DO THAT WOULD BE WORTHY OF A BRONZE STATUE MADE IN MY LIKENESS?
WHY NOT DONATE TO THE U.N. REFUGEE AGENCY?
SPONSOR THE NEXT WORLD FAIR!
BE QUIET!
AH! I HAVE AN IDEA!
THERE'S A CEMETERY A LITTLE WAYS FROM HERE CALLED SITAVANA. IT'S A NICE, QUIET PLACE THAT'S GOOD FOR THINKING. I GO THERE OFTEN JUST FOR A STROLL.
WHY DON'T YOU GO THERE TOMORROW MORNING?
SITAVANA, EH?
YOU'VE GOTTA BE KIDDING ME. WHO COULD EVER COME UP WITH A GOOD IDEA IN SUCH A DESOLATE PLACE?

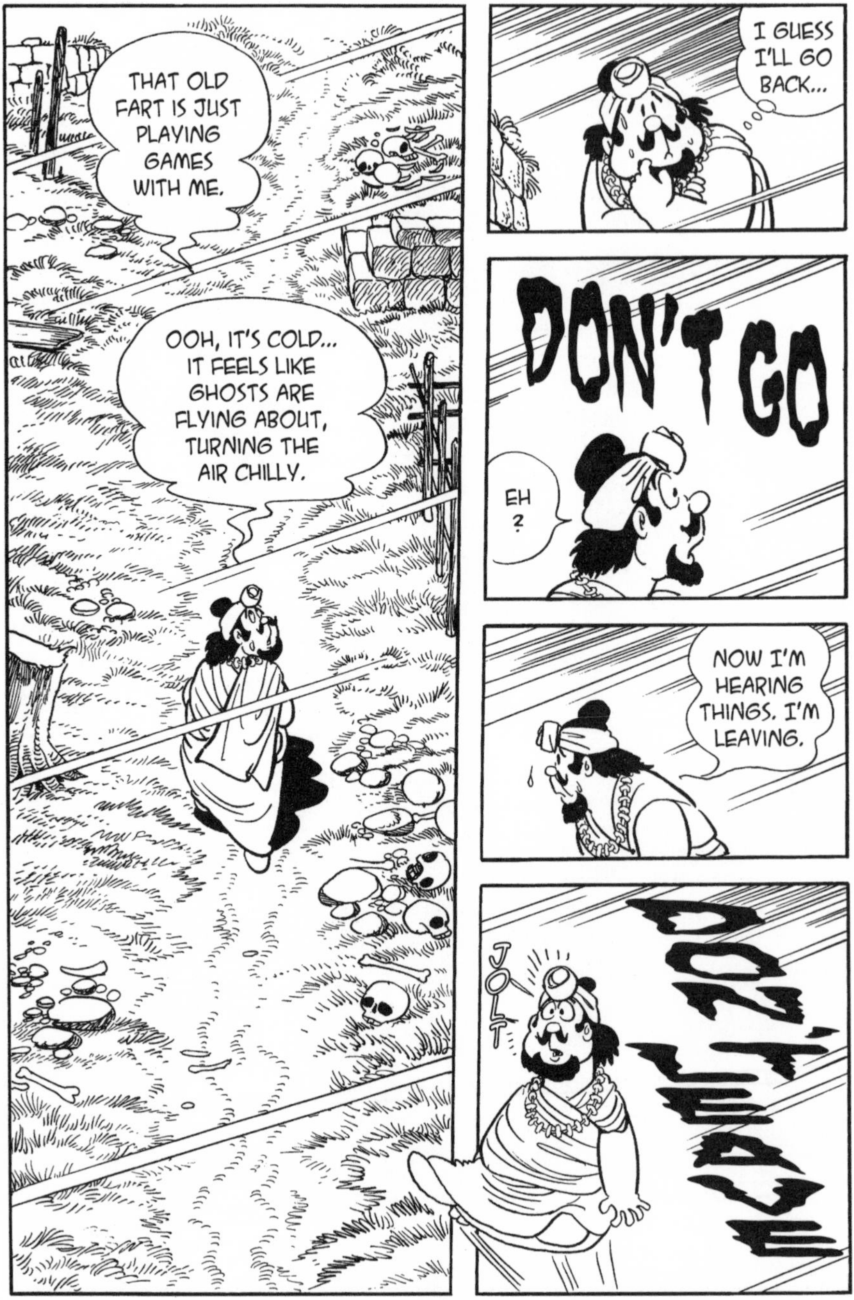
THAT OLD FART IS JUST PLAYING GAMES WITH ME.
OOH, IT'S COLD... IT FEELS LIKE GHOSTS ARE FLYING ABOUT, TURNING THE AIR CHILLY.
I GUESS I'LL GO BACK...
DON'T GO
EH ?
NOW I'M HEARING THINGS. I'M LEAVING.
JOLT
DON'T LEAVE

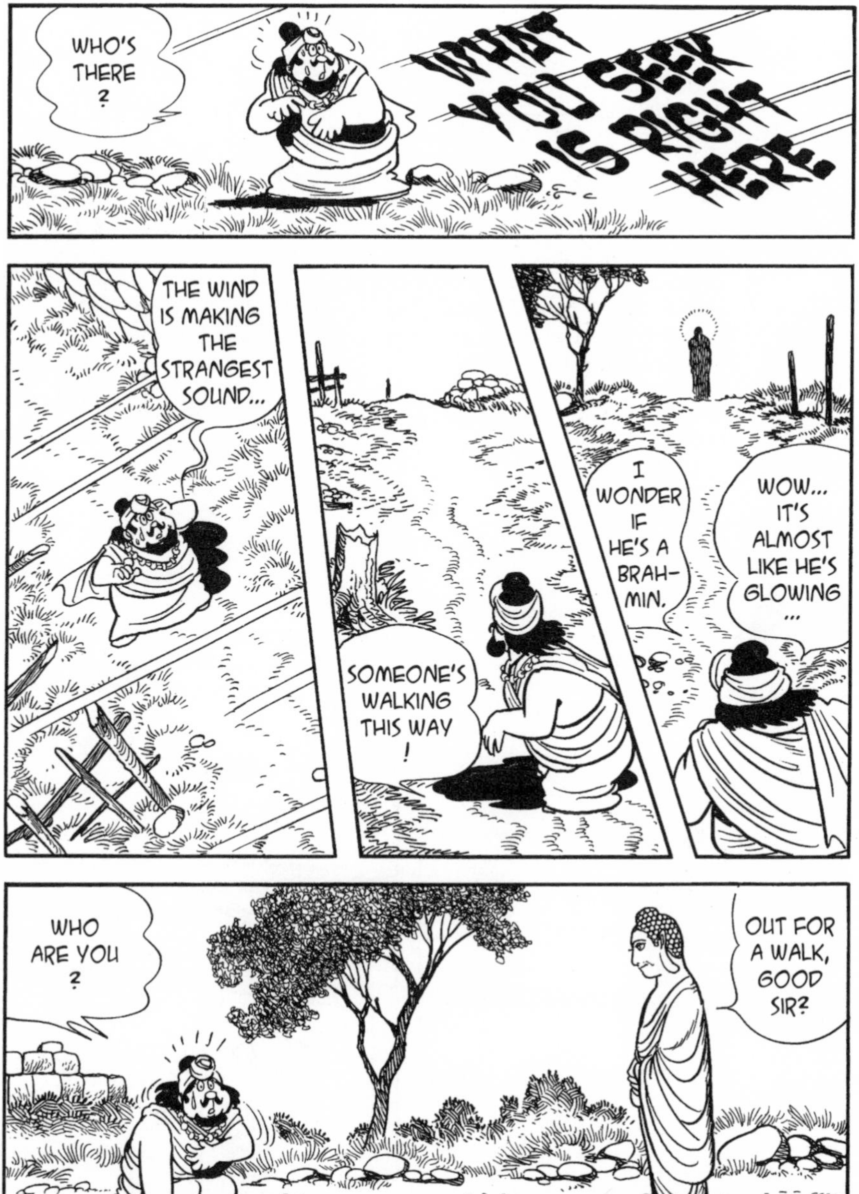
WHO'S THERE ?
WHAT YOU SEEK IS RIGHT HERE.
THE WIND IS MAKING THE STRANGEST SOUND...
SOMEONE'S WALKING THIS WAY !
I WONDER IF HE'S A BRAH-MIN.
WOW... IT'S ALMOST LIKE HE'S GLOWING ...
WHO ARE YOU ?
OUT FOR A WALK, GOOD SIR?

I COME HERE EVERY MORNING TO MEDITATE.

IT'S PEACEFUL HERE. I LIKE TO SIT ON THAT STONE OVER THERE AND LOSE MYSELF IN THOUGHT.

MIGHT I ASK WHAT YOUR NAME IS?

I AM BUDDHA.

AHH!

REALLY? YOU'RE BUDDHA? THE FAMOUS ENLIGHTENED ONE?

TO MEET THE GREAT BUDDHA IN A PLACE LIKE THIS IS SUCH...

AN HONOR!

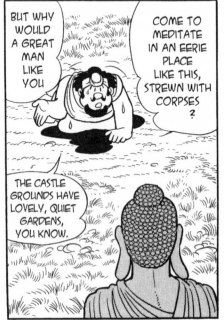

BUT WHY WOULD A GREAT MAN LIKE YOU

COME TO MEDITATE IN AN EERIE PLACE LIKE THIS, STREWN WITH CORPSES?

THE CASTLE GROUNDS HAVE LOVELY, QUIET GARDENS, YOU KNOW.

ARE CORPSES REALLY SO EERIE?

?

94

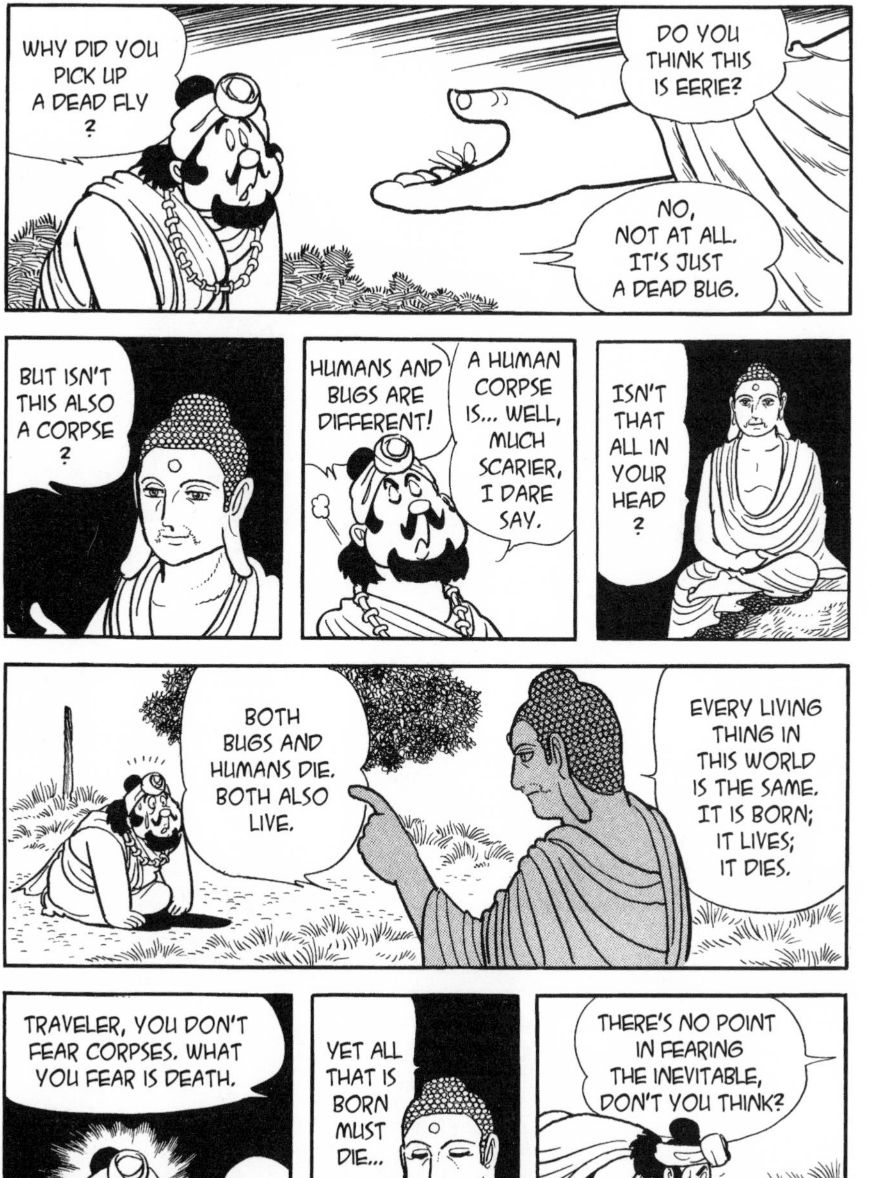
WHY DID YOU PICK UP A DEAD FLY?
DO YOU THINK THIS IS EERIE?
NO, NOT AT ALL. IT'S JUST A DEAD BUG.
BUT ISN'T THIS ALSO A CORPSE?
HUMANS AND BUGS ARE DIFFERENT!
A HUMAN CORPSE IS... WELL, MUCH SCARIER, I DARE SAY.
ISN'T THAT ALL IN YOUR HEAD?
BOTH BUGS AND HUMANS DIE. BOTH ALSO LIVE.
EVERY LIVING THING IN THIS WORLD IS THE SAME. IT IS BORN; IT LIVES; IT DIES.
TRAVELER, YOU DON'T FEAR CORPSES. WHAT YOU FEAR IS DEATH.
YOU'RE RIGHT...
YET ALL THAT IS BORN MUST DIE...
THERE'S NO POINT IN FEARING THE INEVITABLE, DON'T YOU THINK?
TRUE...

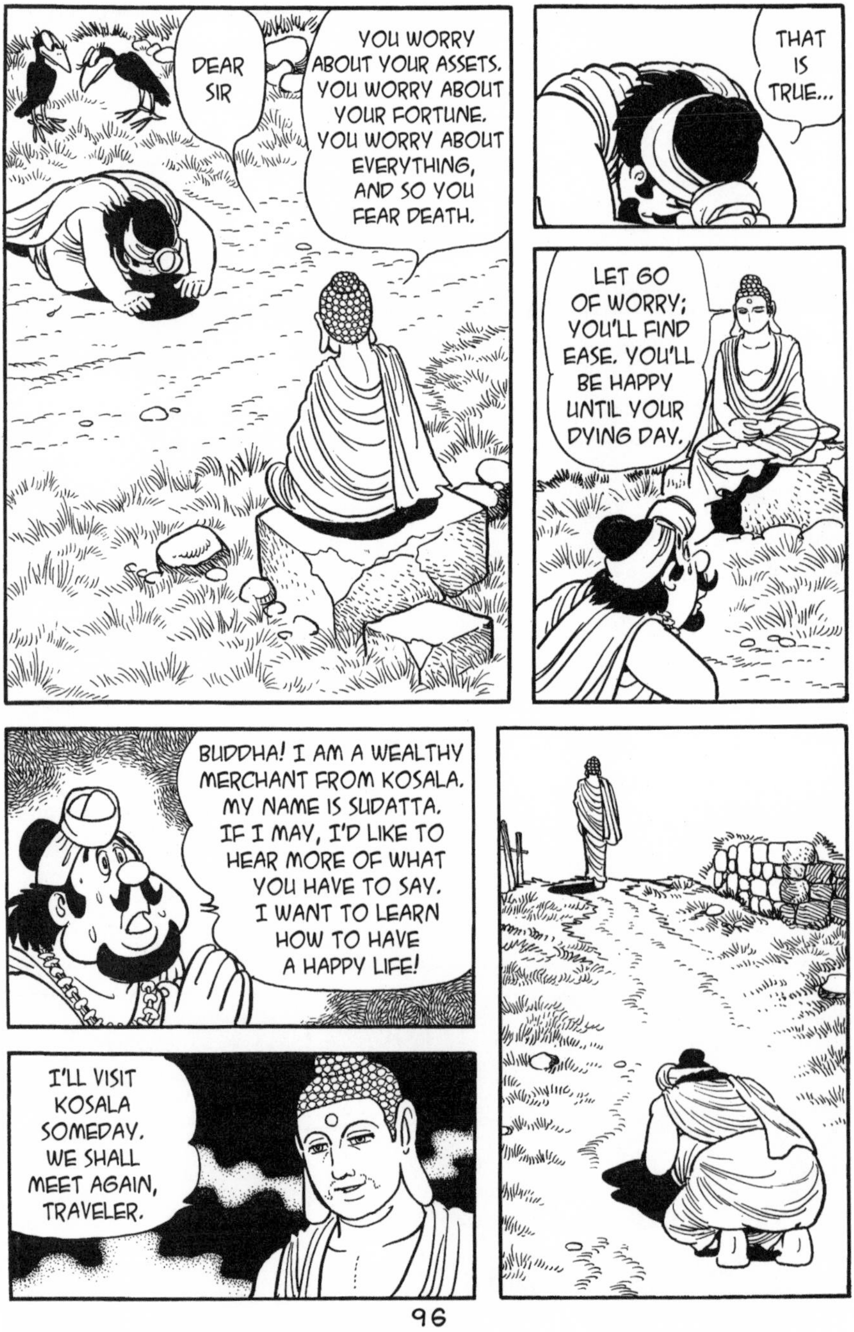
DEAR SIR
YOU WORRY ABOUT YOUR ASSETS. YOU WORRY ABOUT YOUR FORTUNE. YOU WORRY ABOUT EVERYTHING, AND SO YOU FEAR DEATH.
THAT IS TRUE...
LET GO OF WORRY; YOU'LL FIND EASE. YOU'LL BE HAPPY UNTIL YOUR DYING DAY.
BUDDHA! I AM A WEALTHY MERCHANT FROM KOSALA. MY NAME IS SUDATTA. IF I MAY, I'D LIKE TO HEAR MORE OF WHAT YOU HAVE TO SAY. I WANT TO LEARN HOW TO HAVE A HAPPY LIFE!
I'LL VISIT KOSALA SOMEDAY. WE SHALL MEET AGAIN, TRAVELER.

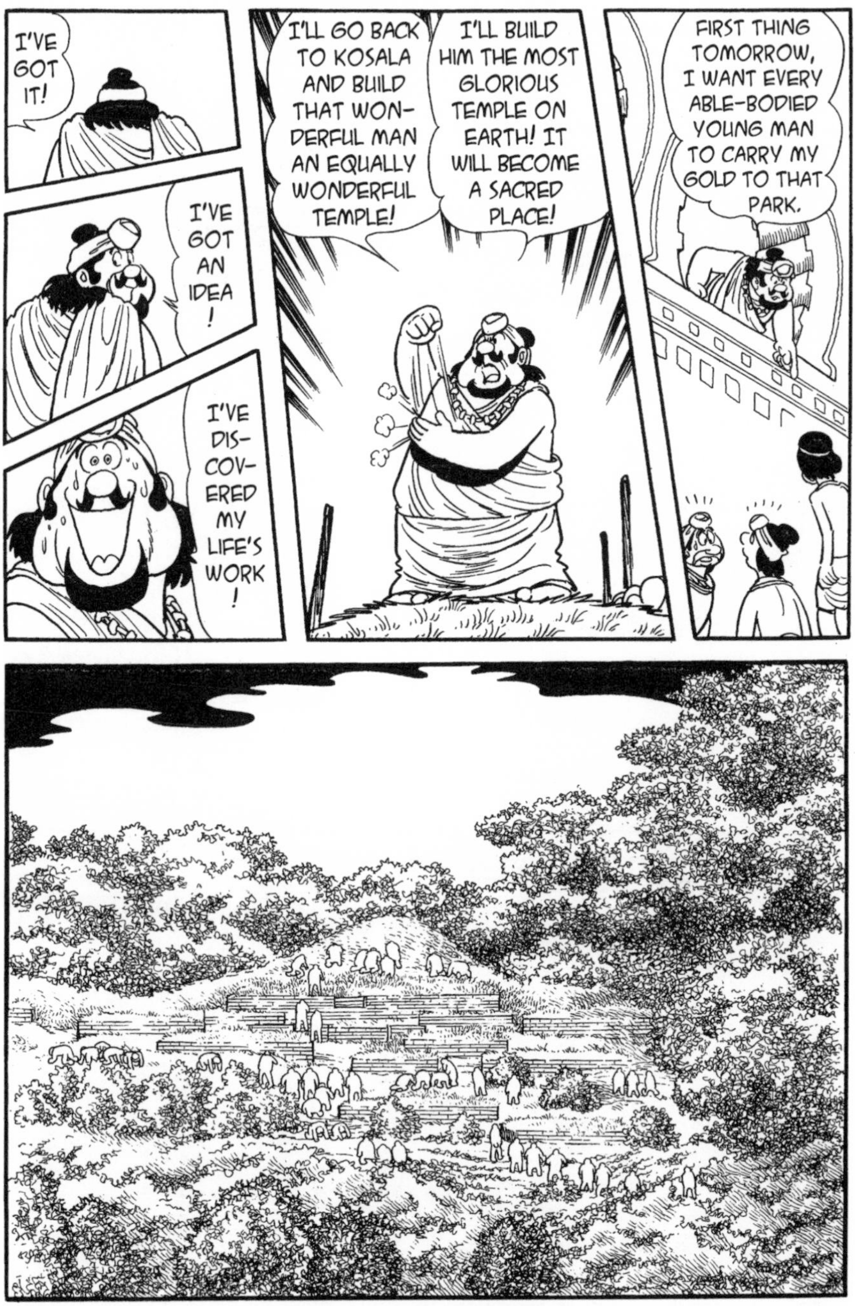
I'VE GOT IT!
I'VE GOT AN IDEA!
I'VE DISCOVERED MY LIFE'S WORK!
I'LL GO BACK TO KOSALA AND BUILD THAT WONDERFUL MAN AN EQUALLY WONDERFUL TEMPLE!
I'LL BUILD HIM THE MOST GLORIOUS TEMPLE ON EARTH! IT WILL BECOME A SACRED PLACE!
FIRST THING TOMORROW, I WANT EVERY ABLE-BODIED YOUNG MAN TO CARRY MY GOLD TO THAT PARK.

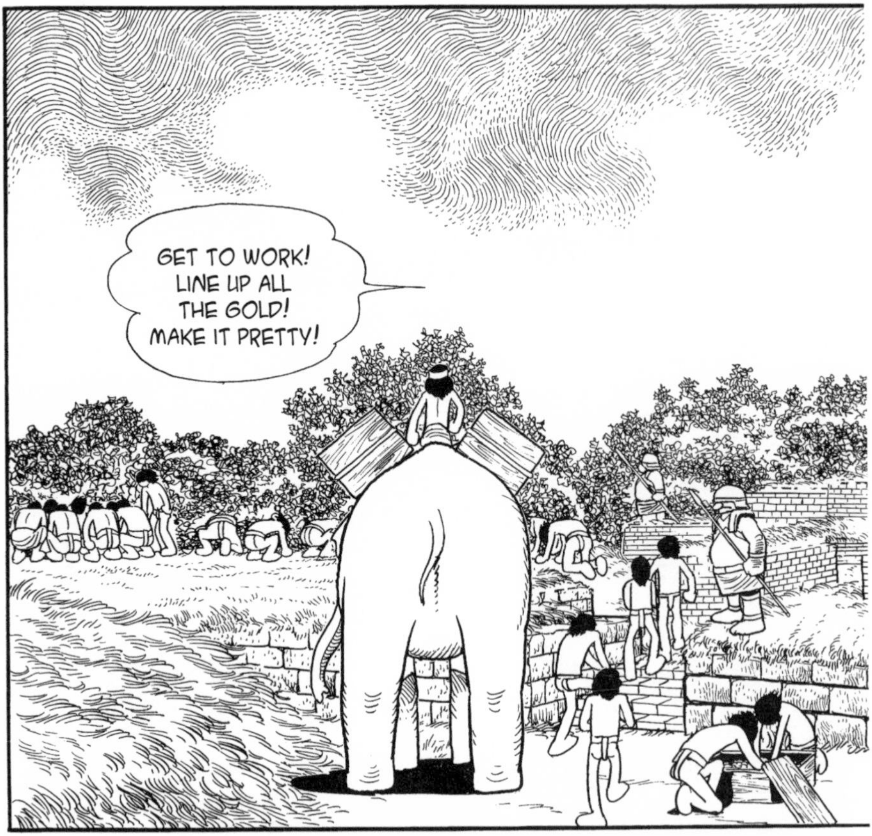
GET TO WORK! LINE UP ALL THE GOLD! MAKE IT PRETTY!
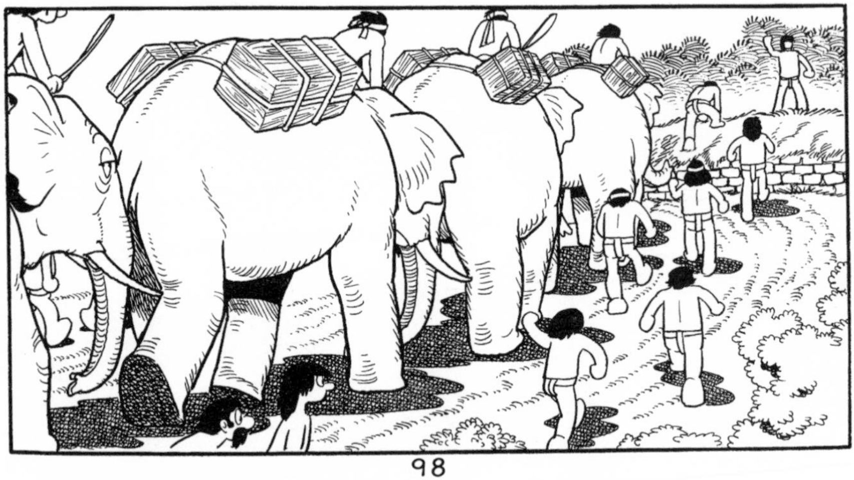

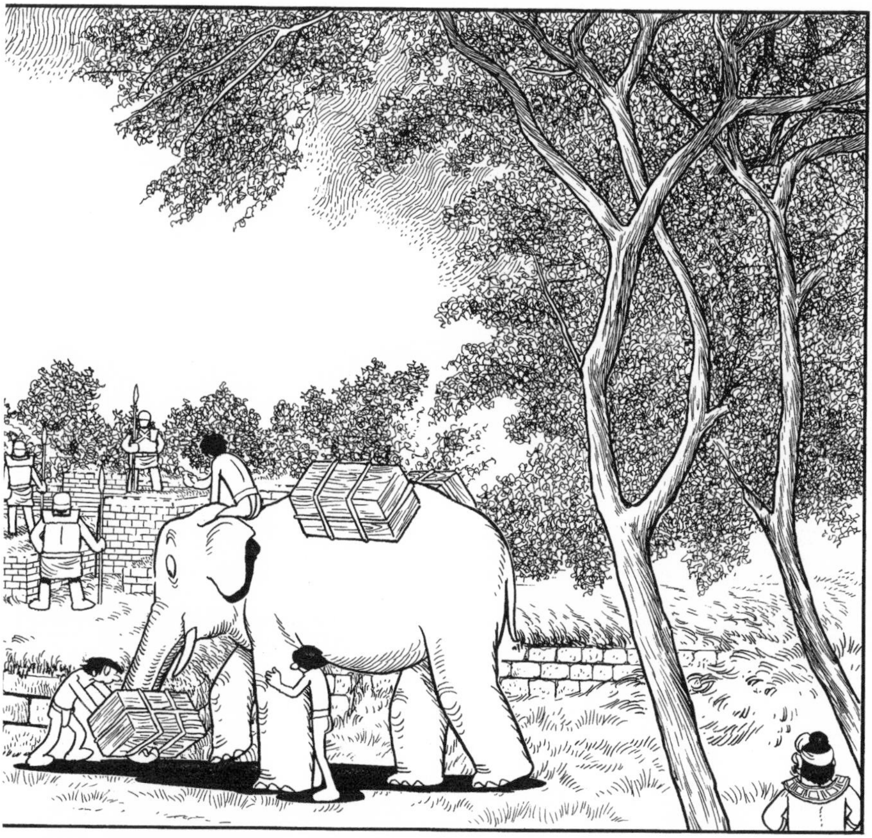

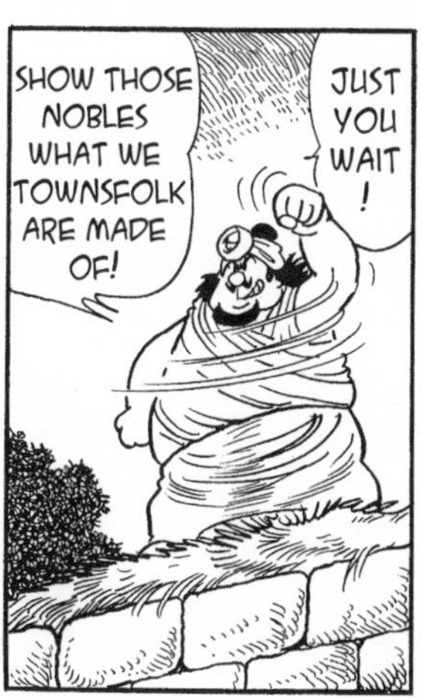
SHOW THOSE NOBLES WHAT WE TOWNSFOLK ARE MADE OF!
JUST YOU WAIT!

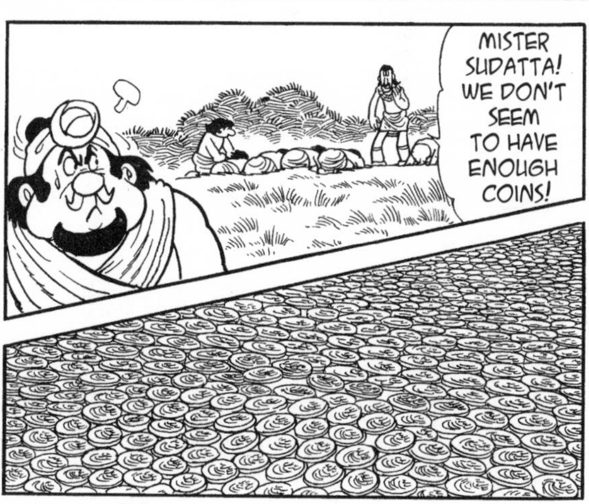
MISTER SUDATTA! WE DON'T SEEM TO HAVE ENOUGH COINS!

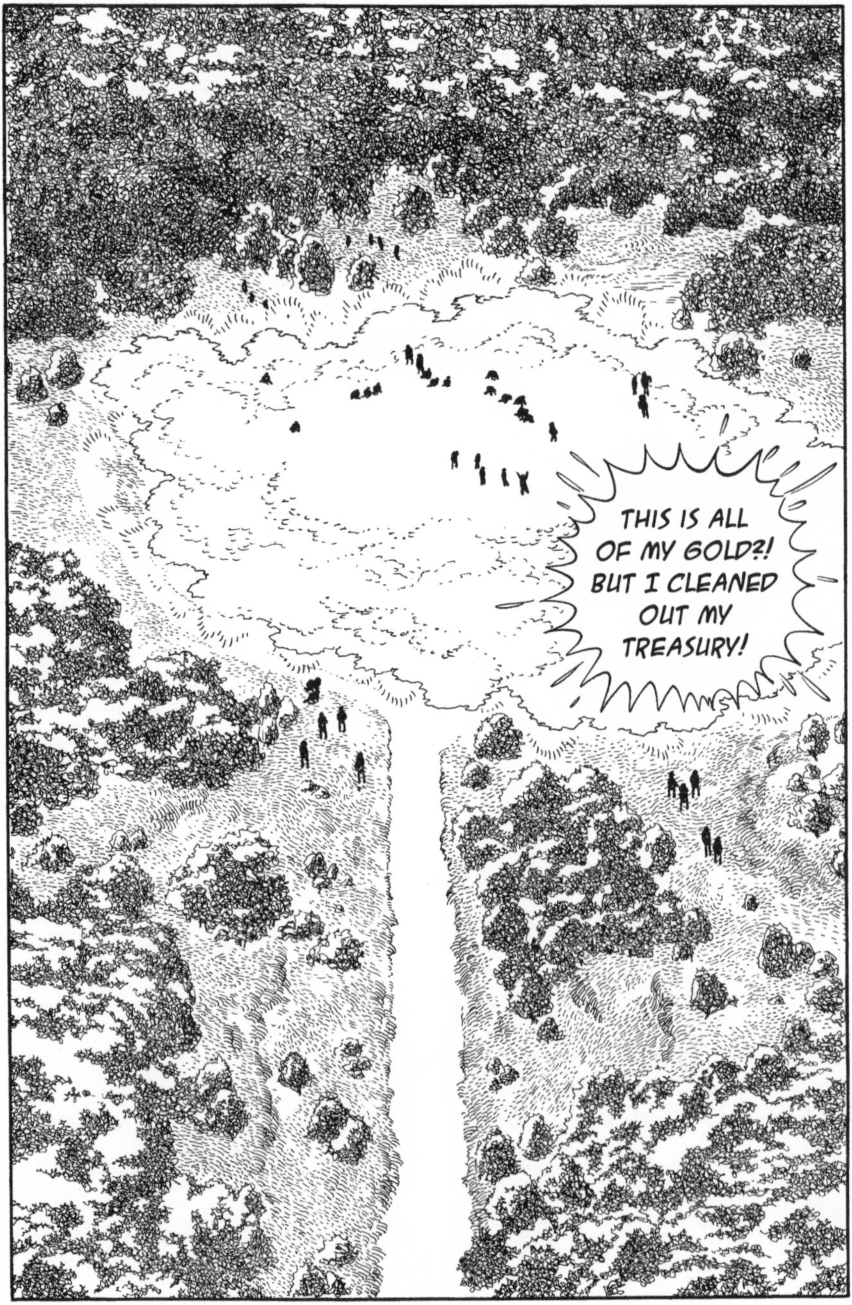
THIS IS ALL OF MY GOLD?! BUT I CLEANED OUT MY TREASURY!

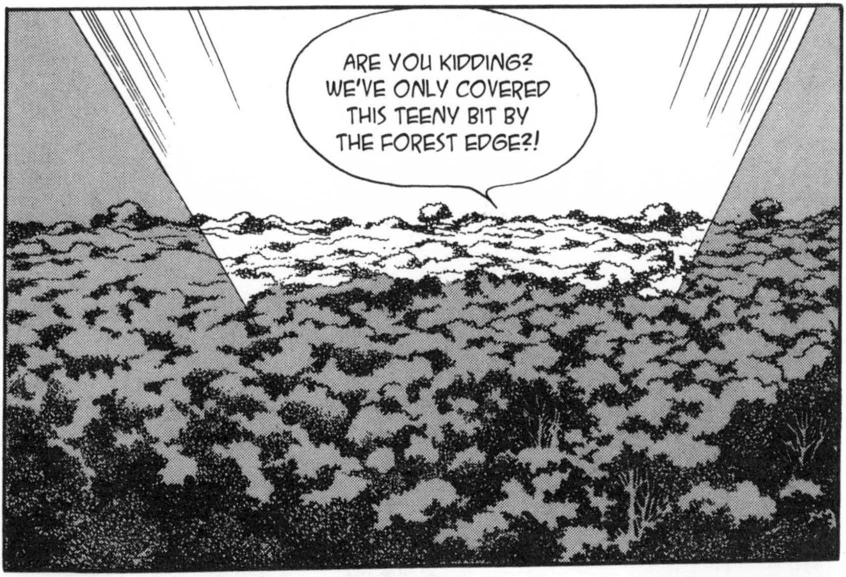
ARE YOU KIDDING? WE'VE ONLY COVERED THIS TEENY BIT BY THE FOREST EDGE?!

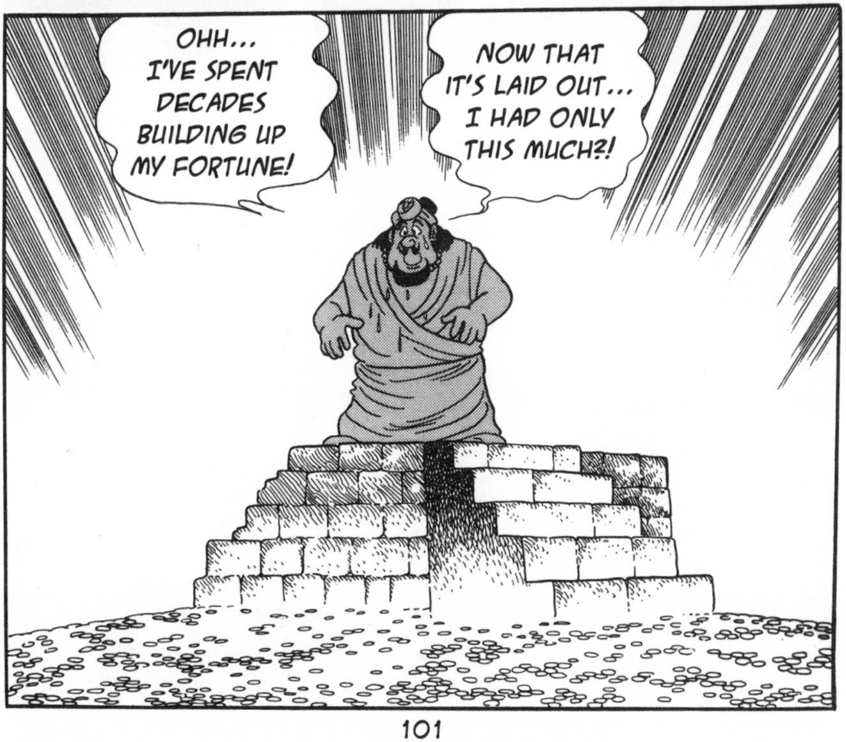
OHH... I'VE SPENT DECADES BUILDING UP MY FORTUNE!
NOW THAT IT'S LAID OUT... I HAD ONLY THIS MUCH?!

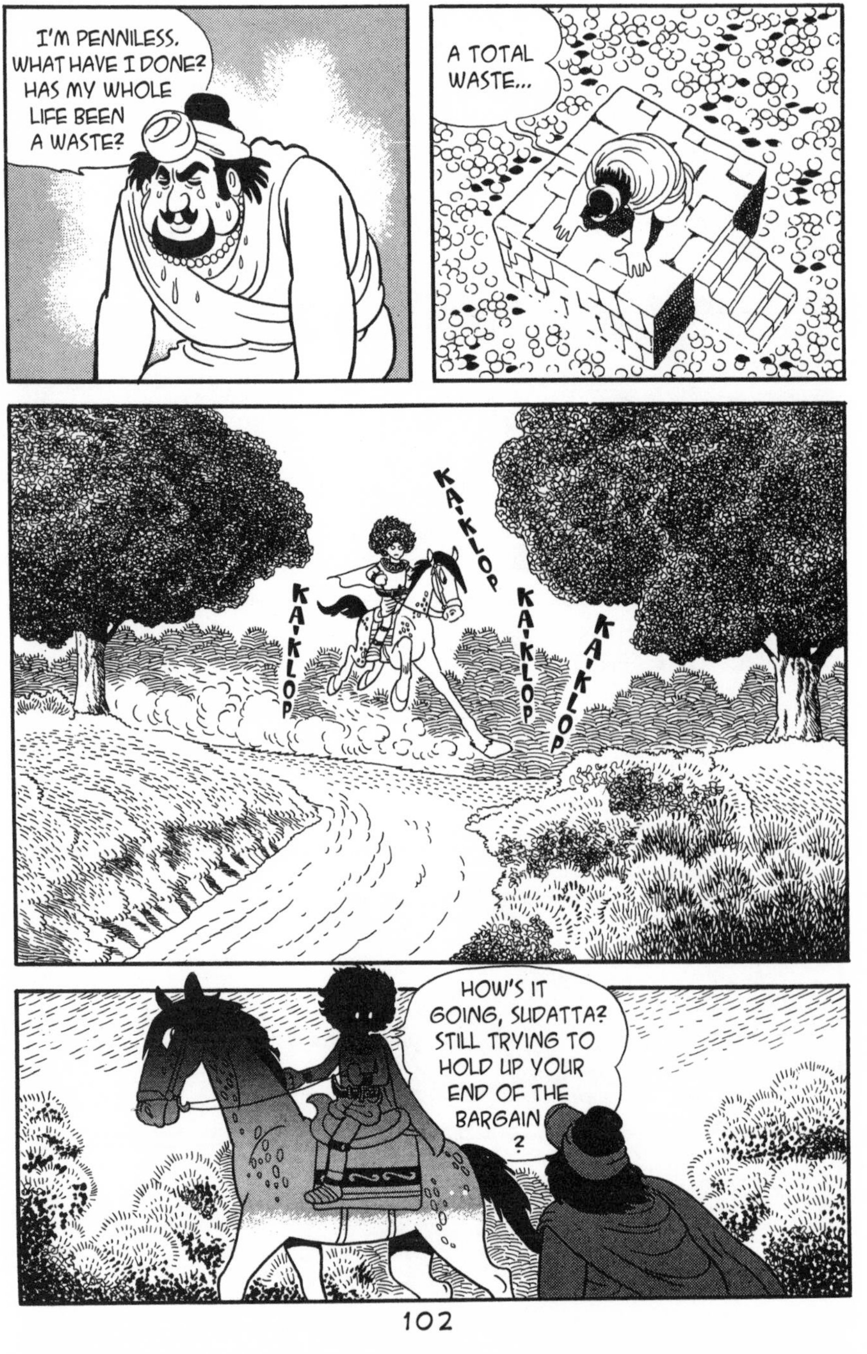
I'M PENNILESS. WHAT HAVE I DONE? HAS MY WHOLE LIFE BEEN A WASTE?
A TOTAL WASTE...
KA-KLOP
KA-KLOP
KA-KLOP
KA-KLOP
HOW'S IT GOING, SUDATTA? STILL TRYING TO HOLD UP YOUR END OF THE BARGAIN?

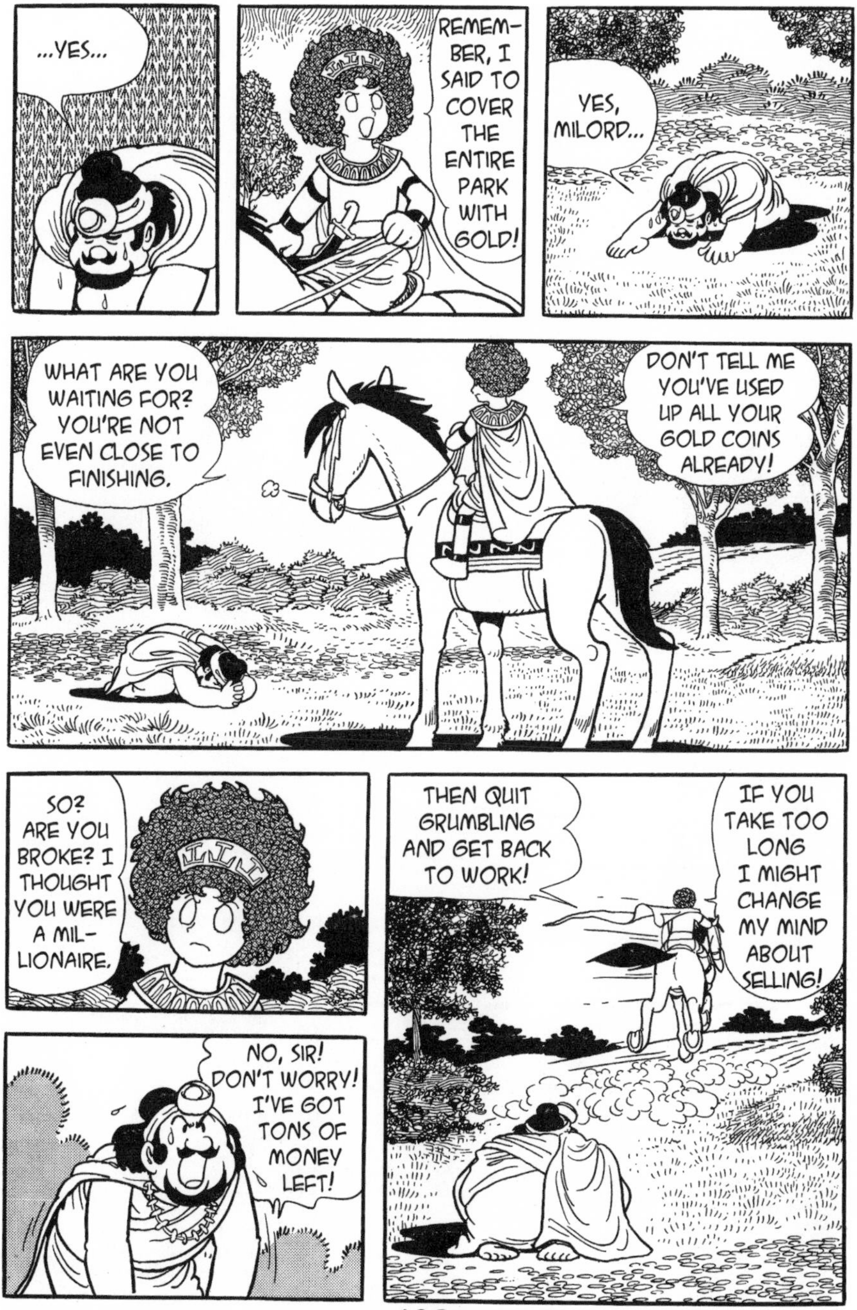
...YES...
REMEMBER, I SAID TO COVER THE ENTIRE PARK WITH GOLD!
YES, MILORD...
WHAT ARE YOU WAITING FOR? YOU'RE NOT EVEN CLOSE TO FINISHING.
DON'T TELL ME YOU'VE USED UP ALL YOUR GOLD COINS ALREADY!
SO? ARE YOU BROKE? I THOUGHT YOU WERE A MILLIONAIRE.
NO, SIR! DON'T WORRY! I'VE GOT TONS OF MONEY LEFT!
THEN QUIT GRUMBLING AND GET BACK TO WORK!
IF YOU TAKE TOO LONG I MIGHT CHANGE MY MIND ABOUT SELLING!

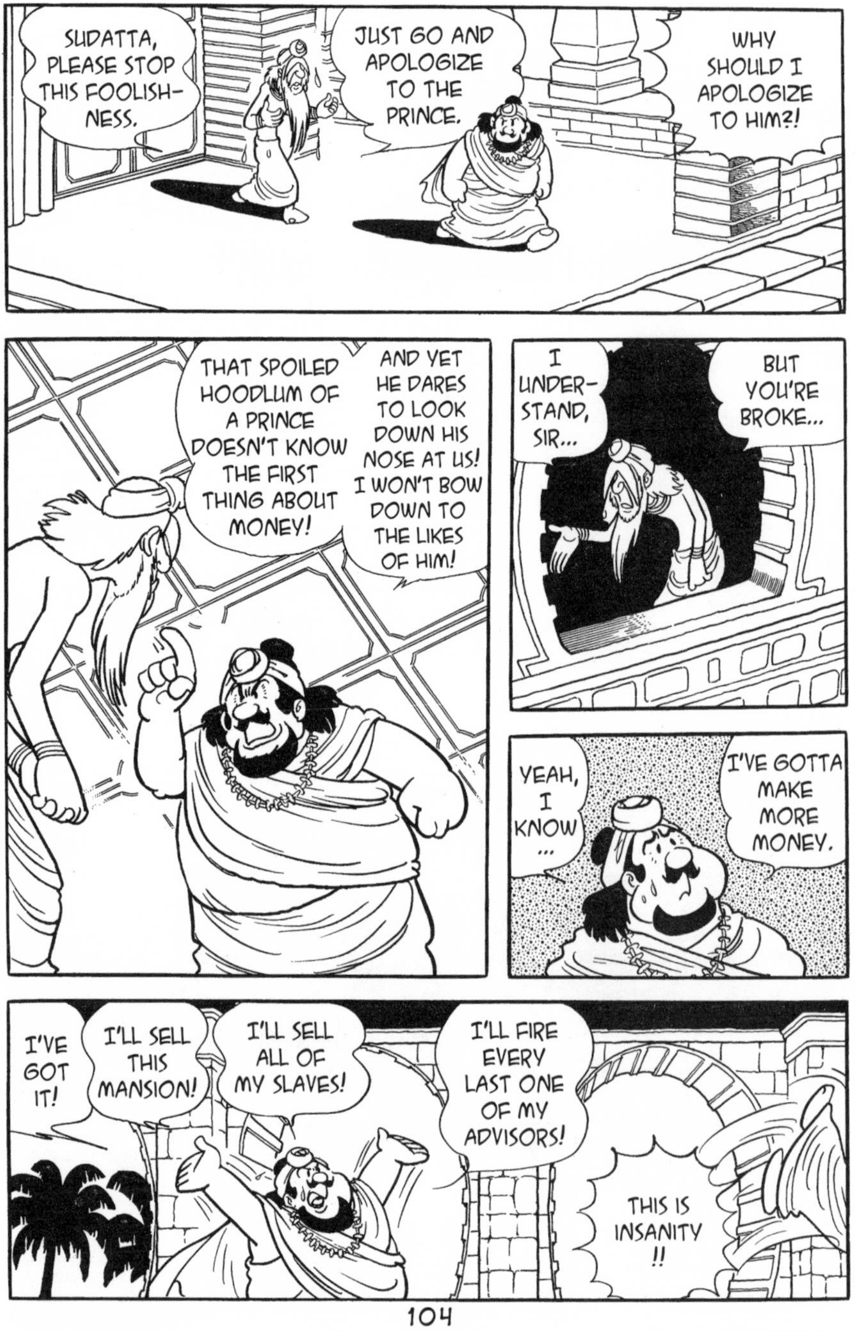
SUDATTA, PLEASE STOP THIS FOOLISH-NESS.
JUST GO AND APOLOGIZE TO THE PRINCE.
WHY SHOULD I APOLOGIZE TO HIM?!
THAT SPOILED HOODLUM OF A PRINCE DOESN'T KNOW THE FIRST THING ABOUT MONEY!
AND YET HE DARES TO LOOK DOWN HIS NOSE AT US! I WON'T BOW DOWN TO THE LIKES OF HIM!
I UNDER-STAND, SIR...
BUT YOU'RE BROKE...
YEAH, I KNOW ...
I'VE GOTTA MAKE MORE MONEY.
I'VE GOT IT!
I'LL SELL THIS MANSION!
I'LL SELL ALL OF MY SLAVES!
I'LL FIRE EVERY LAST ONE OF MY ADVISORS!
THIS IS INSANITY !!

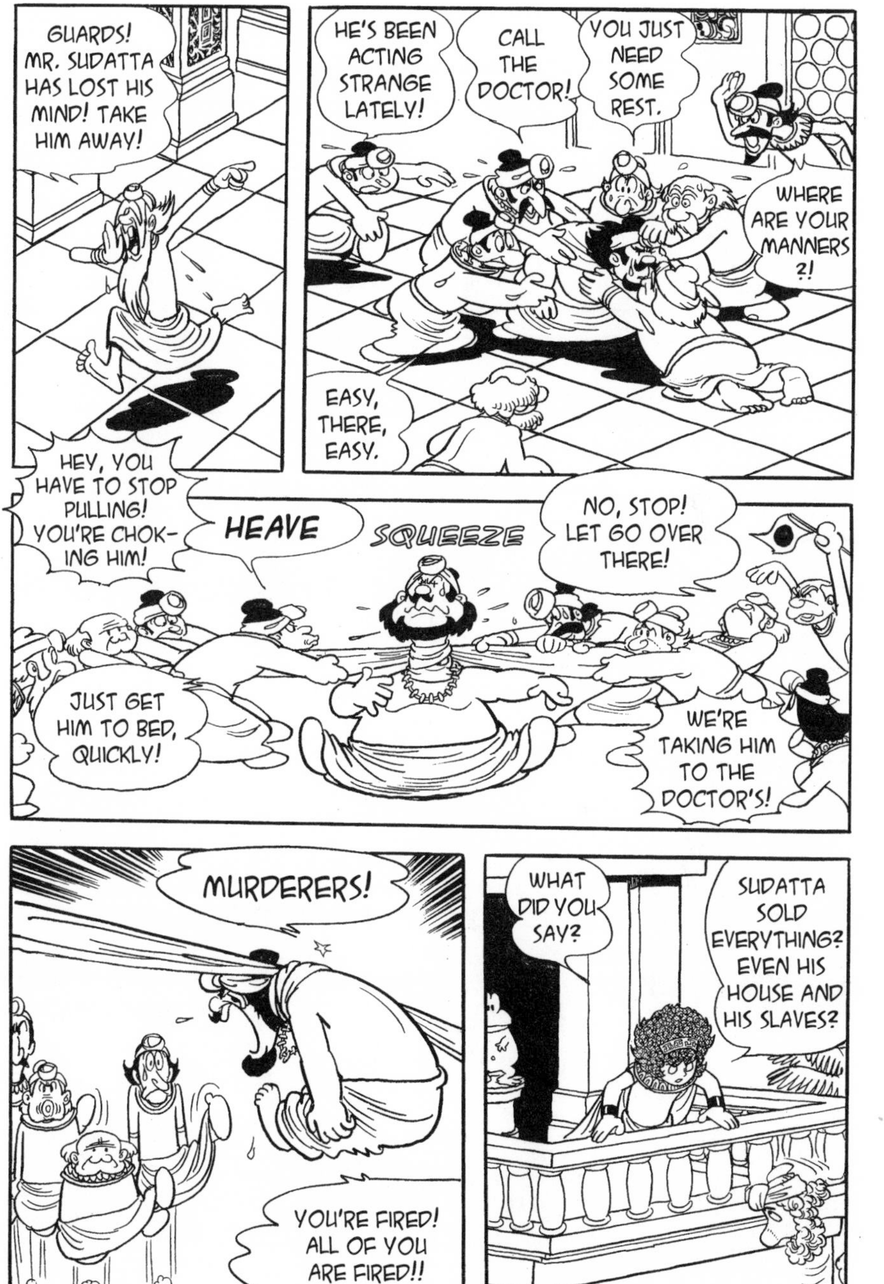
GUARDS! MR. SUDATTA HAS LOST HIS MIND! TAKE HIM AWAY!
HE'S BEEN ACTING STRANGE LATELY!
CALL THE DOCTOR!
YOU JUST NEED SOME REST.
WHERE ARE YOUR MANNERS?!
EASY, THERE, EASY.
HEY, YOU HAVE TO STOP PULLING! YOU'RE CHOKING HIM!
HEAVE
SQUEEZE
NO, STOP! LET GO OVER THERE!
JUST GET HIM TO BED, QUICKLY!
WE'RE TAKING HIM TO THE DOCTOR'S!
MURDERERS!
YOU'RE FIRED! ALL OF YOU ARE FIRED!!
WHAT DID YOU SAY?
SUDATTA SOLD EVERYTHING? EVEN HIS HOUSE AND HIS SLAVES?

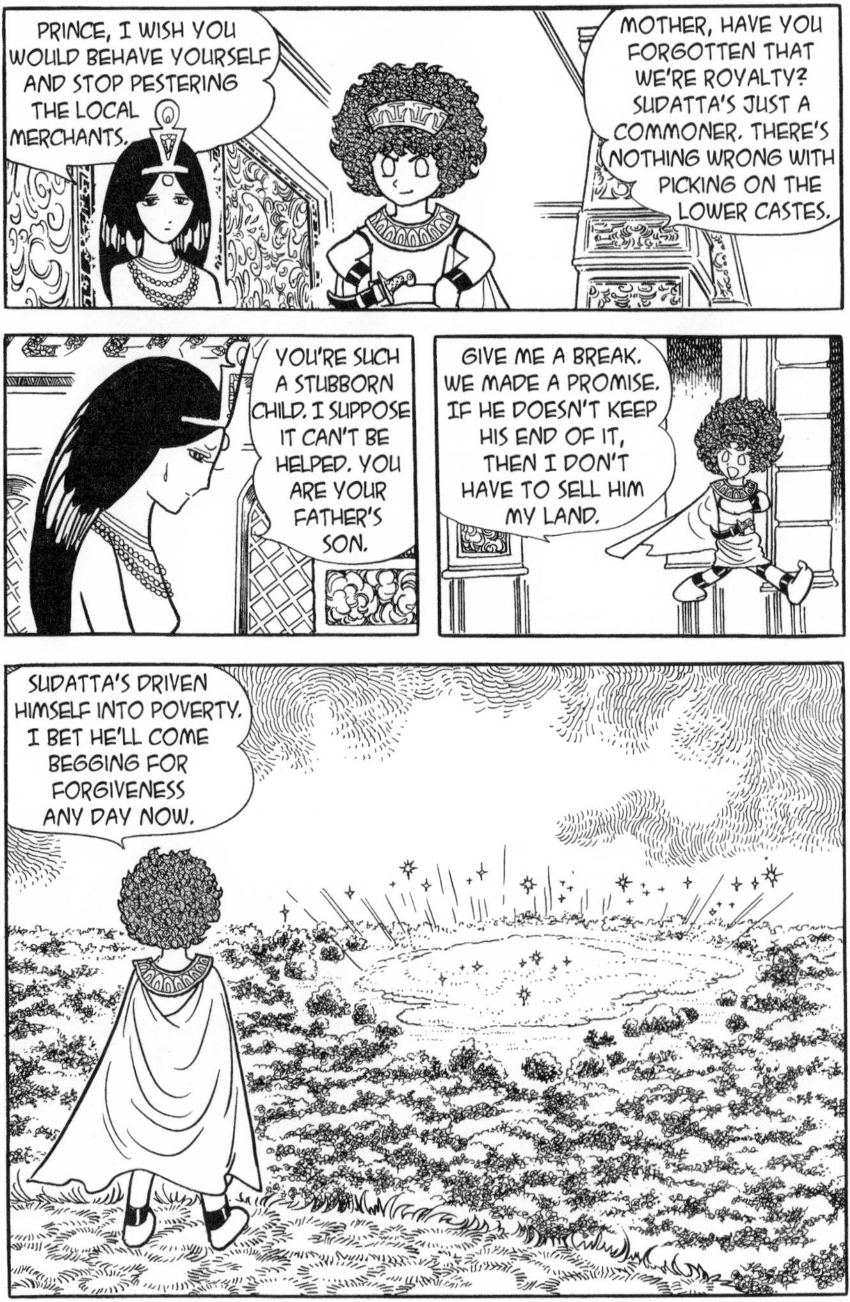
PRINCE, I WISH YOU WOULD BEHAVE YOURSELF AND STOP PESTERING THE LOCAL MERCHANTS.
MOTHER, HAVE YOU FORGOTTEN THAT WE'RE ROYALTY? SUDATTA'S JUST A COMMONER. THERE'S NOTHING WRONG WITH PICKING ON THE LOWER CASTES.
YOU'RE SUCH A STUBBORN CHILD. I SUPPOSE IT CAN'T BE HELPED. YOU ARE YOUR FATHER'S SON.
GIVE ME A BREAK. WE MADE A PROMISE. IF HE DOESN'T KEEP HIS END OF IT, THEN I DON'T HAVE TO SELL HIM MY LAND.
SUDATTA'S DRIVEN HIMSELF INTO POVERTY. I BET HE'LL COME BEGGING FOR FORGIVENESS ANY DAY NOW.

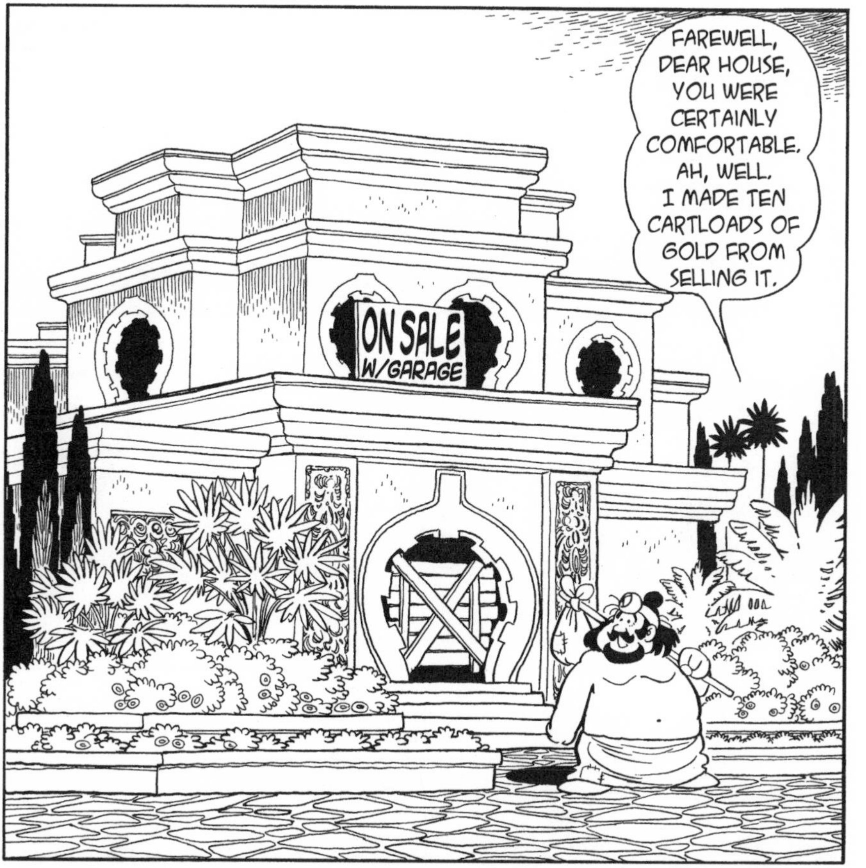
FAREWELL, DEAR HOUSE, YOU WERE CERTAINLY COMFORTABLE. AH, WELL. I MADE TEN CARTLOADS OF GOLD FROM SELLING IT.
ON SALE
W/GARAGE

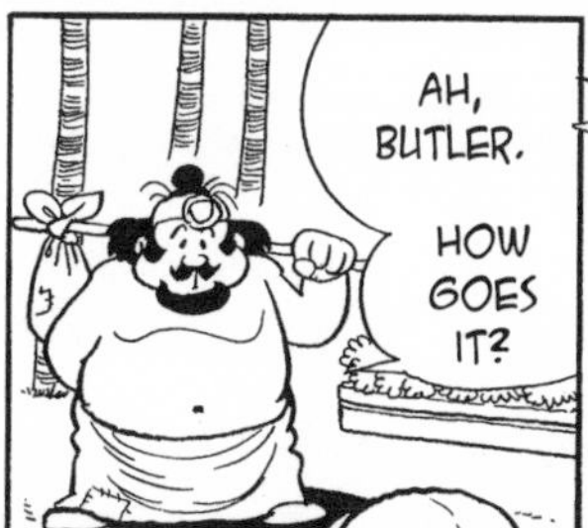
AH, BUTLER.
HOW GOES IT?
WELL, YOU SEE, SIR...

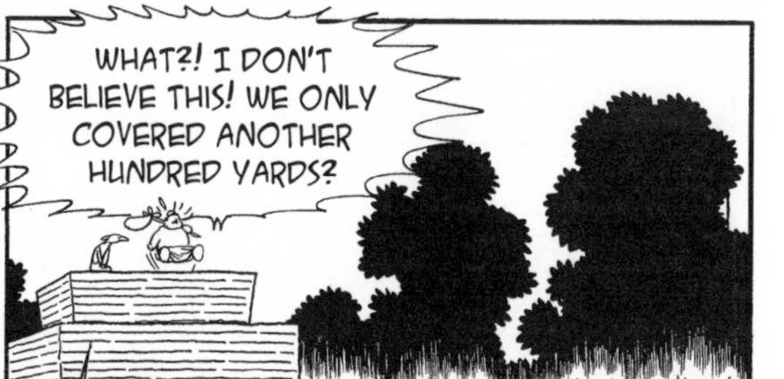
WHAT?! I DON'T BELIEVE THIS! WE ONLY COVERED ANOTHER HUNDRED YARDS?
I'M AFRAID SO, SIR.

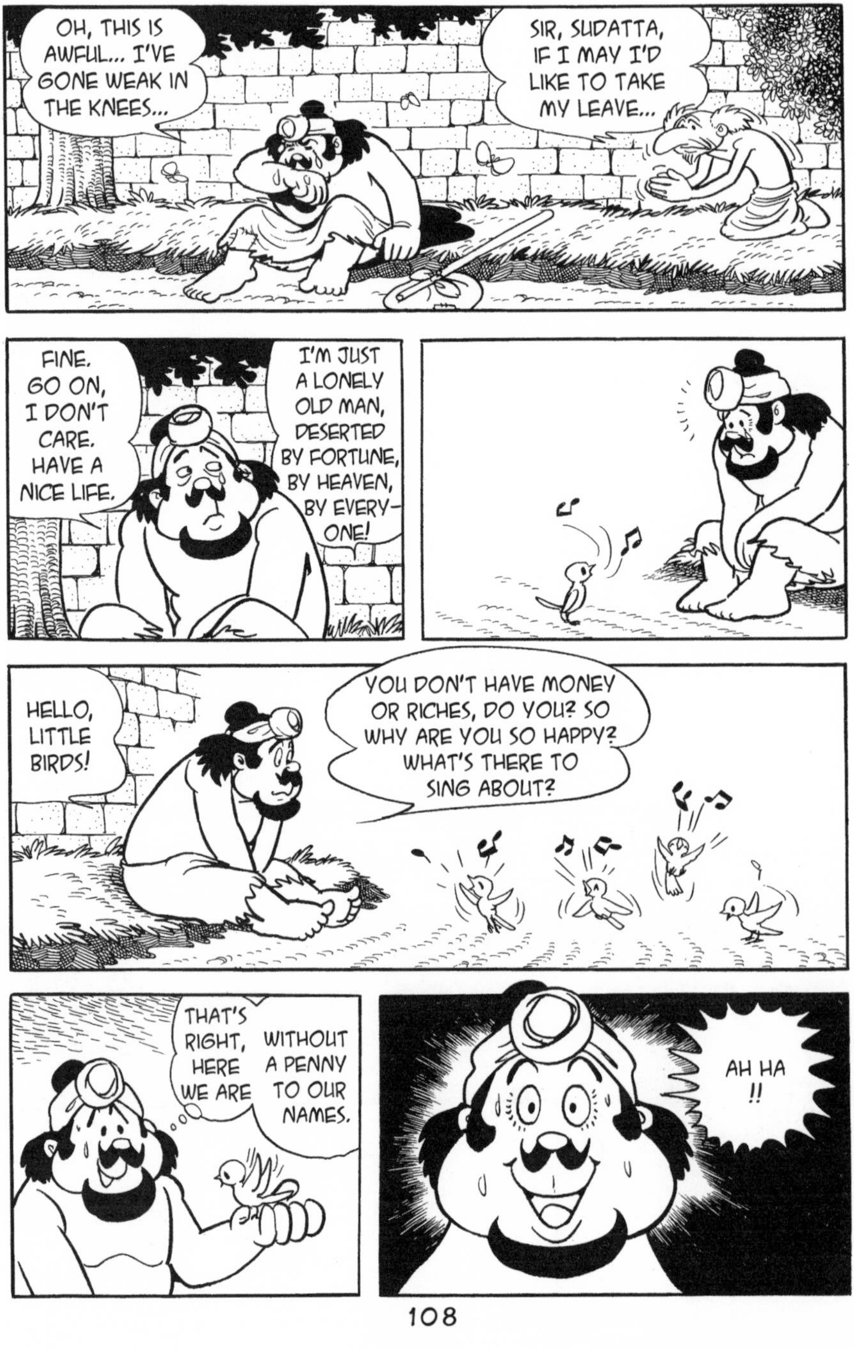
OH, THIS IS AWFUL... I'VE GONE WEAK IN THE KNEES...
SIR, SUDATTA, IF I MAY I'D LIKE TO TAKE MY LEAVE...
FINE. GO ON, I DON'T CARE. HAVE A NICE LIFE.
I'M JUST A LONELY OLD MAN, DESERTED BY FORTUNE, BY HEAVEN, BY EVERY-ONE!
HELLO, LITTLE BIRDS!
YOU DON'T HAVE MONEY OR RICHES, DO YOU? SO WHY ARE YOU SO HAPPY? WHAT'S THERE TO SING ABOUT?
THAT'S RIGHT, HERE WE ARE
WITHOUT A PENNY TO OUR NAMES.
AH HA !!

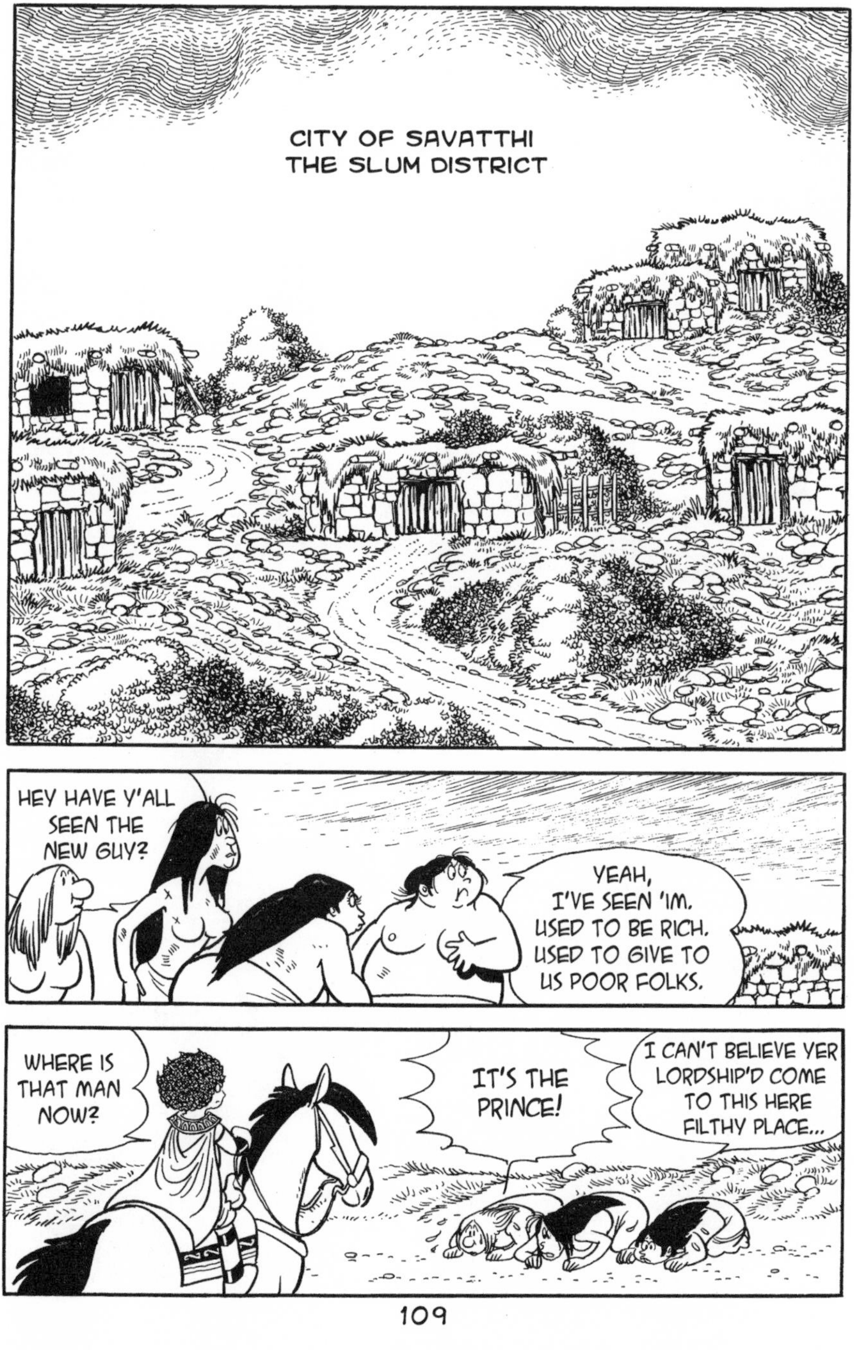
CITY OF SAVATTHI
THE SLUM DISTRICT
HEY HAVE Y'ALL SEEN THE NEW GUY?
YEAH, I'VE SEEN 'IM. USED TO BE RICH. USED TO GIVE TO US POOR FOLKS.
WHERE IS THAT MAN NOW?
IT'S THE PRINCE!
I CAN'T BELIEVE YER LORDSHIP'D COME TO THIS HERE FILTHY PLACE...

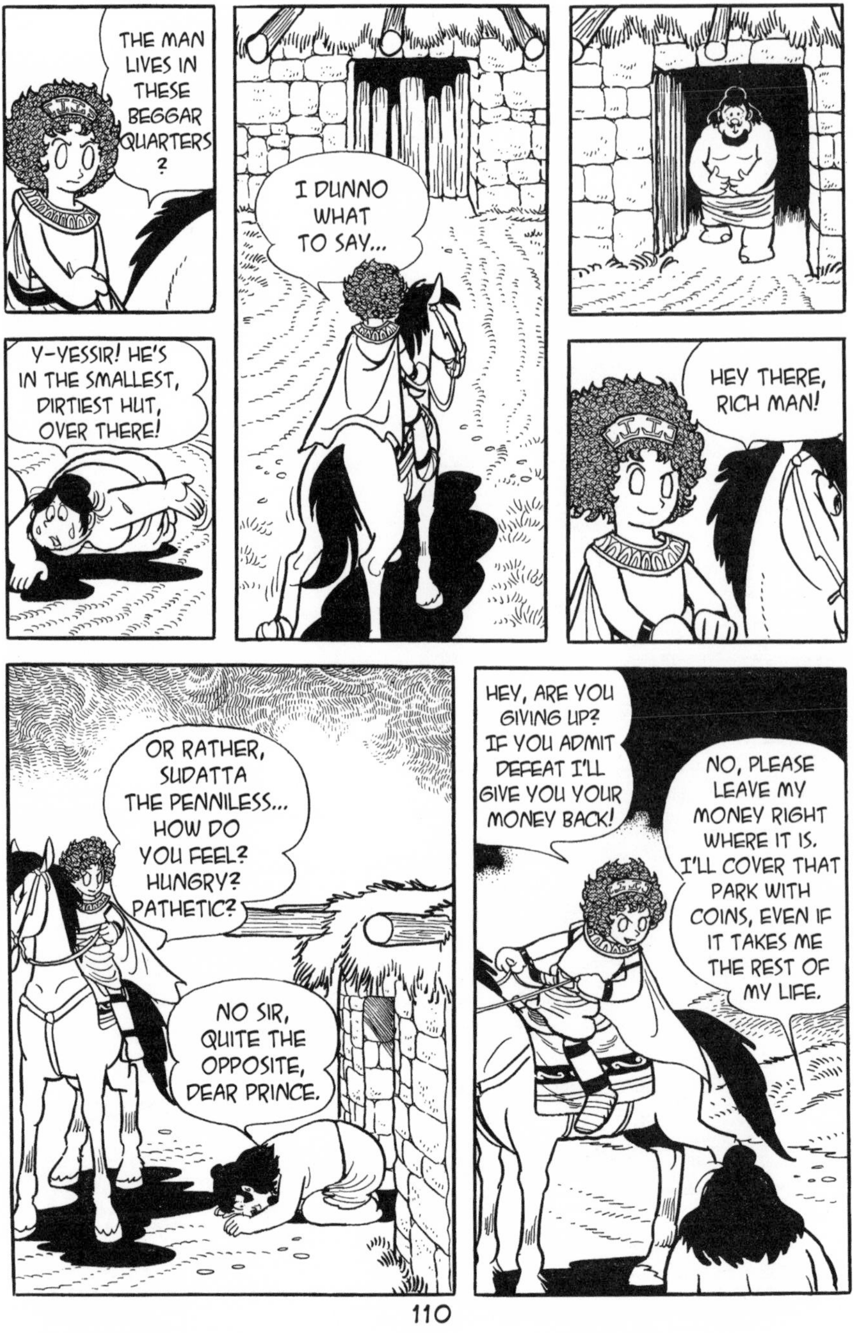
THE MAN LIVES IN THESE BEGGAR QUARTERS?
I DUNNO WHAT TO SAY...
Y-YESSIR! HE'S IN THE SMALLEST, DIRTIEST HUT, OVER THERE!
HEY THERE, RICH MAN!
OR RATHER, SUDATTA THE PENNILESS... HOW DO YOU FEEL? HUNGRY? PATHETIC?
NO SIR, QUITE THE OPPOSITE, DEAR PRINCE.
HEY, ARE YOU GIVING UP? IF YOU ADMIT DEFEAT I'LL GIVE YOU YOUR MONEY BACK!
NO, PLEASE LEAVE MY MONEY RIGHT WHERE IT IS. I'LL COVER THAT PARK WITH COINS, EVEN IF IT TAKES ME THE REST OF MY LIFE.

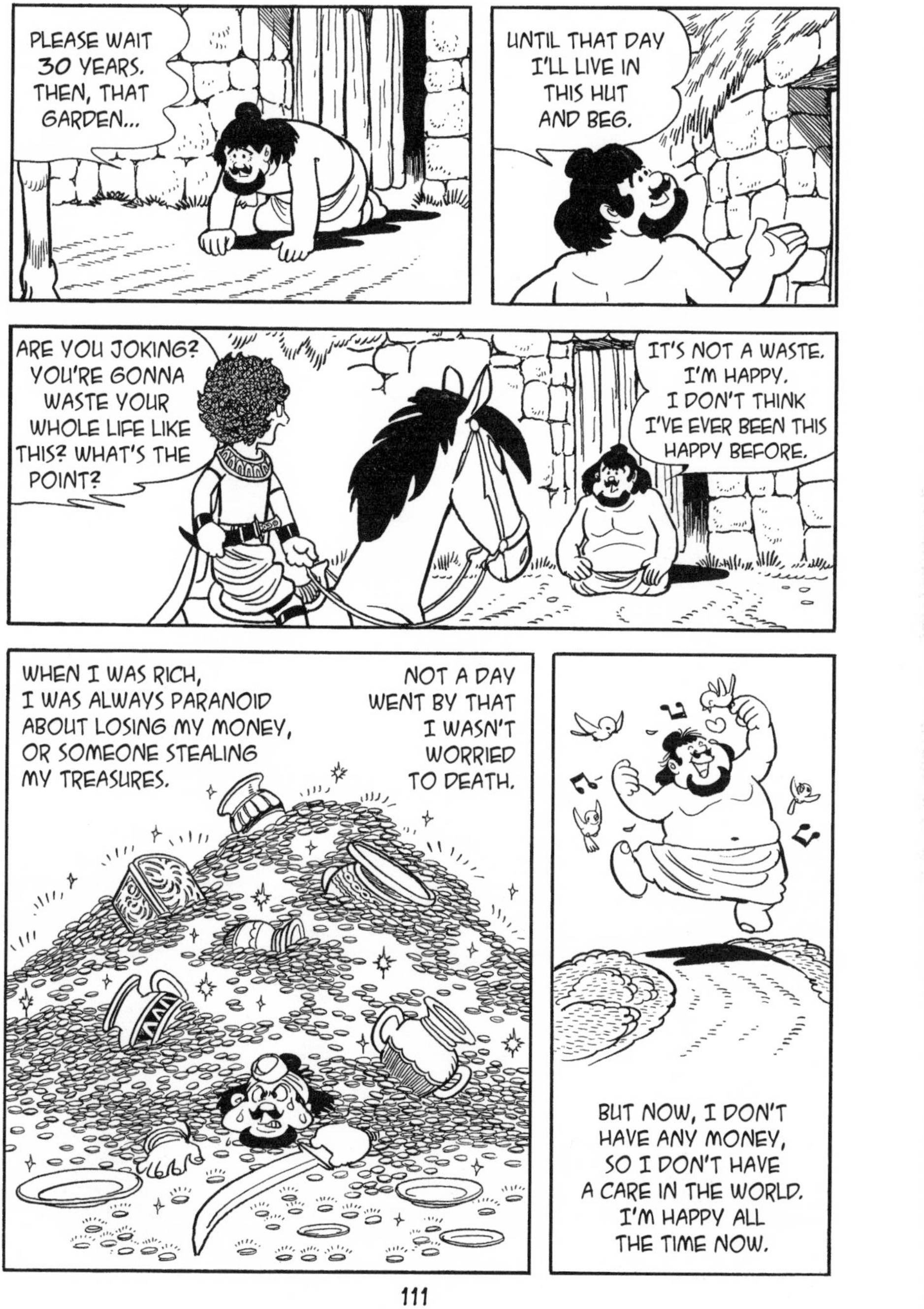
PLEASE WAIT 30 YEARS. THEN, THAT GARDEN...
UNTIL THAT DAY I'LL LIVE IN THIS HUT AND BEG.
ARE YOU JOKING? YOU'RE GONNA WASTE YOUR WHOLE LIFE LIKE THIS? WHAT'S THE POINT?
IT'S NOT A WASTE. I'M HAPPY. I DON'T THINK I'VE EVER BEEN THIS HAPPY BEFORE.
WHEN I WAS RICH, I WAS ALWAYS PARANOID ABOUT LOSING MY MONEY, OR SOMEONE STEALING MY TREASURES.
NOT A DAY WENT BY THAT I WASN'T WORRIED TO DEATH.
BUT NOW, I DON'T HAVE ANY MONEY, SO I DON'T HAVE A CARE IN THE WORLD. I'M HAPPY ALL THE TIME NOW.

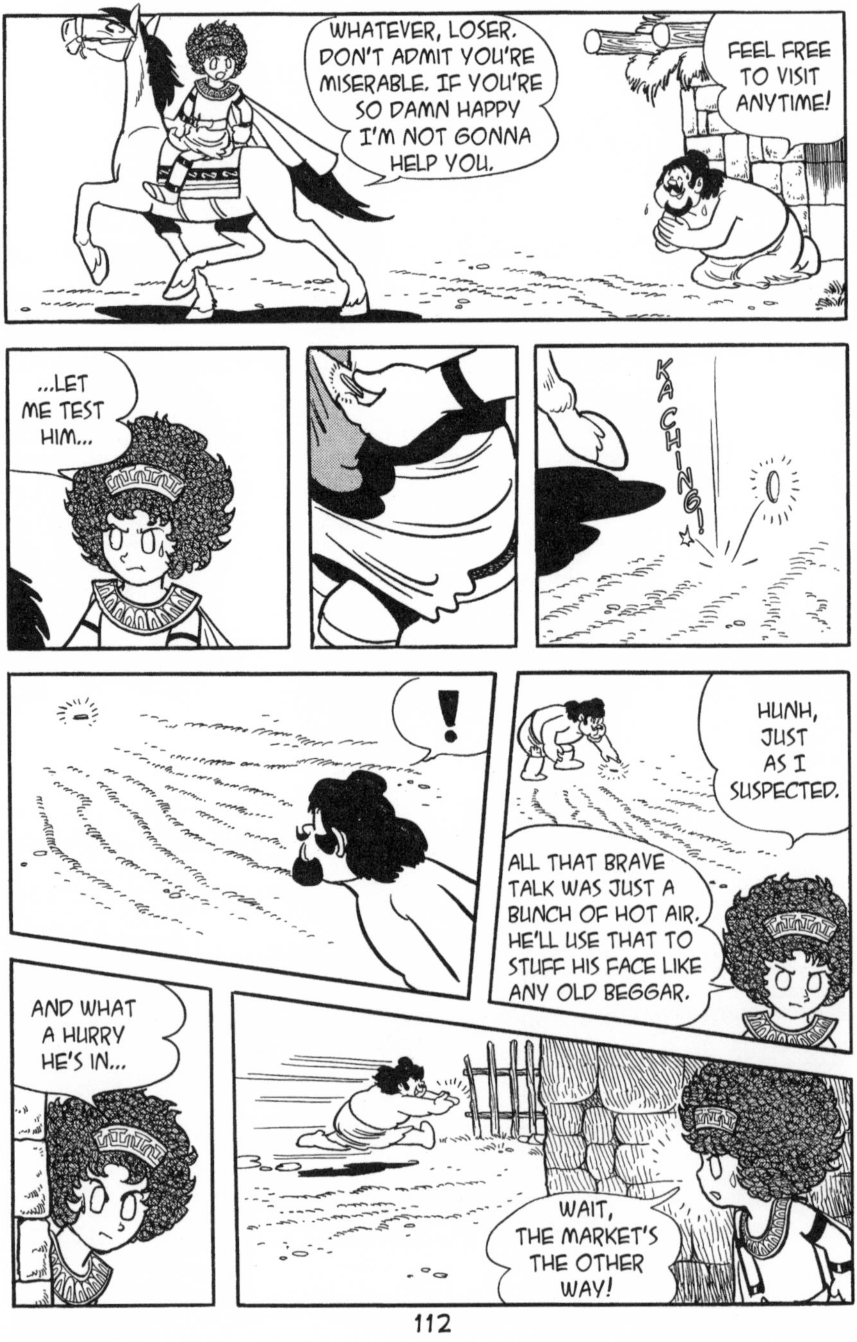
WHATEVER, LOSER. DON'T ADMIT YOU'RE MISERABLE. IF YOU'RE SO DAMN HAPPY I'M NOT GONNA HELP YOU.
FEEL FREE TO VISIT ANYTIME!
...LET ME TEST HIM...
KACHING!
!
HUNH, JUST AS I SUSPECTED.
ALL THAT BRAVE TALK WAS JUST A BUNCH OF HOT AIR. HE'LL USE THAT TO STUFF HIS FACE LIKE ANY OLD BEGGAR.
AND WHAT A HURRY HE'S IN...
WAIT, THE MARKET'S THE OTHER WAY!

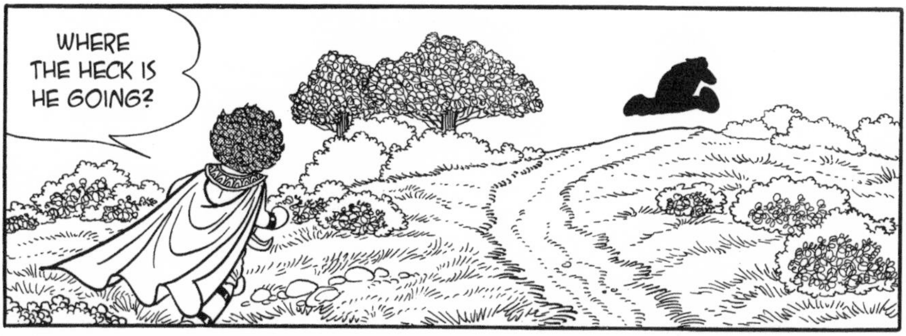
WHERE THE HECK IS HE GOING?

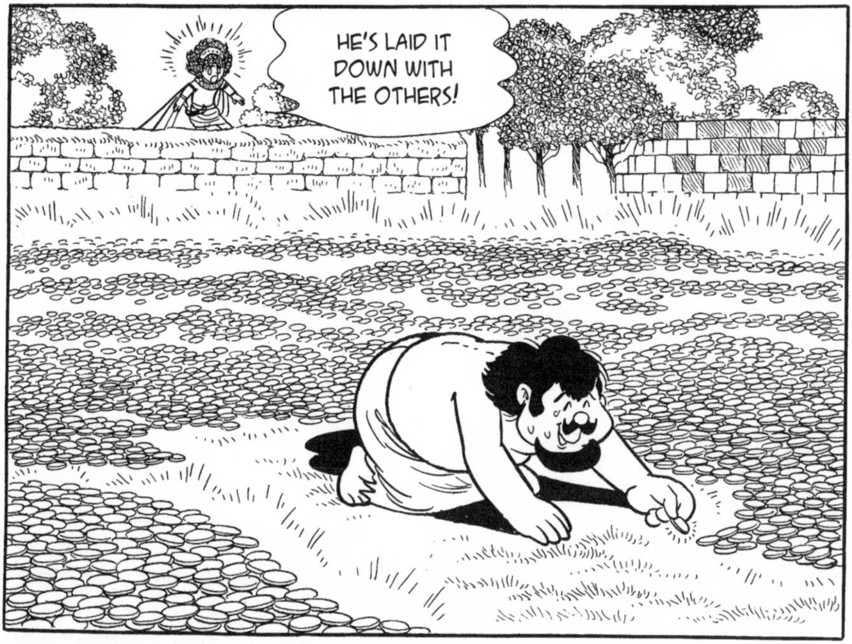
HE'S LAID IT DOWN WITH THE OTHERS!

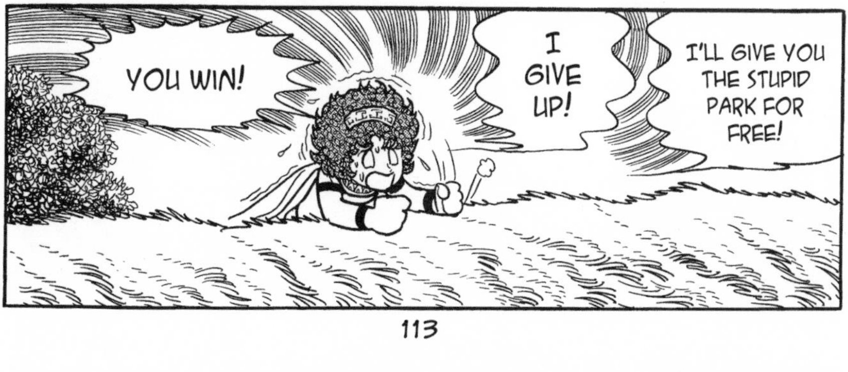
YOU WIN!
I GIVE UP!
I'LL GIVE YOU THE STUPID PARK FOR FREE!

CHAPTER ELEVEN

TRAPPED

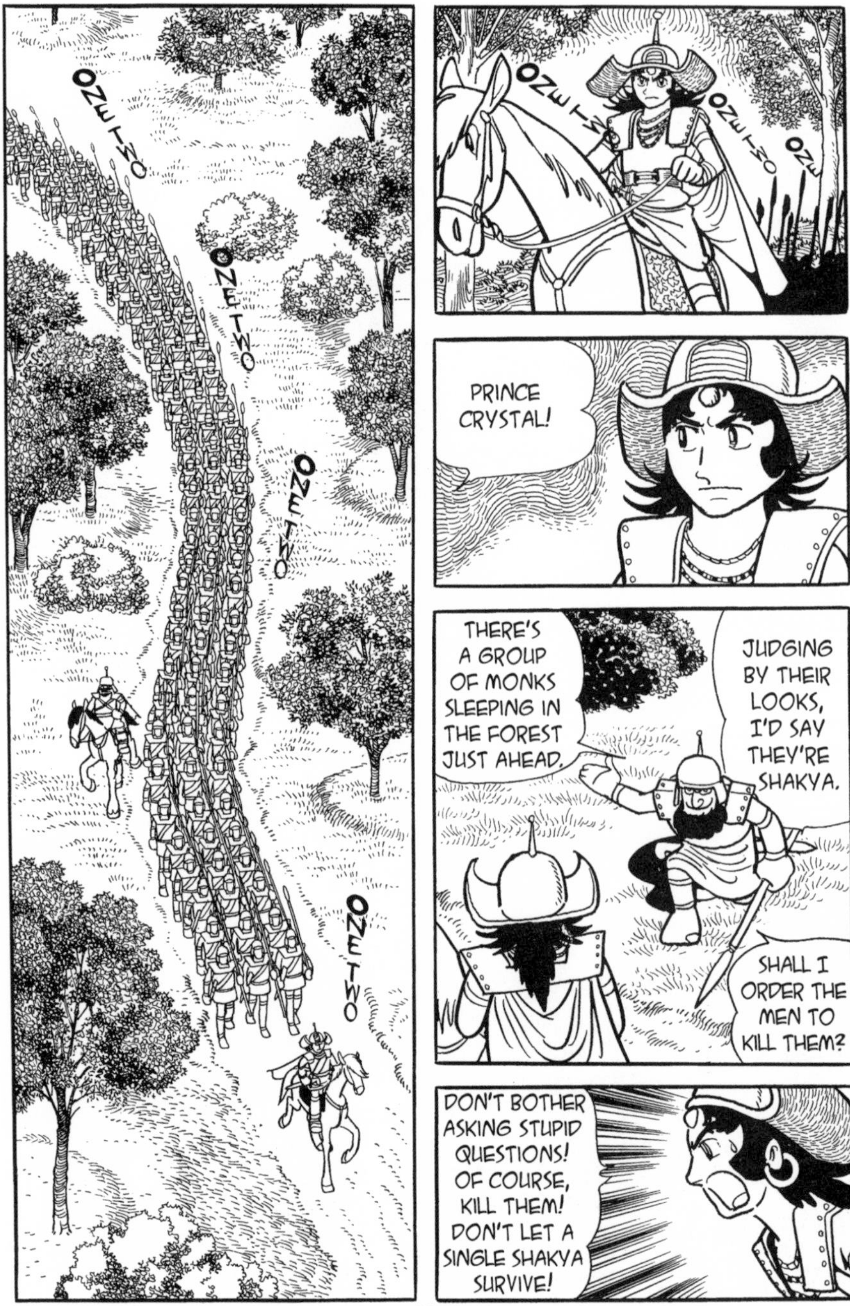

ONE TWO
ONE TWO
ONE TWO
ONE TWO
ONE TWO
ONE TWO
ONE
PRINCE CRYSTAL!
THERE'S A GROUP OF MONKS SLEEPING IN THE FOREST JUST AHEAD.
JUDGING BY THEIR LOOKS, I'D SAY THEY'RE SHAKYA.
SHALL I ORDER THE MEN TO KILL THEM?
DON'T BOTHER ASKING STUPID QUESTIONS! OF COURSE, KILL THEM! DON'T LET A SINGLE SHAKYA SURVIVE!

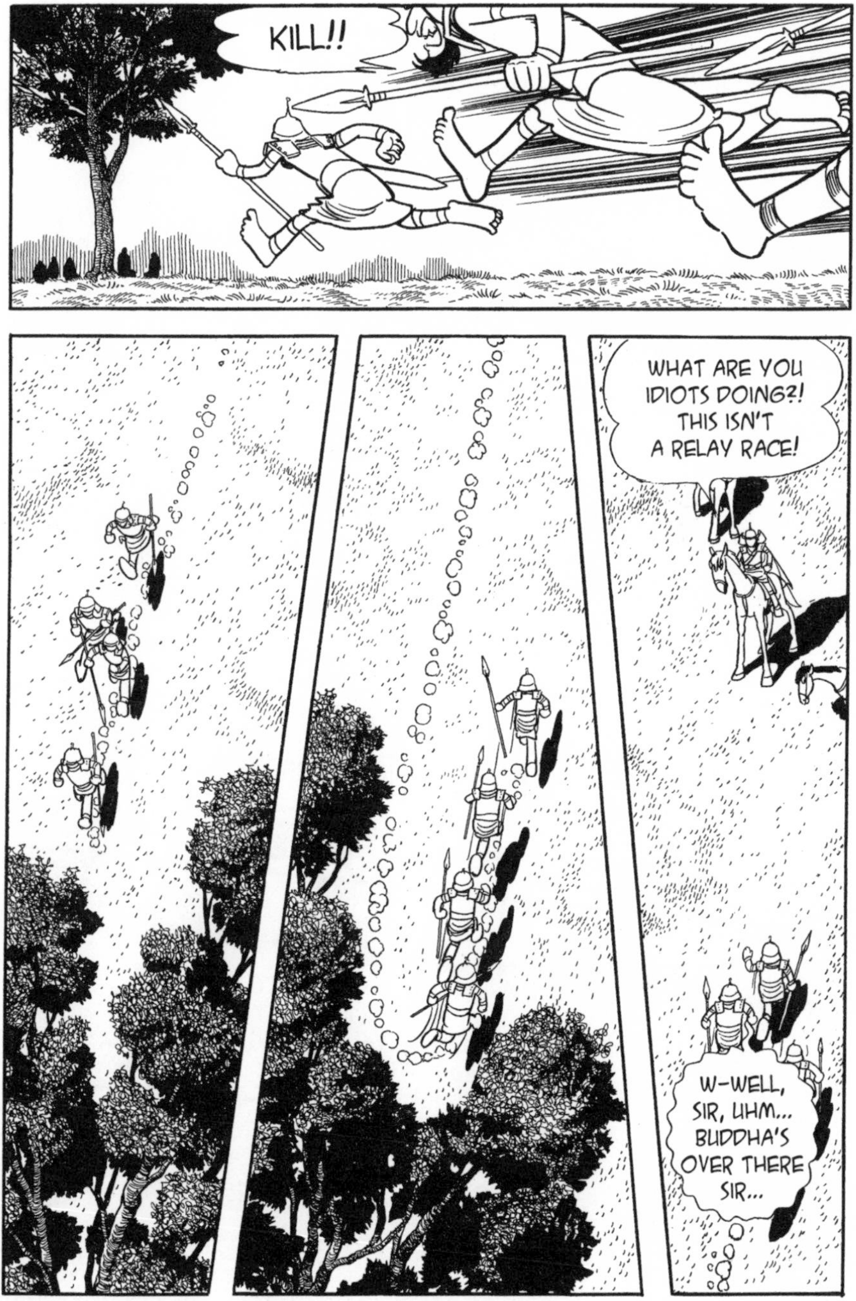
KILL!!
WHAT ARE YOU IDIOTS DOING?! THIS ISN'T A RELAY RACE!
W-WELL, SIR, UHM... BUDDHA'S OVER THERE SIR...

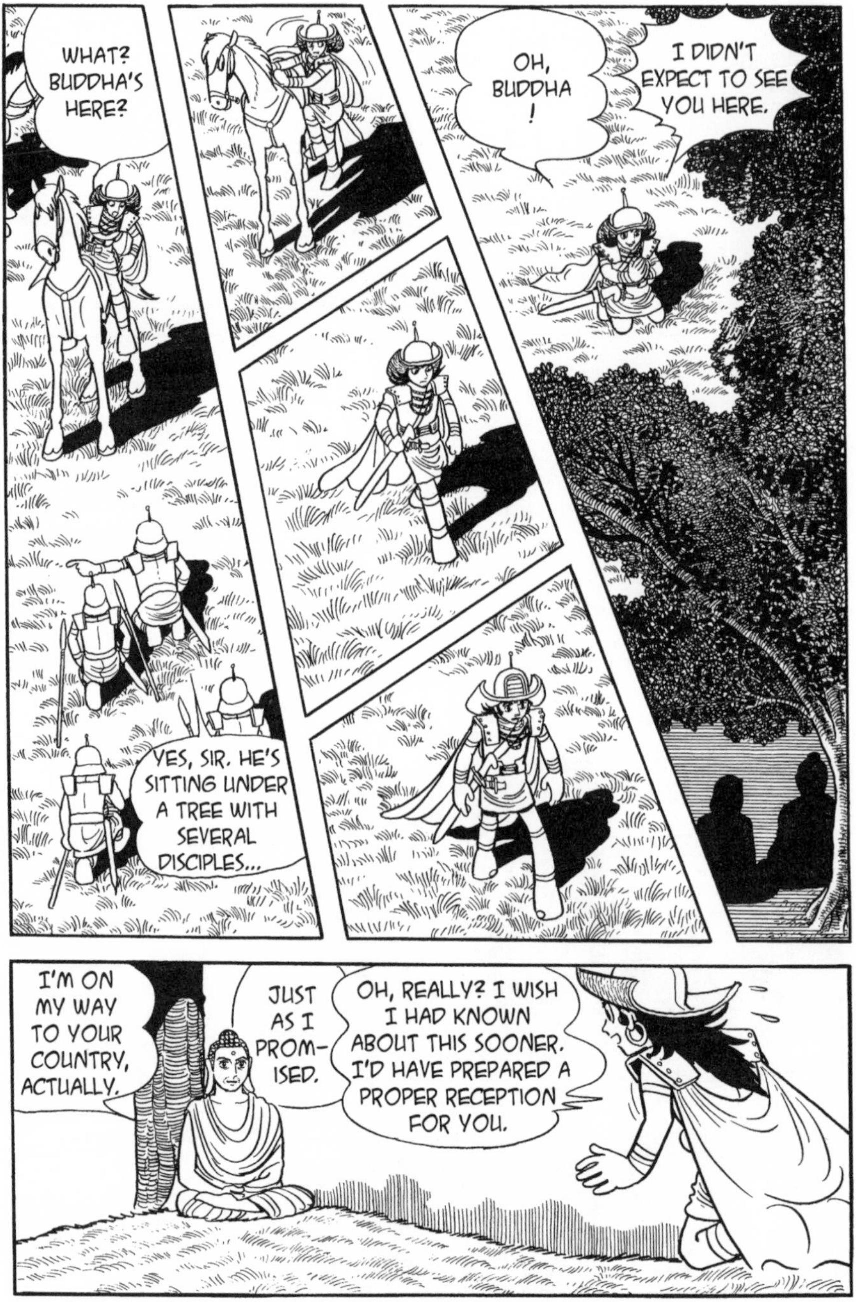
WHAT? BUDDHA'S HERE?
YES, SIR. HE'S SITTING UNDER A TREE WITH SEVERAL DISCIPLES...
OH, BUDDHA !
I DIDN'T EXPECT TO SEE YOU HERE.
I'M ON MY WAY TO YOUR COUNTRY, ACTUALLY.
JUST AS I PROM-ISED.
OH, REALLY? I WISH I HAD KNOWN ABOUT THIS SOONER. I'D HAVE PREPARED A PROPER RECEPTION FOR YOU.

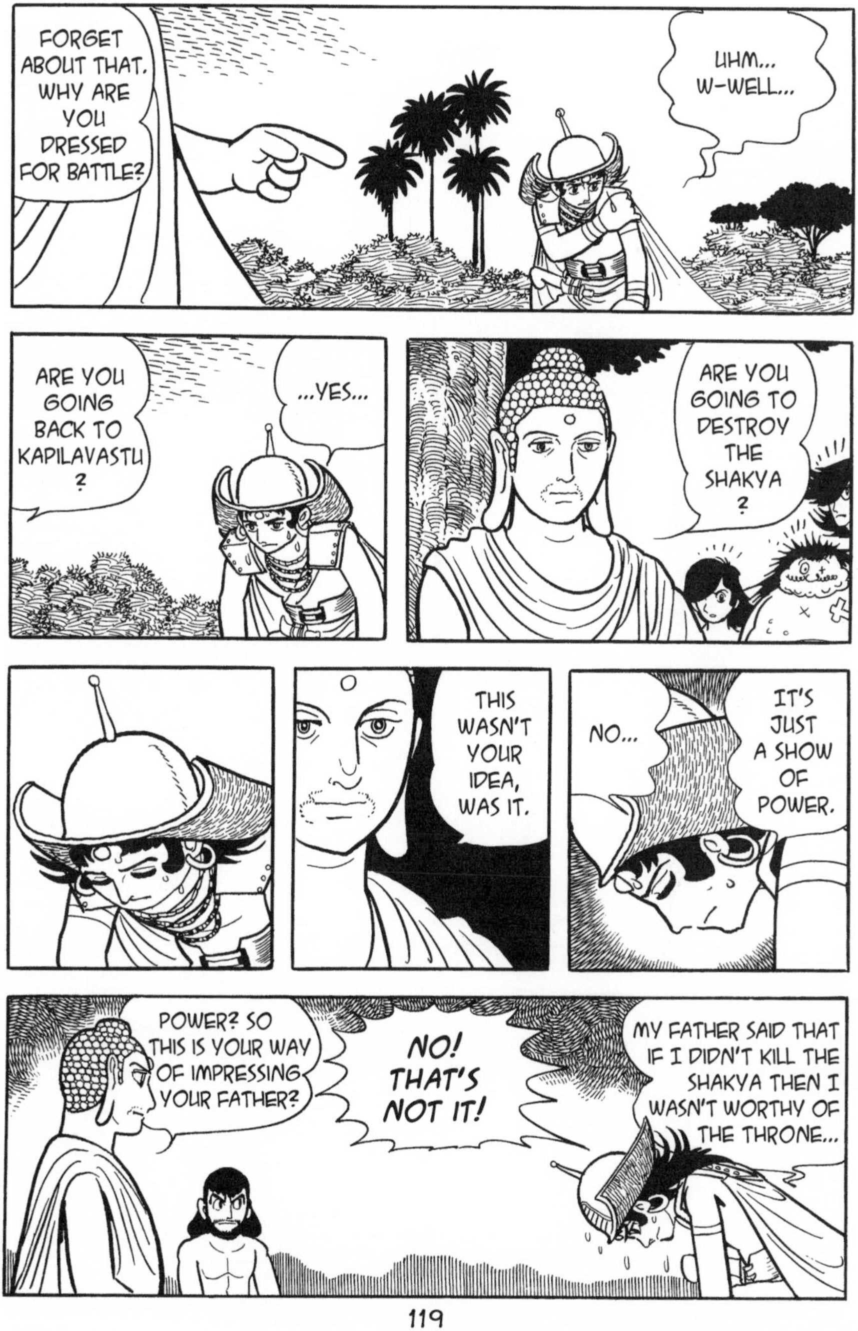
FORGET ABOUT THAT. WHY ARE YOU DRESSED FOR BATTLE?
UHM... W-WELL...
ARE YOU GOING BACK TO KAPILAVASTU?
...YES...
ARE YOU GOING TO DESTROY THE SHAKYA?
THIS WASN'T YOUR IDEA, WAS IT.
NO...
IT'S JUST A SHOW OF POWER.
POWER? SO THIS IS YOUR WAY OF IMPRESSING YOUR FATHER?
NO! THAT'S NOT IT!
MY FATHER SAID THAT IF I DIDN'T KILL THE SHAKYA THEN I WASN'T WORTHY OF THE THRONE...

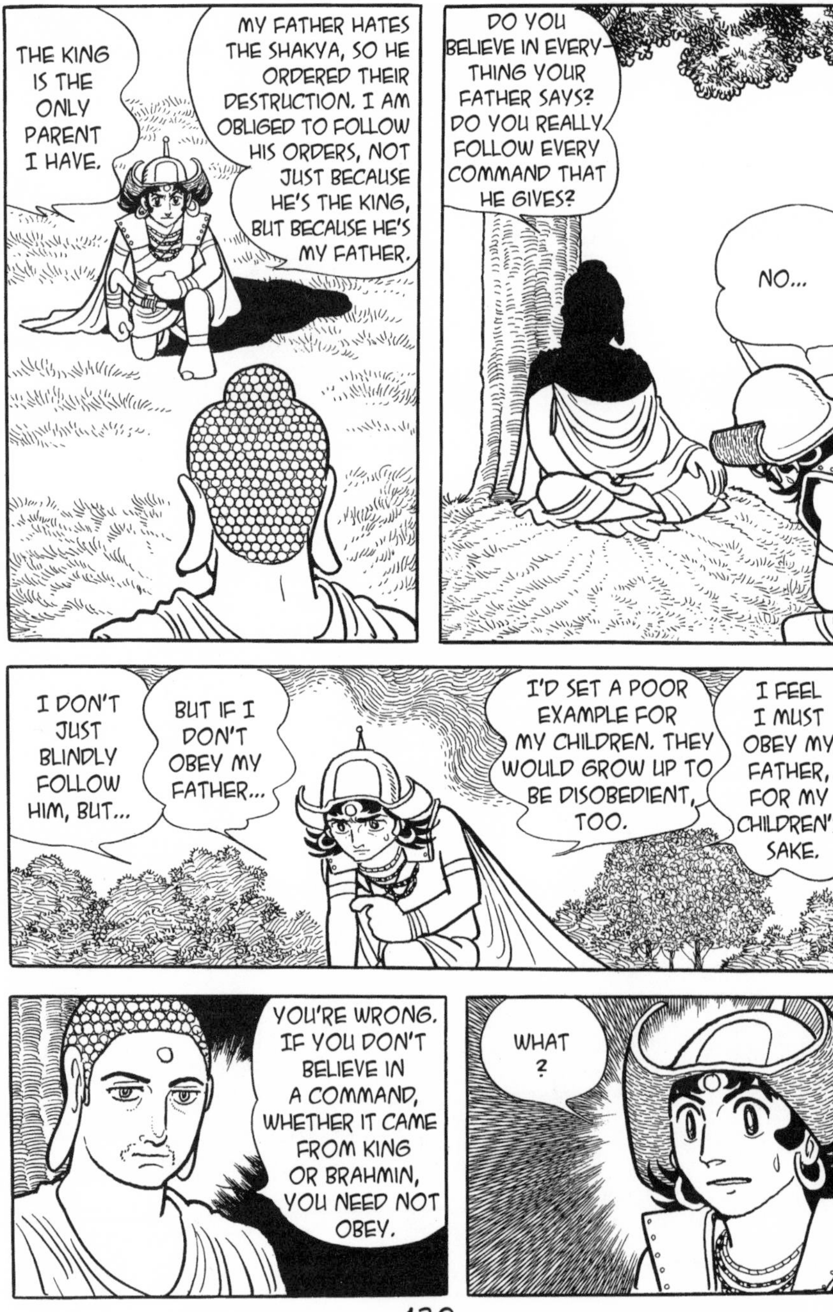
THE KING IS THE ONLY PARENT I HAVE.
MY FATHER HATES THE SHAKYA, SO HE ORDERED THEIR DESTRUCTION. I AM OBLIGED TO FOLLOW HIS ORDERS, NOT JUST BECAUSE HE'S THE KING, BUT BECAUSE HE'S MY FATHER.
DO YOU BELIEVE IN EVERY-THING YOUR FATHER SAYS? DO YOU REALLY FOLLOW EVERY COMMAND THAT HE GIVES?
NO...
I DON'T JUST BLINDLY FOLLOW HIM, BUT...
BUT IF I DON'T OBEY MY FATHER...
I'D SET A POOR EXAMPLE FOR MY CHILDREN. THEY WOULD GROW UP TO BE DISOBEDIENT, TOO.
I FEEL I MUST OBEY MY FATHER, FOR MY CHILDREN'S SAKE.
YOU'RE WRONG. IF YOU DON'T BELIEVE IN A COMMAND, WHETHER IT CAME FROM KING OR BRAHMIN, YOU NEED NOT OBEY.
WHAT ?

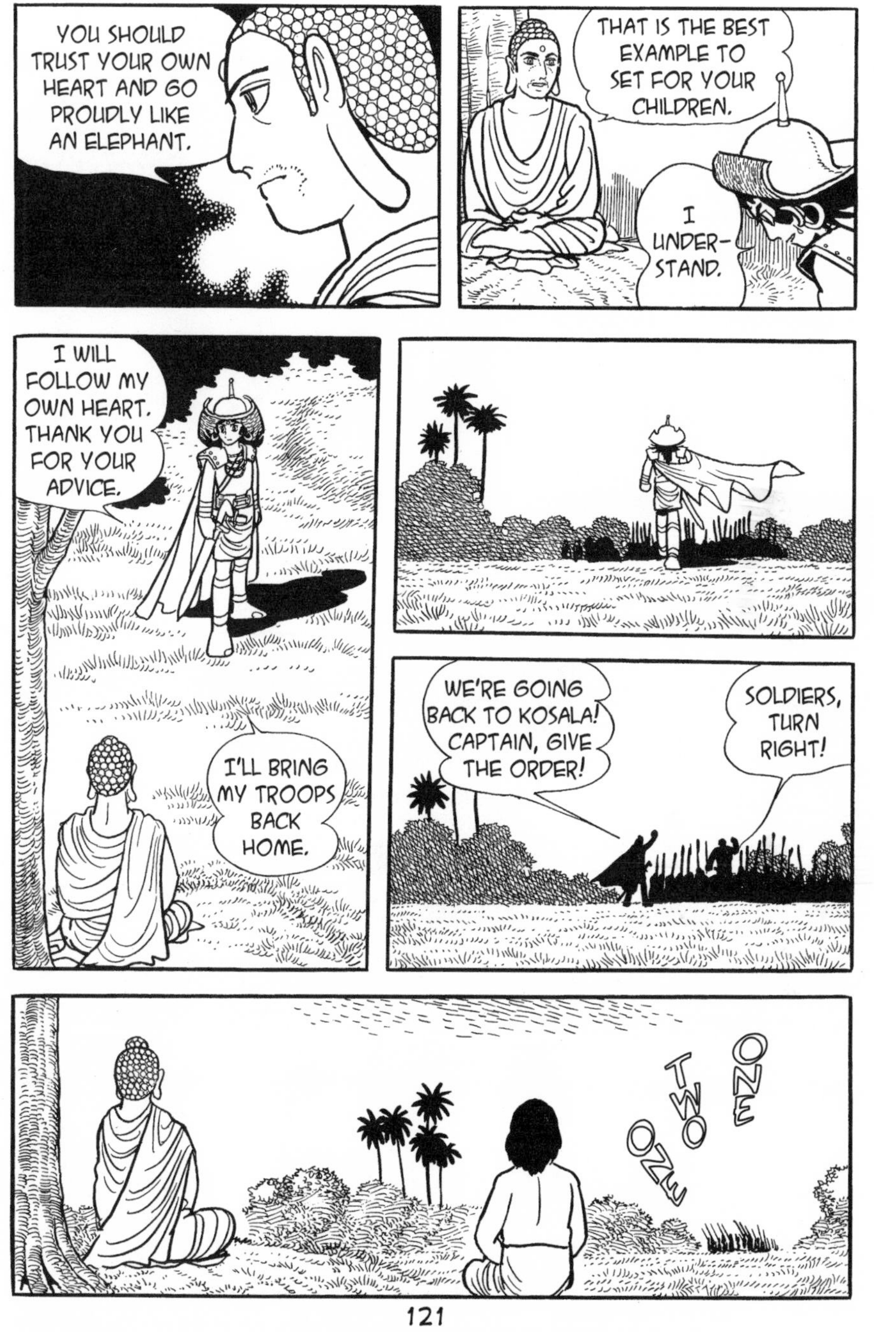
YOU SHOULD TRUST YOUR OWN HEART AND GO PROUDLY LIKE AN ELEPHANT.
THAT IS THE BEST EXAMPLE TO SET FOR YOUR CHILDREN.
I UNDER-STAND.
I WILL FOLLOW MY OWN HEART. THANK YOU FOR YOUR ADVICE.
I'LL BRING MY TROOPS BACK HOME.
WE'RE GOING BACK TO KOSALA! CAPTAIN, GIVE THE ORDER!
SOLDIERS, TURN RIGHT!
ONE TWO ONE

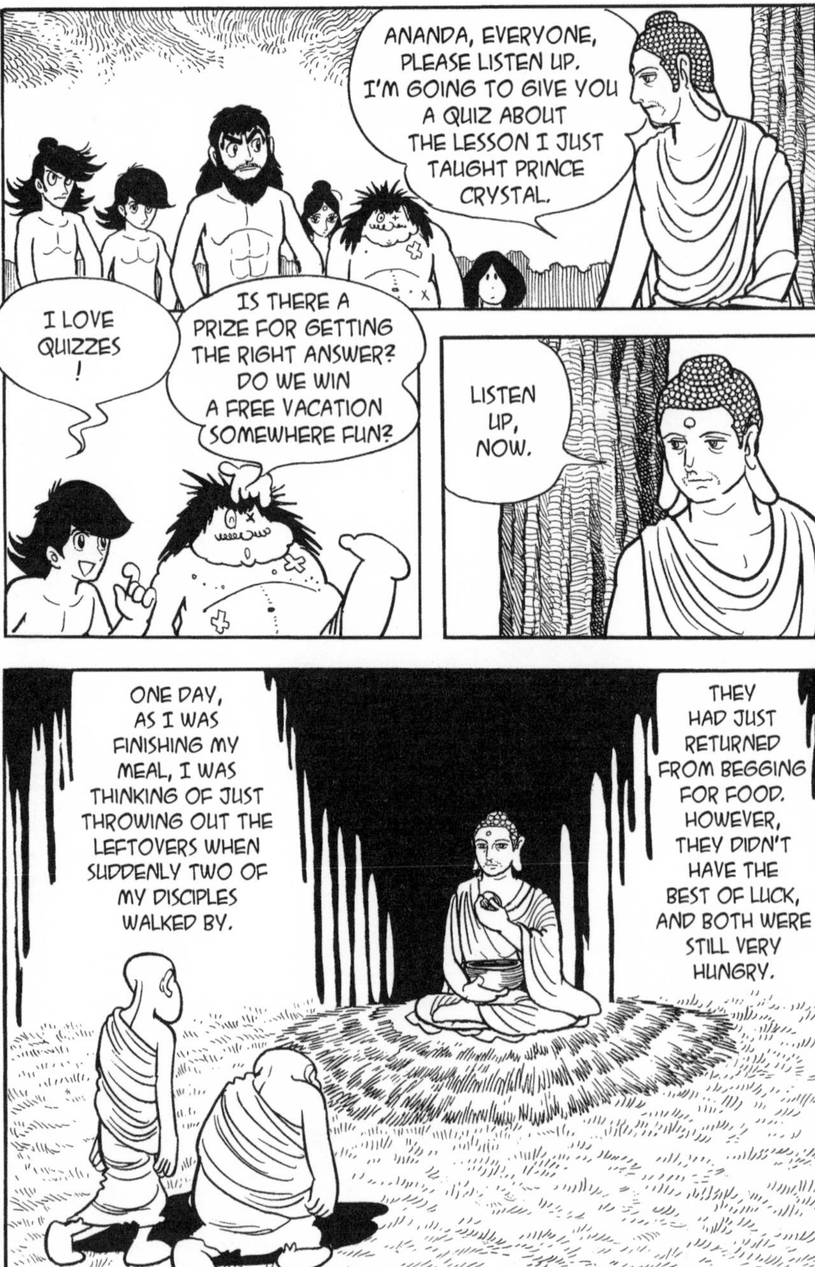
ANANDA, EVERYONE, PLEASE LISTEN UP. I'M GOING TO GIVE YOU A QUIZ ABOUT THE LESSON I JUST TAUGHT PRINCE CRYSTAL.
I LOVE QUIZZES!
IS THERE A PRIZE FOR GETTING THE RIGHT ANSWER? DO WE WIN A FREE VACATION SOMEWHERE FUN?
LISTEN UP, NOW.
ONE DAY, AS I WAS FINISHING MY MEAL, I WAS THINKING OF JUST THROWING OUT THE LEFTOVERS WHEN SUDDENLY TWO OF MY DISCIPLES WALKED BY.
THEY HAD JUST RETURNED FROM BEGGING FOR FOOD. HOWEVER, THEY DIDN'T HAVE THE BEST OF LUCK, AND BOTH WERE STILL VERY HUNGRY.

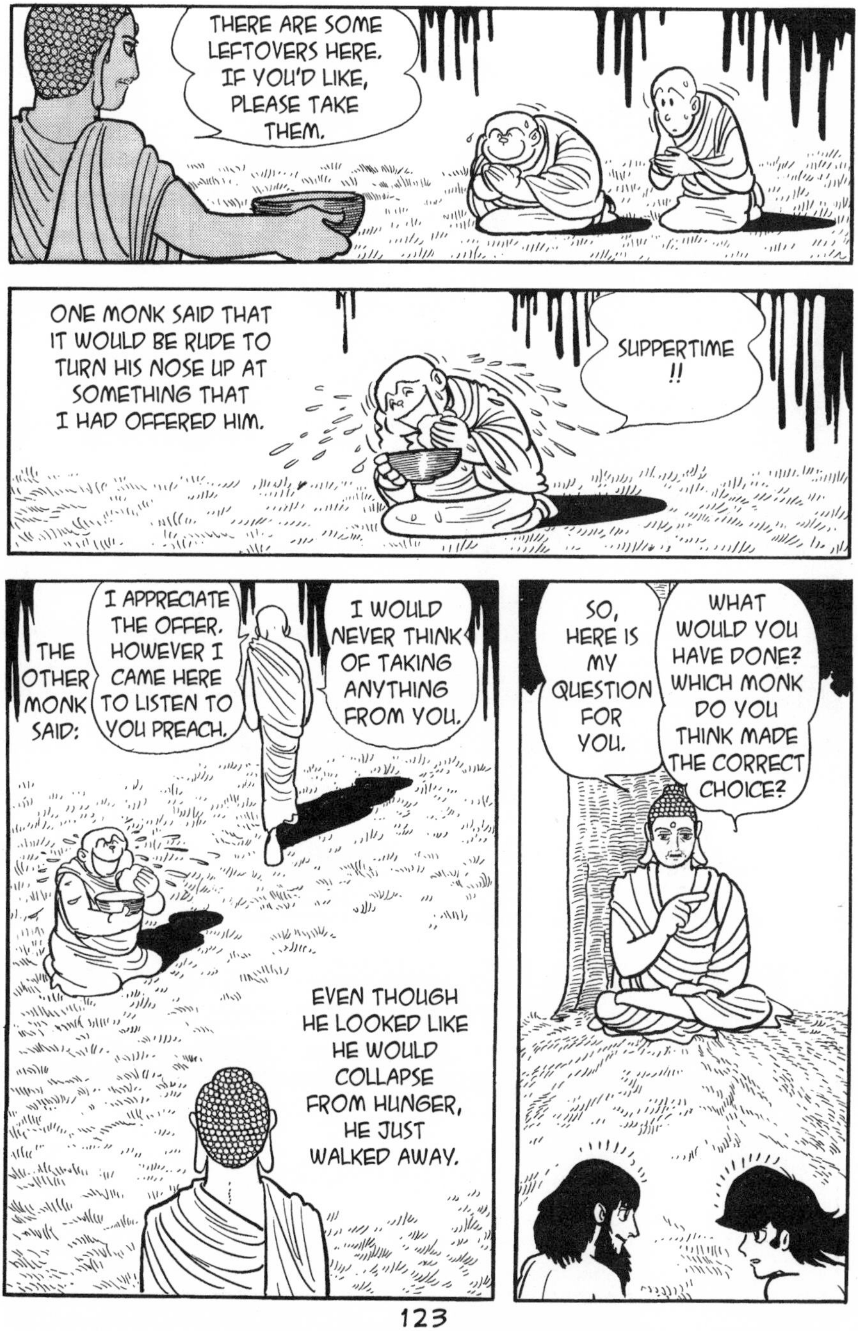
THERE ARE SOME LEFTOVERS HERE. IF YOU'D LIKE, PLEASE TAKE THEM.
ONE MONK SAID THAT IT WOULD BE RUDE TO TURN HIS NOSE UP AT SOMETHING THAT I HAD OFFERED HIM.
SUPPERTIME !!
THE OTHER MONK SAID:
I APPRECIATE THE OFFER. HOWEVER I CAME HERE TO LISTEN TO YOU PREACH.
I WOULD NEVER THINK OF TAKING ANYTHING FROM YOU.
EVEN THOUGH HE LOOKED LIKE HE WOULD COLLAPSE FROM HUNGER, HE JUST WALKED AWAY.
SO, HERE IS MY QUESTION FOR YOU.
WHAT WOULD YOU HAVE DONE? WHICH MONK DO YOU THINK MADE THE CORRECT CHOICE?

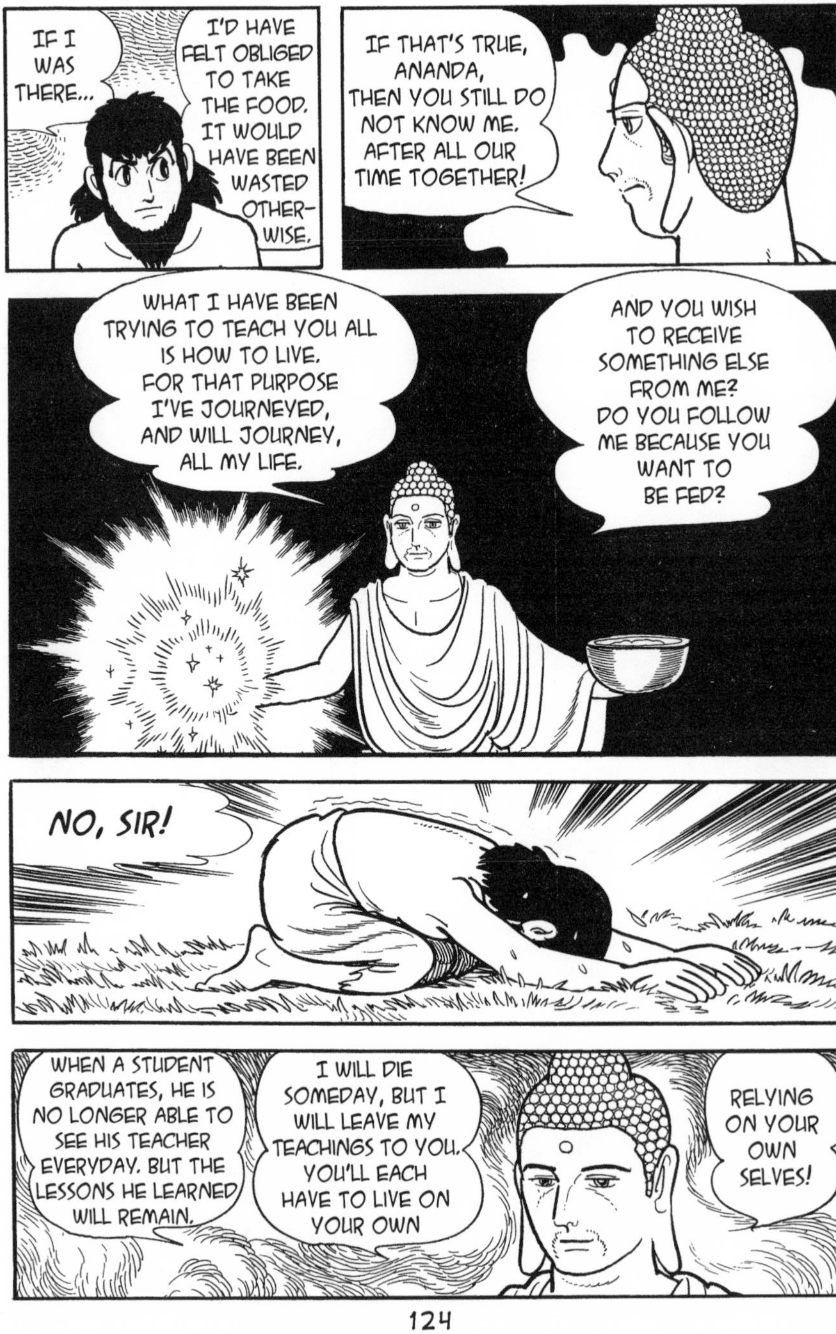
IF I WAS THERE...
I'D HAVE FELT OBLIGED TO TAKE THE FOOD. IT WOULD HAVE BEEN WASTED OTHER-WISE.
IF THAT'S TRUE, ANANDA, THEN YOU STILL DO NOT KNOW ME. AFTER ALL OUR TIME TOGETHER!
WHAT I HAVE BEEN TRYING TO TEACH YOU ALL IS HOW TO LIVE. FOR THAT PURPOSE I'VE JOURNEYED, AND WILL JOURNEY, ALL MY LIFE.
AND YOU WISH TO RECEIVE SOMETHING ELSE FROM ME? DO YOU FOLLOW ME BECAUSE YOU WANT TO BE FED?
NO, SIR!
WHEN A STUDENT GRADUATES, HE IS NO LONGER ABLE TO SEE HIS TEACHER EVERYDAY. BUT THE LESSONS HE LEARNED WILL REMAIN.
I WILL DIE SOMEDAY, BUT I WILL LEAVE MY TEACHINGS TO YOU. YOU'LL EACH HAVE TO LIVE ON YOUR OWN
RELYING ON YOUR OWN SELVES!

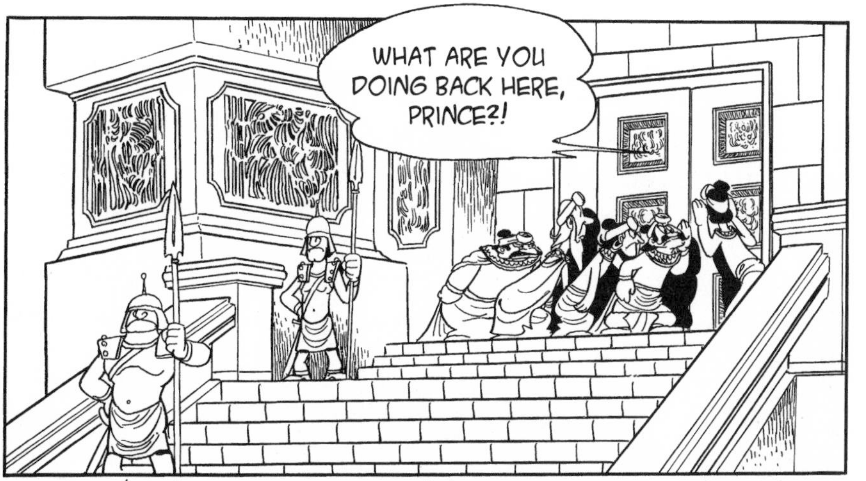
WHAT ARE YOU DOING BACK HERE, PRINCE?!

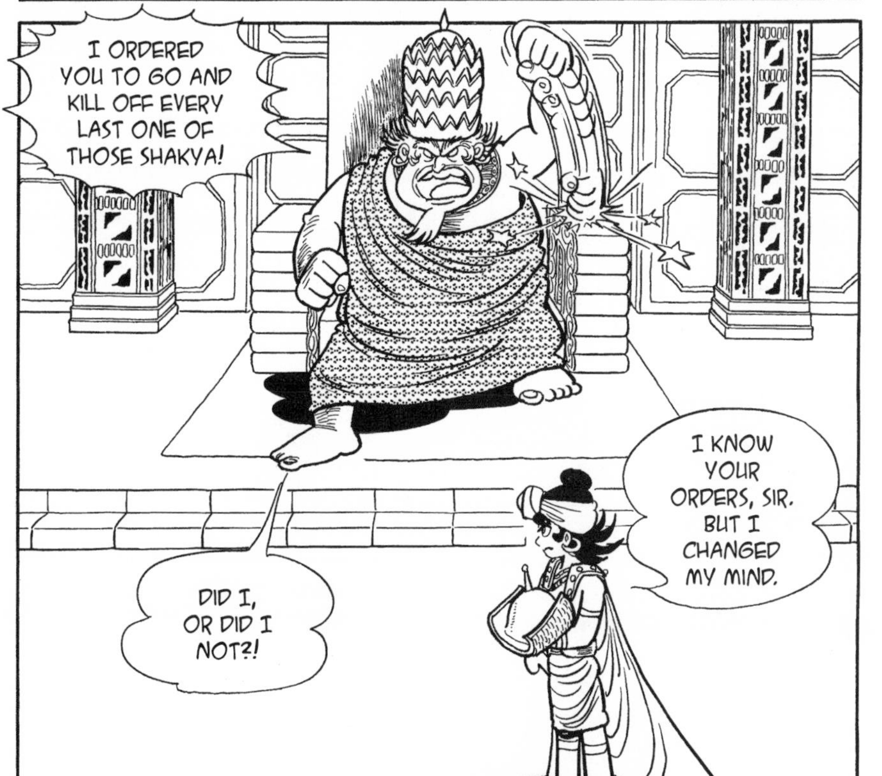
I ORDERED YOU TO GO AND KILL OFF EVERY LAST ONE OF THOSE SHAKYA!
DID I, OR DID I NOT?!
I KNOW YOUR ORDERS, SIR. BUT I CHANGED MY MIND.

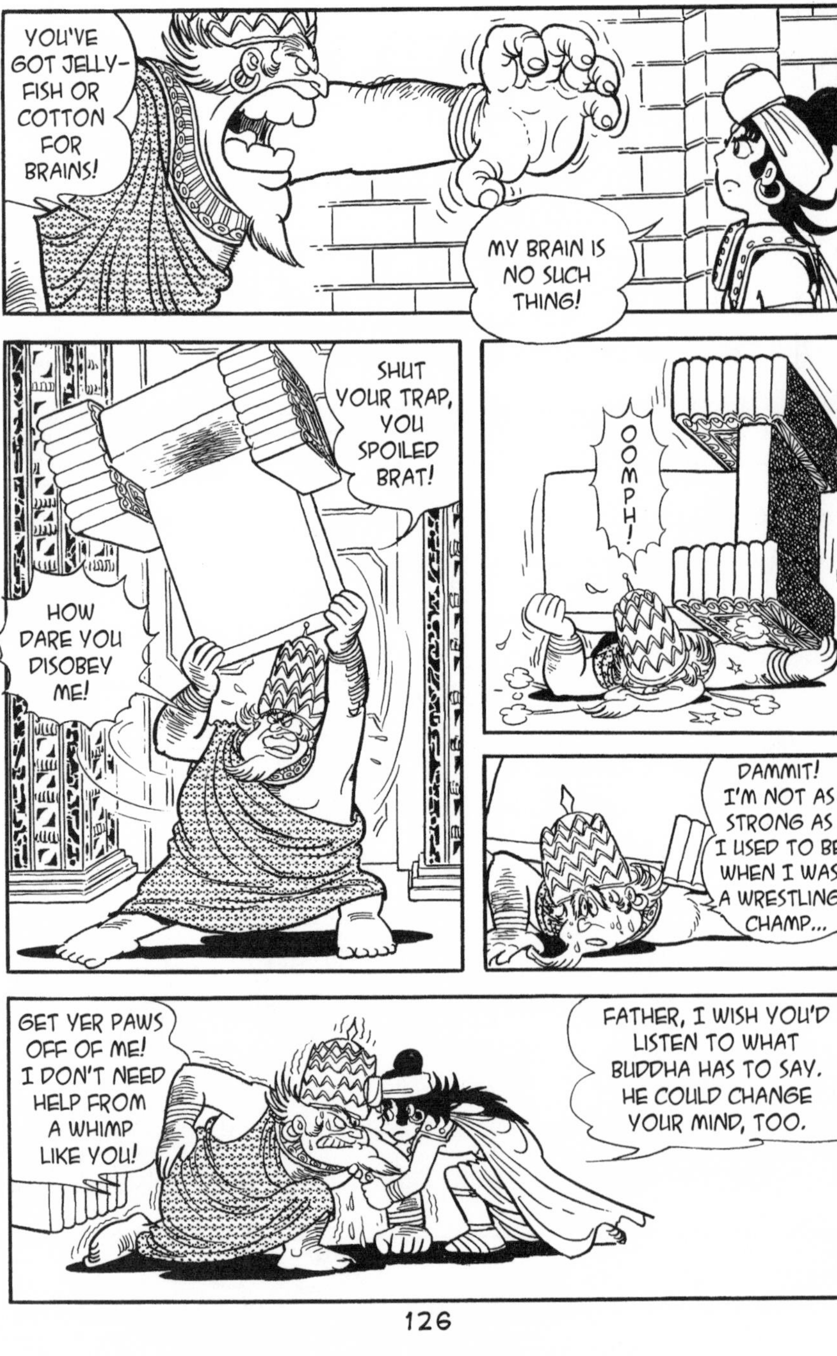
YOU'VE GOT JELLY-FISH OR COTTON FOR BRAINS!
MY BRAIN IS NO SUCH THING!
SHUT YOUR TRAP, YOU SPOILED BRAT!
HOW DARE YOU DISOBEY ME!
OOMPH!
DAMMIT! I'M NOT AS STRONG AS I USED TO BE WHEN I WAS A WRESTLING CHAMP...
GET YER PAWS OFF OF ME! I DON'T NEED HELP FROM A WHIMP LIKE YOU!
FATHER, I WISH YOU'D LISTEN TO WHAT BUDDHA HAS TO SAY. HE COULD CHANGE YOUR MIND, TOO.

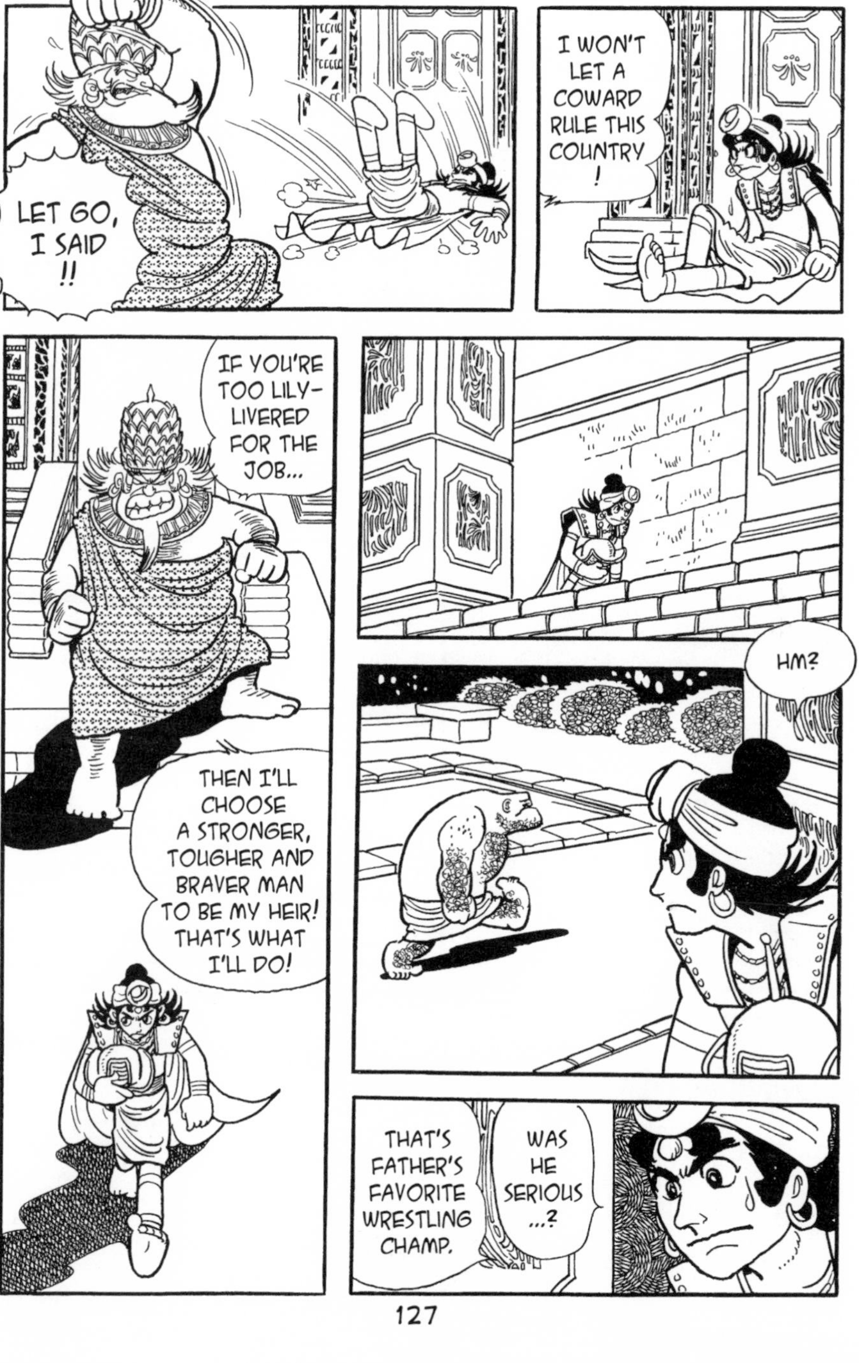
LET GO, I SAID !!
I WON'T LET A COWARD RULE THIS COUNTRY !
IF YOU'RE TOO LILY-LIVERED FOR THE JOB...
THEN I'LL CHOOSE A STRONGER, TOUGHER AND BRAVER MAN TO BE MY HEIR! THAT'S WHAT I'LL DO!
HM?
THAT'S FATHER'S FAVORITE WRESTLING CHAMP.
WAS HE SERIOUS ...?

OOTANG, COME OVER HERE.

BLAAAAAH!

THERE'S NO ONE ANYWHERE NEAR AS STRONG AS YOU ARE IN THE COUNTRY. I'VE GOT BIG PLANS FOR YOU.

I THINK WELL OF YOU. SO MUCH SO THAT I'D LIKE TO ADOPT YOU AS MY SON, HOW'S THAT?

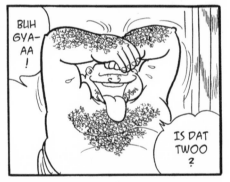

BUH GYA-AA!

IS DAT TWOO?

AHA... OK, STOP LICKING ME...

YA GONNA MAKE ME YA SONNY! GAH! ME SO HAPPEEE!

128

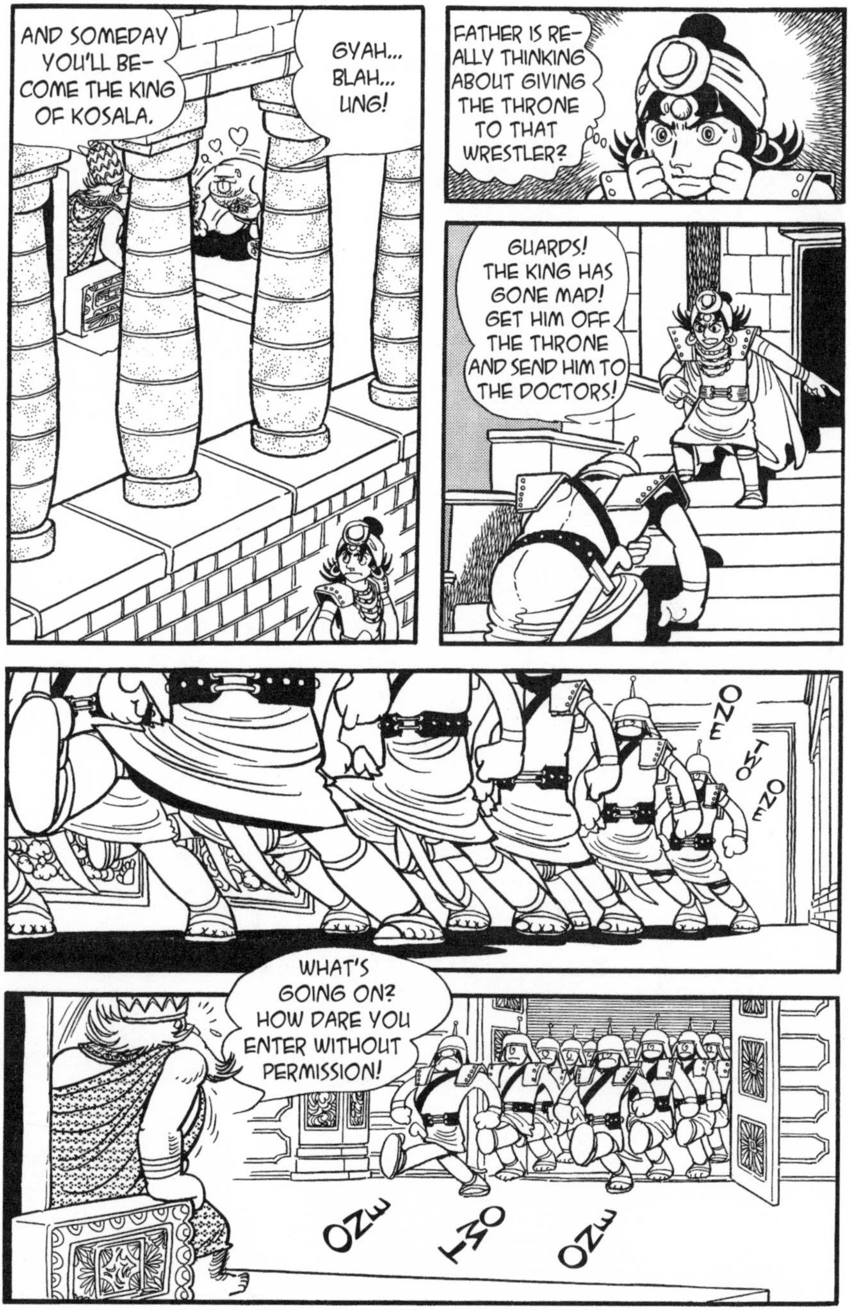
AND SOMEDAY YOU'LL BE-COME THE KING OF KOSALA.
GYAH... BLAH... UNG!
FATHER IS RE-ALLY THINKING ABOUT GIVING THE THRONE TO THAT WRESTLER?
GUARDS! THE KING HAS GONE MAD! GET HIM OFF THE THRONE AND SEND HIM TO THE DOCTORS!
ONE
TWO
ONE
WHAT'S GOING ON? HOW DARE YOU ENTER WITHOUT PERMISSION!
ONE
TWO
ONE

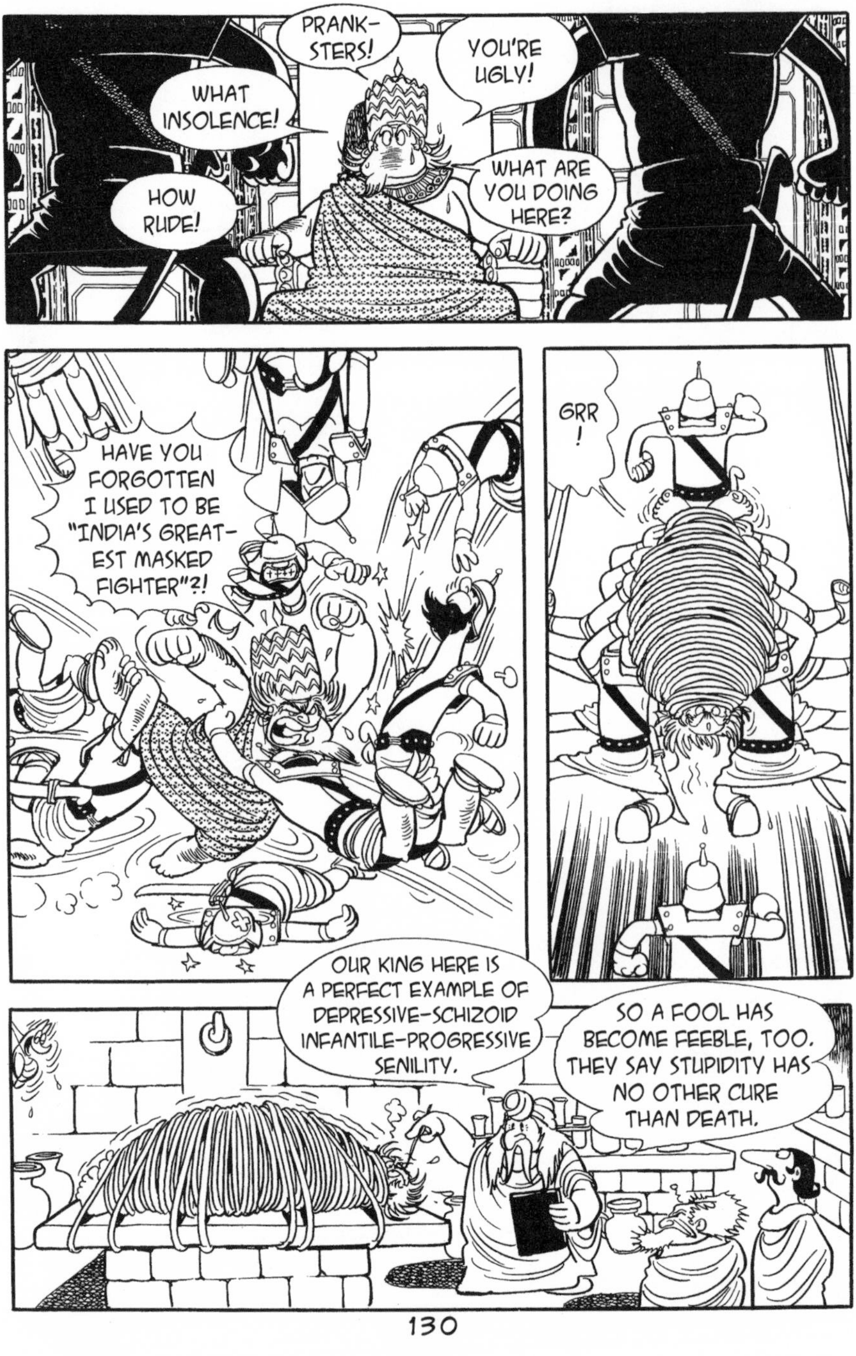
PRANKSTERS!
YOU'RE UGLY!
WHAT INSOLENCE!
HOW RUDE!
WHAT ARE YOU DOING HERE?
HAVE YOU FORGOTTEN I USED TO BE "INDIA'S GREATEST MASKED FIGHTER"?!
GRR!
OUR KING HERE IS A PERFECT EXAMPLE OF DEPRESSIVE-SCHIZOID INFANTILE-PROGRESSIVE SENILITY.
SO A FOOL HAS BECOME FEEBLE, TOO. THEY SAY STUPIDITY HAS NO OTHER CURE THAN DEATH.

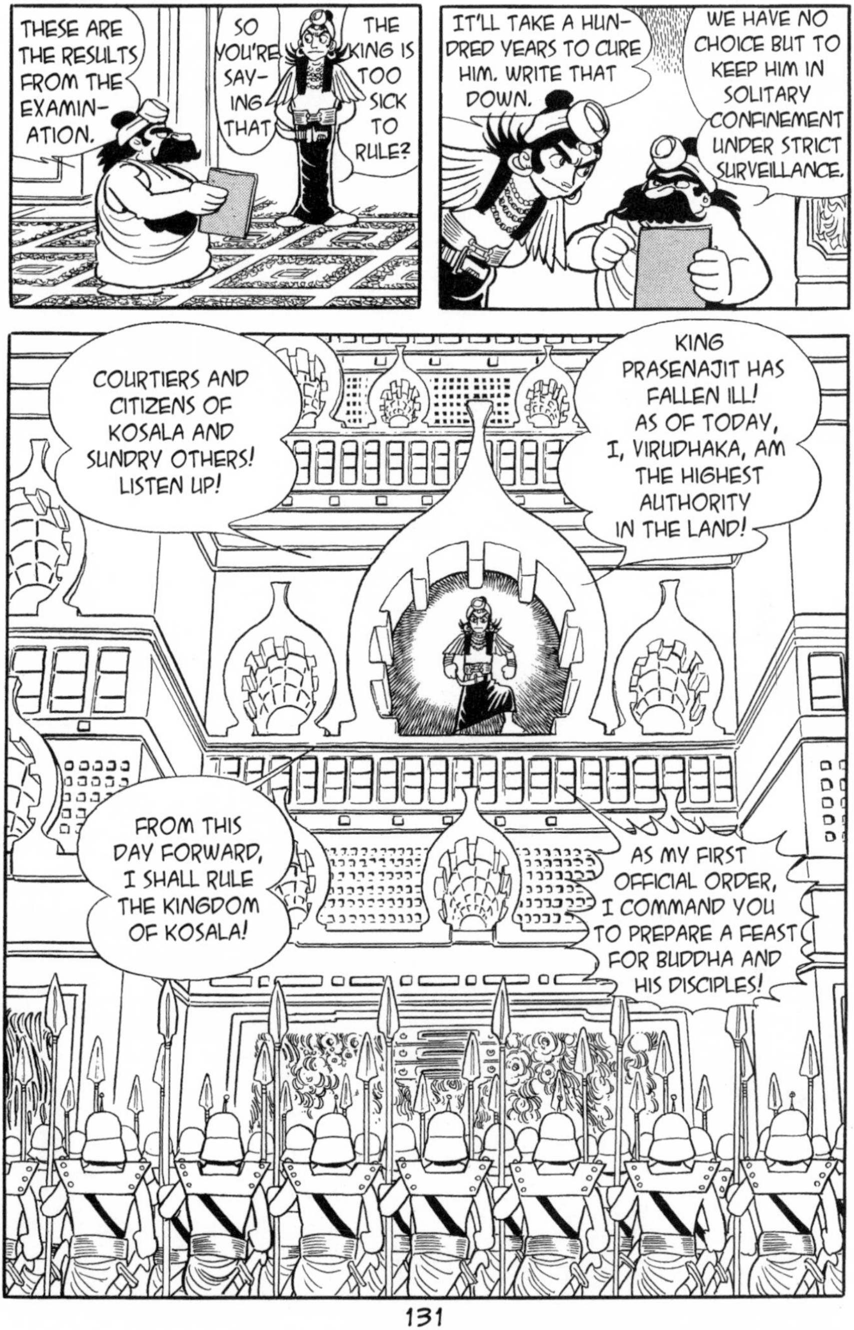
THESE ARE THE RESULTS FROM THE EXAMIN-ATION.
SO YOU'RE SAY-ING THAT
THE KING IS TOO SICK TO RULE?
IT'LL TAKE A HUN-DRED YEARS TO CURE HIM. WRITE THAT DOWN.
WE HAVE NO CHOICE BUT TO KEEP HIM IN SOLITARY CONFINEMENT UNDER STRICT SURVEILLANCE.
COURTIERS AND CITIZENS OF KOSALA AND SUNDRY OTHERS! LISTEN UP!
KING PRASENAJIT HAS FALLEN ILL! AS OF TODAY, I, VIRUDHAKA, AM THE HIGHEST AUTHORITY IN THE LAND!
FROM THIS DAY FORWARD, I SHALL RULE THE KINGDOM OF KOSALA!
AS MY FIRST OFFICIAL ORDER, I COMMAND YOU TO PREPARE A FEAST FOR BUDDHA AND HIS DISCIPLES!

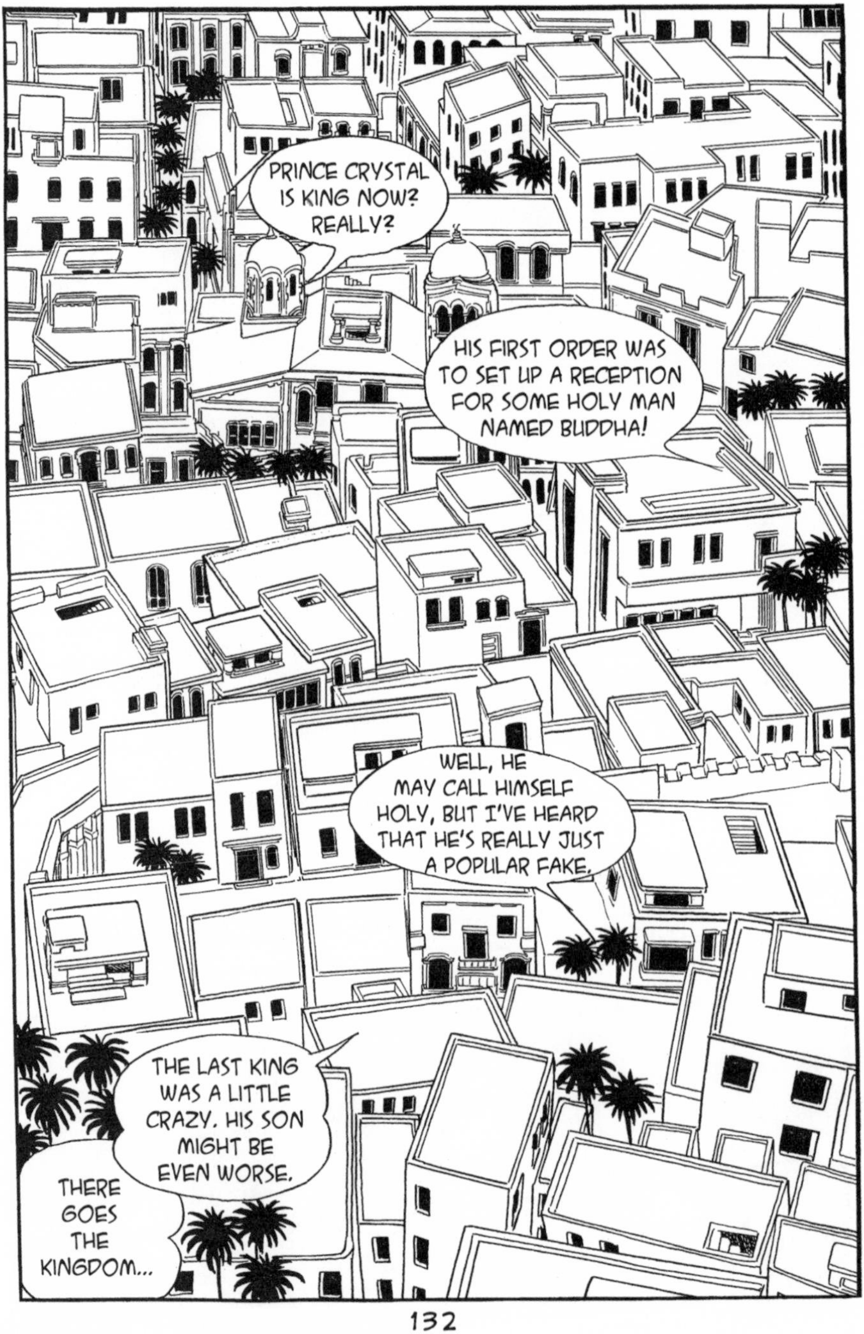
PRINCE CRYSTAL IS KING NOW? REALLY?
HIS FIRST ORDER WAS TO SET UP A RECEPTION FOR SOME HOLY MAN NAMED BUDDHA!
WELL, HE MAY CALL HIMSELF HOLY, BUT I'VE HEARD THAT HE'S REALLY JUST A POPULAR FAKE.
THE LAST KING WAS A LITTLE CRAZY. HIS SON MIGHT BE EVEN WORSE.
THERE GOES THE KINGDOM...

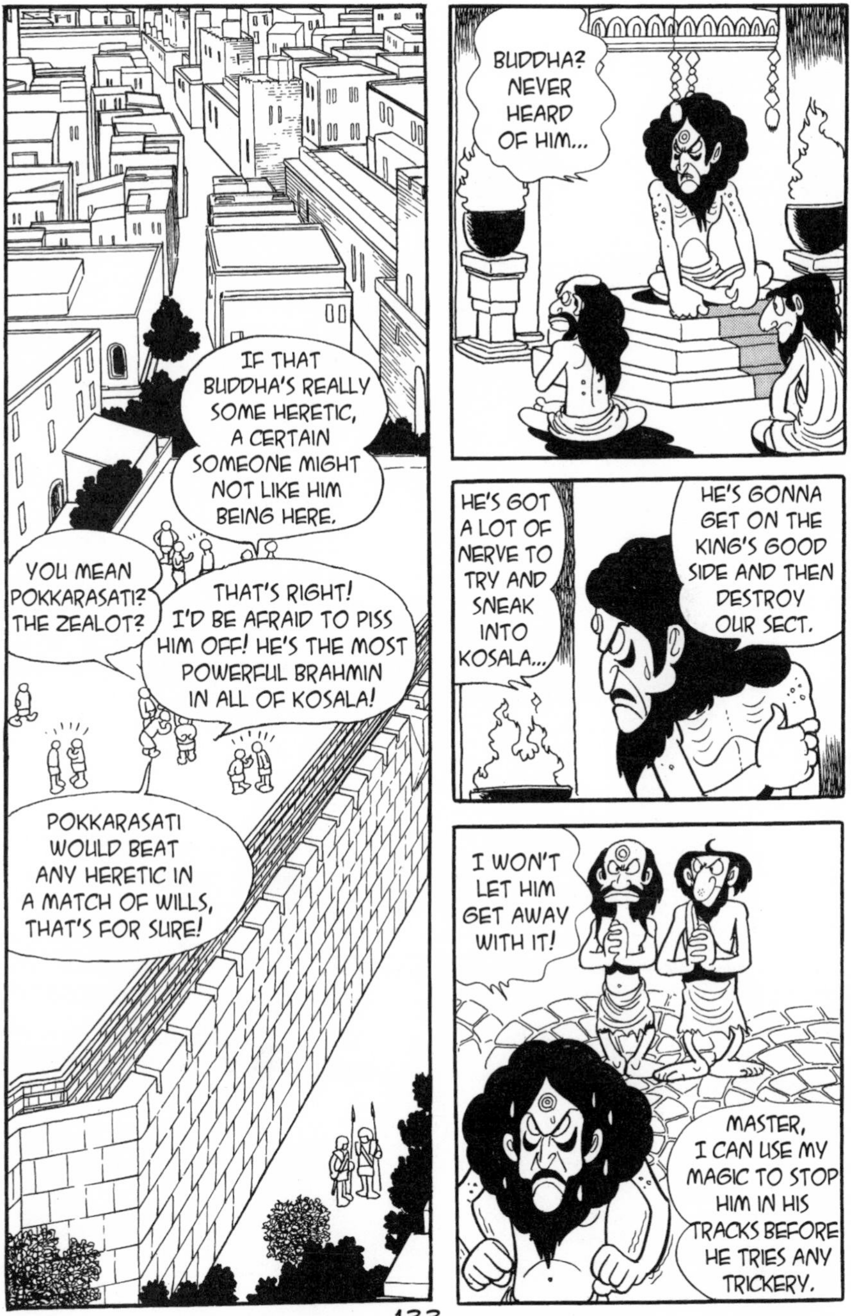
IF THAT BUDDHA'S REALLY SOME HERETIC, A CERTAIN SOMEONE MIGHT NOT LIKE HIM BEING HERE.
YOU MEAN POKKARASATI? THE ZEALOT?
THAT'S RIGHT! I'D BE AFRAID TO PISS HIM OFF! HE'S THE MOST POWERFUL BRAHMIN IN ALL OF KOSALA!
POKKARASATI WOULD BEAT ANY HERETIC IN A MATCH OF WILLS, THAT'S FOR SURE!
BUDDHA? NEVER HEARD OF HIM...
HE'S GOT A LOT OF NERVE TO TRY AND SNEAK INTO KOSALA...
HE'S GONNA GET ON THE KING'S GOOD SIDE AND THEN DESTROY OUR SECT.
I WON'T LET HIM GET AWAY WITH IT!
MASTER, I CAN USE MY MAGIC TO STOP HIM IN HIS TRACKS BEFORE HE TRIES ANY TRICKERY.

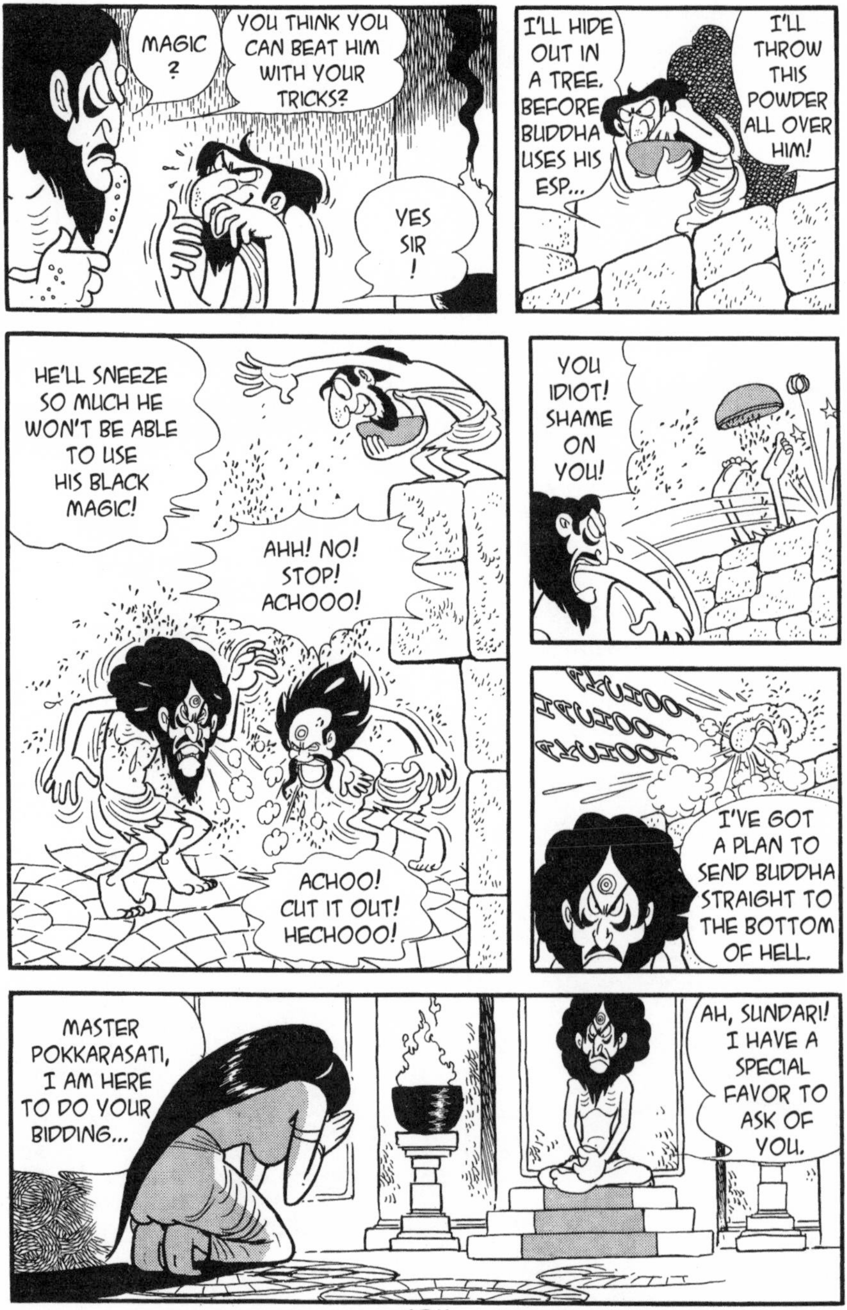
MAGIC?
YOU THINK YOU CAN BEAT HIM WITH YOUR TRICKS?
YES SIR!
I'LL HIDE OUT IN A TREE. BEFORE BUDDHA USES HIS ESP...
I'LL THROW THIS POWDER ALL OVER HIM!
HE'LL SNEEZE SO MUCH HE WON'T BE ABLE TO USE HIS BLACK MAGIC!
AHH! NO! STOP! ACHOOO!
ACHOO! CUT IT OUT! HECHOOO!
YOU IDIOT! SHAME ON YOU!
I'VE GOT A PLAN TO SEND BUDDHA STRAIGHT TO THE BOTTOM OF HELL.
MASTER POKKARASATI, I AM HERE TO DO YOUR BIDDING...
AH, SUNDARI! I HAVE A SPECIAL FAVOR TO ASK OF YOU.

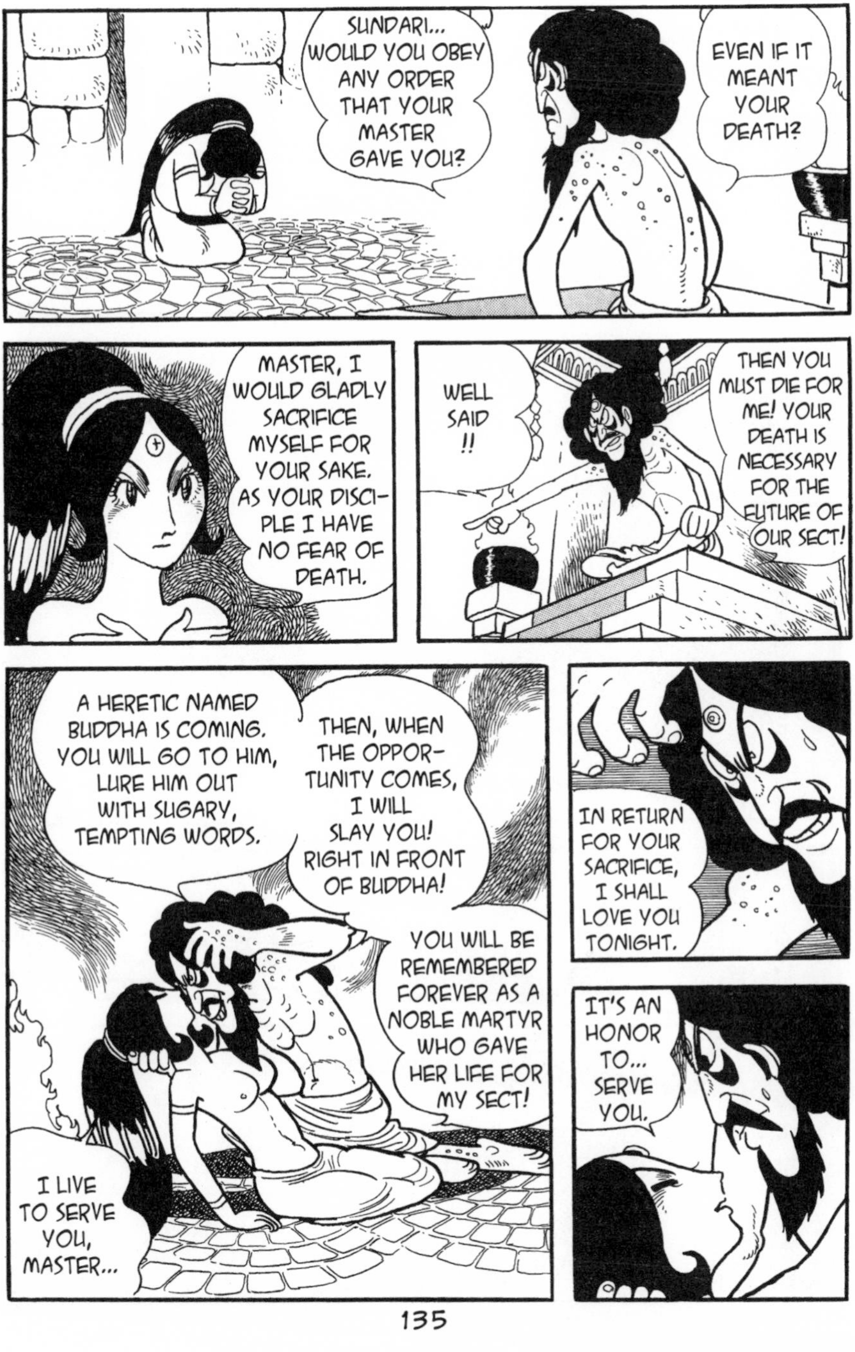
SUNDARI... WOULD YOU OBEY ANY ORDER THAT YOUR MASTER GAVE YOU?
EVEN IF IT MEANT YOUR DEATH?
MASTER, I WOULD GLADLY SACRIFICE MYSELF FOR YOUR SAKE. AS YOUR DISCI-PLE I HAVE NO FEAR OF DEATH.
WELL SAID !!
THEN YOU MUST DIE FOR ME! YOUR DEATH IS NECESSARY FOR THE FUTURE OF OUR SECT!
A HERETIC NAMED BUDDHA IS COMING. YOU WILL GO TO HIM, LURE HIM OUT WITH SUGARY, TEMPTING WORDS.
THEN, WHEN THE OPPOR-TUNITY COMES, I WILL SLAY YOU! RIGHT IN FRONT OF BUDDHA!
YOU WILL BE REMEMBERED FOREVER AS A NOBLE MARTYR WHO GAVE HER LIFE FOR MY SECT!
I LIVE TO SERVE YOU, MASTER...
IN RETURN FOR YOUR SACRIFICE, I SHALL LOVE YOU TONIGHT.
IT'S AN HONOR TO... SERVE YOU.

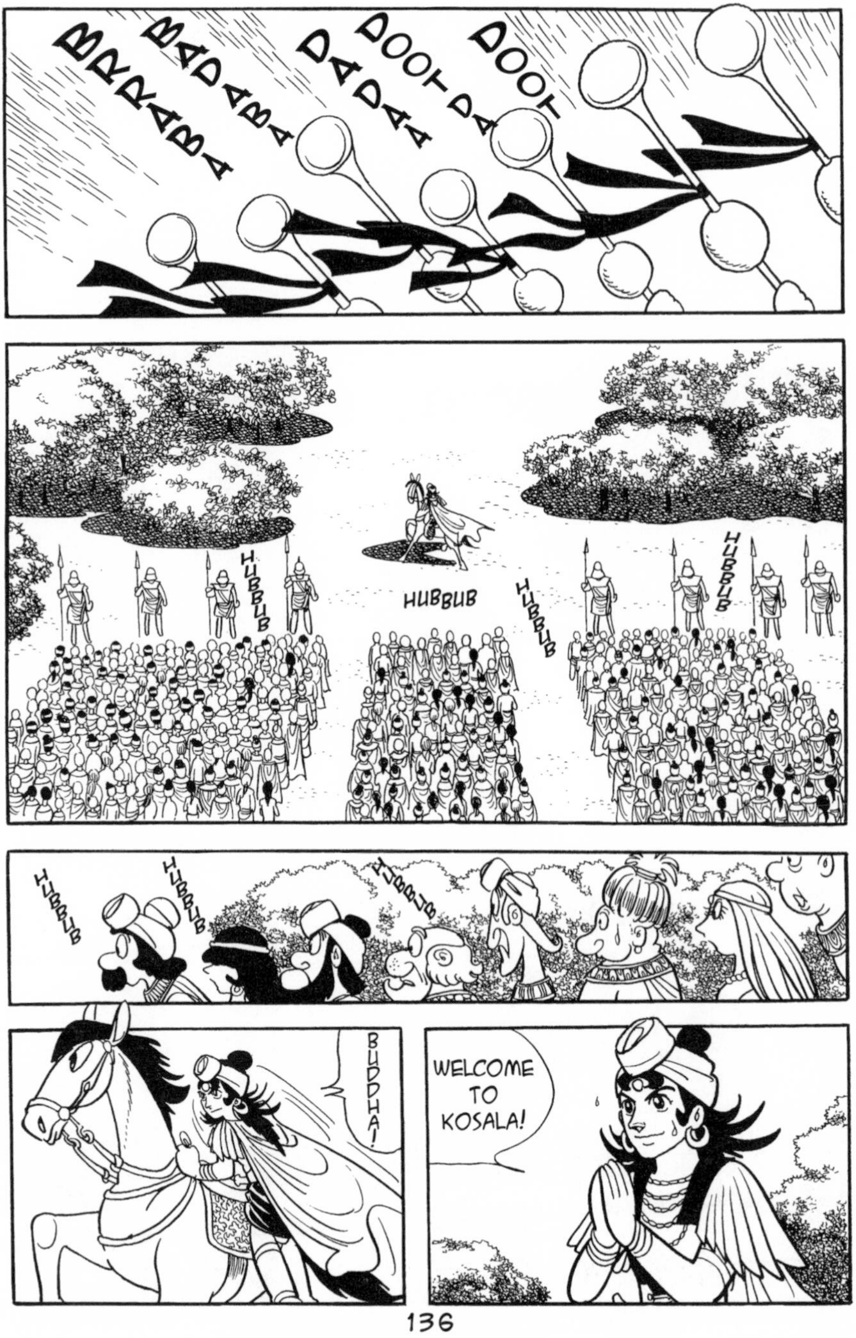
BRRABA
BADABA
DADAA
DOOTDA
DOOT
HUBBUB
HUBBUB
HUBBUB
HUBBUB
HUBBUB
HUBBUB
HUBBUB
HUBBUB
BUDDHA!
WELCOME TO KOSALA!

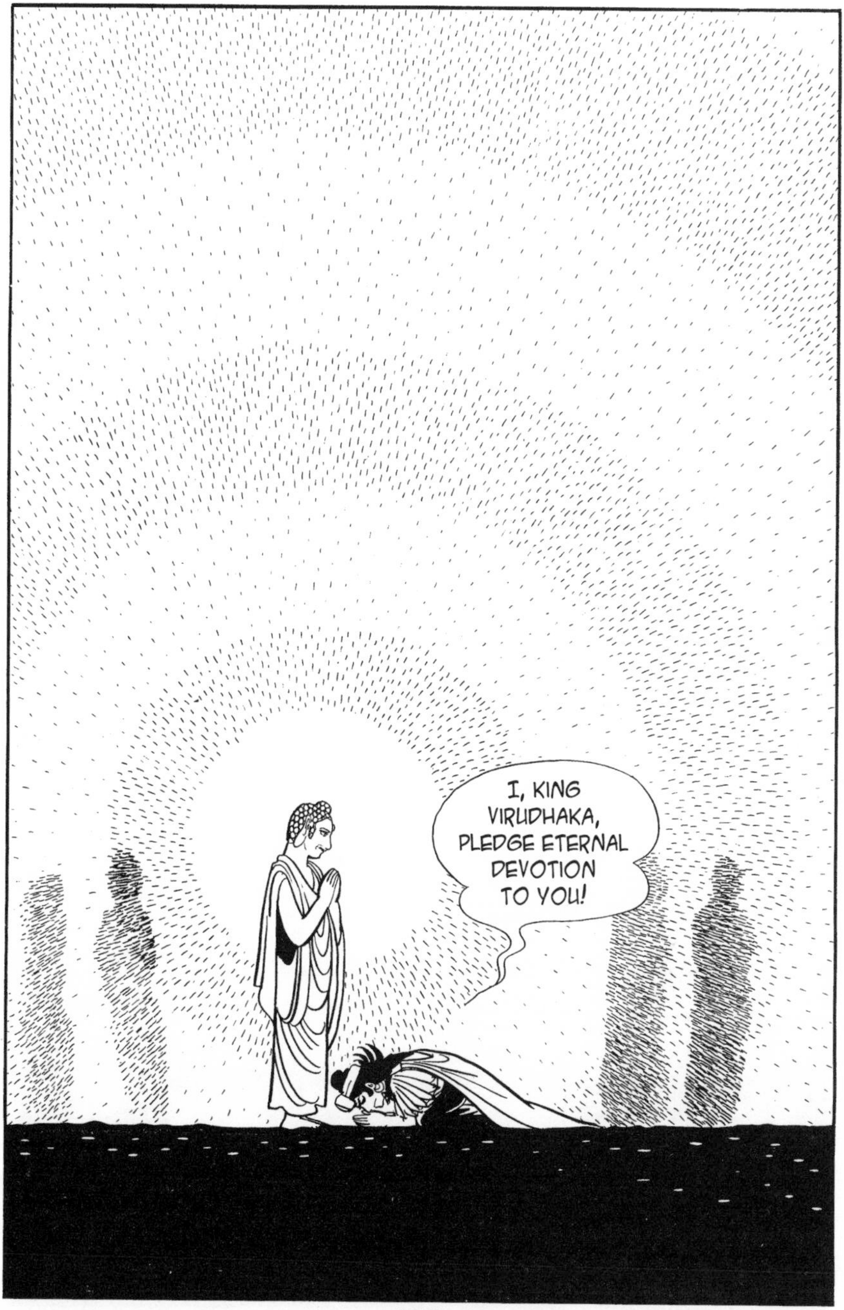
I, KING VIRUDHAKA, PLEDGE ETERNAL DEVOTION TO YOU!

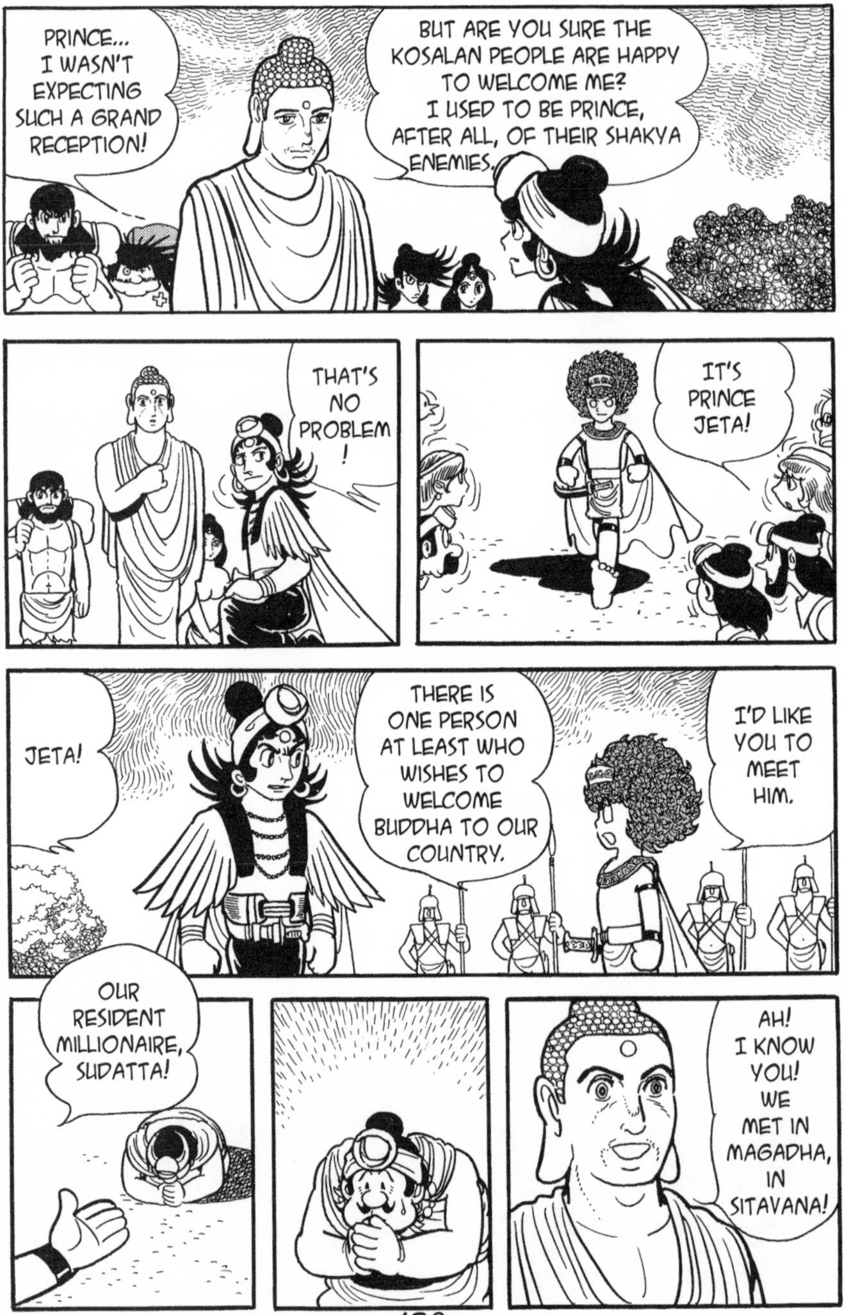
PRINCE... I WASN'T EXPECTING SUCH A GRAND RECEPTION!
BUT ARE YOU SURE THE KOSALAN PEOPLE ARE HAPPY TO WELCOME ME? I USED TO BE PRINCE, AFTER ALL, OF THEIR SHAKYA ENEMIES.
THAT'S NO PROBLEM!
IT'S PRINCE JETA!
JETA!
THERE IS ONE PERSON AT LEAST WHO WISHES TO WELCOME BUDDHA TO OUR COUNTRY.
I'D LIKE YOU TO MEET HIM.
OUR RESIDENT MILLIONAIRE, SUDATTA!
AH! I KNOW YOU! WE MET IN MAGADHA, IN SITAVANA!

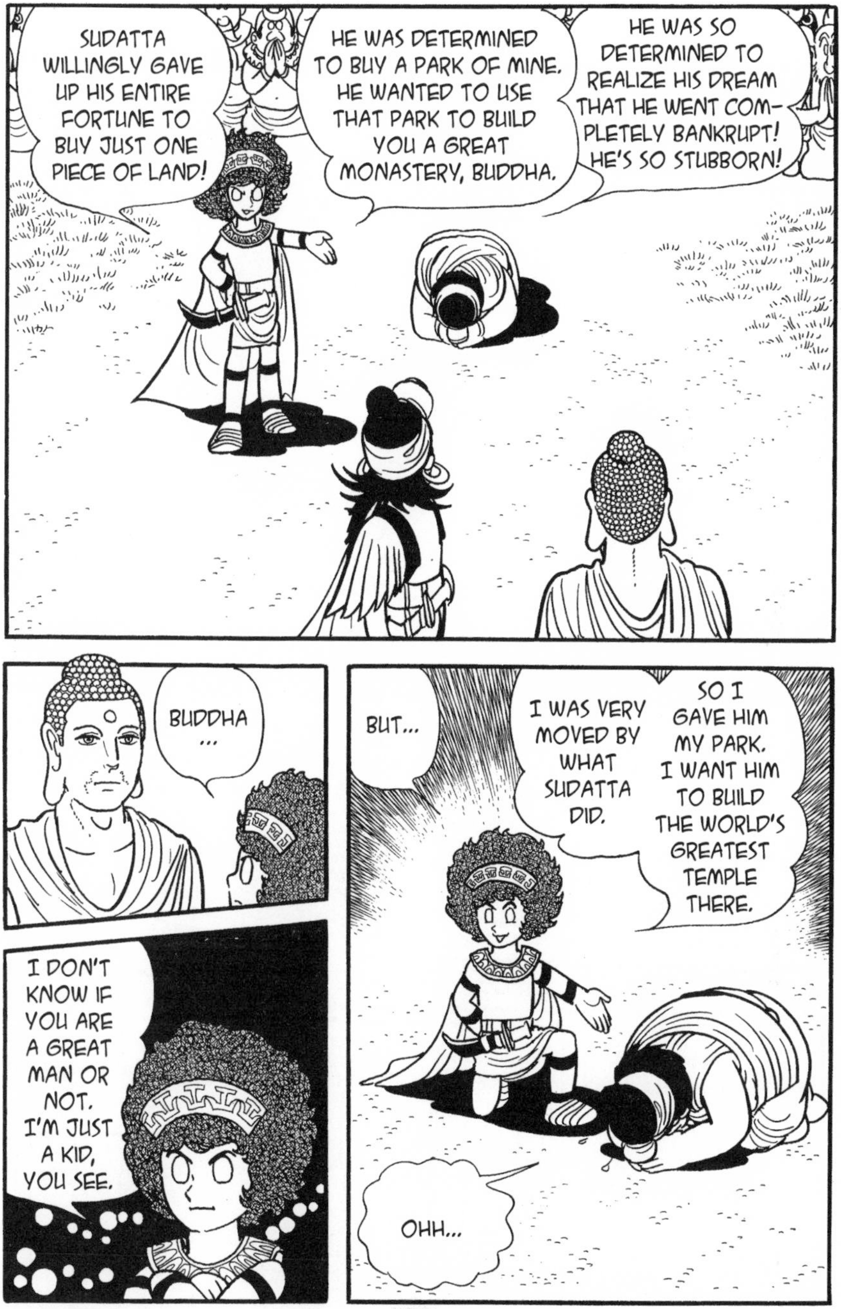
SUDATTA WILLINGLY GAVE UP HIS ENTIRE FORTUNE TO BUY JUST ONE PIECE OF LAND!
HE WAS DETERMINED TO BUY A PARK OF MINE. HE WANTED TO USE THAT PARK TO BUILD YOU A GREAT MONASTERY, BUDDHA.
HE WAS SO DETERMINED TO REALIZE HIS DREAM THAT HE WENT COM-PLETELY BANKRUPT! HE'S SO STUBBORN!
BUDDHA ...
I DON'T KNOW IF YOU ARE A GREAT MAN OR NOT. I'M JUST A KID, YOU SEE.
BUT...
I WAS VERY MOVED BY WHAT SUDATTA DID.
SO I GAVE HIM MY PARK. I WANT HIM TO BUILD THE WORLD'S GREATEST TEMPLE THERE.
OHH...

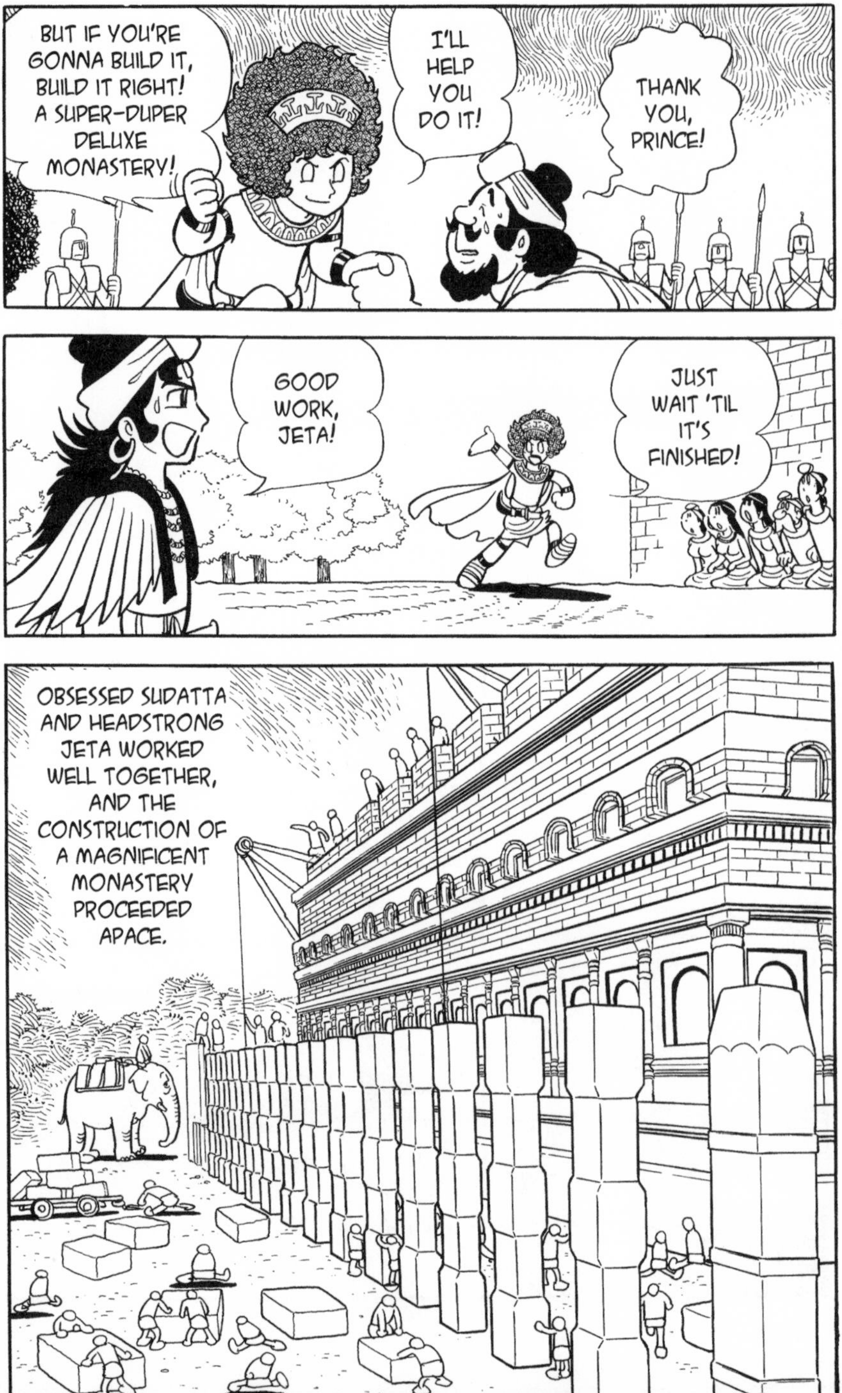
BUT IF YOU'RE GONNA BUILD IT, BUILD IT RIGHT! A SUPER-DUPER DELUXE MONASTERY!
I'LL HELP YOU DO IT!
THANK YOU, PRINCE!
GOOD WORK, JETA!
JUST WAIT 'TIL IT'S FINISHED!
OBSESSED SUDATTA AND HEADSTRONG JETA WORKED WELL TOGETHER, AND THE CONSTRUCTION OF A MAGNIFICENT MONASTERY PROCEEDED APACE.

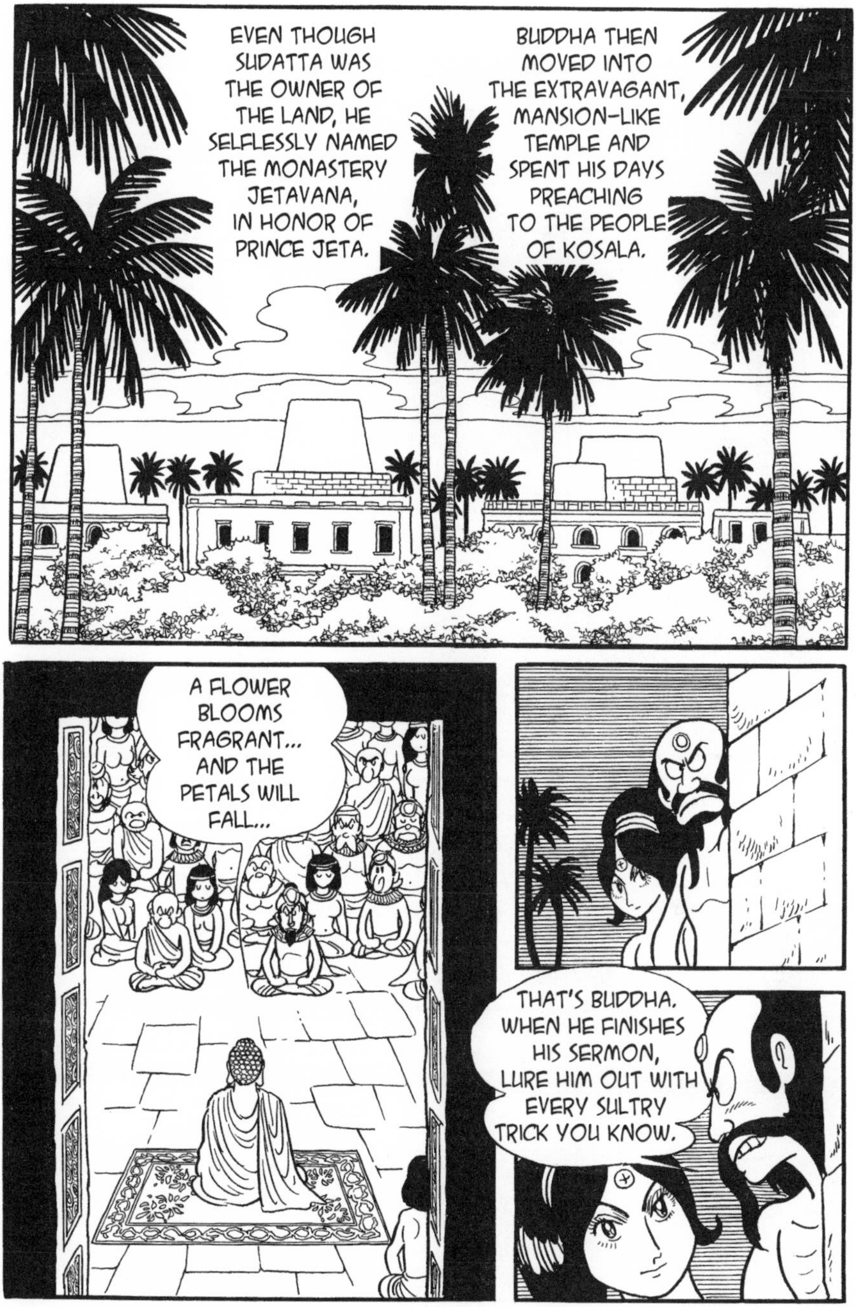
EVEN THOUGH SUDATTA WAS THE OWNER OF THE LAND, HE SELFLESSLY NAMED THE MONASTERY JETAVANA, IN HONOR OF PRINCE JETA.
BUDDHA THEN MOVED INTO THE EXTRAVAGANT, MANSION-LIKE TEMPLE AND SPENT HIS DAYS PREACHING TO THE PEOPLE OF KOSALA.
A FLOWER BLOOMS FRAGRANT... AND THE PETALS WILL FALL...
THAT'S BUDDHA. WHEN HE FINISHES HIS SERMON, LURE HIM OUT WITH EVERY SULTRY TRICK YOU KNOW.

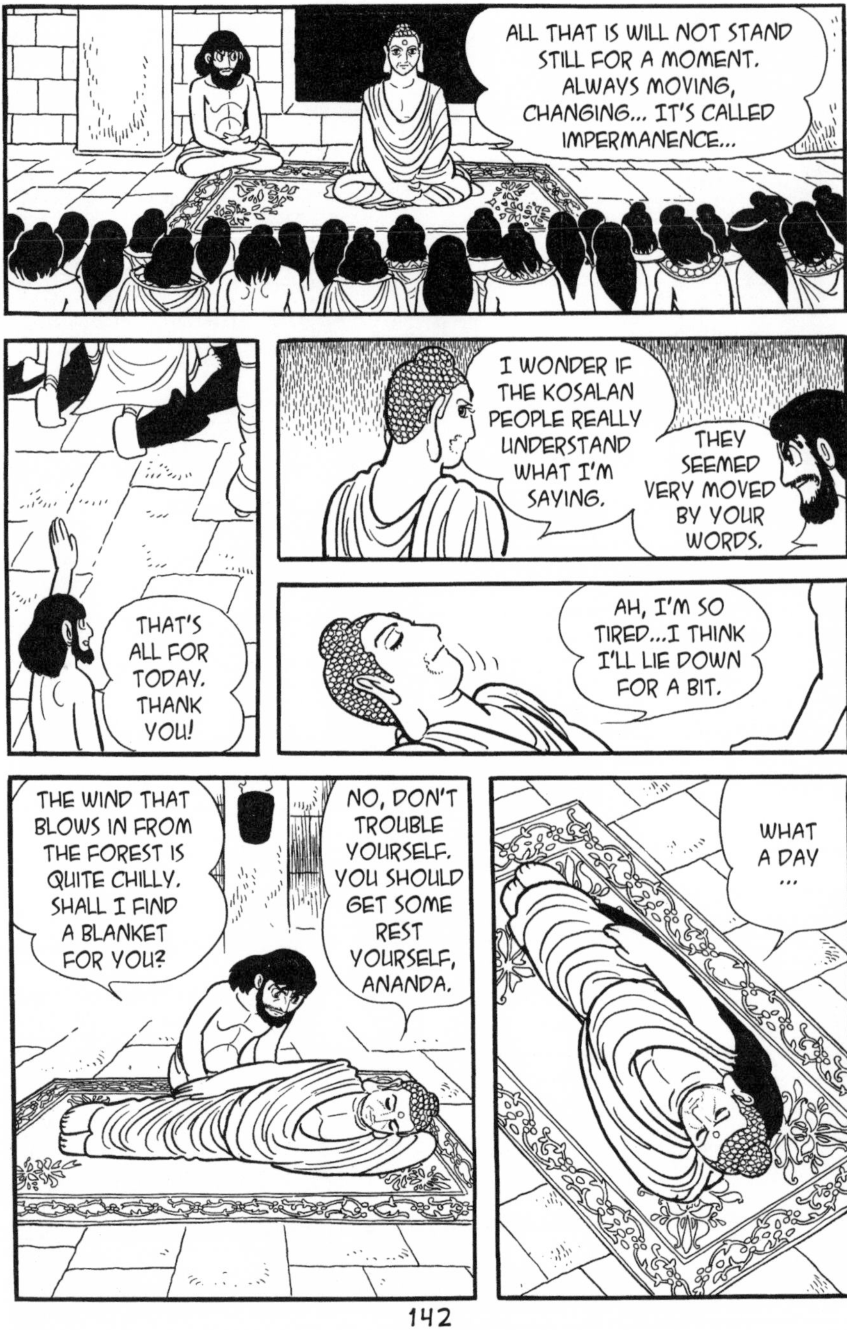
ALL THAT IS WILL NOT STAND STILL FOR A MOMENT. ALWAYS MOVING, CHANGING... IT'S CALLED IMPERMANENCE...
THAT'S ALL FOR TODAY. THANK YOU!
I WONDER IF THE KOSALAN PEOPLE REALLY UNDERSTAND WHAT I'M SAYING.
THEY SEEMED VERY MOVED BY YOUR WORDS.
AH, I'M SO TIRED...I THINK I'LL LIE DOWN FOR A BIT.
THE WIND THAT BLOWS IN FROM THE FOREST IS QUITE CHILLY. SHALL I FIND A BLANKET FOR YOU?
NO, DON'T TROUBLE YOURSELF. YOU SHOULD GET SOME REST YOURSELF, ANANDA.
WHAT A DAY ...

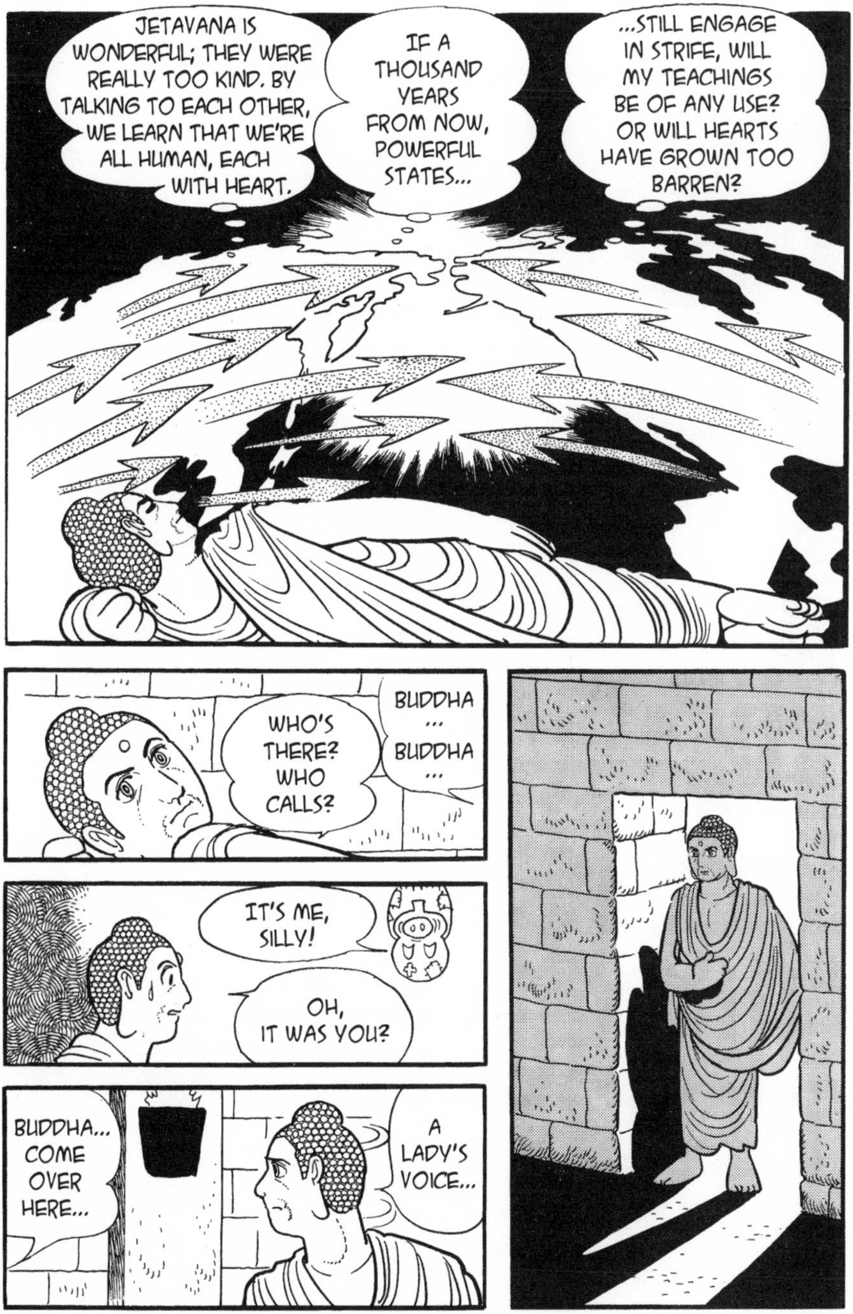
JETAVANA IS WONDERFUL; THEY WERE REALLY TOO KIND. BY TALKING TO EACH OTHER, WE LEARN THAT WE'RE ALL HUMAN, EACH WITH HEART.
IF A THOUSAND YEARS FROM NOW, POWERFUL STATES...
...STILL ENGAGE IN STRIFE, WILL MY TEACHINGS BE OF ANY USE? OR WILL HEARTS HAVE GROWN TOO BARREN?
WHO'S THERE? WHO CALLS?
BUDDHA ... BUDDHA ...
IT'S ME, SILLY!
OH, IT WAS YOU?
BUDDHA... COME OVER HERE...
A LADY'S VOICE...

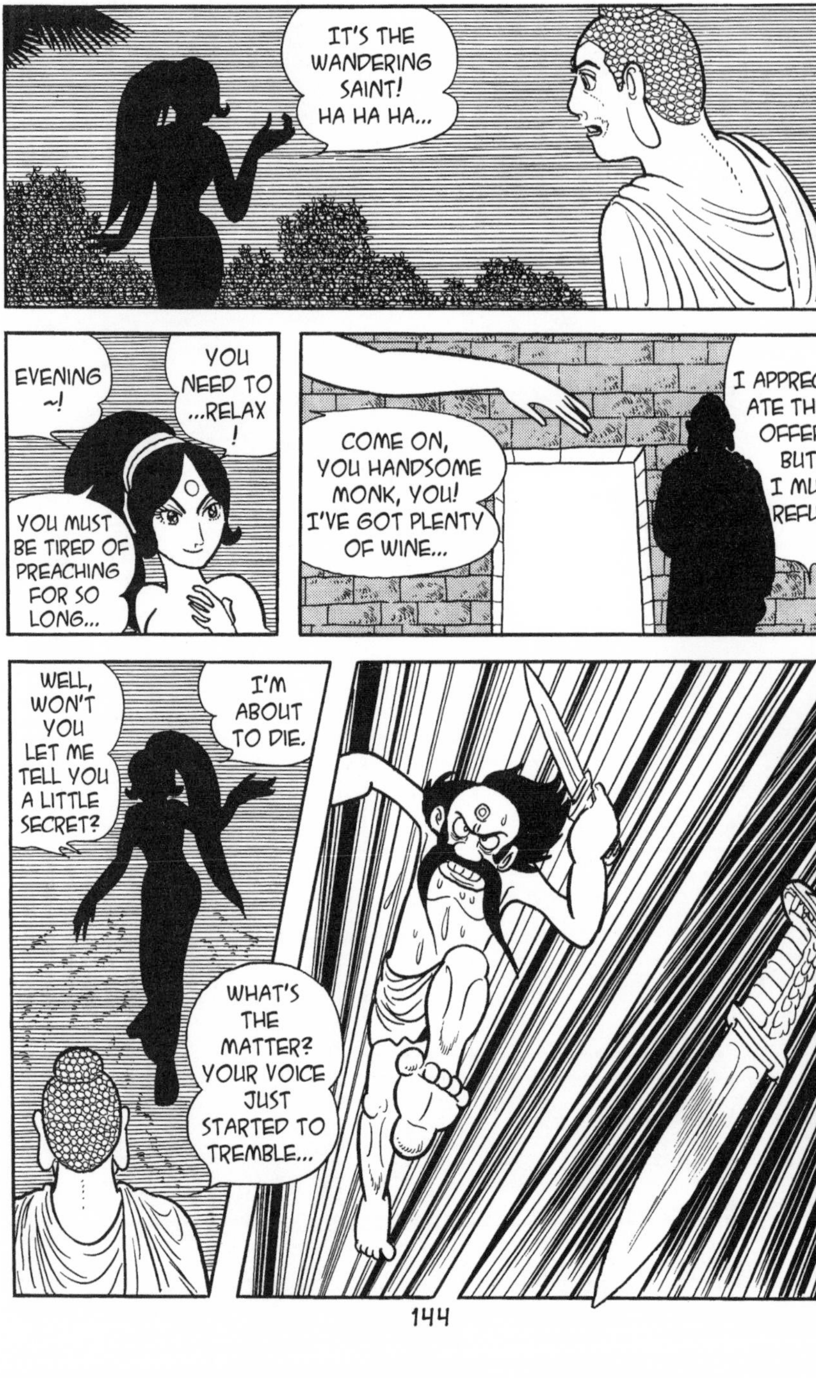
IT'S THE WANDERING SAINT! HA HA HA...
EVENING ~!
YOU NEED TO ...RELAX !
YOU MUST BE TIRED OF PREACHING FOR SO LONG...
COME ON, YOU HANDSOME MONK, YOU! I'VE GOT PLENTY OF WINE...
I APPRECIATE THE OFFER, BUT I MUST REFUSE.
WELL, WON'T YOU LET ME TELL YOU A LITTLE SECRET? ~!
I'M ABOUT TO DIE.
WHAT'S THE MATTER? YOUR VOICE JUST STARTED TO TREMBLE...

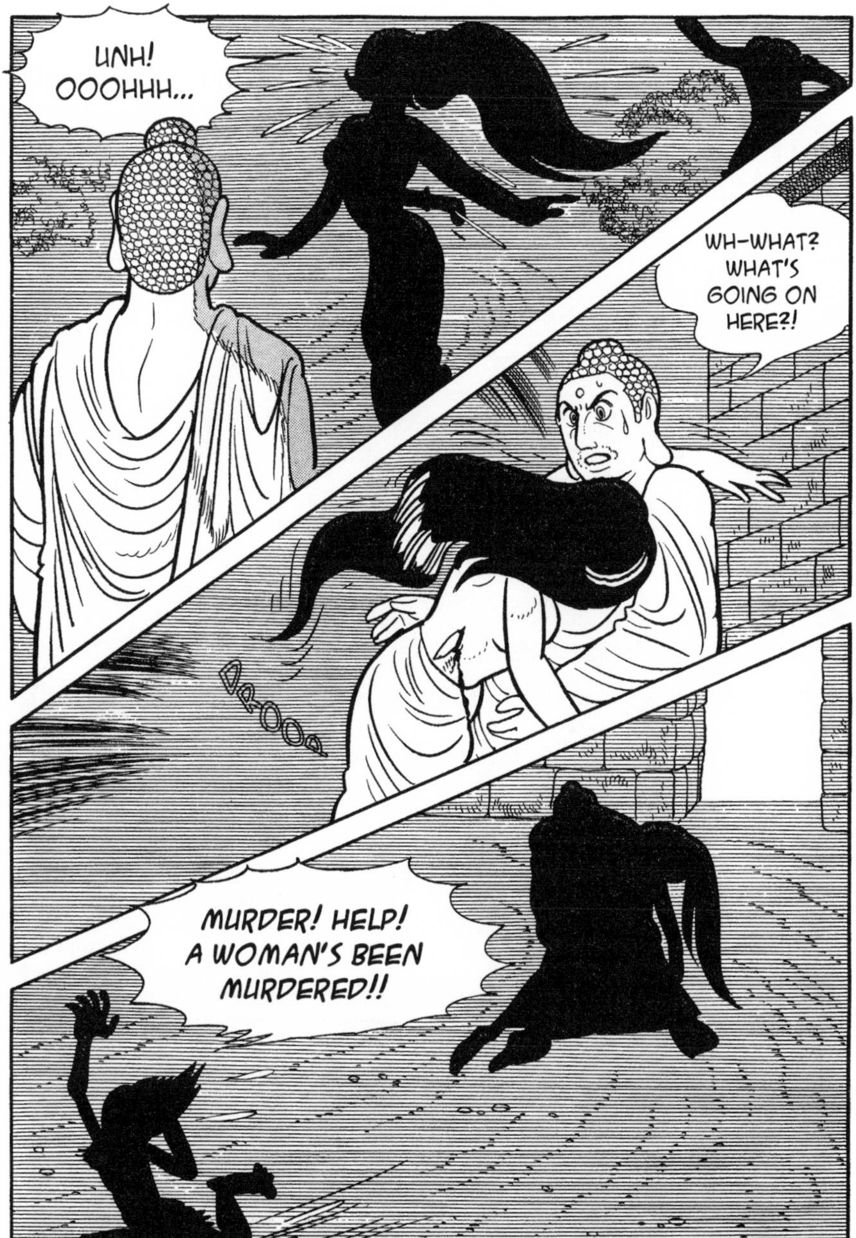
UNH! OOOHHH...
WH-WHAT? WHAT'S GOING ON HERE?!
DROOP
MURDER! HELP! A WOMAN'S BEEN MURDERED!!

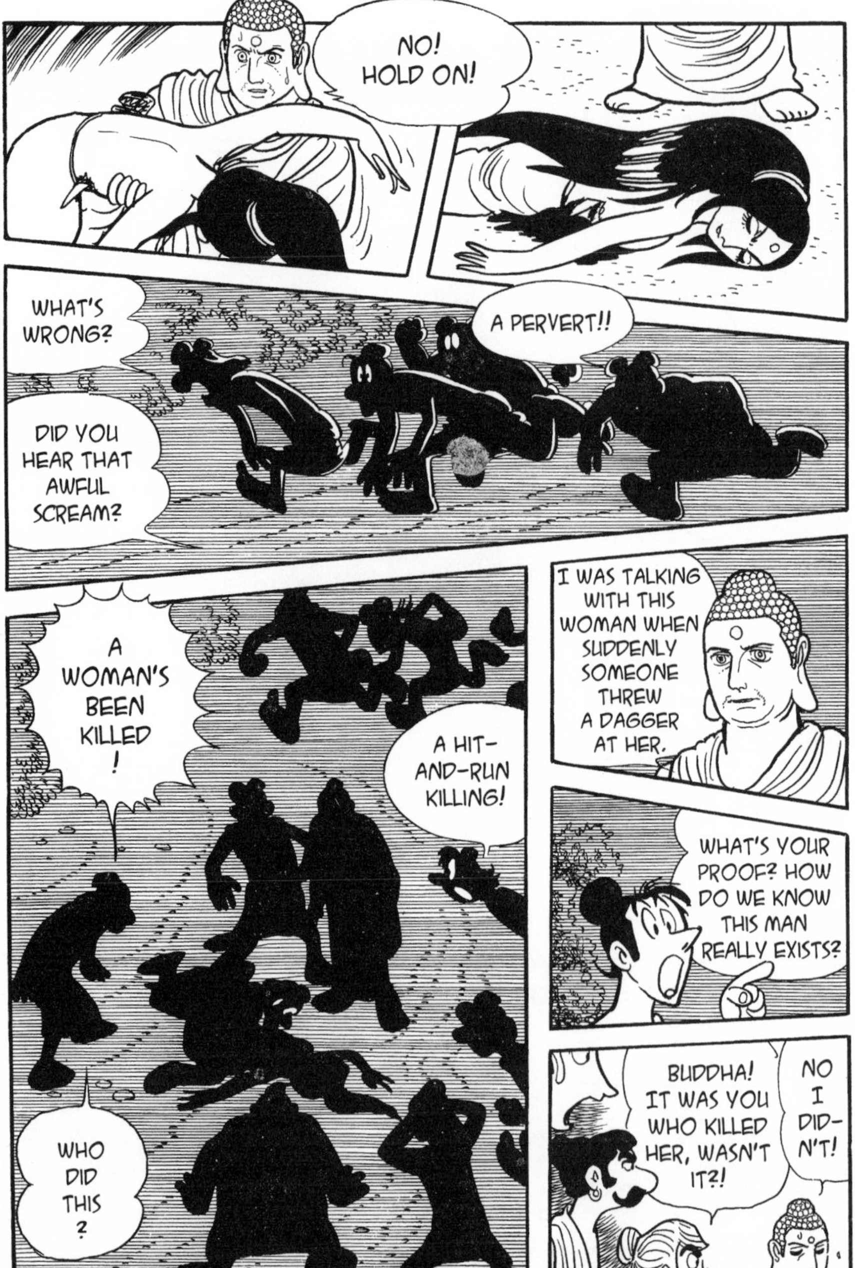
NO! HOLD ON!
WHAT'S WRONG?
DID YOU HEAR THAT AWFUL SCREAM?
A PERVERT!!
A WOMAN'S BEEN KILLED !
A HIT-AND-RUN KILLING!
WHO DID THIS ?
I WAS TALKING WITH THIS WOMAN WHEN SUDDENLY SOMEONE THREW A DAGGER AT HER.
WHAT'S YOUR PROOF? HOW DO WE KNOW THIS MAN REALLY EXISTS?
BUDDHA! IT WAS YOU WHO KILLED HER, WASN'T IT?!
NO I DID-N'T!

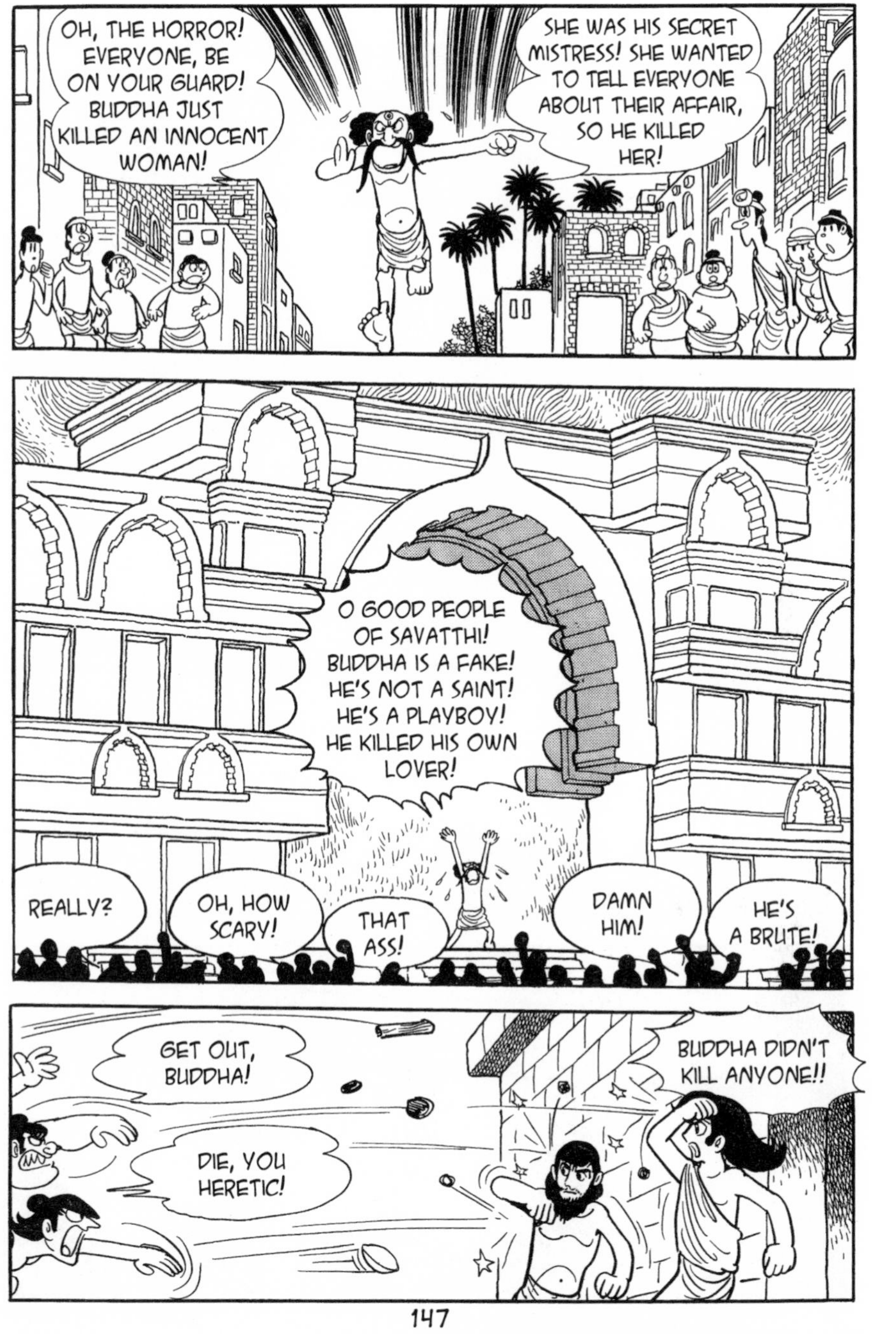
OH, THE HORROR! EVERYONE, BE ON YOUR GUARD! BUDDHA JUST KILLED AN INNOCENT WOMAN!
SHE WAS HIS SECRET MISTRESS! SHE WANTED TO TELL EVERYONE ABOUT THEIR AFFAIR, SO HE KILLED HER!
O GOOD PEOPLE OF SAVATTHI! BUDDHA IS A FAKE! HE'S NOT A SAINT! HE'S A PLAYBOY! HE KILLED HIS OWN LOVER!
REALLY?
OH, HOW SCARY!
THAT ASS!
DAMN HIM!
HE'S A BRUTE!
GET OUT, BUDDHA!
DIE, YOU HERETIC!
BUDDHA DIDN'T KILL ANYONE!!

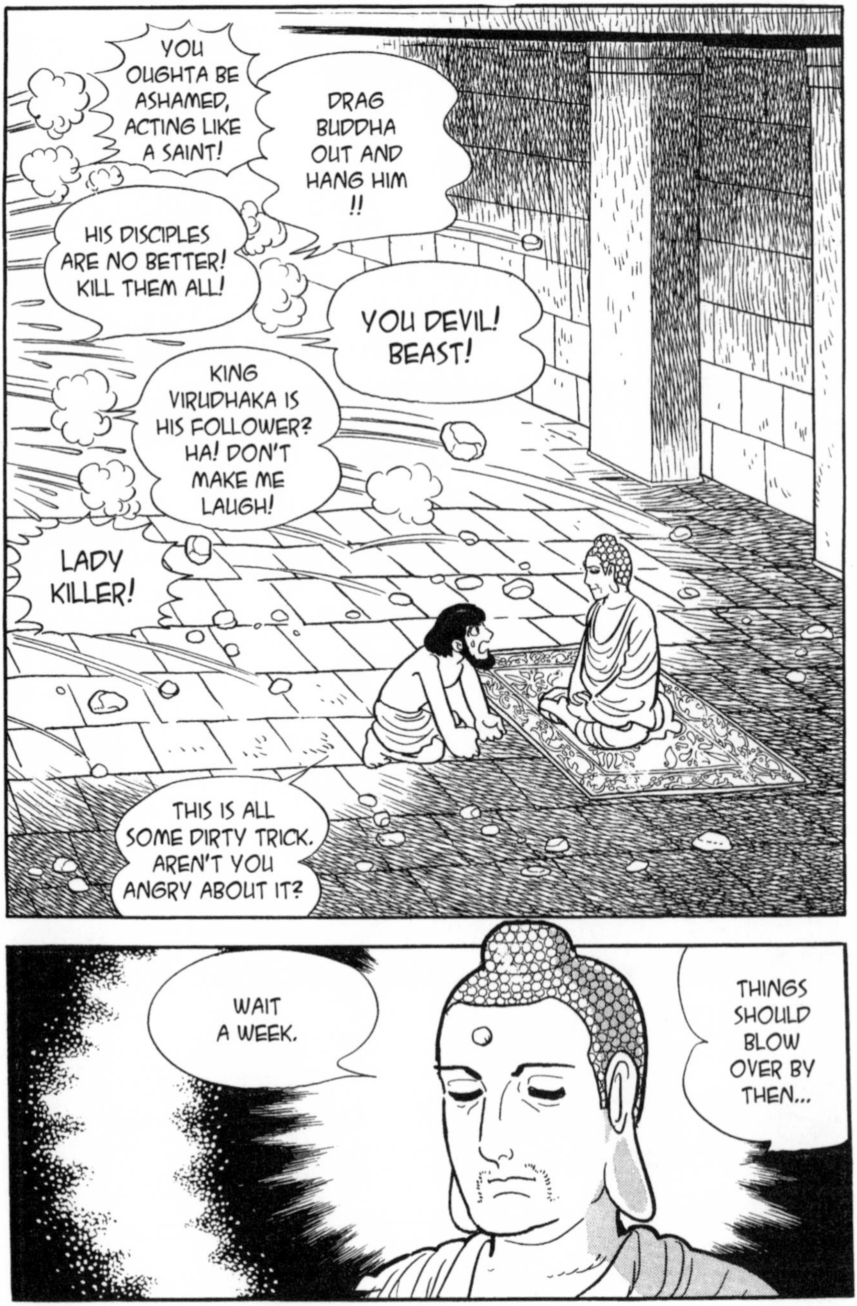
YOU OUGHTA BE ASHAMED, ACTING LIKE A SAINT!
DRAG BUDDHA OUT AND HANG HIM !!
HIS DISCIPLES ARE NO BETTER! KILL THEM ALL!
YOU DEVIL! BEAST!
KING VIRUDHAKA IS HIS FOLLOWER? HA! DON'T MAKE ME LAUGH!
LADY KILLER!
THIS IS ALL SOME DIRTY TRICK. AREN'T YOU ANGRY ABOUT IT?
WAIT A WEEK.
THINGS SHOULD BLOW OVER BY THEN...

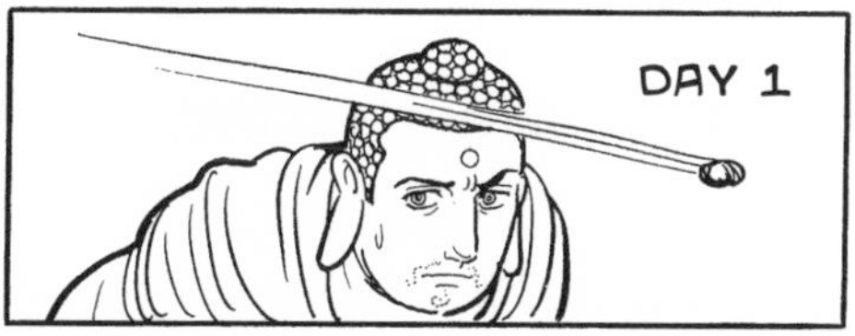
DAY 1

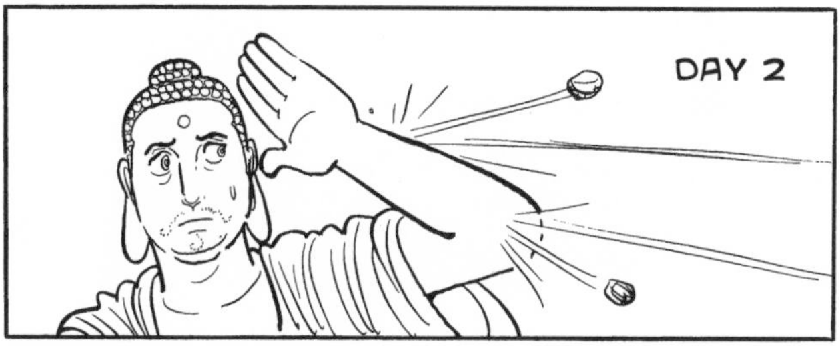
DAY 2

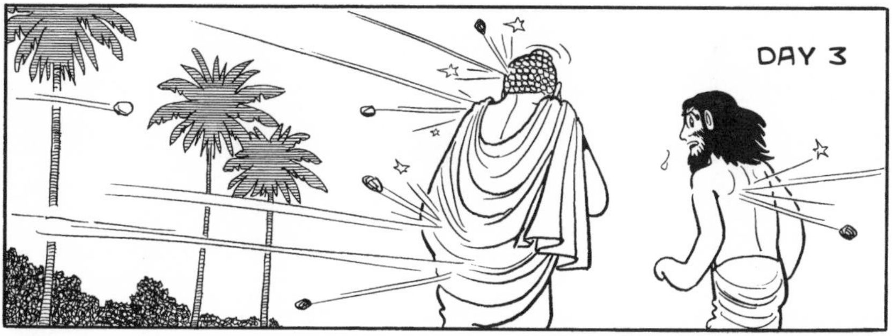
DAY 3

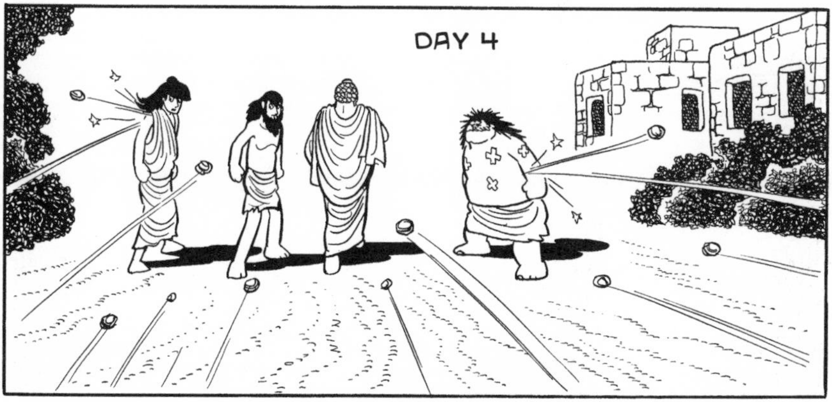
DAY 4

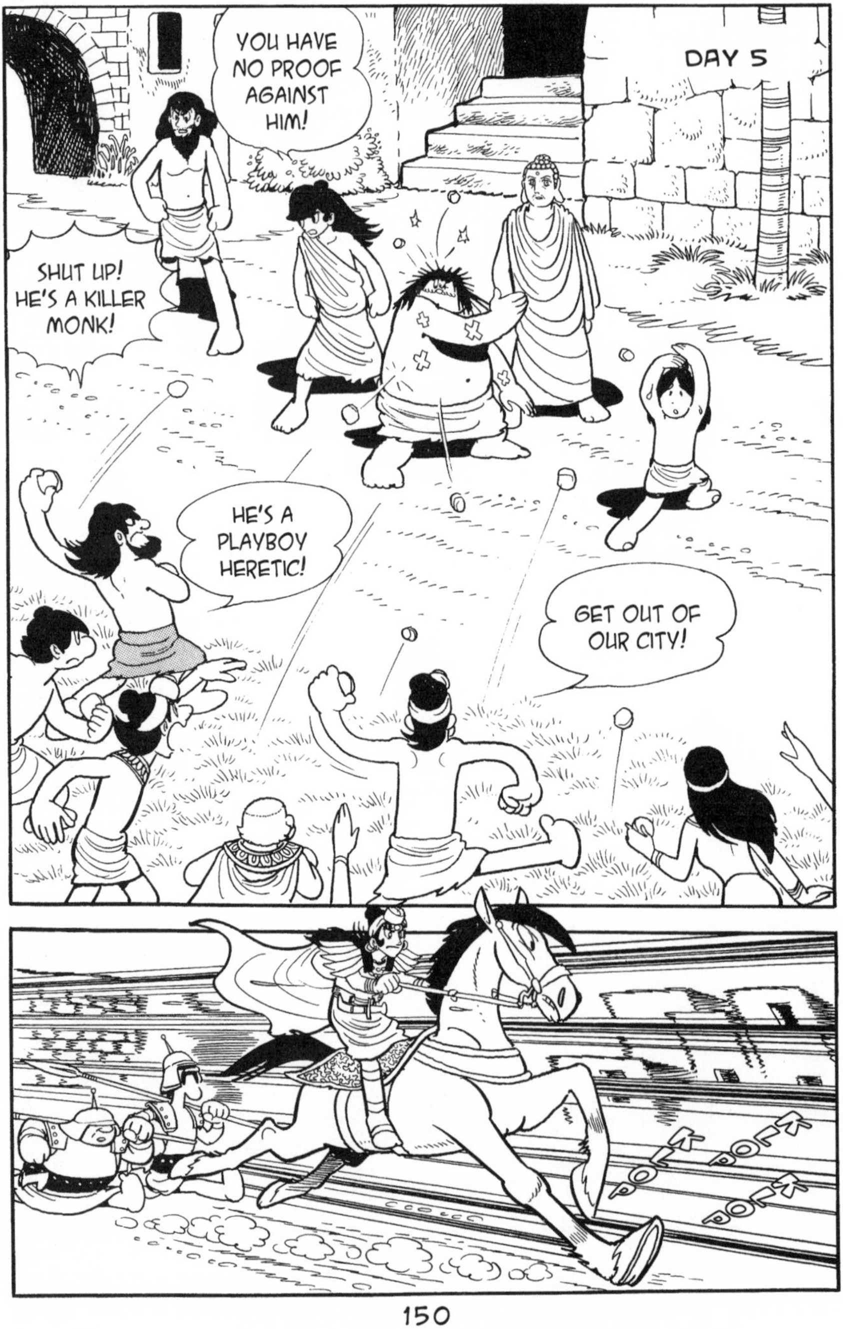
DAY 5
YOU HAVE NO PROOF AGAINST HIM!
SHUT UP! HE'S A KILLER MONK!
HE'S A PLAYBOY HERETIC!
GET OUT OF OUR CITY!
POLK POLK POLK

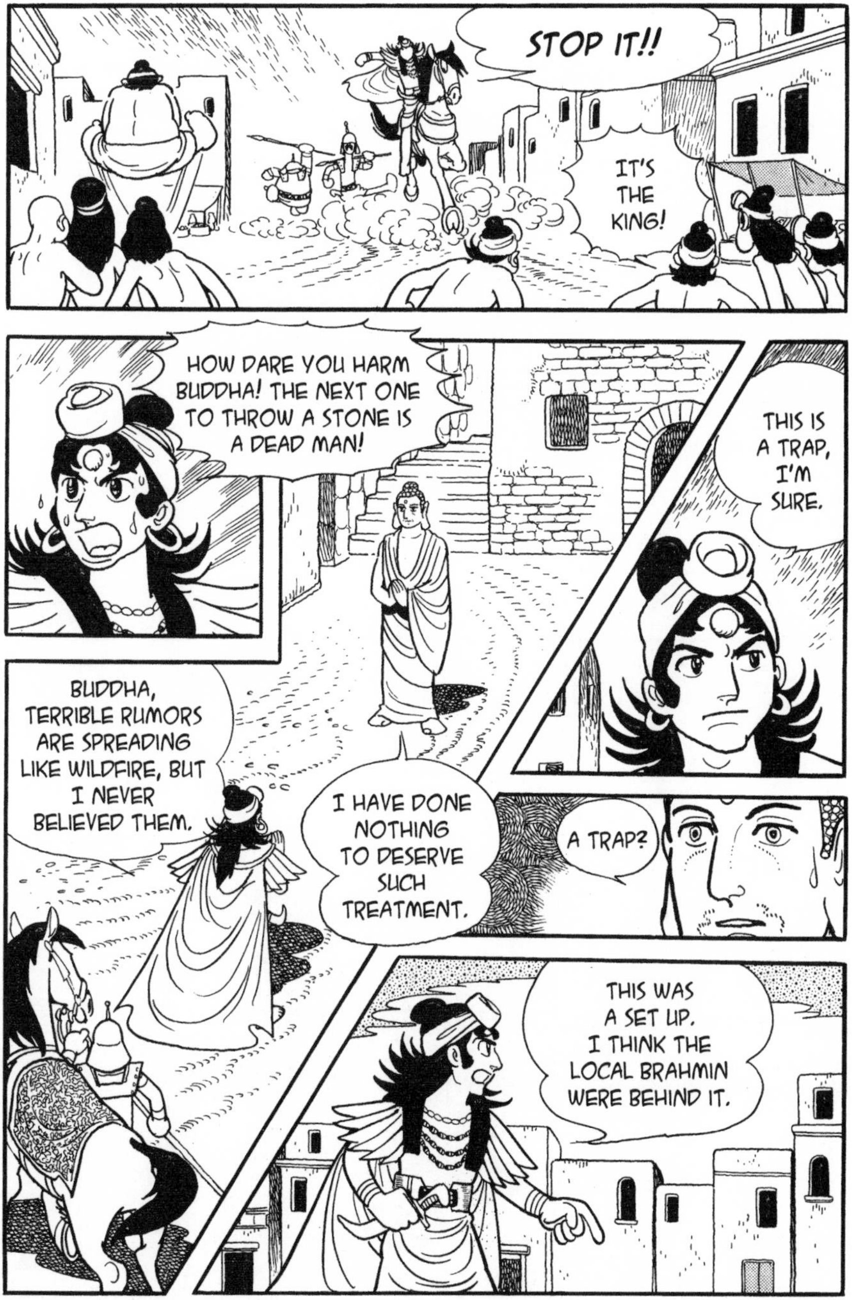
STOP IT!!
IT'S THE KING!
HOW DARE YOU HARM BUDDHA! THE NEXT ONE TO THROW A STONE IS A DEAD MAN!
THIS IS A TRAP, I'M SURE.
BUDDHA, TERRIBLE RUMORS ARE SPREADING LIKE WILDFIRE, BUT I NEVER BELIEVED THEM.
I HAVE DONE NOTHING TO DESERVE SUCH TREATMENT.
A TRAP?
THIS WAS A SET UP. I THINK THE LOCAL BRAHMIN WERE BEHIND IT.

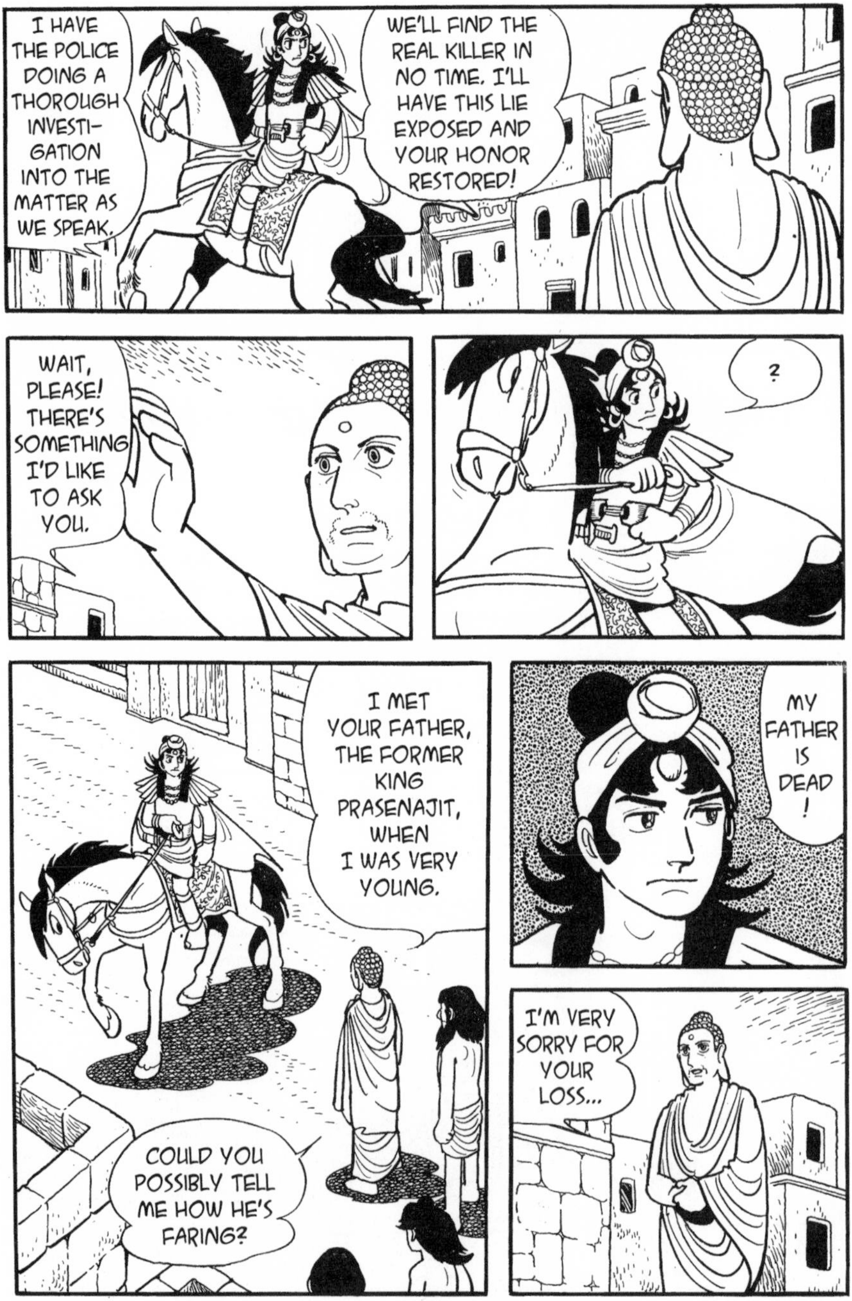
I HAVE THE POLICE DOING A THOROUGH INVESTIGATION INTO THE MATTER AS WE SPEAK.
WE'LL FIND THE REAL KILLER IN NO TIME. I'LL HAVE THIS LIE EXPOSED AND YOUR HONOR RESTORED!
WAIT, PLEASE! THERE'S SOMETHING I'D LIKE TO ASK YOU.
?
I MET YOUR FATHER, THE FORMER KING PRASENAJIT, WHEN I WAS VERY YOUNG.
COULD YOU POSSIBLY TELL ME HOW HE'S FARING?
MY FATHER IS DEAD!
I'M VERY SORRY FOR YOUR LOSS...

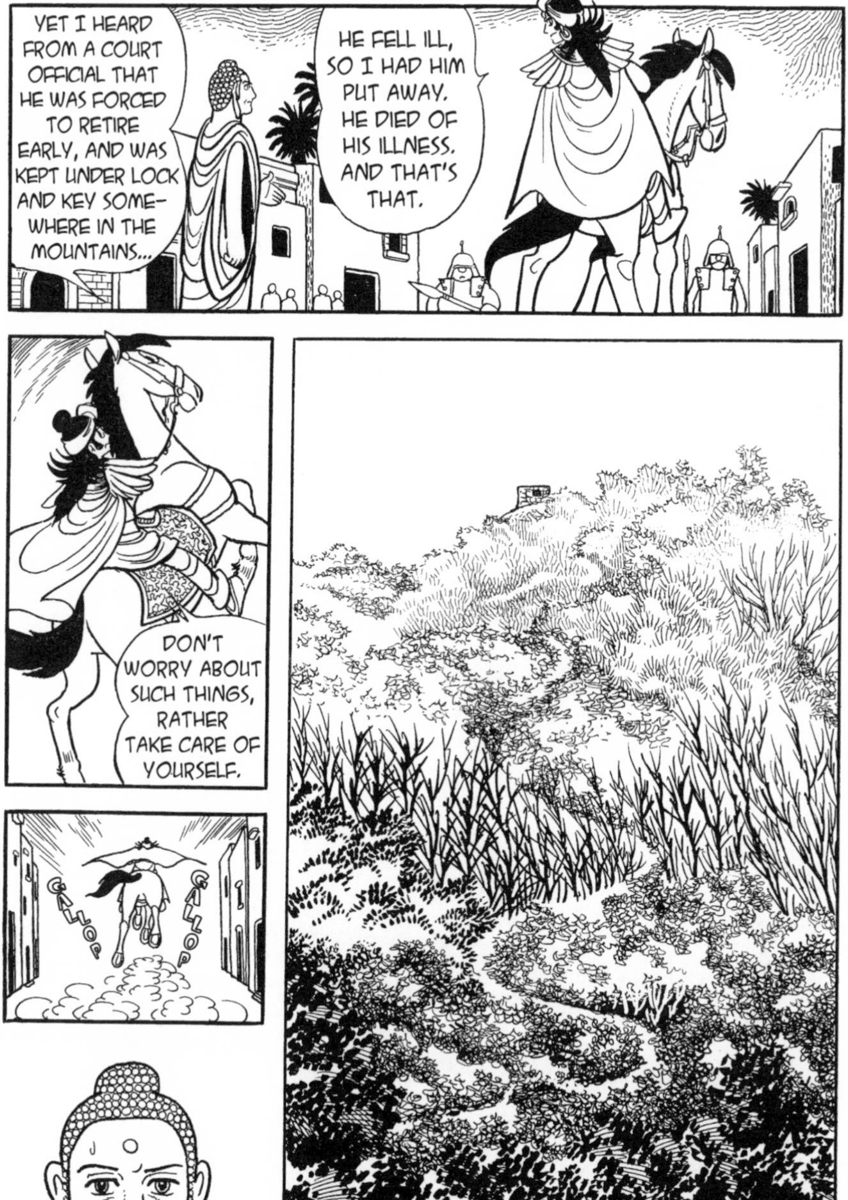
YET I HEARD FROM A COURT OFFICIAL THAT HE WAS FORCED TO RETIRE EARLY, AND WAS KEPT UNDER LOCK AND KEY SOME-WHERE IN THE MOUNTAINS...
HE FELL ILL, SO I HAD HIM PUT AWAY. HE DIED OF HIS ILLNESS. AND THAT'S THAT.
DON'T WORRY ABOUT SUCH THINGS, RATHER TAKE CARE OF YOURSELF.
GALLOP
GALLOP

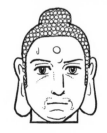

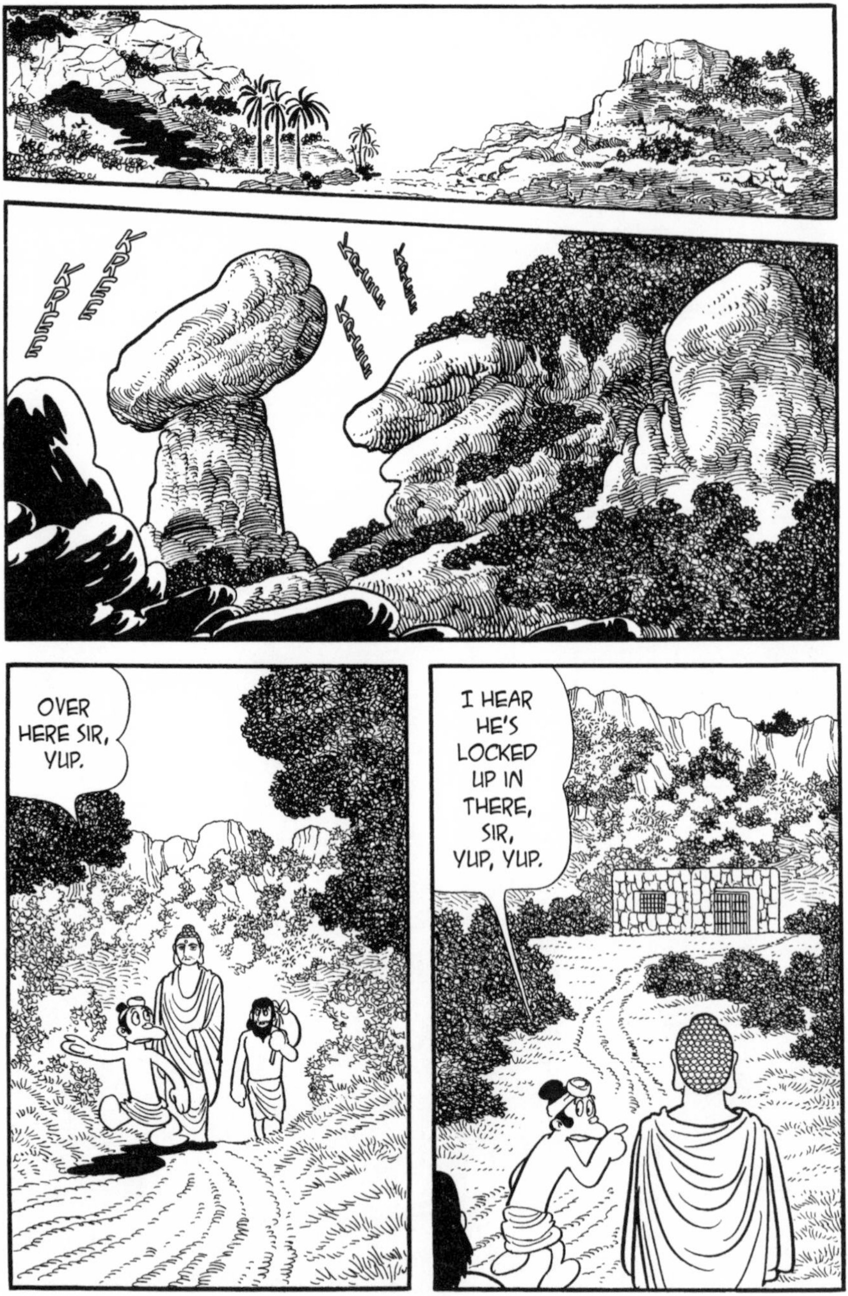
KREEEE
KREEE
OVER HERE SIR, YUP.
I HEAR HE'S LOCKED UP IN THERE, SIR, YUP, YUP.

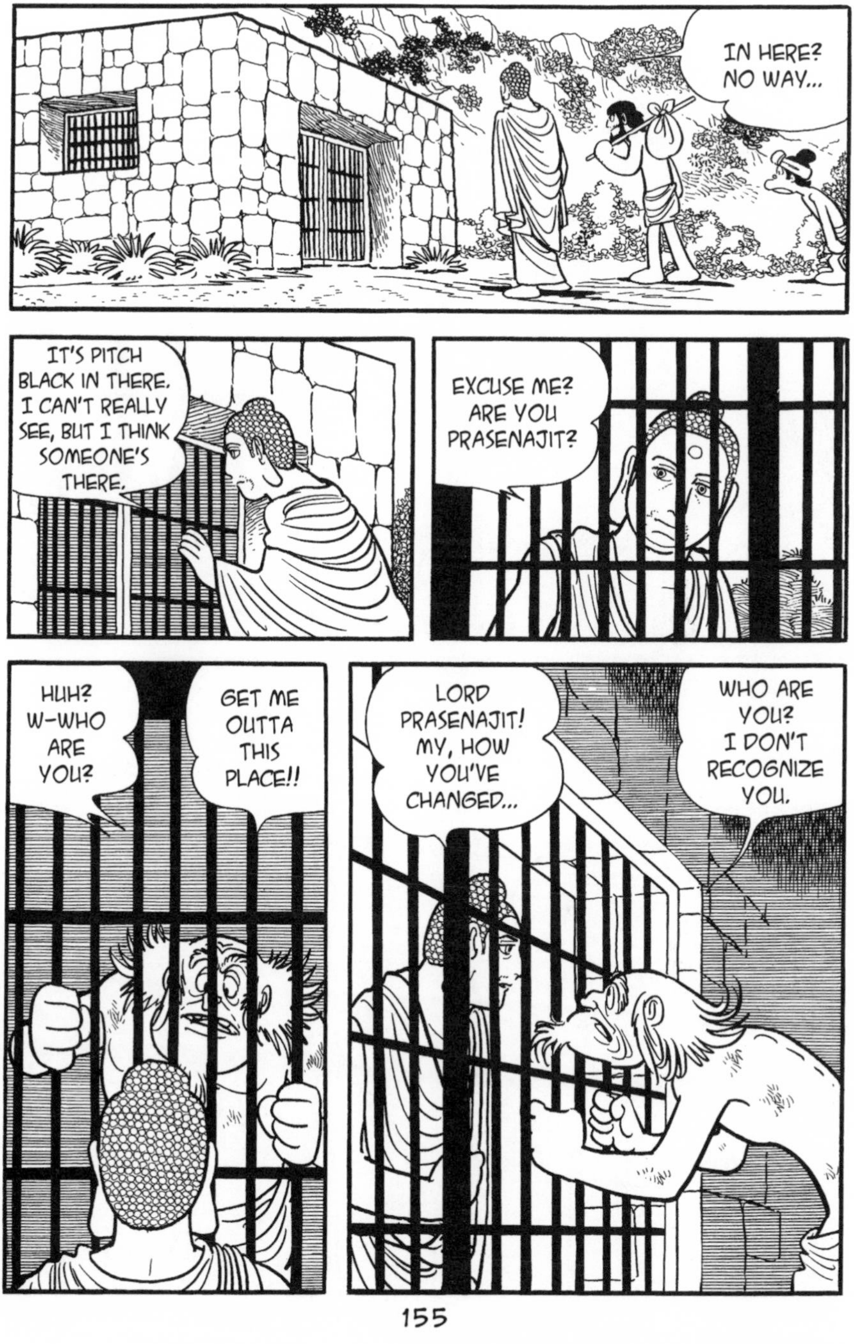
IN HERE? NO WAY...
IT'S PITCH BLACK IN THERE. I CAN'T REALLY SEE, BUT I THINK SOMEONE'S THERE.
EXCUSE ME? ARE YOU PRASENAJIT?
HUH? W-WHO ARE YOU?
GET ME OUTTA THIS PLACE!!
LORD PRASENAJIT! MY, HOW YOU'VE CHANGED...
WHO ARE YOU? I DON'T RECOGNIZE YOU.

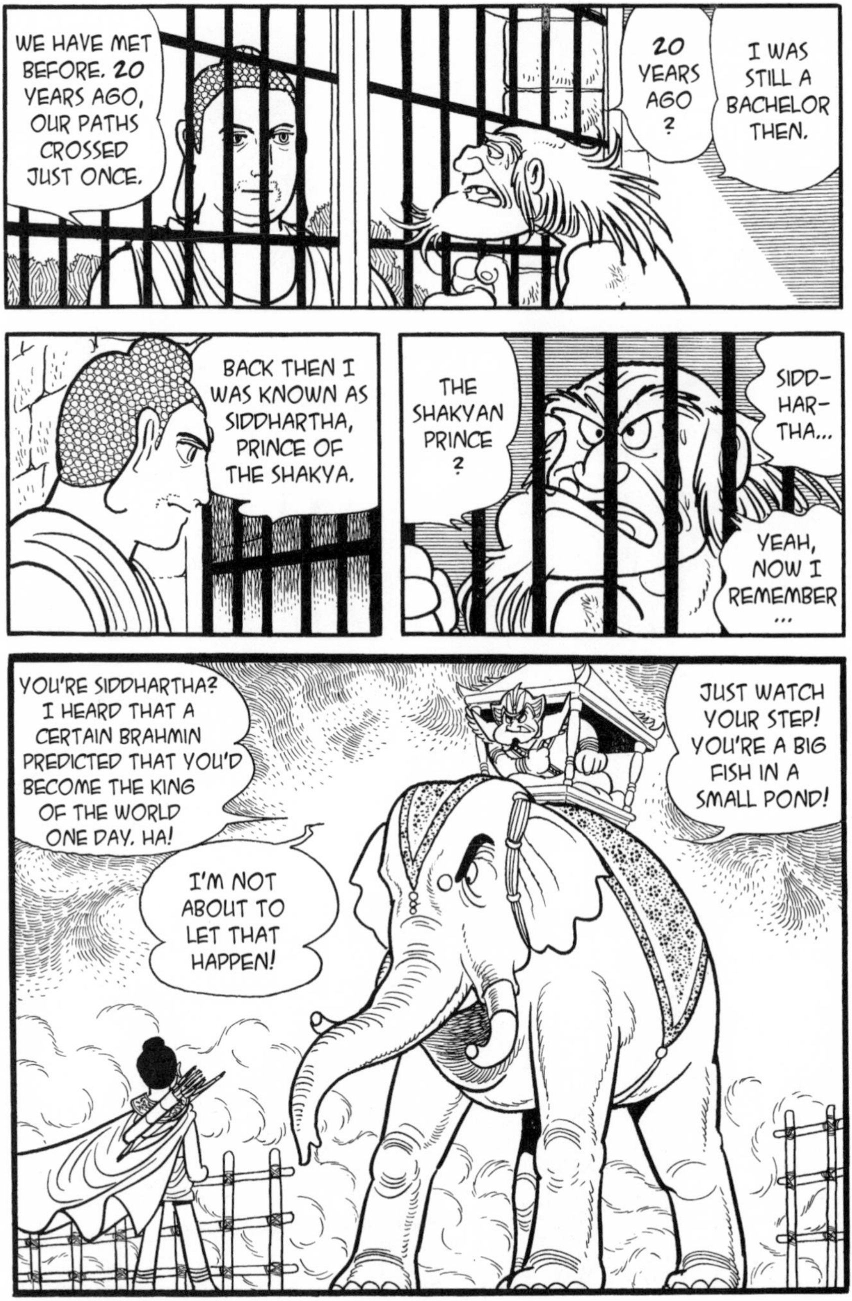
WE HAVE MET BEFORE. 20 YEARS AGO, OUR PATHS CROSSED JUST ONCE.
20 YEARS AGO ?
I WAS STILL A BACHELOR THEN.
BACK THEN I WAS KNOWN AS SIDDHARTHA, PRINCE OF THE SHAKYA.
THE SHAKYAN PRINCE ?
SIDD-HAR-THA...
YEAH, NOW I REMEMBER ...
YOU'RE SIDDHARTHA? I HEARD THAT A CERTAIN BRAHMIN PREDICTED THAT YOU'D BECOME THE KING OF THE WORLD ONE DAY. HA!
I'M NOT ABOUT TO LET THAT HAPPEN!
JUST WATCH YOUR STEP! YOU'RE A BIG FISH IN A SMALL POND!

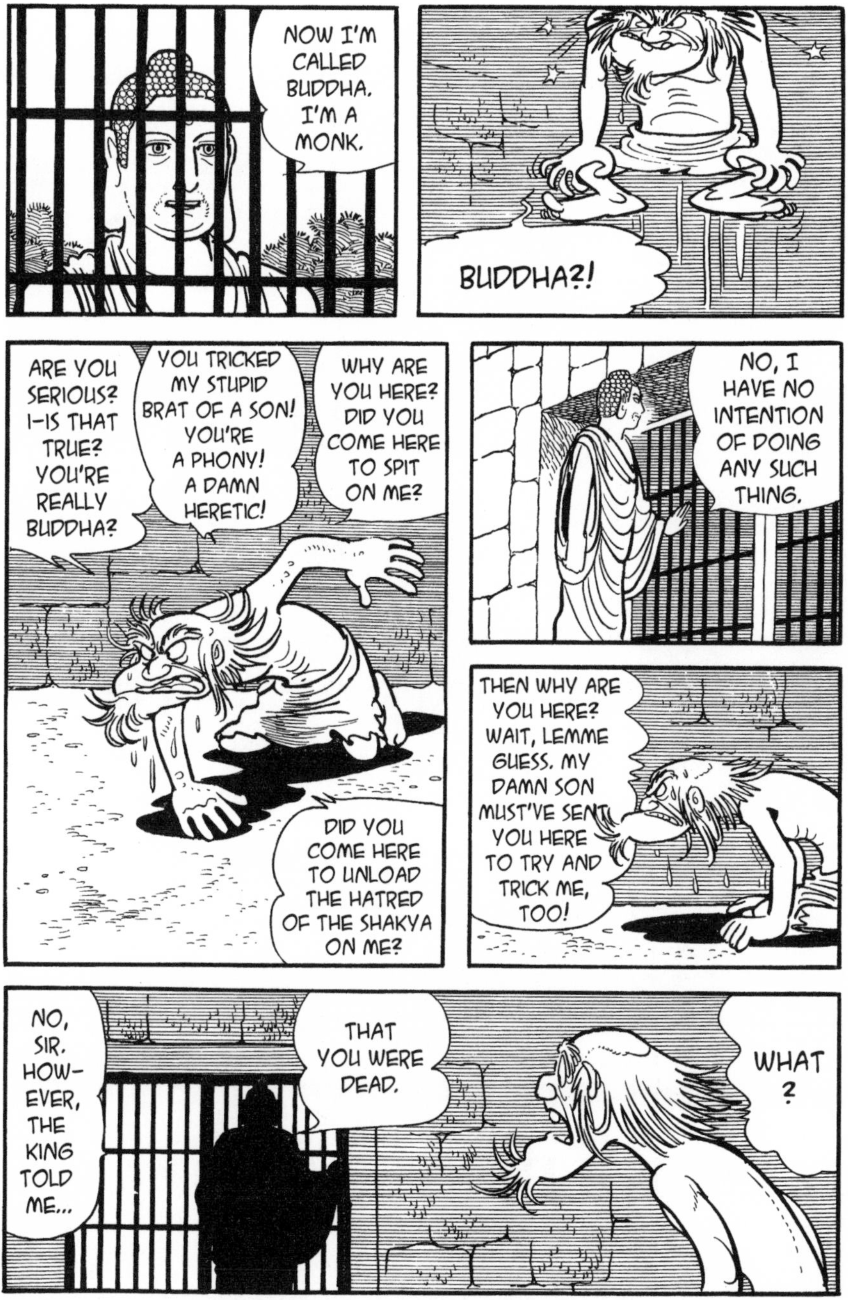
NOW I'M CALLED BUDDHA. I'M A MONK.
BUDDHA?!
ARE YOU SERIOUS? I-IS THAT TRUE? YOU'RE REALLY BUDDHA?
YOU TRICKED MY STUPID BRAT OF A SON! YOU'RE A PHONY! A DAMN HERETIC!
WHY ARE YOU HERE? DID YOU COME HERE TO SPIT ON ME?
DID YOU COME HERE TO UNLOAD THE HATRED OF THE SHAKYA ON ME?
NO, I HAVE NO INTENTION OF DOING ANY SUCH THING.
THEN WHY ARE YOU HERE? WAIT, LEMME GUESS. MY DAMN SON MUST'VE SENT YOU HERE TO TRY AND TRICK ME, TOO!
NO, SIR. HOW-EVER, THE KING TOLD ME...
THAT YOU WERE DEAD.
WHAT?

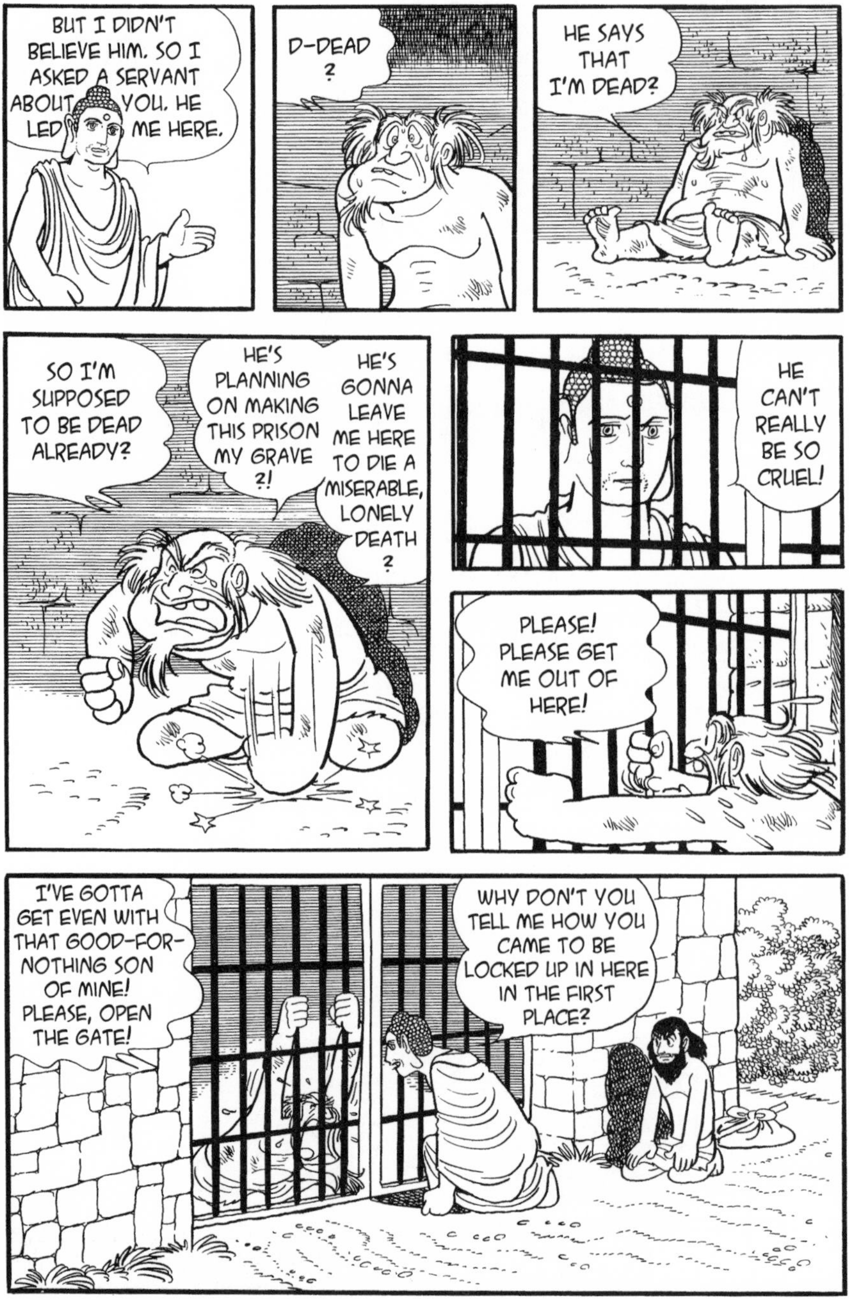

BUT I DIDN'T BELIEVE HIM. SO I ASKED A SERVANT ABOUT YOU. HE LED ME HERE.
D-DEAD?
HE SAYS THAT I'M DEAD?
SO I'M SUPPOSED TO BE DEAD ALREADY?
HE'S PLANNING ON MAKING THIS PRISON MY GRAVE?!
HE'S GONNA LEAVE ME HERE TO DIE A MISERABLE, LONELY DEATH?
HE CAN'T REALLY BE SO CRUEL!
PLEASE! PLEASE GET ME OUT OF HERE!
I'VE GOTTA GET EVEN WITH THAT GOOD-FOR-NOTHING SON OF MINE! PLEASE, OPEN THE GATE!
WHY DON'T YOU TELL ME HOW YOU CAME TO BE LOCKED UP IN HERE IN THE FIRST PLACE?

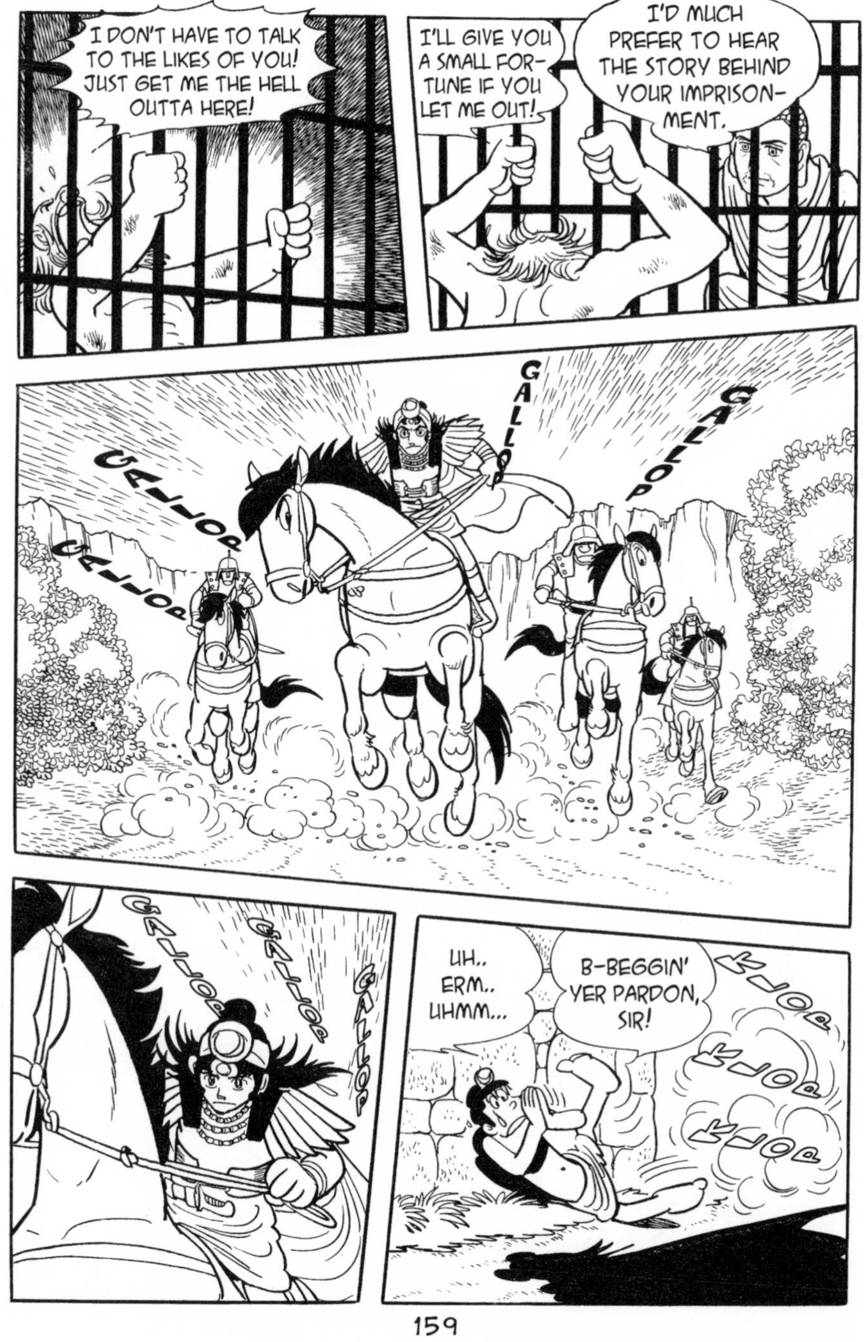
I DON'T HAVE TO TALK TO THE LIKES OF YOU! JUST GET ME THE HELL OUTTA HERE!
I'LL GIVE YOU A SMALL FOR-TUNE IF YOU LET ME OUT!
I'D MUCH PREFER TO HEAR THE STORY BEHIND YOUR IMPRISON-MENT.
GALLOP
GALLOP
GALLOP
GALLOP
GALLOP
GALLOP
GALLOP
UH.. ERM.. UHMM...
B-BEGGIN' YER PARDON, SIR!
GALLOP
GALLOP
GALLOP

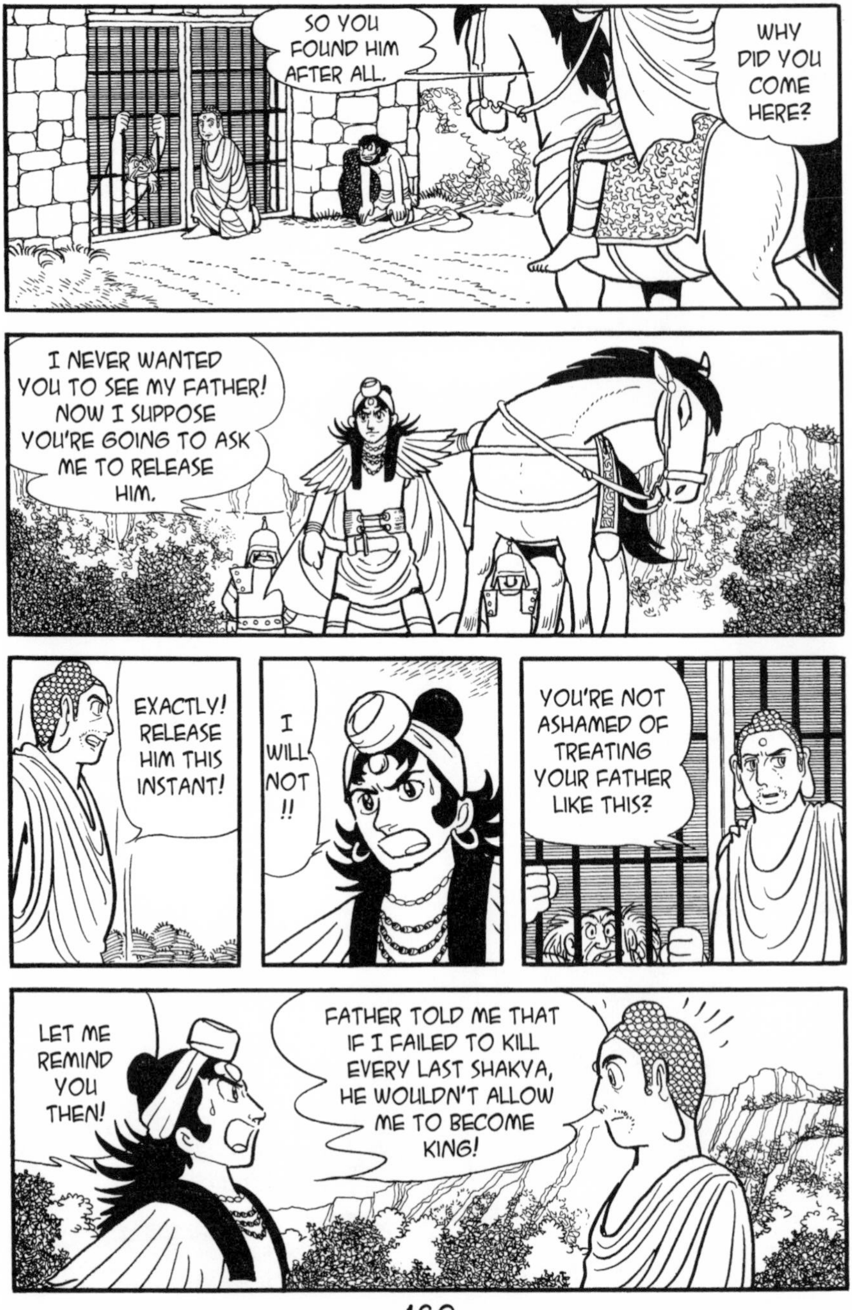

SO YOU FOUND HIM AFTER ALL.
WHY DID YOU COME HERE?
I NEVER WANTED YOU TO SEE MY FATHER! NOW I SUPPOSE YOU'RE GOING TO ASK ME TO RELEASE HIM.
EXACTLY! RELEASE HIM THIS INSTANT!
I WILL NOT !!
YOU'RE NOT ASHAMED OF TREATING YOUR FATHER LIKE THIS?
LET ME REMIND YOU THEN!
FATHER TOLD ME THAT IF I FAILED TO KILL EVERY LAST SHAKYA, HE WOULDN'T ALLOW ME TO BECOME KING!

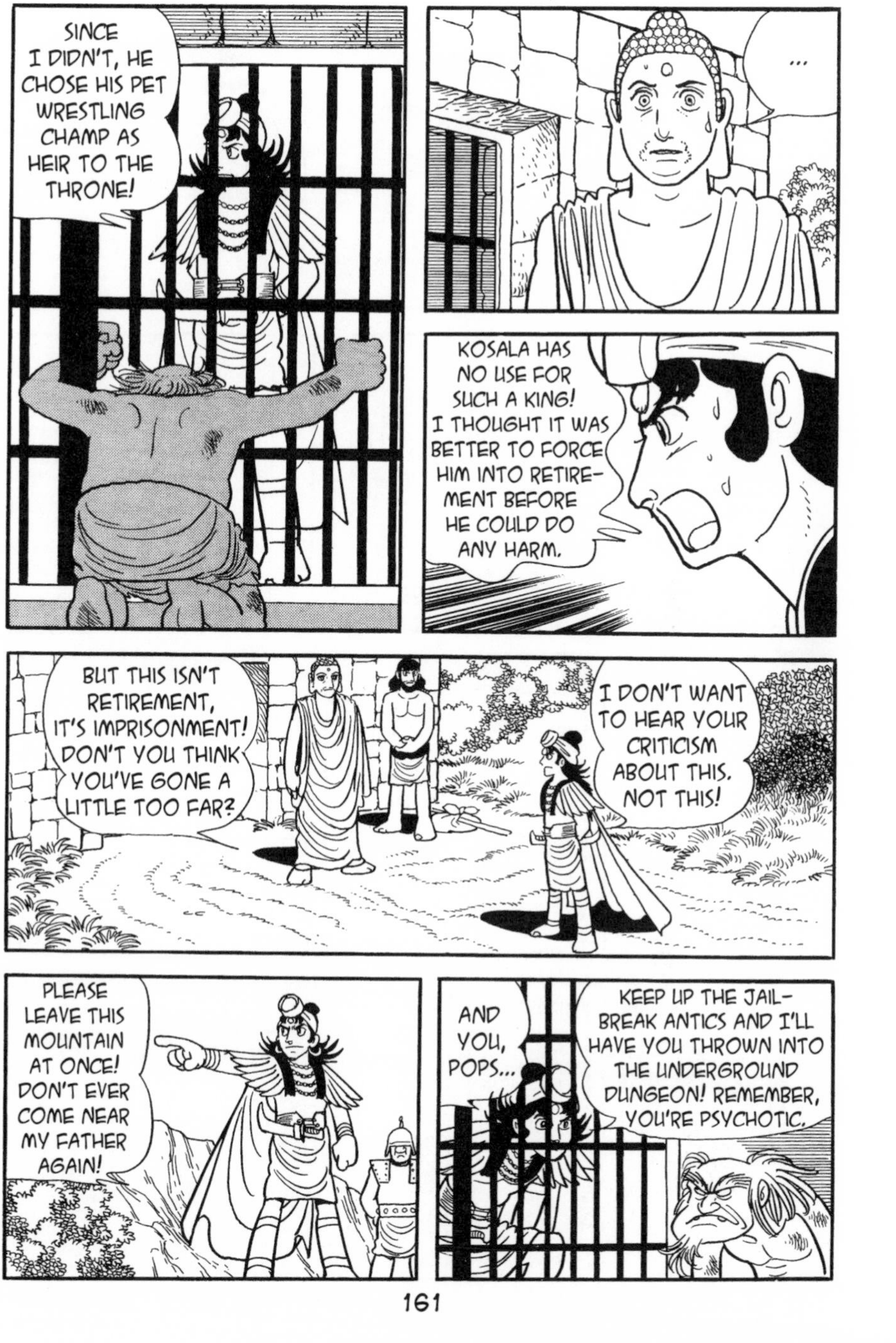

SINCE I DIDN'T, HE CHOSE HIS PET WRESTLING CHAMP AS HEIR TO THE THRONE!
...
KOSALA HAS NO USE FOR SUCH A KING! I THOUGHT IT WAS BETTER TO FORCE HIM INTO RETIRE-MENT BEFORE HE COULD DO ANY HARM.
BUT THIS ISN'T RETIREMENT, IT'S IMPRISONMENT! DON'T YOU THINK YOU'VE GONE A LITTLE TOO FAR?
I DON'T WANT TO HEAR YOUR CRITICISM ABOUT THIS. NOT THIS!
PLEASE LEAVE THIS MOUNTAIN AT ONCE! DON'T EVER COME NEAR MY FATHER AGAIN!
AND YOU, POPS...
KEEP UP THE JAIL-BREAK ANTICS AND I'LL HAVE YOU THROWN INTO THE UNDERGROUND DUNGEON! REMEMBER, YOU'RE PSYCHOTIC.

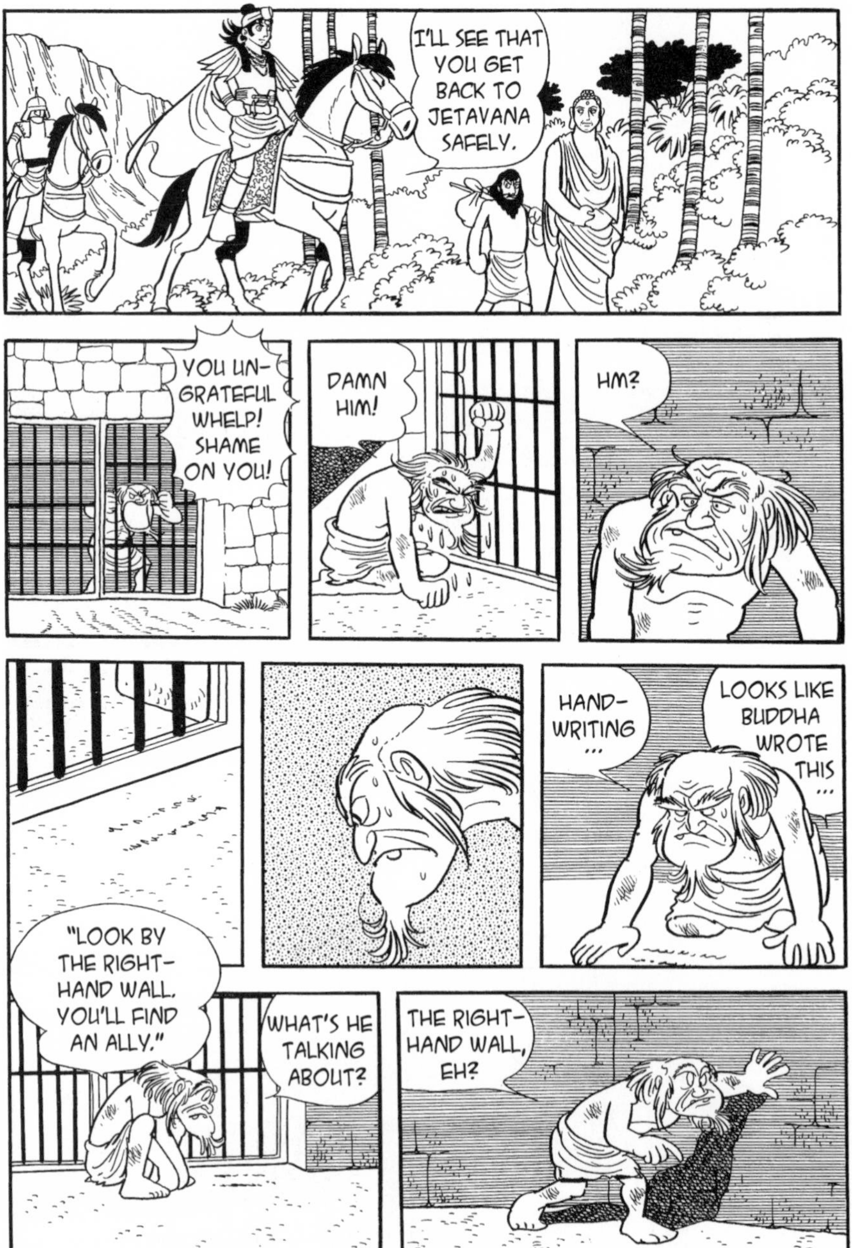
I'LL SEE THAT YOU GET BACK TO JETAVANA SAFELY.
YOU UN-GRATEFUL WHELP! SHAME ON YOU!
DAMN HIM!
HM?
HAND-WRITING ...
LOOKS LIKE BUDDHA WROTE THIS ...
"LOOK BY THE RIGHT-HAND WALL. YOU'LL FIND AN ALLY."
WHAT'S HE TALKING ABOUT?
THE RIGHT-HAND WALL, EH?

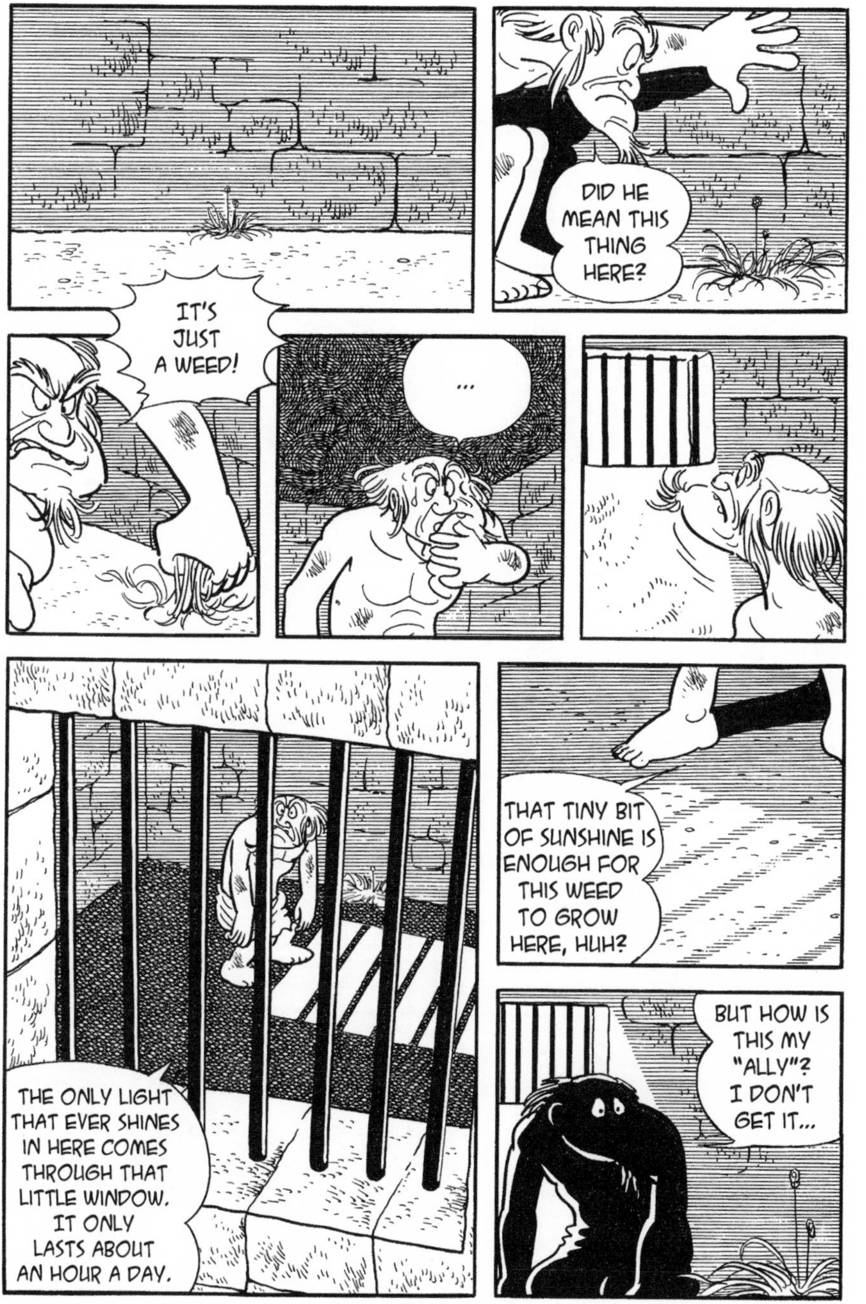
DID HE MEAN THIS THING HERE?
IT'S JUST A WEED!
...
THE ONLY LIGHT THAT EVER SHINES IN HERE COMES THROUGH THAT LITTLE WINDOW. IT ONLY LASTS ABOUT AN HOUR A DAY.
THAT TINY BIT OF SUNSHINE IS ENOUGH FOR THIS WEED TO GROW HERE, HUH?
BUT HOW IS THIS MY "ALLY"? I DON'T GET IT...

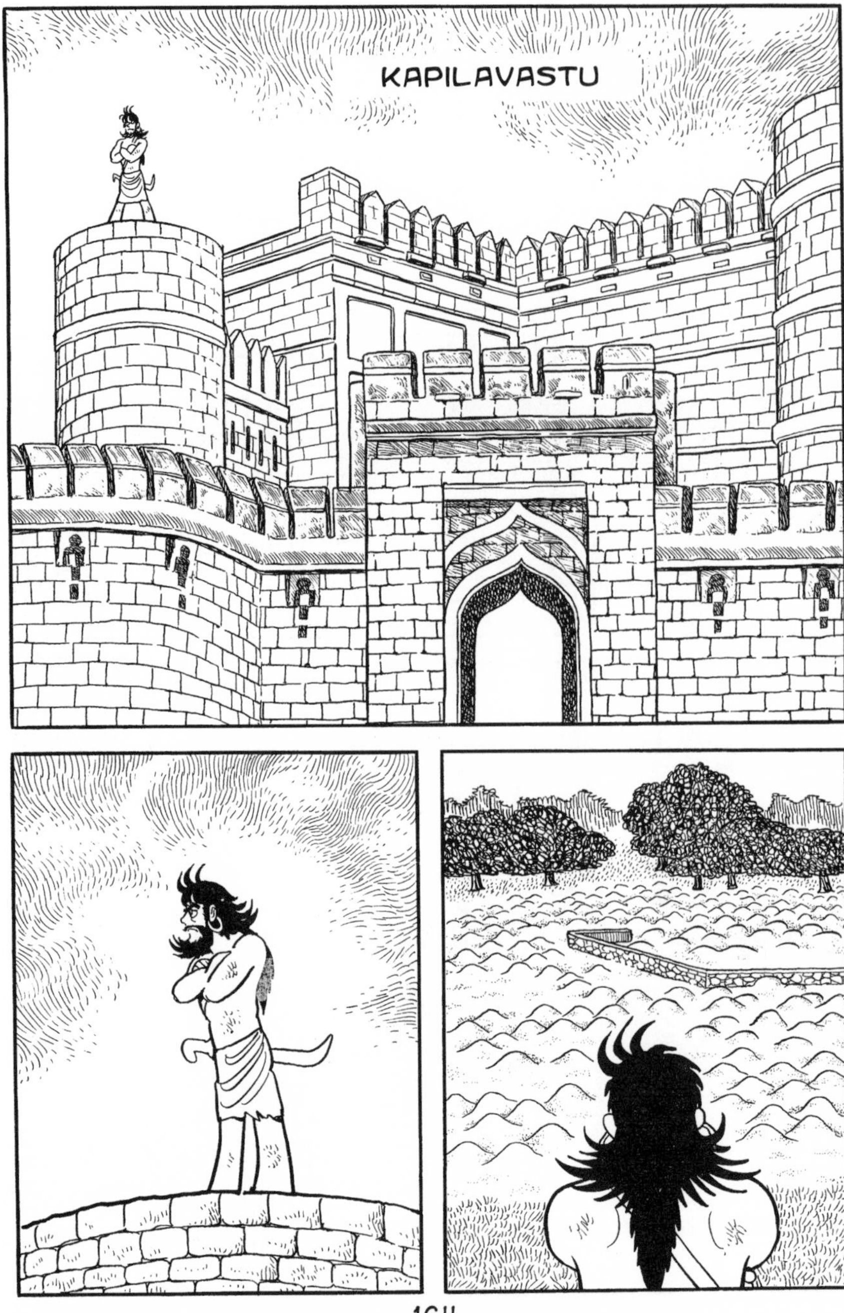
KAPILAVASTU

TATTA, I'VE BEEN SEARCHING FOR CLUES FOR DAYS NOW, BUT I CAN'T FIND OUT WHERE BUDDHA AND HIS PARTY HAVE GONE.

IT'S A SHAME, REALLY. YOU JUST BARELY MISSED HIM. IF ONLY YOU'D COME BACK FROM MAGADHA SOONER...

WHATEVER, IT'S FINE. DO YOU KNOW WHAT ALL THOSE LUMPS ARE?

THOSE ARE GRAVES. THE ONLY THINGS LEFT AFTER THE KOSALAN ARMY CAME AND SLAUGHTERED THE PEOPLE OF KAPILAVASTU.

THEY KILLED THAT MANY PEOPLE? DAMN THOSE KOSALANS!

WHY GET ANGRY? THE ARMY WAS SENT BACK TO KOSALA...

AND YOU'RE COOL WITH THAT?!

165

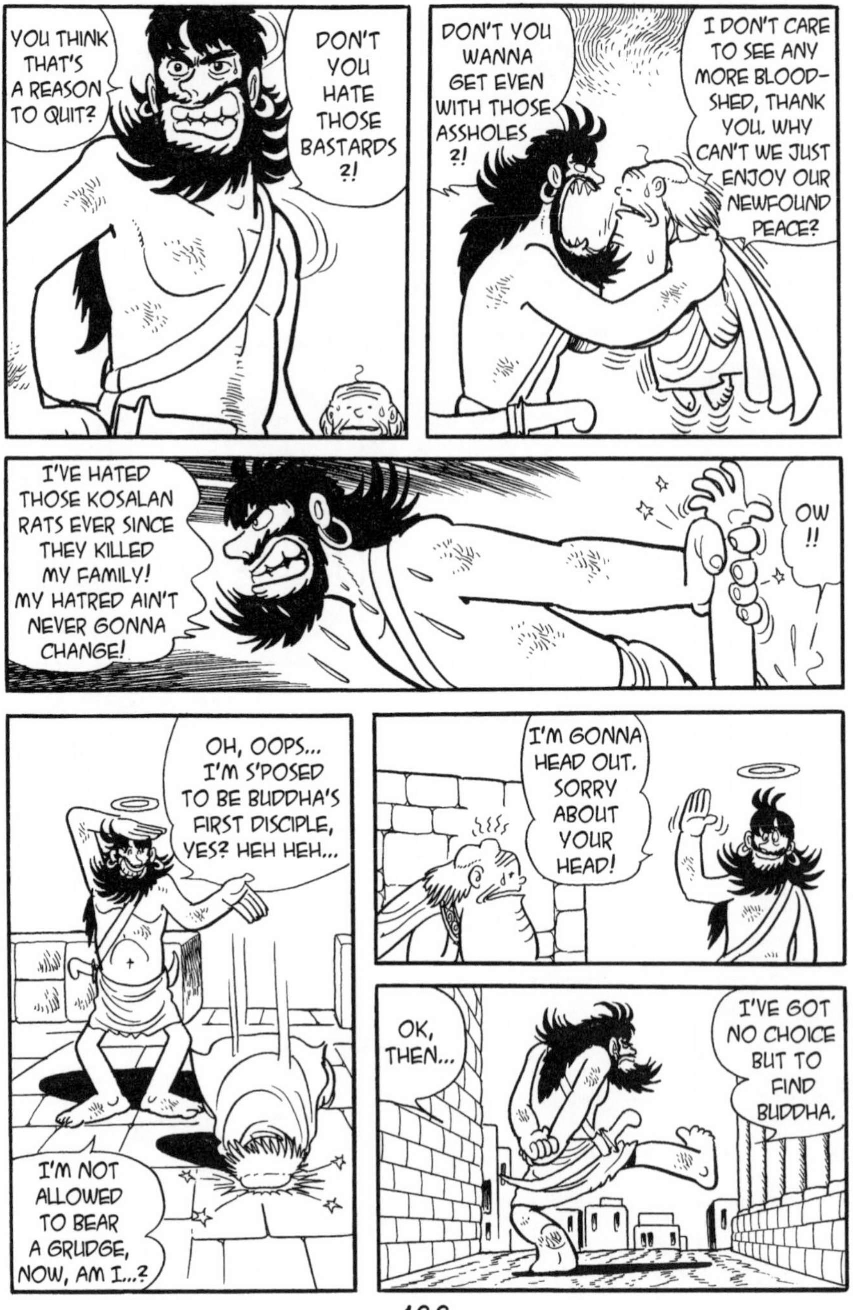
YOU THINK THAT'S A REASON TO QUIT?
DON'T YOU HATE THOSE BASTARDS ?!
DON'T YOU WANNA GET EVEN WITH THOSE ASSHOLES ?!
I DON'T CARE TO SEE ANY MORE BLOODSHED, THANK YOU. WHY CAN'T WE JUST ENJOY OUR NEWFOUND PEACE?
I'VE HATED THOSE KOSALAN RATS EVER SINCE THEY KILLED MY FAMILY! MY HATRED AIN'T NEVER GONNA CHANGE!
OW !!
OH, OOPS... I'M S'POSED TO BE BUDDHA'S FIRST DISCIPLE, YES? HEH HEH...
I'M NOT ALLOWED TO BEAR A GRUDGE, NOW, AM I...?
I'M GONNA HEAD OUT. SORRY ABOUT YOUR HEAD!
OK, THEN...
I'VE GOT NO CHOICE BUT TO FIND BUDDHA.

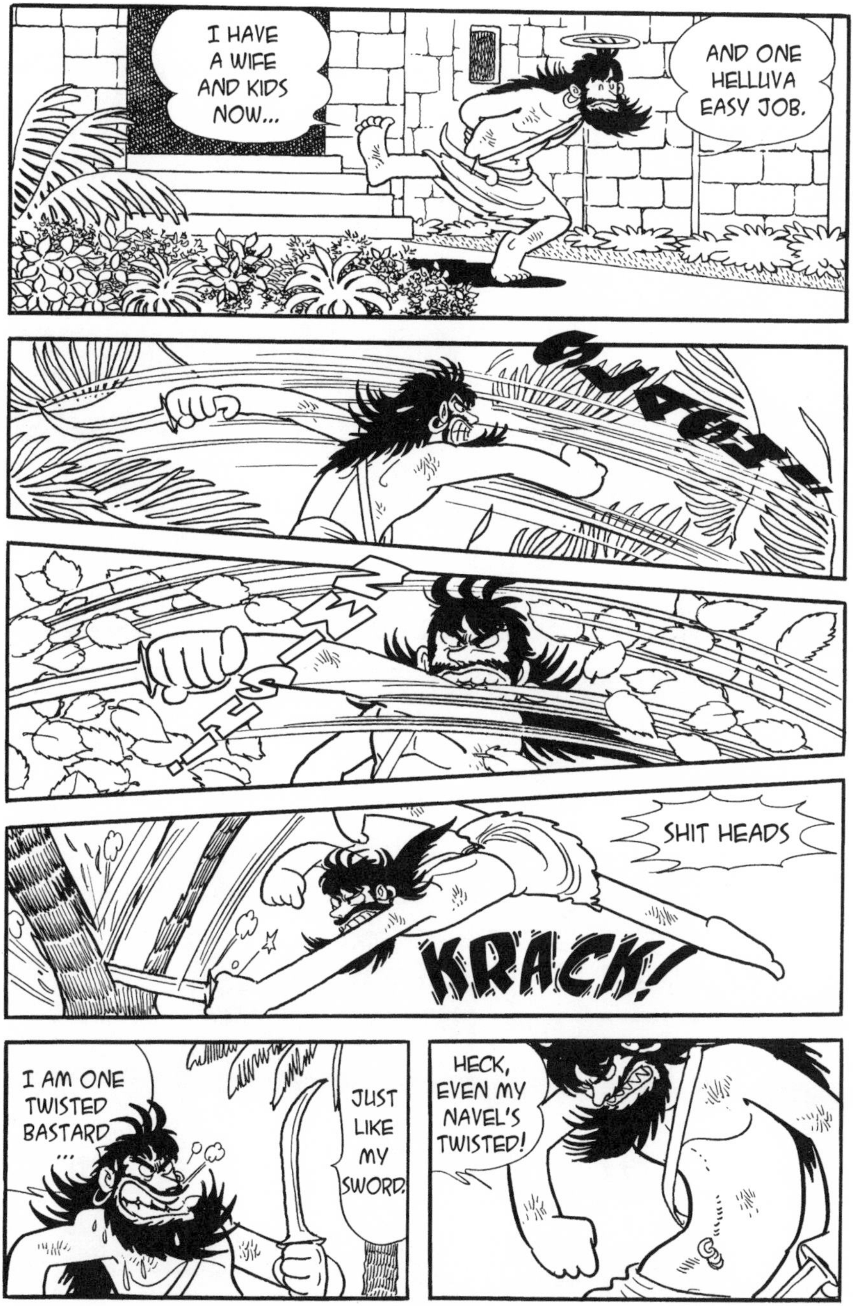
I HAVE A WIFE AND KIDS NOW...
AND ONE HELLUVA EASY JOB.
SLASH!!
SWISH!!
SHIT HEADS
KRACK!
I AM ONE TWISTED BASTARD ...
JUST LIKE MY SWORD.
HECK, EVEN MY NAVEL'S TWISTED!

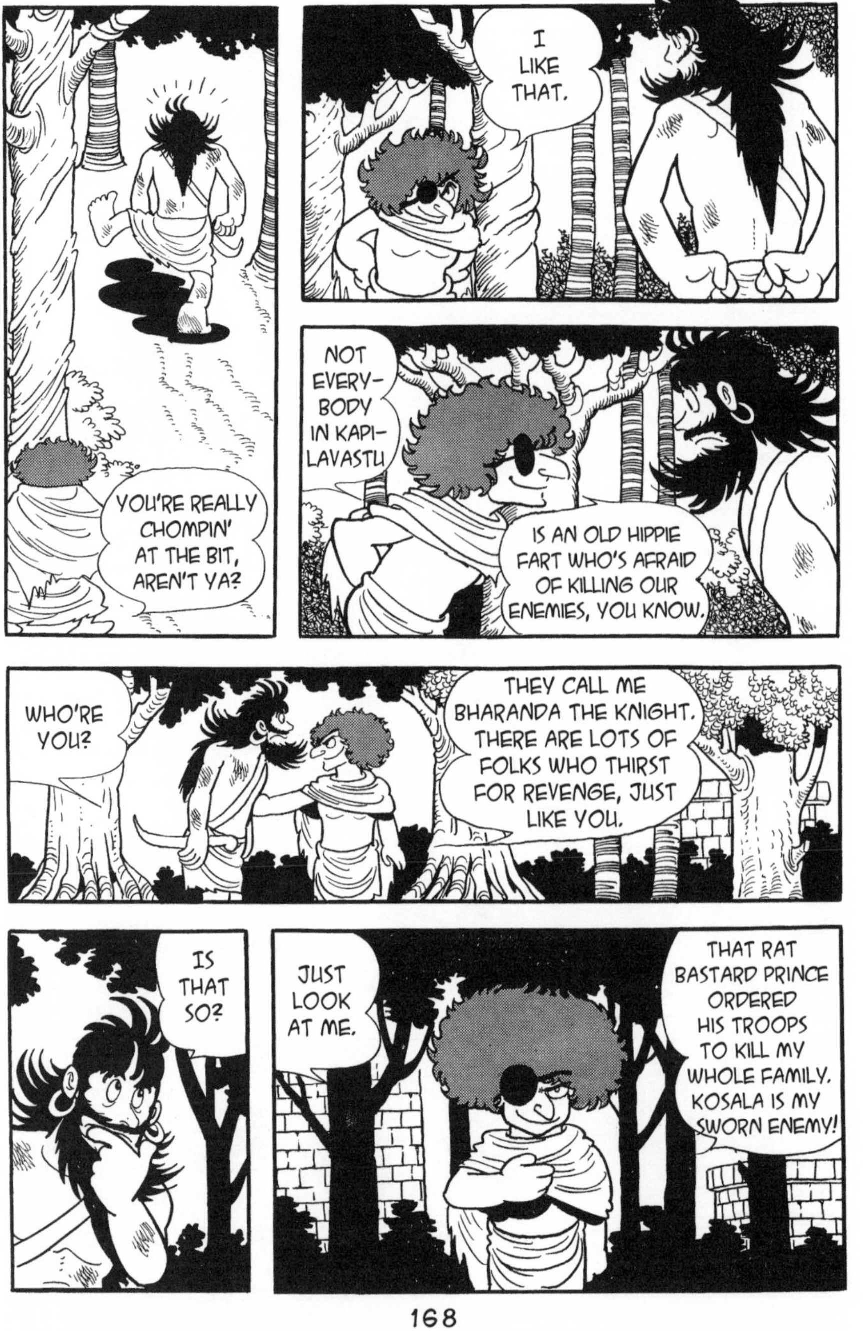
YOU'RE REALLY CHOMPIN' AT THE BIT, AREN'T YA?
I LIKE THAT.
NOT EVERY-BODY IN KAPI-LAVASTU
IS AN OLD HIPPIE FART WHO'S AFRAID OF KILLING OUR ENEMIES, YOU KNOW.
WHO'RE YOU?
THEY CALL ME BHARANDA THE KNIGHT. THERE ARE LOTS OF FOLKS WHO THIRST FOR REVENGE, JUST LIKE YOU.
IS THAT SO?
JUST LOOK AT ME.
THAT RAT BASTARD PRINCE ORDERED HIS TROOPS TO KILL MY WHOLE FAMILY. KOSALA IS MY SWORN ENEMY!

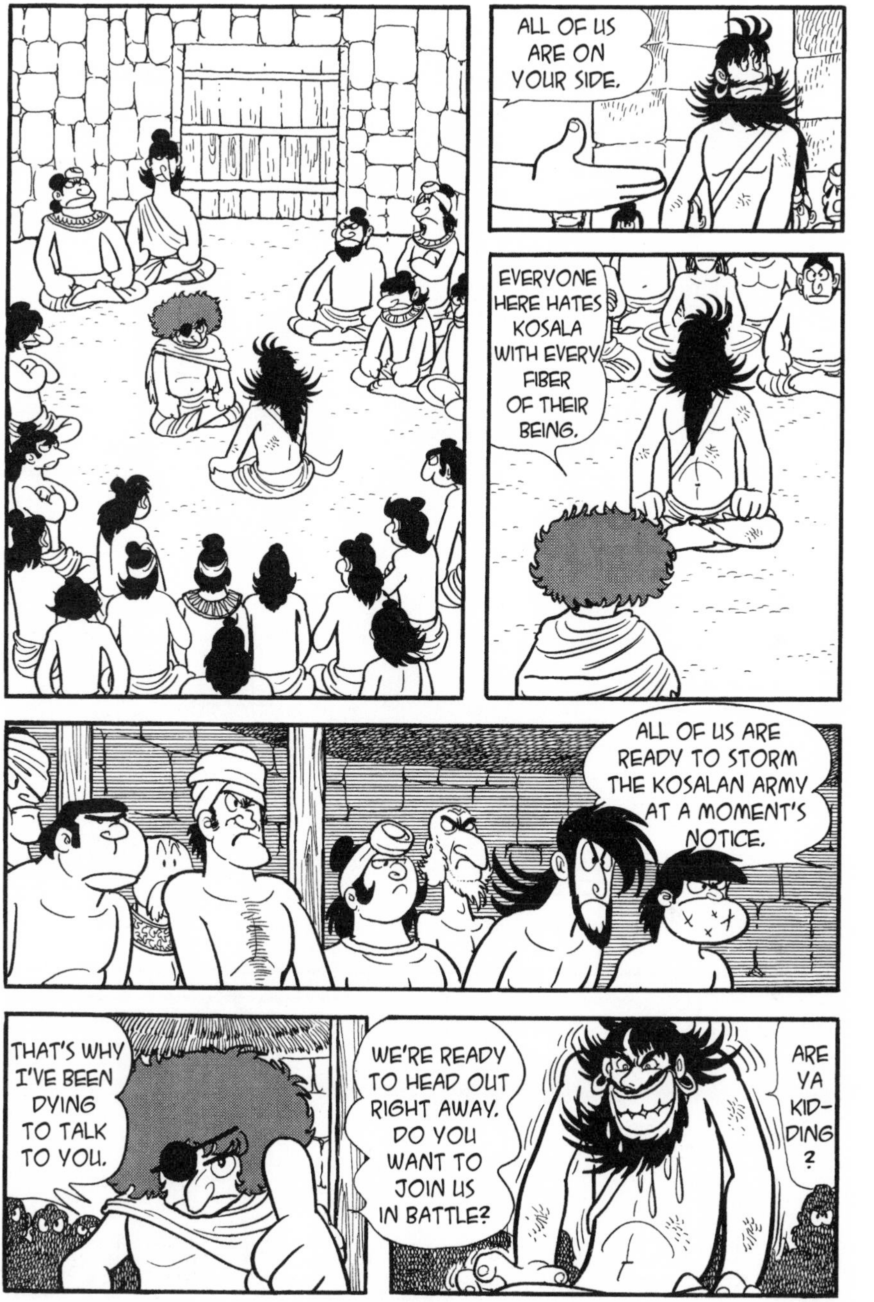
ALL OF US ARE ON YOUR SIDE.
EVERYONE HERE HATES KOSALA WITH EVERY FIBER OF THEIR BEING.
ALL OF US ARE READY TO STORM THE KOSALAN ARMY AT A MOMENT'S NOTICE.
THAT'S WHY I'VE BEEN DYING TO TALK TO YOU.
WE'RE READY TO HEAD OUT RIGHT AWAY. DO YOU WANT TO JOIN US IN BATTLE?
ARE YA KID-DING?

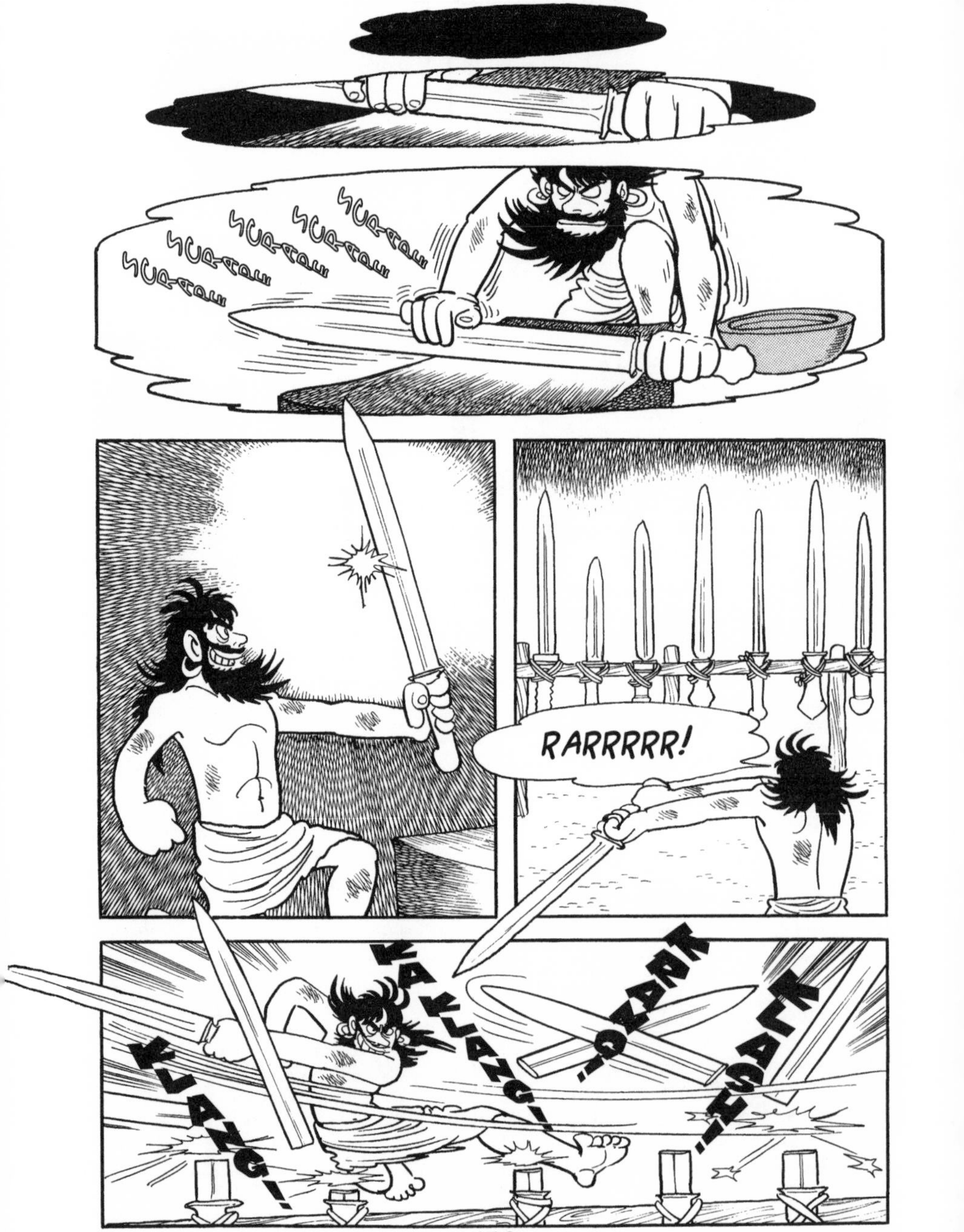
SCR-APE!!
SCR-APE!!
SCR-APE!!
SCR-APE!!
RARRRRR!
KLANG!!
KAKLANG!!

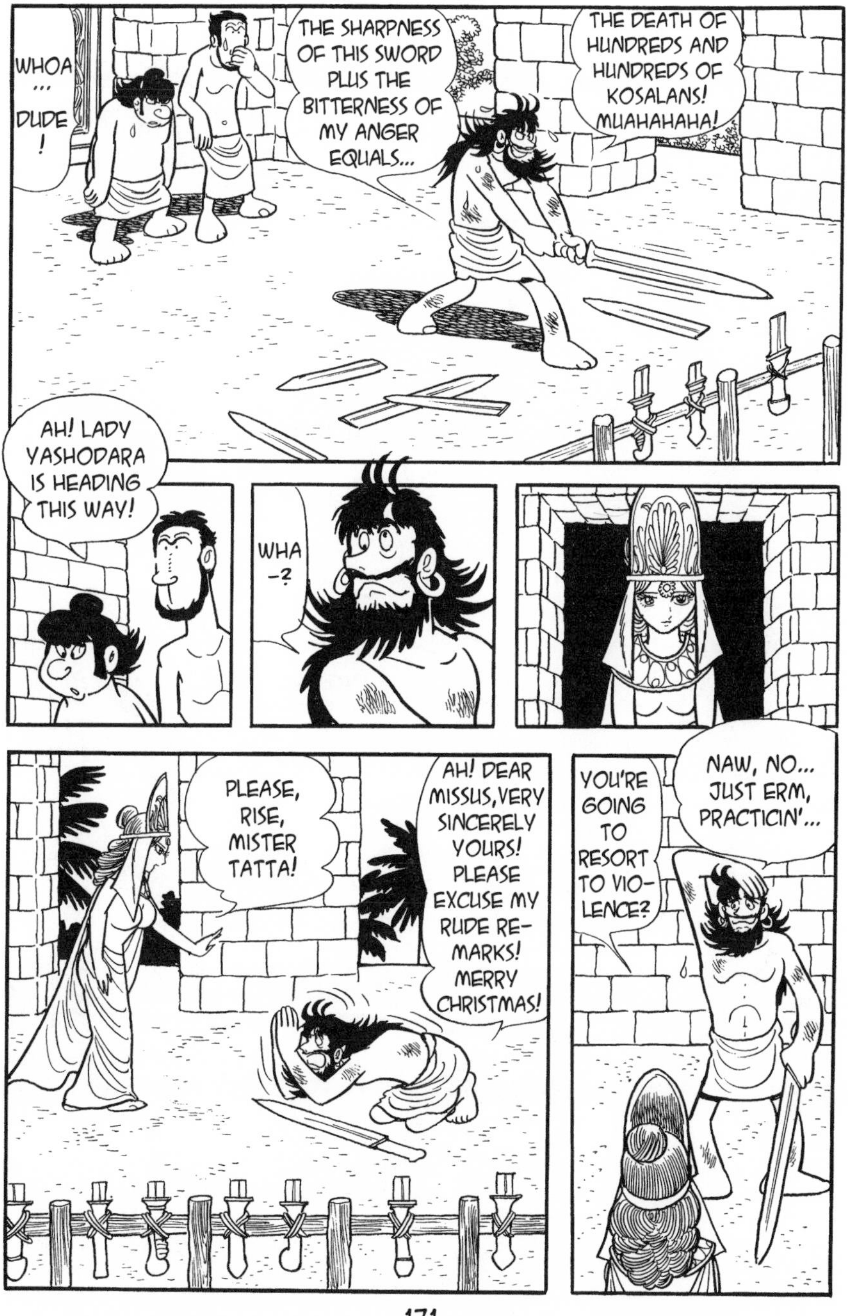
WHOA ... DUDE!
THE SHARPNESS OF THIS SWORD PLUS THE BITTERNESS OF MY ANGER EQUALS...
THE DEATH OF HUNDREDS AND HUNDREDS OF KOSALANS! MUAHAHAHA!
AH! LADY YASHODARA IS HEADING THIS WAY!
WHA-?
PLEASE, RISE, MISTER TATTA!
AH! DEAR MISSUS, VERY SINCERELY YOURS! PLEASE EXCUSE MY RUDE RE-MARKS! MERRY CHRISTMAS!
YOU'RE GOING TO RESORT TO VIO-LENCE?
NAW, NO... JUST ERM, PRACTICIN'...

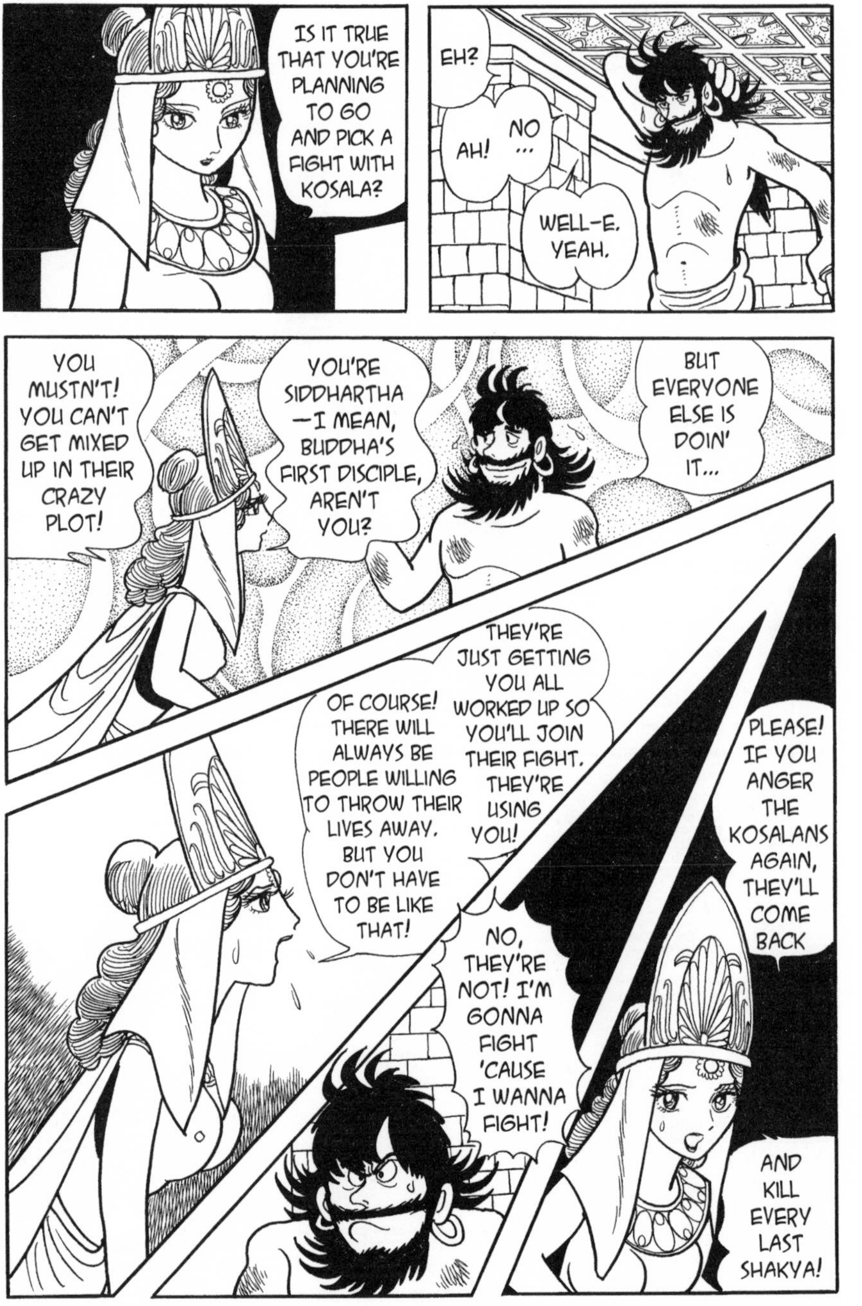

IS IT TRUE THAT YOU'RE PLANNING TO GO AND PICK A FIGHT WITH KOSALA?
EH?
AH!
NO ...
WELL—E. YEAH.
YOU MUSTN'T! YOU CAN'T GET MIXED UP IN THEIR CRAZY PLOT!
YOU'RE SIDDHARTHA—I MEAN, BUDDHA'S FIRST DISCIPLE, AREN'T YOU?
BUT EVERYONE ELSE IS DOIN' IT...
OF COURSE! THERE WILL ALWAYS BE PEOPLE WILLING TO THROW THEIR LIVES AWAY. BUT YOU DON'T HAVE TO BE LIKE THAT!
THEY'RE JUST GETTING YOU ALL WORKED UP SO YOU'LL JOIN THEIR FIGHT. THEY'RE USING YOU!
NO, THEY'RE NOT! I'M GONNA FIGHT 'CAUSE I WANNA FIGHT!
PLEASE! IF YOU ANGER THE KOSALANS AGAIN, THEY'LL COME BACK
AND KILL EVERY LAST SHAKYA!

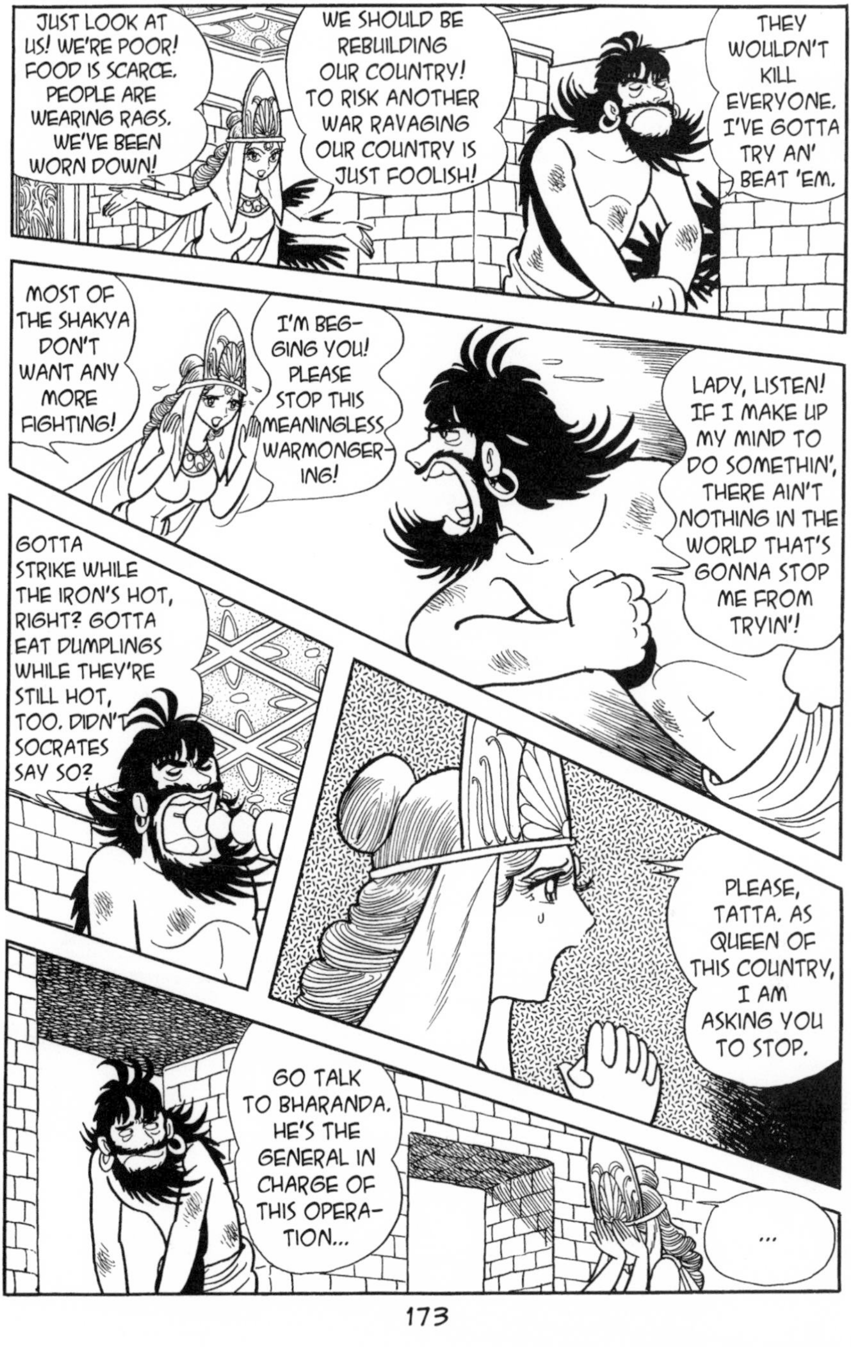
JUST LOOK AT US! WE'RE POOR! FOOD IS SCARCE. PEOPLE ARE WEARING RAGS. WE'VE BEEN WORN DOWN!
WE SHOULD BE REBUILDING OUR COUNTRY! TO RISK ANOTHER WAR RAVAGING OUR COUNTRY IS JUST FOOLISH!
THEY WOULDN'T KILL EVERYONE. I'VE GOTTA TRY AN' BEAT 'EM.
MOST OF THE SHAKYA DON'T WANT ANY MORE FIGHTING!
I'M BEG-GING YOU! PLEASE STOP THIS MEANINGLESS WARMONGER-ING!
LADY, LISTEN! IF I MAKE UP MY MIND TO DO SOMETHIN', THERE AIN'T NOTHING IN THE WORLD THAT'S GONNA STOP ME FROM TRYIN'!
GOTTA STRIKE WHILE THE IRON'S HOT, RIGHT? GOTTA EAT DUMPLINGS WHILE THEY'RE STILL HOT, TOO. DIDN'T SOCRATES SAY SO?
PLEASE, TATTA. AS QUEEN OF THIS COUNTRY, I AM ASKING YOU TO STOP.
GO TALK TO BHARANDA. HE'S THE GENERAL IN CHARGE OF THIS OPERA-TION...
...

CHAPTER TWELVE

DESTRUCTION OF THE SHAKYA

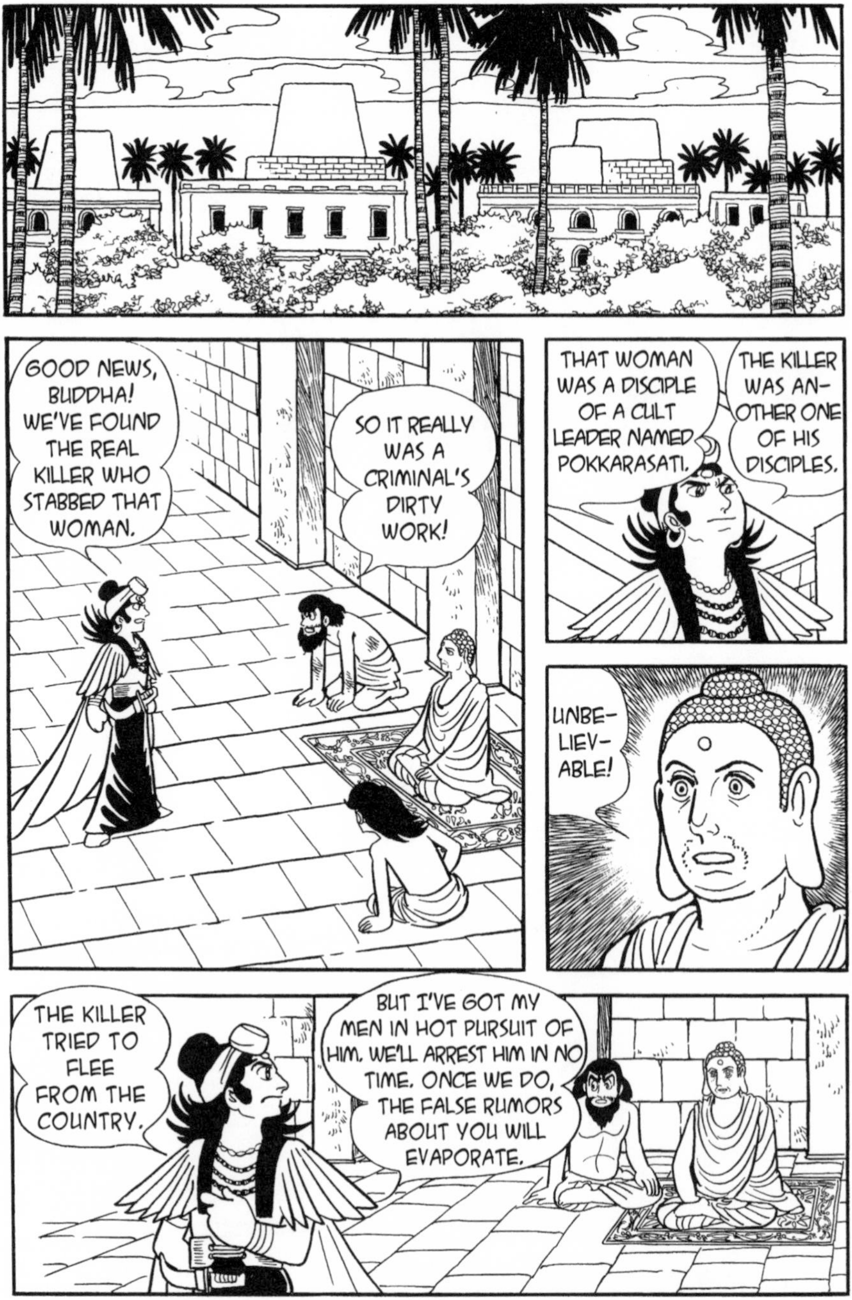
GOOD NEWS, BUDDHA! WE'VE FOUND THE REAL KILLER WHO STABBED THAT WOMAN.
SO IT REALLY WAS A CRIMINAL'S DIRTY WORK!
THAT WOMAN WAS A DISCIPLE OF A CULT LEADER NAMED POKKARASATI.
THE KILLER WAS AN-OTHER ONE OF HIS DISCIPLES.
UNBE-LIEV-ABLE!
THE KILLER TRIED TO FLEE FROM THE COUNTRY.
BUT I'VE GOT MY MEN IN HOT PURSUIT OF HIM. WE'LL ARREST HIM IN NO TIME. ONCE WE DO, THE FALSE RUMORS ABOUT YOU WILL EVAPORATE.

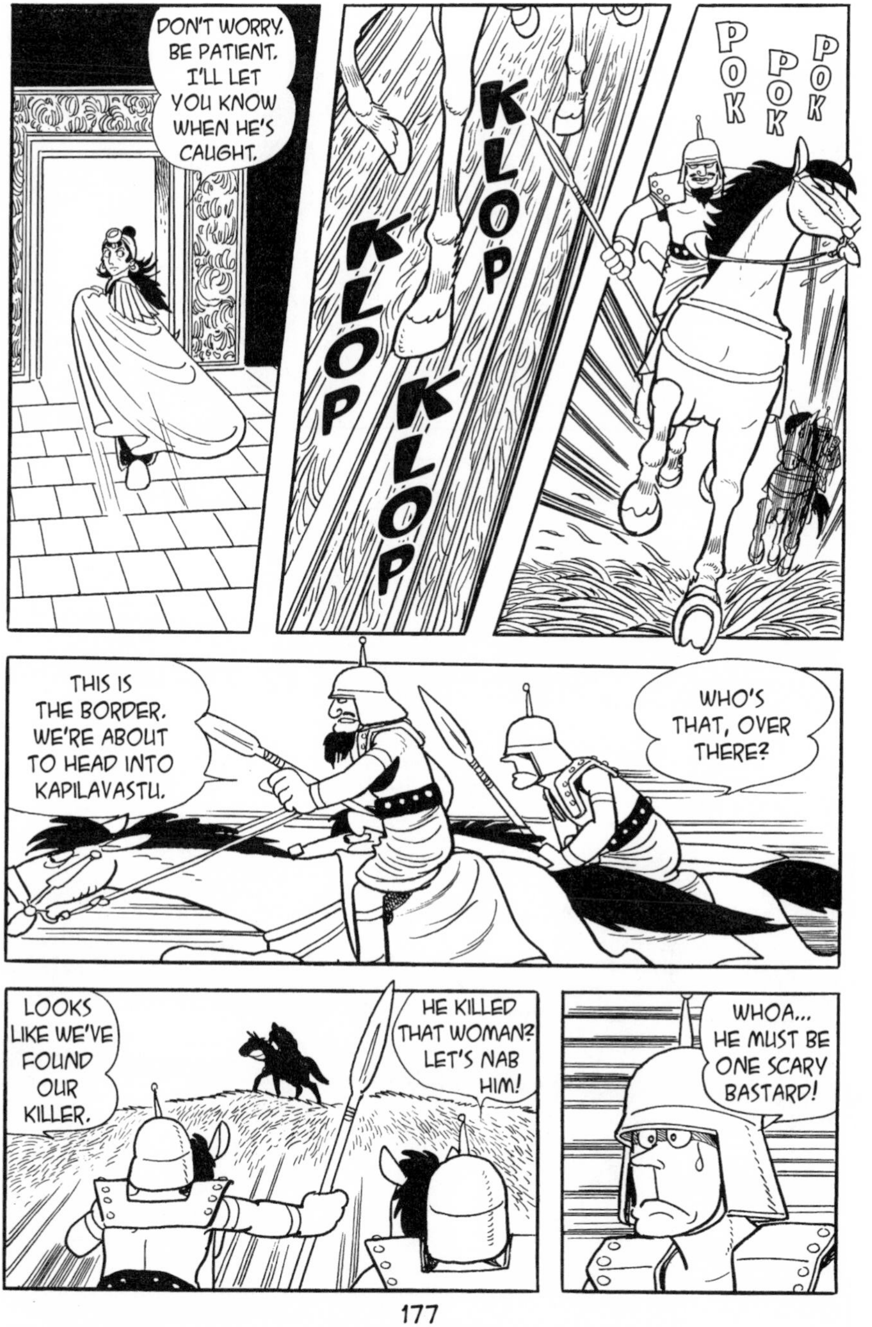
DON'T WORRY. BE PATIENT. I'LL LET YOU KNOW WHEN HE'S CAUGHT.
KLOP KLOP
KLOP KLOP
POK POK POK
THIS IS THE BORDER. WE'RE ABOUT TO HEAD INTO KAPILAVASTU.
WHO'S THAT, OVER THERE?
LOOKS LIKE WE'VE FOUND OUR KILLER.
HE KILLED THAT WOMAN? LET'S NAB HIM!
WHOA... HE MUST BE ONE SCARY BASTARD!

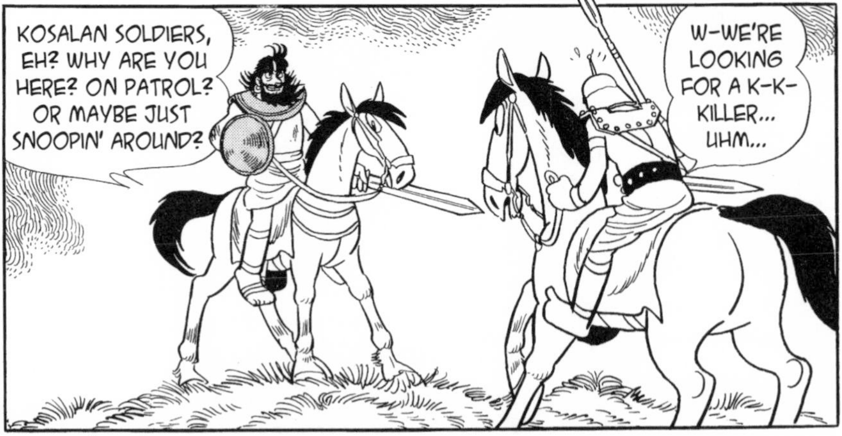
KOSALAN SOLDIERS, EH? WHY ARE YOU HERE? ON PATROL? OR MAYBE JUST SNOOPIN' AROUND?
W-WE'RE LOOKING FOR A K-K-KILLER... UHM...

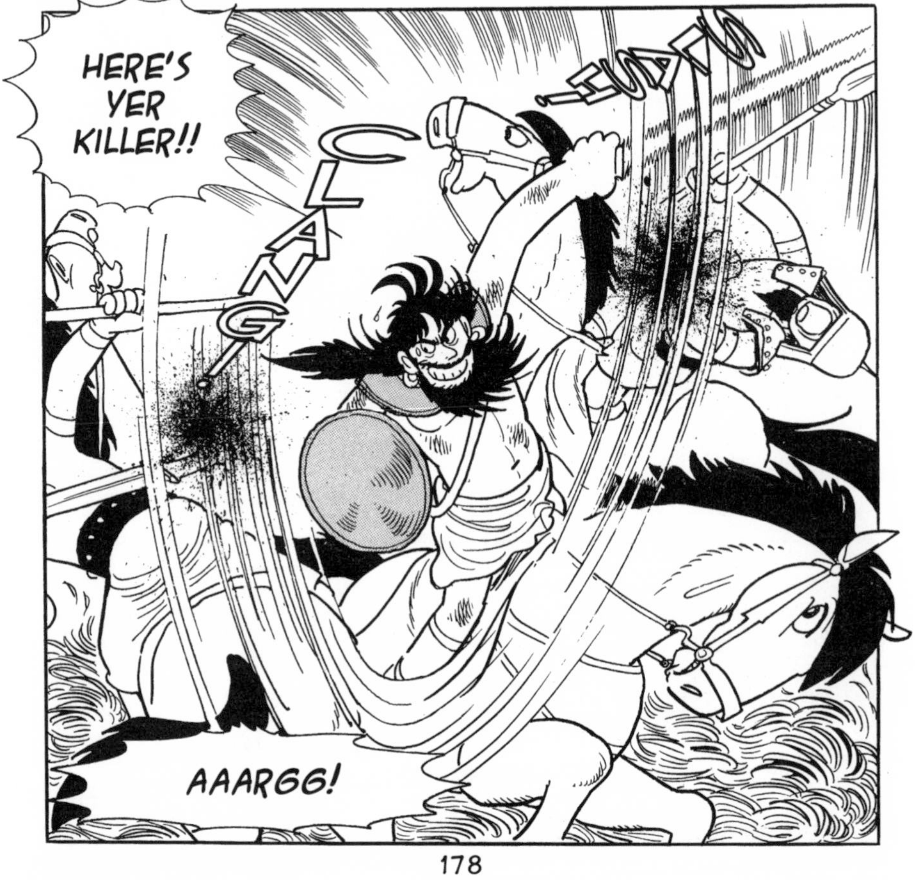
HERE'S YER KILLER!!
CLANG
SMASH!
AAARGG!

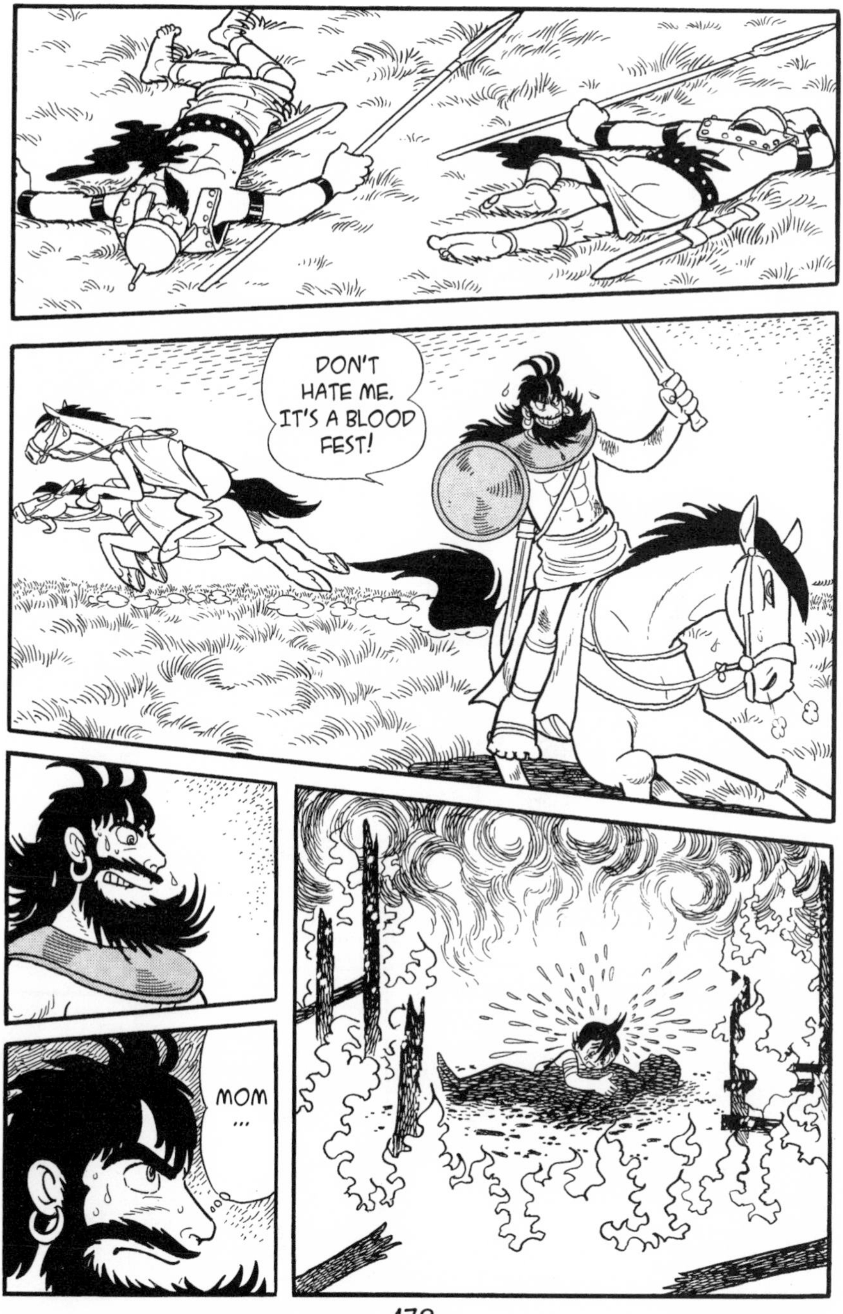

DON'T HATE ME. IT'S A BLOOD FEST!
MOM ...

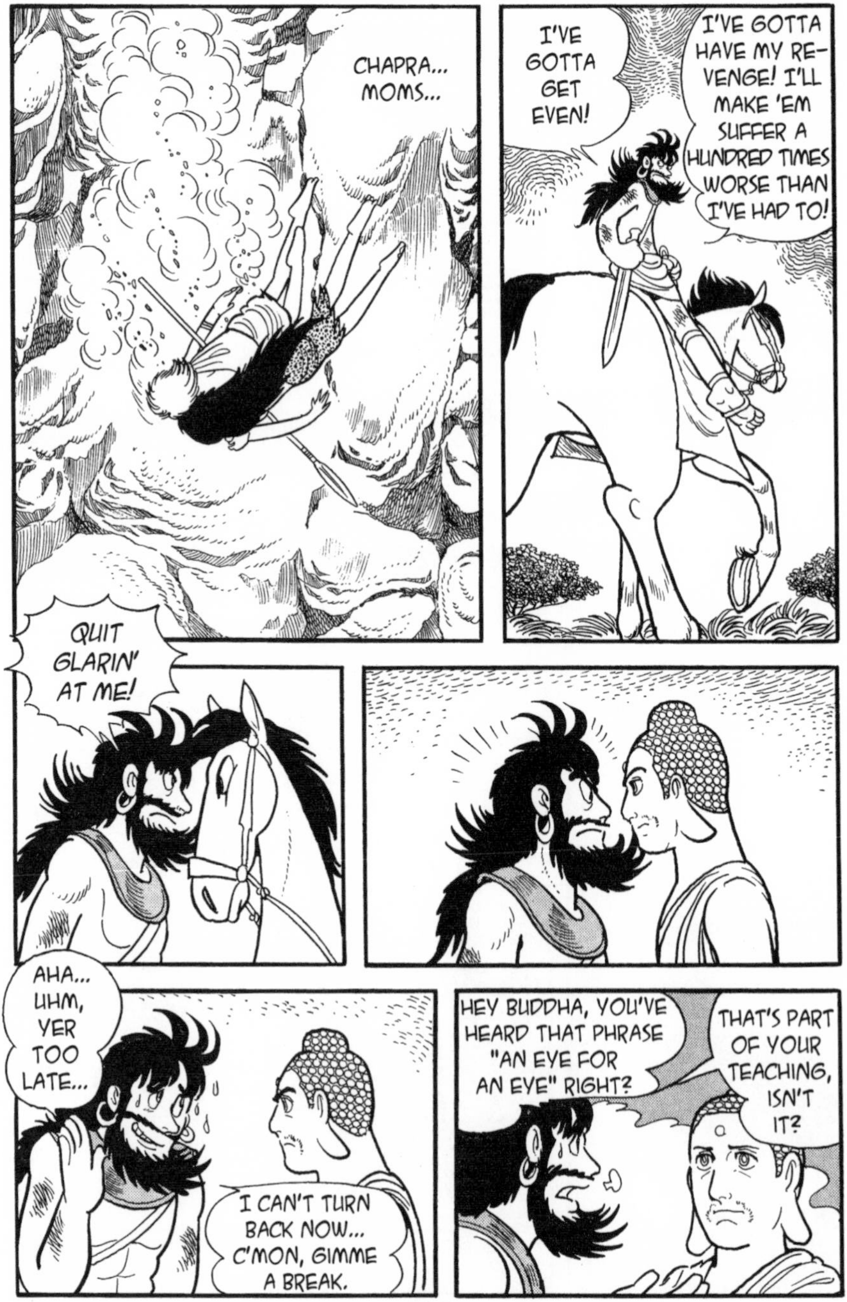
CHAPRA... MOMS...
I'VE GOTTA GET EVEN!
I'VE GOTTA HAVE MY RE-VENGE! I'LL MAKE 'EM SUFFER A HUNDRED TIMES WORSE THAN I'VE HAD TO!
QUIT GLARIN' AT ME!
AHA... UHM, YER TOO LATE...
I CAN'T TURN BACK NOW... C'MON, GIMME A BREAK.
HEY BUDDHA, YOU'VE HEARD THAT PHRASE "AN EYE FOR AN EYE" RIGHT?
THAT'S PART OF YOUR TEACHING, ISN'T IT?

NO, WAIT, THAT'S FROM THE BIBLE? WAS IT? WRONG RELIGION?

AW, COME ON, STOP POUTIN' ALREADY.

I'VE ALREADY KILLED **2** KOSALAN RATS. WHAT DIFFERENCE DOES IT MAKE IF I KILL HUNDREDS MORE?

AAARG! DON'T BITE ME!

DAMMIT! DUMB HORSE...

I THOUGHT YOU WERE BUDDHA...

WHY DID I THINK MY HORSE WAS BUDDHA?

HERE THEY COME, DAMN KOSALANS!

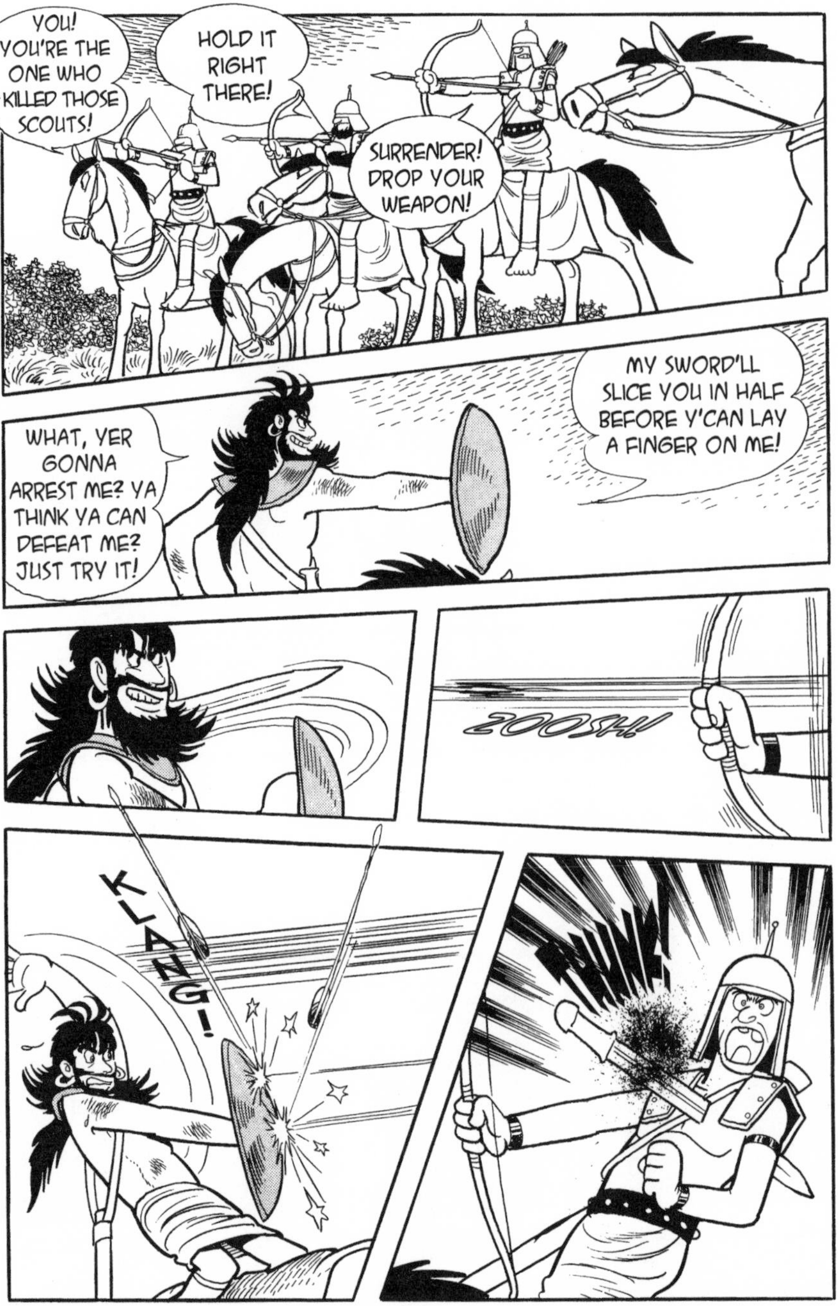
YOU! YOU'RE THE ONE WHO KILLED THOSE SCOUTS!
HOLD IT RIGHT THERE!
SURRENDER! DROP YOUR WEAPON!
WHAT, YER GONNA ARREST ME? YA THINK YA CAN DEFEAT ME? JUST TRY IT!
MY SWORD'LL SLICE YOU IN HALF BEFORE Y'CAN LAY A FINGER ON ME!
ZOOSH!
KLANG!

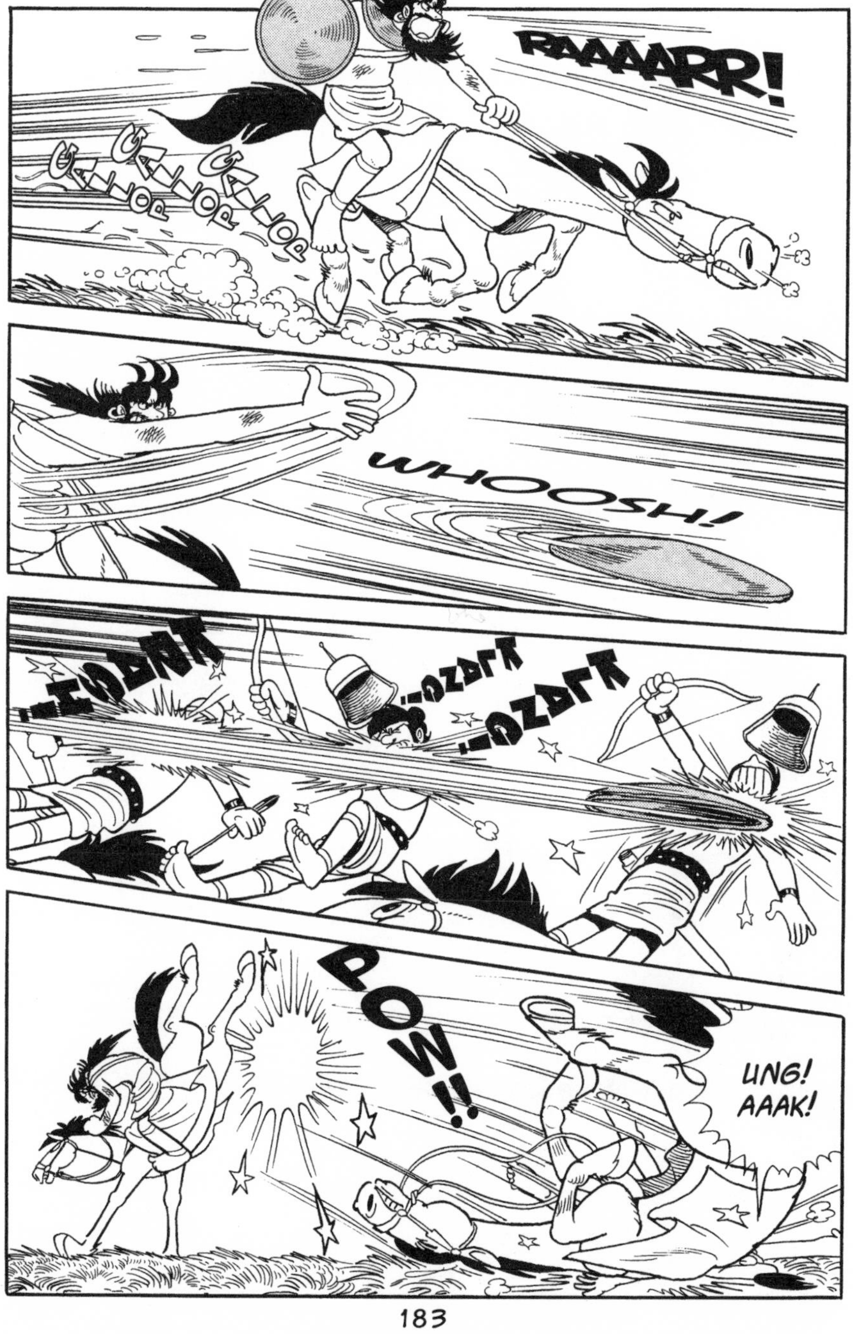
RAAAARR!
GALLOP GALLOP
WHOOSH!
KRASH!!
KLANG!!
KLANG!!
POW!!
UNG!
AAAK!

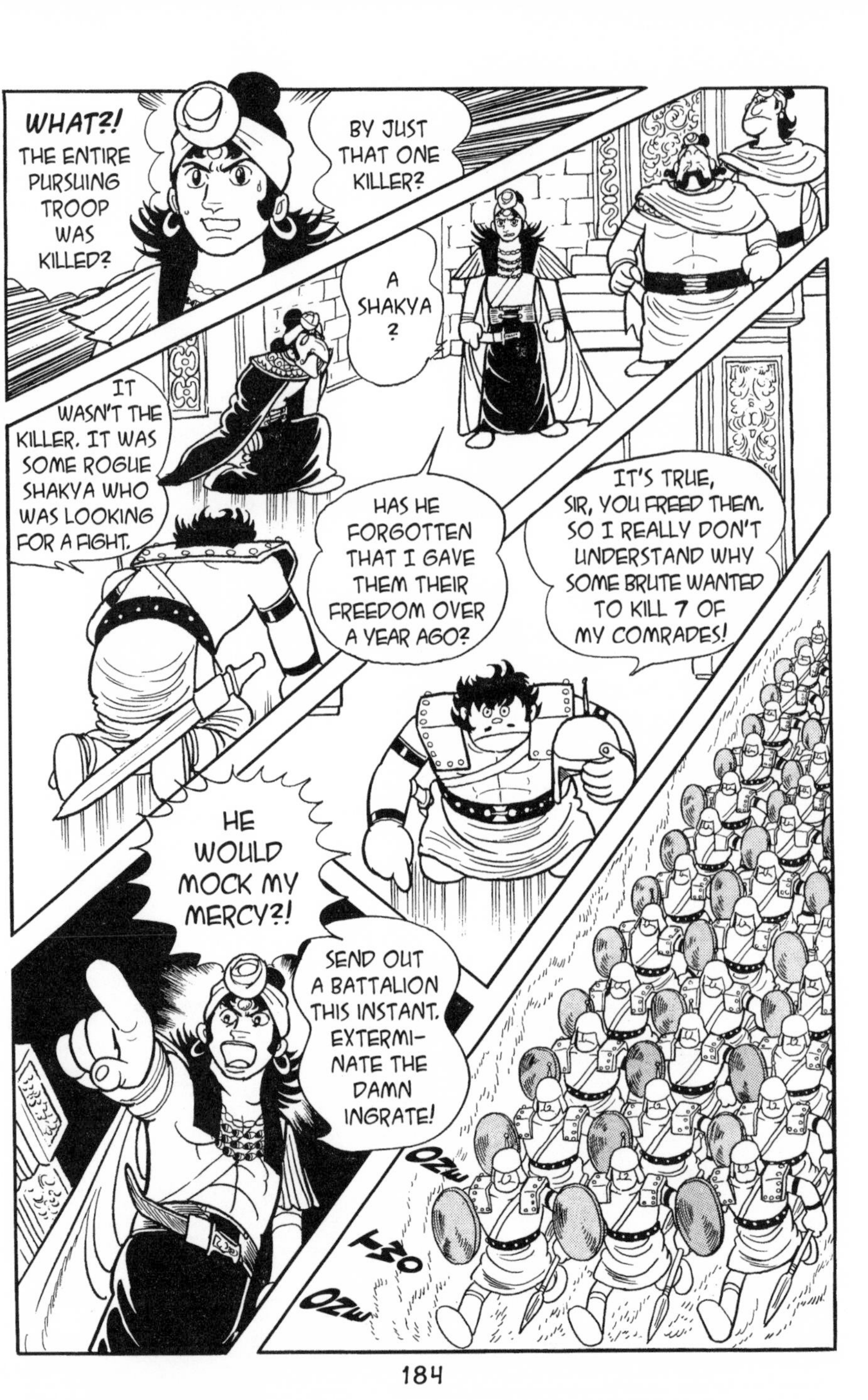
WHAT?! THE ENTIRE PURSUING TROOP WAS KILLED?
BY JUST THAT ONE KILLER?
A SHAKYA?
IT WASN'T THE KILLER. IT WAS SOME ROGUE SHAKYA WHO WAS LOOKING FOR A FIGHT.
HAS HE FORGOTTEN THAT I GAVE THEM THEIR FREEDOM OVER A YEAR AGO?
IT'S TRUE, SIR, YOU FREED THEM. SO I REALLY DON'T UNDERSTAND WHY SOME BRUTE WANTED TO KILL 7 OF MY COMRADES!
HE WOULD MOCK MY MERCY?!
SEND OUT A BATTALION THIS INSTANT. EXTERMI-NATE THE DAMN INGRATE!

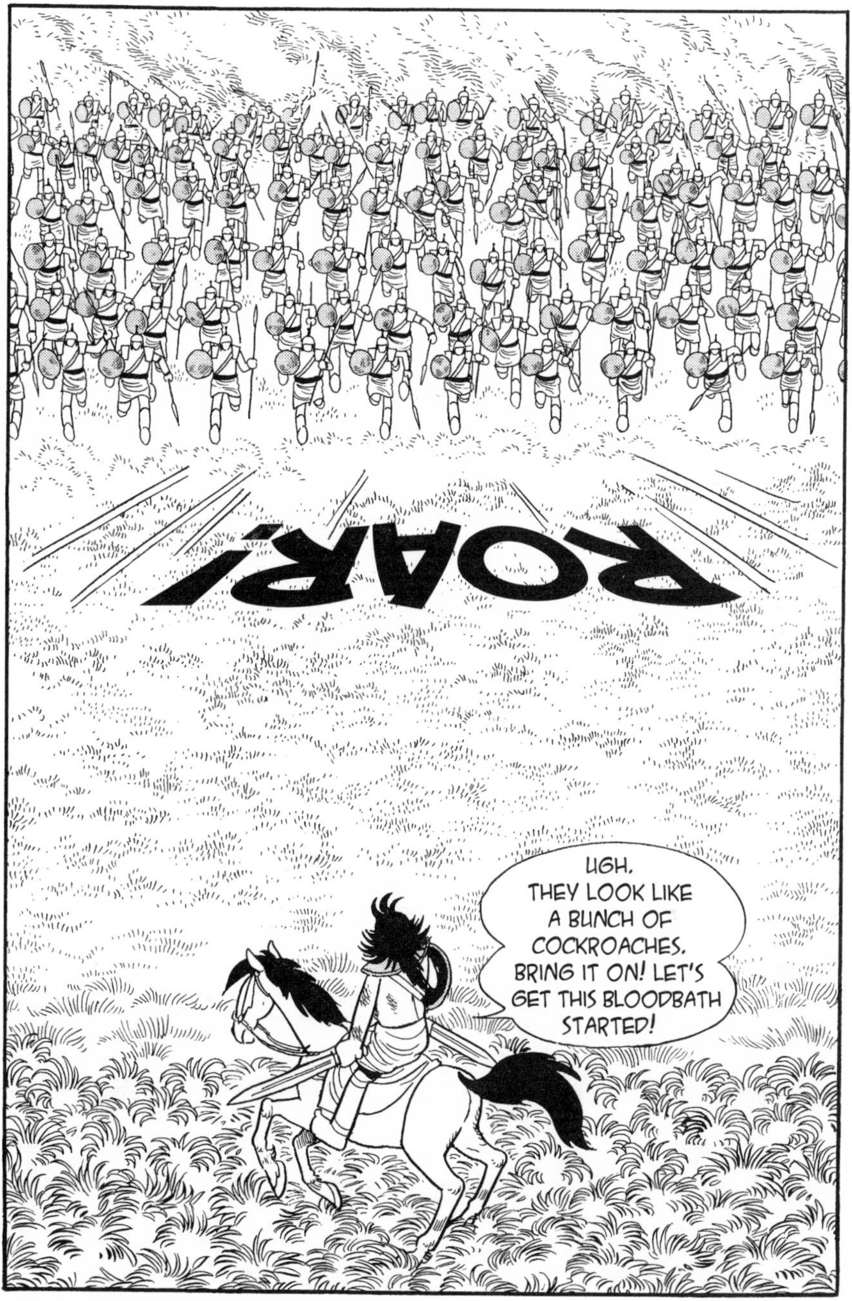
ROAR!
UGH. THEY LOOK LIKE A BUNCH OF COCKROACHES. BRING IT ON! LET'S GET THIS BLOODBATH STARTED!

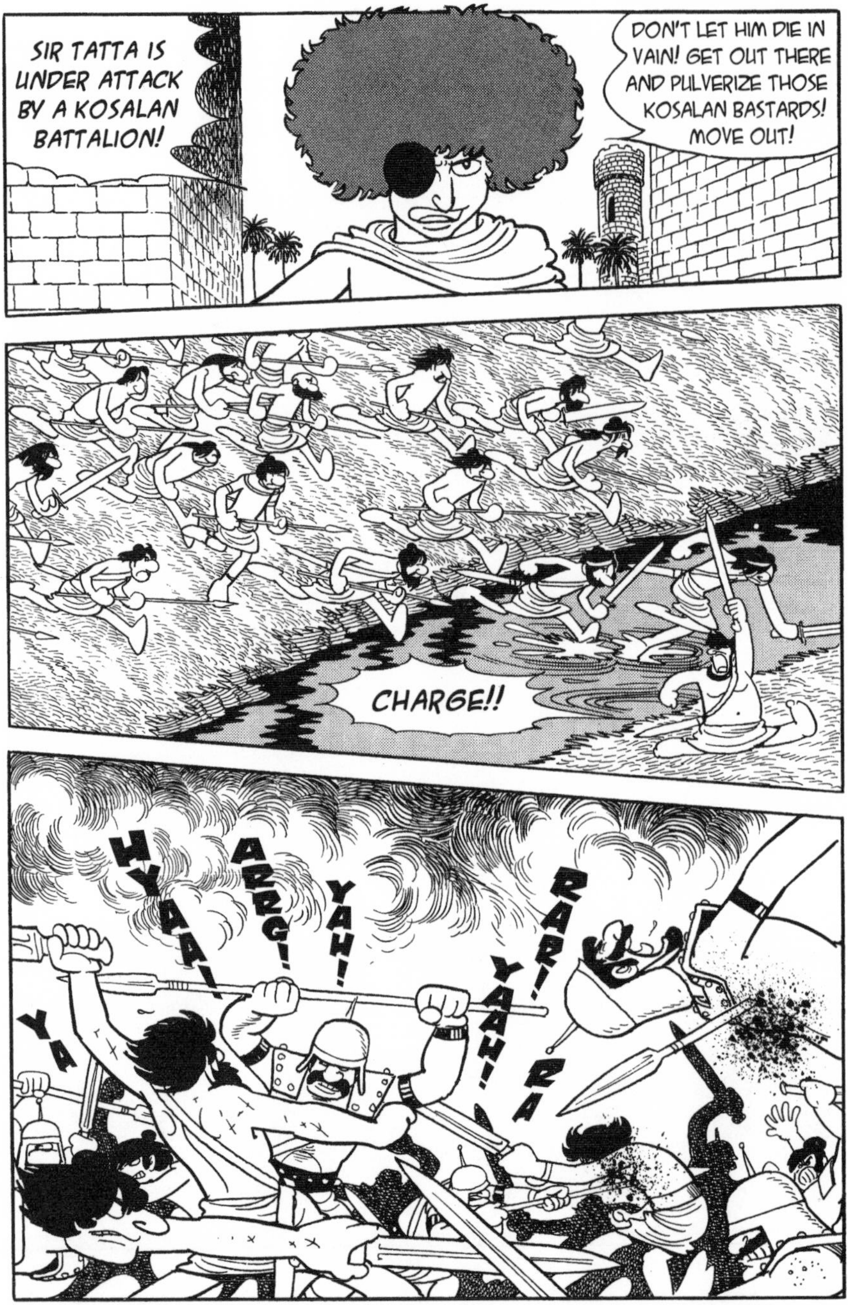
SIR TATTA IS UNDER ATTACK BY A KOSALAN BATTALION!
DON'T LET HIM DIE IN VAIN! GET OUT THERE AND PULVERIZE THOSE KOSALAN BASTARDS! MOVE OUT!
CHARGE!!
YA
HYAAA!
ARRG!
YAH!
YAAAH!
RARI!
RA

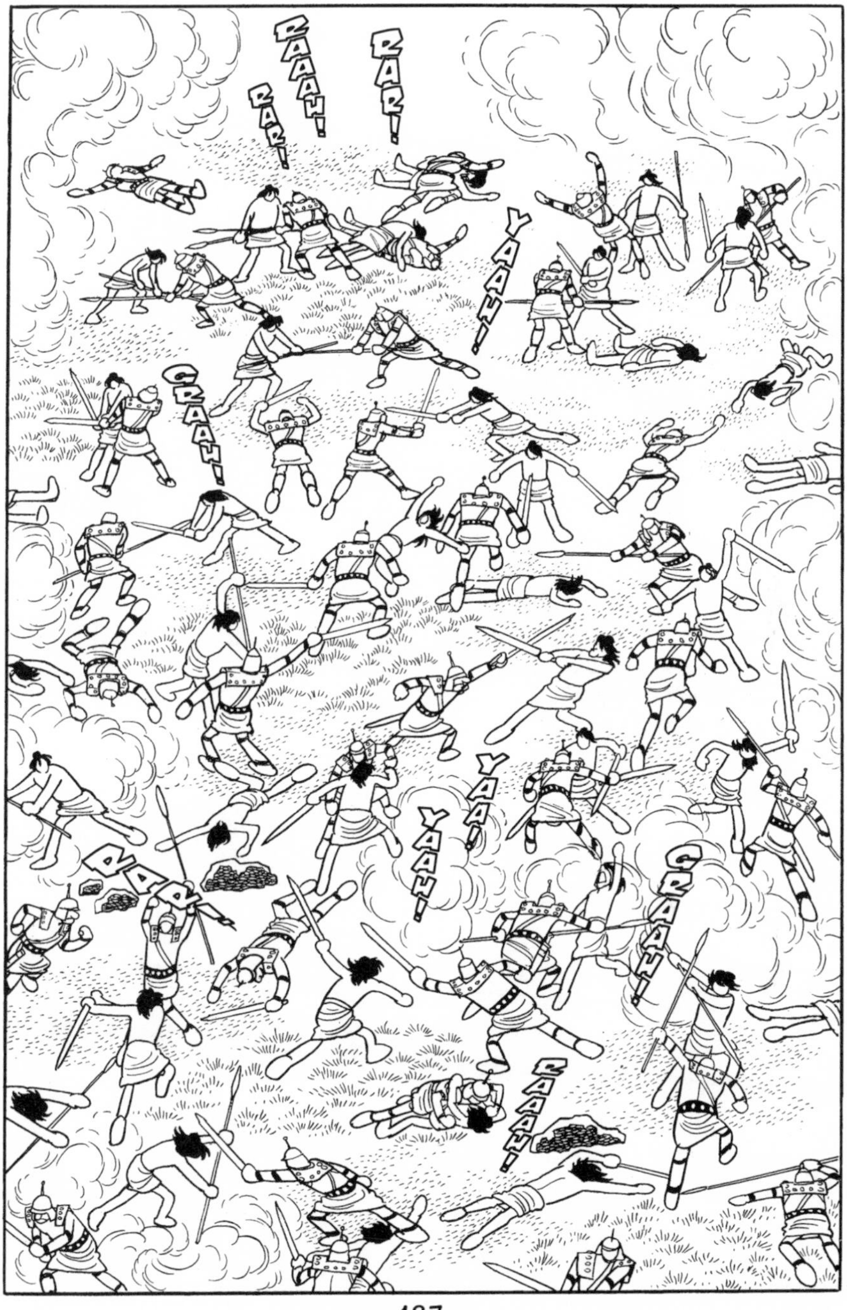
RAR!
RAAAH!
RAR!
YAAAH!
GRAAAH!
YAAA!
YAAAH!
RAR
GRAAAH!
RAAAAH!

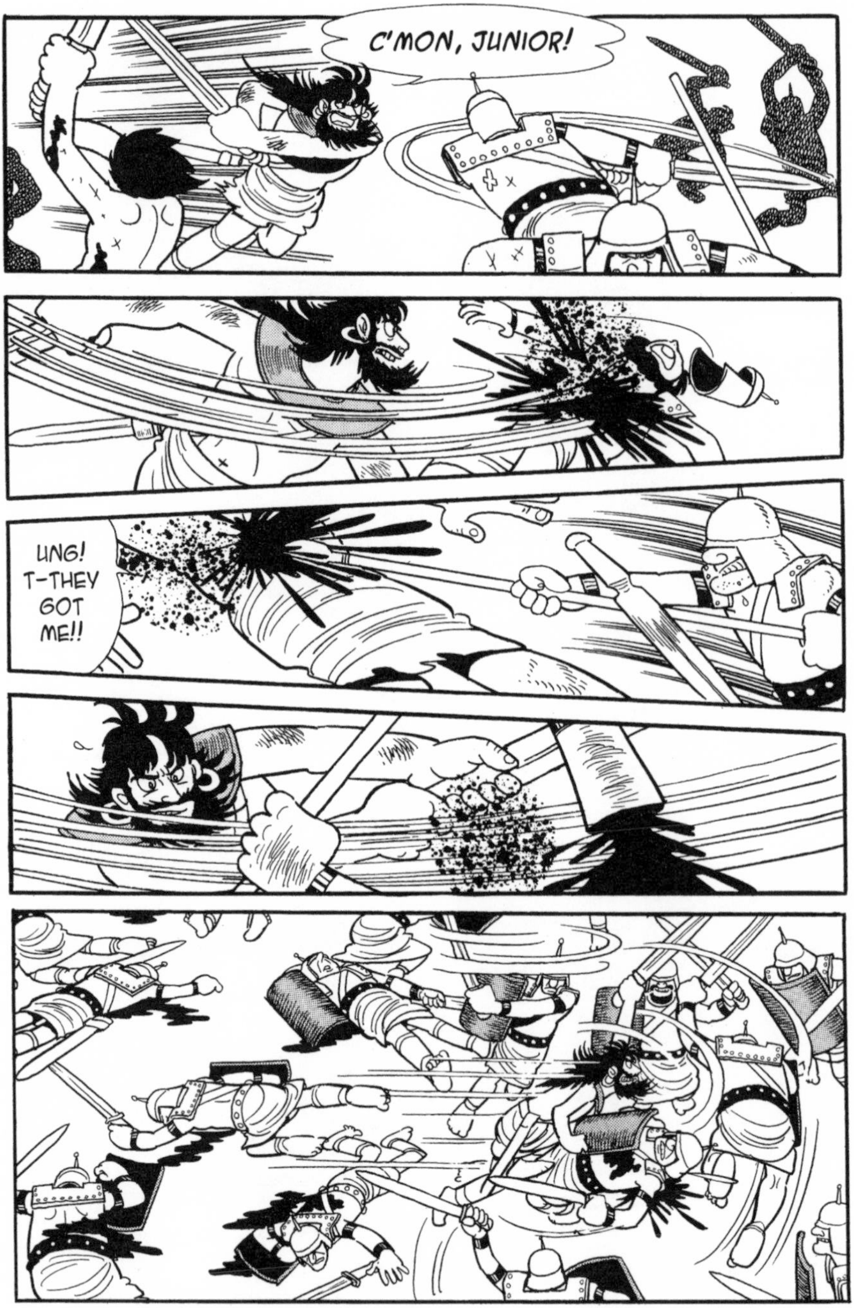
C'MON, JUNIOR!
UNG! T-THEY GOT ME!!

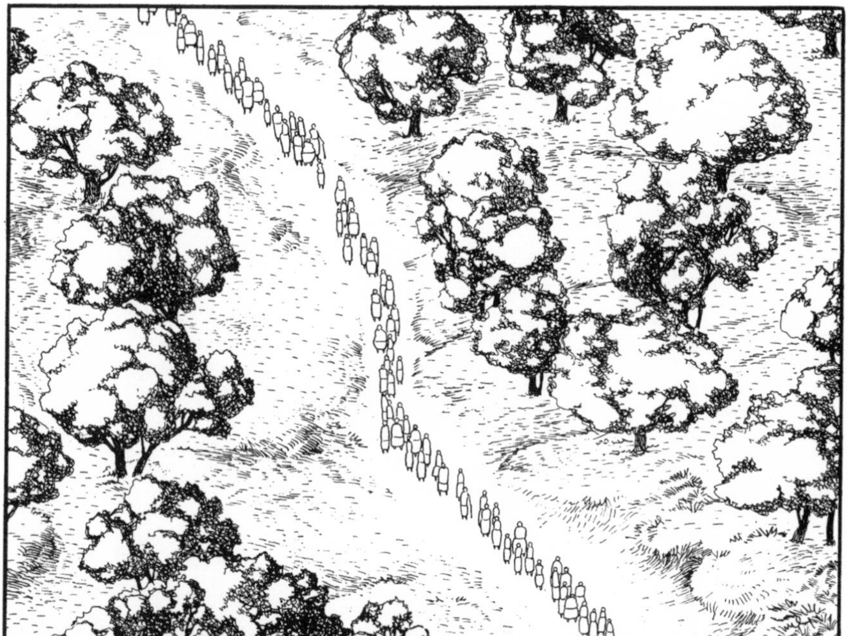
AS THE BATTLE BETWEEN THE KOSALAN TROOPS AND THE REBELLIOUS SHAKYA RAGED ON, THOSE WHO WERE FED UP WITH FIGHTING FLED THE COUNTRY AND HEADED TO KOSALA.

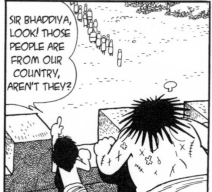

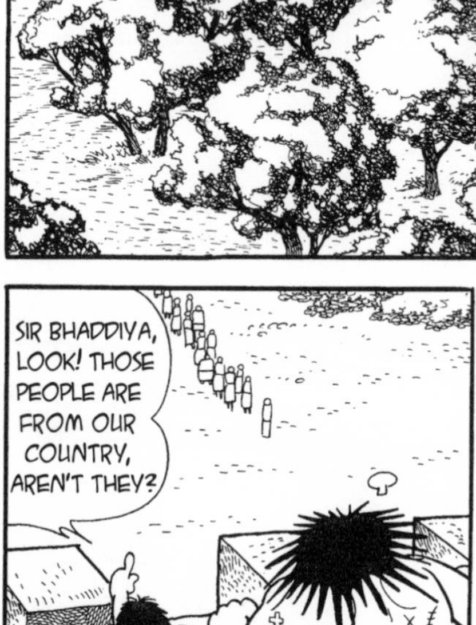
SIR BHADDIYA, LOOK! THOSE PEOPLE ARE FROM OUR COUNTRY, AREN'T THEY?

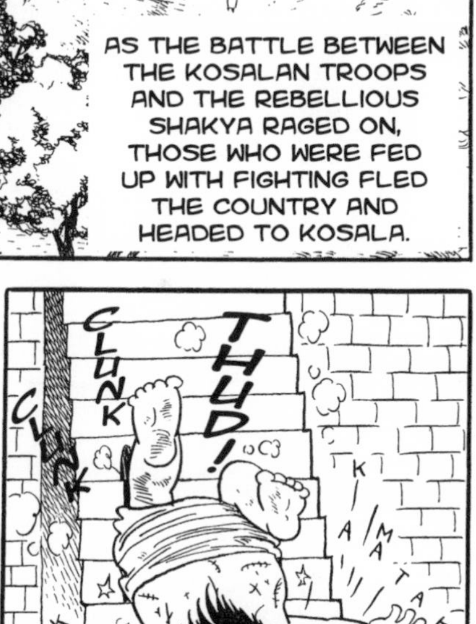
CLUNK
THUD!
CLUNK

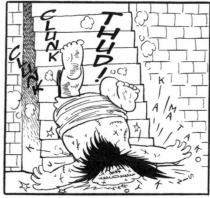

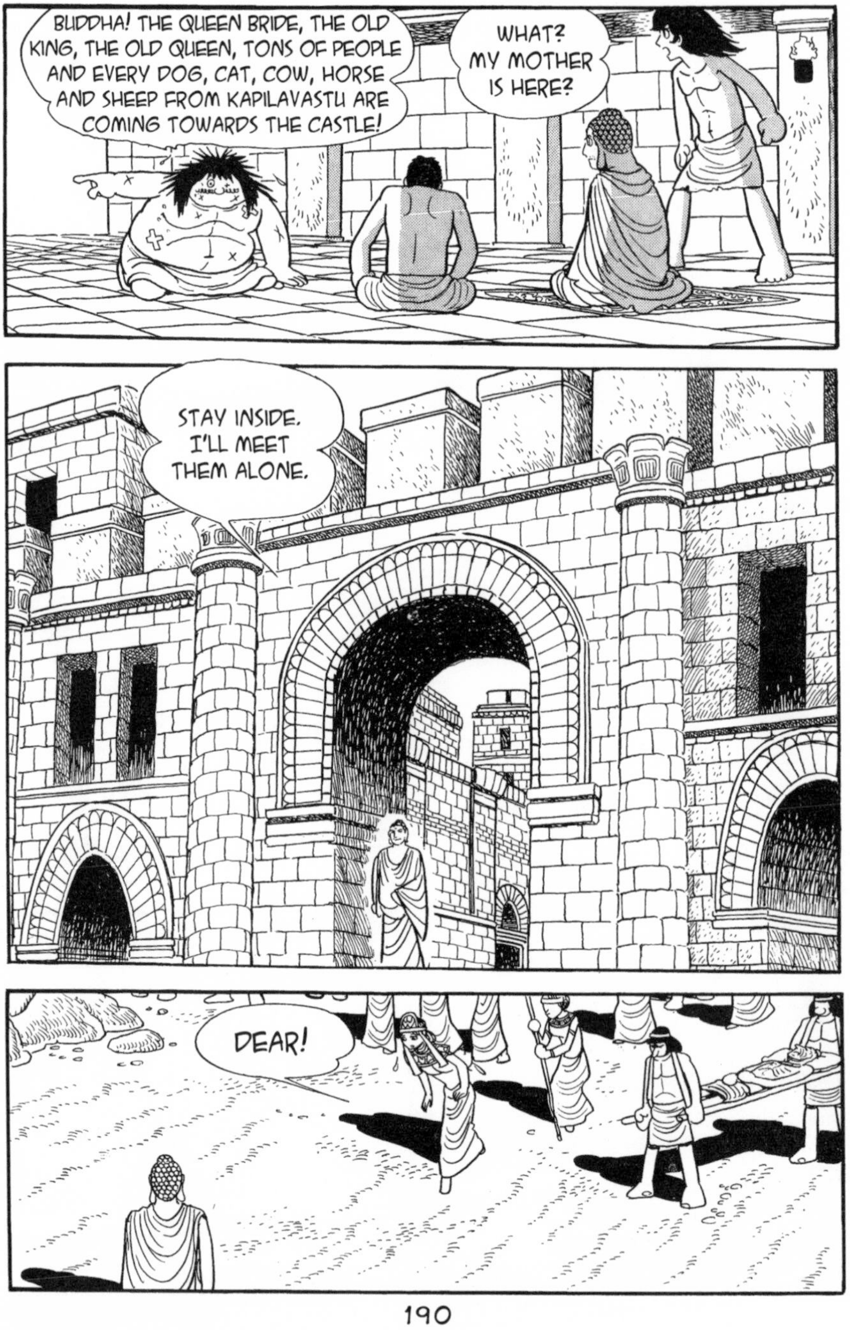
BUDDHA! THE QUEEN BRIDE, THE OLD KING, THE OLD QUEEN, TONS OF PEOPLE AND EVERY DOG, CAT, COW, HORSE AND SHEEP FROM KAPILAVASTU ARE COMING TOWARDS THE CASTLE!
WHAT? MY MOTHER IS HERE?
STAY INSIDE. I'LL MEET THEM ALONE.
DEAR!

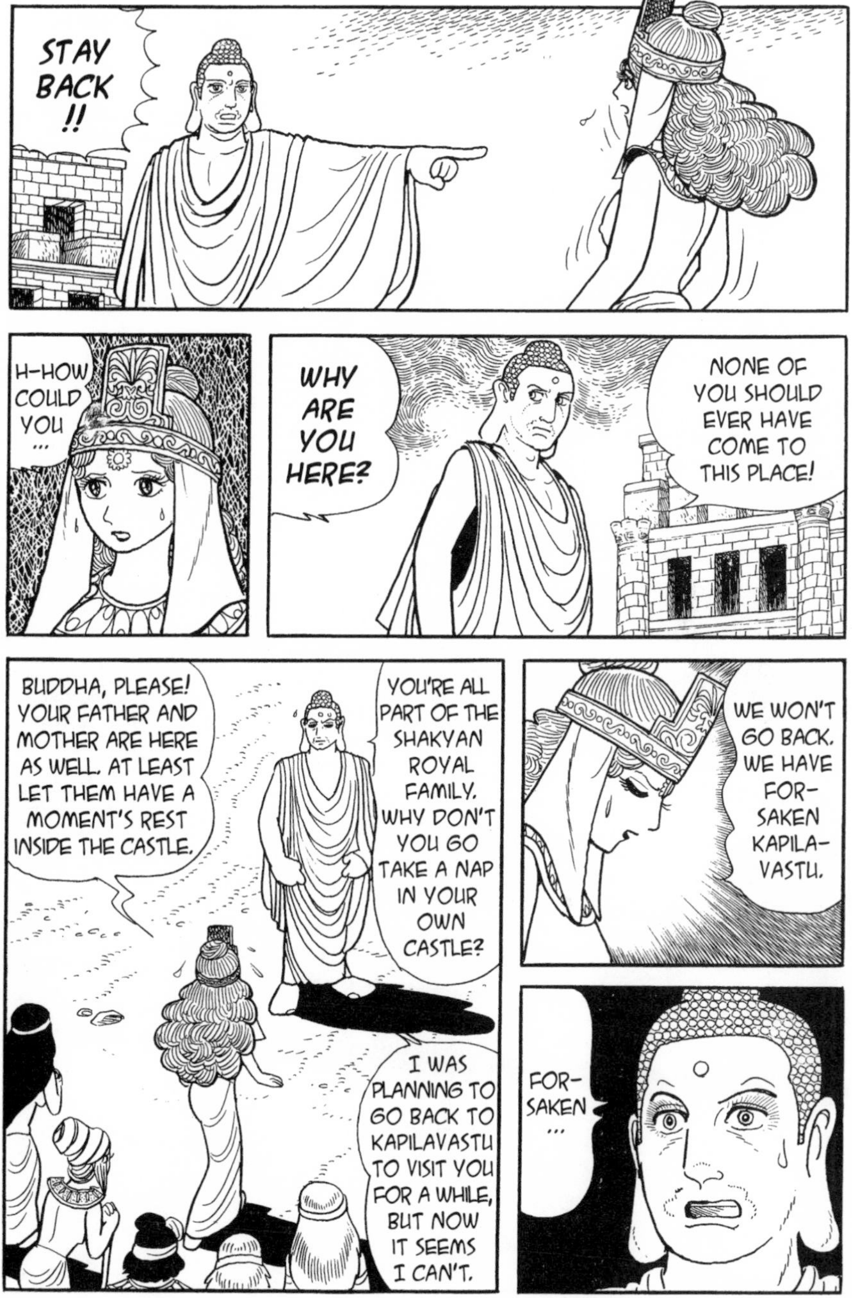
STAY BACK !!
H-HOW COULD YOU ...
WHY ARE YOU HERE?
NONE OF YOU SHOULD EVER HAVE COME TO THIS PLACE!
BUDDHA, PLEASE! YOUR FATHER AND MOTHER ARE HERE AS WELL. AT LEAST LET THEM HAVE A MOMENT'S REST INSIDE THE CASTLE.
YOU'RE ALL PART OF THE SHAKYAN ROYAL FAMILY. WHY DON'T YOU GO TAKE A NAP IN YOUR OWN CASTLE?
I WAS PLANNING TO GO BACK TO KAPILAVASTU TO VISIT YOU FOR A WHILE, BUT NOW IT SEEMS I CAN'T.
WE WON'T GO BACK. WE HAVE FOR-SAKEN KAPILA-VASTU.
FOR-SAKEN ...

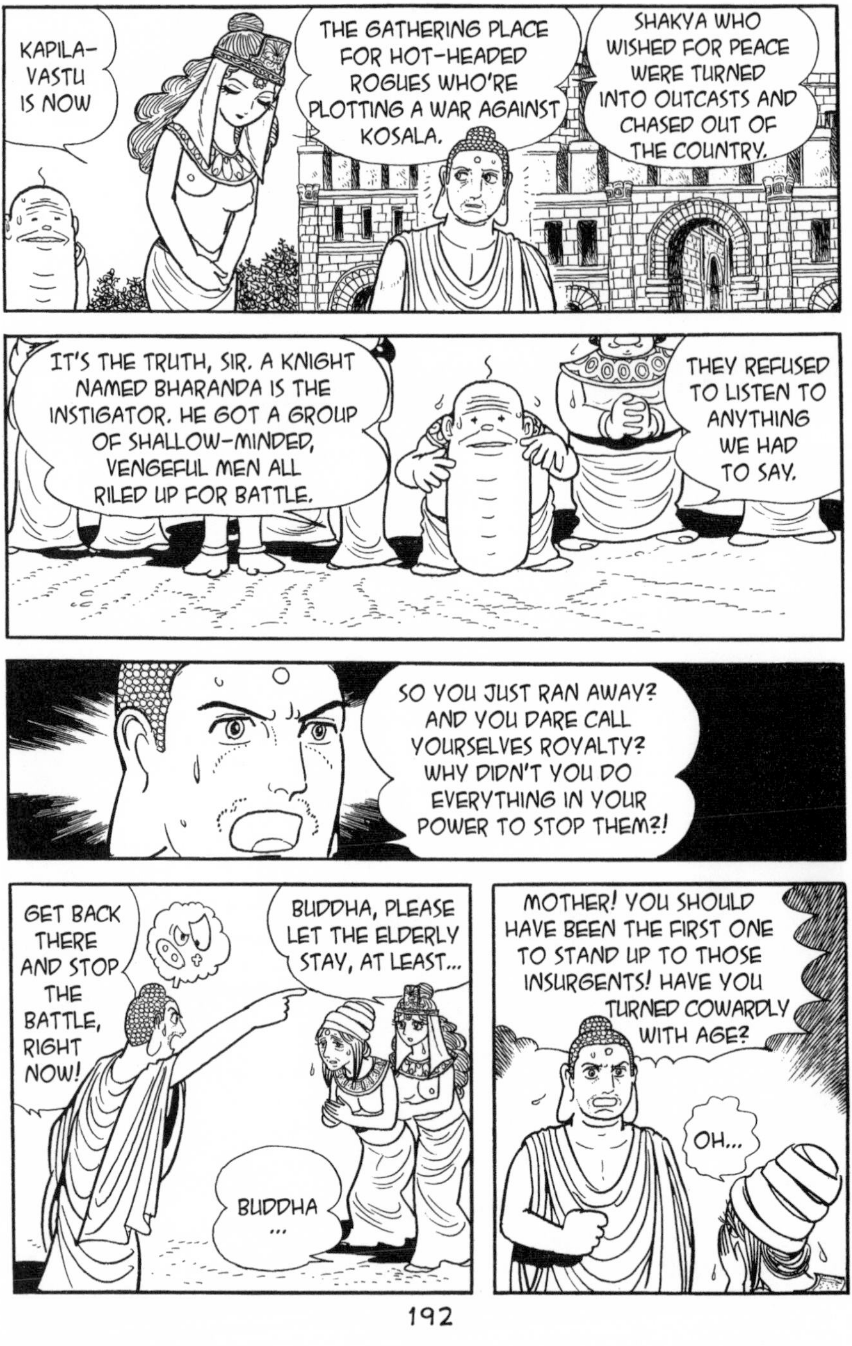
KAPILA-VASTU IS NOW
THE GATHERING PLACE FOR HOT-HEADED ROGUES WHO'RE PLOTTING A WAR AGAINST KOSALA.
SHAKYA WHO WISHED FOR PEACE WERE TURNED INTO OUTCASTS AND CHASED OUT OF THE COUNTRY.
IT'S THE TRUTH, SIR. A KNIGHT NAMED BHARANDA IS THE INSTIGATOR. HE GOT A GROUP OF SHALLOW-MINDED, VENGEFUL MEN ALL RILED UP FOR BATTLE.
THEY REFUSED TO LISTEN TO ANYTHING WE HAD TO SAY.
SO YOU JUST RAN AWAY? AND YOU DARE CALL YOURSELVES ROYALTY? WHY DIDN'T YOU DO EVERYTHING IN YOUR POWER TO STOP THEM?!
GET BACK THERE AND STOP THE BATTLE, RIGHT NOW!
BUDDHA, PLEASE LET THE ELDERLY STAY, AT LEAST...
BUDDHA ...
MOTHER! YOU SHOULD HAVE BEEN THE FIRST ONE TO STAND UP TO THOSE INSURGENTS! HAVE YOU TURNED COWARDLY WITH AGE?
OH...

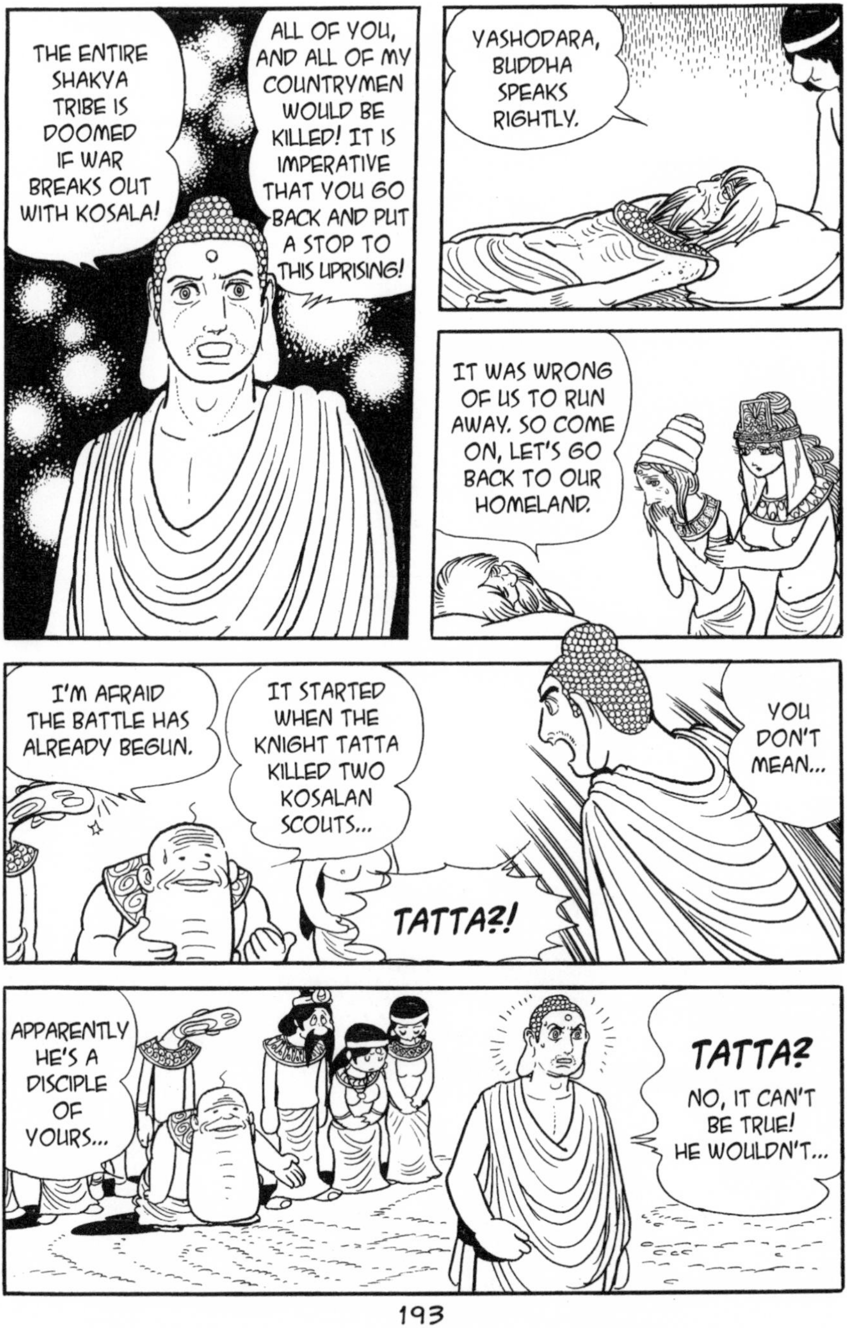
THE ENTIRE SHAKYA TRIBE IS DOOMED IF WAR BREAKS OUT WITH KOSALA!
ALL OF YOU, AND ALL OF MY COUNTRYMEN WOULD BE KILLED! IT IS IMPERATIVE THAT YOU GO BACK AND PUT A STOP TO THIS UPRISING!
YASHODARA, BUDDHA SPEAKS RIGHTLY.
IT WAS WRONG OF US TO RUN AWAY. SO COME ON, LET'S GO BACK TO OUR HOMELAND.
I'M AFRAID THE BATTLE HAS ALREADY BEGUN.
IT STARTED WHEN THE KNIGHT TATTA KILLED TWO KOSALAN SCOUTS...
YOU DON'T MEAN...
TATTA?!
APPARENTLY HE'S A DISCIPLE OF YOURS...
TATTA?
NO, IT CAN'T BE TRUE! HE WOULDN'T...

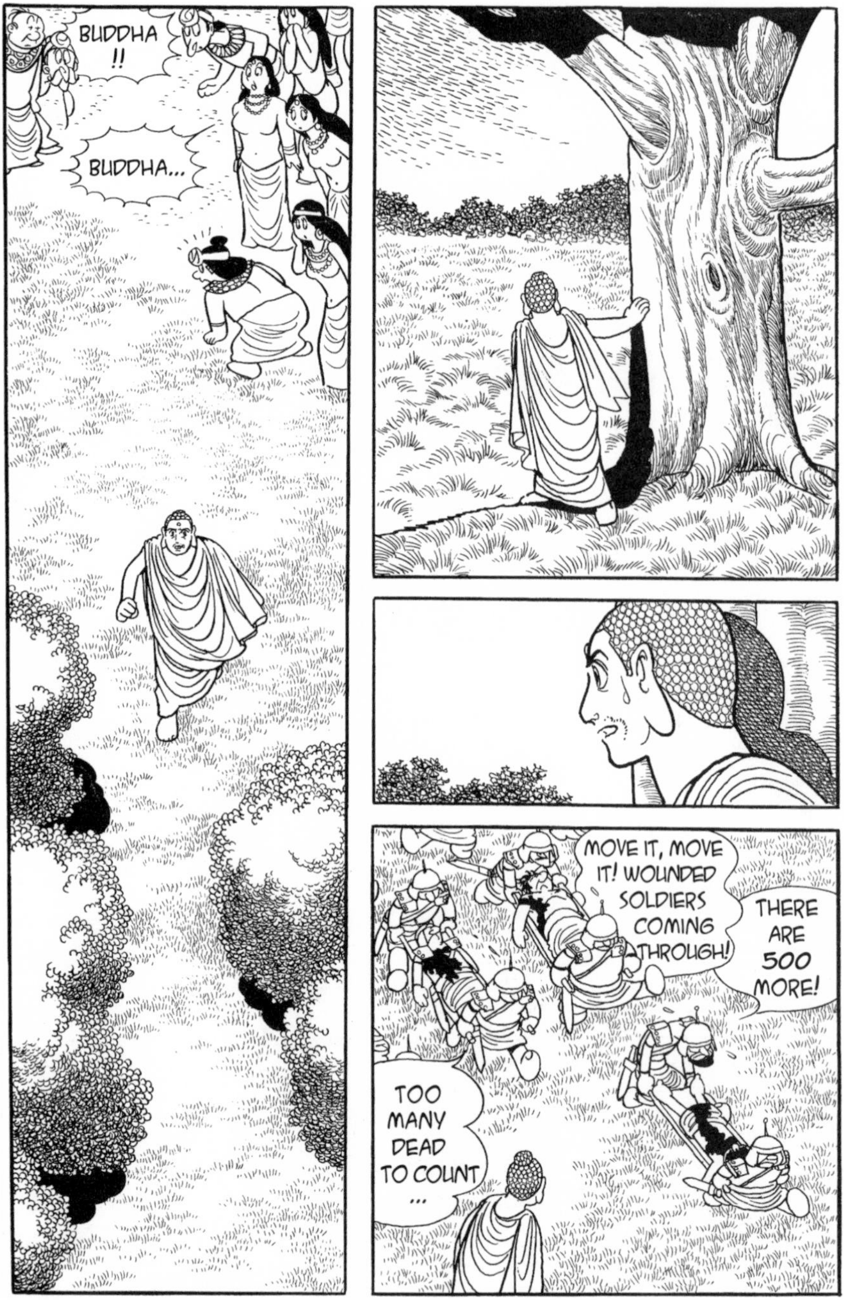
BUDDHA !!
BUDDHA...
MOVE IT, MOVE IT! WOUNDED SOLDIERS COMING THROUGH!
THERE ARE 500 MORE!
TOO MANY DEAD TO COUNT ...

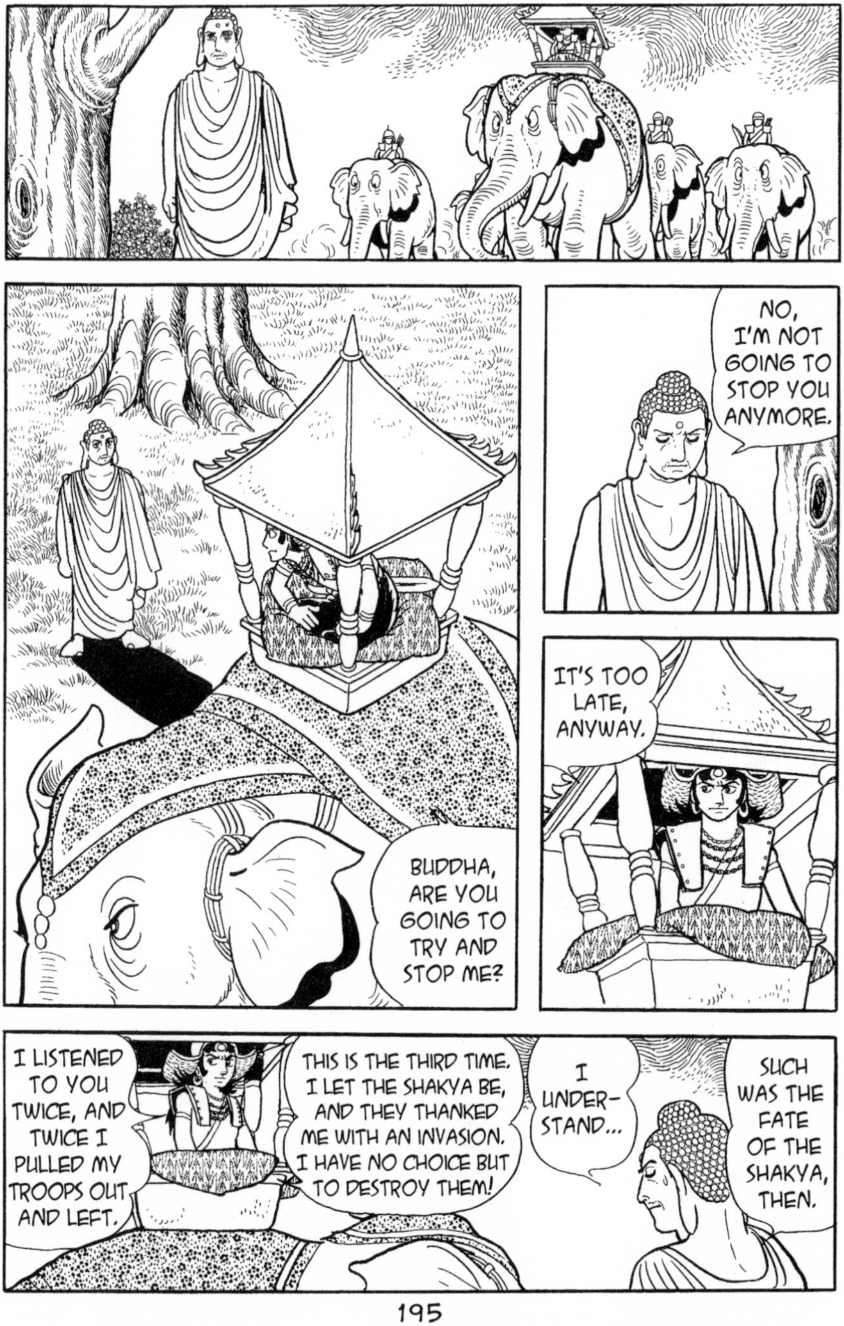
BUDDHA, ARE YOU GOING TO TRY AND STOP ME?
NO, I'M NOT GOING TO STOP YOU ANYMORE.
IT'S TOO LATE, ANYWAY.
I LISTENED TO YOU TWICE, AND TWICE I PULLED MY TROOPS OUT AND LEFT.
THIS IS THE THIRD TIME. I LET THE SHAKYA BE, AND THEY THANKED ME WITH AN INVASION. I HAVE NO CHOICE BUT TO DESTROY THEM!
I UNDER-STAND...
SUCH WAS THE FATE OF THE SHAKYA, THEN.

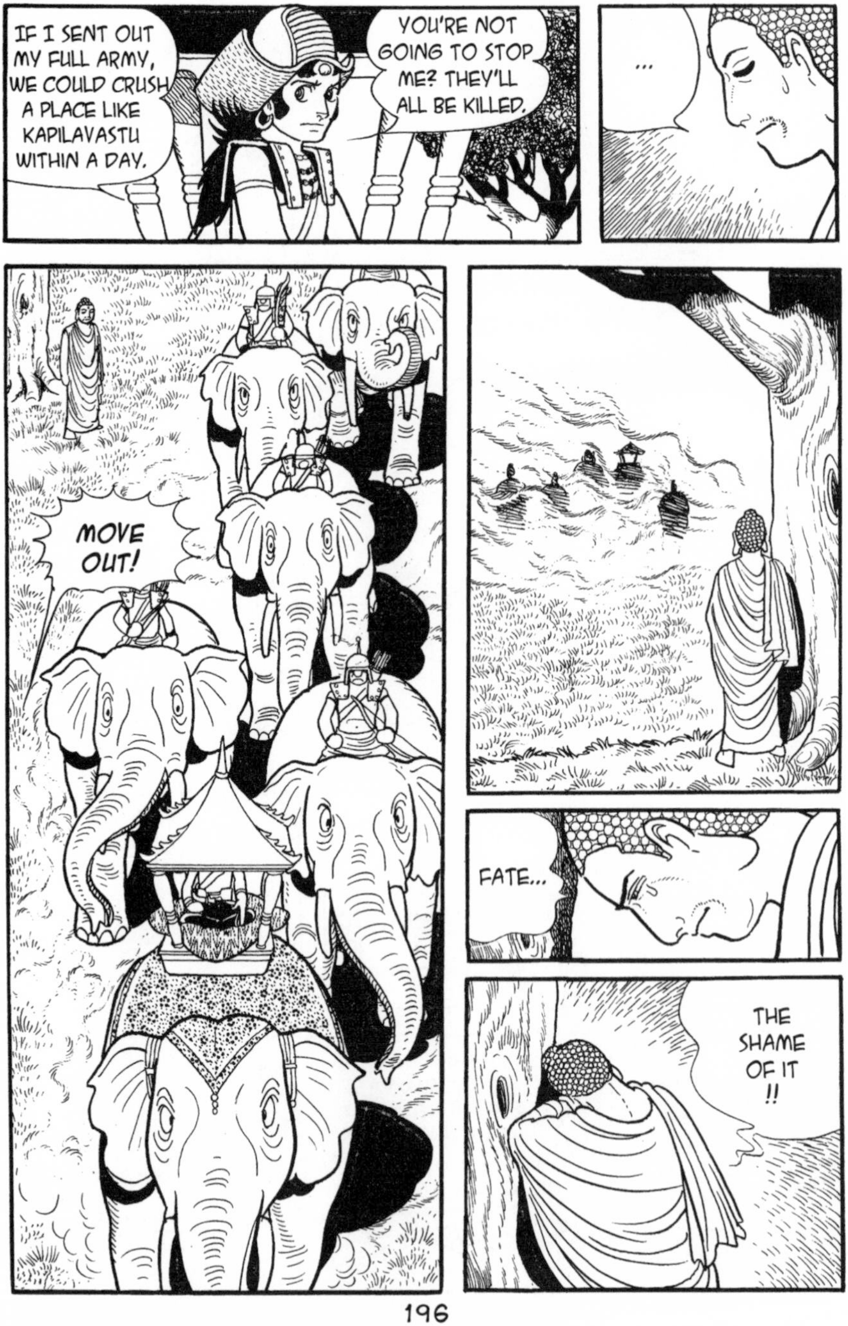
IF I SENT OUT MY FULL ARMY, WE COULD CRUSH A PLACE LIKE KAPILAVASTU WITHIN A DAY.
YOU'RE NOT GOING TO STOP ME? THEY'LL ALL BE KILLED.
...
MOVE OUT!
FATE...
THE SHAME OF IT !!

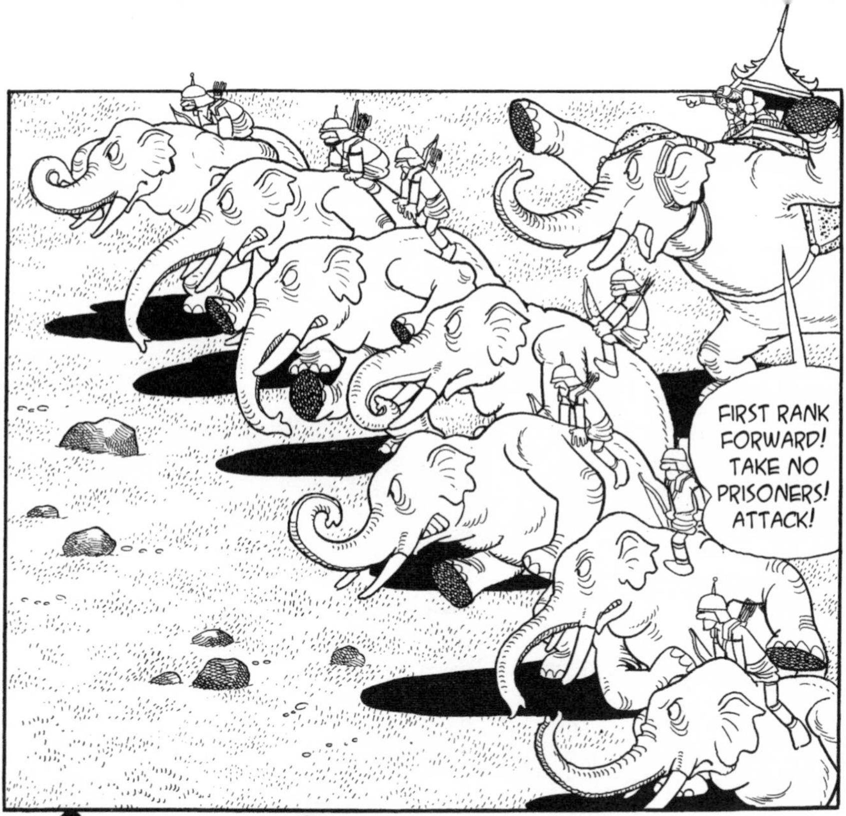
FIRST RANK FORWARD! TAKE NO PRISONERS! ATTACK!

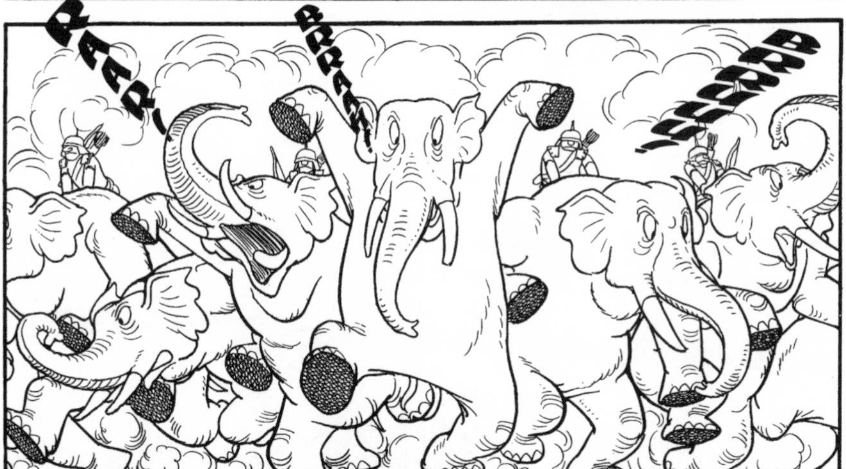
RAAR-!
BRRAAH!

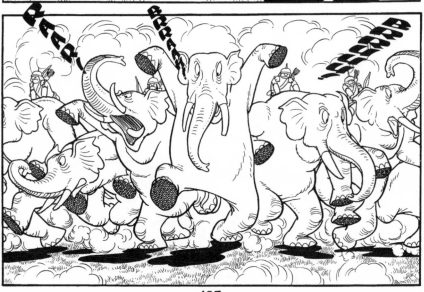

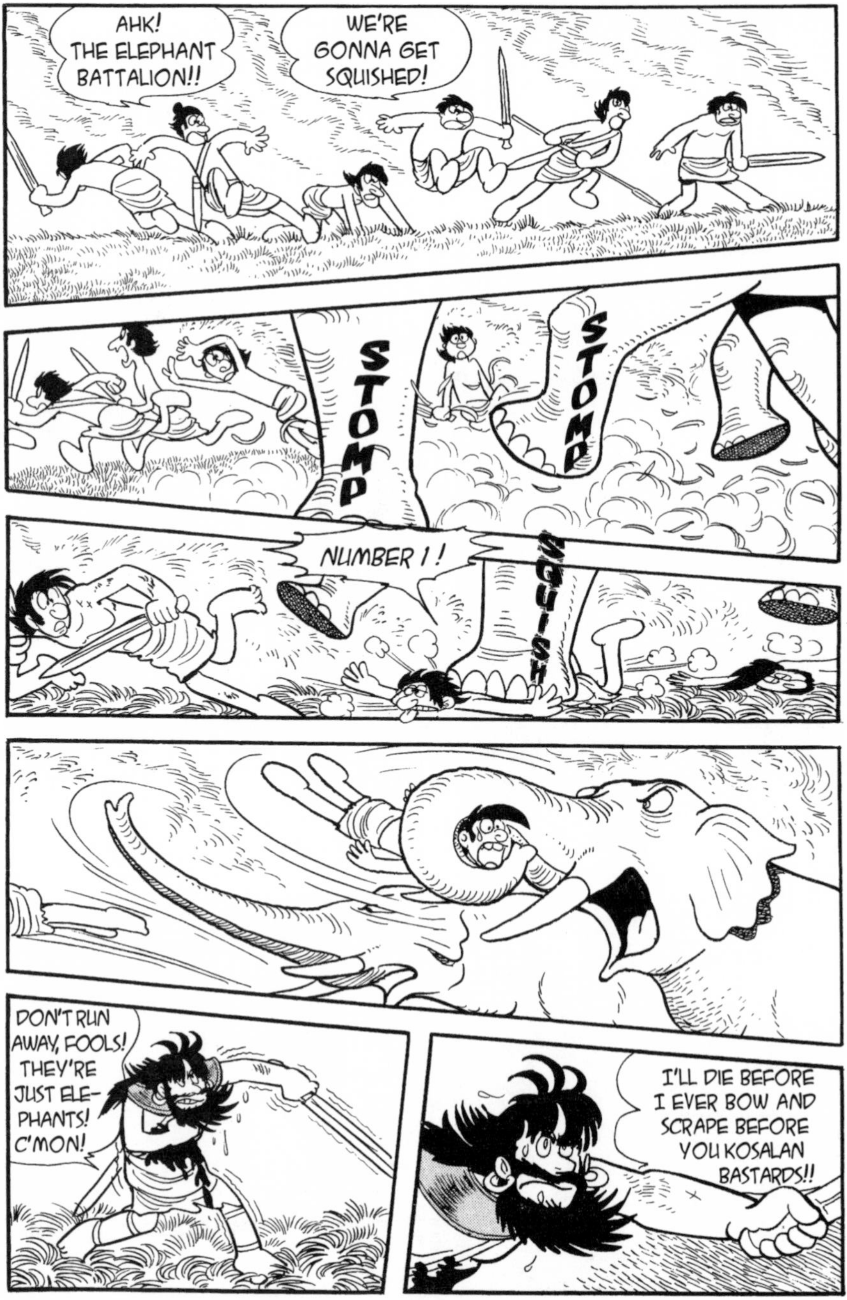
AHK! THE ELEPHANT BATTALION!!
WE'RE GONNA GET SQUISHED!
STOMP
STOMP
NUMBER 1!
SQUISH
DON'T RUN AWAY, FOOLS! THEY'RE JUST ELE-PHANTS! C'MON!
I'LL DIE BEFORE I EVER BOW AND SCRAPE BEFORE YOU KOSALAN BASTARDS!!

DAMMIT. IF I WASN'T HIT IN THE CHEST I COULDA TAKEN OUT 2 OR 3 OF THESE FAT SUCKERS...

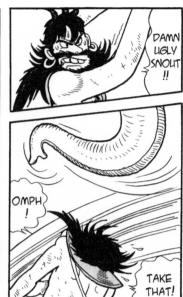

DAMN UGLY SNOUT!!

OMPH!

TAKE THAT!

OOOH...

OH, MAN. I'M SO TIRED ALREADY...

BRING IT ON, YOU RAT BASTARD KOSALAN GENERAL!

YOU... I'VE SEEN YOU BEFORE...

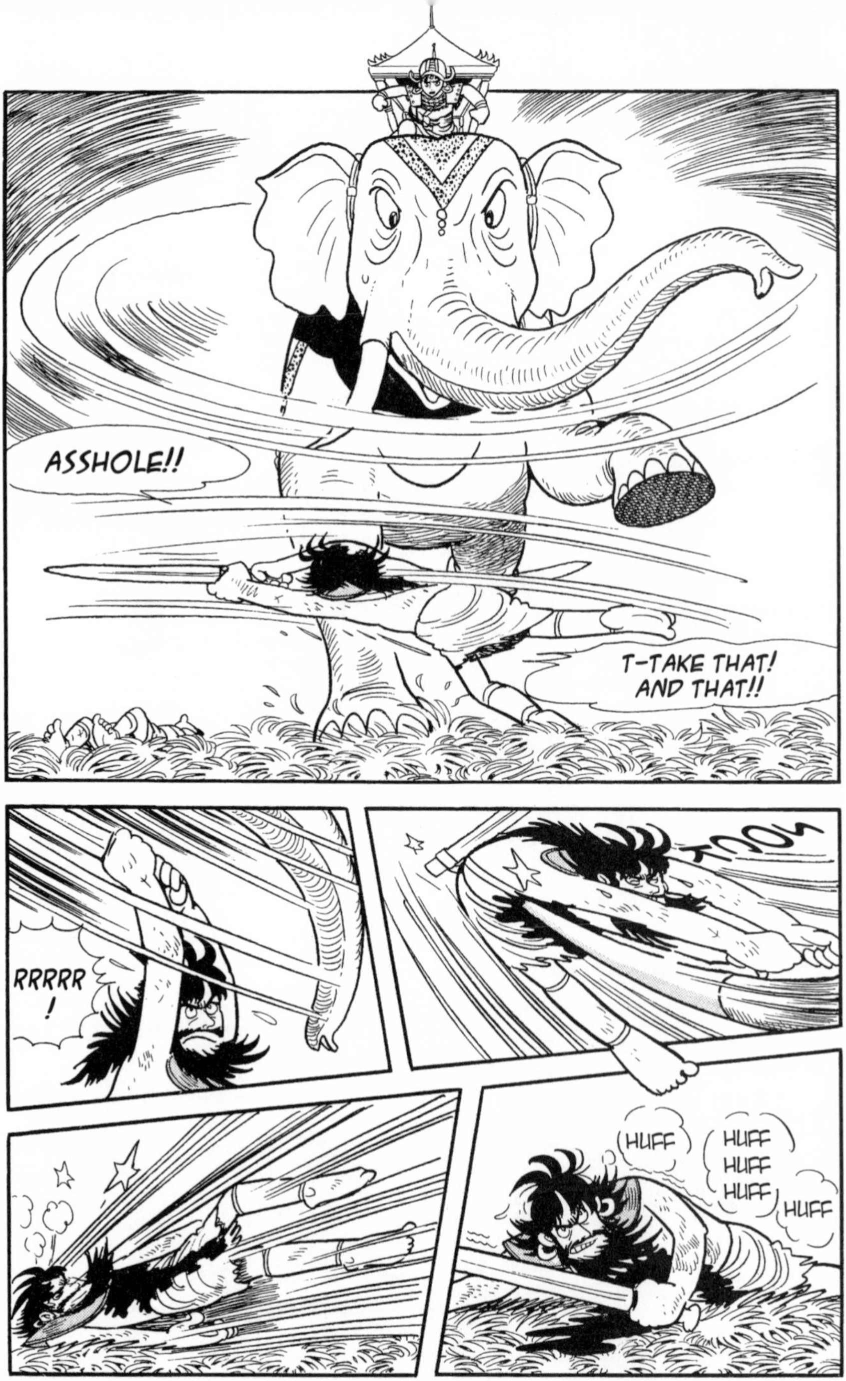
ASSHOLE!!
T-TAKE THAT! AND THAT!!
RRRRR !
HUFF
HUFF HUFF HUFF
HUFF

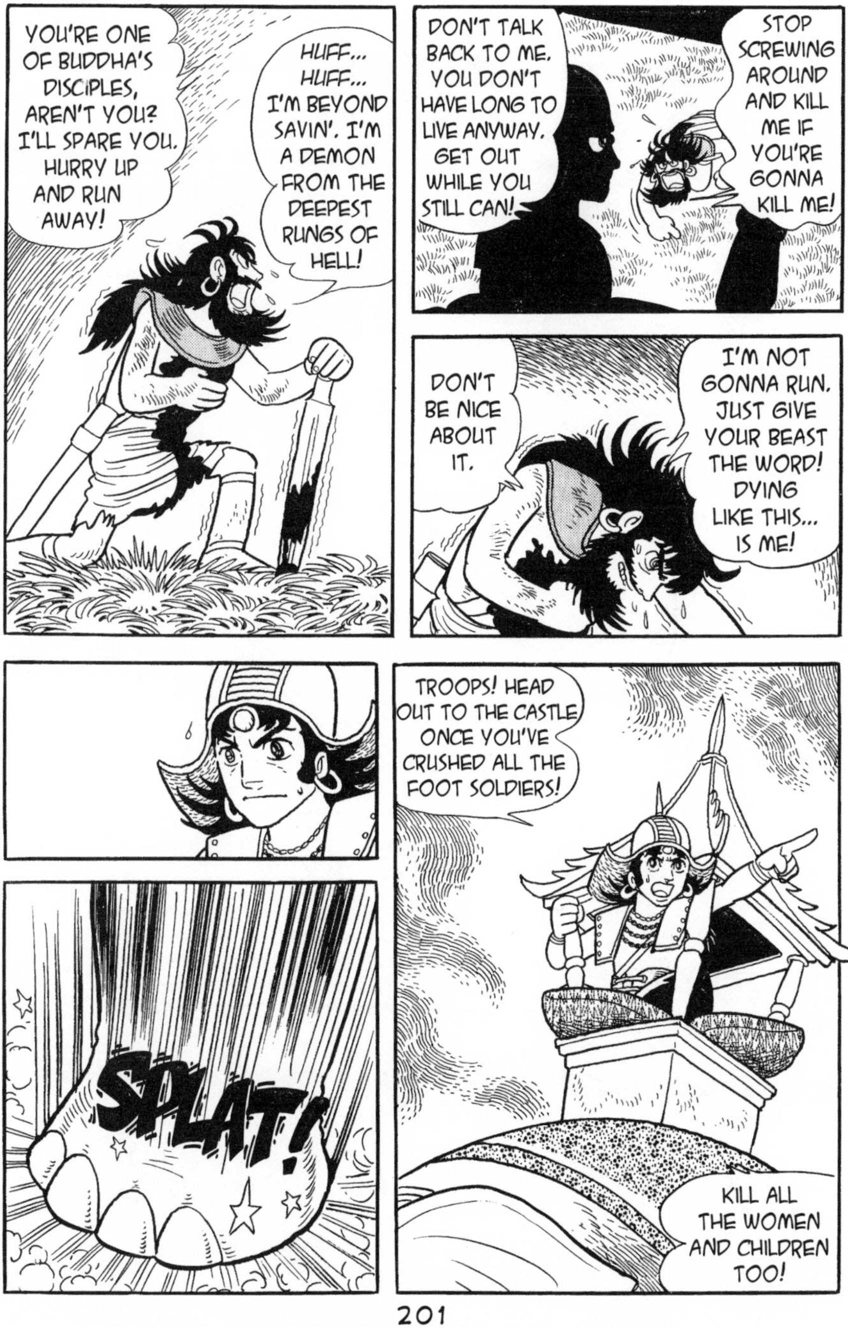

YOU'RE ONE OF BUDDHA'S DISCIPLES, AREN'T YOU? I'LL SPARE YOU. HURRY UP AND RUN AWAY!
HUFF... HUFF... I'M BEYOND SAVIN'. I'M A DEMON FROM THE DEEPEST RUNGS OF HELL!
DON'T TALK BACK TO ME. YOU DON'T HAVE LONG TO LIVE ANYWAY. GET OUT WHILE YOU STILL CAN!
STOP SCREWING AROUND AND KILL ME IF YOU'RE GONNA KILL ME!
DON'T BE NICE ABOUT IT.
I'M NOT GONNA RUN. JUST GIVE YOUR BEAST THE WORD! DYING LIKE THIS... IS ME!
SPLAT!
TROOPS! HEAD OUT TO THE CASTLE ONCE YOU'VE CRUSHED ALL THE FOOT SOLDIERS!
KILL ALL THE WOMEN AND CHILDREN TOO!

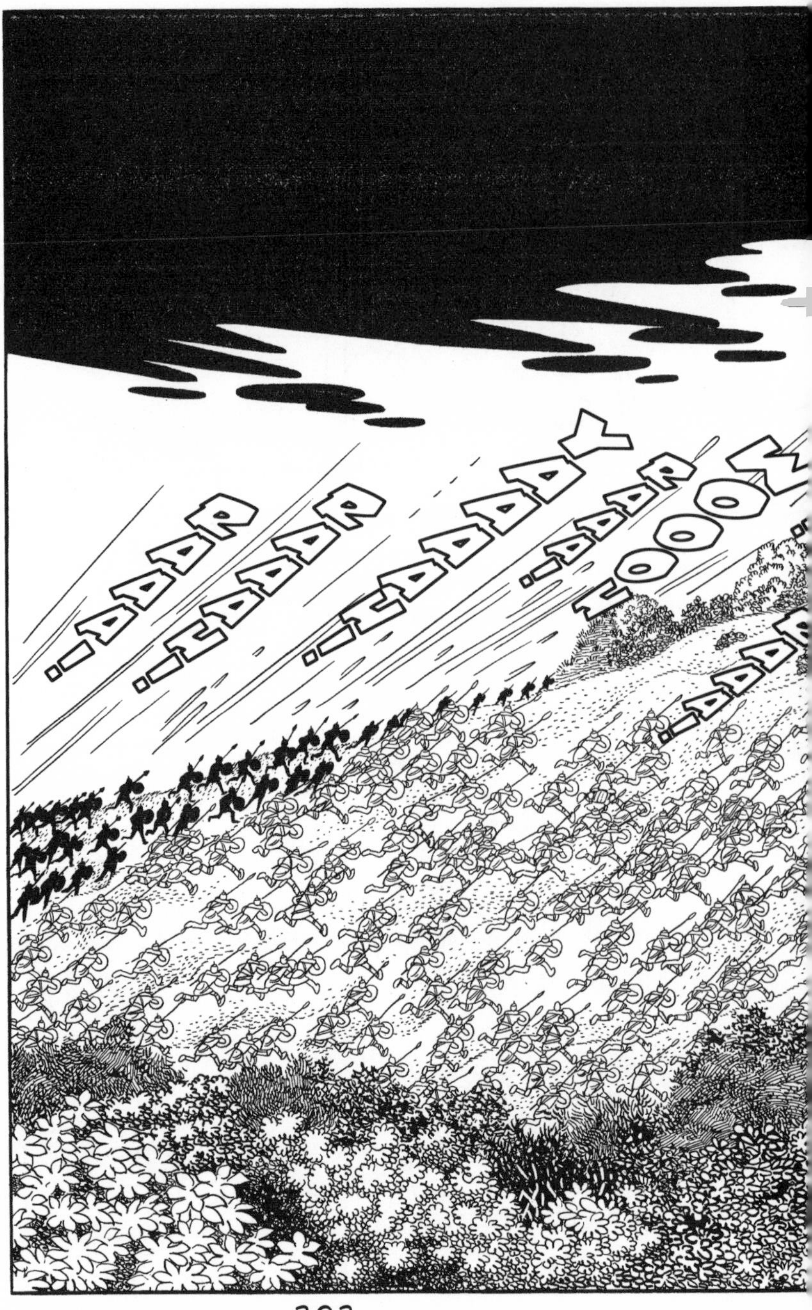
RAAA-!
RAAAH-!
YAAAAH-!
RAAA-!

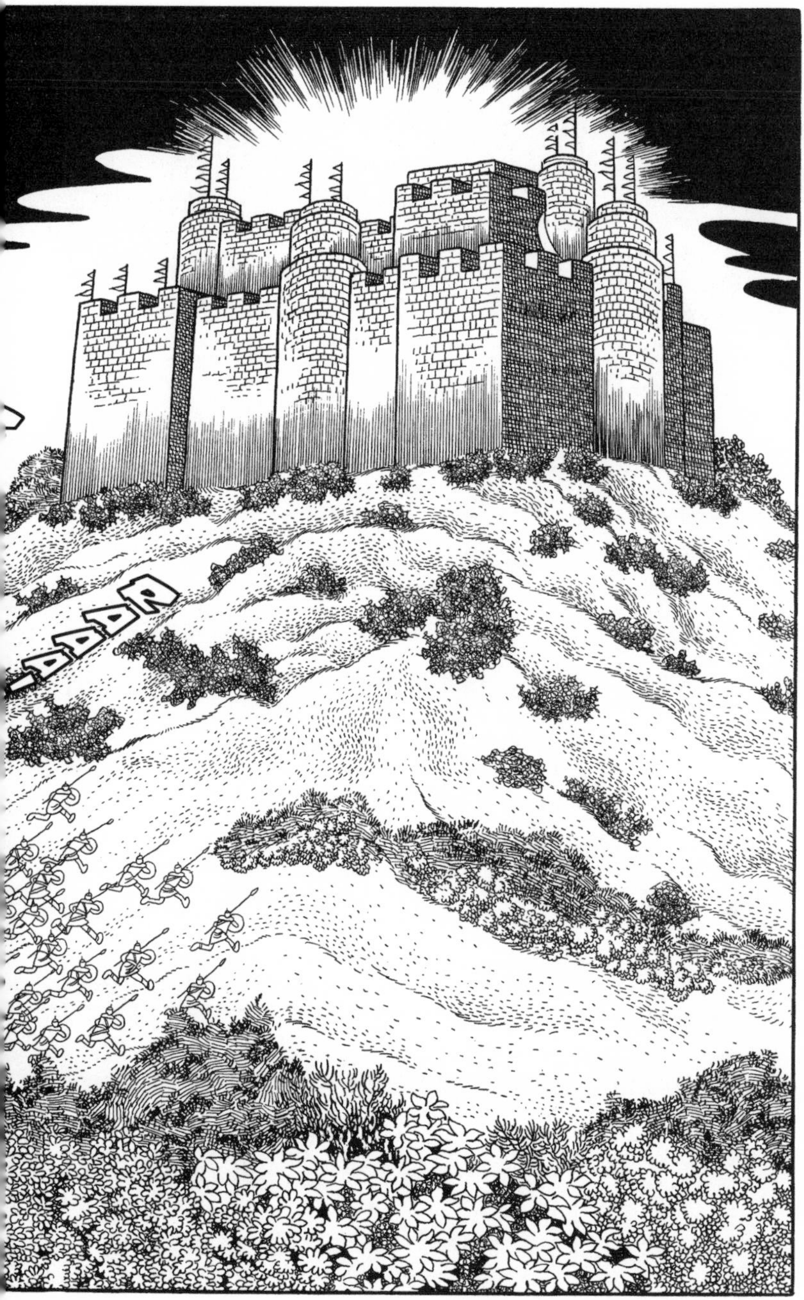
RAAA-

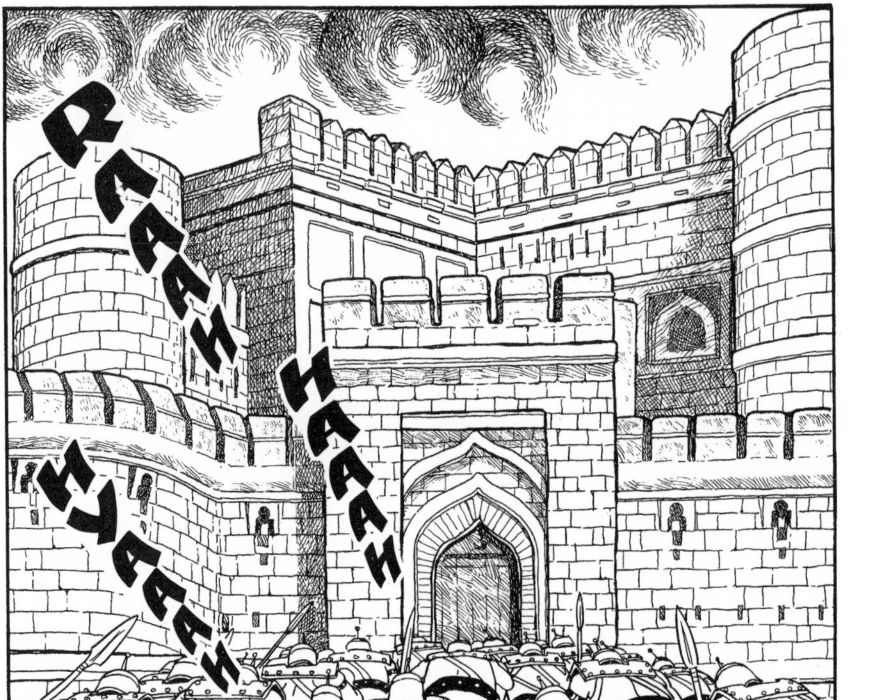
RAAAH
HYAAAH
HAAAAH

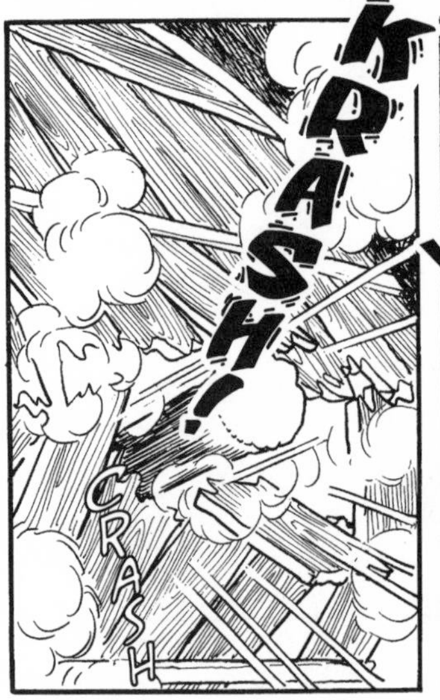
KRASH!
CRASH

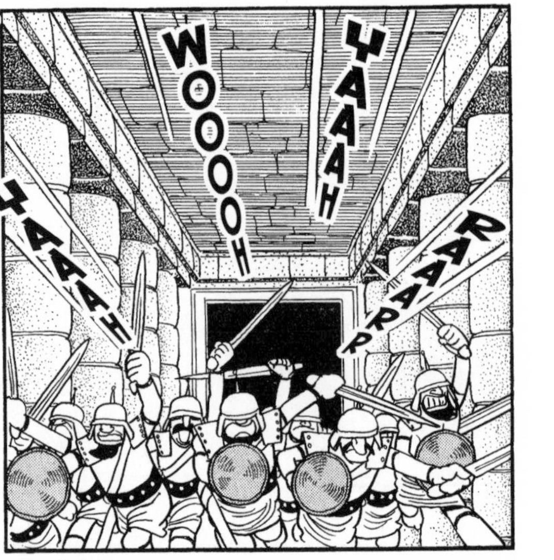
YAAAAH
WOOOOH
YAAAAH
RAAARP

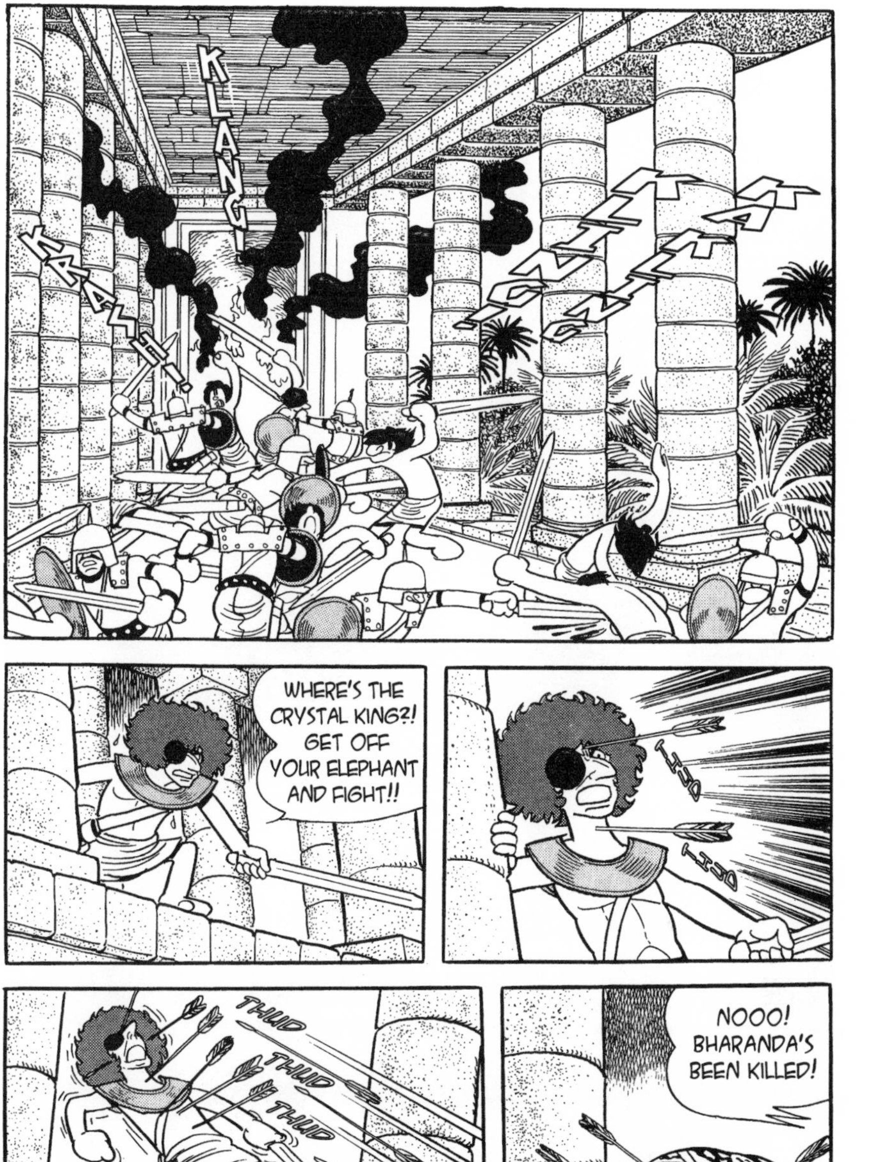
KLANG!
KRASH!
KLING
WHERE'S THE CRYSTAL KING?! GET OFF YOUR ELEPHANT AND FIGHT!!
THUD
THUD
THUD
NOOO! BHARANDA'S BEEN KILLED!

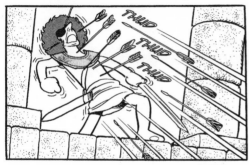

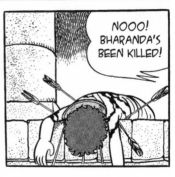

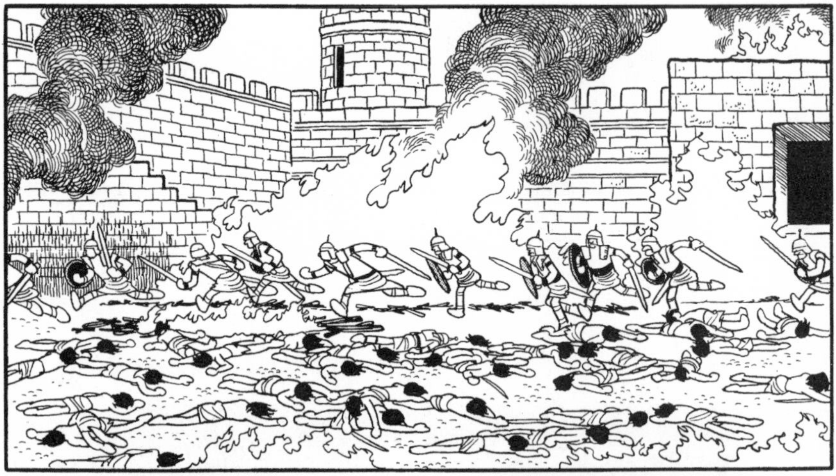
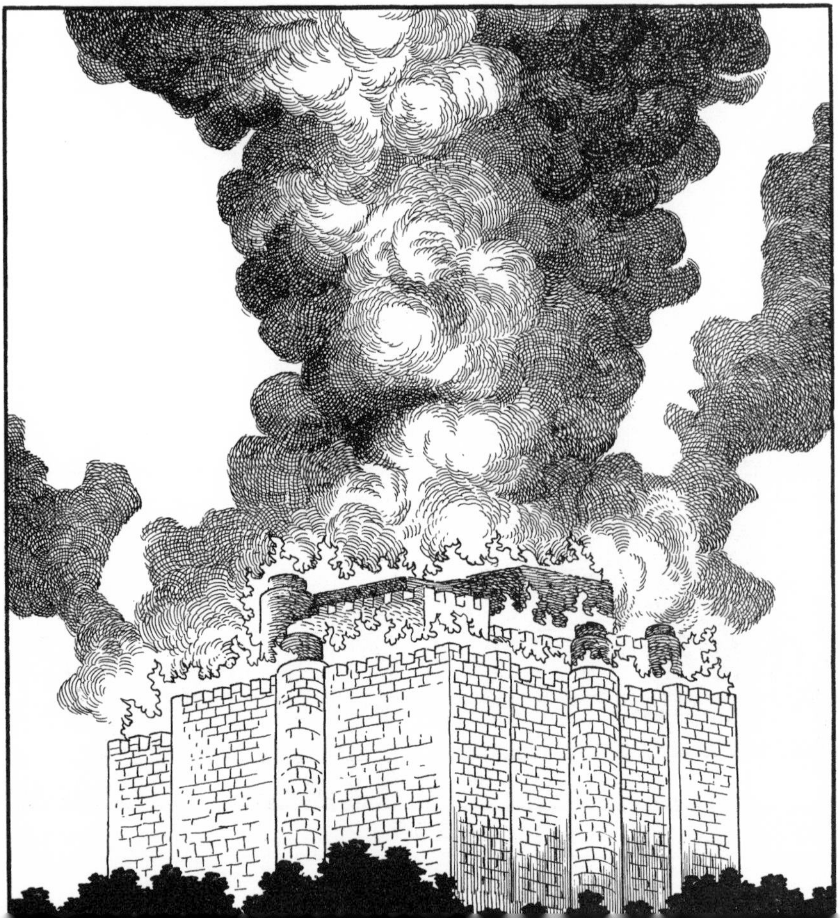

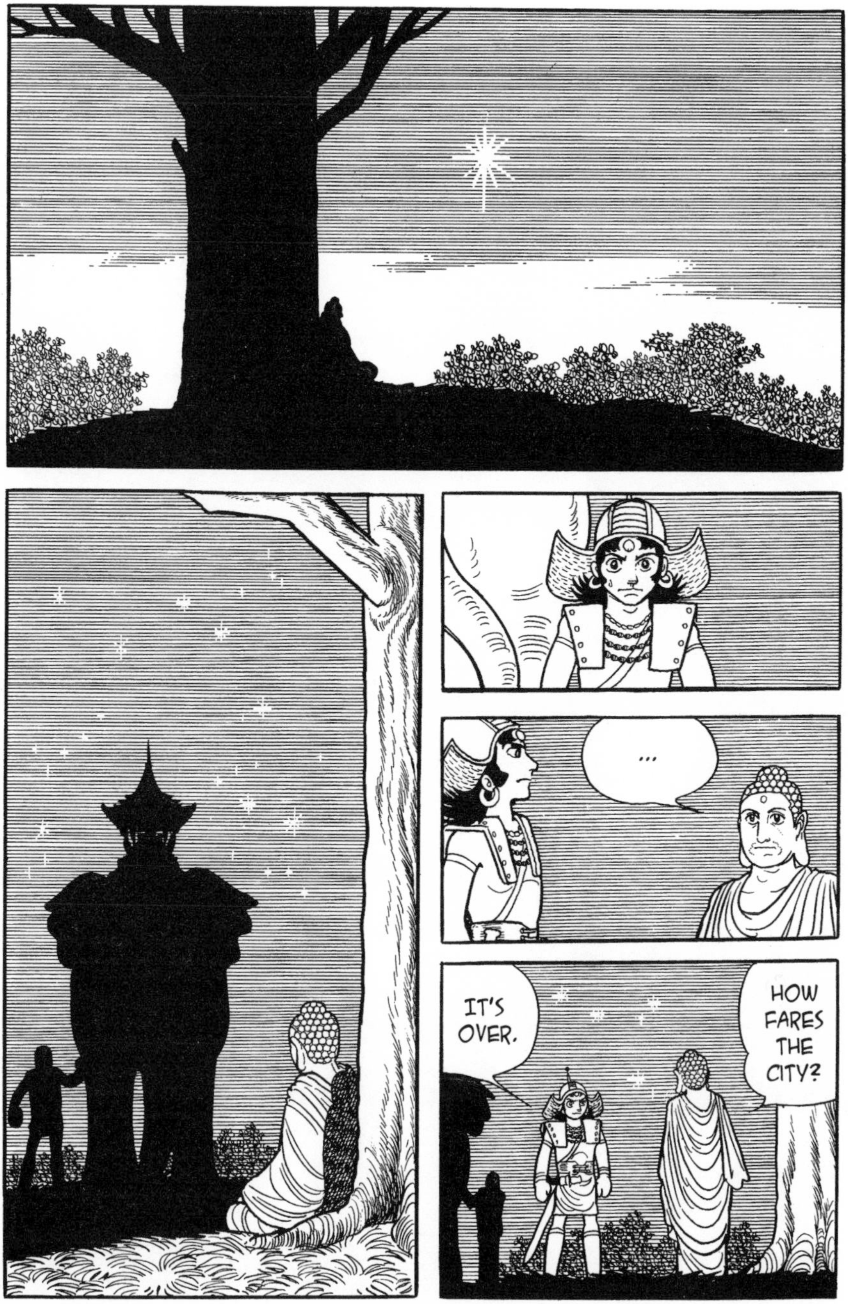
...
HOW FARES THE CITY?
IT'S OVER.

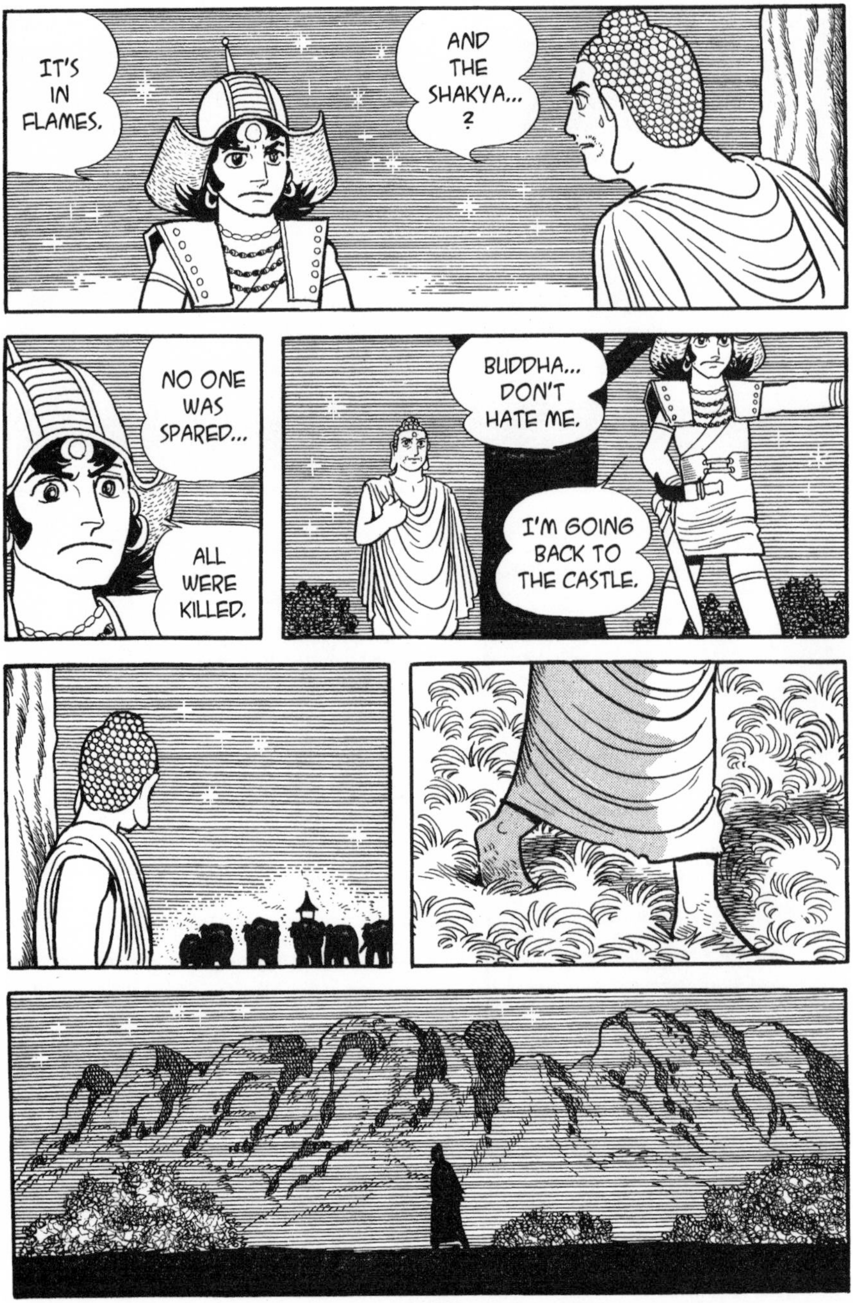
IT'S IN FLAMES.
AND THE SHAKYA...?
NO ONE WAS SPARED...
ALL WERE KILLED.
BUDDHA... DON'T HATE ME.
I'M GOING BACK TO THE CASTLE.

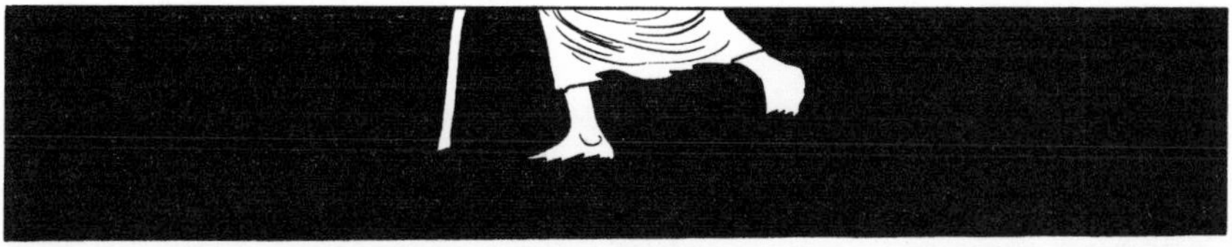
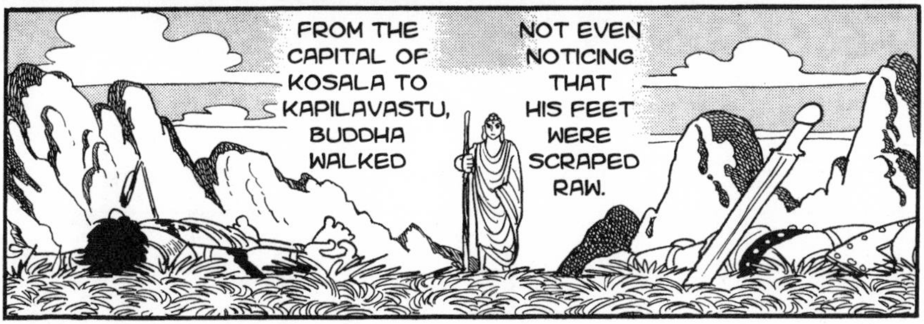
FROM THE CAPITAL OF KOSALA TO KAPILAVASTU, BUDDHA WALKED
NOT EVEN NOTICING THAT HIS FEET WERE SCRAPED RAW.
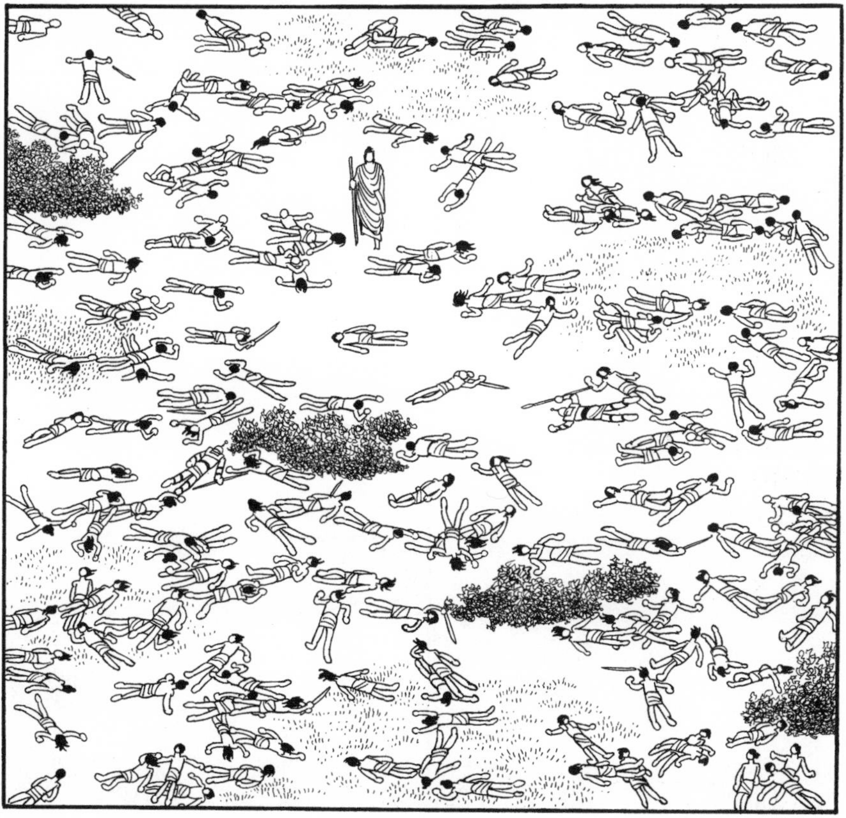

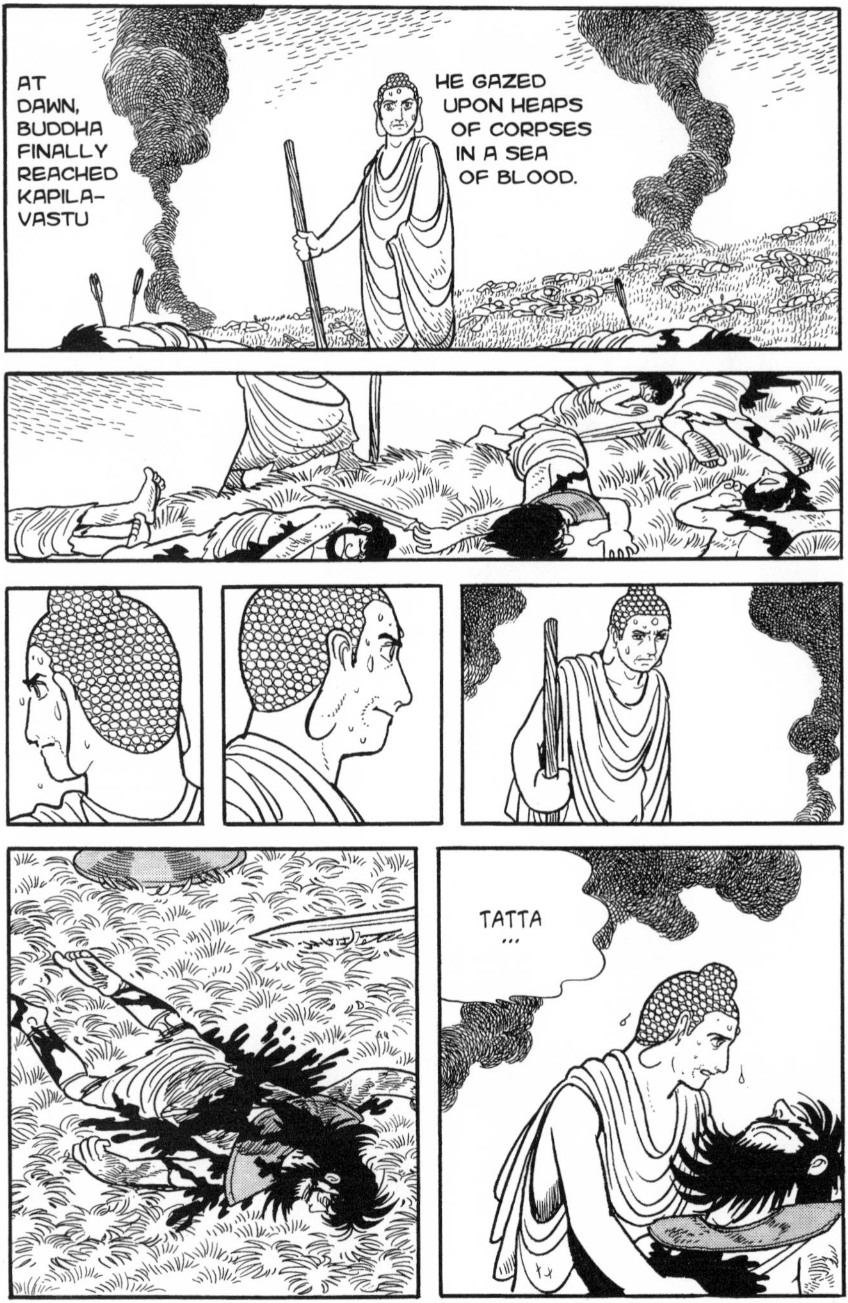
AT DAWN, BUDDHA FINALLY REACHED KAPILA-VASTU
HE GAZED UPON HEAPS OF CORPSES IN A SEA OF BLOOD.
TATTA ...

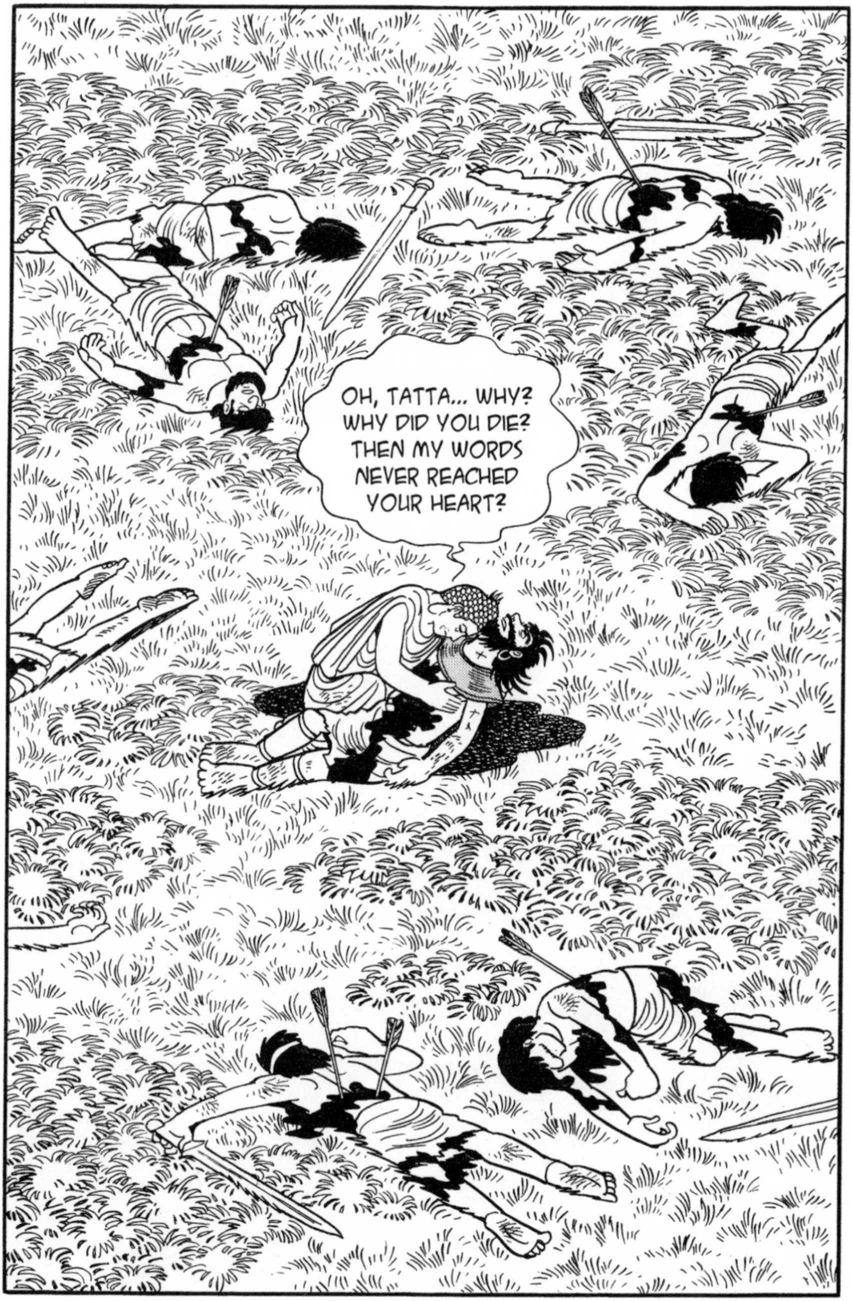
OH, TATTA... WHY? WHY DID YOU DIE? THEN MY WORDS NEVER REACHED YOUR HEART?

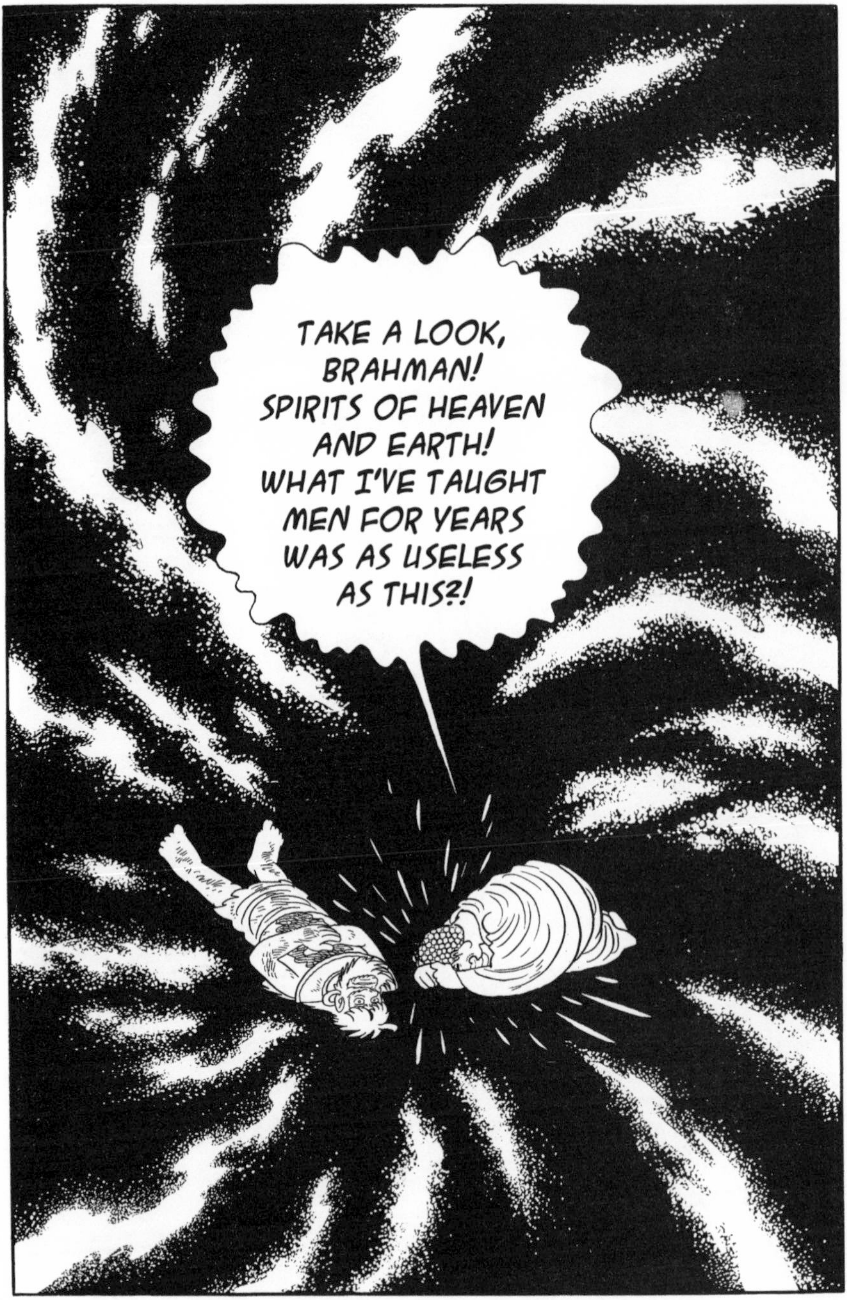
TAKE A LOOK, BRAHMAN! SPIRITS OF HEAVEN AND EARTH! WHAT I'VE TAUGHT MEN FOR YEARS WAS AS USELESS AS THIS?!

PART SEVEN

CHAPTER ONE

SAD NEWS

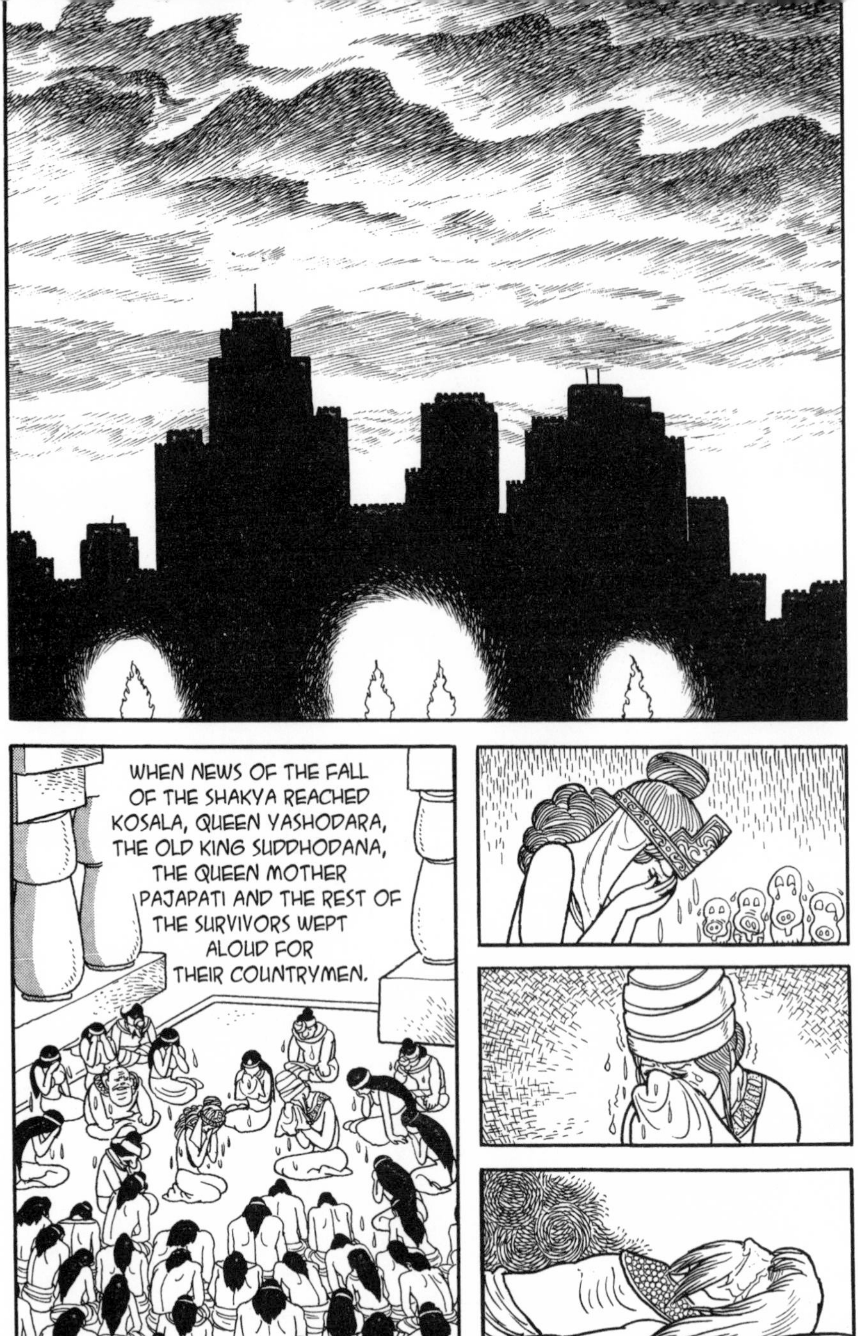
WHEN NEWS OF THE FALL OF THE SHAKYA REACHED KOSALA, QUEEN YASHODARA, THE OLD KING SUDDHODANA, THE QUEEN MOTHER PAJAPATI AND THE REST OF THE SURVIVORS WEPT ALOUD FOR THEIR COUNTRYMEN.

BUT BUDDHA WAS THE MOST ANGUISHED AND GRIEF-STRICKEN OF THEM ALL. NOT ONLY HAD HIS PEOPLE BEEN EXTERMINATED, BUT IN THE END, IT SEEMED THAT NOT A SINGLE WORD OF HIS TEACHINGS HAD DONE ANY GOOD. NOT FOR THE SHAKYA, NOT FOR TATTA, HIS VERY FIRST FOLLOWER.

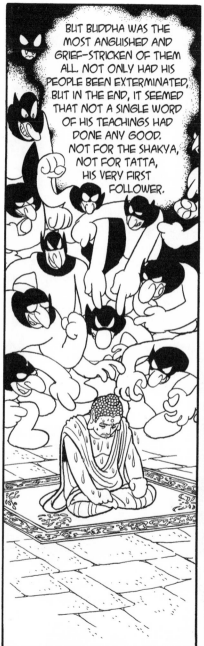

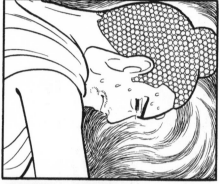

FOR 30 YEARS, I HAVE TAUGHT PEOPLE ABOUT THE LAWS OF HEAVEN AND NATURE. WHAT FOR? WHAT WAS THE PURPOSE? ALL MY EFFORTS PROVED FRUITLESS, IN THE END.

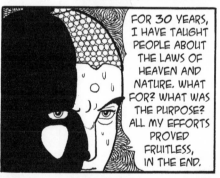

TATTA! EVEN YOU, MY FRIEND!... WHY DID YOU HAVE TO DIE?

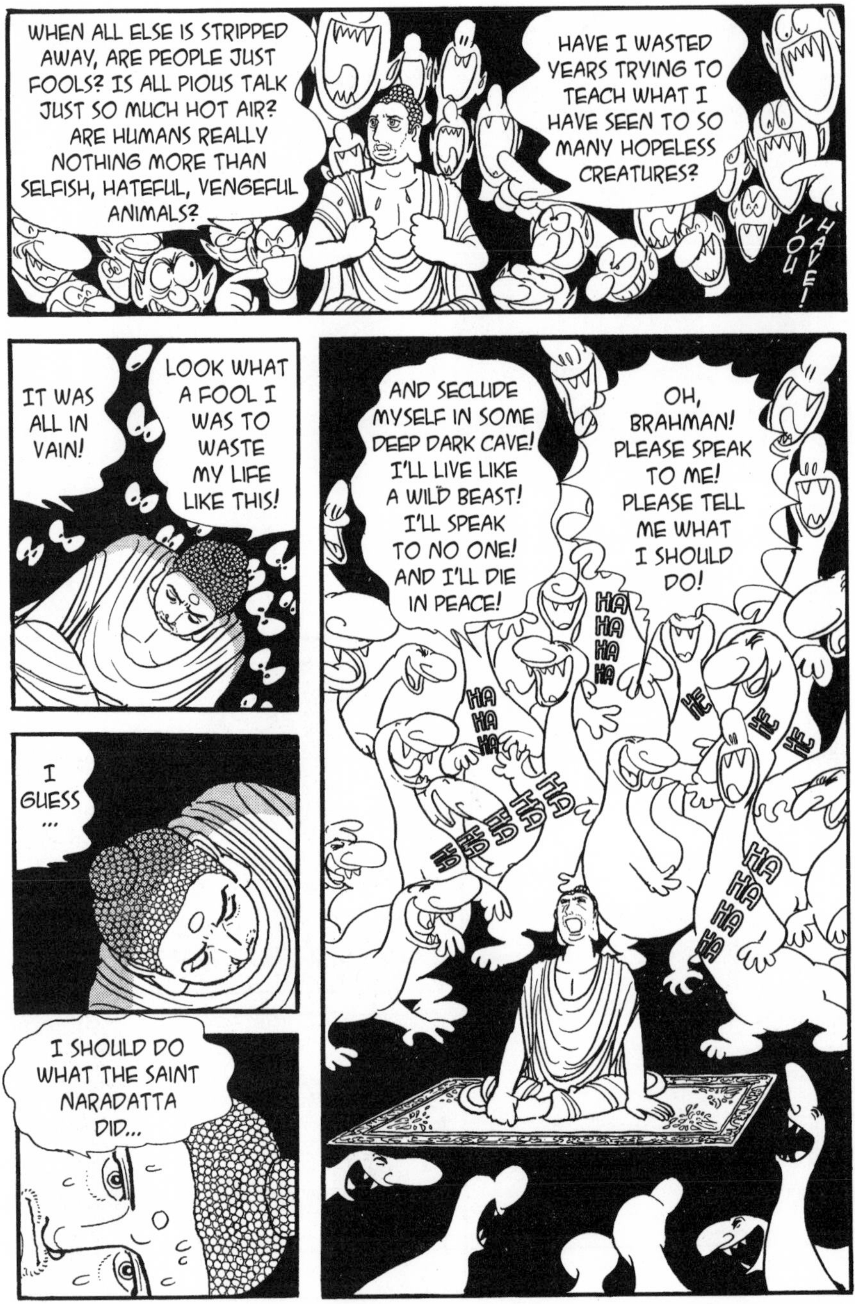
WHEN ALL ELSE IS STRIPPED AWAY, ARE PEOPLE JUST FOOLS? IS ALL PIOUS TALK JUST SO MUCH HOT AIR? ARE HUMANS REALLY NOTHING MORE THAN SELFISH, HATEFUL, VENGEFUL ANIMALS?
HAVE I WASTED YEARS TRYING TO TEACH WHAT I HAVE SEEN TO SO MANY HOPELESS CREATURES?
YOU HAVE!
IT WAS ALL IN VAIN!
LOOK WHAT A FOOL I WAS TO WASTE MY LIFE LIKE THIS!
I GUESS ...
I SHOULD DO WHAT THE SAINT NARADATTA DID...
AND SECLUDE MYSELF IN SOME DEEP DARK CAVE! I'LL LIVE LIKE A WILD BEAST! I'LL SPEAK TO NO ONE! AND I'LL DIE IN PEACE!
OH, BRAHMAN! PLEASE SPEAK TO ME! PLEASE TELL ME WHAT I SHOULD DO!
HA HA HA HA
HA HA HA
HE HE HE
HA HA HA HA HA
HA HA HA HA HA

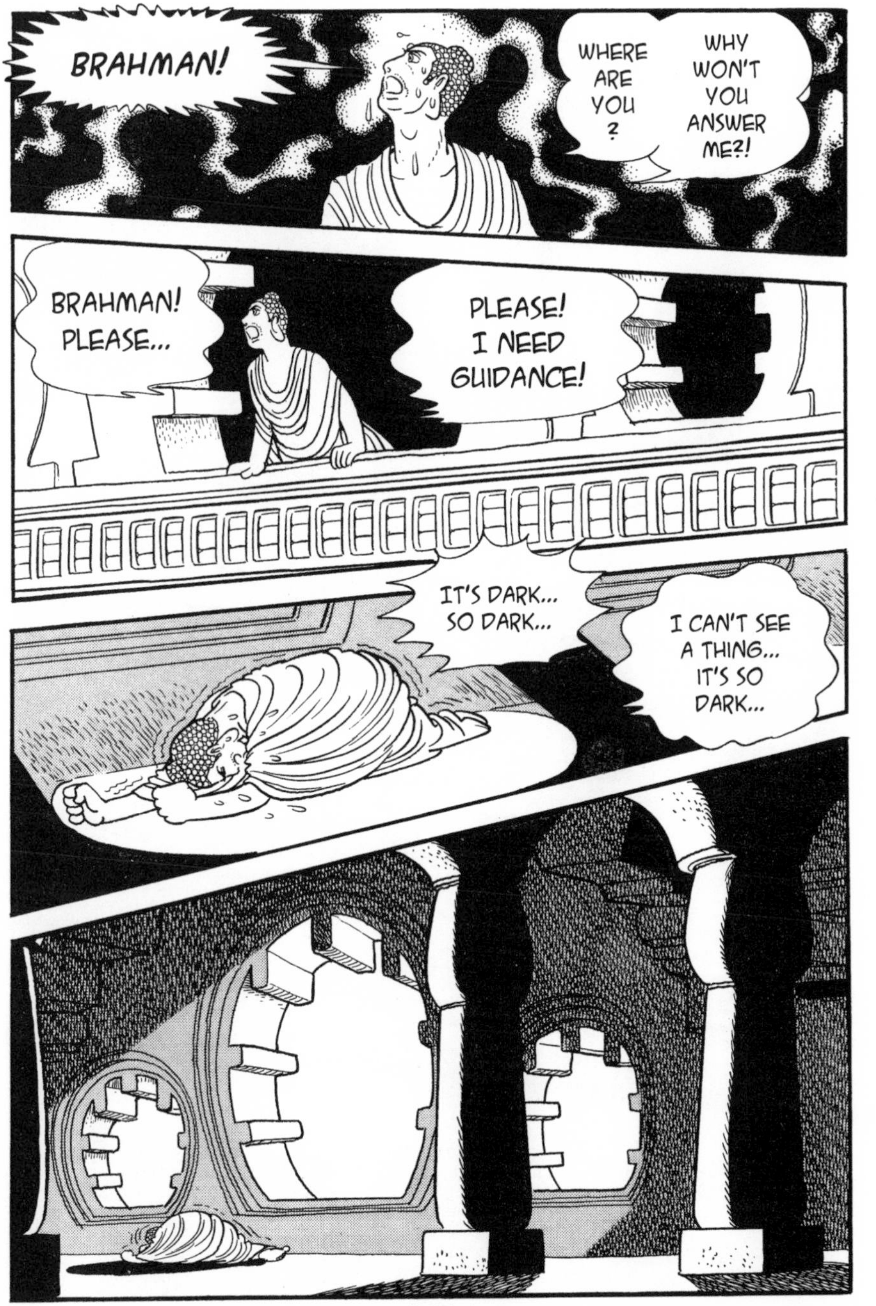
BRAHMAN!
WHERE ARE YOU?
WHY WON'T YOU ANSWER ME?!
BRAHMAN! PLEASE...
PLEASE! I NEED GUIDANCE!
IT'S DARK... SO DARK...
I CAN'T SEE A THING... IT'S SO DARK...

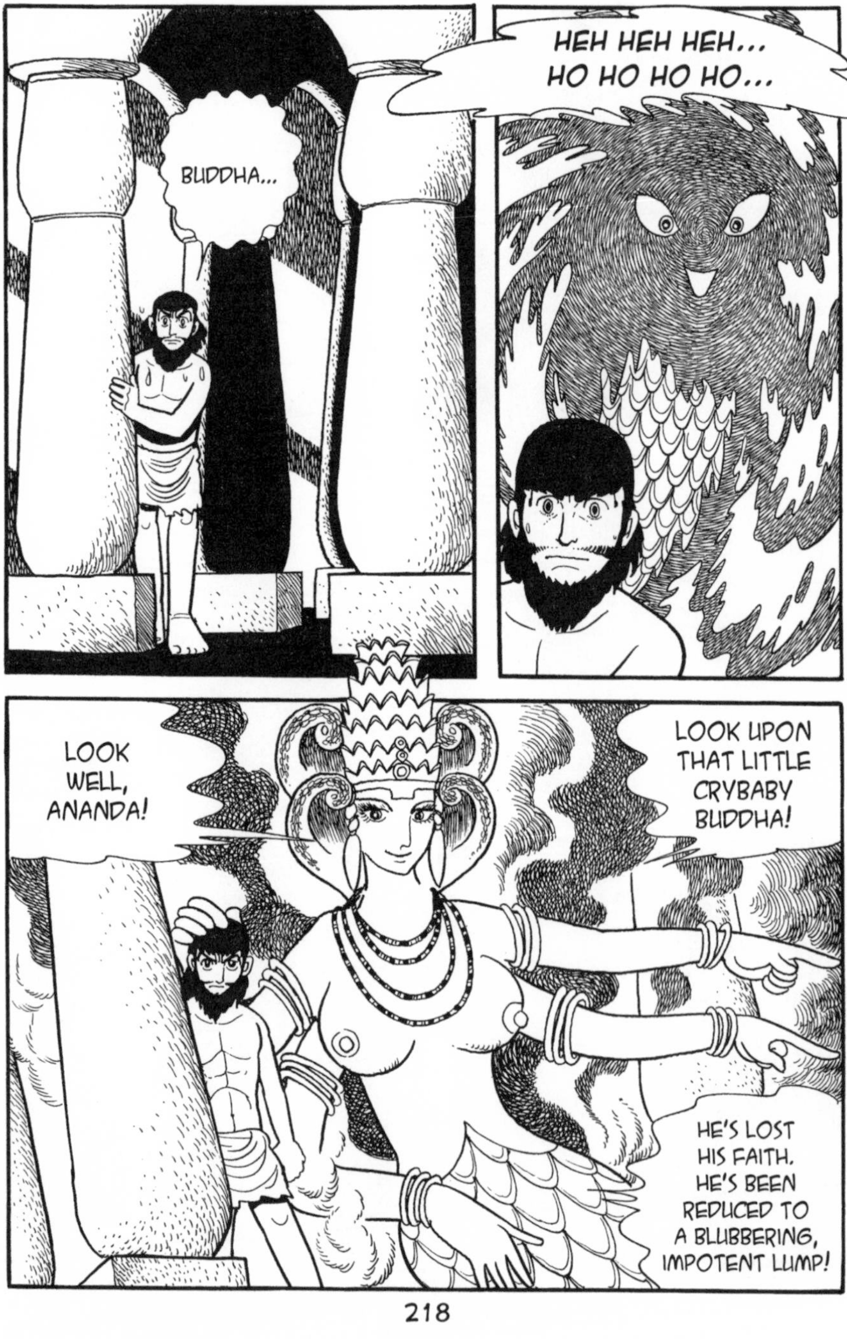
BUDDHA...
HEH HEH HEH... HO HO HO HO...
LOOK WELL, ANANDA!
LOOK UPON THAT LITTLE CRYBABY BUDDHA!
HE'S LOST HIS FAITH. HE'S BEEN REDUCED TO A BLUBBERING, IMPOTENT LUMP!

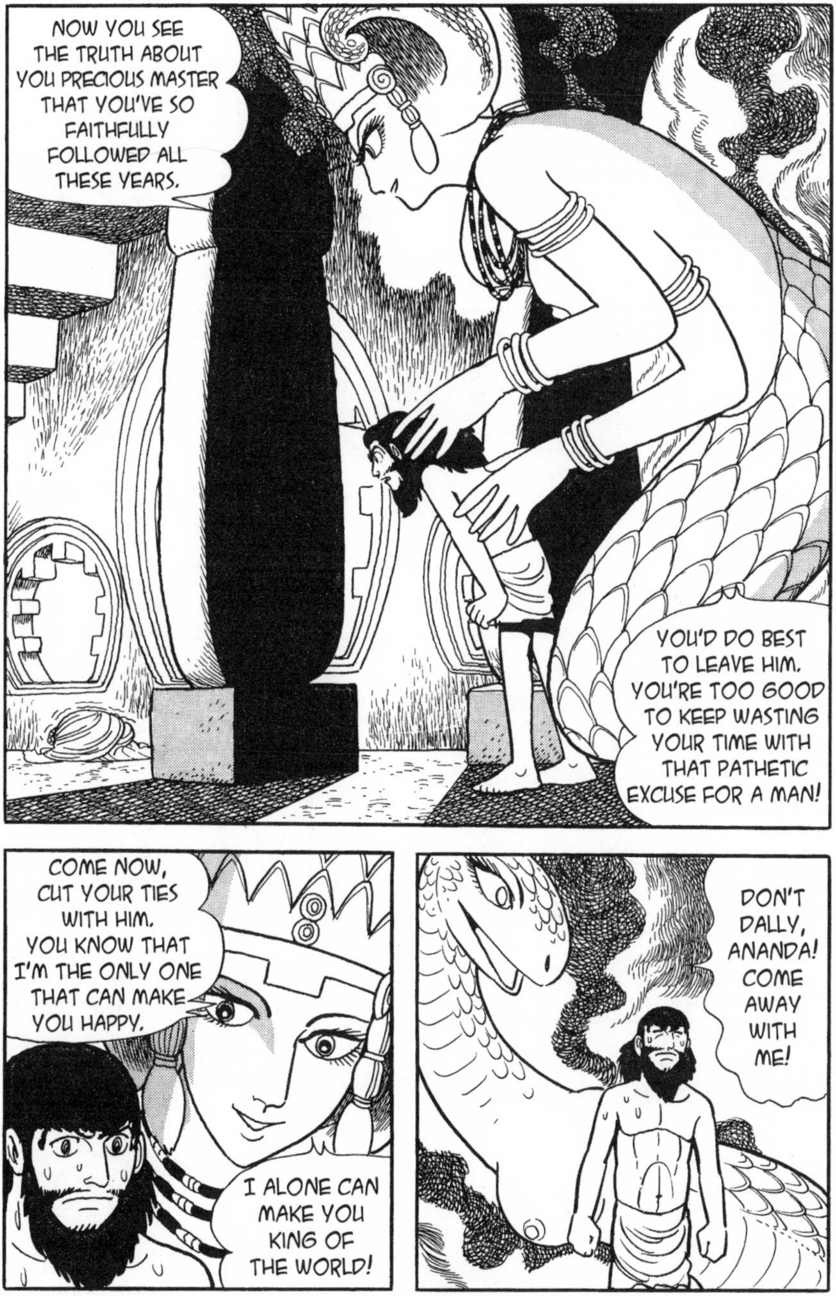
NOW YOU SEE THE TRUTH ABOUT YOU PRECIOUS MASTER THAT YOU'VE SO FAITHFULLY FOLLOWED ALL THESE YEARS.
YOU'D DO BEST TO LEAVE HIM. YOU'RE TOO GOOD TO KEEP WASTING YOUR TIME WITH THAT PATHETIC EXCUSE FOR A MAN!
COME NOW, CUT YOUR TIES WITH HIM. YOU KNOW THAT I'M THE ONLY ONE THAT CAN MAKE YOU HAPPY.
I ALONE CAN MAKE YOU KING OF THE WORLD!
DON'T DALLY, ANANDA! COME AWAY WITH ME!

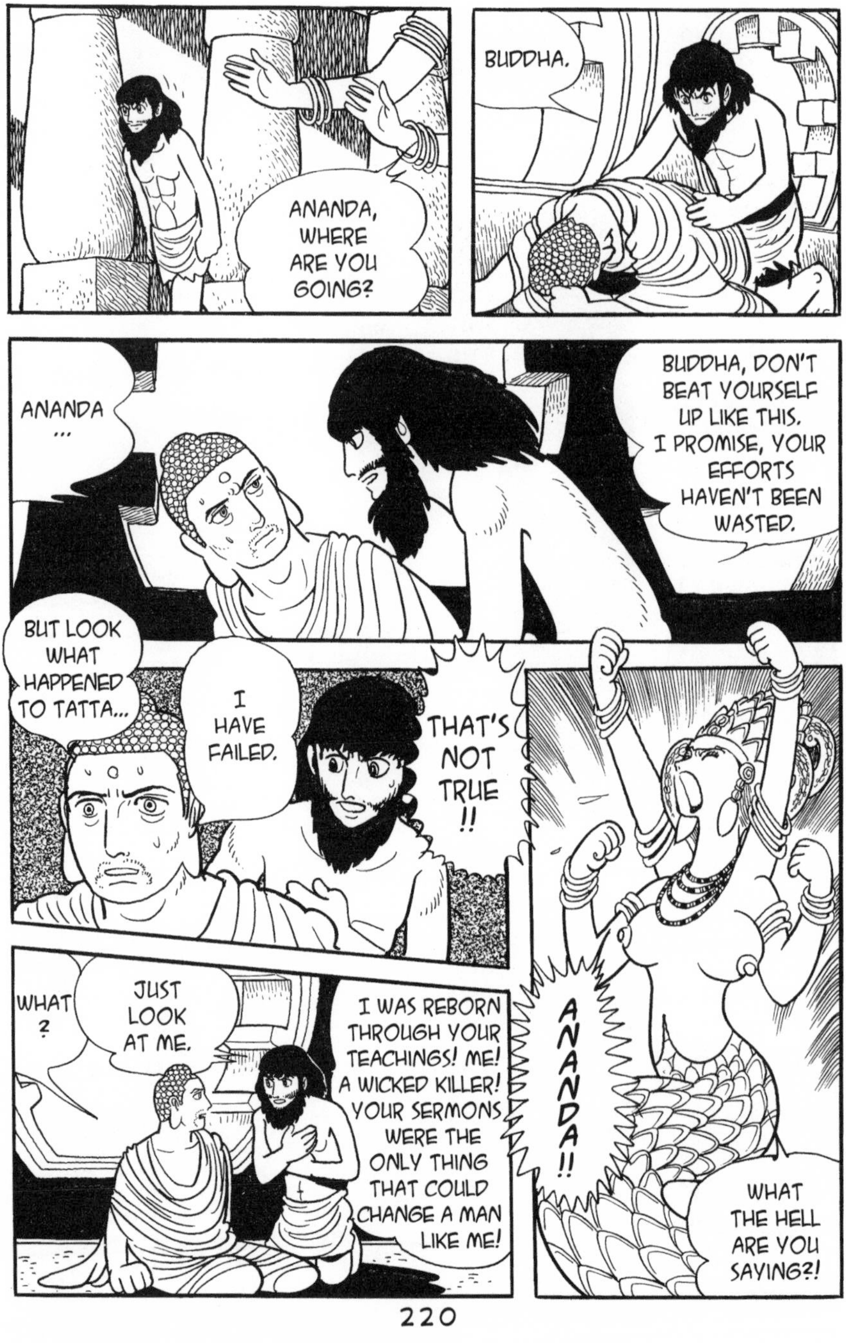

ANANDA, WHERE ARE YOU GOING?
BUDDHA.
ANANDA ...
BUDDHA, DON'T BEAT YOURSELF UP LIKE THIS. I PROMISE, YOUR EFFORTS HAVEN'T BEEN WASTED.
BUT LOOK WHAT HAPPENED TO TATTA...
I HAVE FAILED.
THAT'S NOT TRUE!!
WHAT?
JUST LOOK AT ME.
I WAS REBORN THROUGH YOUR TEACHINGS! ME! A WICKED KILLER! YOUR SERMONS WERE THE ONLY THING THAT COULD CHANGE A MAN LIKE ME!
ANANDA!!
WHAT THE HELL ARE YOU SAYING?!

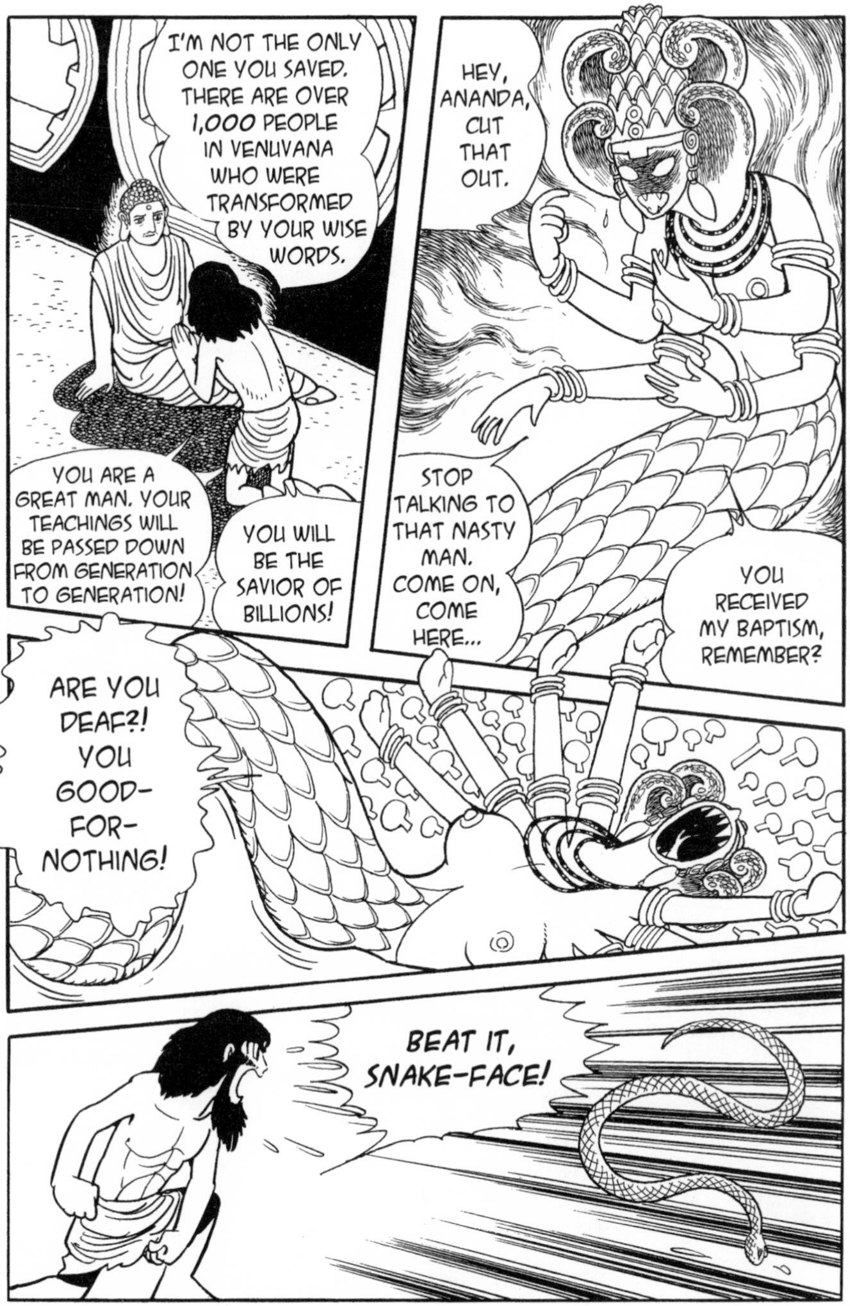
I'M NOT THE ONLY ONE YOU SAVED. THERE ARE OVER 1,000 PEOPLE IN VENUVANA WHO WERE TRANSFORMED BY YOUR WISE WORDS.
YOU ARE A GREAT MAN. YOUR TEACHINGS WILL BE PASSED DOWN FROM GENERATION TO GENERATION!
YOU WILL BE THE SAVIOR OF BILLIONS!
HEY, ANANDA, CUT THAT OUT.
STOP TALKING TO THAT NASTY MAN. COME ON, COME HERE...
YOU RECEIVED MY BAPTISM, REMEMBER?
ARE YOU DEAF?! YOU GOOD-FOR-NOTHING!
BEAT IT, SNAKE-FACE!

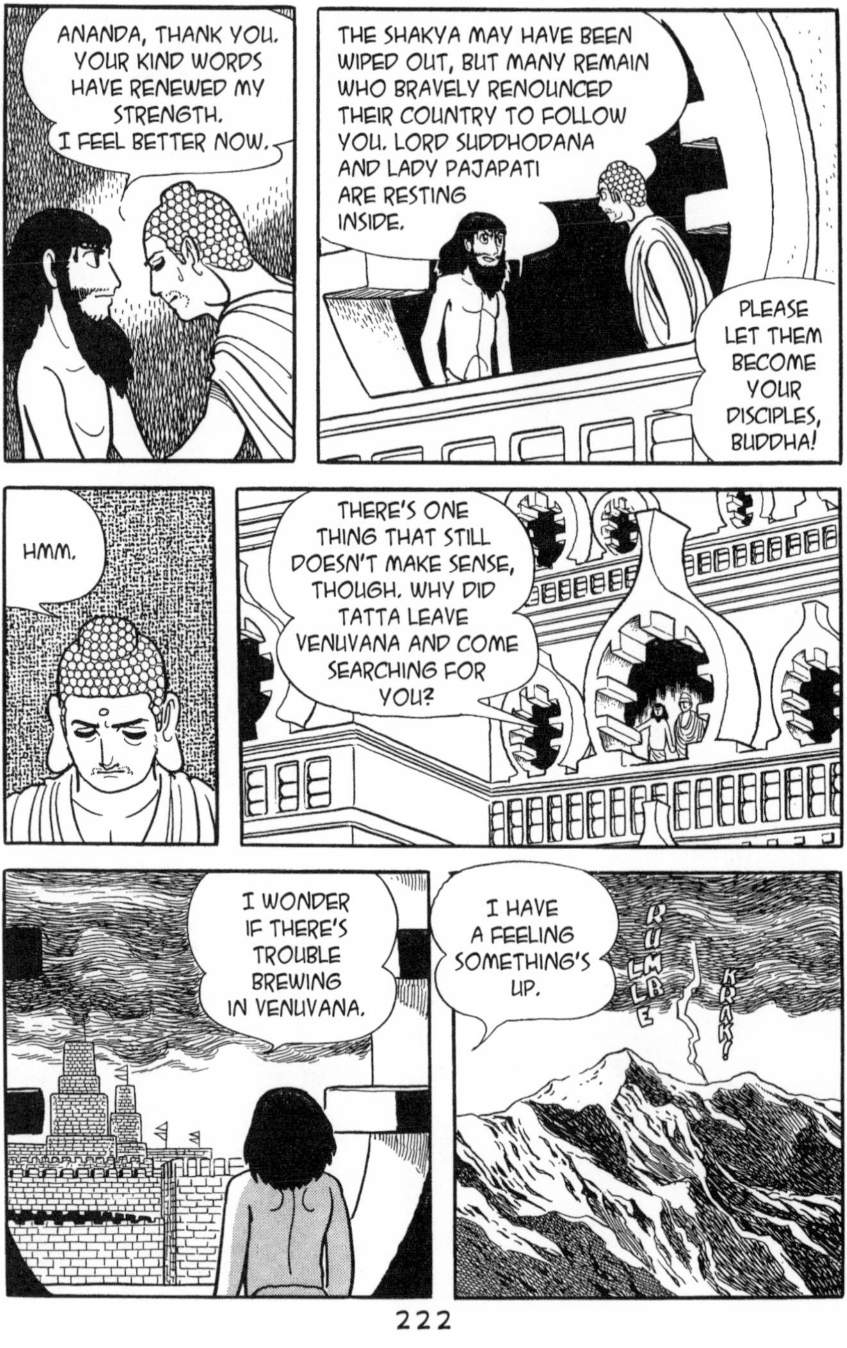
ANANDA, THANK YOU. YOUR KIND WORDS HAVE RENEWED MY STRENGTH. I FEEL BETTER NOW.
THE SHAKYA MAY HAVE BEEN WIPED OUT, BUT MANY REMAIN WHO BRAVELY RENOUNCED THEIR COUNTRY TO FOLLOW YOU. LORD SUDDHODANA AND LADY PAJAPATI ARE RESTING INSIDE.
PLEASE LET THEM BECOME YOUR DISCIPLES, BUDDHA!
HMM.
THERE'S ONE THING THAT STILL DOESN'T MAKE SENSE, THOUGH. WHY DID TATTA LEAVE VENUVANA AND COME SEARCHING FOR YOU?
I WONDER IF THERE'S TROUBLE BREWING IN VENUVANA.
I HAVE A FEELING SOMETHING'S UP.
RUMBLE
KRAK!

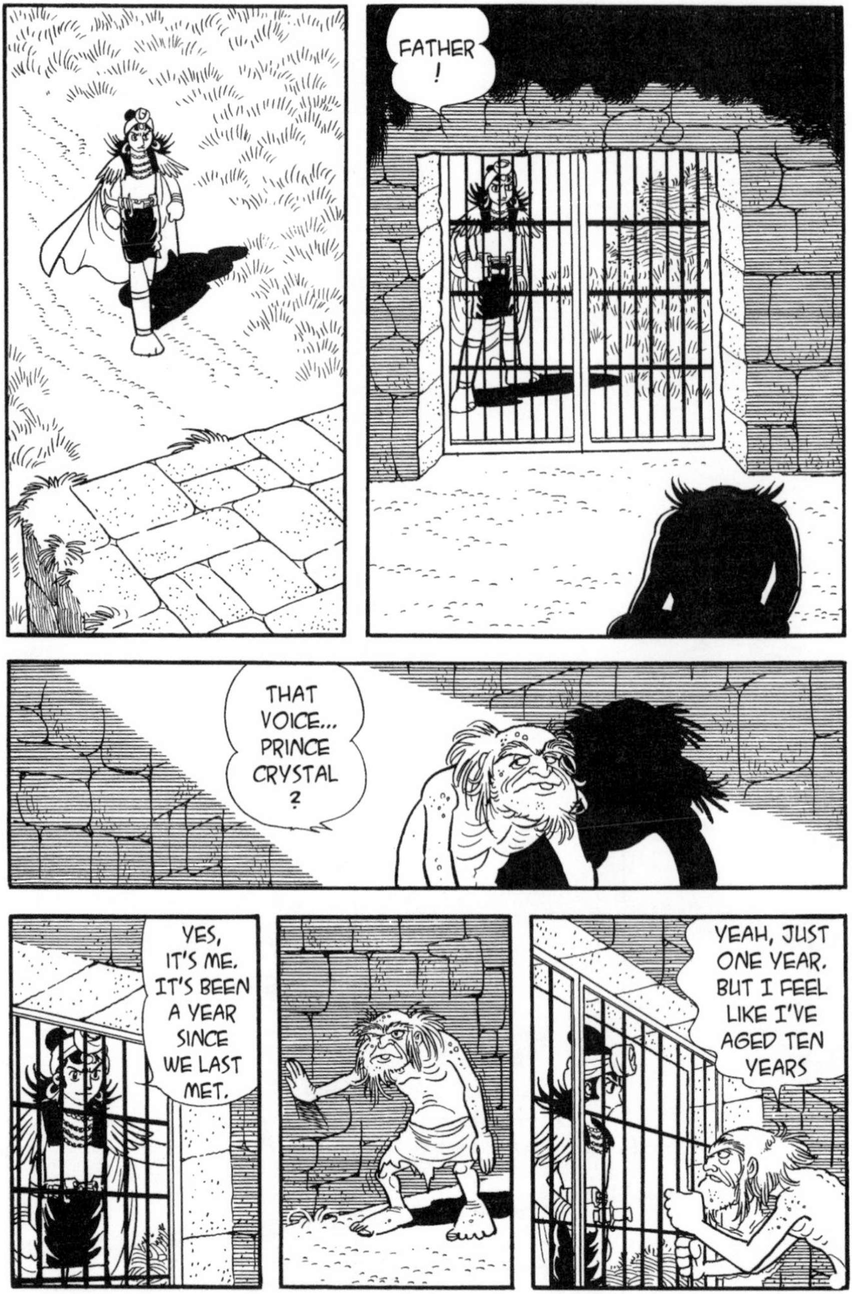
FATHER !
THAT VOICE... PRINCE CRYSTAL ?
YES, IT'S ME. IT'S BEEN A YEAR SINCE WE LAST MET.
YEAH, JUST ONE YEAR. BUT I FEEL LIKE I'VE AGED TEN YEARS

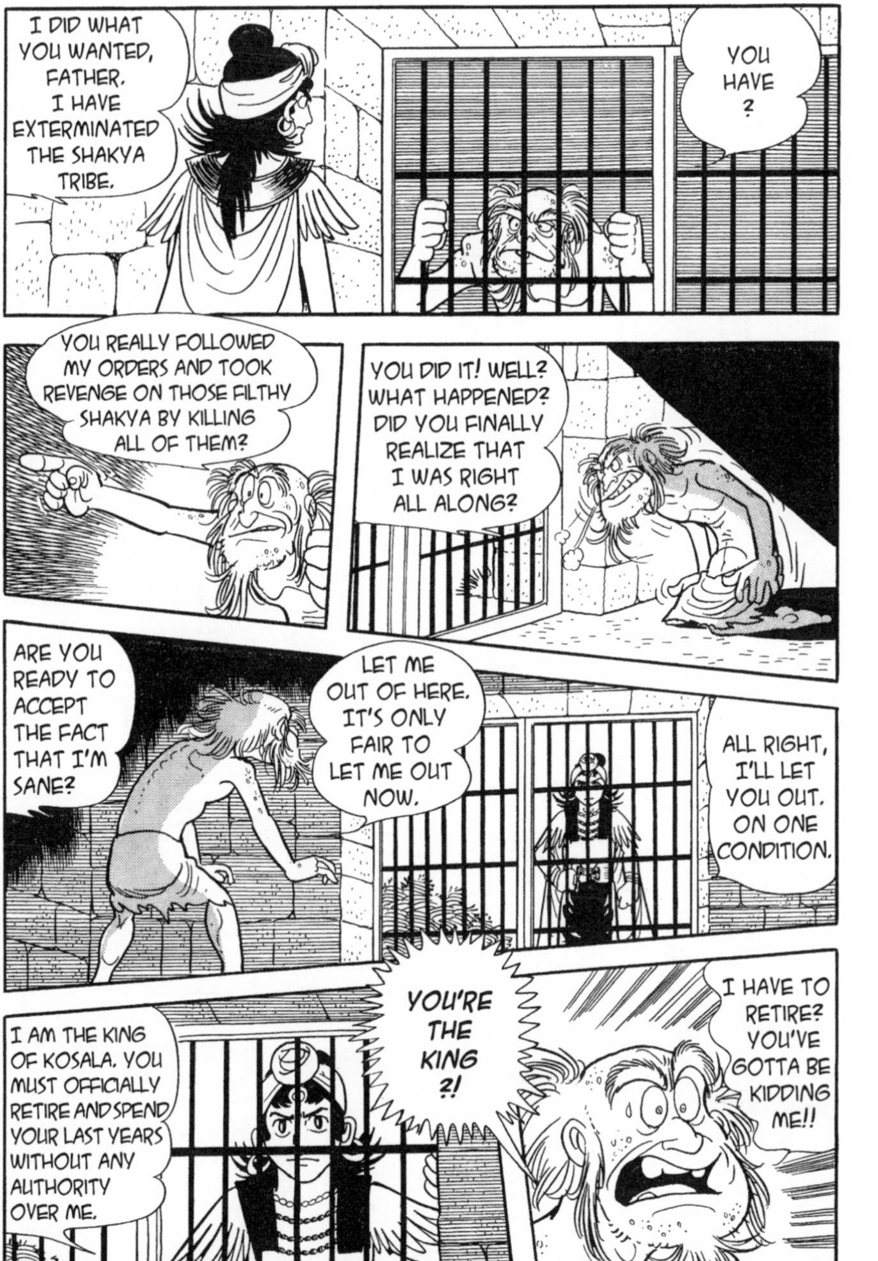
I DID WHAT YOU WANTED, FATHER. I HAVE EXTERMINATED THE SHAKYA TRIBE.
YOU HAVE ?
YOU REALLY FOLLOWED MY ORDERS AND TOOK REVENGE ON THOSE FILTHY SHAKYA BY KILLING ALL OF THEM?
YOU DID IT! WELL? WHAT HAPPENED? DID YOU FINALLY REALIZE THAT I WAS RIGHT ALL ALONG?
ARE YOU READY TO ACCEPT THE FACT THAT I'M SANE?
LET ME OUT OF HERE. IT'S ONLY FAIR TO LET ME OUT NOW.
ALL RIGHT, I'LL LET YOU OUT. ON ONE CONDITION.
I AM THE KING OF KOSALA. YOU MUST OFFICIALLY RETIRE AND SPEND YOUR LAST YEARS WITHOUT ANY AUTHORITY OVER ME.
YOU'RE THE KING ?!
I HAVE TO RETIRE? YOU'VE GOTTA BE KIDDING ME!!

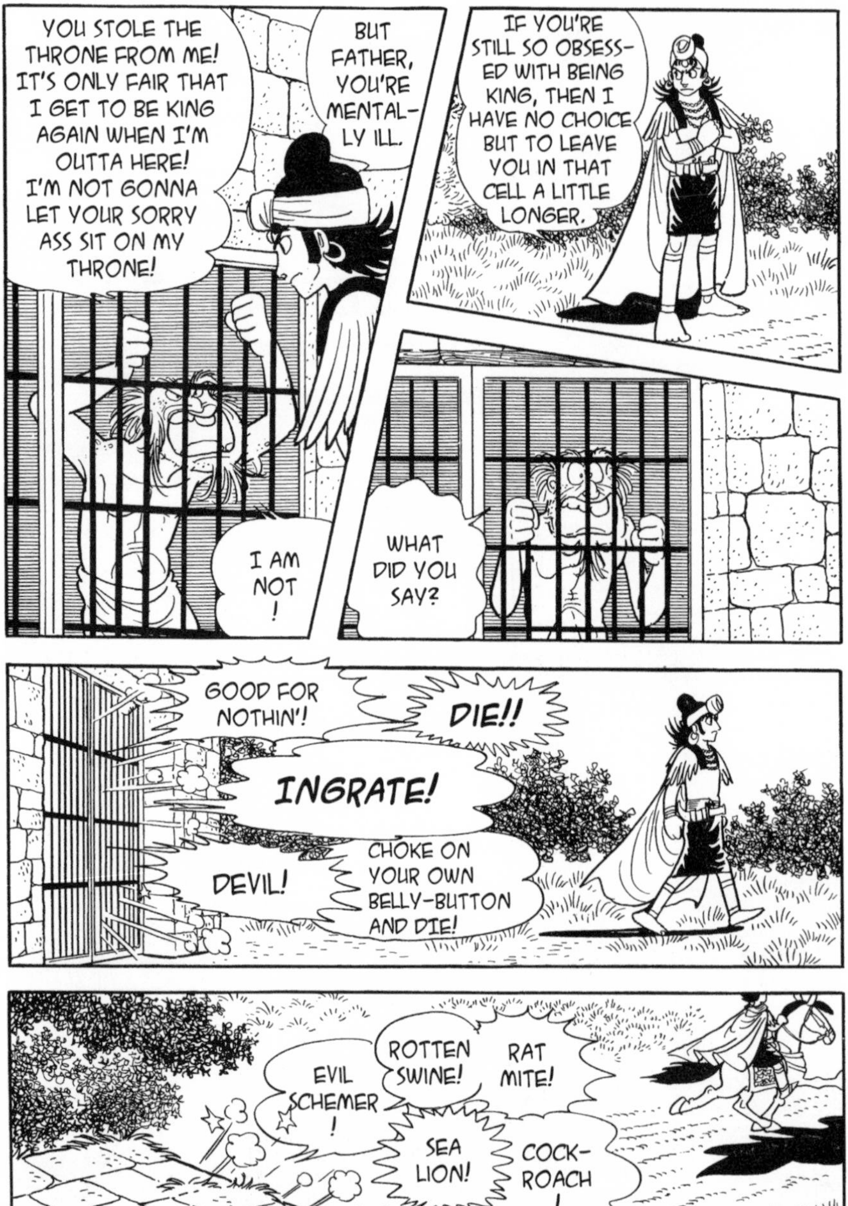
YOU STOLE THE THRONE FROM ME! IT'S ONLY FAIR THAT I GET TO BE KING AGAIN WHEN I'M OUTTA HERE! I'M NOT GONNA LET YOUR SORRY ASS SIT ON MY THRONE!
BUT FATHER, YOU'RE MENTAL-LY ILL.
I AM NOT!
IF YOU'RE STILL SO OBSESS-ED WITH BEING KING, THEN I HAVE NO CHOICE BUT TO LEAVE YOU IN THAT CELL A LITTLE LONGER.
WHAT DID YOU SAY?
GOOD FOR NOTHIN'!
DIE!!
INGRATE!
DEVIL!
CHOKE ON YOUR OWN BELLY-BUTTON AND DIE!
EVIL SCHEMER!
ROTTEN SWINE!
RAT MITE!
SEA LION!
COCK-ROACH!

LEMME OUT! YOU ROTTEN SON OF A WHORE!

SLAVE BRAT!

WAAAAH! I DON'T WANNA GIVE UP THE THRONE!!

I DON'T CARE IF IT TAKES YEARS, IF IT TAKES DECADES... I'LL FIND A WAY OUT OF THIS HELL-HOLE.

KING BIMBISARA OF MAGADHA WOULD TAKE MY SIDE. I'LL GET OUT OF HERE AND GO ASK FOR HIS HELP.

AND THEN...

I'LL HAVE HIM SEND HIS ARMY HERE AND HAVE HIM CAPTURE PRINCE CRYSTAL.

UNTIL THEN...

I'VE GOTTA STAY ALIVE. I WILL SIT ON THE THRONE ONCE MORE...

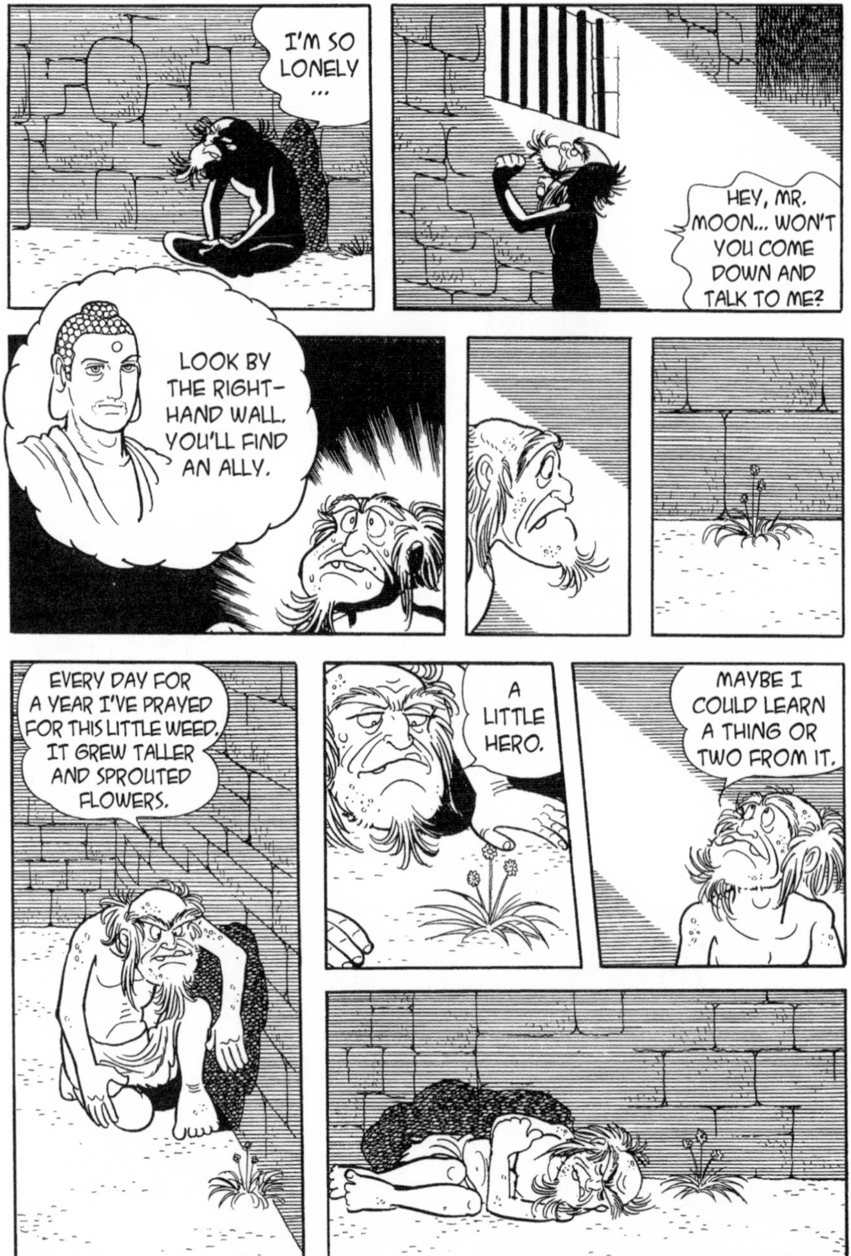
I'M SO LONELY ...
HEY, MR. MOON... WON'T YOU COME DOWN AND TALK TO ME?
LOOK BY THE RIGHT-HAND WALL. YOU'LL FIND AN ALLY.
EVERY DAY FOR A YEAR I'VE PRAYED FOR THIS LITTLE WEED. IT GREW TALLER AND SPROUTED FLOWERS.
A LITTLE HERO.
MAYBE I COULD LEARN A THING OR TWO FROM IT.

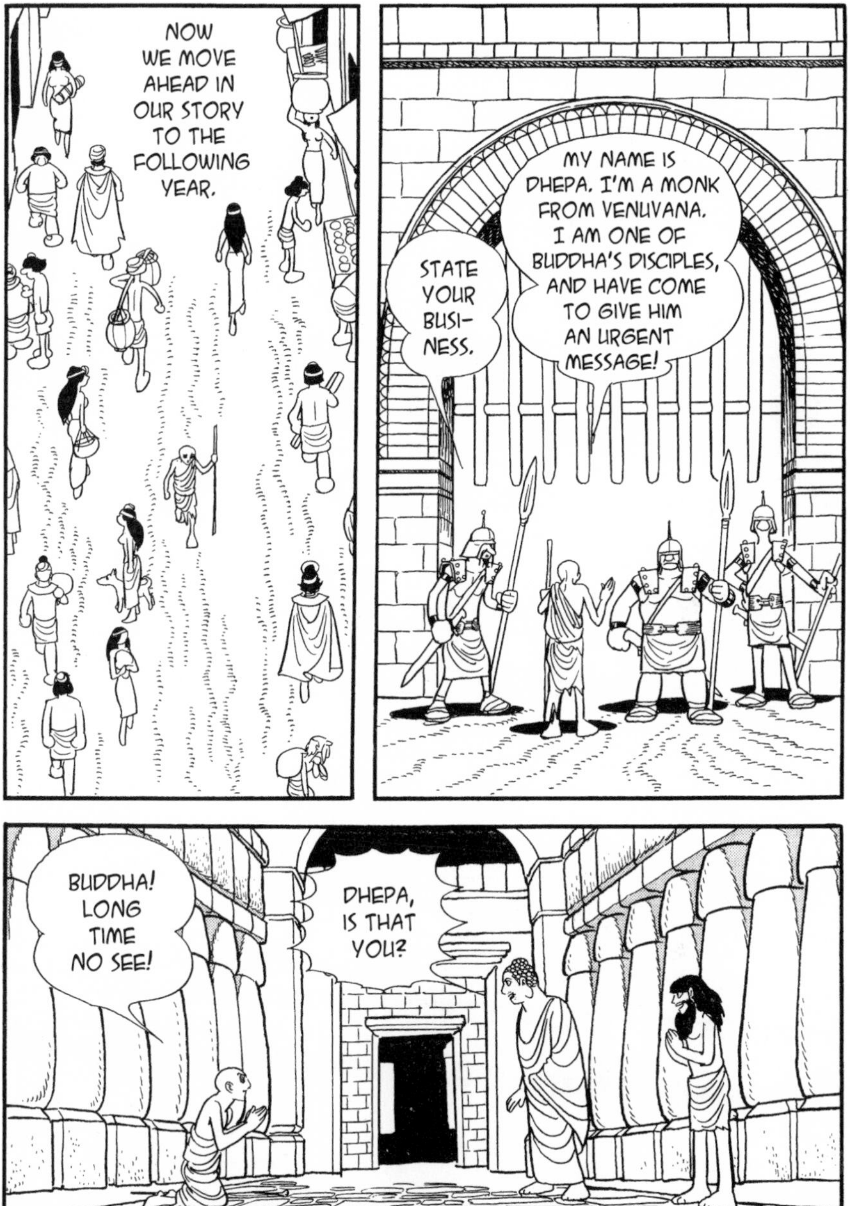
NOW WE MOVE AHEAD IN OUR STORY TO THE FOLLOWING YEAR.
STATE YOUR BUSI-NESS.
MY NAME IS DHEPA. I'M A MONK FROM VENUVANA. I AM ONE OF BUDDHA'S DISCIPLES, AND HAVE COME TO GIVE HIM AN URGENT MESSAGE!
BUDDHA! LONG TIME NO SEE!
DHEPA, IS THAT YOU?

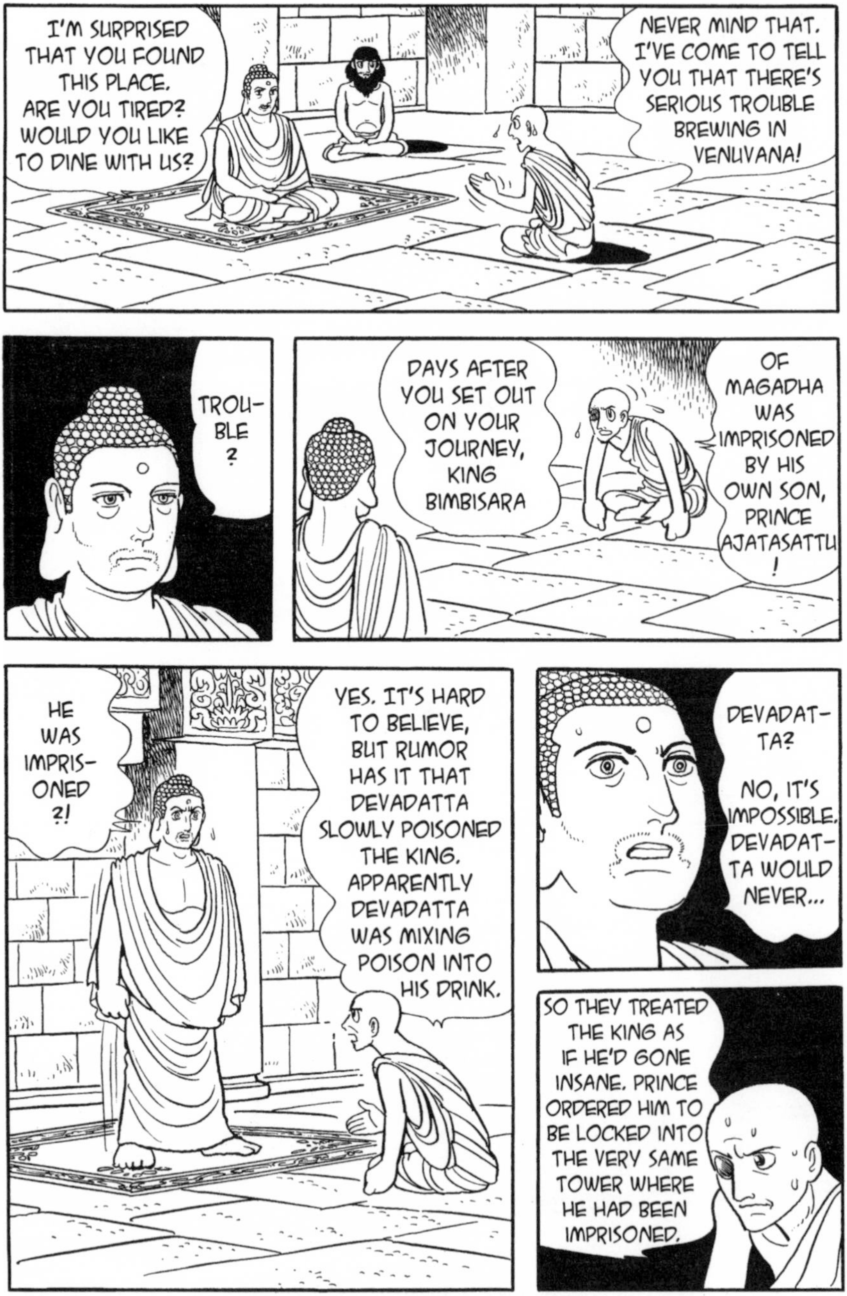
I'M SURPRISED THAT YOU FOUND THIS PLACE. ARE YOU TIRED? WOULD YOU LIKE TO DINE WITH US?
NEVER MIND THAT. I'VE COME TO TELL YOU THAT THERE'S SERIOUS TROUBLE BREWING IN VENUVANA!
TROU-BLE?
DAYS AFTER YOU SET OUT ON YOUR JOURNEY, KING BIMBISARA
OF MAGADHA WAS IMPRISONED BY HIS OWN SON, PRINCE AJATASATTU!
HE WAS IMPRIS-ONED?!
YES. IT'S HARD TO BELIEVE, BUT RUMOR HAS IT THAT DEVADATTA SLOWLY POISONED THE KING. APPARENTLY DEVADATTA WAS MIXING POISON INTO HIS DRINK.
DEVADAT-TA?
NO, IT'S IMPOSSIBLE. DEVADAT-TA WOULD NEVER...
SO THEY TREATED THE KING AS IF HE'D GONE INSANE. PRINCE ORDERED HIM TO BE LOCKED INTO THE VERY SAME TOWER WHERE HE HAD BEEN IMPRISONED.

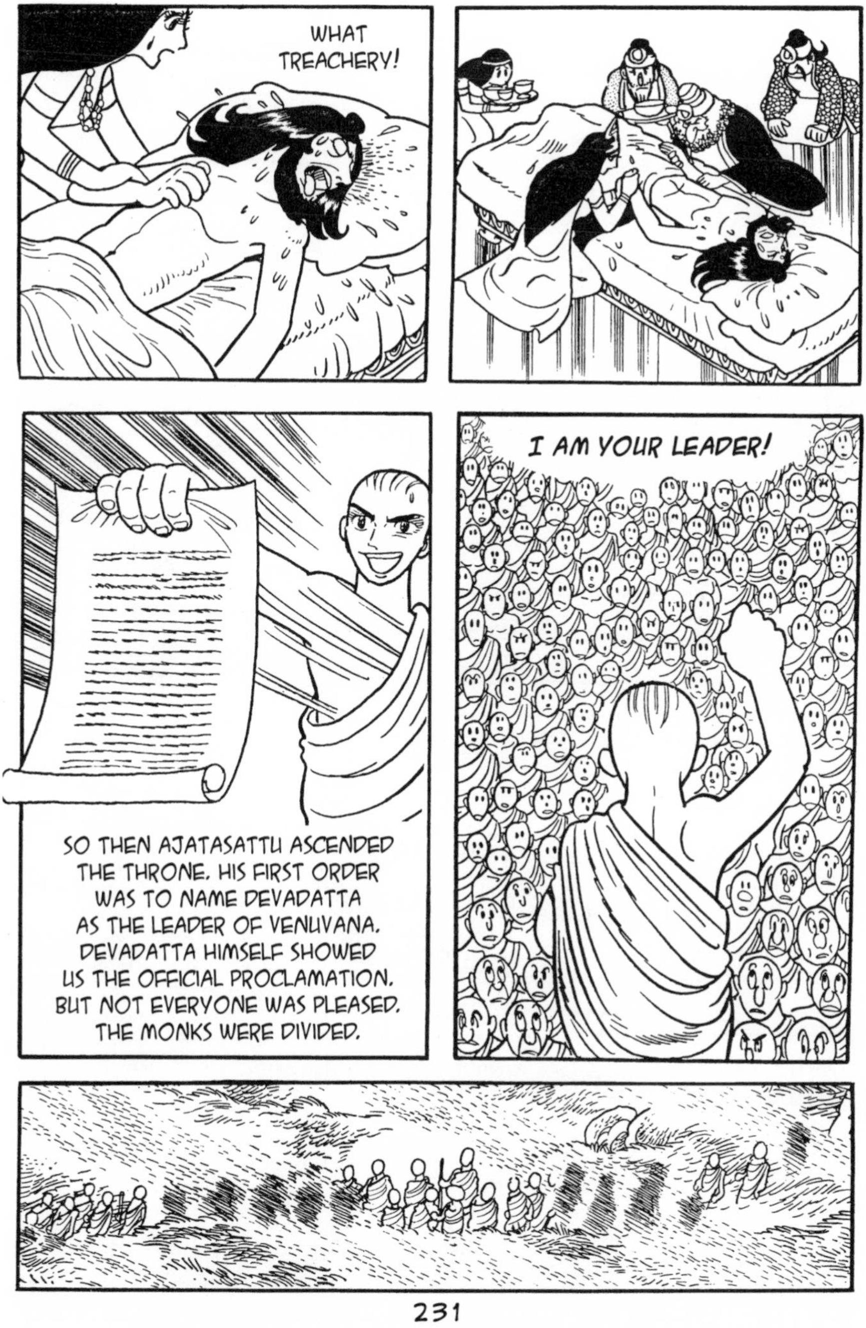
WHAT TREACHERY!
SO THEN AJATASATTU ASCENDED THE THRONE. HIS FIRST ORDER WAS TO NAME DEVADATTA AS THE LEADER OF VENUVANA. DEVADATTA HIMSELF SHOWED US THE OFFICIAL PROCLAMATION. BUT NOT EVERYONE WAS PLEASED. THE MONKS WERE DIVIDED.
I AM YOUR LEADER!

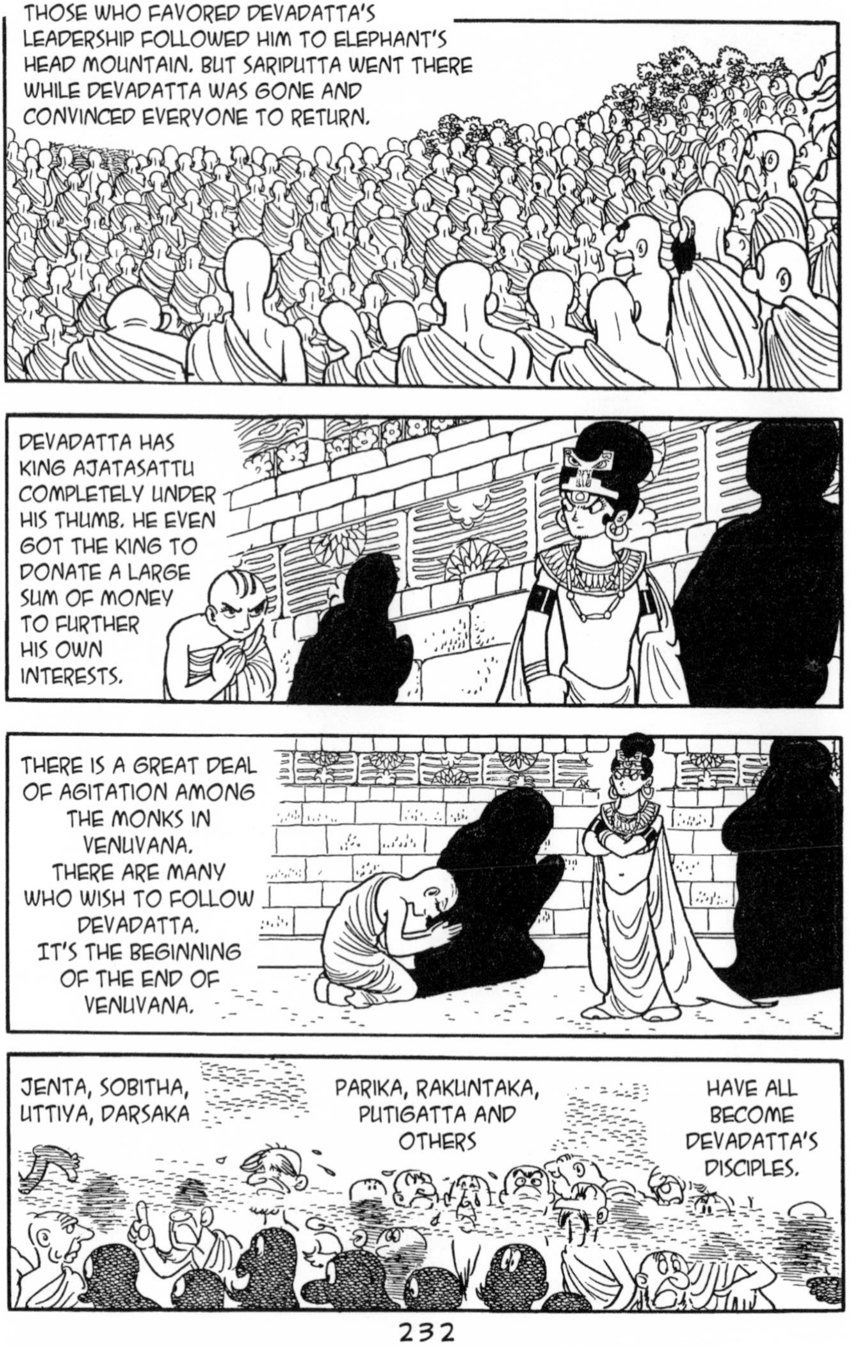
THOSE WHO FAVORED DEVADATTA'S LEADERSHIP FOLLOWED HIM TO ELEPHANT'S HEAD MOUNTAIN. BUT SARIPUTTA WENT THERE WHILE DEVADATTA WAS GONE AND CONVINCED EVERYONE TO RETURN.
DEVADATTA HAS KING AJATASATTU COMPLETELY UNDER HIS THUMB. HE EVEN GOT THE KING TO DONATE A LARGE SUM OF MONEY TO FURTHER HIS OWN INTERESTS.
THERE IS A GREAT DEAL OF AGITATION AMONG THE MONKS IN VENUVANA.
THERE ARE MANY WHO WISH TO FOLLOW DEVADATTA.
IT'S THE BEGINNING OF THE END OF VENUVANA.
JENTA, SOBITHA, UTTIYA, DARSAKA
PARIKA, RAKUNTAKA, PUTIGATTA AND OTHERS
HAVE ALL BECOME DEVADATTA'S DISCIPLES.

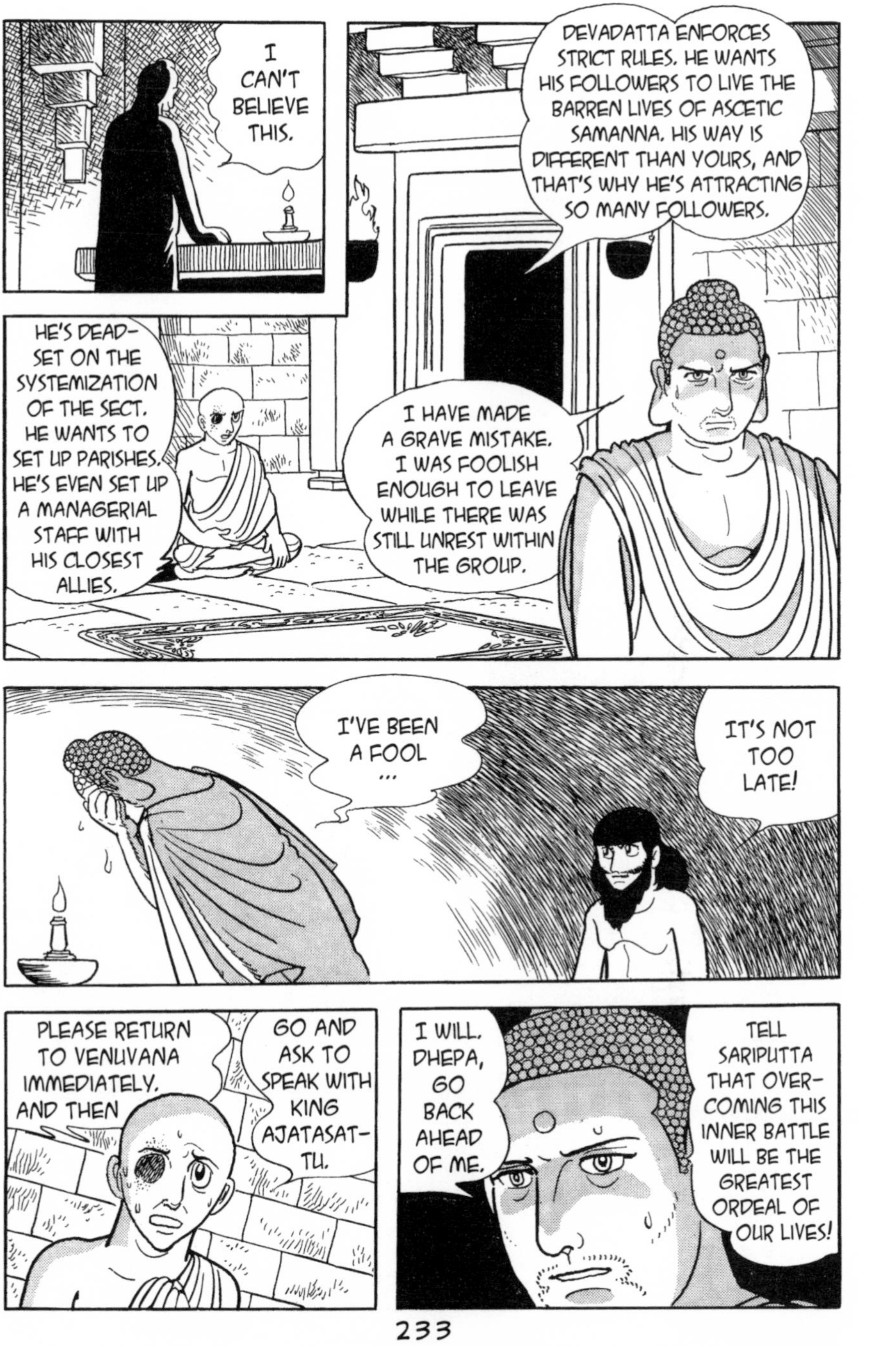
I CAN'T BELIEVE THIS.
DEVADATTA ENFORCES STRICT RULES. HE WANTS HIS FOLLOWERS TO LIVE THE BARREN LIVES OF ASCETIC SAMANNA. HIS WAY IS DIFFERENT THAN YOURS, AND THAT'S WHY HE'S ATTRACTING SO MANY FOLLOWERS.
HE'S DEAD-SET ON THE SYSTEMIZATION OF THE SECT. HE WANTS TO SET UP PARISHES. HE'S EVEN SET UP A MANAGERIAL STAFF WITH HIS CLOSEST ALLIES.
I HAVE MADE A GRAVE MISTAKE. I WAS FOOLISH ENOUGH TO LEAVE WHILE THERE WAS STILL UNREST WITHIN THE GROUP.
I'VE BEEN A FOOL ...
IT'S NOT TOO LATE!
PLEASE RETURN TO VENUVANA IMMEDIATELY. AND THEN
GO AND ASK TO SPEAK WITH KING AJATASAT-TU.
I WILL. DHEPA, GO BACK AHEAD OF ME.
TELL SARIPUTTA THAT OVER-COMING THIS INNER BATTLE WILL BE THE GREATEST ORDEAL OF OUR LIVES!

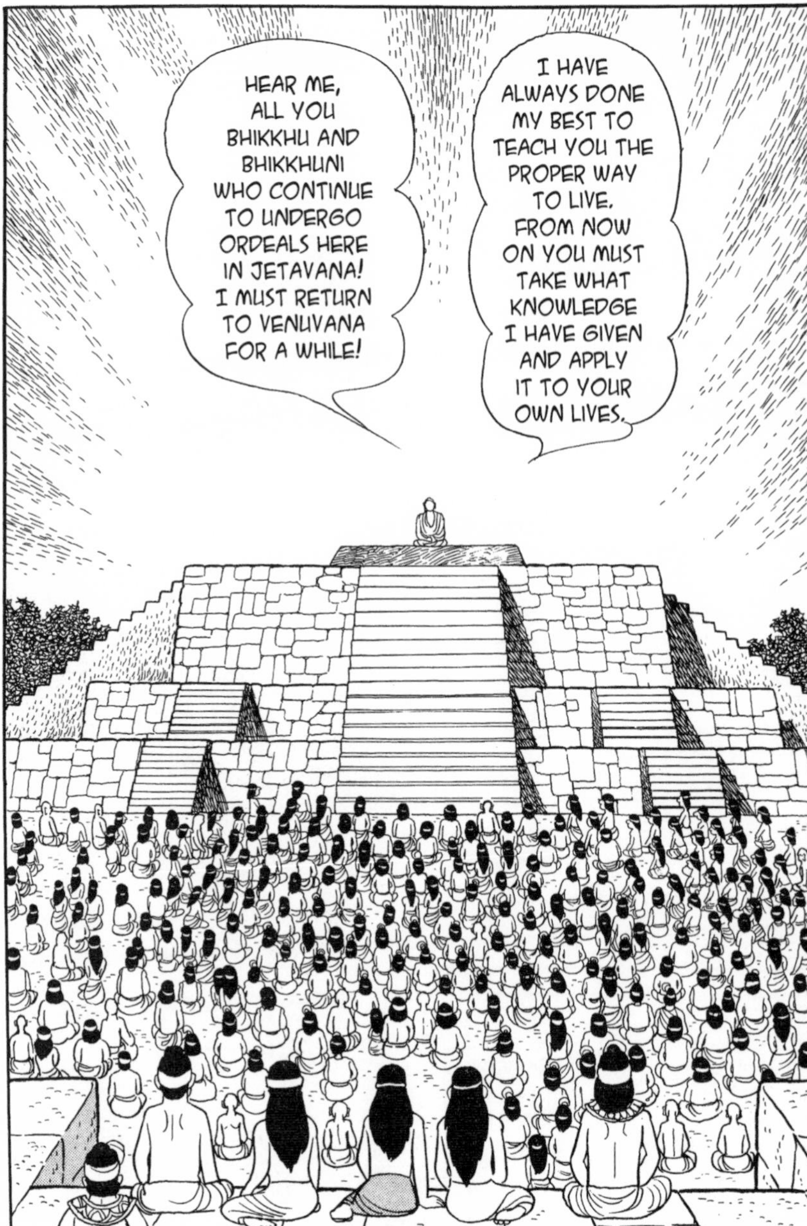
HEAR ME, ALL YOU BHIKKHU AND BHIKKHUNI WHO CONTINUE TO UNDERGO ORDEALS HERE IN JETAVANA! I MUST RETURN TO VENUVANA FOR A WHILE!
I HAVE ALWAYS DONE MY BEST TO TEACH YOU THE PROPER WAY TO LIVE. FROM NOW ON YOU MUST TAKE WHAT KNOWLEDGE I HAVE GIVEN AND APPLY IT TO YOUR OWN LIVES.

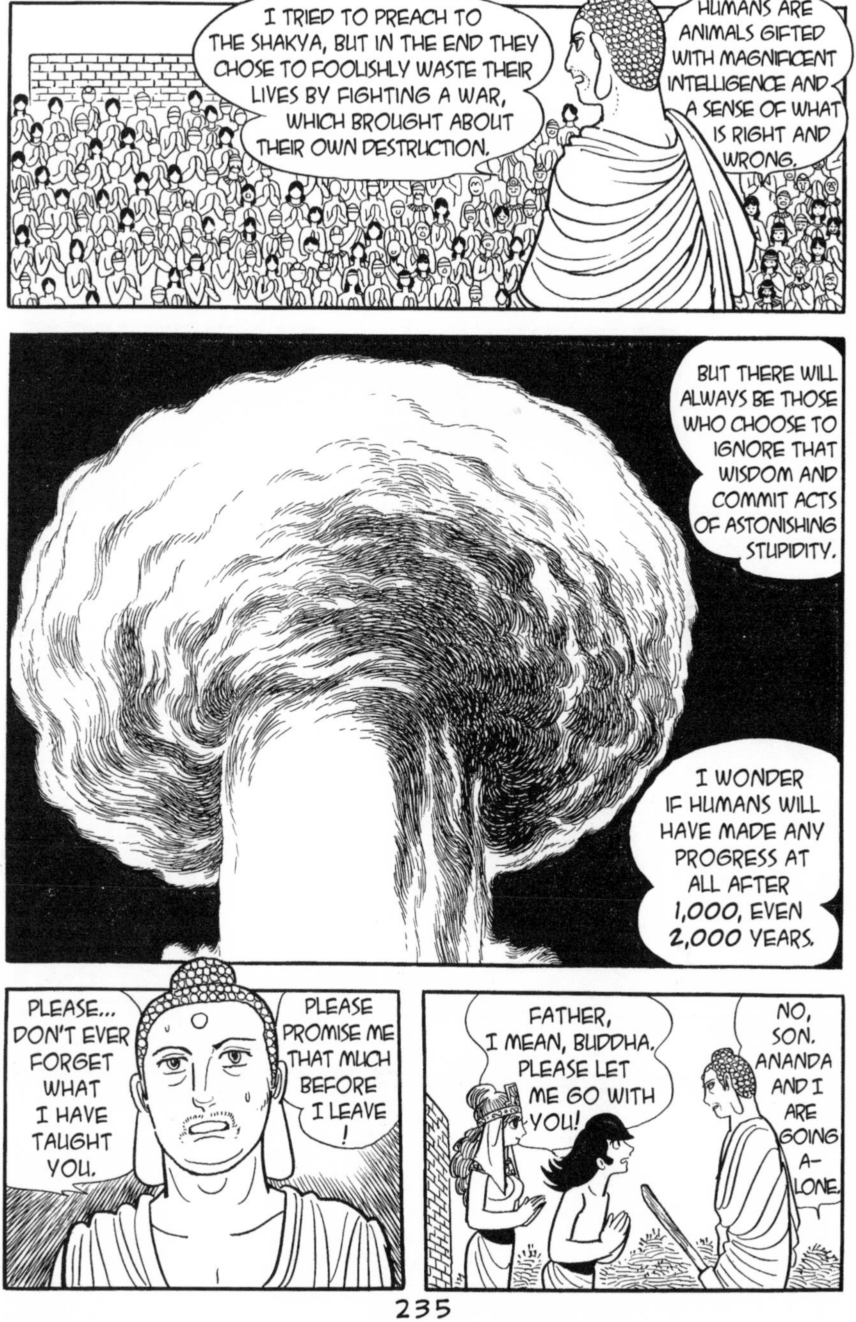

I TRIED TO PREACH TO THE SHAKYA, BUT IN THE END THEY CHOSE TO FOOLISHLY WASTE THEIR LIVES BY FIGHTING A WAR, WHICH BROUGHT ABOUT THEIR OWN DESTRUCTION.
HUMANS ARE ANIMALS GIFTED WITH MAGNIFICENT INTELLIGENCE AND A SENSE OF WHAT IS RIGHT AND WRONG.
BUT THERE WILL ALWAYS BE THOSE WHO CHOOSE TO IGNORE THAT WISDOM AND COMMIT ACTS OF ASTONISHING STUPIDITY.
I WONDER IF HUMANS WILL HAVE MADE ANY PROGRESS AT ALL AFTER 1,000, EVEN 2,000 YEARS.
PLEASE... DON'T EVER FORGET WHAT I HAVE TAUGHT YOU.
PLEASE PROMISE ME THAT MUCH BEFORE I LEAVE!
FATHER, I MEAN, BUDDHA. PLEASE LET ME GO WITH YOU!
NO, SON. ANANDA AND I ARE GOING A-LONE.

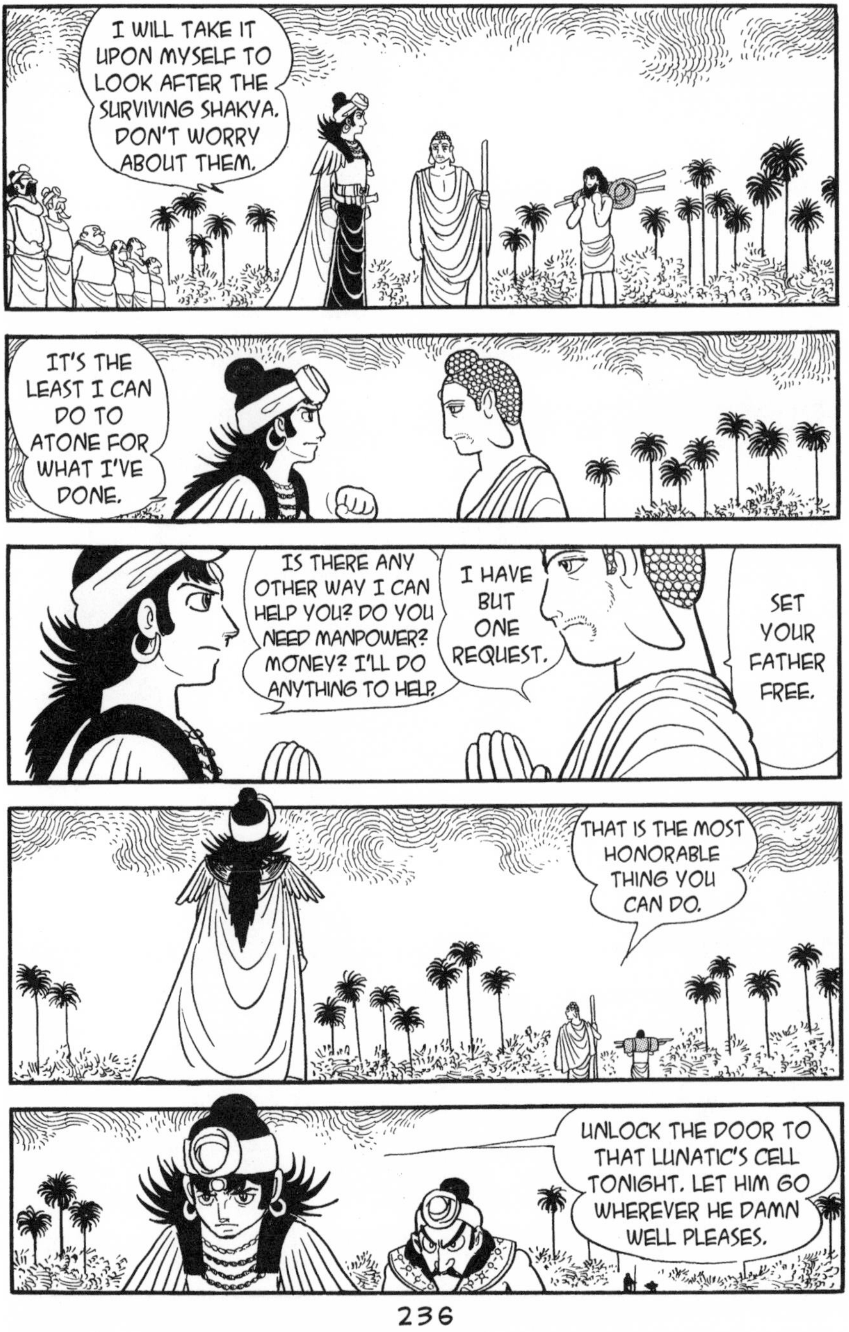
I WILL TAKE IT UPON MYSELF TO LOOK AFTER THE SURVIVING SHAKYA. DON'T WORRY ABOUT THEM.
IT'S THE LEAST I CAN DO TO ATONE FOR WHAT I'VE DONE.
IS THERE ANY OTHER WAY I CAN HELP YOU? DO YOU NEED MANPOWER? MONEY? I'LL DO ANYTHING TO HELP.
I HAVE BUT ONE REQUEST.
SET YOUR FATHER FREE.
THAT IS THE MOST HONORABLE THING YOU CAN DO.
UNLOCK THE DOOR TO THAT LUNATIC'S CELL TONIGHT. LET HIM GO WHEREVER HE DAMN WELL PLEASES.

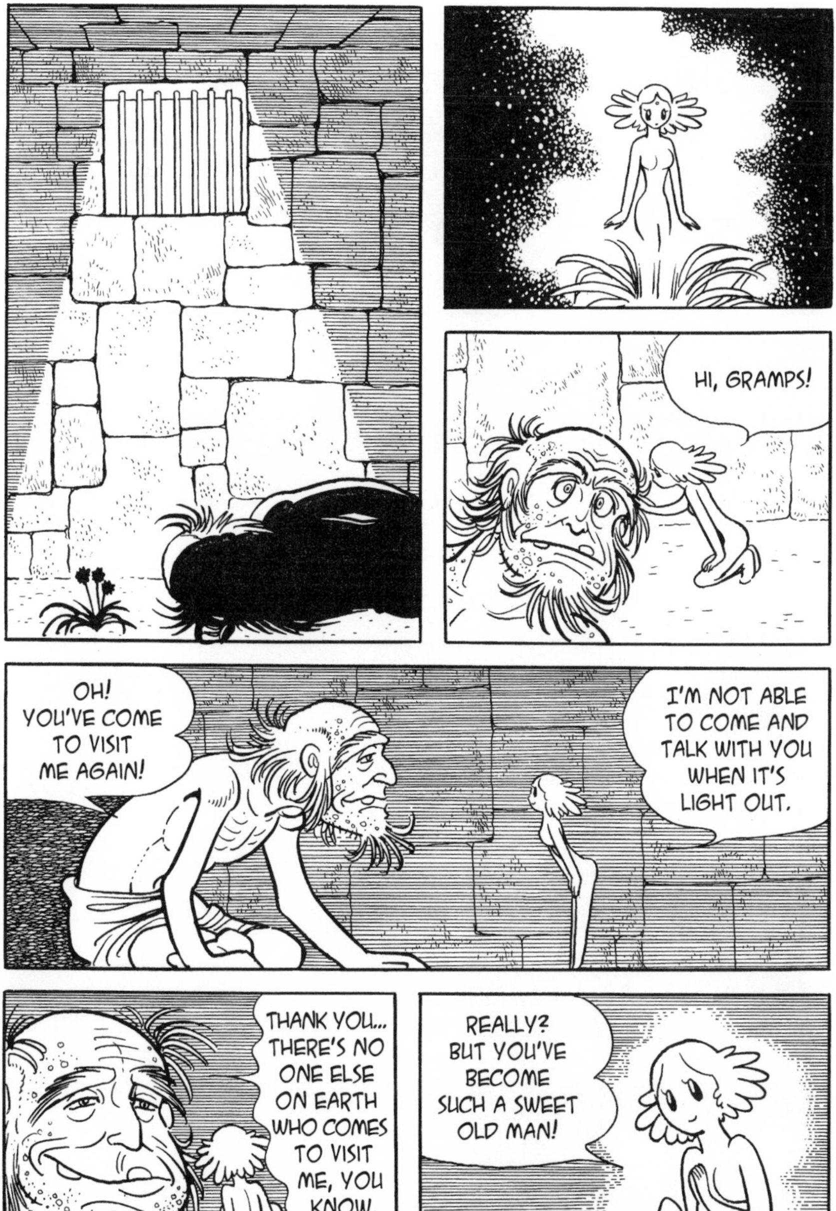
HI, GRAMPS!
OH! YOU'VE COME TO VISIT ME AGAIN!
I'M NOT ABLE TO COME AND TALK WITH YOU WHEN IT'S LIGHT OUT.
THANK YOU... THERE'S NO ONE ELSE ON EARTH WHO COMES TO VISIT ME, YOU KNOW.
REALLY? BUT YOU'VE BECOME SUCH A SWEET OLD MAN!

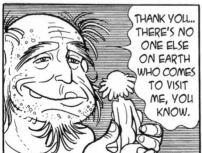

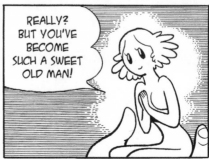

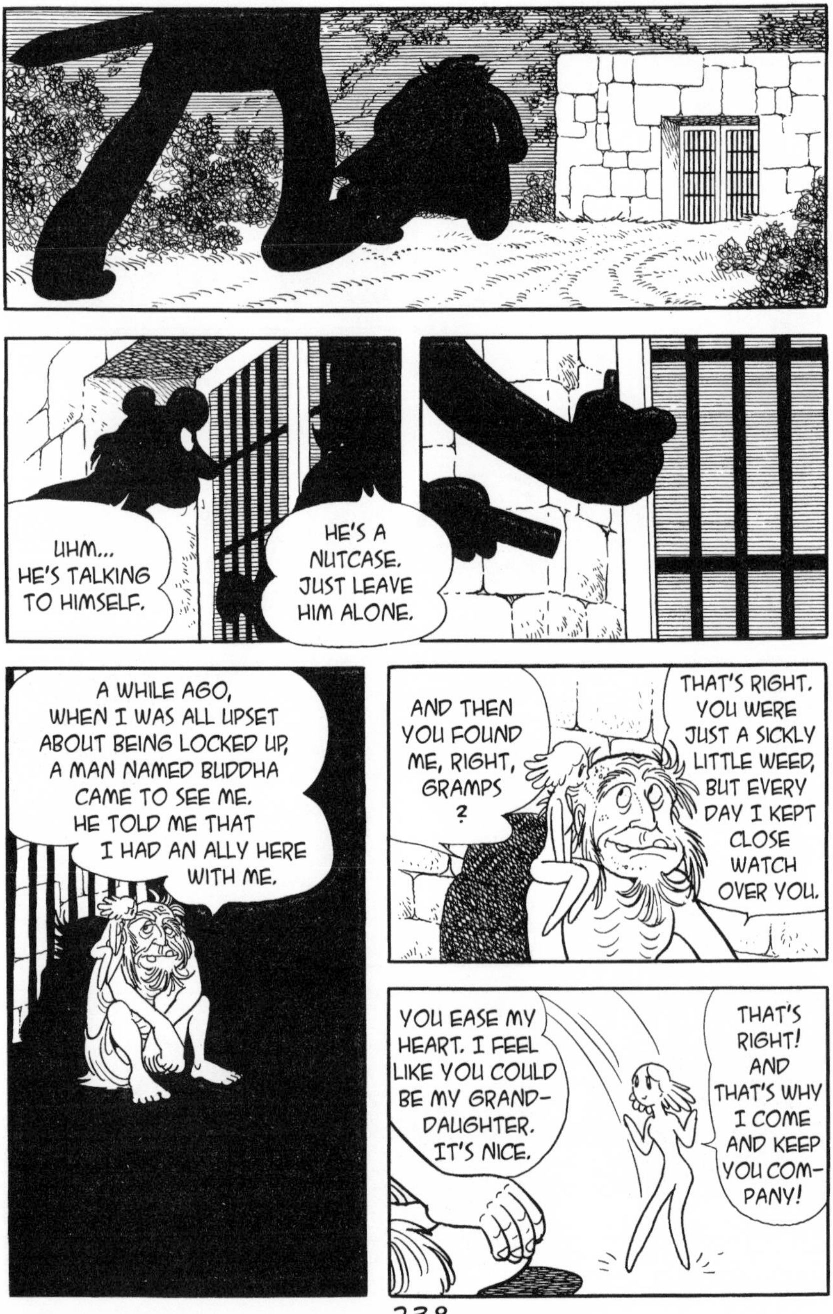
UHM... HE'S TALKING TO HIMSELF.
HE'S A NUTCASE. JUST LEAVE HIM ALONE.
A WHILE AGO, WHEN I WAS ALL UPSET ABOUT BEING LOCKED UP, A MAN NAMED BUDDHA CAME TO SEE ME. HE TOLD ME THAT I HAD AN ALLY HERE WITH ME.
AND THEN YOU FOUND ME, RIGHT, GRAMPS?
THAT'S RIGHT. YOU WERE JUST A SICKLY LITTLE WEED, BUT EVERY DAY I KEPT CLOSE WATCH OVER YOU.
YOU EASE MY HEART. I FEEL LIKE YOU COULD BE MY GRAND-DAUGHTER. IT'S NICE.
THAT'S RIGHT! AND THAT'S WHY I COME AND KEEP YOU COM-PANY!

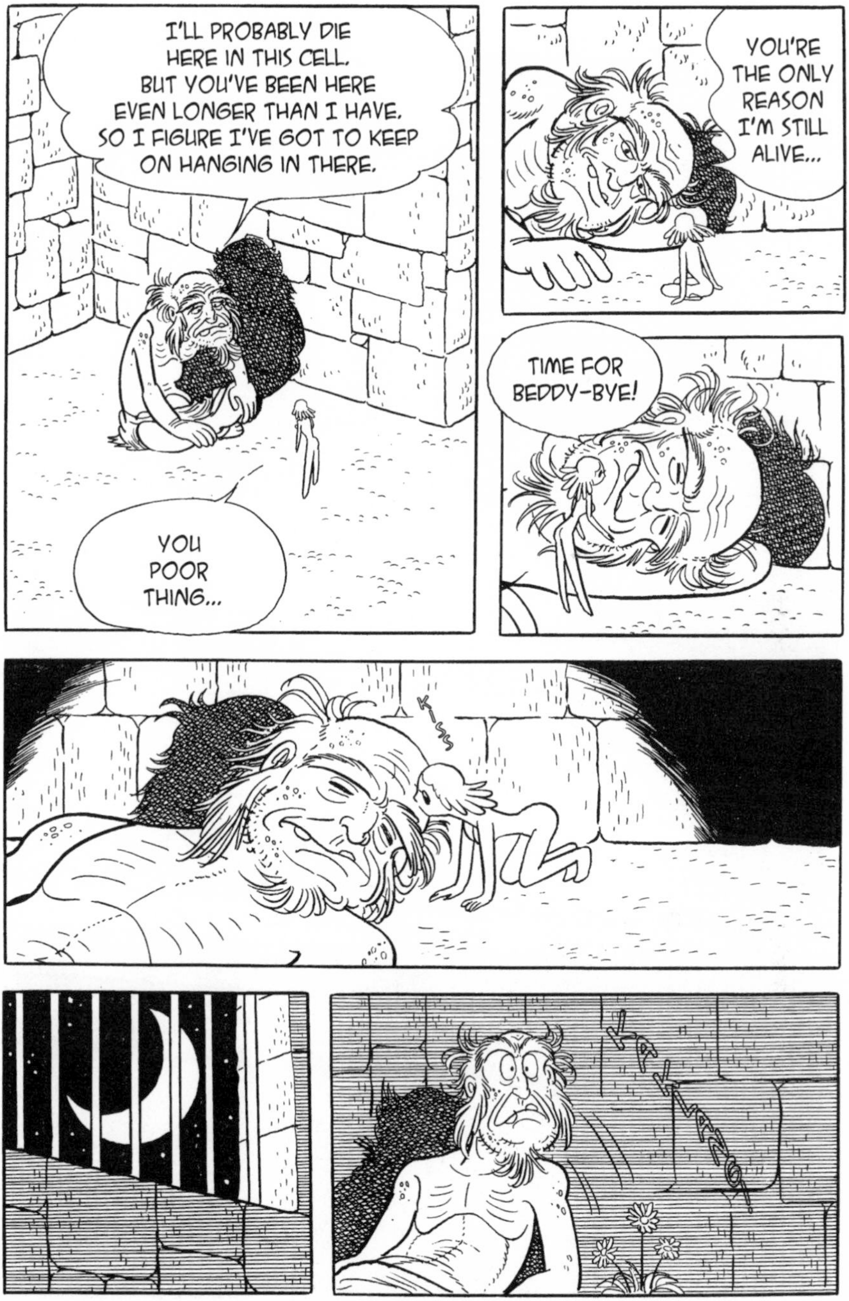
I'LL PROBABLY DIE HERE IN THIS CELL. BUT YOU'VE BEEN HERE EVEN LONGER THAN I HAVE. SO I FIGURE I'VE GOT TO KEEP ON HANGING IN THERE.
YOU POOR THING...
YOU'RE THE ONLY REASON I'M STILL ALIVE...
TIME FOR BEDDY-BYE!
KISS
KAKLANG!

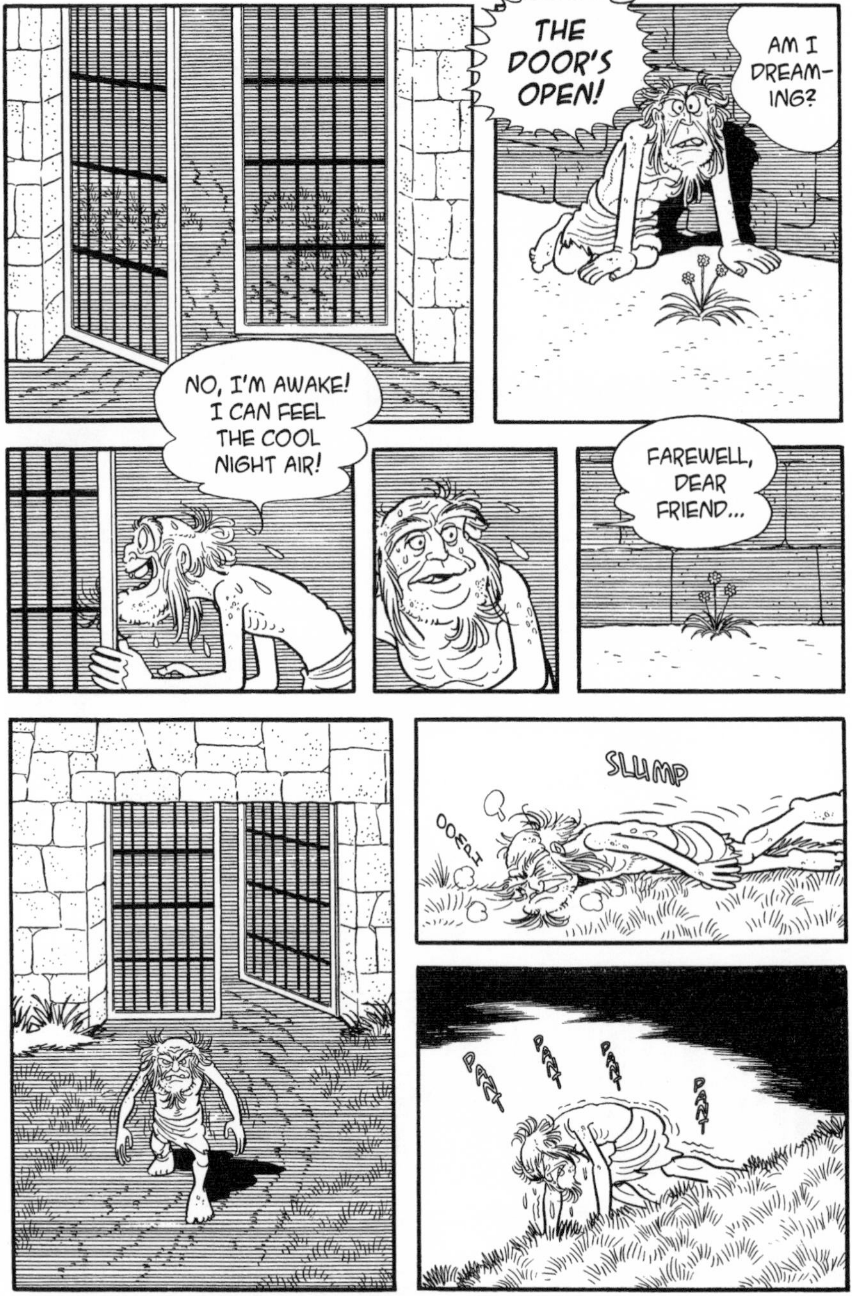
THE DOOR'S OPEN!
AM I DREAMING?
NO, I'M AWAKE! I CAN FEEL THE COOL NIGHT AIR!
FAREWELL, DEAR FRIEND...
SLUMP
OOF!
PANT
PANT
PANT
PANT

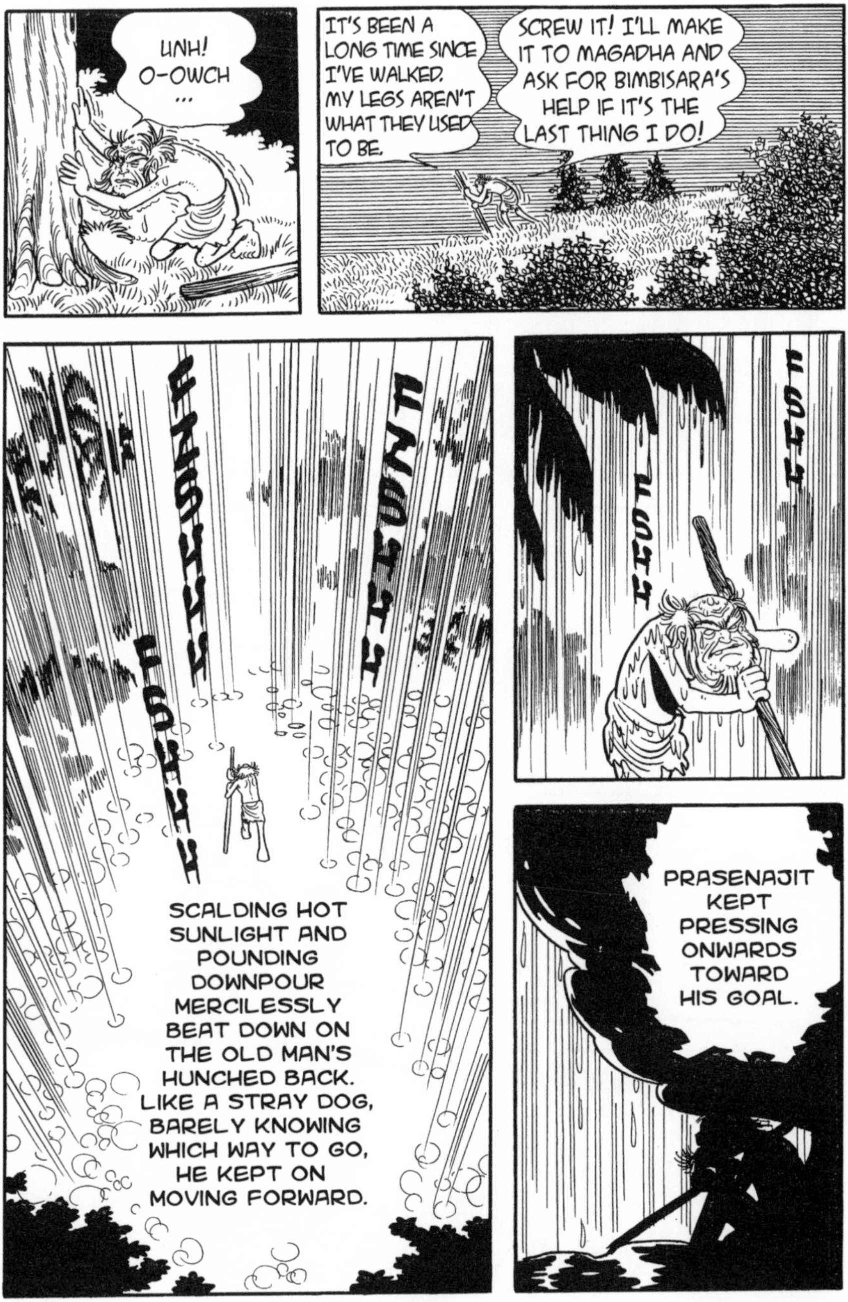
UNH! O-OWCH ...
IT'S BEEN A LONG TIME SINCE I'VE WALKED. MY LEGS AREN'T WHAT THEY USED TO BE.
SCREW IT! I'LL MAKE IT TO MAGADHA AND ASK FOR BIMBISARA'S HELP IF IT'S THE LAST THING I DO!
SCALDING HOT SUNLIGHT AND POUNDING DOWNPOUR MERCILESSLY BEAT DOWN ON THE OLD MAN'S HUNCHED BACK. LIKE A STRAY DOG, BARELY KNOWING WHICH WAY TO GO, HE KEPT ON MOVING FORWARD.
PRASENAJIT KEPT PRESSING ONWARDS TOWARD HIS GOAL.

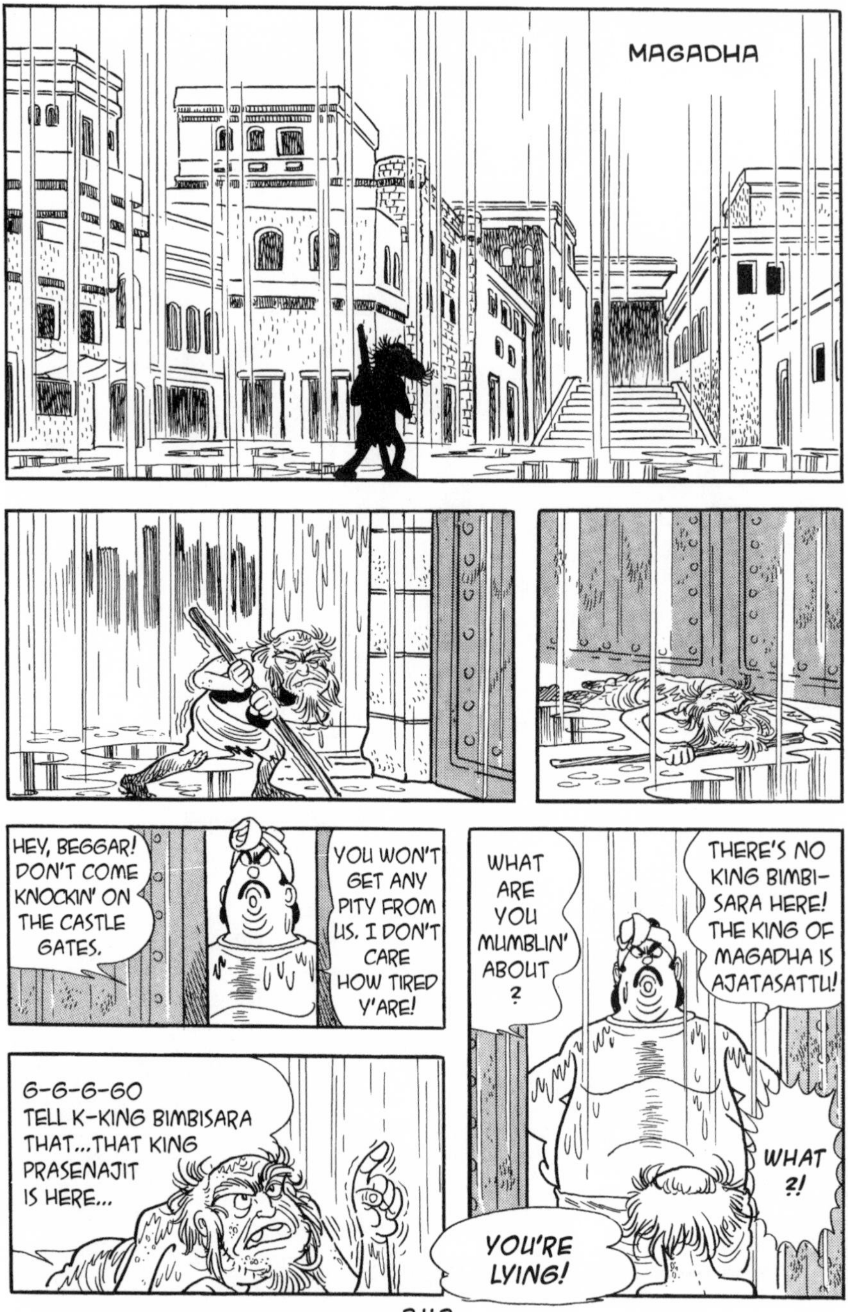
MAGADHA
HEY, BEGGAR! DON'T COME KNOCKIN' ON THE CASTLE GATES.
YOU WON'T GET ANY PITY FROM US. I DON'T CARE HOW TIRED Y'ARE!
6-6-6-60 TELL K-KING BIMBISARA THAT...THAT KING PRASENAJIT IS HERE...
WHAT ARE YOU MUMBLIN' ABOUT ?
THERE'S NO KING BIMBI-SARA HERE! THE KING OF MAGADHA IS AJATASATTU!
WHAT ?!
YOU'RE LYING!

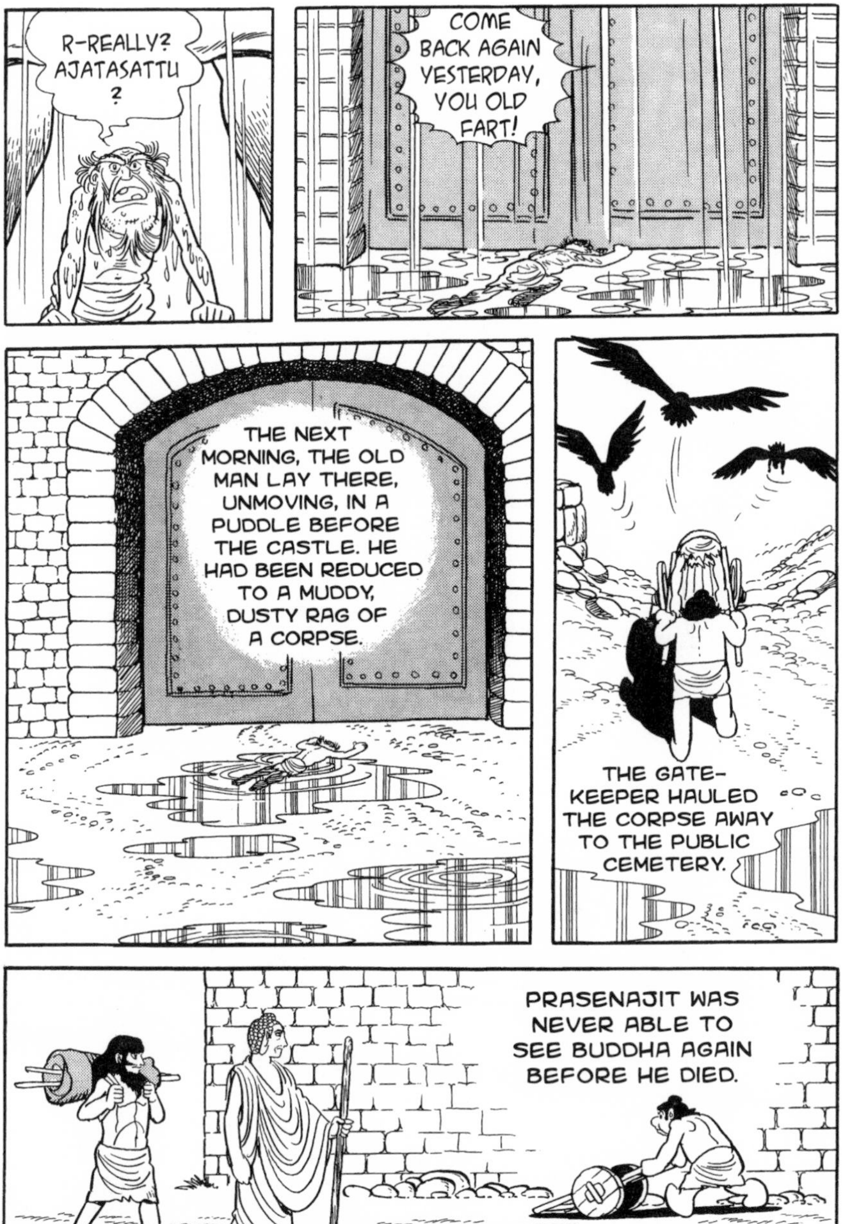
R-REALLY? AJATASATTU ?
COME BACK AGAIN YESTERDAY, YOU OLD FART!
THE NEXT MORNING, THE OLD MAN LAY THERE, UNMOVING, IN A PUDDLE BEFORE THE CASTLE. HE HAD BEEN REDUCED TO A MUDDY, DUSTY RAG OF A CORPSE.
THE GATE-KEEPER HAULED THE CORPSE AWAY TO THE PUBLIC CEMETERY.
PRASENAJIT WAS NEVER ABLE TO SEE BUDDHA AGAIN BEFORE HE DIED.

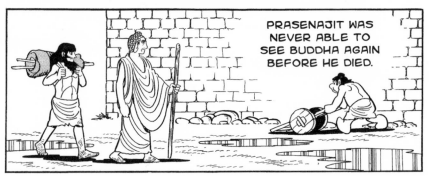

CHAPTER TWO

DEVADATTA

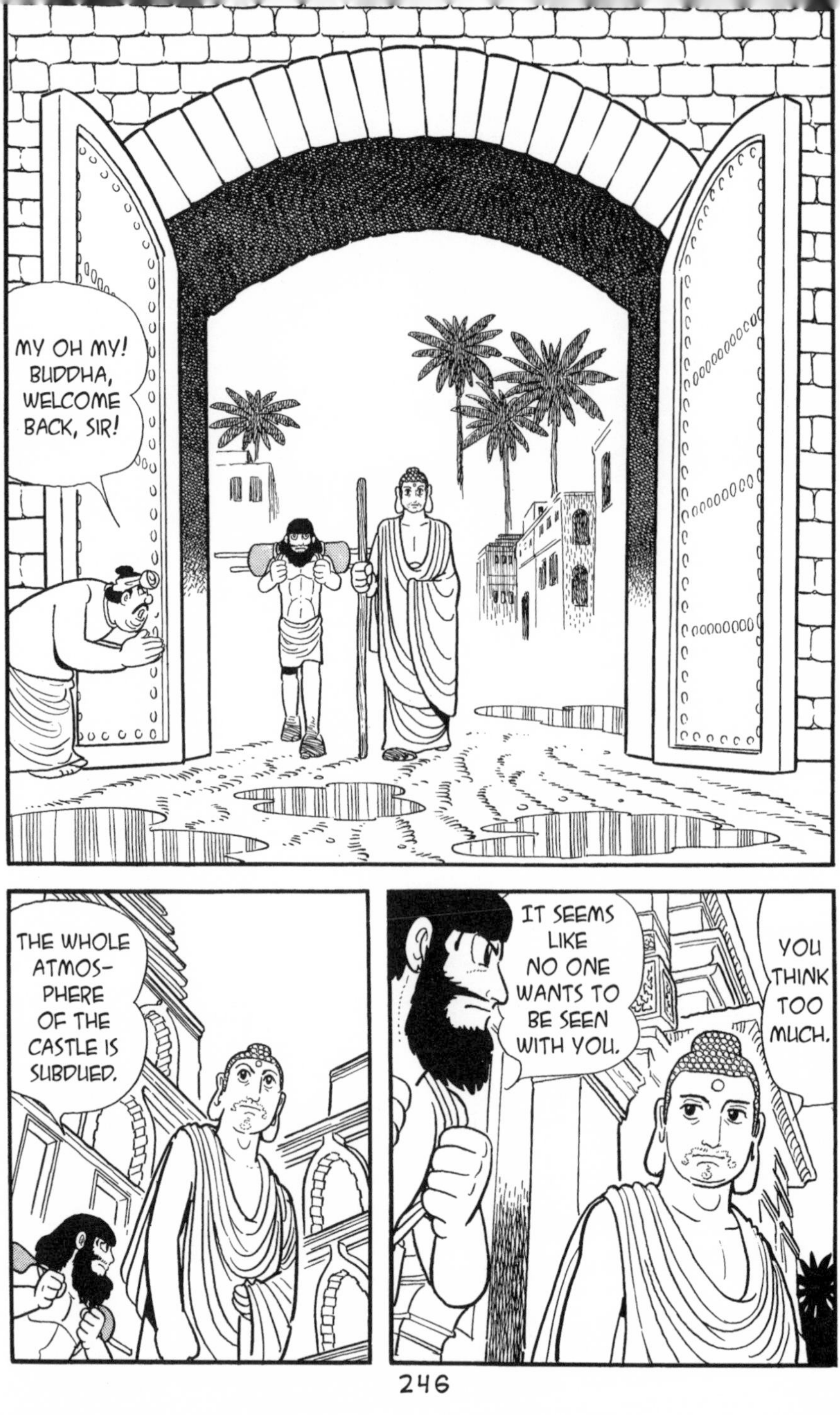
MY OH MY! BUDDHA, WELCOME BACK, SIR!
THE WHOLE ATMOS-PHERE OF THE CASTLE IS SUBDUED.
IT SEEMS LIKE NO ONE WANTS TO BE SEEN WITH YOU.
YOU THINK TOO MUCH.

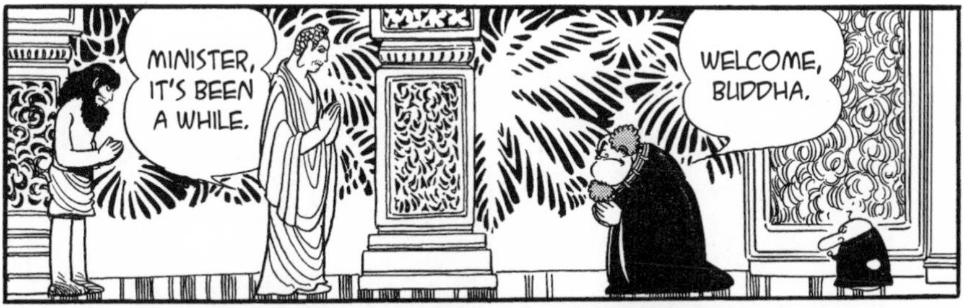
MINISTER, IT'S BEEN A WHILE.
WELCOME, BUDDHA.

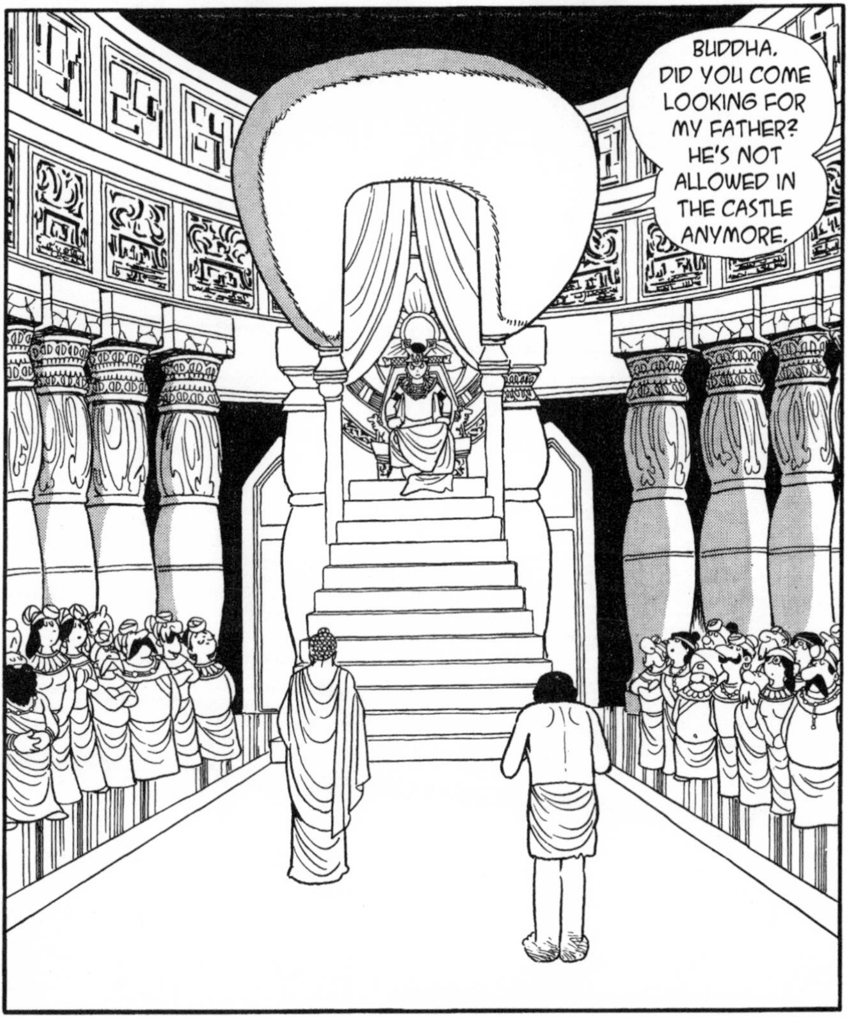
BUDDHA. DID YOU COME LOOKING FOR MY FATHER? HE'S NOT ALLOWED IN THE CASTLE ANYMORE.

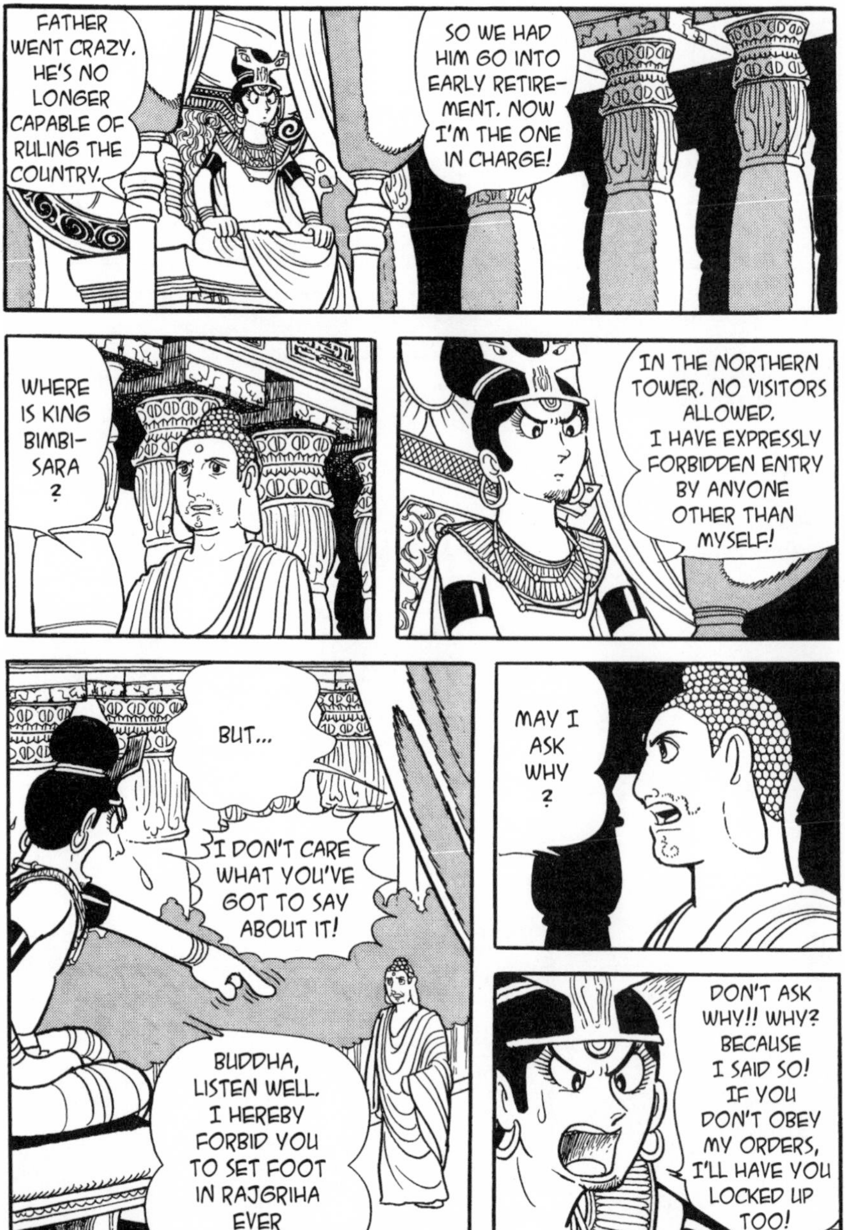
FATHER WENT CRAZY. HE'S NO LONGER CAPABLE OF RULING THE COUNTRY.
SO WE HAD HIM GO INTO EARLY RETIREMENT. NOW I'M THE ONE IN CHARGE!
WHERE IS KING BIMBISARA?
IN THE NORTHERN TOWER. NO VISITORS ALLOWED. I HAVE EXPRESSLY FORBIDDEN ENTRY BY ANYONE OTHER THAN MYSELF!
BUT...
I DON'T CARE WHAT YOU'VE GOT TO SAY ABOUT IT!
BUDDHA, LISTEN WELL. I HEREBY FORBID YOU TO SET FOOT IN RAJGRIHA EVER AGAIN!!
MAY I ASK WHY?
DON'T ASK WHY!! WHY? BECAUSE I SAID SO! IF YOU DON'T OBEY MY ORDERS, I'LL HAVE YOU LOCKED UP TOO!

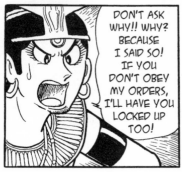

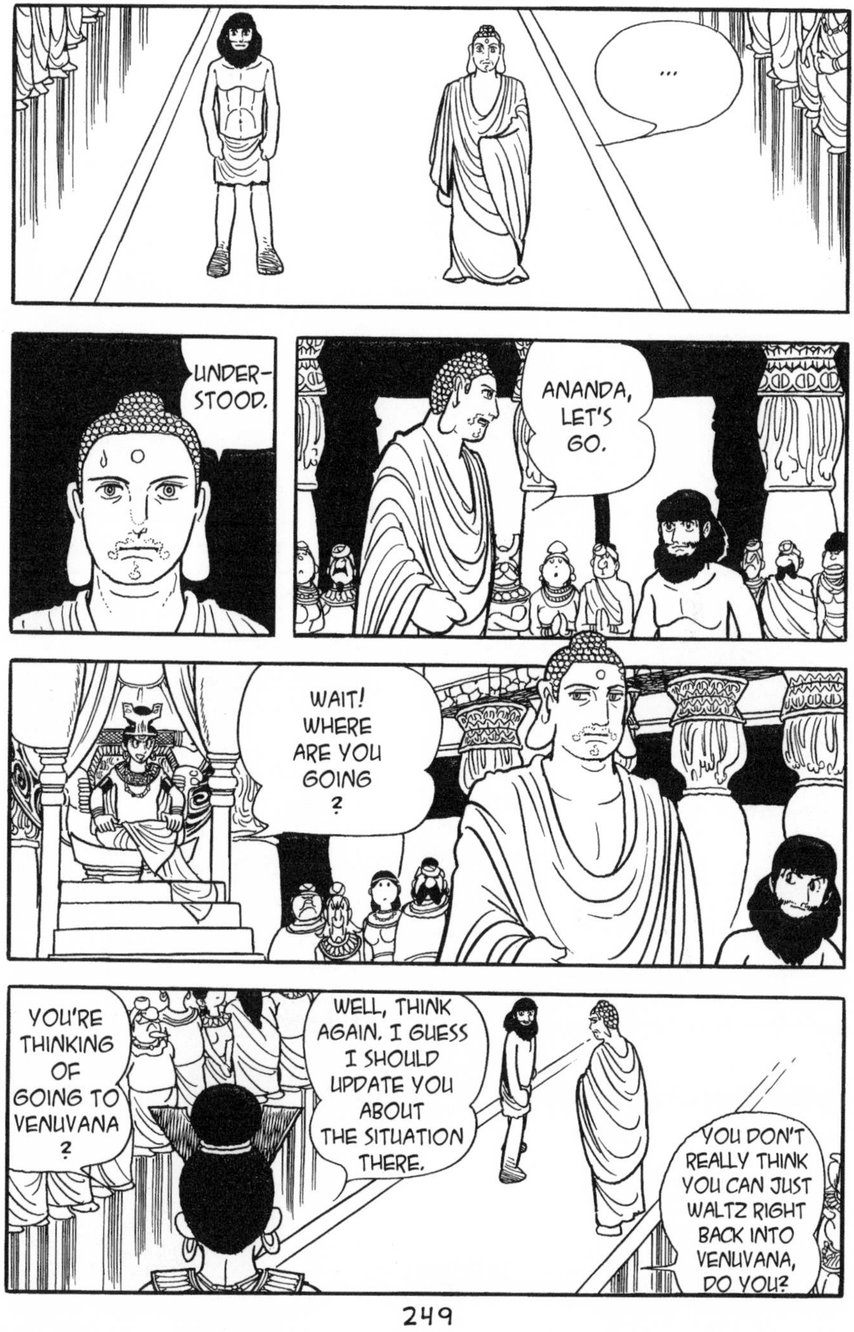
...
UNDER-STOOD.
ANANDA, LET'S GO.
WAIT! WHERE ARE YOU GOING?
YOU'RE THINKING OF GOING TO VENUVANA?
WELL, THINK AGAIN. I GUESS I SHOULD UPDATE YOU ABOUT THE SITUATION THERE.
YOU DON'T REALLY THINK YOU CAN JUST WALTZ RIGHT BACK INTO VENUVANA, DO YOU?

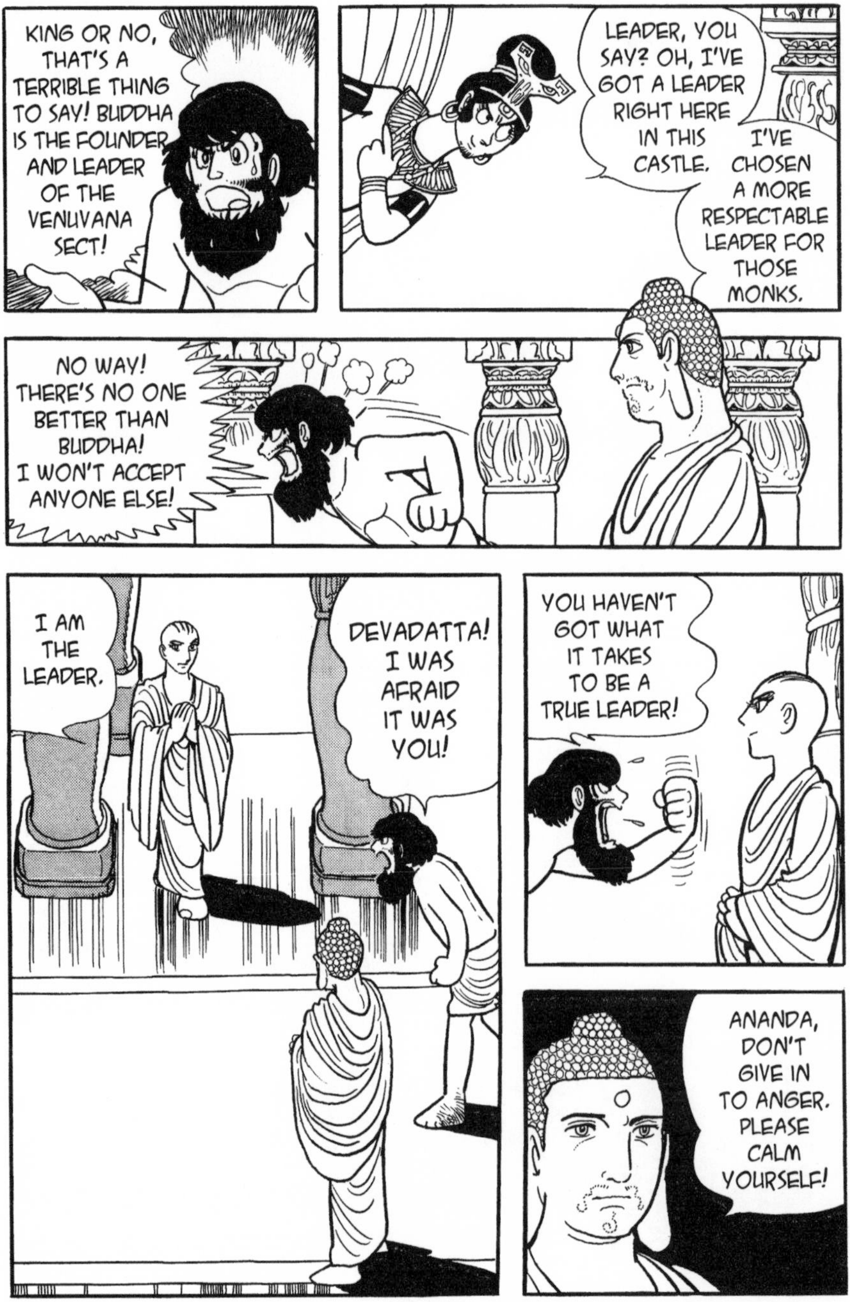
KING OR NO, THAT'S A TERRIBLE THING TO SAY! BUDDHA IS THE FOUNDER AND LEADER OF THE VENUVANA SECT!
LEADER, YOU SAY? OH, I'VE GOT A LEADER RIGHT HERE IN THIS CASTLE.
I'VE CHOSEN A MORE RESPECTABLE LEADER FOR THOSE MONKS.
NO WAY! THERE'S NO ONE BETTER THAN BUDDHA! I WON'T ACCEPT ANYONE ELSE!
I AM THE LEADER.
DEVADATTA! I WAS AFRAID IT WAS YOU!
YOU HAVEN'T GOT WHAT IT TAKES TO BE A TRUE LEADER!
ANANDA, DON'T GIVE IN TO ANGER. PLEASE CALM YOURSELF!

SO THE RUMORS WERE TRUE. DEVADATTA, WHY DID YOU DISOBEY ME? WHY DID YOU DO SUCH A THING?

DISOBEY YOU? HOW DARE YOU TALK LIKE THAT. THIS IS WHAT WE CALL PROGRESS!

BUDDHA, FACE IT. YOU'RE OLD. TO BE QUITE FRANK, I THINK YOU'RE GETTING SENILE.

THE SECT NEEDS NEW, YOUNG ENERGY. I WAS THINKING OF MAKING YOU CHAIRMAN OR SOMETHING, BUT YOU MIGHT AS WELL RETIRE, DON'T YOU THINK?

IF YOU LIKE, I COULD ASK THE KING TO GIVE YOU A PASS SO THAT YOU CAN COME AND GO FROM VENUVANA AS YOU PLEASE.

DEVADATTA HAS ONLY YOUR WELFARE IN MIND, BUDDHA.

THE KING MAY VERY WELL HAVE CHOSEN YOU AS THE LEADER. BUT NEITHER BRAHMAN NOR NATURE WOULD EVER CHOOSE THE LIKES OF YOU. YOU'RE NOT WORTHY OF SUCH A ROLE.

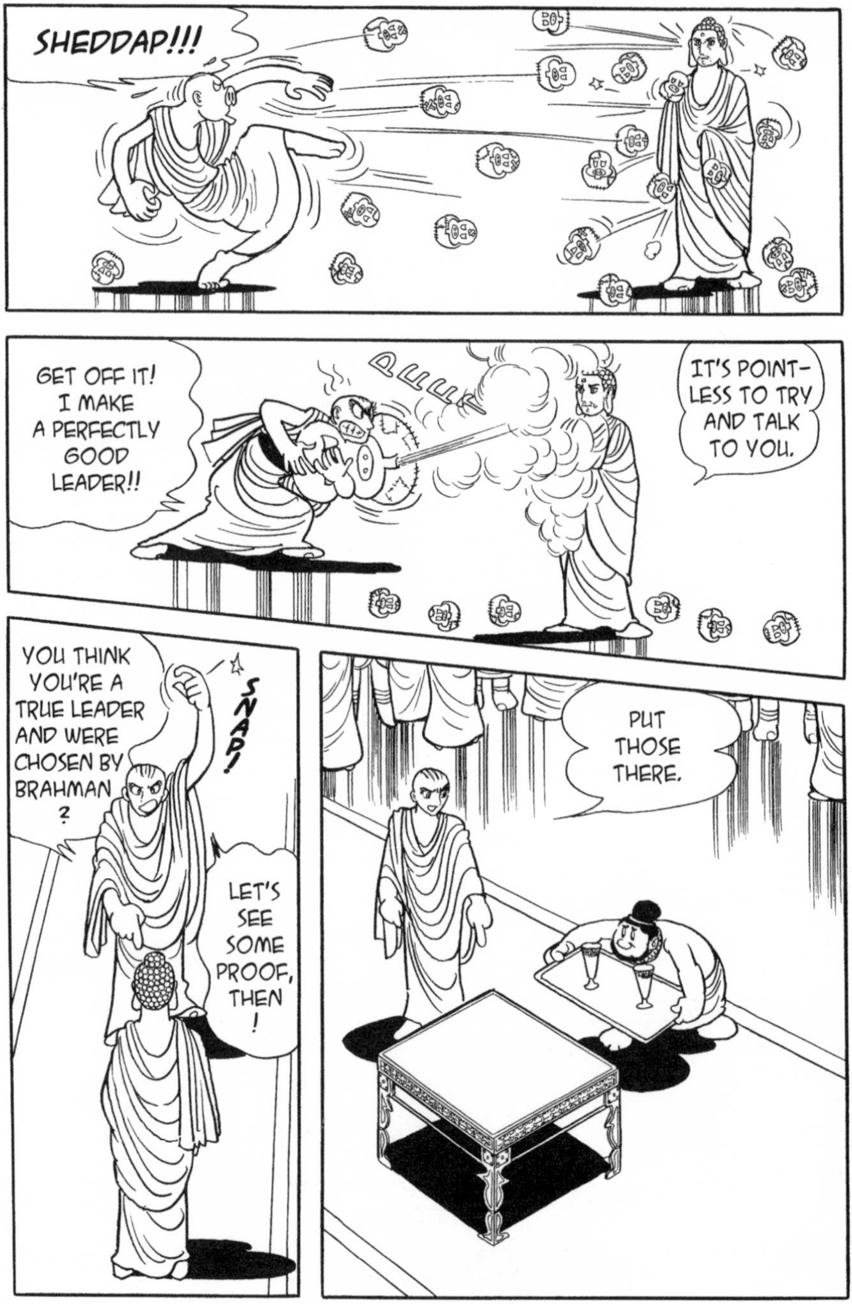
SHEDDAP!!!
GET OFF IT! I MAKE A PERFECTLY GOOD LEADER!!
PFFFT
IT'S POINTLESS TO TRY AND TALK TO YOU.
YOU THINK YOU'RE A TRUE LEADER AND WERE CHOSEN BY BRAHMAN?
SNAP!
LET'S SEE SOME PROOF, THEN!
PUT THOSE THERE.

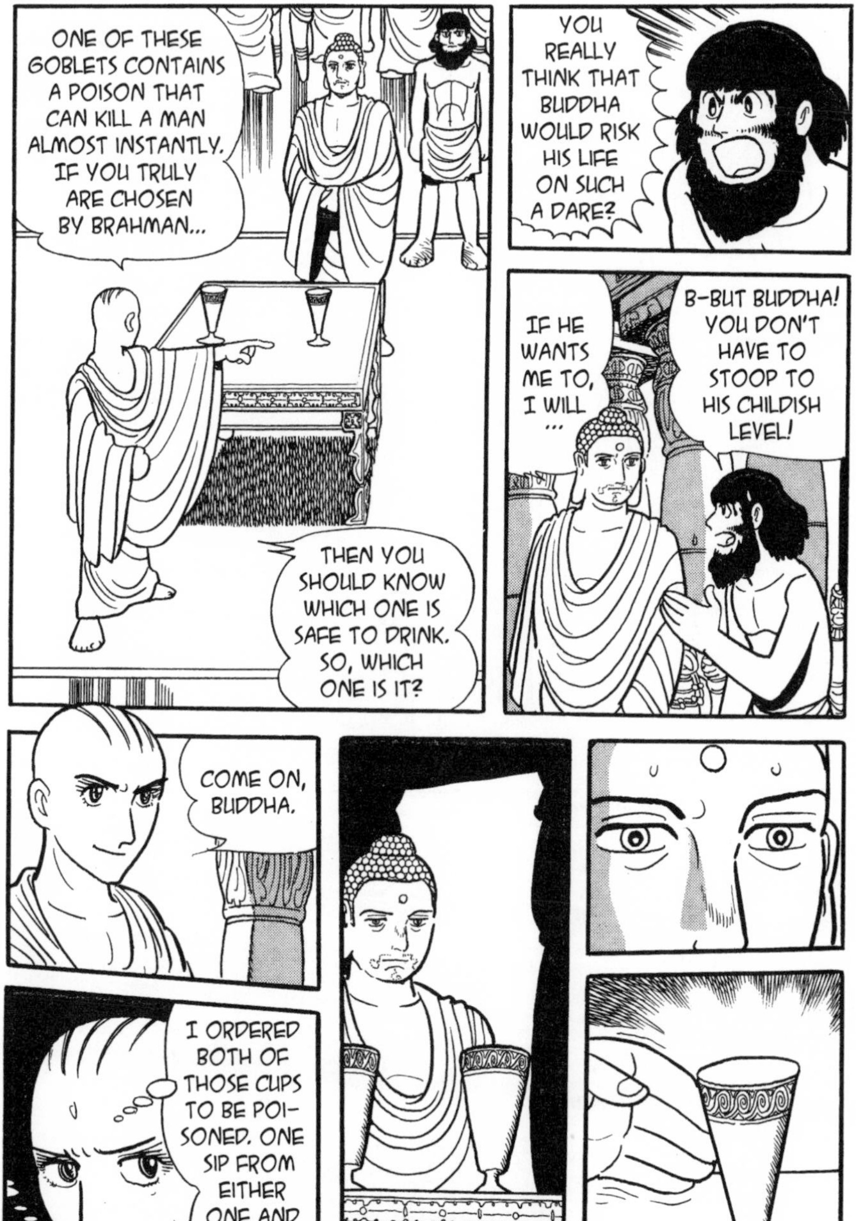
ONE OF THESE GOBLETS CONTAINS A POISON THAT CAN KILL A MAN ALMOST INSTANTLY. IF YOU TRULY ARE CHOSEN BY BRAHMAN...
THEN YOU SHOULD KNOW WHICH ONE IS SAFE TO DRINK. SO, WHICH ONE IS IT?
YOU REALLY THINK THAT BUDDHA WOULD RISK HIS LIFE ON SUCH A DARE?
IF HE WANTS ME TO, I WILL ...
B-BUT BUDDHA! YOU DON'T HAVE TO STOOP TO HIS CHILDISH LEVEL!
COME ON, BUDDHA.
I ORDERED BOTH OF THOSE CUPS TO BE POI-SONED. ONE SIP FROM EITHER ONE AND HE'S DONE FOR.

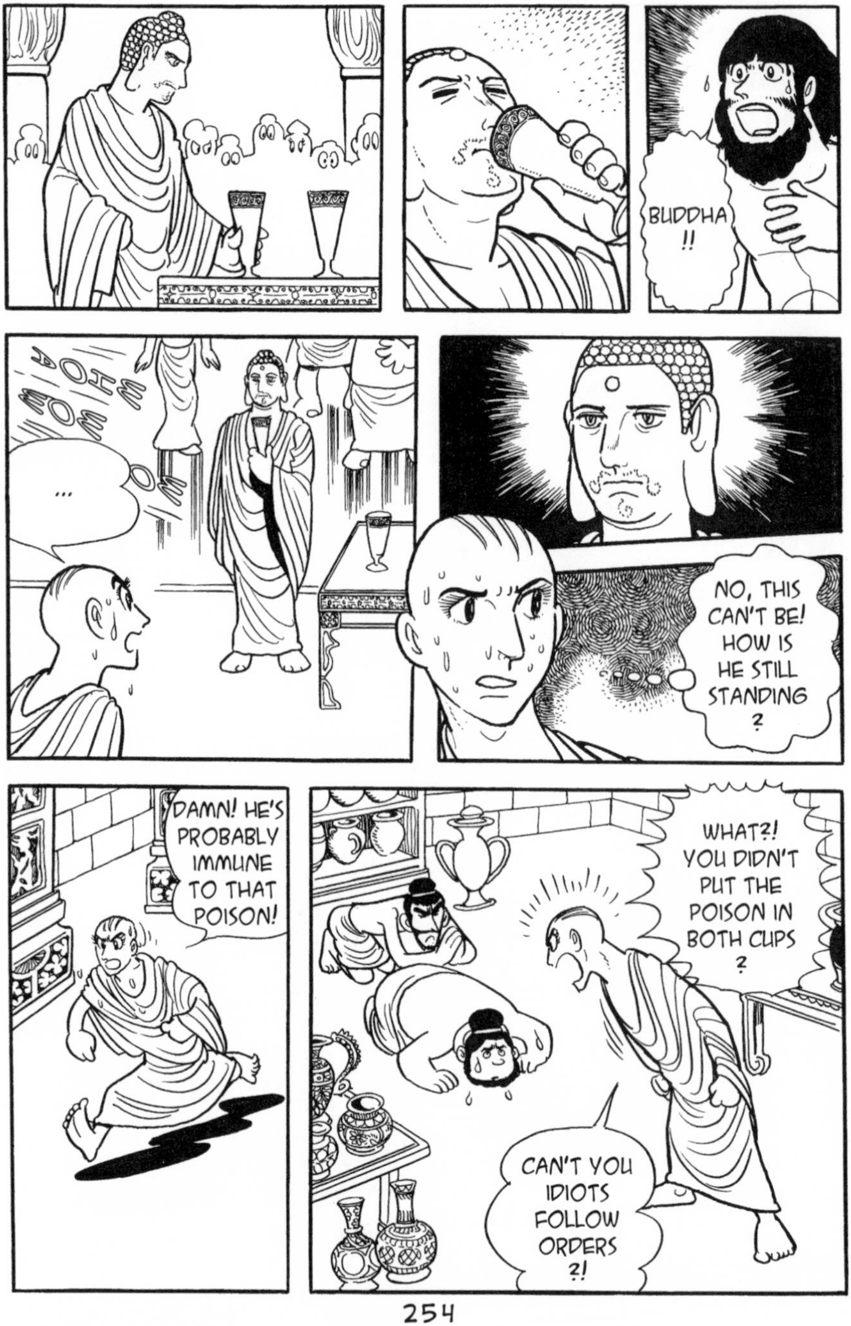
BUDDHA !!
WHOA
WOW
WOW
...
NO, THIS CAN'T BE! HOW IS HE STILL STANDING?
DAMN! HE'S PROBABLY IMMUNE TO THAT POISON!
WHAT?! YOU DIDN'T PUT THE POISON IN BOTH CUPS?
CAN'T YOU IDIOTS FOLLOW ORDERS?!

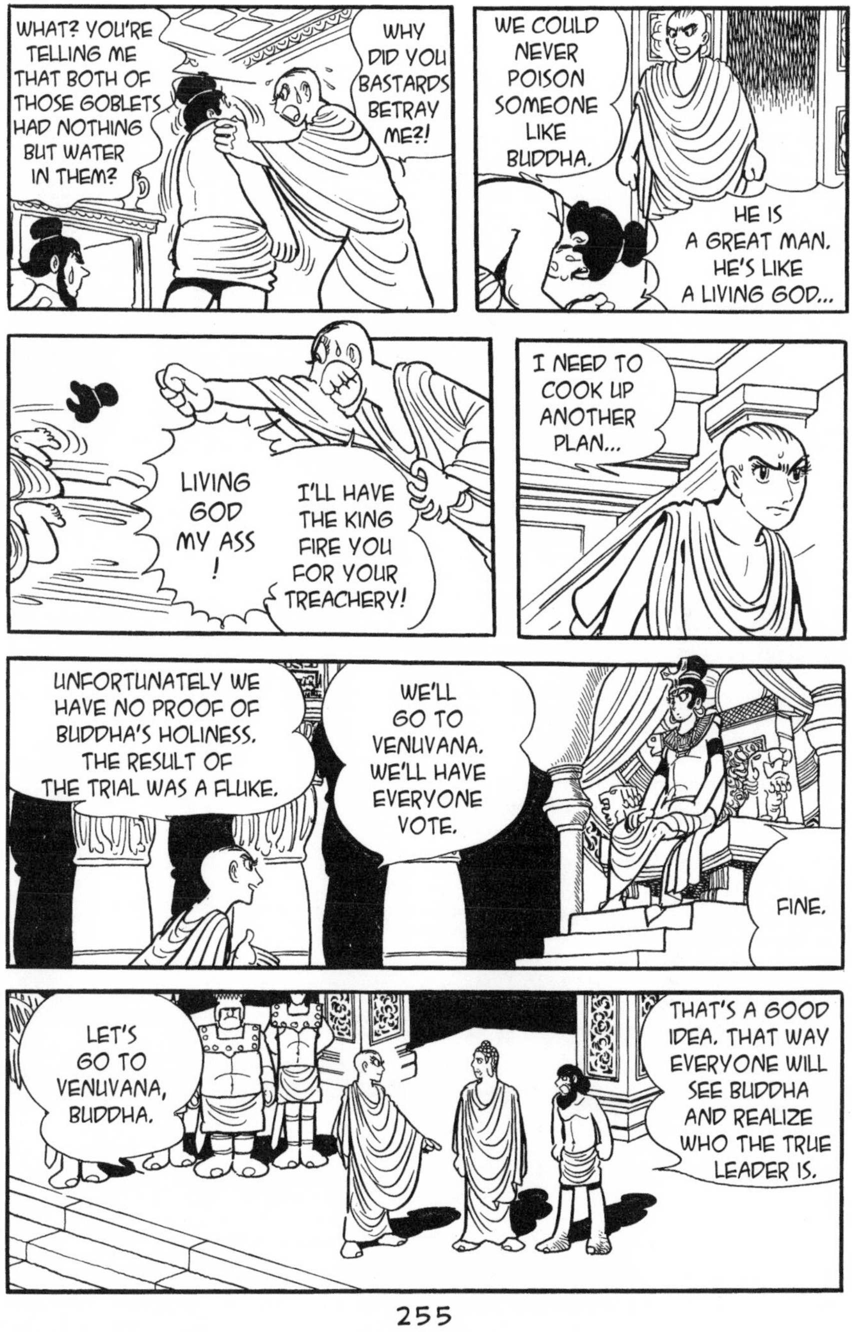
WHAT? YOU'RE TELLING ME THAT BOTH OF THOSE GOBLETS HAD NOTHING BUT WATER IN THEM?
WHY DID YOU BASTARDS BETRAY ME?!
WE COULD NEVER POISON SOMEONE LIKE BUDDHA.
HE IS A GREAT MAN. HE'S LIKE A LIVING GOD...
LIVING GOD MY ASS!
I'LL HAVE THE KING FIRE YOU FOR YOUR TREACHERY!
I NEED TO COOK UP ANOTHER PLAN...
UNFORTUNATELY WE HAVE NO PROOF OF BUDDHA'S HOLINESS. THE RESULT OF THE TRIAL WAS A FLUKE.
WE'LL GO TO VENUVANA. WE'LL HAVE EVERYONE VOTE.
FINE.
LET'S GO TO VENUVANA, BUDDHA.
THAT'S A GOOD IDEA. THAT WAY EVERYONE WILL SEE BUDDHA AND REALIZE WHO THE TRUE LEADER IS.

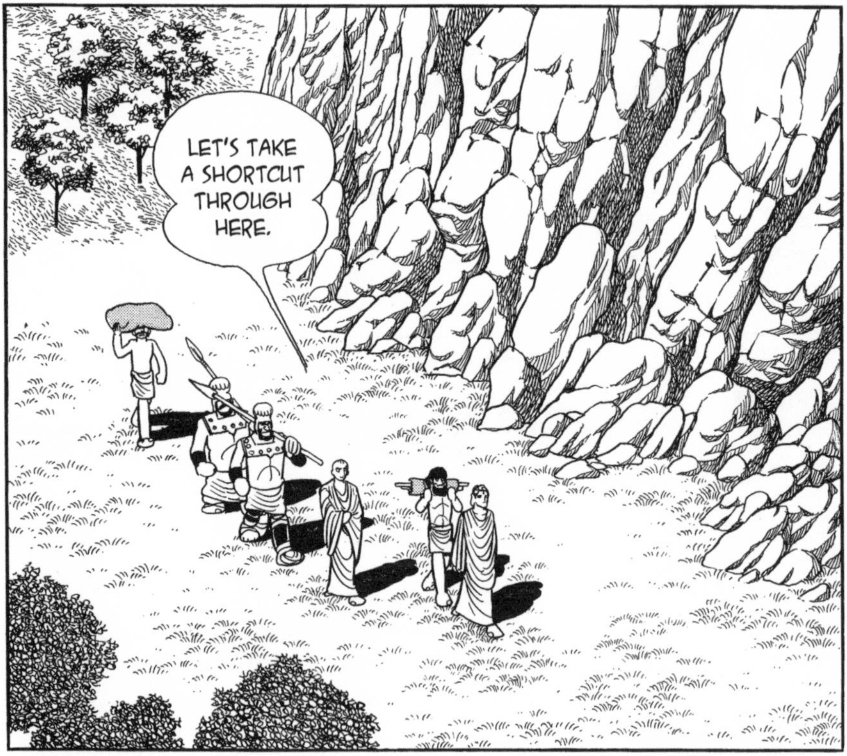
LET'S TAKE A SHORTCUT THROUGH HERE.

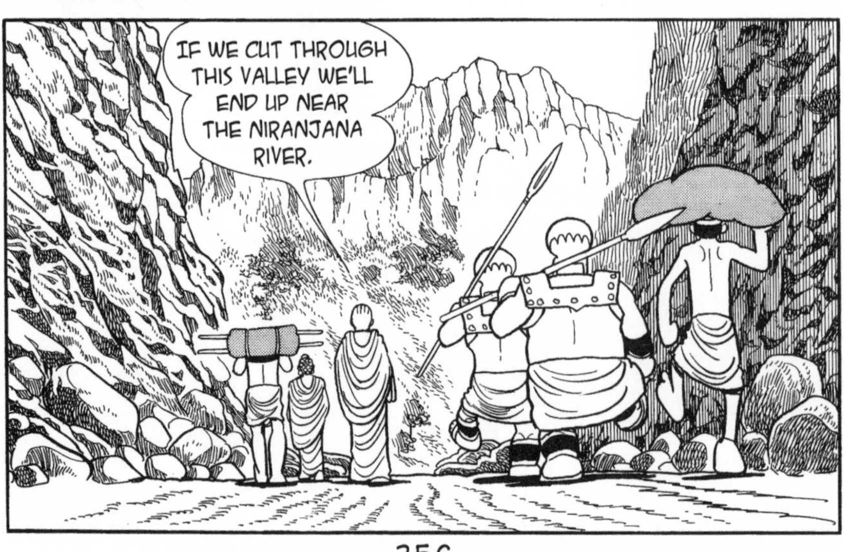
IF WE CUT THROUGH THIS VALLEY WE'LL END UP NEAR THE NIRANJANA RIVER.

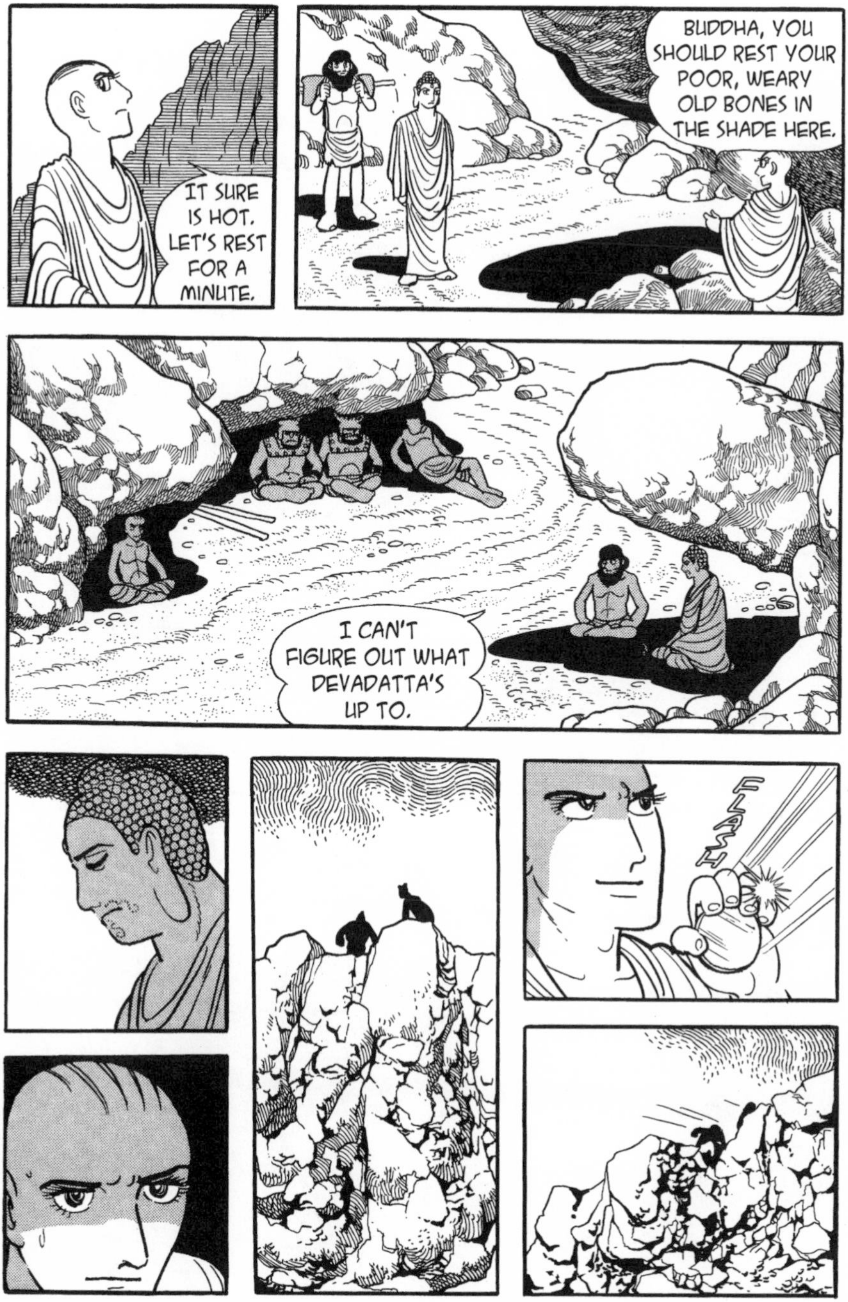
IT SURE IS HOT. LET'S REST FOR A MINUTE.
BUDDHA, YOU SHOULD REST YOUR POOR, WEARY OLD BONES IN THE SHADE HERE.
I CAN'T FIGURE OUT WHAT DEVADATTA'S UP TO.
FLASH

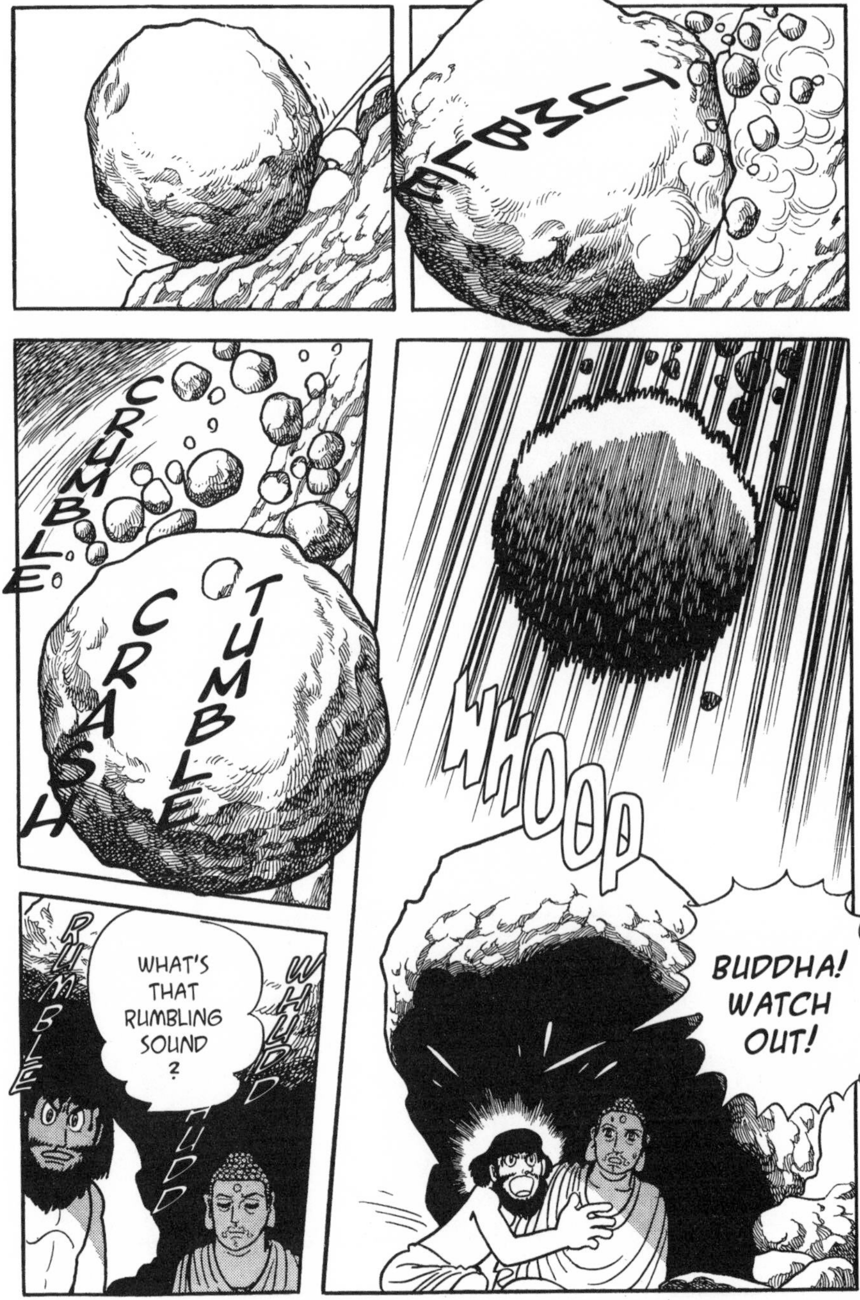
TUMBLE
CRUMBLE
CRASH
TUMBLE
WHOOP
RUMBLE
WHAT'S THAT RUMBLING SOUND?
THUDD
THUDD
BUDDHA! WATCH OUT!

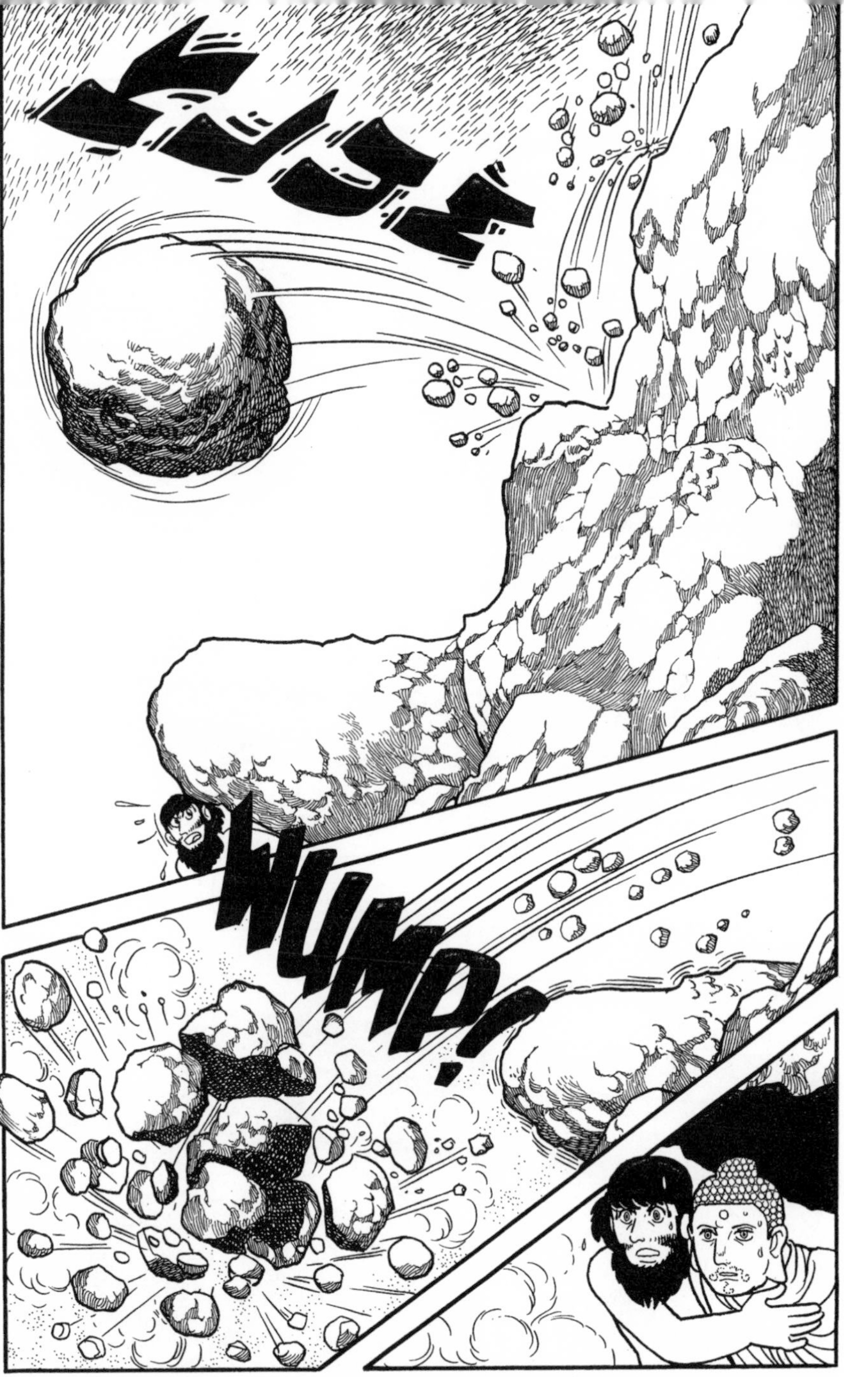
WUMP!

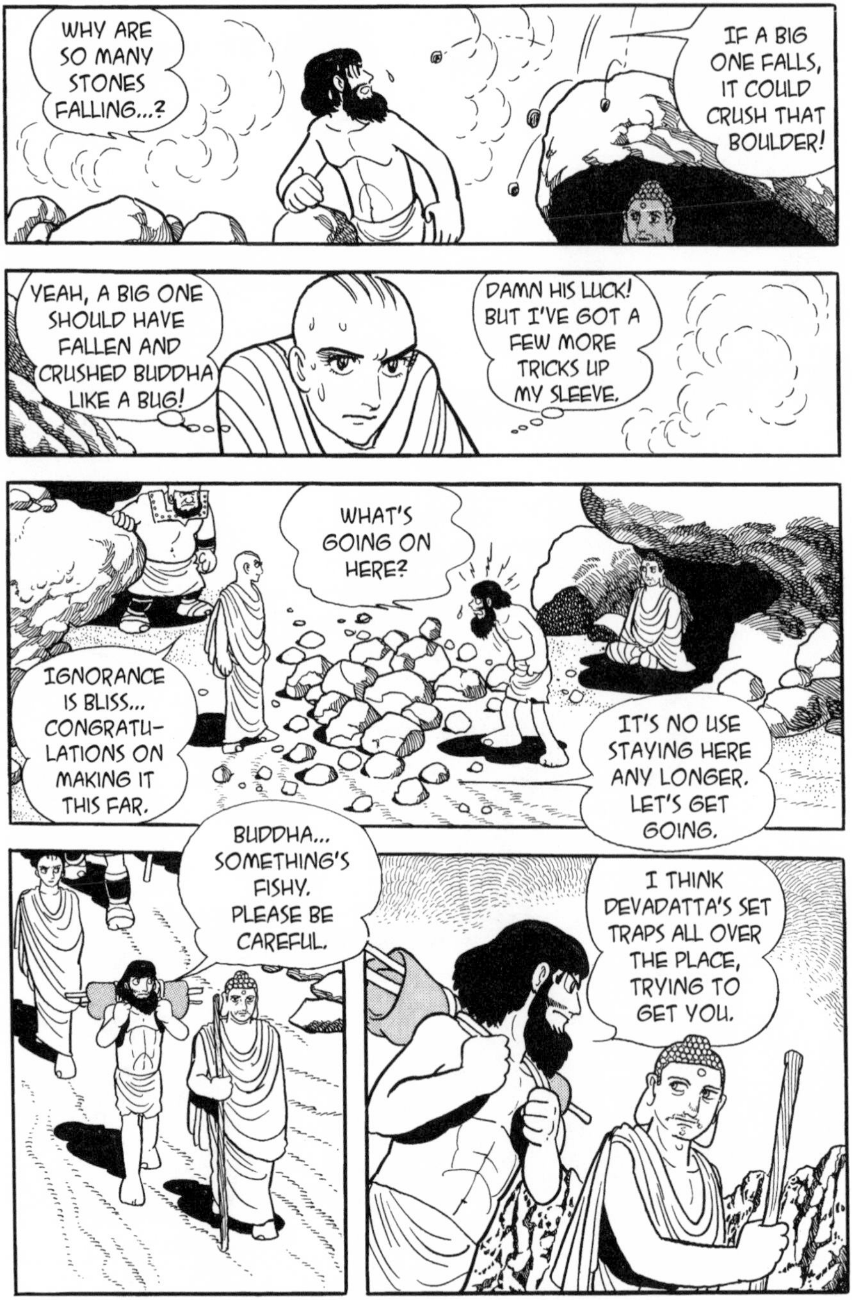
WHY ARE SO MANY STONES FALLING...?
IF A BIG ONE FALLS, IT COULD CRUSH THAT BOULDER!
YEAH, A BIG ONE SHOULD HAVE FALLEN AND CRUSHED BUDDHA LIKE A BUG!
DAMN HIS LUCK! BUT I'VE GOT A FEW MORE TRICKS UP MY SLEEVE.
WHAT'S GOING ON HERE?
IGNORANCE IS BLISS... CONGRATU-LATIONS ON MAKING IT THIS FAR.
IT'S NO USE STAYING HERE ANY LONGER. LET'S GET GOING.
BUDDHA... SOMETHING'S FISHY. PLEASE BE CAREFUL.
I THINK DEVADATTA'S SET TRAPS ALL OVER THE PLACE, TRYING TO GET YOU.

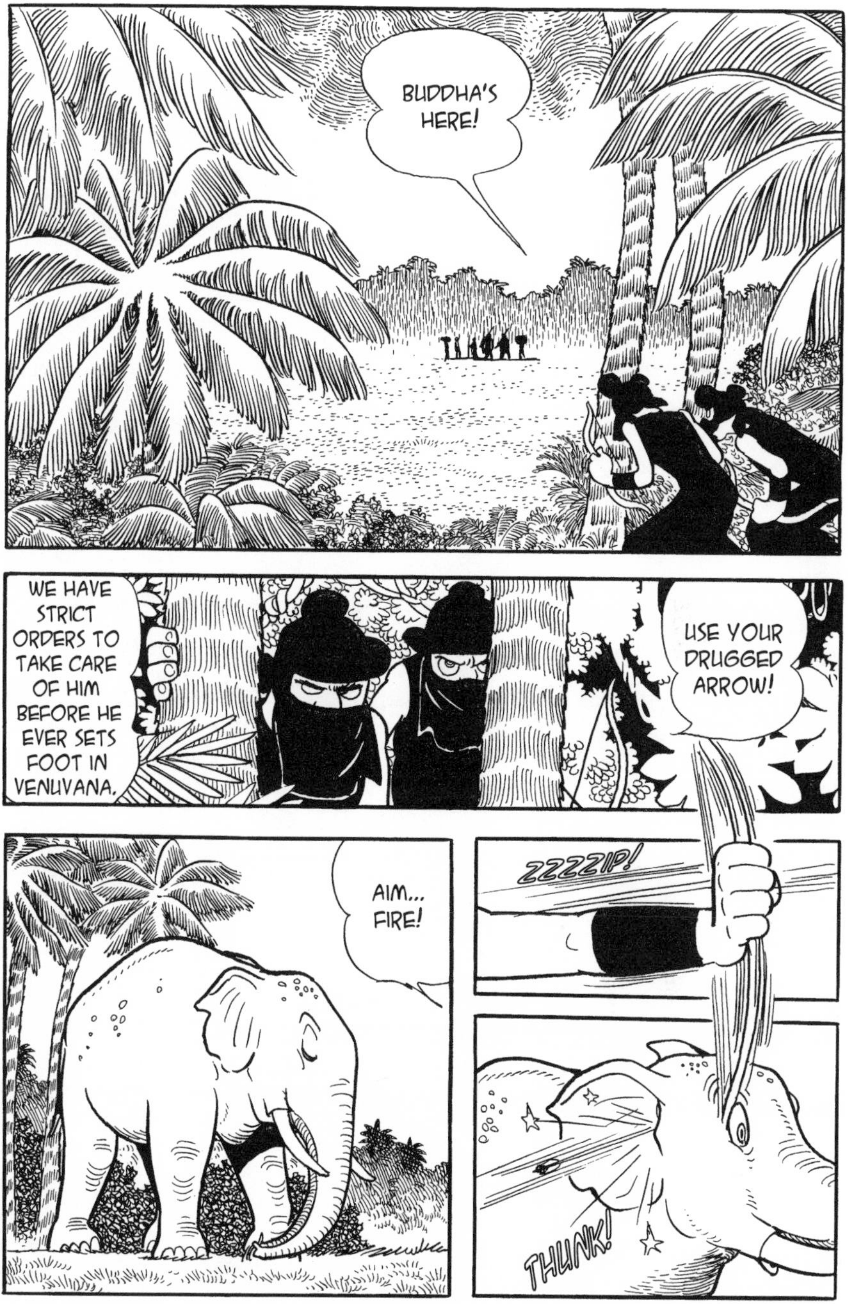
BUDDHA'S HERE!
WE HAVE STRICT ORDERS TO TAKE CARE OF HIM BEFORE HE EVER SETS FOOT IN VENUVANA.
USE YOUR DRUGGED ARROW!
AIM... FIRE!
ZZZZZIP!
THUNK!

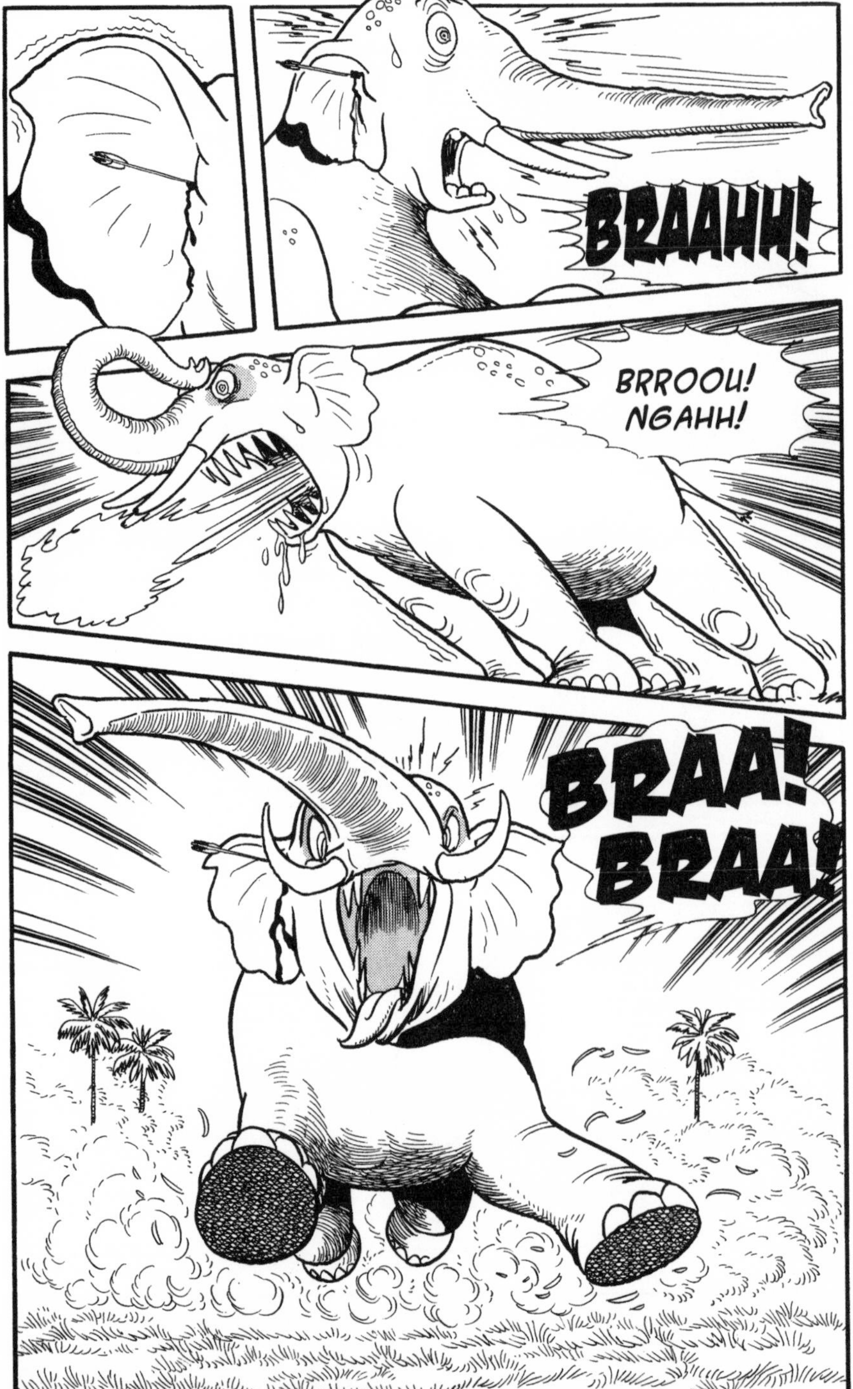
BRAAHH!
BRROOU! NGAHH!
BRAA! BRAA!

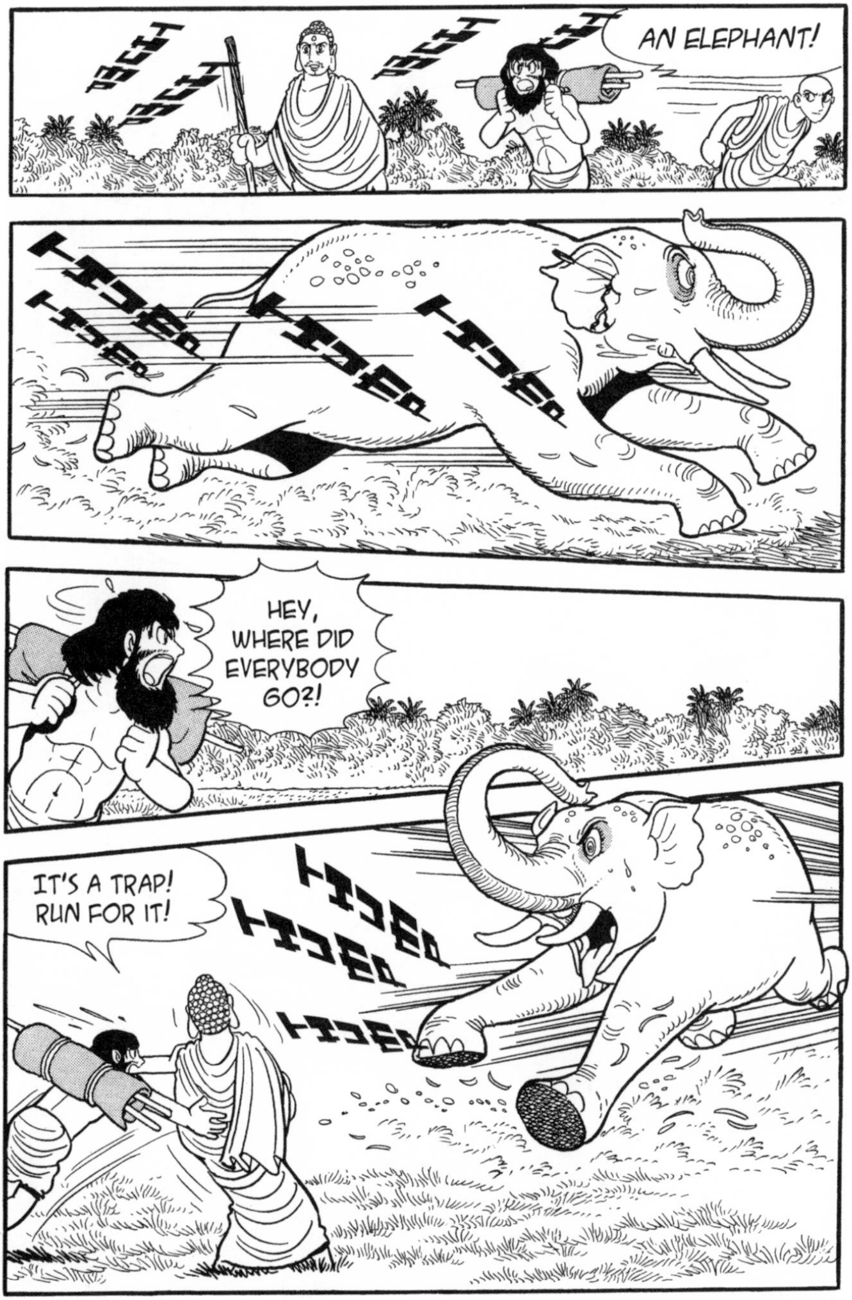
AN ELEPHANT!
HEY, WHERE DID EVERYBODY GO?!
IT'S A TRAP! RUN FOR IT!

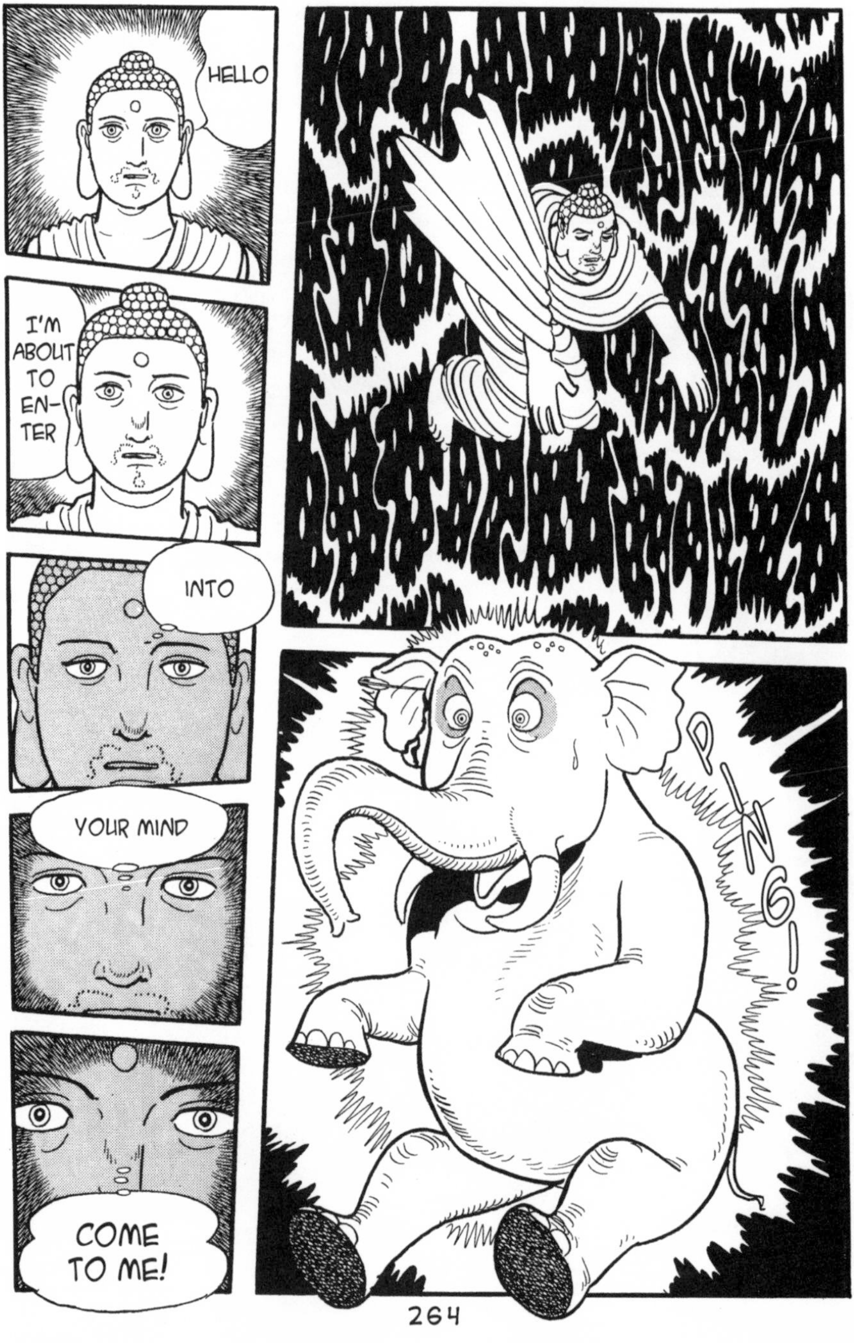
HELLO
I'M ABOUT TO EN-TER
INTO
YOUR MIND
COME TO ME!
PINGG!

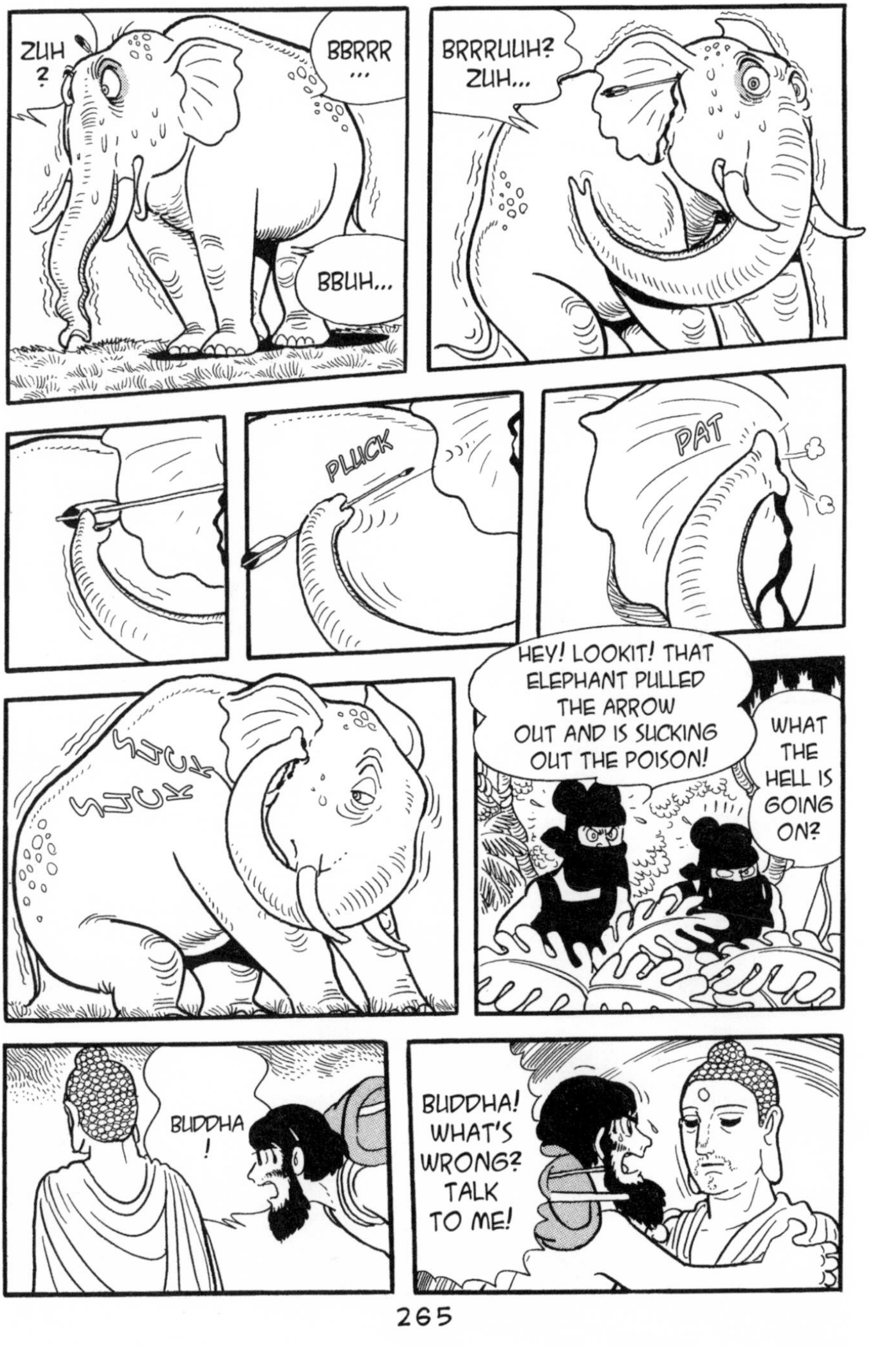
ZUH ?
BBRRR ...
BBUH...
BRRRUUH? ZUH...
PLUCK
PAT
SUCK SUCK
HEY! LOOKIT! THAT ELEPHANT PULLED THE ARROW OUT AND IS SUCKING OUT THE POISON!
WHAT THE HELL IS GOING ON?
BUDDHA !
BUDDHA! WHAT'S WRONG? TALK TO ME!

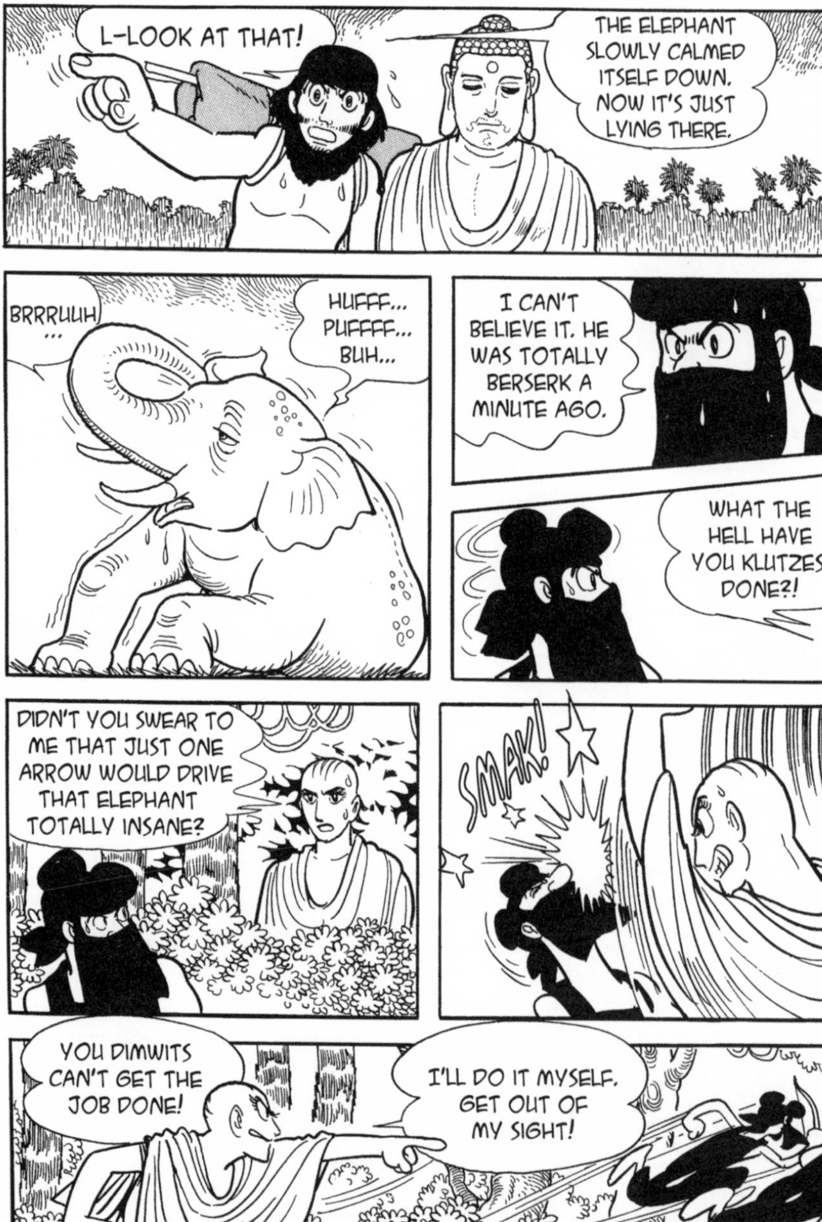
L-LOOK AT THAT!
THE ELEPHANT SLOWLY CALMED ITSELF DOWN. NOW IT'S JUST LYING THERE.
BRRRUUH ...
HUFFF... PUFFFF... BUH...
I CAN'T BELIEVE IT. HE WAS TOTALLY BERSERK A MINUTE AGO.
WHAT THE HELL HAVE YOU KLUTZES DONE?!
DIDN'T YOU SWEAR TO ME THAT JUST ONE ARROW WOULD DRIVE THAT ELEPHANT TOTALLY INSANE?
SMAK!
YOU DIMWITS CAN'T GET THE JOB DONE!
I'LL DO IT MYSELF. GET OUT OF MY SIGHT!

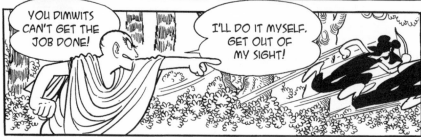

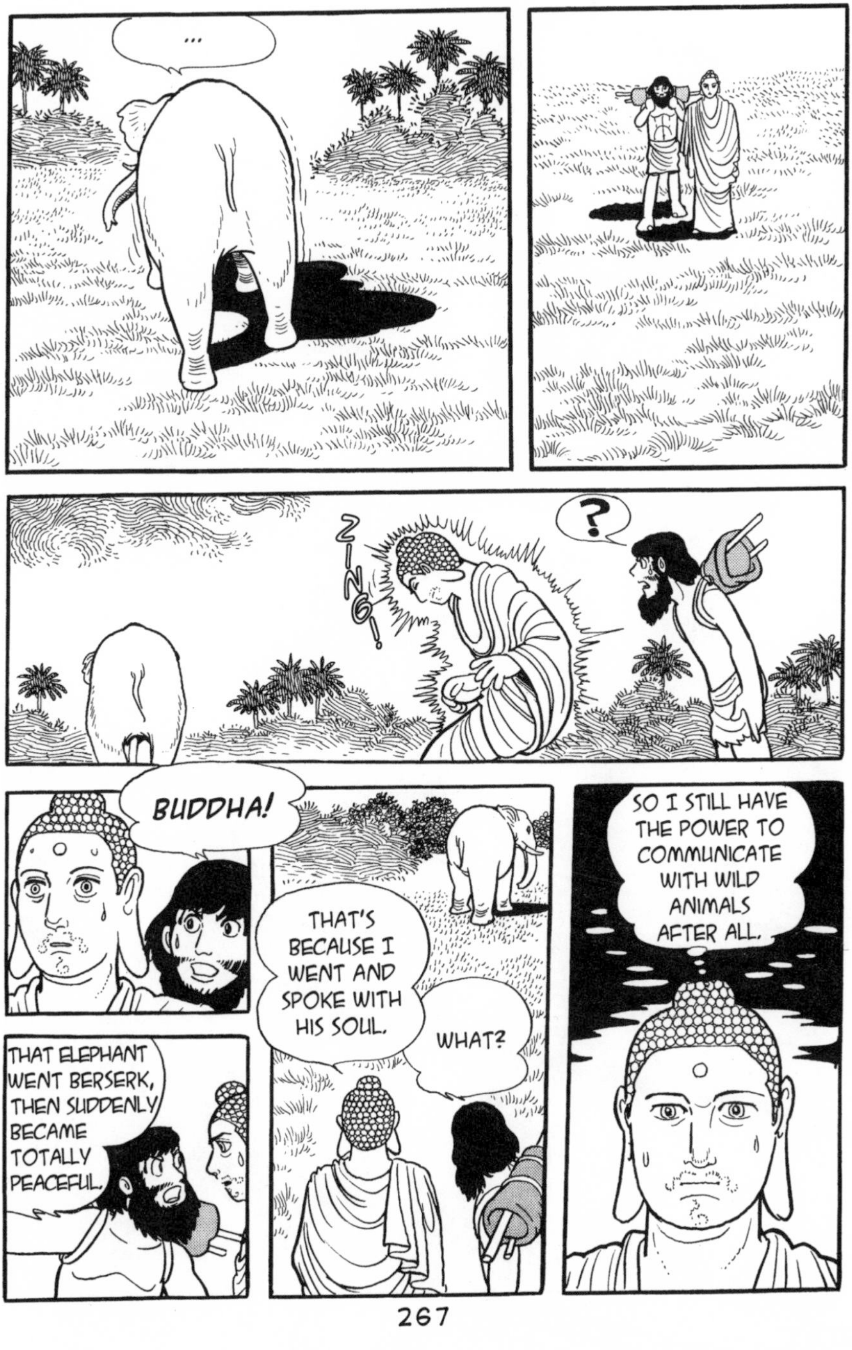
...
?
ZING!
BUDDHA!
THAT ELEPHANT WENT BERSERK, THEN SUDDENLY BECAME TOTALLY PEACEFUL.
THAT'S BECAUSE I WENT AND SPOKE WITH HIS SOUL.
WHAT?
SO I STILL HAVE THE POWER TO COMMUNICATE WITH WILD ANIMALS AFTER ALL.

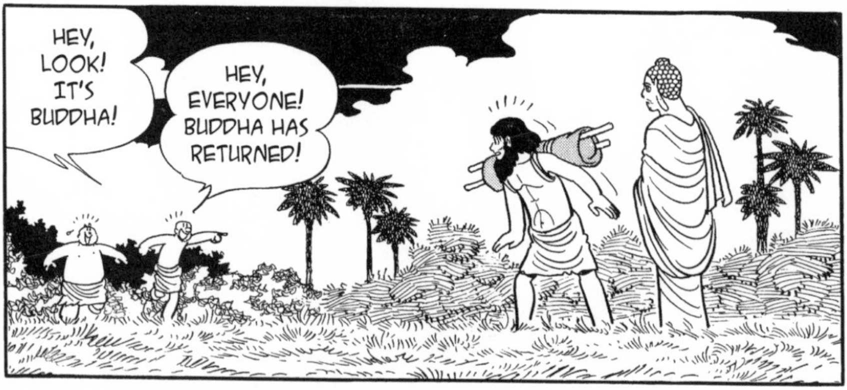
HEY, LOOK! IT'S BUDDHA!
HEY, EVERYONE! BUDDHA HAS RETURNED!

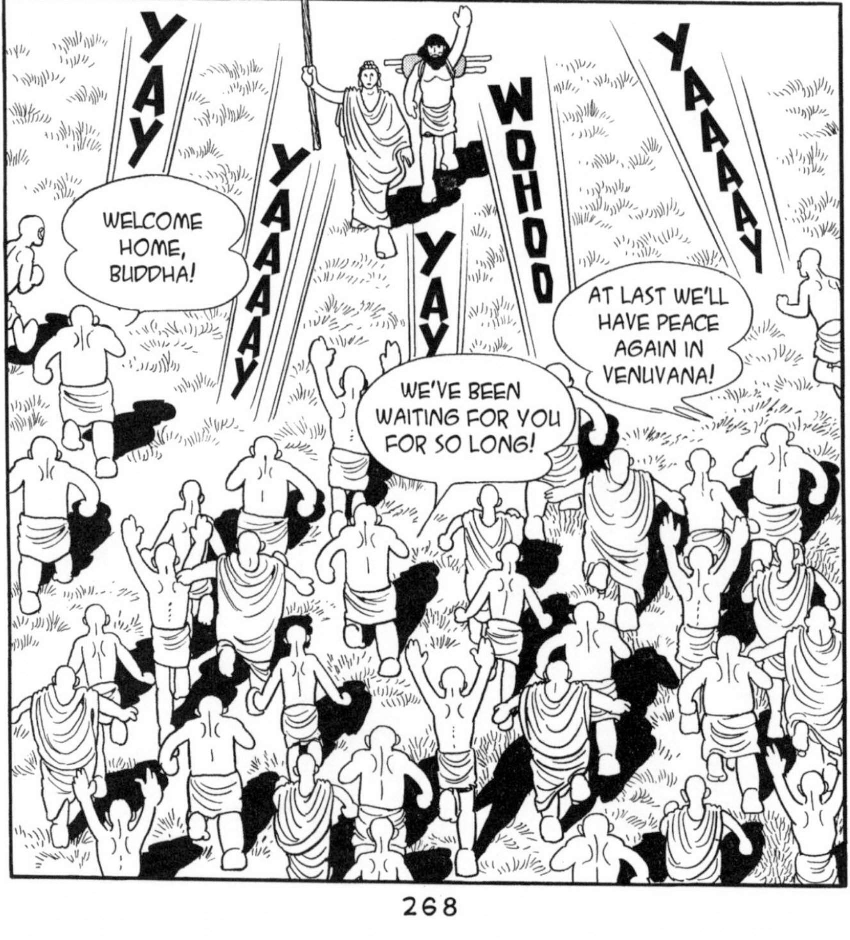
YAY
YAAAAAY
WELCOME HOME, BUDDHA!
YAY
WOHOOO
YAAAAAY
AT LAST WE'LL HAVE PEACE AGAIN IN VENUVANA!
WE'VE BEEN WAITING FOR YOU FOR SO LONG!

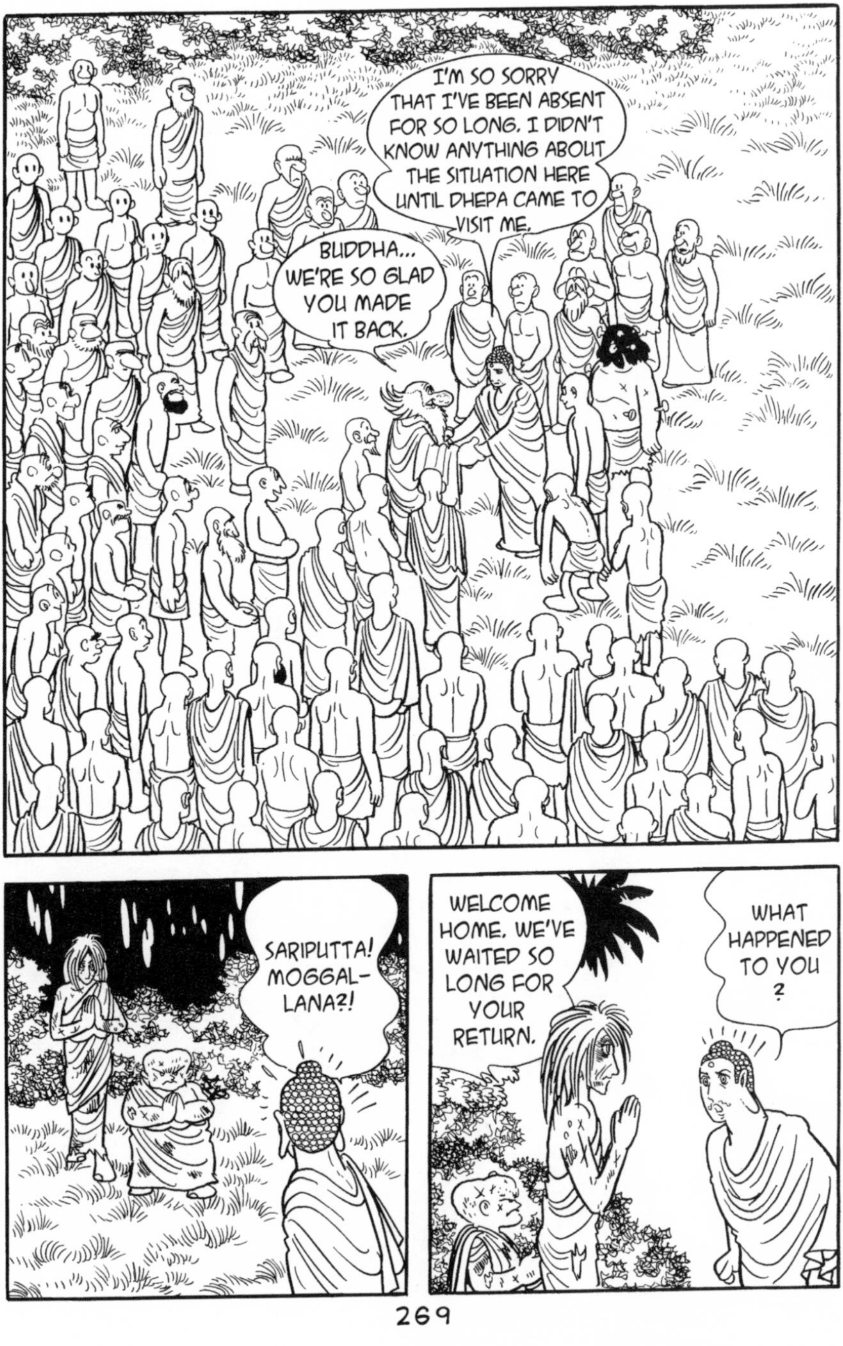
I'M SO SORRY THAT I'VE BEEN ABSENT FOR SO LONG. I DIDN'T KNOW ANYTHING ABOUT THE SITUATION HERE UNTIL DHEPA CAME TO VISIT ME.
BUDDHA... WE'RE SO GLAD YOU MADE IT BACK.
SARIPUTTA! MOGGAL-LANA?!
WELCOME HOME. WE'VE WAITED SO LONG FOR YOUR RETURN.
WHAT HAPPENED TO YOU ?

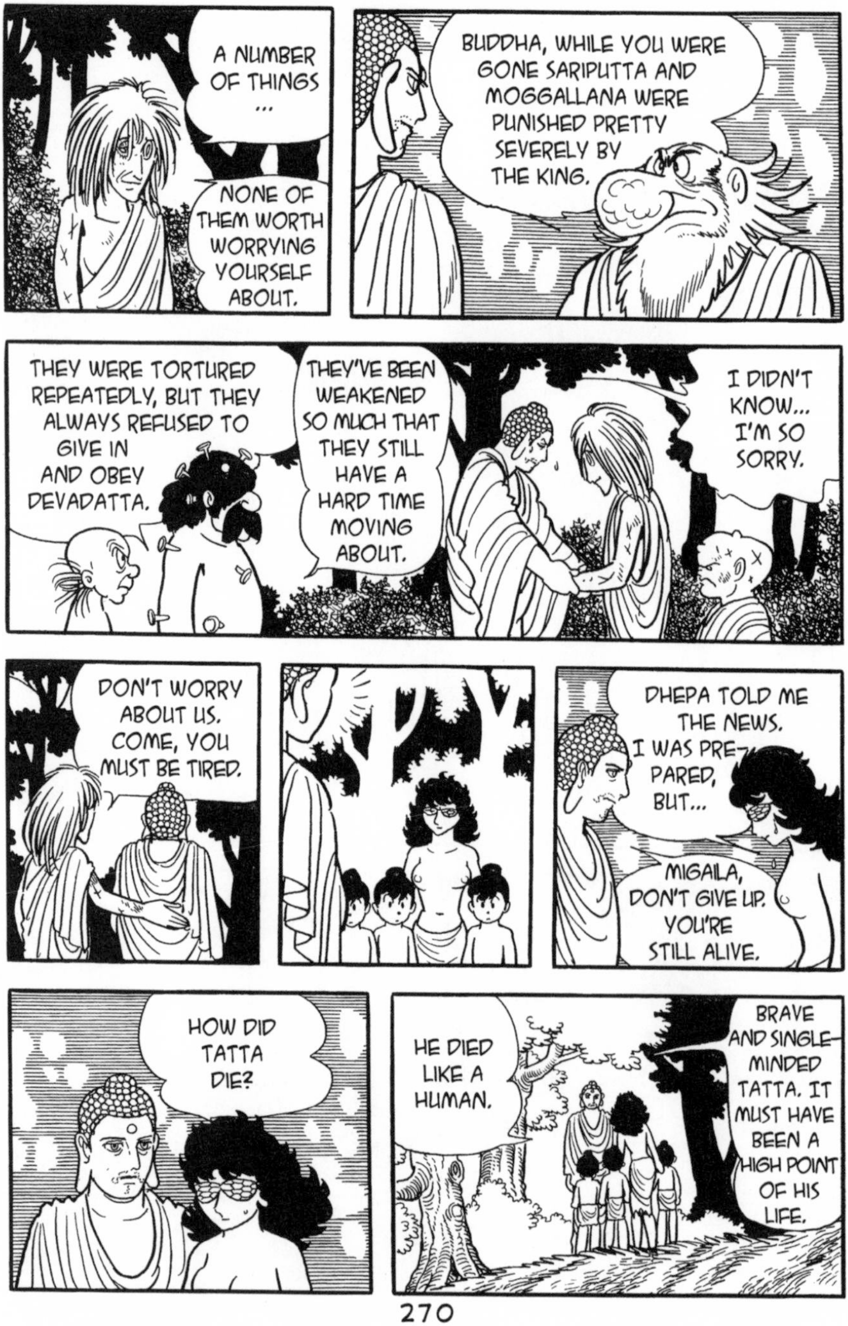
A NUMBER OF THINGS ...
NONE OF THEM WORTH WORRYING YOURSELF ABOUT.
BUDDHA, WHILE YOU WERE GONE SARIPUTTA AND MOGGALLANA WERE PUNISHED PRETTY SEVERELY BY THE KING.
THEY WERE TORTURED REPEATEDLY, BUT THEY ALWAYS REFUSED TO GIVE IN AND OBEY DEVADATTA.
THEY'VE BEEN WEAKENED SO MUCH THAT THEY STILL HAVE A HARD TIME MOVING ABOUT.
I DIDN'T KNOW... I'M SO SORRY.
DON'T WORRY ABOUT US. COME, YOU MUST BE TIRED.
DHEPA TOLD ME THE NEWS. I WAS PRE-PARED, BUT...
MIGAILA, DON'T GIVE UP. YOU'RE STILL ALIVE.
HOW DID TATTA DIE?
HE DIED LIKE A HUMAN.
BRAVE AND SINGLE-MINDED TATTA. IT MUST HAVE BEEN A HIGH POINT OF HIS LIFE.

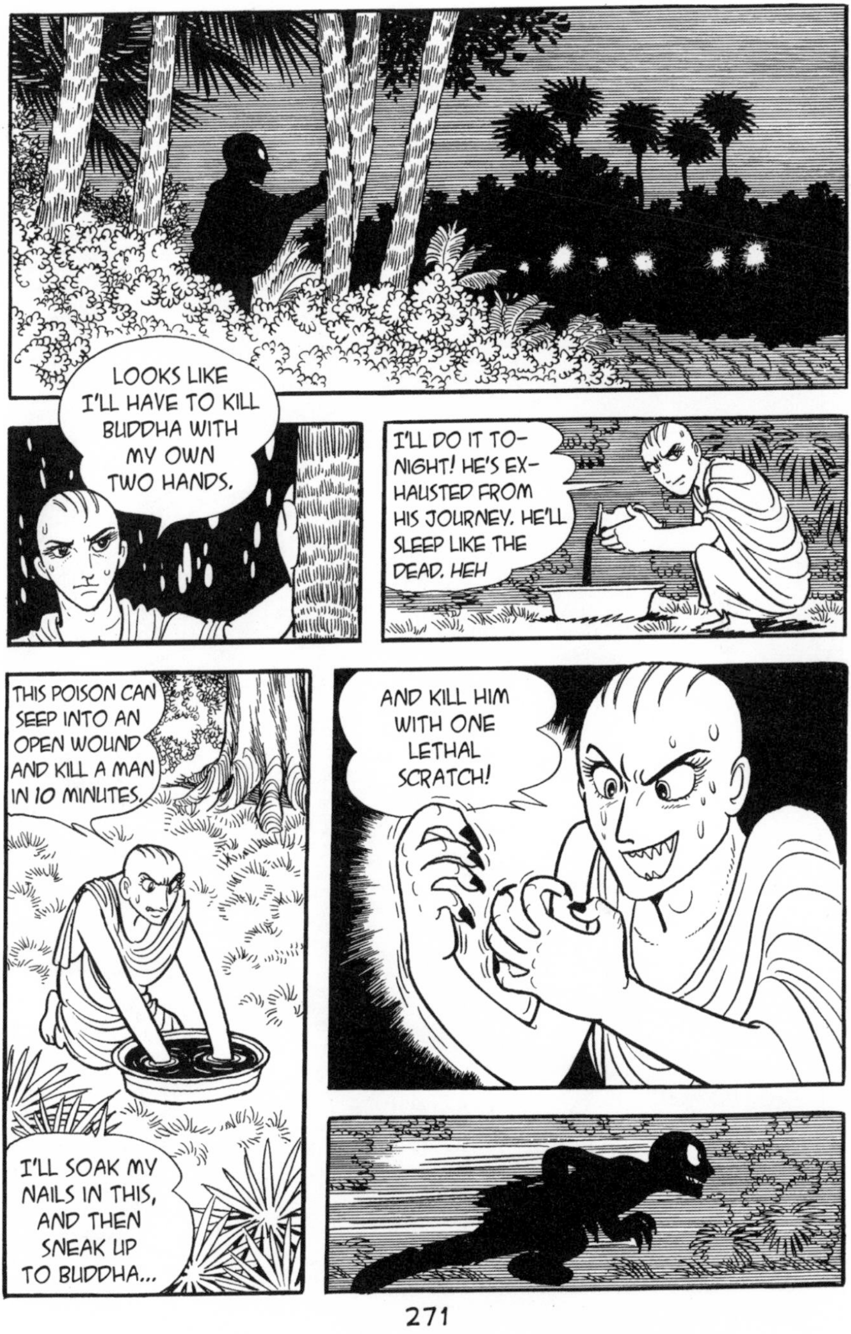
LOOKS LIKE I'LL HAVE TO KILL BUDDHA WITH MY OWN TWO HANDS.
I'LL DO IT TO-NIGHT! HE'S EX-HAUSTED FROM HIS JOURNEY. HE'LL SLEEP LIKE THE DEAD. HEH
THIS POISON CAN SEEP INTO AN OPEN WOUND AND KILL A MAN IN 10 MINUTES.
I'LL SOAK MY NAILS IN THIS, AND THEN SNEAK UP TO BUDDHA...
AND KILL HIM WITH ONE LETHAL SCRATCH!

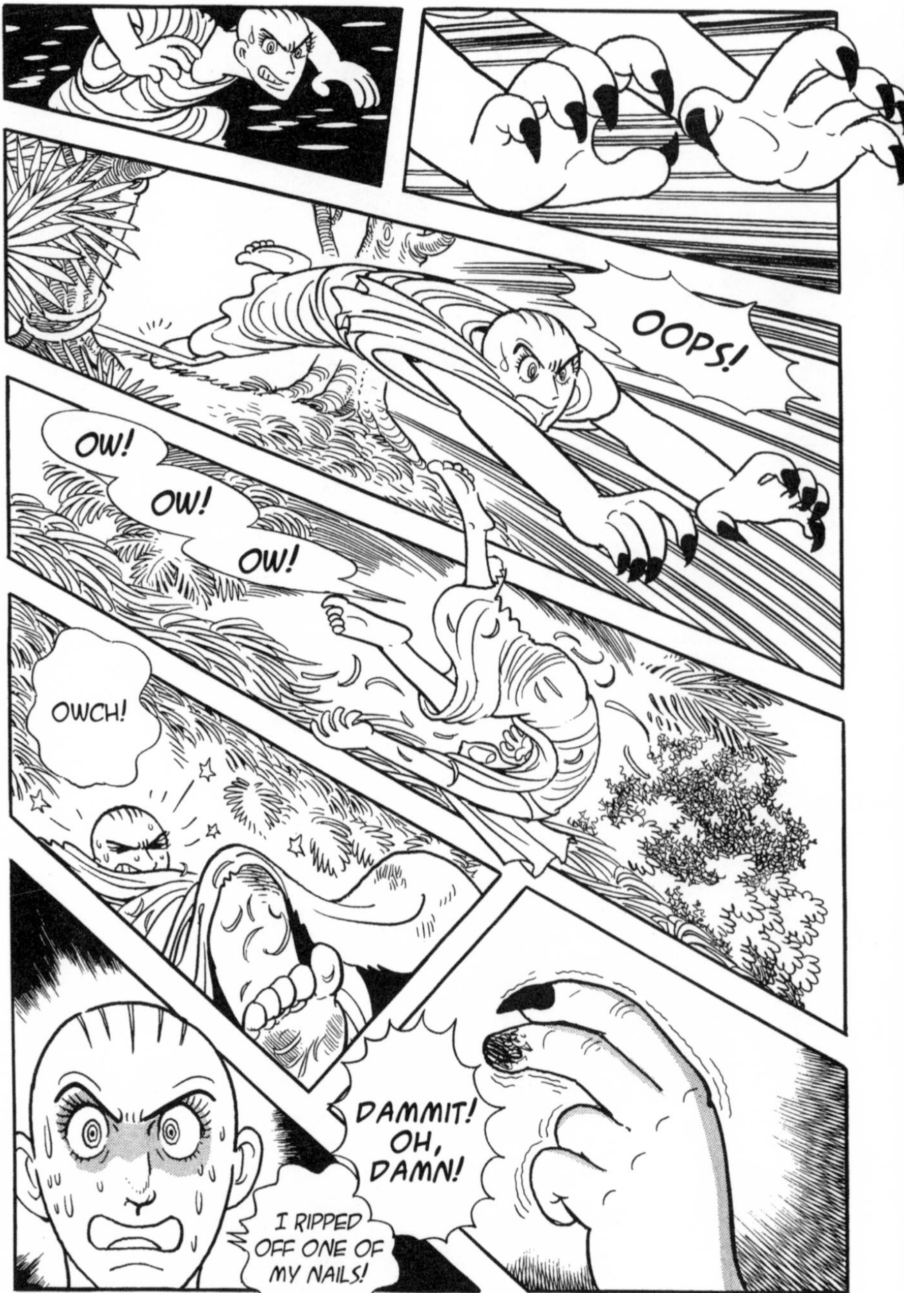
OOPS!
OW!
OW!
OW!
OWCH!
DAMMIT! OH, DAMN!
I RIPPED OFF ONE OF MY NAILS!

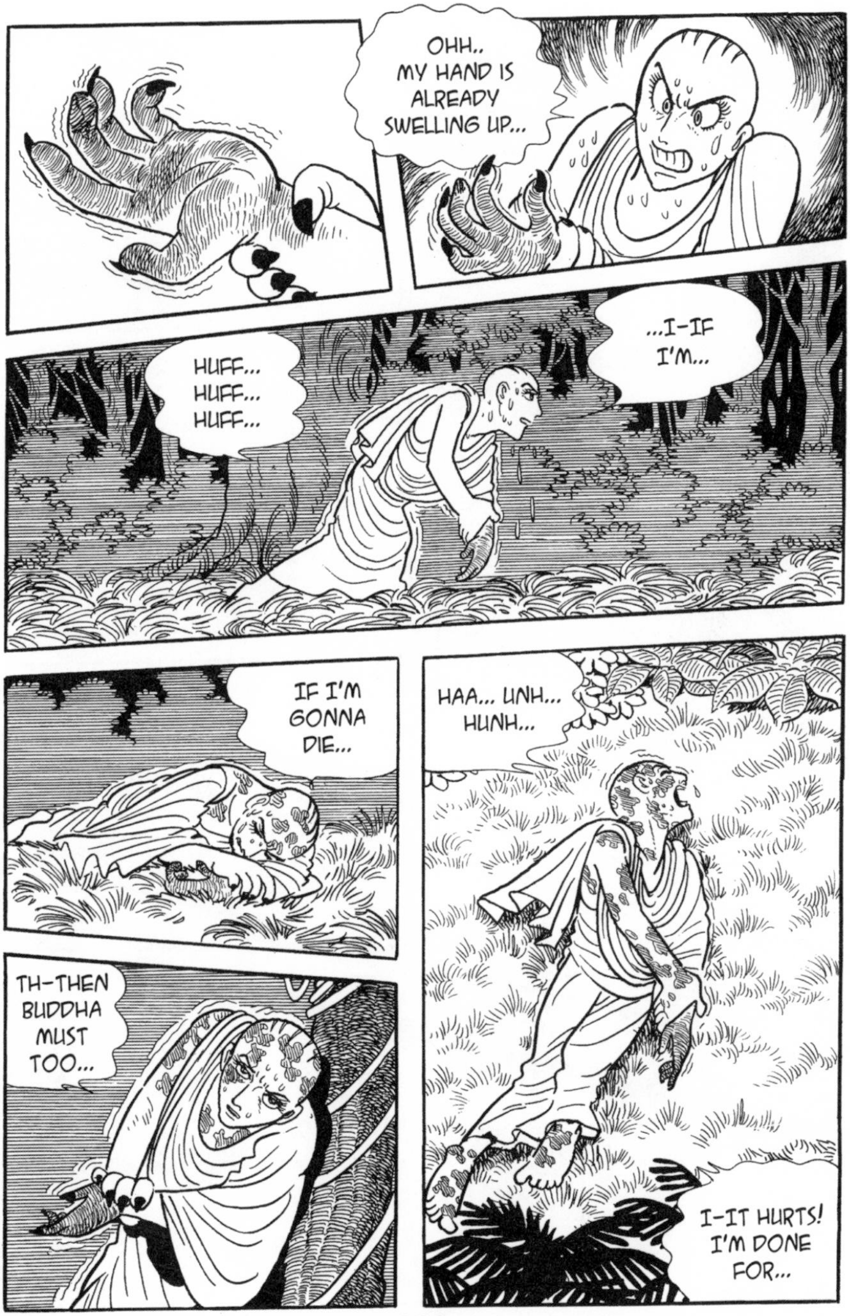
OHH.. MY HAND IS ALREADY SWELLING UP...
HUFF... HUFF... HUFF...
...I-IF I'M...
IF I'M GONNA DIE...
TH-THEN BUDDHA MUST TOO...
HAA... UNH... HUNH...
I-IT HURTS! I'M DONE FOR...

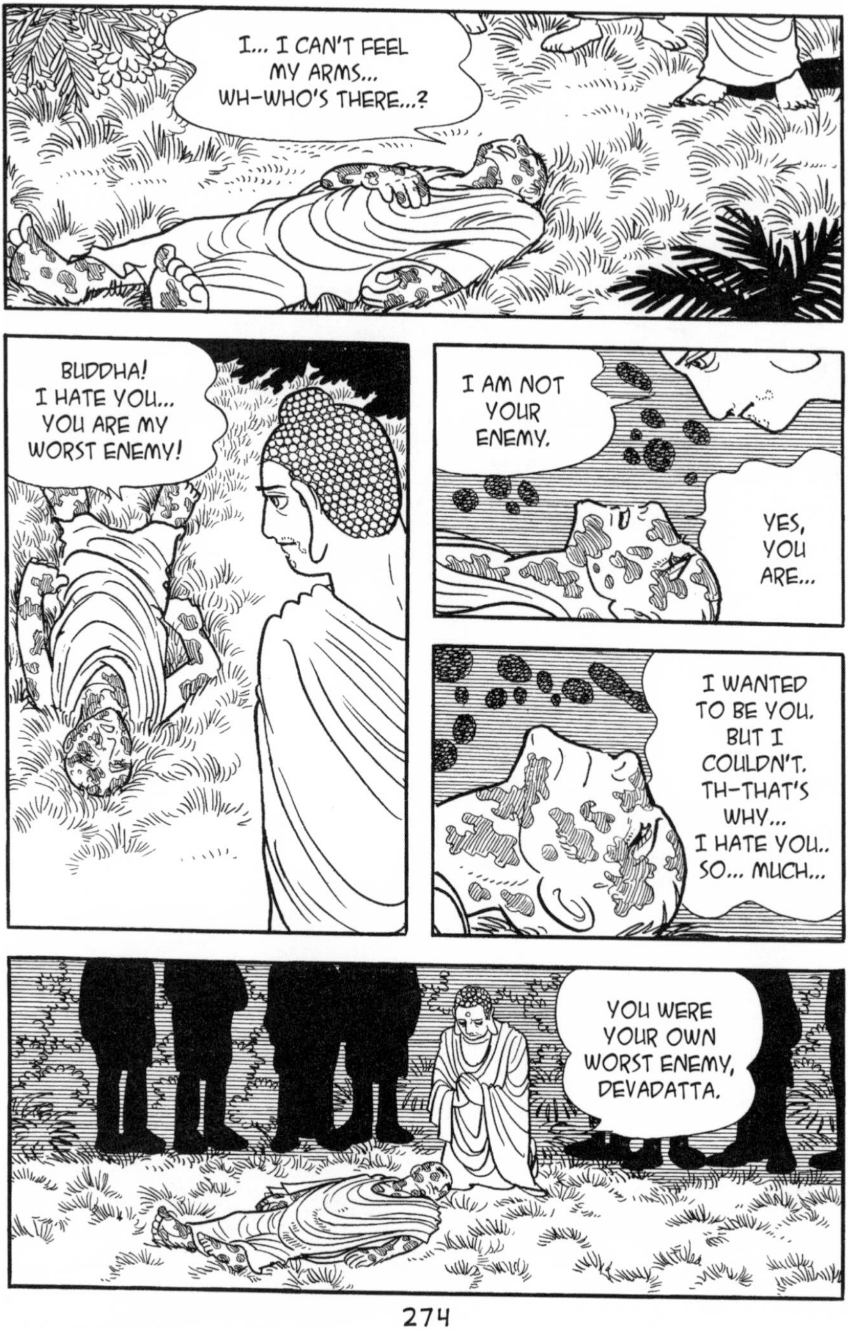
I... I CAN'T FEEL MY ARMS... WH-WHO'S THERE...?
BUDDHA! I HATE YOU... YOU ARE MY WORST ENEMY!
I AM NOT YOUR ENEMY.
YES, YOU ARE...
I WANTED TO BE YOU. BUT I COULDN'T. TH-THAT'S WHY... I HATE YOU.. SO... MUCH...
YOU WERE YOUR OWN WORST ENEMY, DEVADATTA.

CHAPTER THREE

KING AJATASATTU'S SMILE

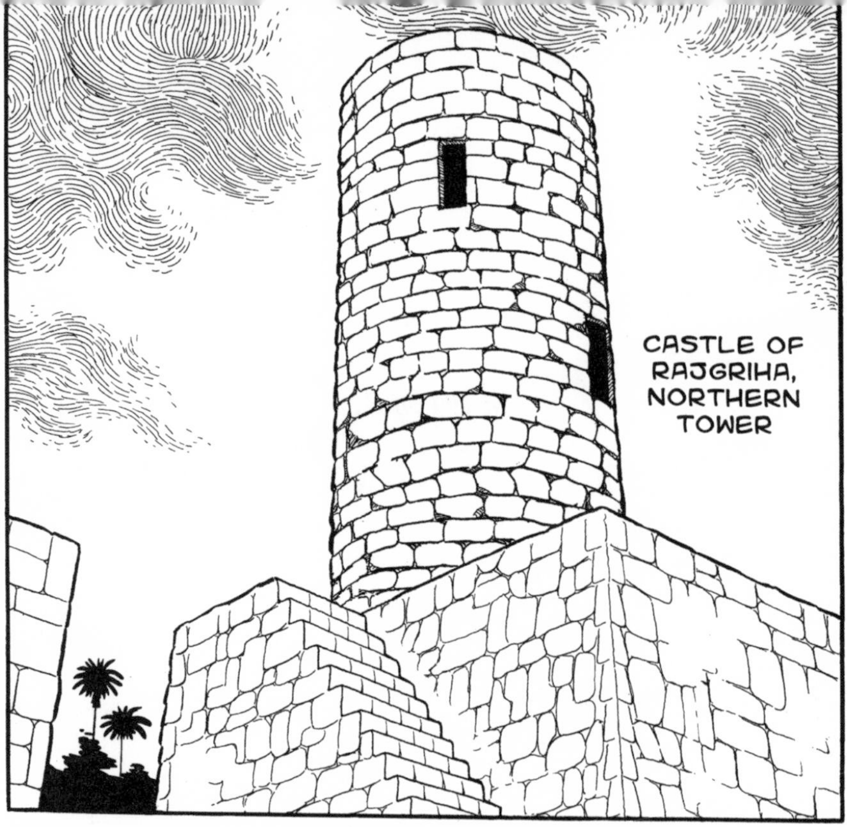
CASTLE OF RAJGRIHA, NORTHERN TOWER

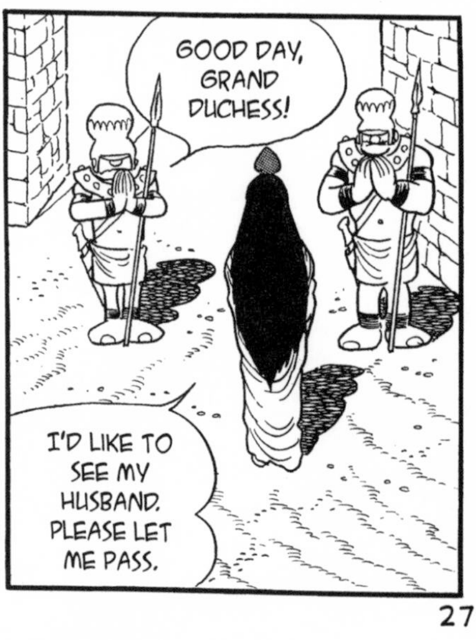
GOOD DAY, GRAND DUCHESS!
I'D LIKE TO SEE MY HUSBAND. PLEASE LET ME PASS.

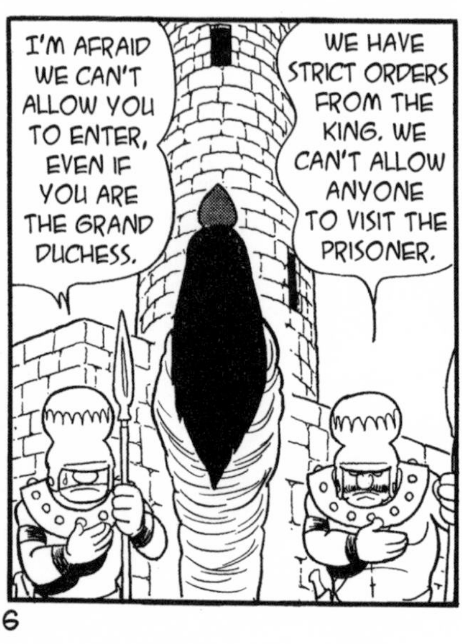
I'M AFRAID WE CAN'T ALLOW YOU TO ENTER, EVEN IF YOU ARE THE GRAND DUCHESS.
WE HAVE STRICT ORDERS FROM THE KING. WE CAN'T ALLOW ANYONE TO VISIT THE PRISONER.

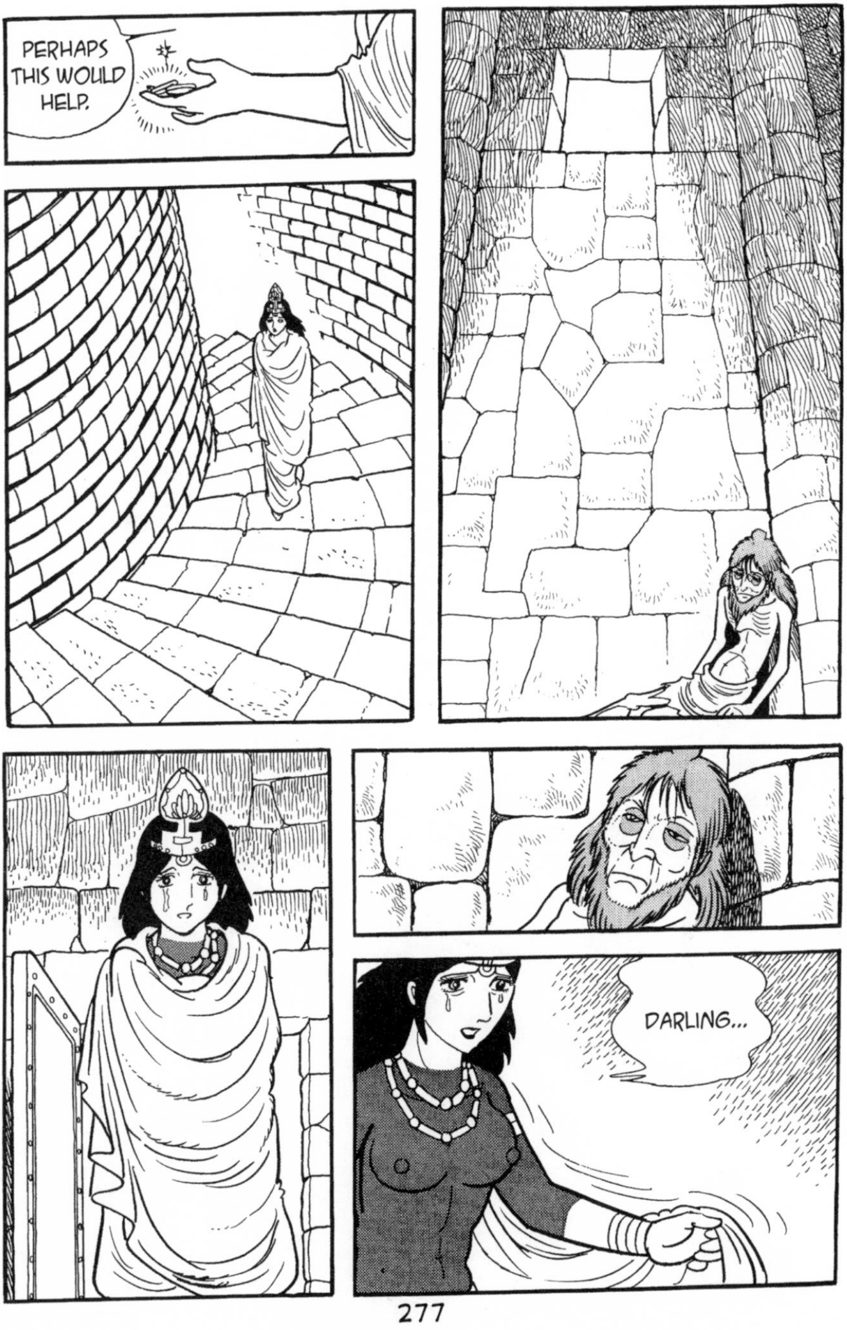
PERHAPS THIS WOULD HELP.
DARLING...

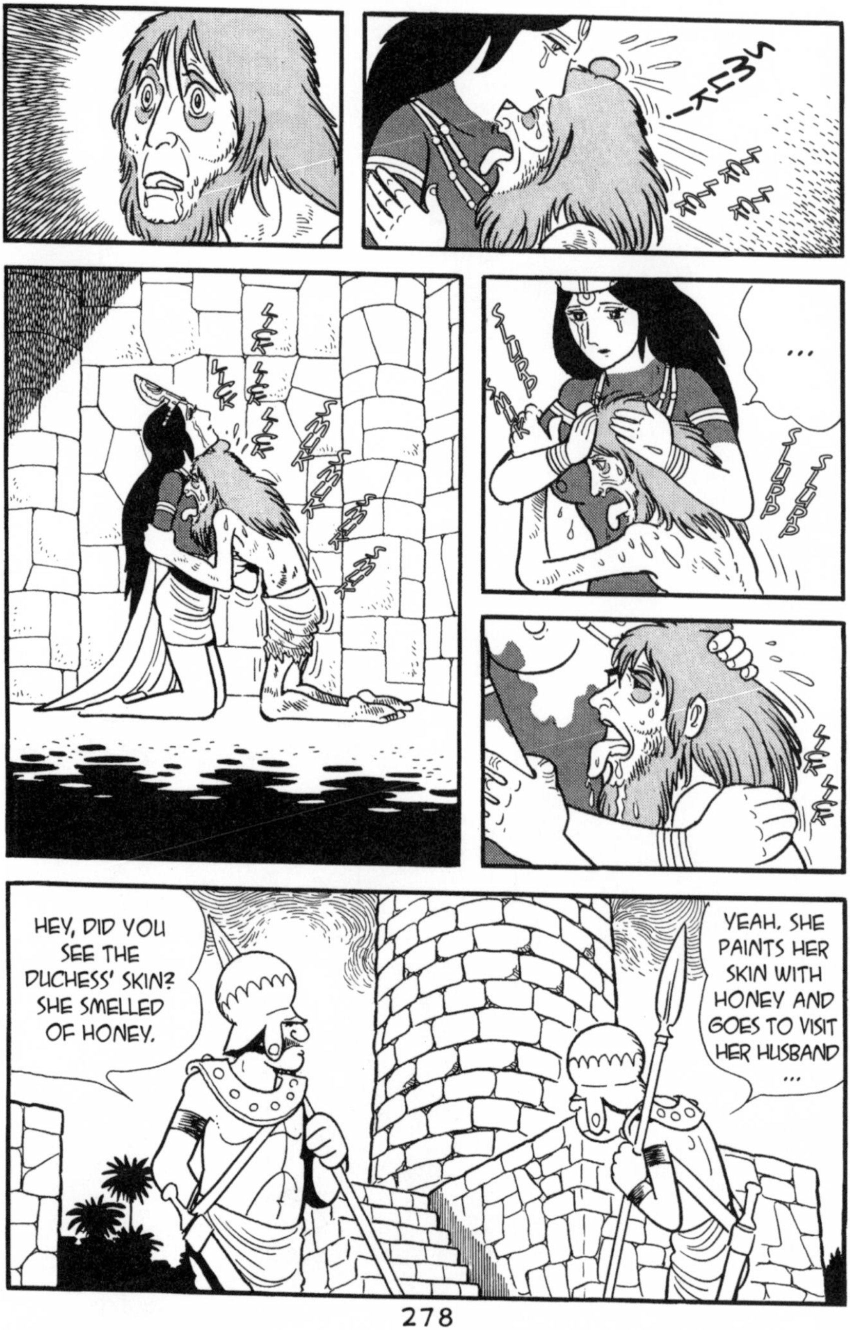
LICK LICK LICK
LICK LICK LICK LICK LICK
SLURP
...
SLURP SLURP
LICK LICK
HEY, DID YOU SEE THE DUCHESS' SKIN? SHE SMELLED OF HONEY.
YEAH. SHE PAINTS HER SKIN WITH HONEY AND GOES TO VISIT HER HUSBAND ...

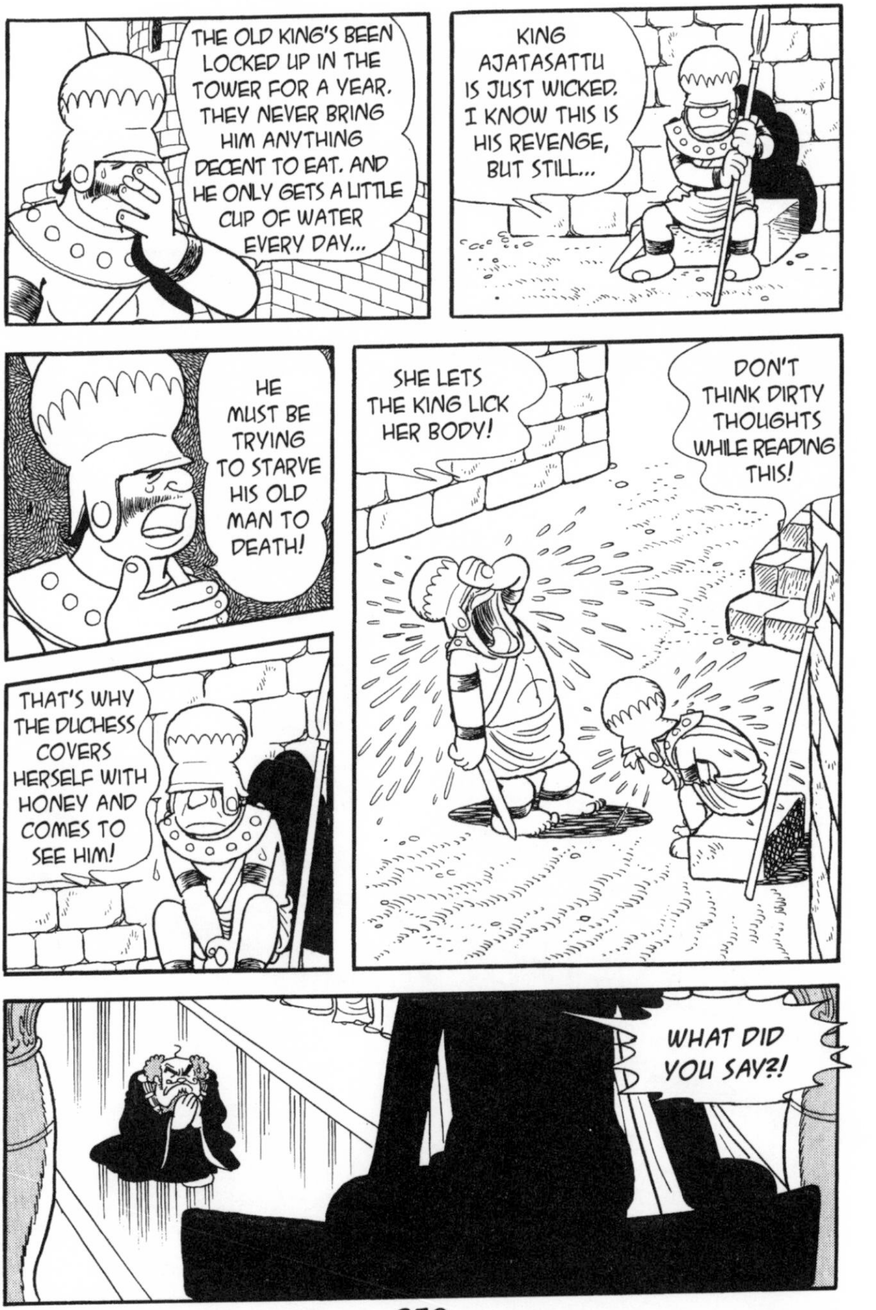
THE OLD KING'S BEEN LOCKED UP IN THE TOWER FOR A YEAR. THEY NEVER BRING HIM ANYTHING DECENT TO EAT. AND HE ONLY GETS A LITTLE CUP OF WATER EVERY DAY...
KING AJATASATTU IS JUST WICKED. I KNOW THIS IS HIS REVENGE, BUT STILL...
HE MUST BE TRYING TO STARVE HIS OLD MAN TO DEATH!
THAT'S WHY THE DUCHESS COVERS HERSELF WITH HONEY AND COMES TO SEE HIM!
SHE LETS THE KING LICK HER BODY!
DON'T THINK DIRTY THOUGHTS WHILE READING THIS!
WHAT DID YOU SAY?!

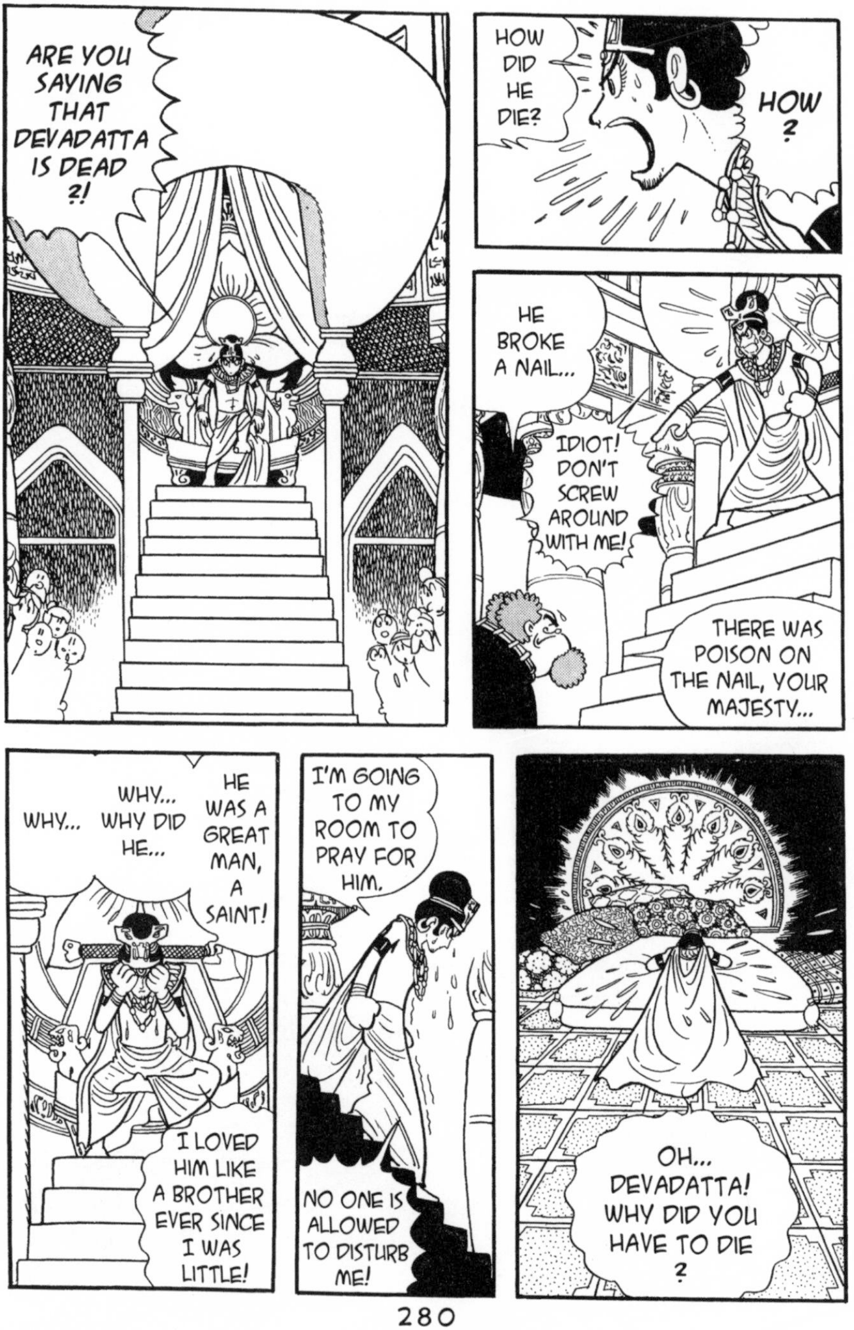

ARE YOU SAYING THAT DEVADATTA IS DEAD ?!
HOW DID HE DIE?
HOW ?
HE BROKE A NAIL...
IDIOT! DON'T SCREW AROUND WITH ME!
THERE WAS POISON ON THE NAIL, YOUR MAJESTY...
WHY...
WHY... WHY DID HE...
HE WAS A GREAT MAN, A SAINT!
I LOVED HIM LIKE A BROTHER EVER SINCE I WAS LITTLE!
I'M GOING TO MY ROOM TO PRAY FOR HIM.
NO ONE IS ALLOWED TO DISTURB ME!
OH... DEVADATTA! WHY DID YOU HAVE TO DIE ?

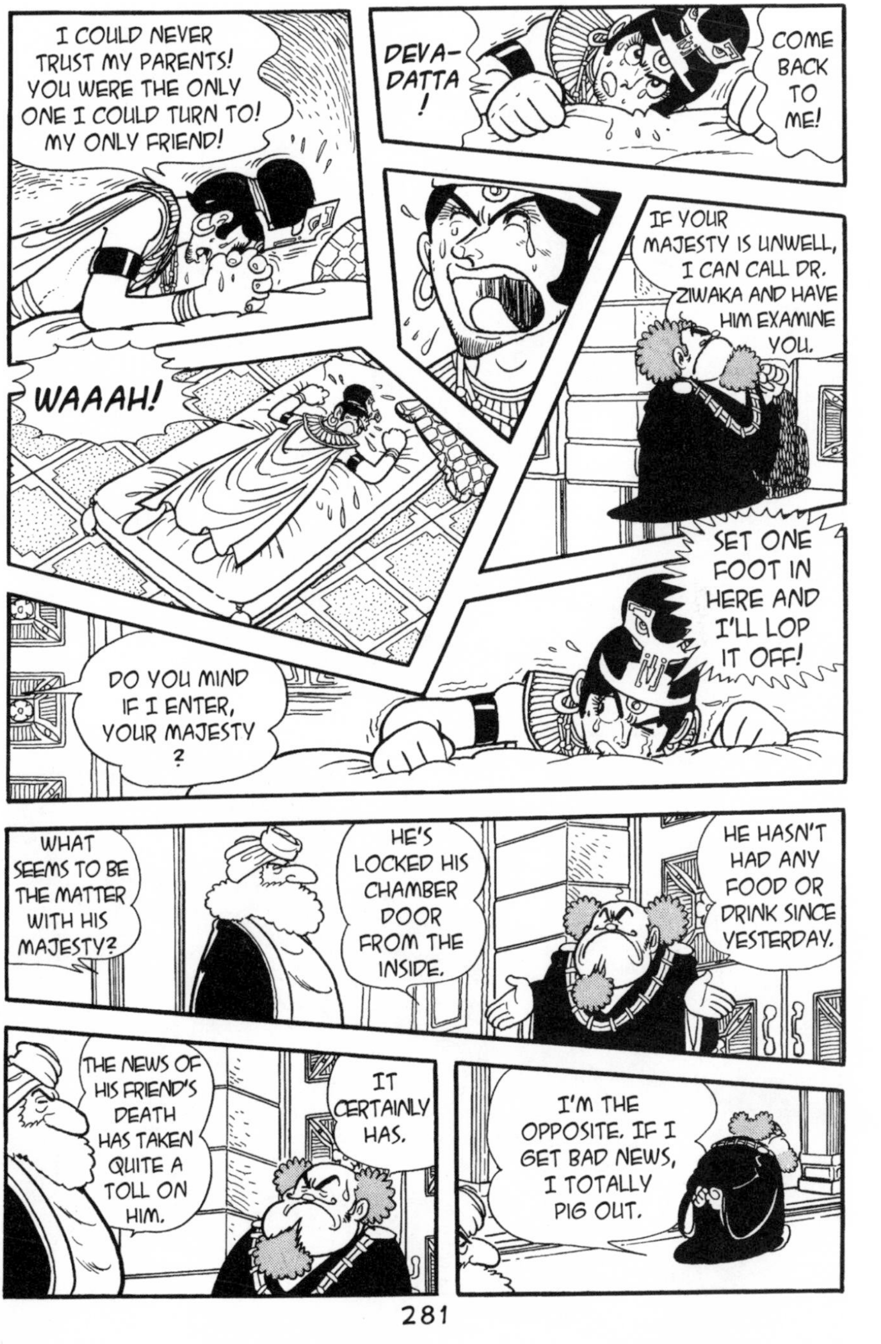
I COULD NEVER TRUST MY PARENTS! YOU WERE THE ONLY ONE I COULD TURN TO! MY ONLY FRIEND!
DEVA-DATTA!
COME BACK TO ME!
WAAAH!
IF YOUR MAJESTY IS UNWELL, I CAN CALL DR. ZIWAKA AND HAVE HIM EXAMINE YOU.
DO YOU MIND IF I ENTER, YOUR MAJESTY?
SET ONE FOOT IN HERE AND I'LL LOP IT OFF!
WHAT SEEMS TO BE THE MATTER WITH HIS MAJESTY?
HE'S LOCKED HIS CHAMBER DOOR FROM THE INSIDE.
HE HASN'T HAD ANY FOOD OR DRINK SINCE YESTERDAY.
THE NEWS OF HIS FRIEND'S DEATH HAS TAKEN QUITE A TOLL ON HIM.
IT CERTAINLY HAS.
I'M THE OPPOSITE. IF I GET BAD NEWS, I TOTALLY PIG OUT.

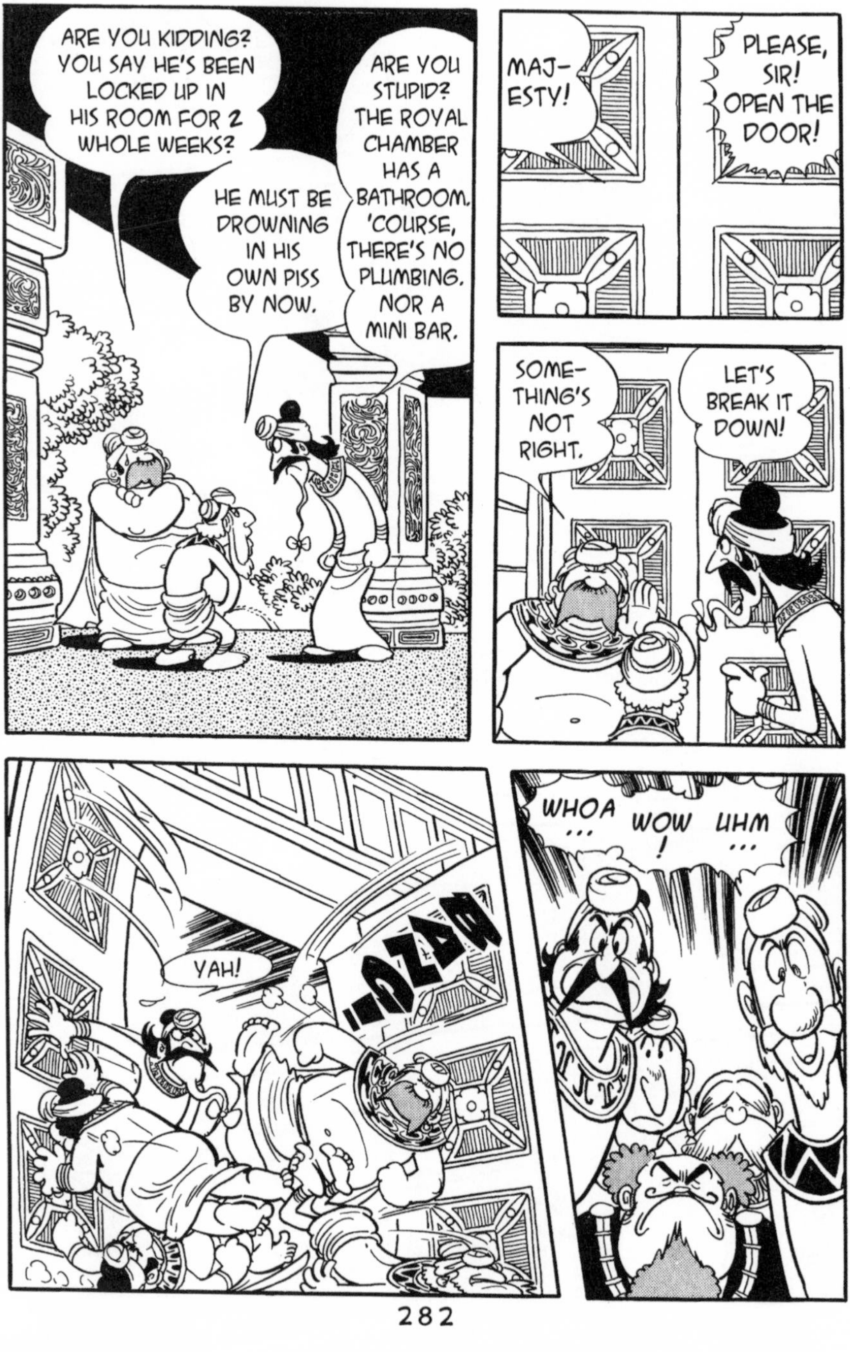
ARE YOU KIDDING? YOU SAY HE'S BEEN LOCKED UP IN HIS ROOM FOR 2 WHOLE WEEKS?
HE MUST BE DROWNING IN HIS OWN PISS BY NOW.
ARE YOU STUPID? THE ROYAL CHAMBER HAS A BATHROOM. 'COURSE, THERE'S NO PLUMBING. NOR A MINI BAR.
MAJ-ESTY!
PLEASE, SIR! OPEN THE DOOR!
SOME-THING'S NOT RIGHT.
LET'S BREAK IT DOWN!
YAH!
WHOA ...
WOW !
UHM ...

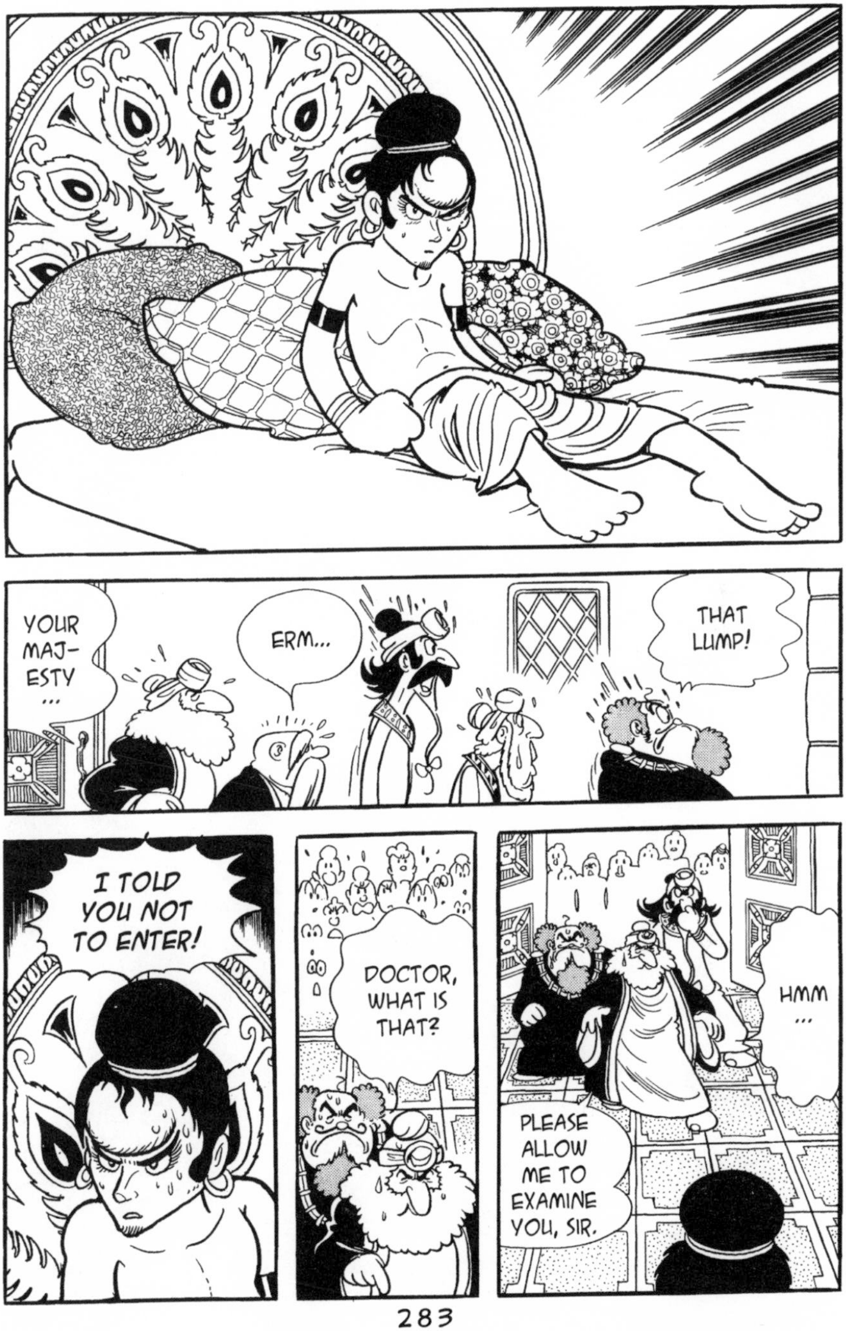
YOUR MAJ-ESTY ...
ERM...
THAT LUMP!
I TOLD YOU NOT TO ENTER!
DOCTOR, WHAT IS THAT?
HMM ...
PLEASE ALLOW ME TO EXAMINE YOU, SIR.

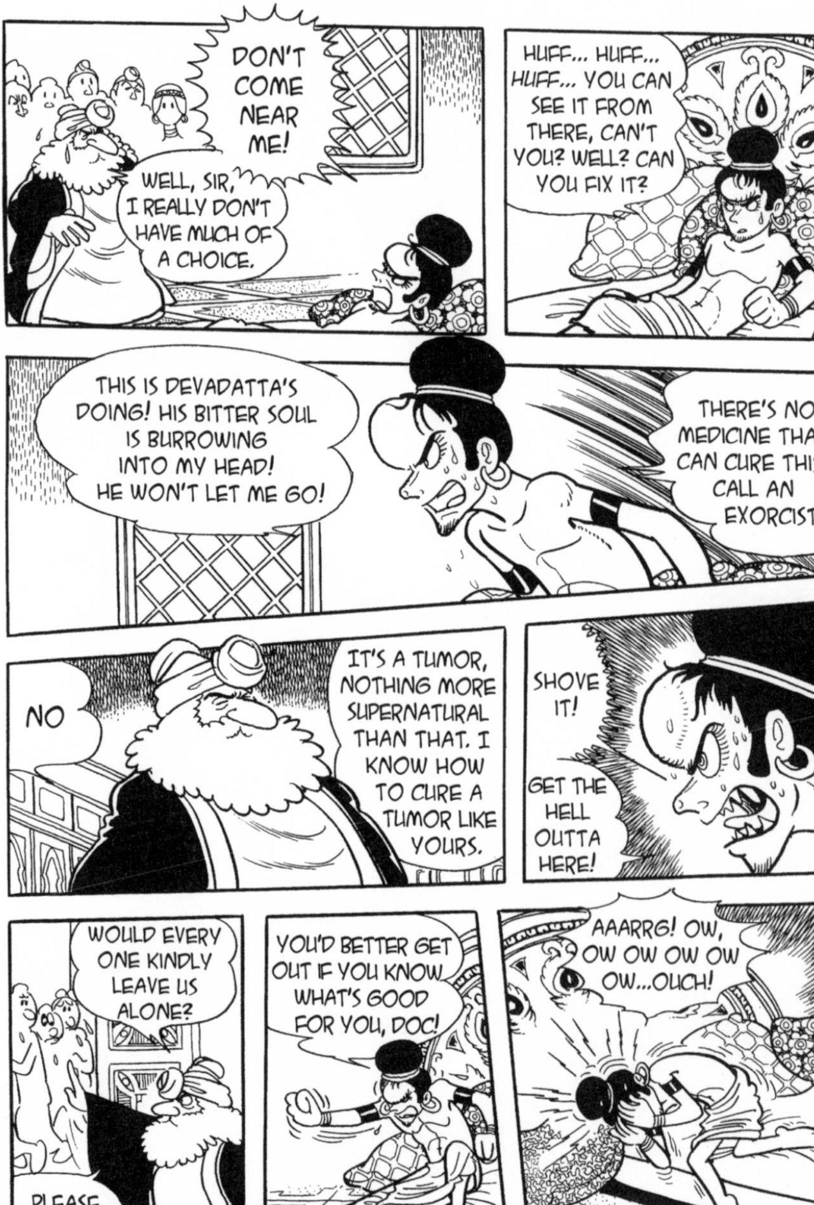
DON'T COME NEAR ME!
WELL, SIR, I REALLY DON'T HAVE MUCH OF A CHOICE.
HUFF... HUFF... HUFF... YOU CAN SEE IT FROM THERE, CAN'T YOU? WELL? CAN YOU FIX IT?
THIS IS DEVADATTA'S DOING! HIS BITTER SOUL IS BURROWING INTO MY HEAD! HE WON'T LET ME GO!
THERE'S NO MEDICINE THAT CAN CURE THIS! CALL AN EXORCIST!
NO
IT'S A TUMOR, NOTHING MORE SUPERNATURAL THAN THAT. I KNOW HOW TO CURE A TUMOR LIKE YOURS.
SHOVE IT!
GET THE HELL OUTTA HERE!
WOULD EVERY ONE KINDLY LEAVE US ALONE?
PLEASE LEAVE THIS TO ME.
YOU'D BETTER GET OUT IF YOU KNOW WHAT'S GOOD FOR YOU, DOC!
AAARRG! OW, OW OW OW OW OW...OUCH!

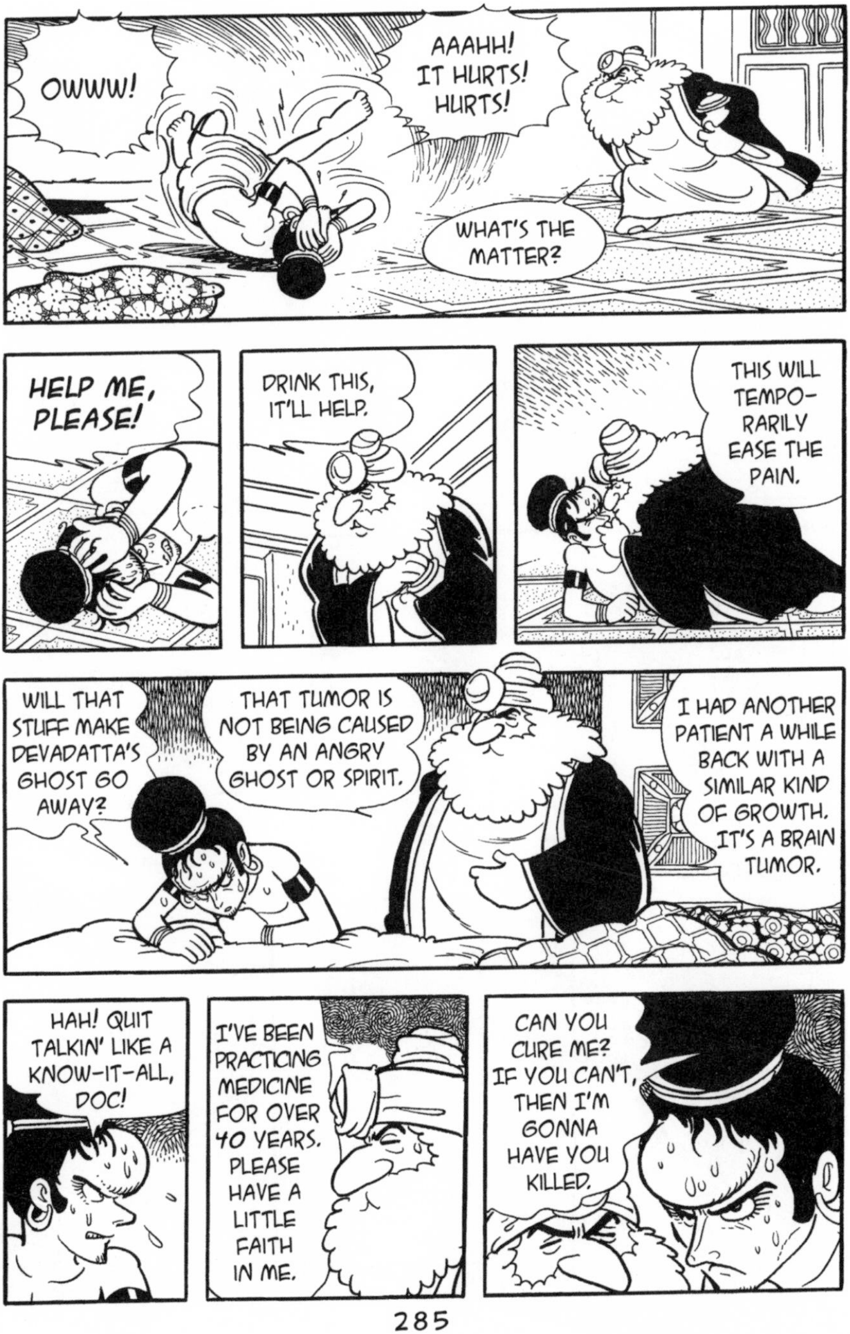
OWWW!
AAAHH! IT HURTS! HURTS!
WHAT'S THE MATTER?
HELP ME, PLEASE!
DRINK THIS, IT'LL HELP.
THIS WILL TEMPO-RARILY EASE THE PAIN.
WILL THAT STUFF MAKE DEVADATTA'S GHOST GO AWAY?
THAT TUMOR IS NOT BEING CAUSED BY AN ANGRY GHOST OR SPIRIT.
I HAD ANOTHER PATIENT A WHILE BACK WITH A SIMILAR KIND OF GROWTH. IT'S A BRAIN TUMOR.
HAH! QUIT TALKIN' LIKE A KNOW-IT-ALL, DOC!
I'VE BEEN PRACTICING MEDICINE FOR OVER 40 YEARS. PLEASE HAVE A LITTLE FAITH IN ME.
CAN YOU CURE ME? IF YOU CAN'T, THEN I'M GONNA HAVE YOU KILLED.

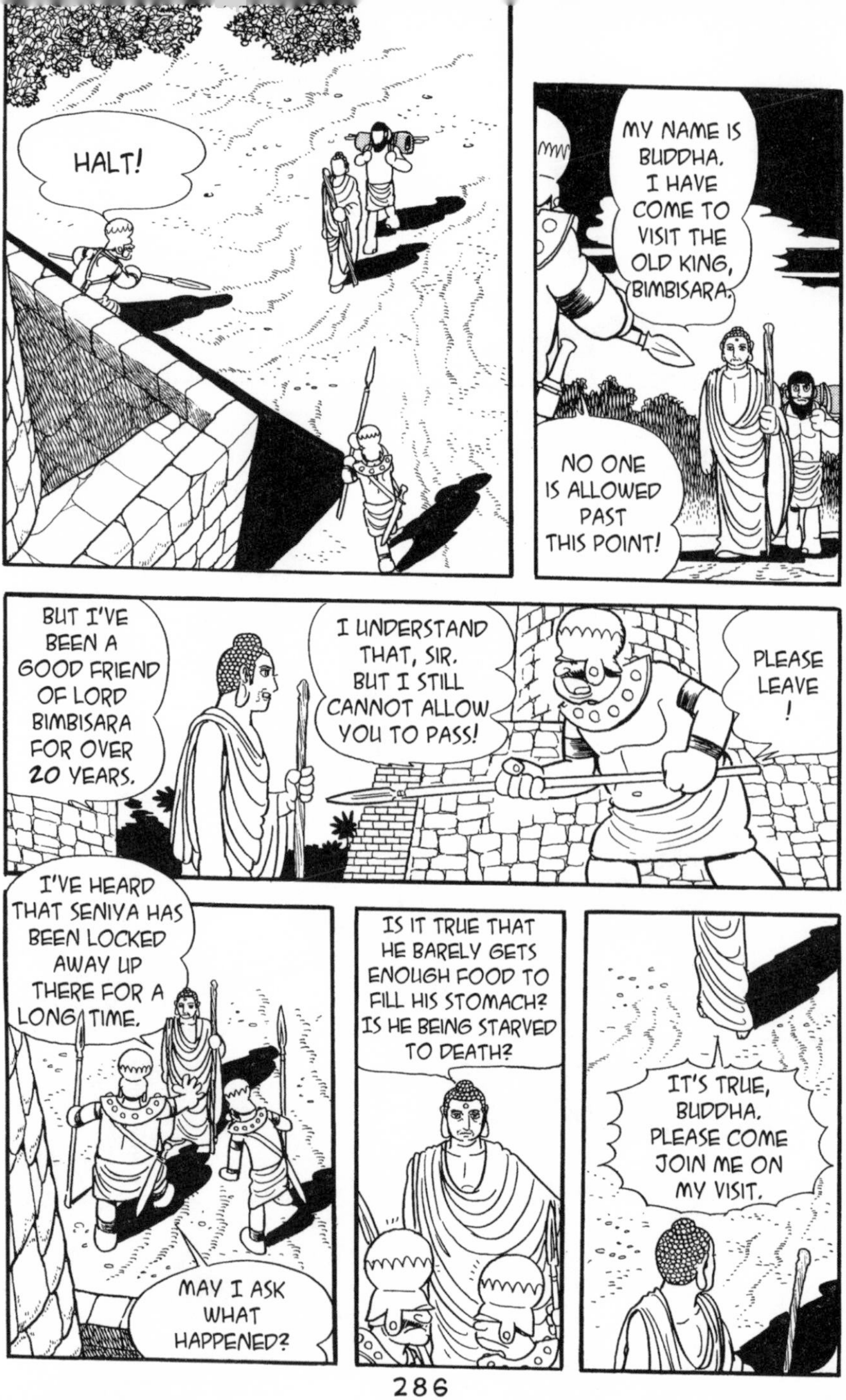
HALT!
MY NAME IS BUDDHA. I HAVE COME TO VISIT THE OLD KING, BIMBISARA.
NO ONE IS ALLOWED PAST THIS POINT!
BUT I'VE BEEN A GOOD FRIEND OF LORD BIMBISARA FOR OVER 20 YEARS.
I UNDERSTAND THAT, SIR. BUT I STILL CANNOT ALLOW YOU TO PASS!
PLEASE LEAVE!
I'VE HEARD THAT SENIYA HAS BEEN LOCKED AWAY UP THERE FOR A LONG TIME.
MAY I ASK WHAT HAPPENED?
IS IT TRUE THAT HE BARELY GETS ENOUGH FOOD TO FILL HIS STOMACH? IS HE BEING STARVED TO DEATH?
IT'S TRUE, BUDDHA. PLEASE COME JOIN ME ON MY VISIT.

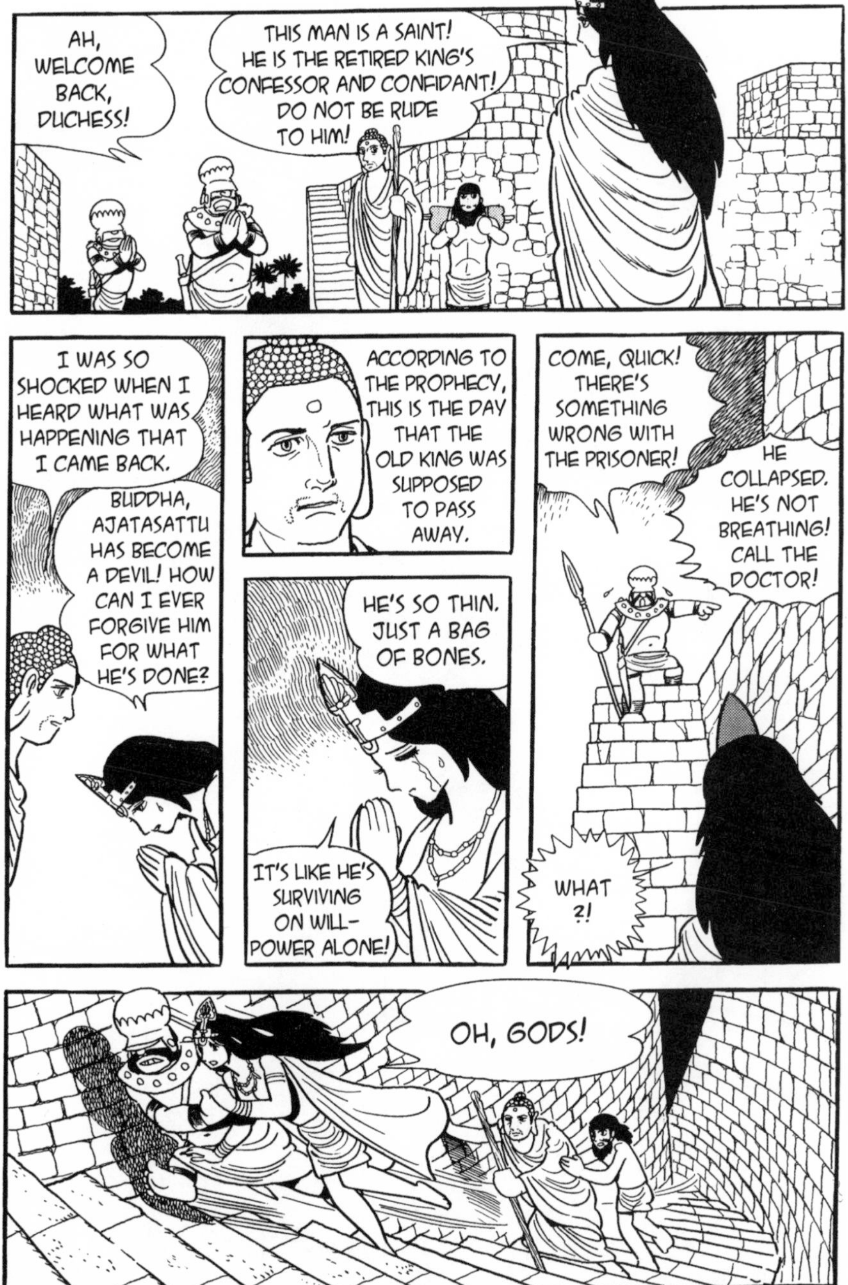
AH, WELCOME BACK, DUCHESS!
THIS MAN IS A SAINT! HE IS THE RETIRED KING'S CONFESSOR AND CONFIDANT! DO NOT BE RUDE TO HIM!
I WAS SO SHOCKED WHEN I HEARD WHAT WAS HAPPENING THAT I CAME BACK.
BUDDHA, AJATASATTU HAS BECOME A DEVIL! HOW CAN I EVER FORGIVE HIM FOR WHAT HE'S DONE?
ACCORDING TO THE PROPHECY, THIS IS THE DAY THAT THE OLD KING WAS SUPPOSED TO PASS AWAY.
HE'S SO THIN. JUST A BAG OF BONES.
IT'S LIKE HE'S SURVIVING ON WILL-POWER ALONE!
COME, QUICK! THERE'S SOMETHING WRONG WITH THE PRISONER!
HE COLLAPSED. HE'S NOT BREATHING! CALL THE DOCTOR!
WHAT?!
OH, GODS!

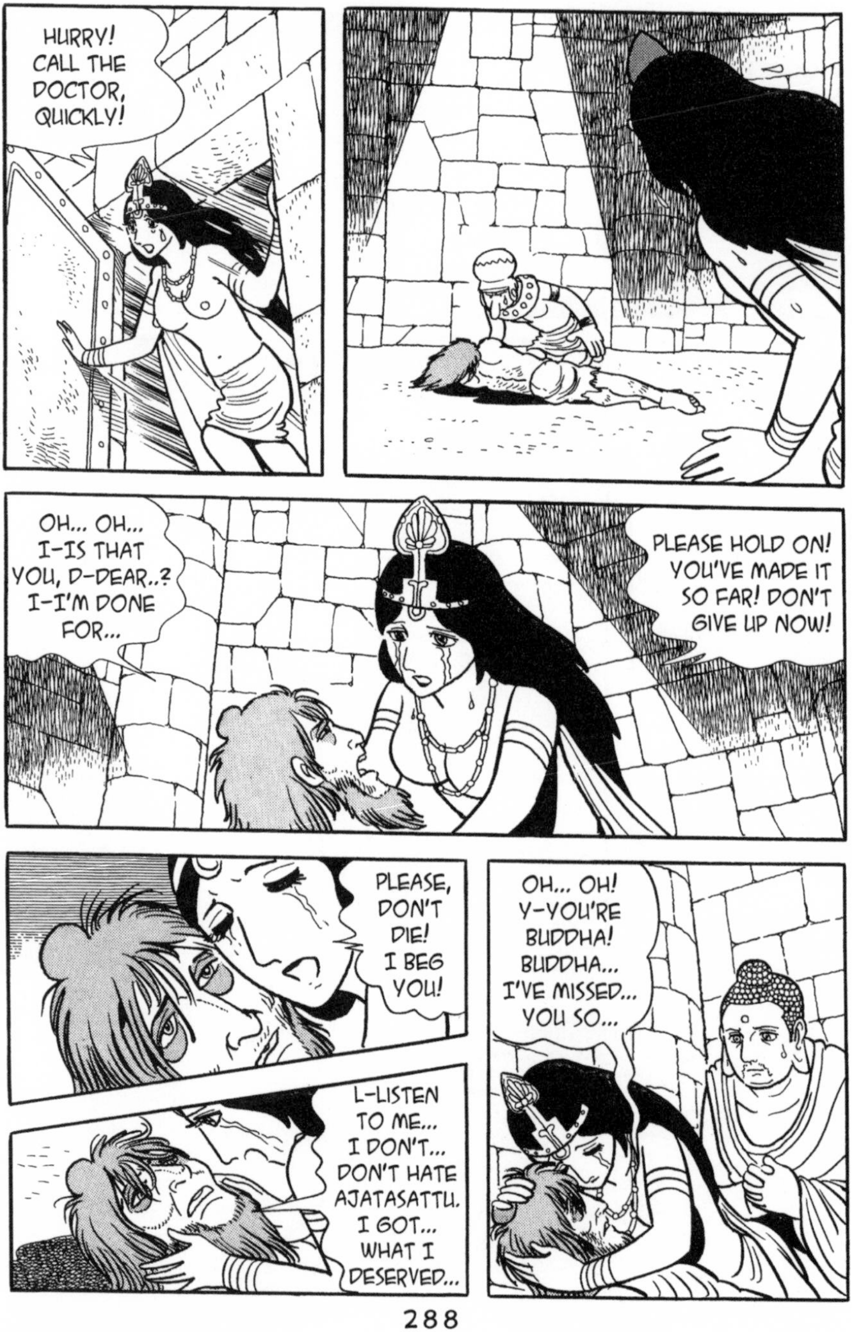
HURRY! CALL THE DOCTOR, QUICKLY!
OH... OH... I-IS THAT YOU, D-DEAR..? I-I'M DONE FOR...
PLEASE HOLD ON! YOU'VE MADE IT SO FAR! DON'T GIVE UP NOW!
PLEASE, DON'T DIE! I BEG YOU!
L-LISTEN TO ME... I DON'T... DON'T HATE AJATASATTU. I GOT... WHAT I DESERVED...
OH... OH! Y-YOU'RE BUDDHA! BUDDHA... I'VE MISSED... YOU SO...

TH-THERE'S SOMETHING... I NEED T-TO ASK... YOU... BEFORE I D-DIE...

WHAT IS IT? I'M LISTENING.

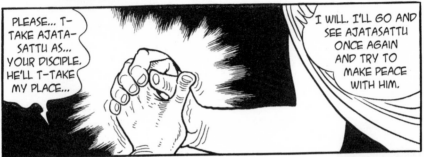

PLEASE... T-TAKE AJATA-SATTU AS... YOUR DISCIPLE. HE'LL T-TAKE MY PLACE...

I WILL. I'LL GO AND SEE AJATASATTU ONCE AGAIN AND TRY TO MAKE PEACE WITH HIM.

I FEEL SORRY FOR HIM. I...WAS WRONG TO...AVOID HIM LIKE I DID... I MADE A TERRIBLE... MISTAKE...

P-PLEASE... I BEG YOU... SAVE MY BOY... AJATA-SATTU

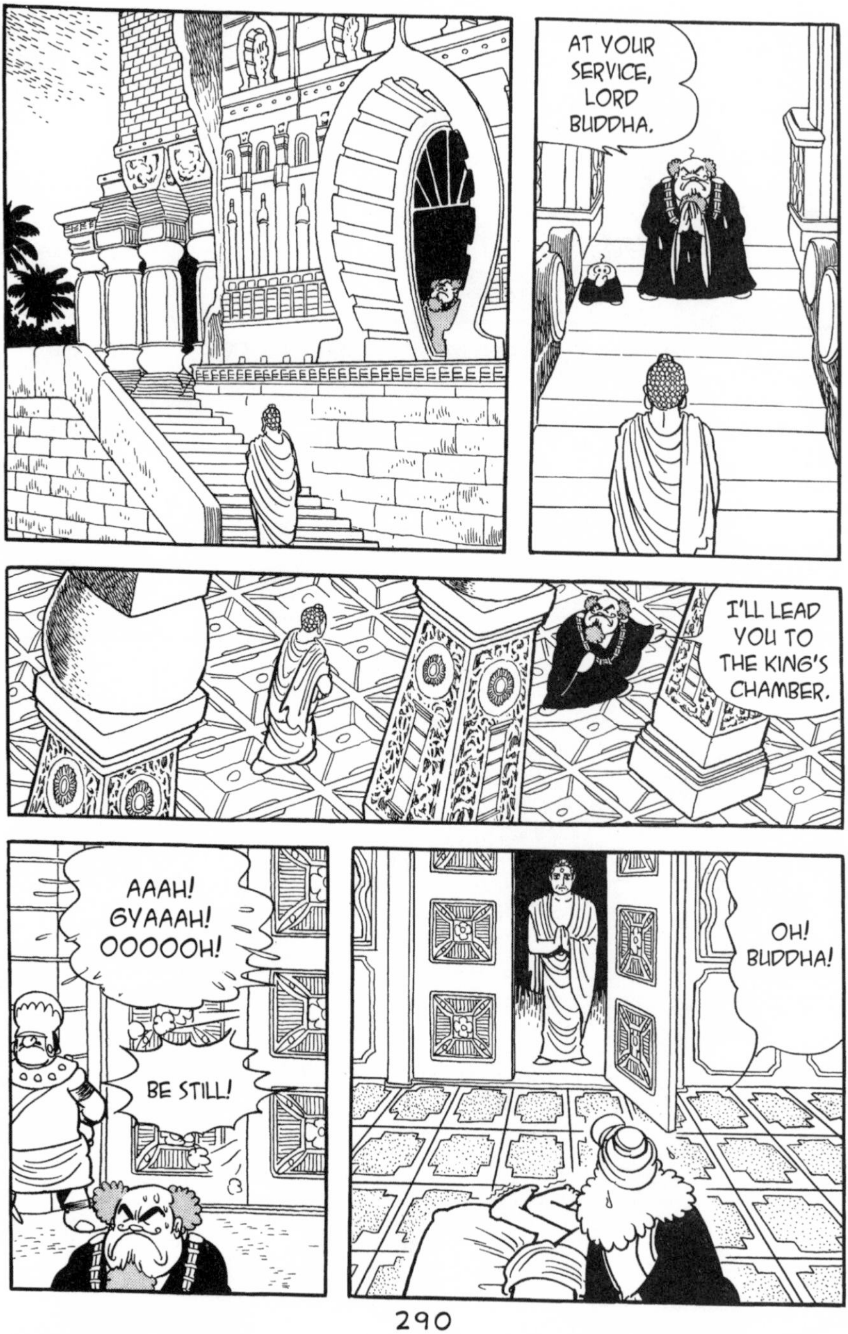
AT YOUR SERVICE, LORD BUDDHA.
I'LL LEAD YOU TO THE KING'S CHAMBER.
AAAH! GYAAAH! OOOOOH!
BE STILL!
OH! BUDDHA!

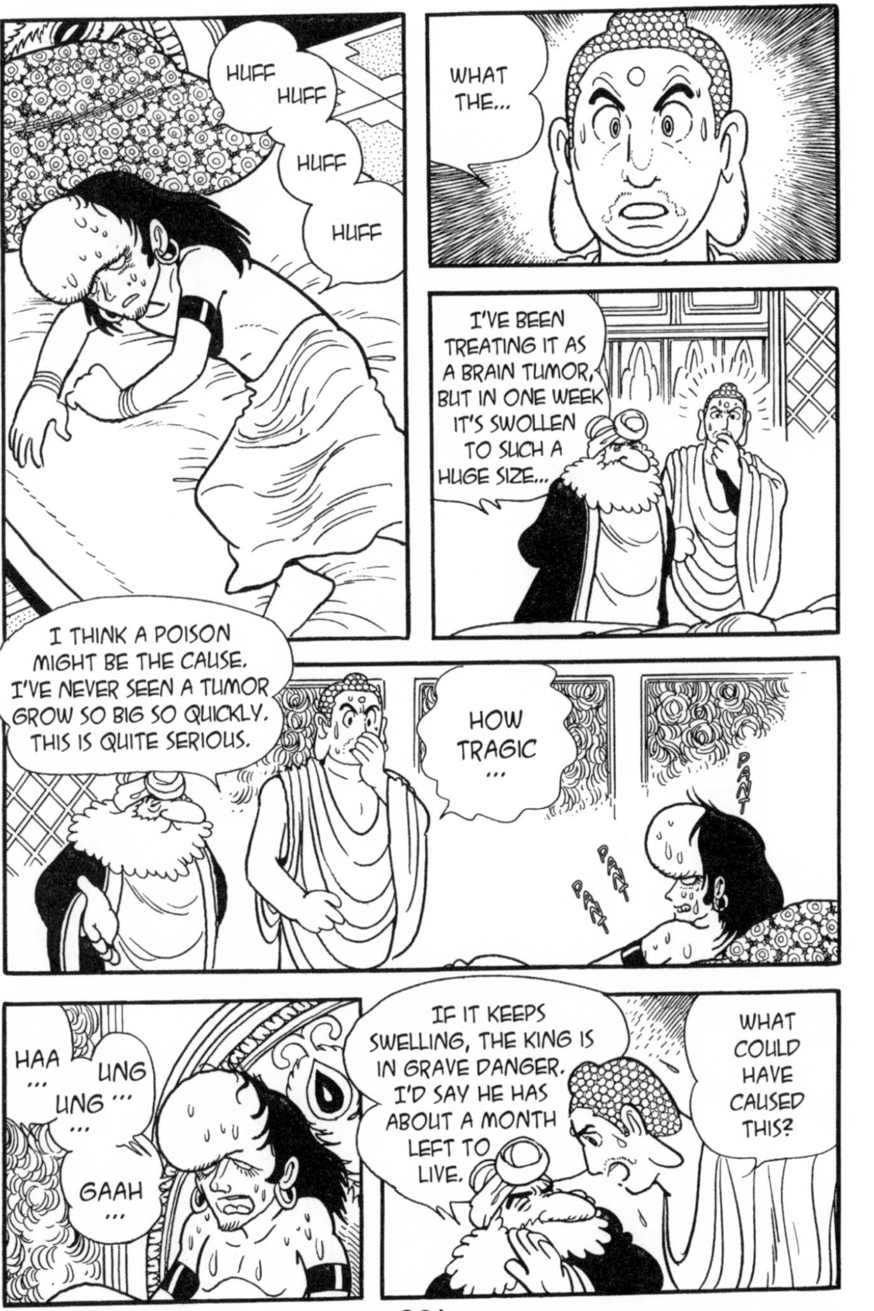
HUFF HUFF
HUFF
HUFF
WHAT THE...
I'VE BEEN TREATING IT AS A BRAIN TUMOR, BUT IN ONE WEEK IT'S SWOLLEN TO SUCH A HUGE SIZE...
I THINK A POISON MIGHT BE THE CAUSE. I'VE NEVER SEEN A TUMOR GROW SO BIG SO QUICKLY. THIS IS QUITE SERIOUS.
HOW TRAGIC ...
PANT
PANT
PANT
HAA ...
UNG ...
UNG ...
GAAH ...
IF IT KEEPS SWELLING, THE KING IS IN GRAVE DANGER. I'D SAY HE HAS ABOUT A MONTH LEFT TO LIVE.
WHAT COULD HAVE CAUSED THIS?

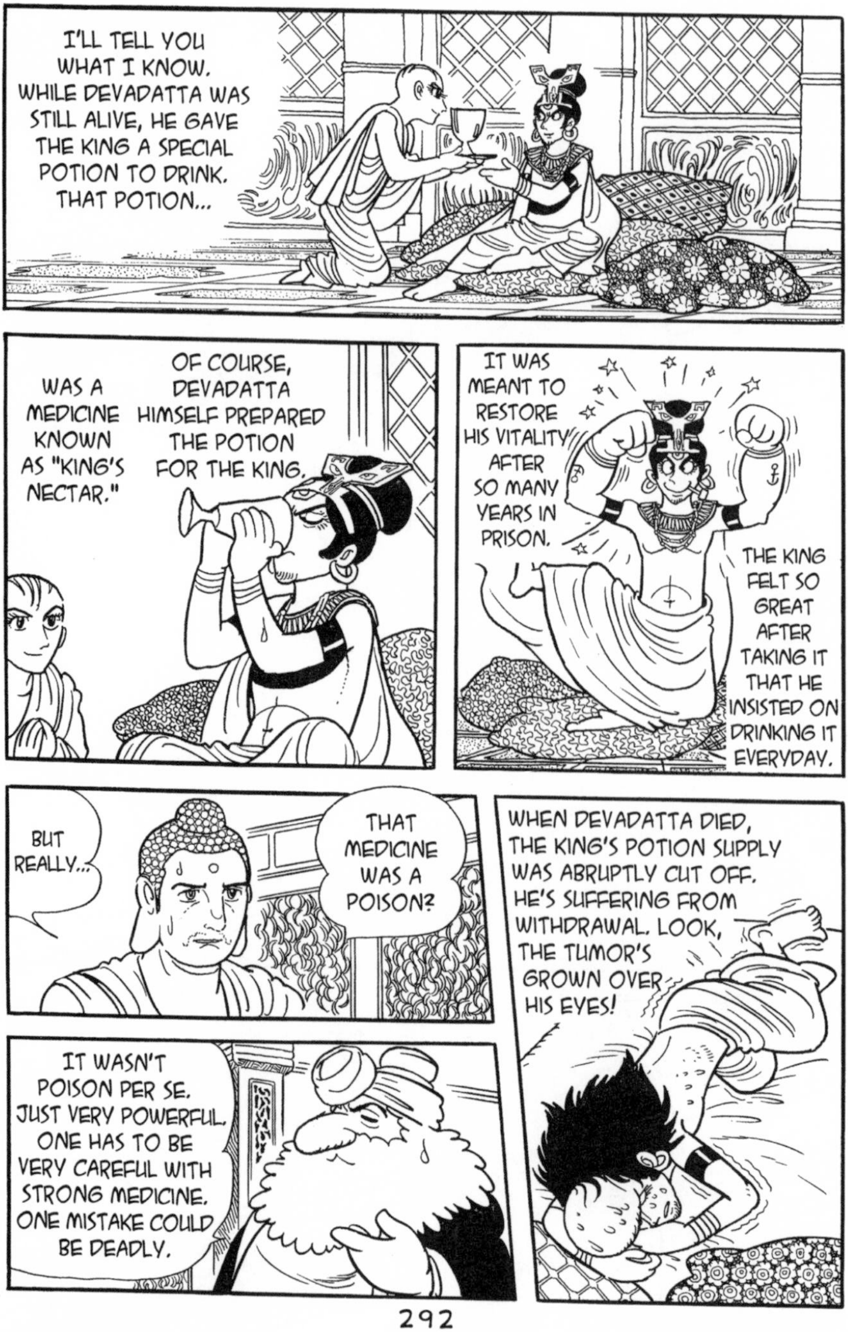
I'LL TELL YOU WHAT I KNOW. WHILE DEVADATTA WAS STILL ALIVE, HE GAVE THE KING A SPECIAL POTION TO DRINK. THAT POTION...
WAS A MEDICINE KNOWN AS "KING'S NECTAR."
OF COURSE, DEVADATTA HIMSELF PREPARED THE POTION FOR THE KING.
IT WAS MEANT TO RESTORE HIS VITALITY AFTER SO MANY YEARS IN PRISON.
THE KING FELT SO GREAT AFTER TAKING IT THAT HE INSISTED ON DRINKING IT EVERYDAY.
BUT REALLY...
THAT MEDICINE WAS A POISON?
IT WASN'T POISON PER SE. JUST VERY POWERFUL. ONE HAS TO BE VERY CAREFUL WITH STRONG MEDICINE. ONE MISTAKE COULD BE DEADLY.
WHEN DEVADATTA DIED, THE KING'S POTION SUPPLY WAS ABRUPTLY CUT OFF. HE'S SUFFERING FROM WITHDRAWAL. LOOK, THE TUMOR'S GROWN OVER HIS EYES!

WE COULD TRY MIXING A BATCH OF THE SAME POTION FOR HIM TO DRINK, BUT I'VE NEVER WORKED WITH THAT MEDICINE BEFORE...

IS THERE ANYTHING ELSE WE CAN DO?

WELL, WE COULD TRY TO CUT OPEN AND DRAIN THE TUMOR, BUT THAT COULD PROVE DANGEROUS.

THERE ARE OTHER DRUGS TO REDUCE SWELLING, BUT HE MIGHT HAVE A BAD REACTION.

AHAN!

GHUH... UNH!

UNGG!

AH!

GUH... UNG...

OOHH... UNG!

GUH!

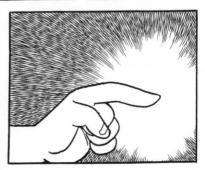

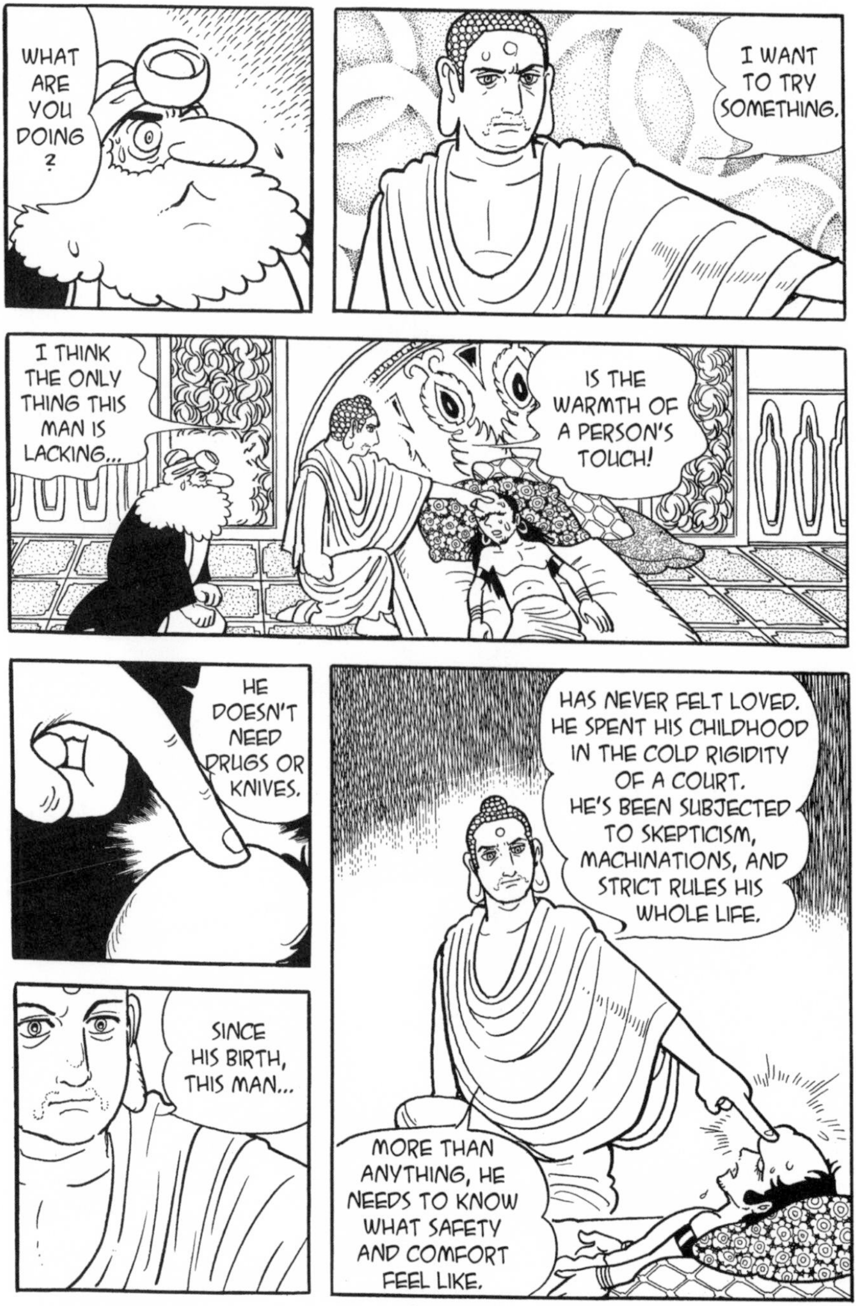
WHAT ARE YOU DOING?
I WANT TO TRY SOMETHING.
I THINK THE ONLY THING THIS MAN IS LACKING...
IS THE WARMTH OF A PERSON'S TOUCH!
HE DOESN'T NEED DRUGS OR KNIVES.
SINCE HIS BIRTH, THIS MAN...
HAS NEVER FELT LOVED. HE SPENT HIS CHILDHOOD IN THE COLD RIGIDITY OF A COURT. HE'S BEEN SUBJECTED TO SKEPTICISM, MACHINATIONS, AND STRICT RULES HIS WHOLE LIFE.
MORE THAN ANYTHING, HE NEEDS TO KNOW WHAT SAFETY AND COMFORT FEEL LIKE.

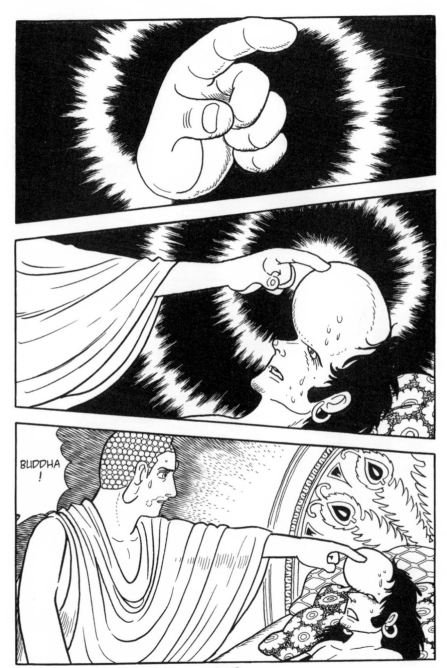

BUDDHA
!

295

IF I CONTINUE THIS, MY WARMTH WILL EVENTUALLY COURSE THROUGH HIS ENTIRE BODY.

WITH JUST ONE FINGER?

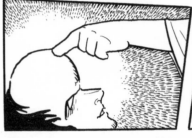

I DON'T BELIEVE IT... THE KING JUST DROPPED OFF INTO A PEACEFUL SLEEP.

IT IS BELIEVED THAT THERE IS A FIELD OF ENERGY THAT SURROUNDS THE BODY. THIS ENERGY IS CALLED AN AURA. PEOPLE WITH VITALITY HAVE STRONG AURAS.
THE WARMTH THAT PASSED FROM BUDDHA TO AJATASATTU WAS PROBABLY ENERGY FROM HIS AURA.

HE'S SOUND ASLEEP. I'LL COME BACK TOMORROW. I'LL COME EVERY DAY IF I HAVE TO.

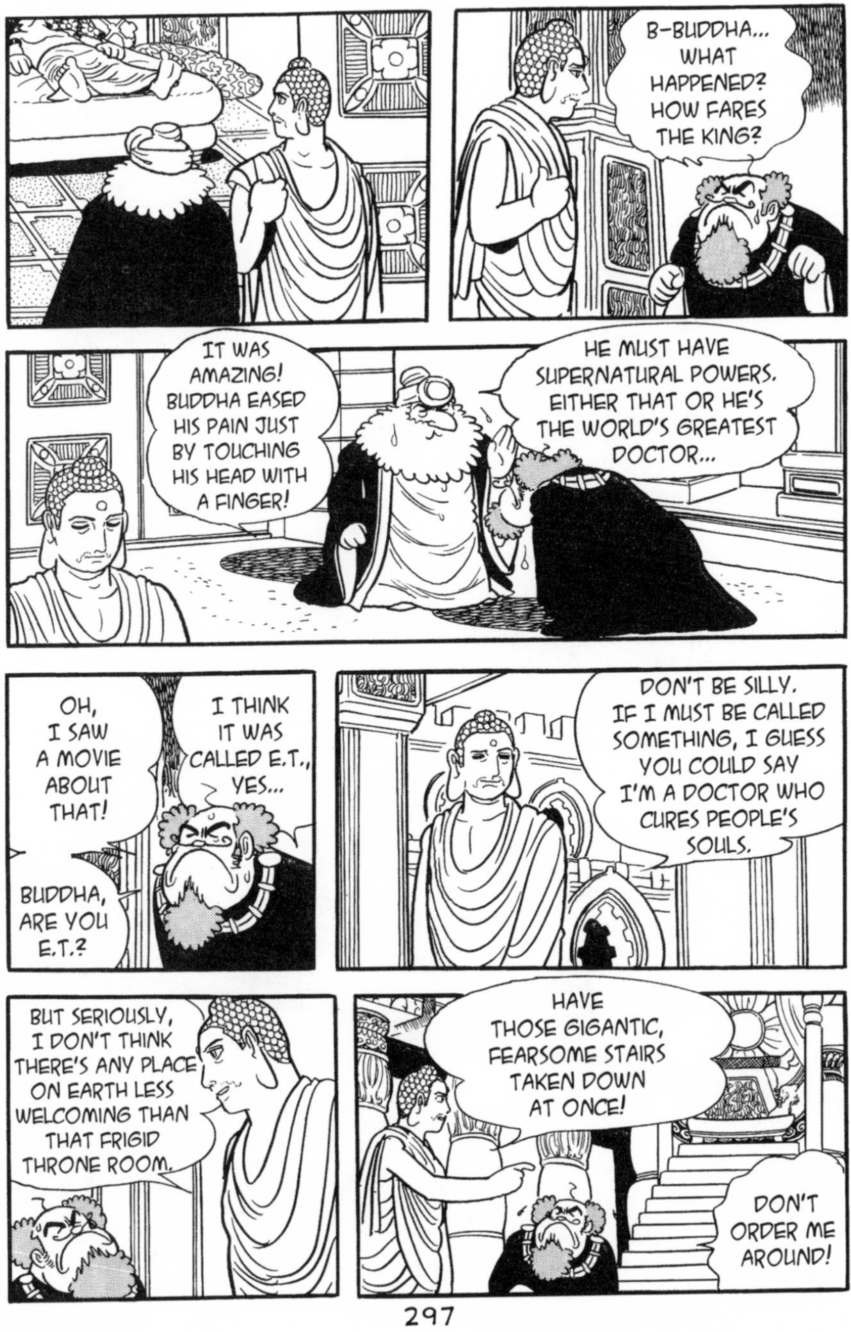
B-BUDDHA... WHAT HAPPENED? HOW FARES THE KING?
IT WAS AMAZING! BUDDHA EASED HIS PAIN JUST BY TOUCHING HIS HEAD WITH A FINGER!
HE MUST HAVE SUPERNATURAL POWERS. EITHER THAT OR HE'S THE WORLD'S GREATEST DOCTOR...
OH, I SAW A MOVIE ABOUT THAT!
I THINK IT WAS CALLED E.T., YES...
BUDDHA, ARE YOU E.T.?
DON'T BE SILLY. IF I MUST BE CALLED SOMETHING, I GUESS YOU COULD SAY I'M A DOCTOR WHO CURES PEOPLE'S SOULS.
BUT SERIOUSLY, I DON'T THINK THERE'S ANY PLACE ON EARTH LESS WELCOMING THAN THAT FRIGID THRONE ROOM.
HAVE THOSE GIGANTIC, FEARSOME STAIRS TAKEN DOWN AT ONCE!
DON'T ORDER ME AROUND!

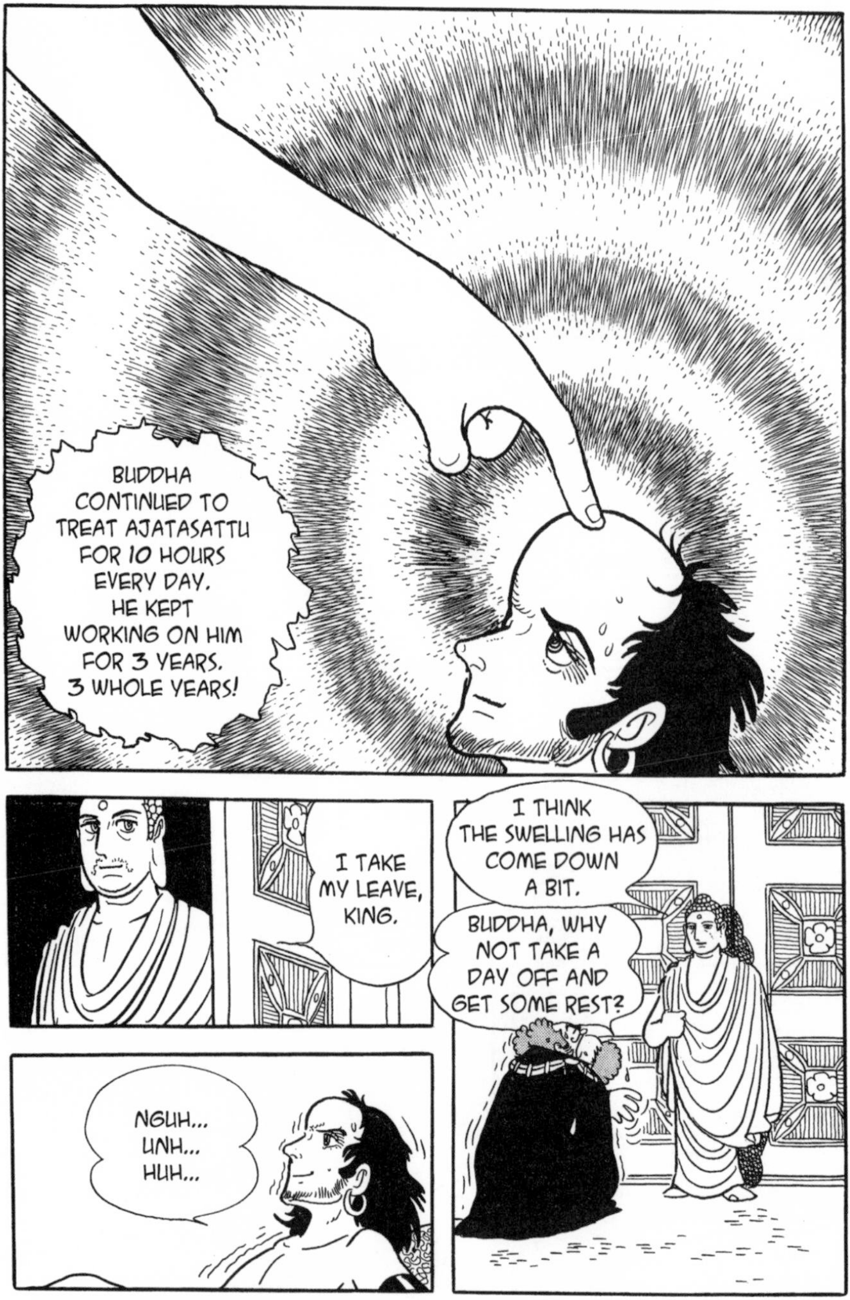
BUDDHA CONTINUED TO TREAT AJATASATTU FOR 10 HOURS EVERY DAY. HE KEPT WORKING ON HIM FOR 3 YEARS. 3 WHOLE YEARS!
I TAKE MY LEAVE, KING.
NGUH... UNH... HUH...
I THINK THE SWELLING HAS COME DOWN A BIT.
BUDDHA, WHY NOT TAKE A DAY OFF AND GET SOME REST?

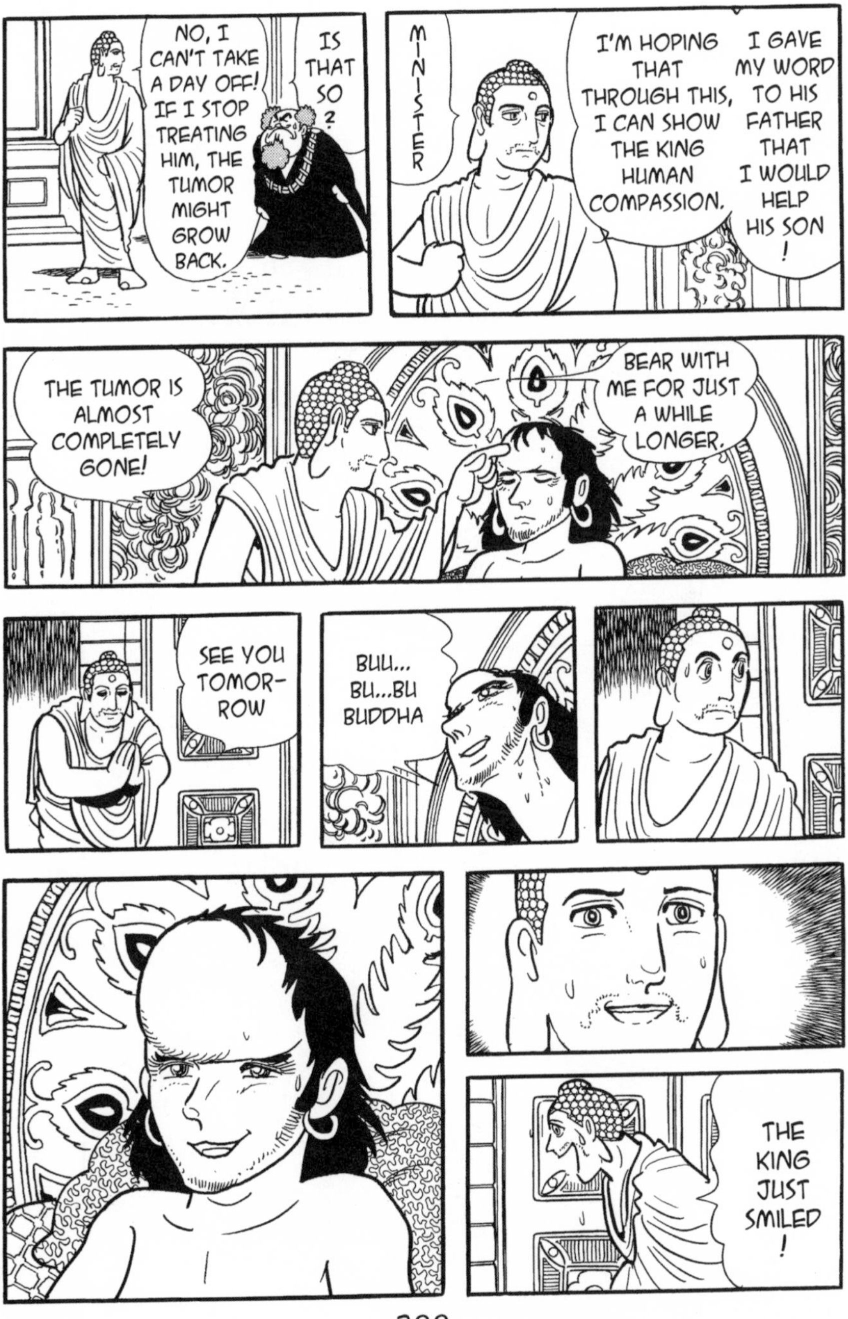
NO, I CAN'T TAKE A DAY OFF! IF I STOP TREATING HIM, THE TUMOR MIGHT GROW BACK.
IS THAT SO?
MINISTER
I'M HOPING THAT THROUGH THIS, I CAN SHOW THE KING HUMAN COMPASSION.
I GAVE MY WORD TO HIS FATHER THAT I WOULD HELP HIS SON!
THE TUMOR IS ALMOST COMPLETELY GONE!
BEAR WITH ME FOR JUST A WHILE LONGER.
SEE YOU TOMOR-ROW
BUU... BU...BU BUDDHA
THE KING JUST SMILED!

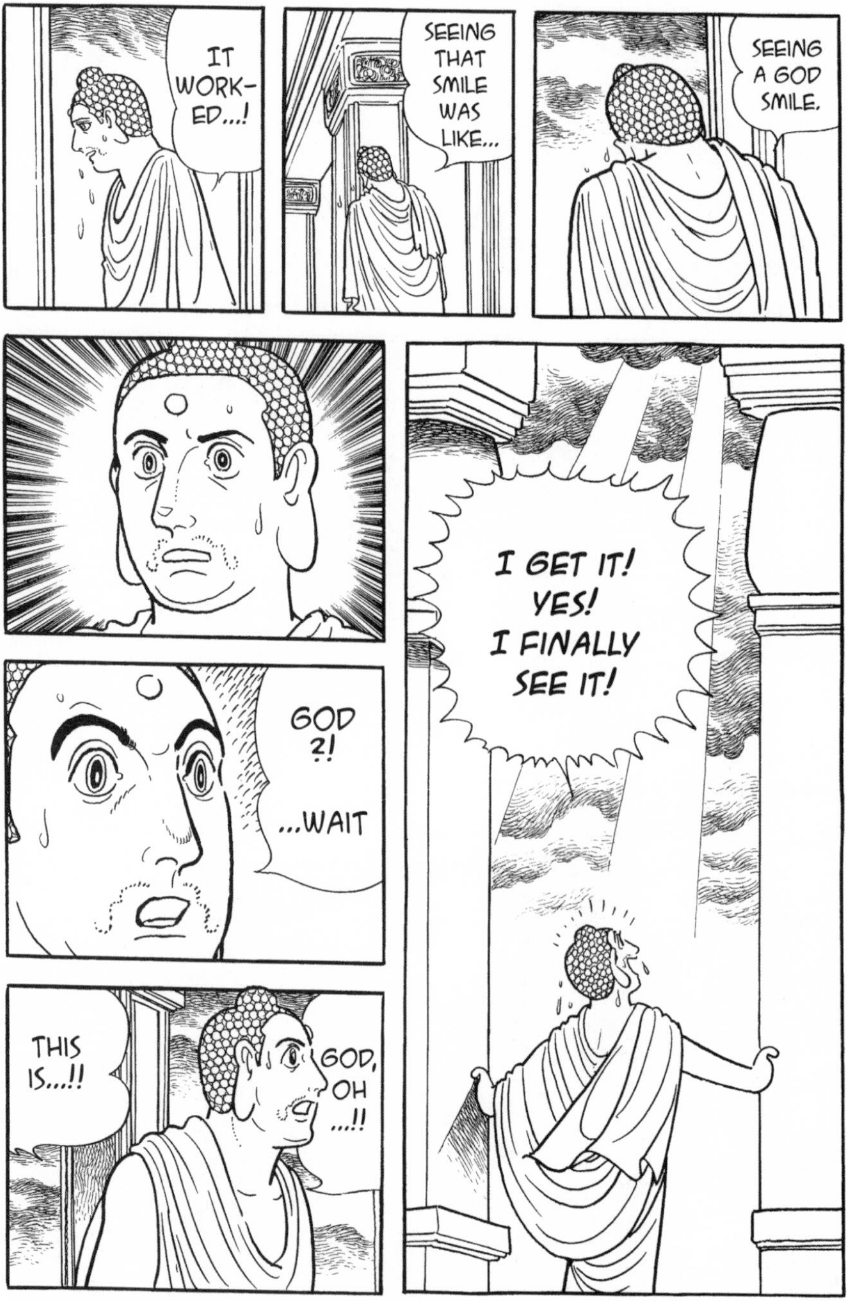
IT WORKED...!
SEEING THAT SMILE WAS LIKE...
SEEING A GOD SMILE.
GOD ?!
...WAIT
THIS IS...!!
GOD, OH ...!!
I GET IT! YES! I FINALLY SEE IT!

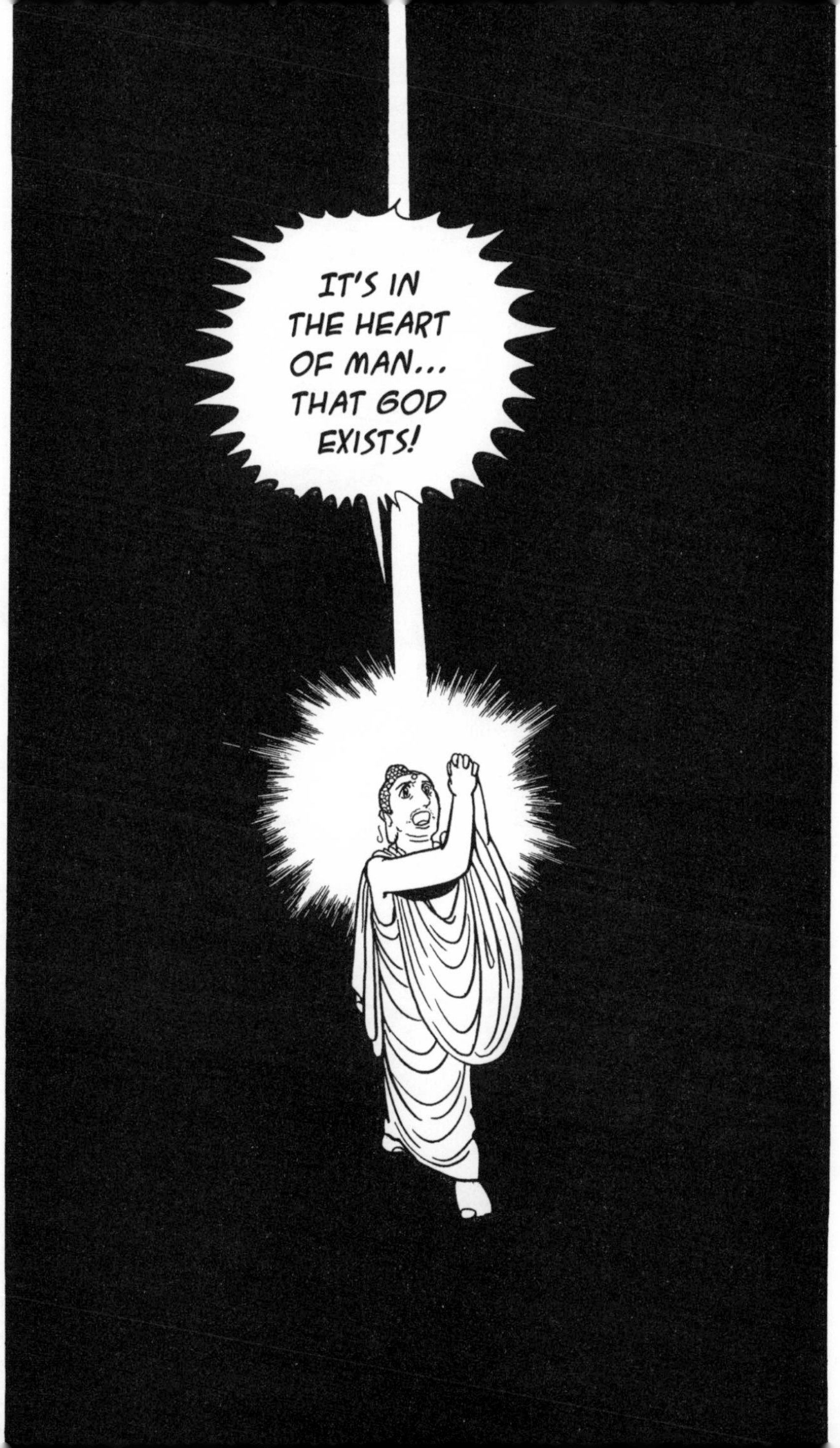
IT'S IN THE HEART OF MAN... THAT GOD EXISTS!

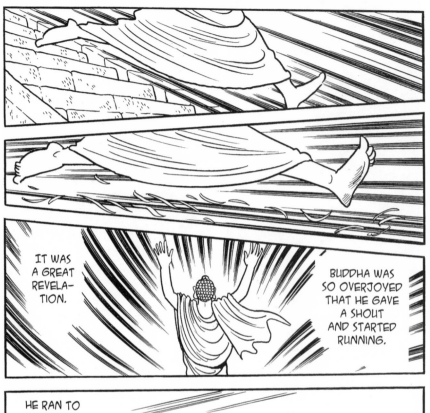

IT WAS A GREAT REVELATION.

BUDDHA WAS SO OVERJOYED THAT HE GAVE A SHOUT AND STARTED RUNNING.

HE RAN TO A NEARBY MOUNTAIN AND SHOUTED HIS JOYOUS INSIGHT TO THE HEAVENS

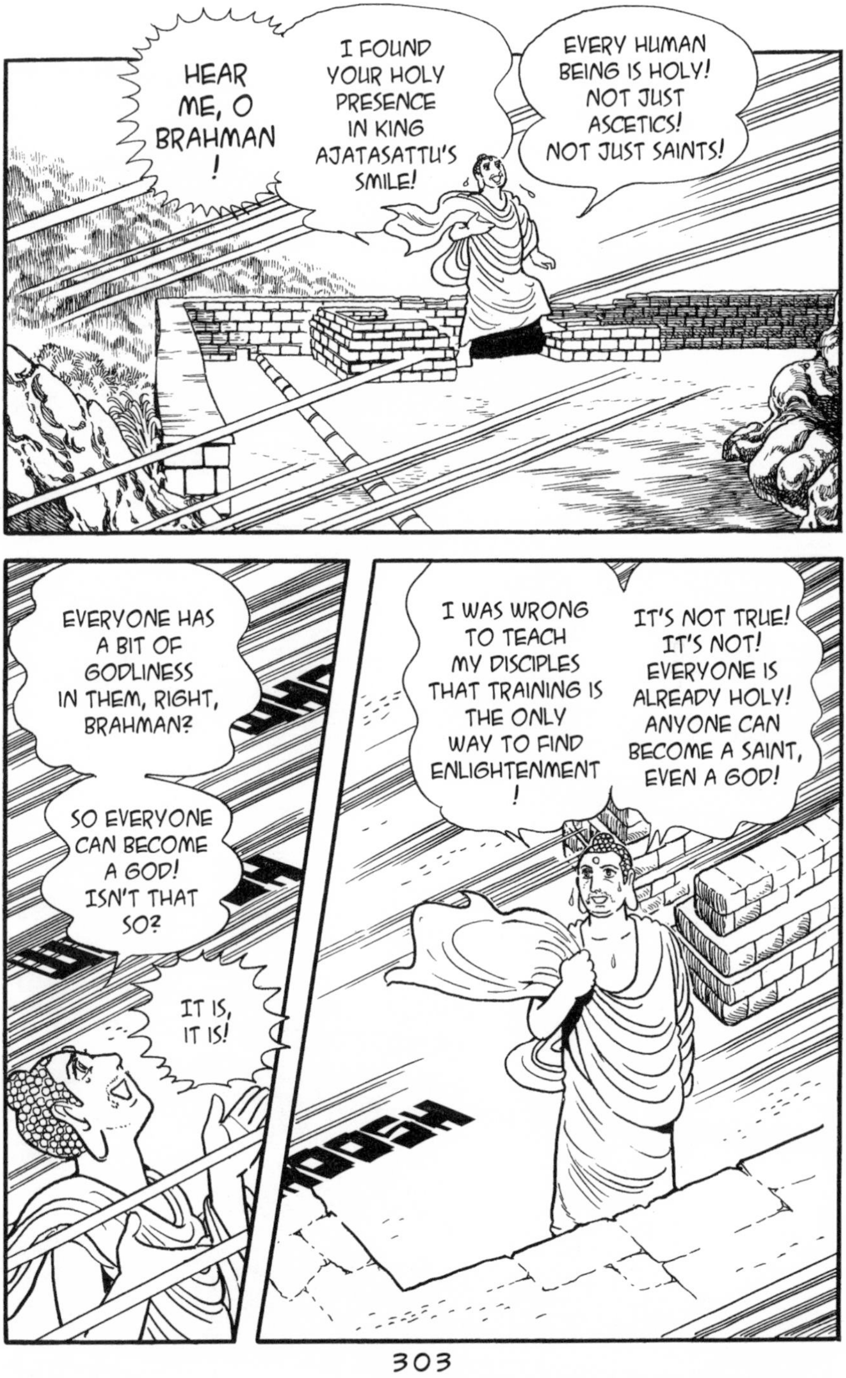
HEAR ME, O BRAHMAN!
I FOUND YOUR HOLY PRESENCE IN KING AJATASATTU'S SMILE!
EVERY HUMAN BEING IS HOLY! NOT JUST ASCETICS! NOT JUST SAINTS!
EVERYONE HAS A BIT OF GODLINESS IN THEM, RIGHT, BRAHMAN?
SO EVERYONE CAN BECOME A GOD! ISN'T THAT SO?
IT IS, IT IS!
I WAS WRONG TO TEACH MY DISCIPLES THAT TRAINING IS THE ONLY WAY TO FIND ENLIGHTENMENT!
IT'S NOT TRUE! IT'S NOT! EVERYONE IS ALREADY HOLY! ANYONE CAN BECOME A SAINT, EVEN A GOD!

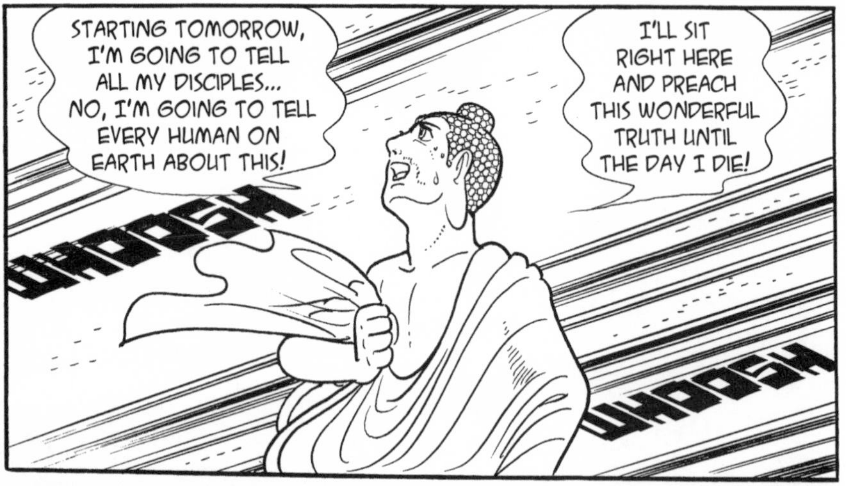
STARTING TOMORROW, I'M GOING TO TELL ALL MY DISCIPLES... NO, I'M GOING TO TELL EVERY HUMAN ON EARTH ABOUT THIS!
I'LL SIT RIGHT HERE AND PREACH THIS WONDERFUL TRUTH UNTIL THE DAY I DIE!
WHOOSH
WHOOSH

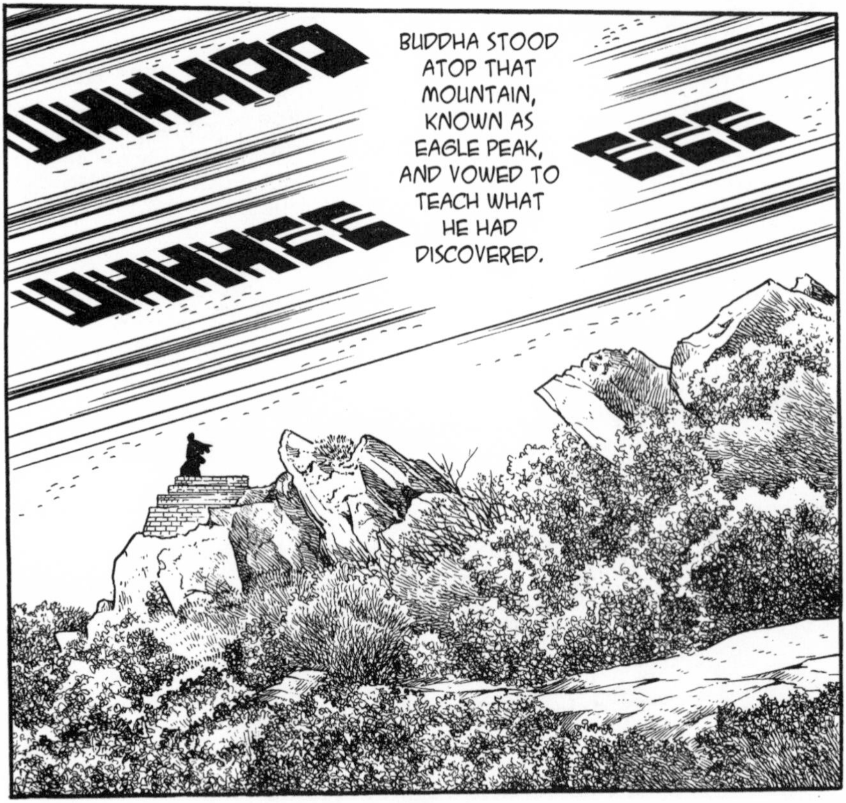
WHHHOO
BUDDHA STOOD ATOP THAT MOUNTAIN, KNOWN AS EAGLE PEAK, AND VOWED TO TEACH WHAT HE HAD DISCOVERED.
EEEE
WHHHEE

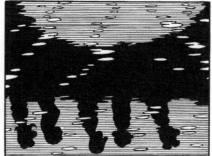

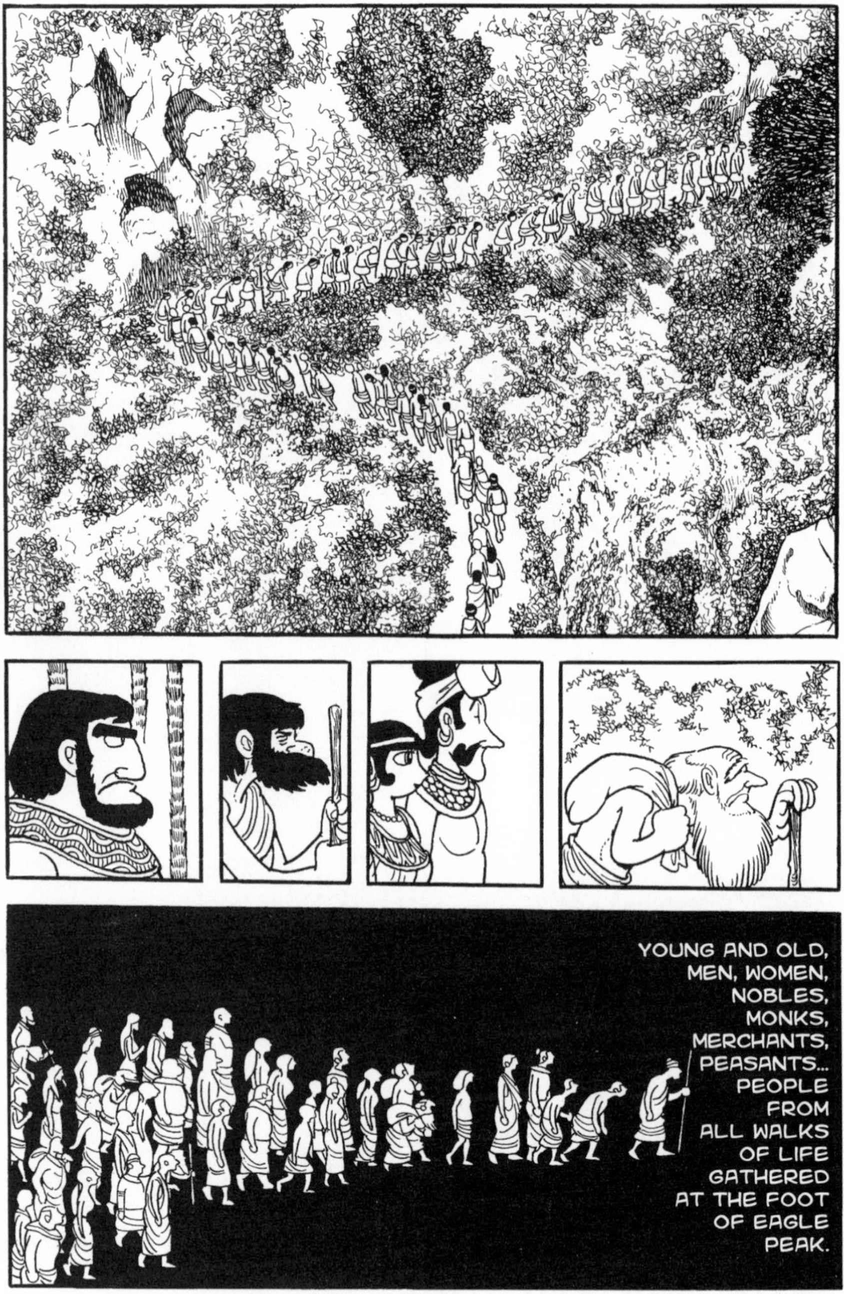
YOUNG AND OLD,
MEN, WOMEN,
NOBLES,
MONKS,
MERCHANTS,
PEASANTS...
PEOPLE
FROM
ALL WALKS
OF LIFE
GATHERED
AT THE FOOT
OF EAGLE
PEAK.

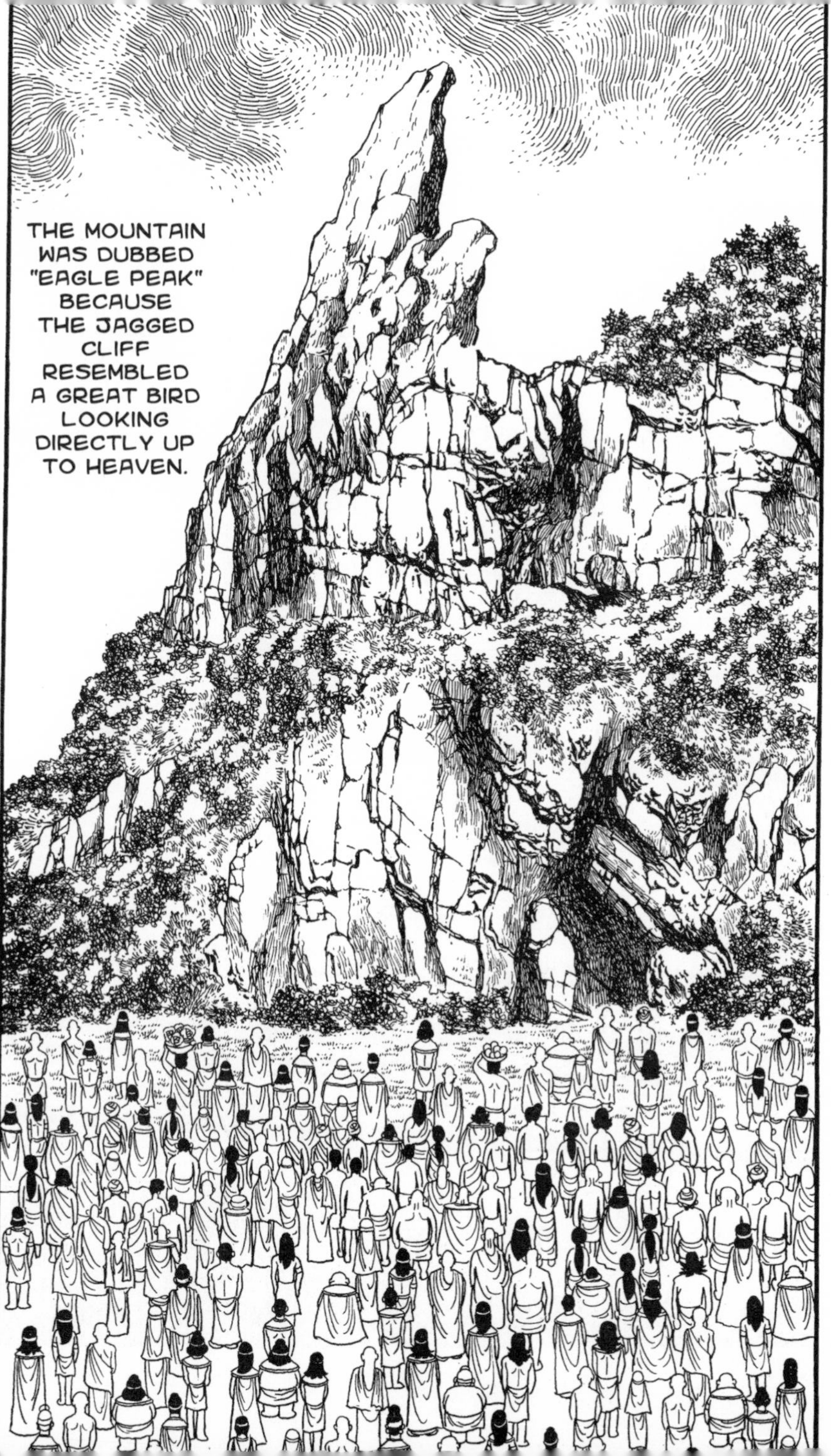
THE MOUNTAIN WAS DUBBED "EAGLE PEAK" BECAUSE THE JAGGED CLIFF RESEMBLED A GREAT BIRD LOOKING DIRECTLY UP TO HEAVEN.

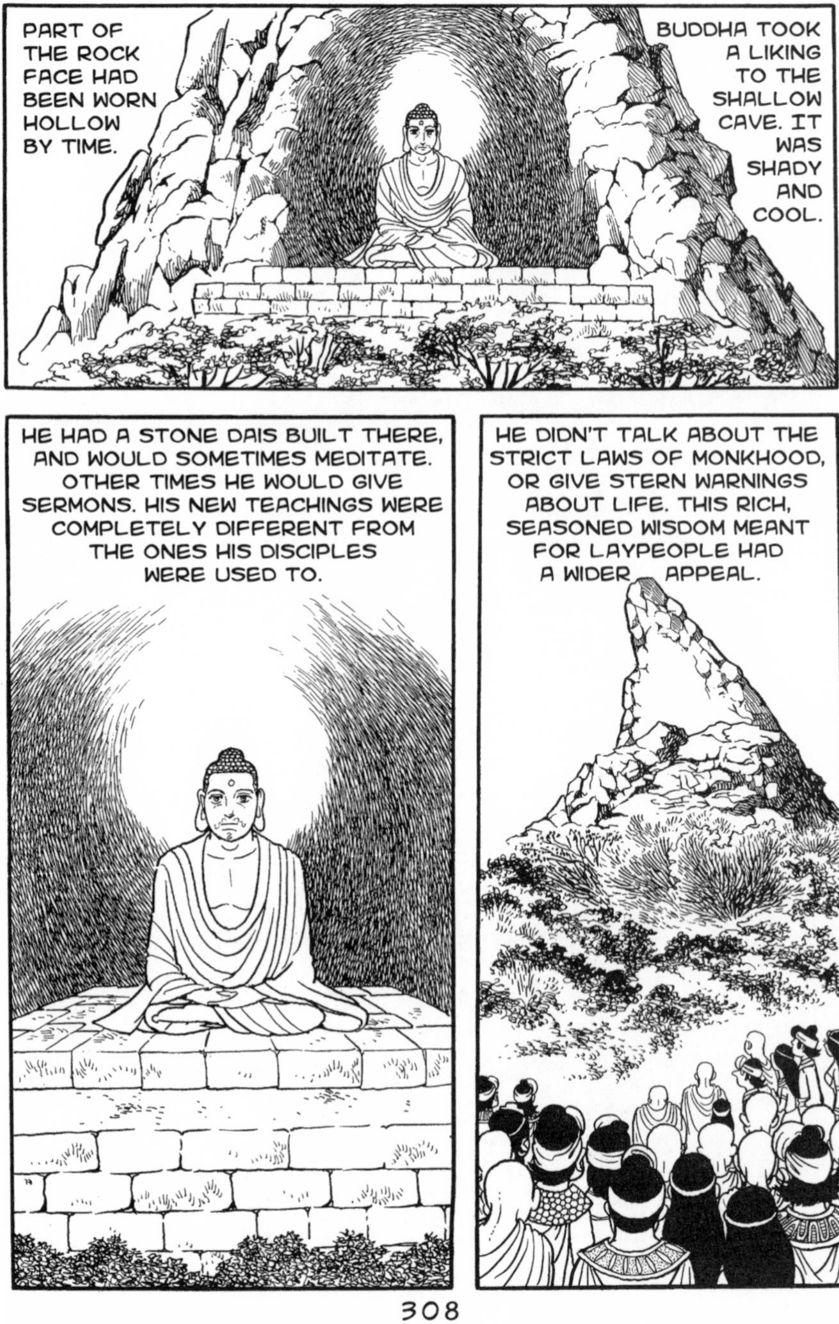
PART OF THE ROCK FACE HAD BEEN WORN HOLLOW BY TIME.
BUDDHA TOOK A LIKING TO THE SHALLOW CAVE. IT WAS SHADY AND COOL.
HE HAD A STONE DAIS BUILT THERE, AND WOULD SOMETIMES MEDITATE. OTHER TIMES HE WOULD GIVE SERMONS. HIS NEW TEACHINGS WERE COMPLETELY DIFFERENT FROM THE ONES HIS DISCIPLES WERE USED TO.
HE DIDN'T TALK ABOUT THE STRICT LAWS OF MONKHOOD, OR GIVE STERN WARNINGS ABOUT LIFE. THIS RICH, SEASONED WISDOM MEANT FOR LAYPEOPLE HAD A WIDER APPEAL.

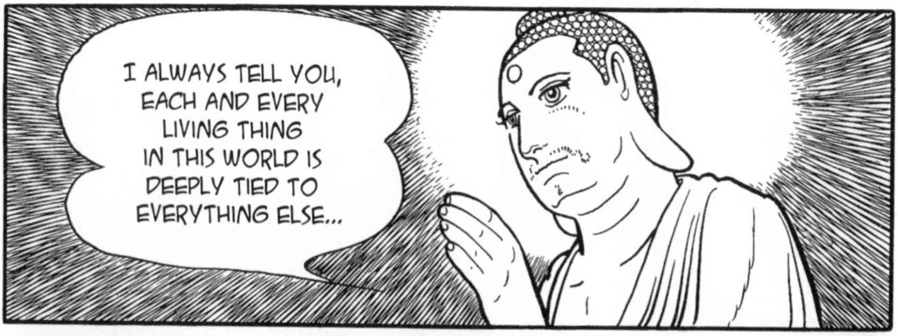
I ALWAYS TELL YOU, EACH AND EVERY LIVING THING IN THIS WORLD IS DEEPLY TIED TO EVERYTHING ELSE...

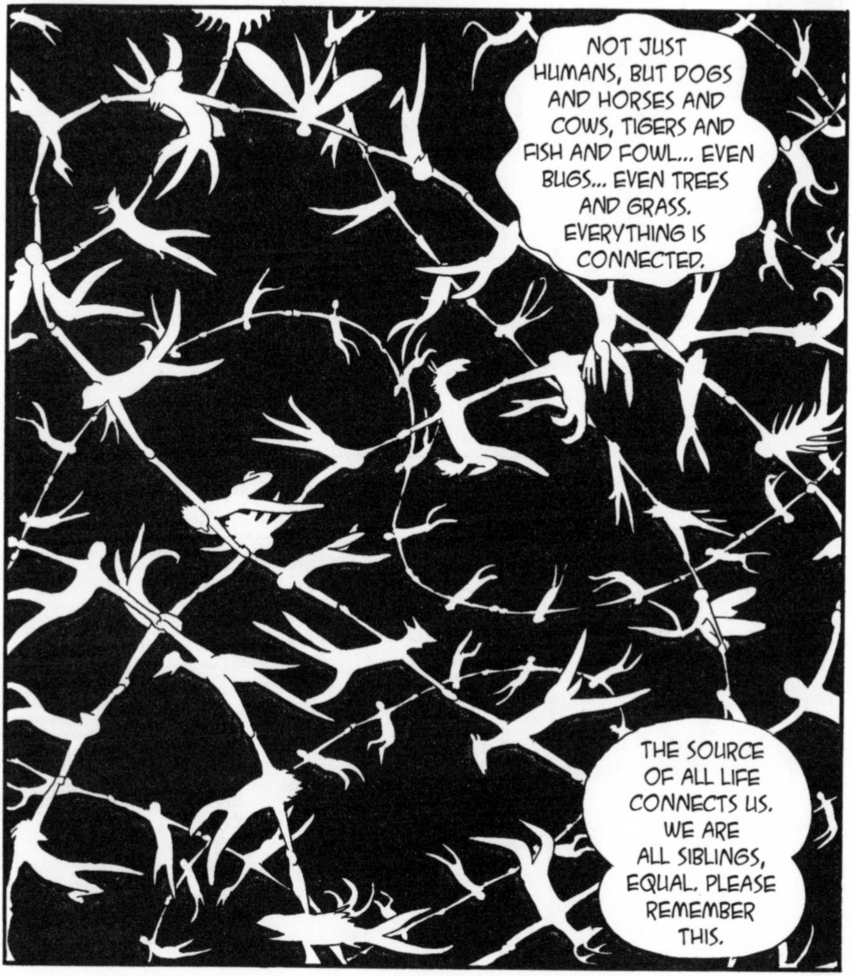
NOT JUST HUMANS, BUT DOGS AND HORSES AND COWS, TIGERS AND FISH AND FOWL... EVEN BUGS... EVEN TREES AND GRASS. EVERYTHING IS CONNECTED.
THE SOURCE OF ALL LIFE CONNECTS US. WE ARE ALL SIBLINGS, EQUAL. PLEASE REMEMBER THIS.

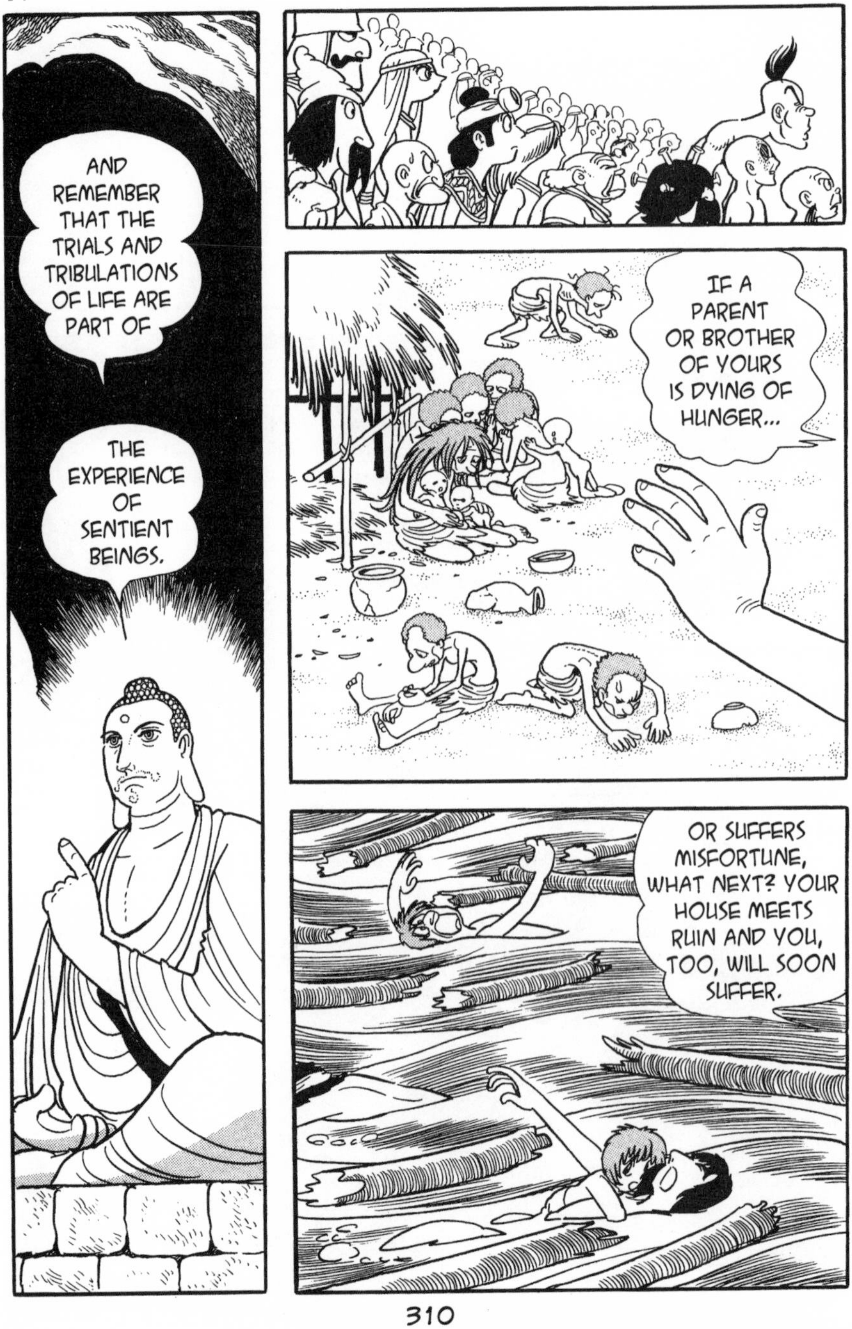
AND REMEMBER THAT THE TRIALS AND TRIBULATIONS OF LIFE ARE PART OF
THE EXPERIENCE OF SENTIENT BEINGS.
IF A PARENT OR BROTHER OF YOURS IS DYING OF HUNGER...
OR SUFFERS MISFORTUNE, WHAT NEXT? YOUR HOUSE MEETS RUIN AND YOU, TOO, WILL SOON SUFFER.

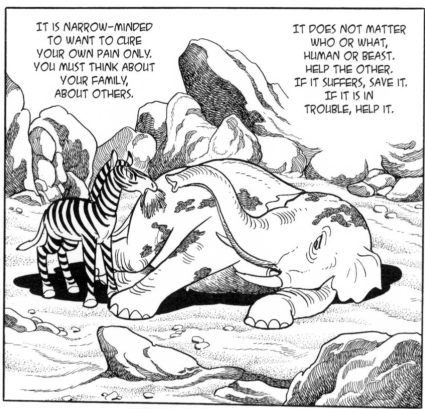

IT IS NARROW-MINDED TO WANT TO CURE YOUR OWN PAIN ONLY. YOU MUST THINK ABOUT YOUR FAMILY, ABOUT OTHERS.

IT DOES NOT MATTER WHO OR WHAT, HUMAN OR BEAST. HELP THE OTHER. IF IT SUFFERS, SAVE IT. IF IT IS IN TROUBLE, HELP IT.

WHY? BECAUSE ALL LIVING CREATURES ARE KIN IN THE HOUSE OF NATURE!

AT TIMES, YOU MIGHT SACRIFICE YOURSELF TO SAVE OTHERS.

311

LET ME TELL YOU A STORY...

WHEE

WHOO

AN OLD MAN

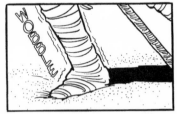

WOOOM

COLLAPSED IN THE MIDDLE OF A DESERT.

THUMP

HE WAS TOO HUNGRY, THIRSTY AND TIRED TO GO ON. THEN...

312

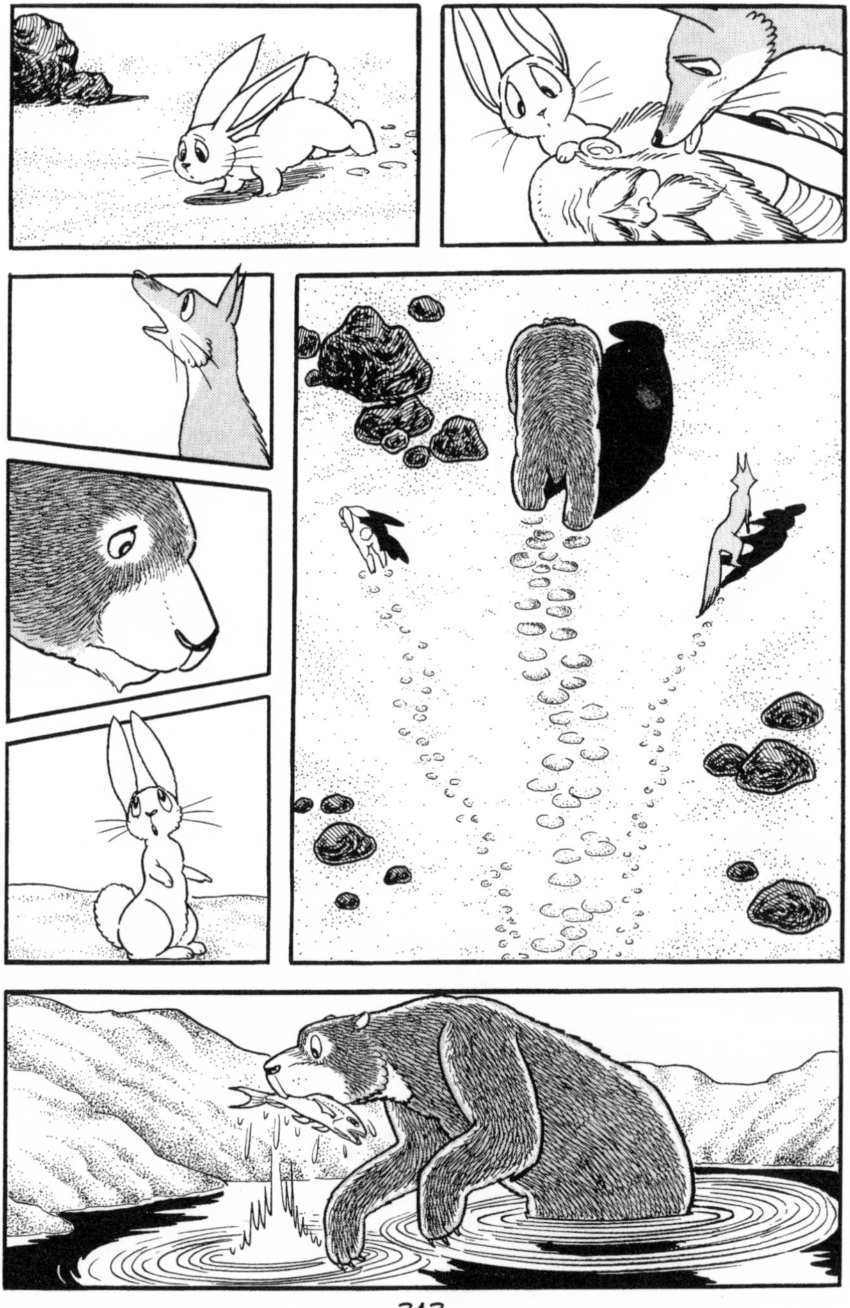

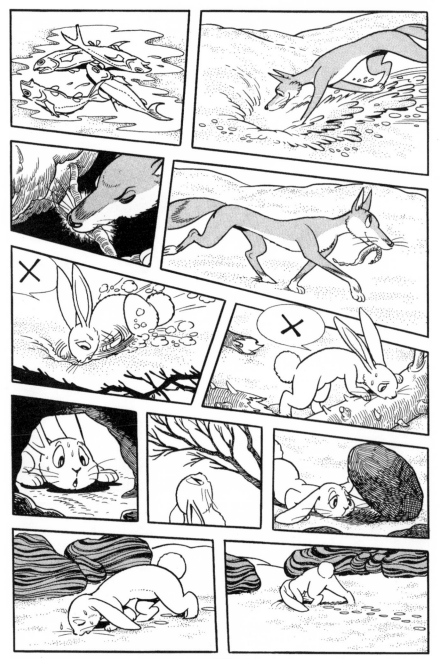

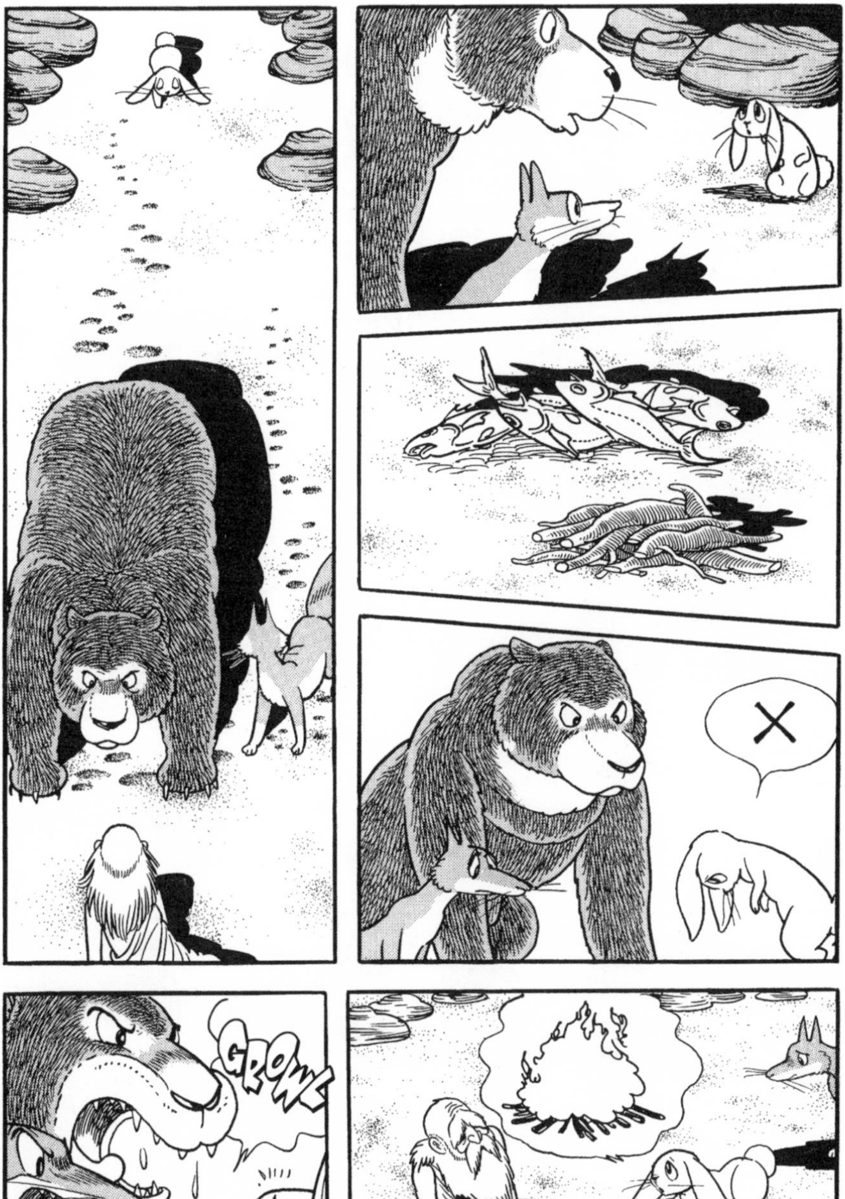
GROWL

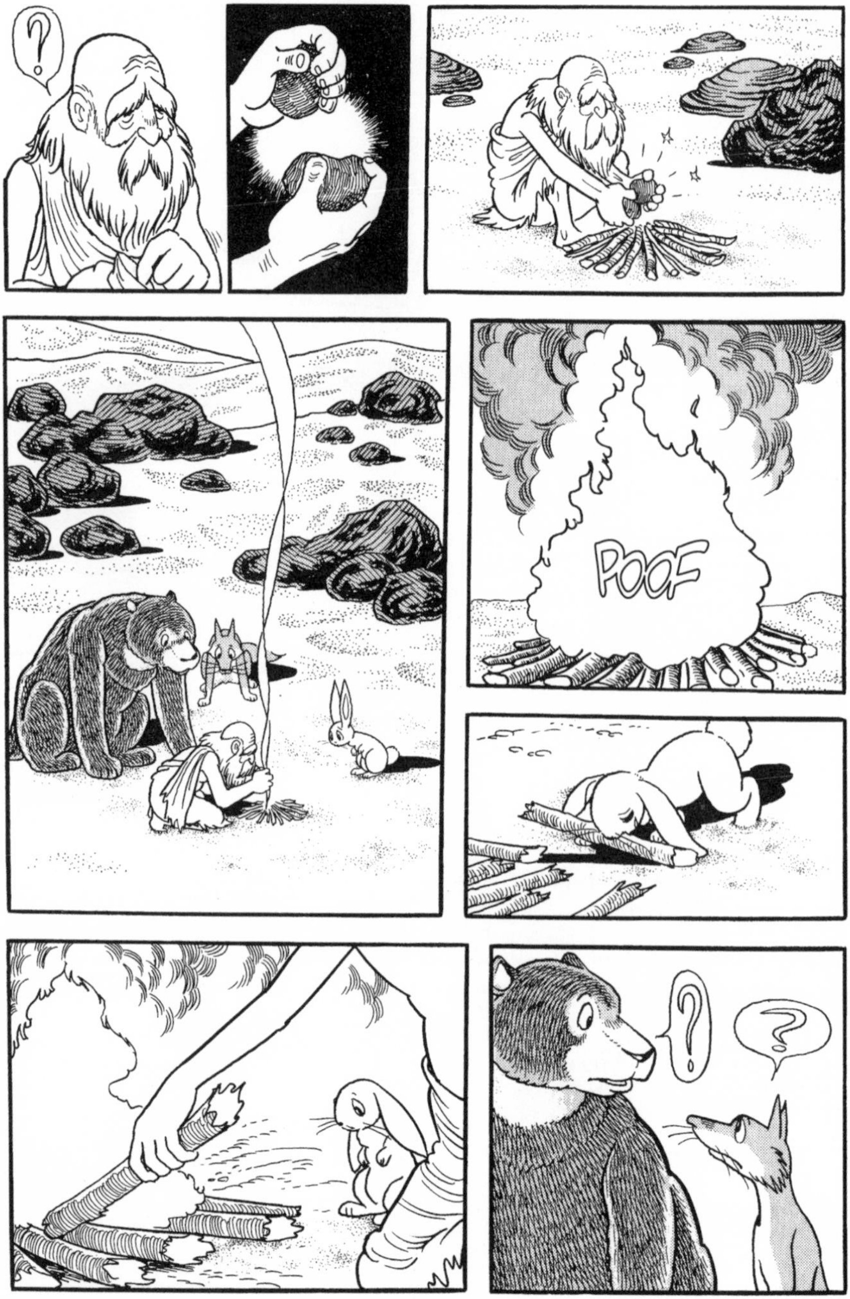
?
POOF
?
?

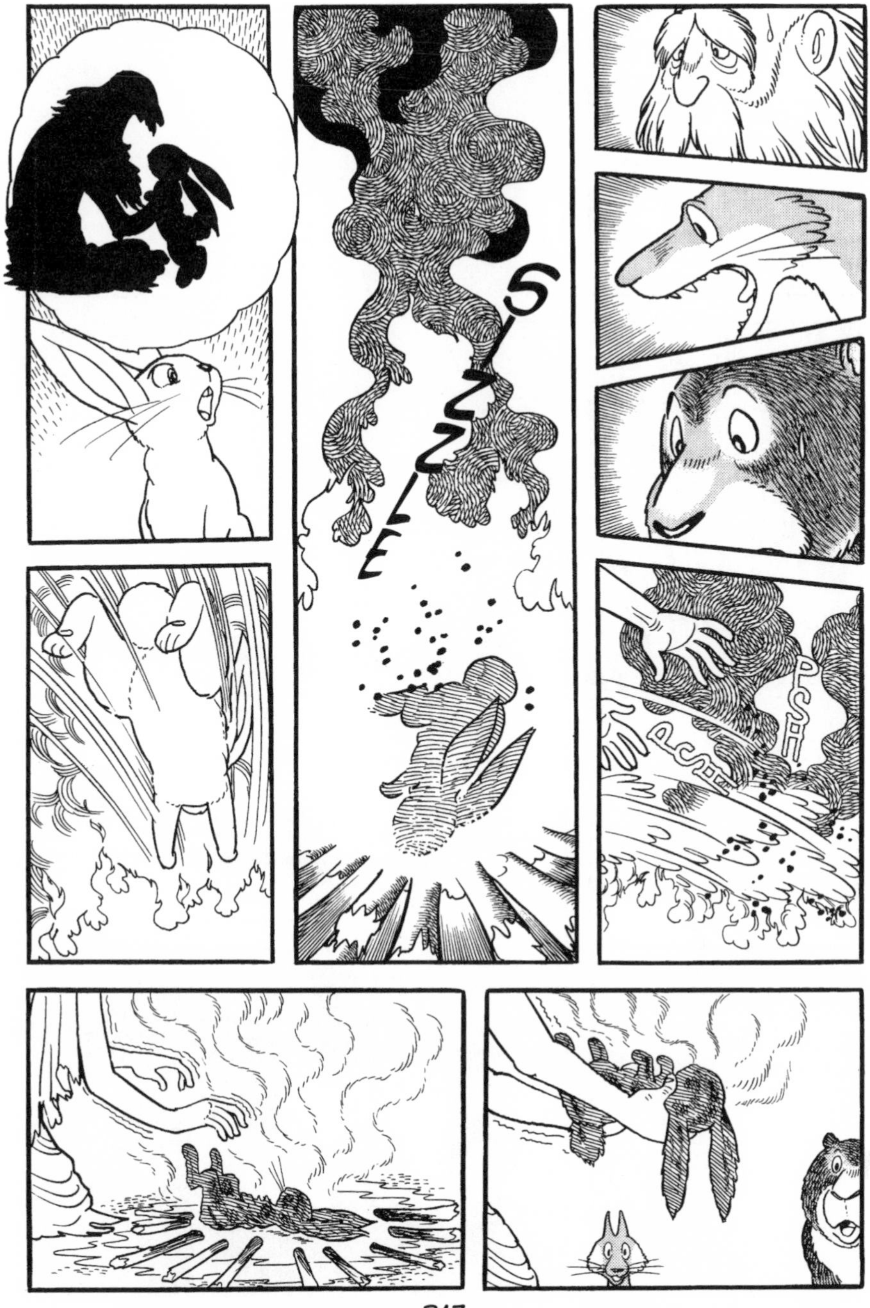
SIZZLE
PSH!
PSH

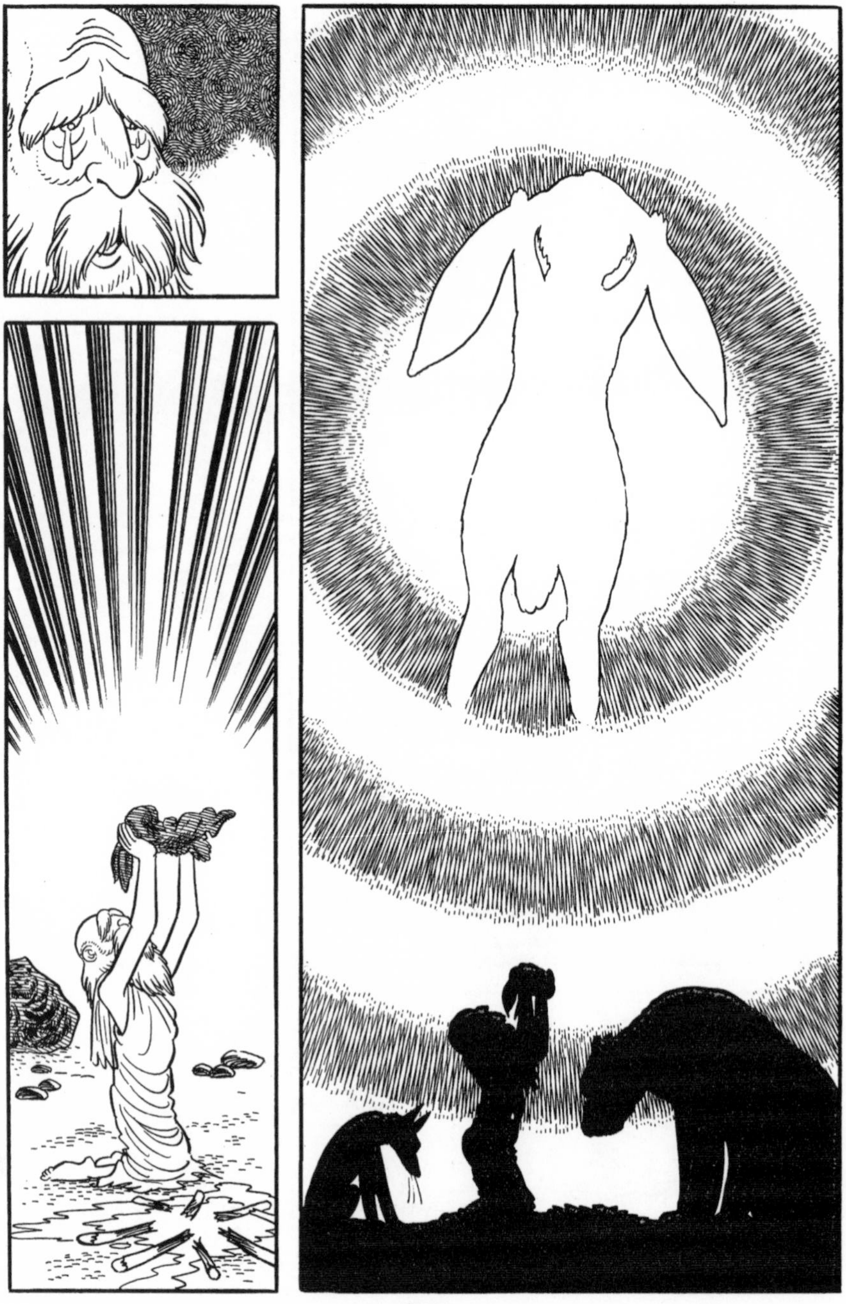

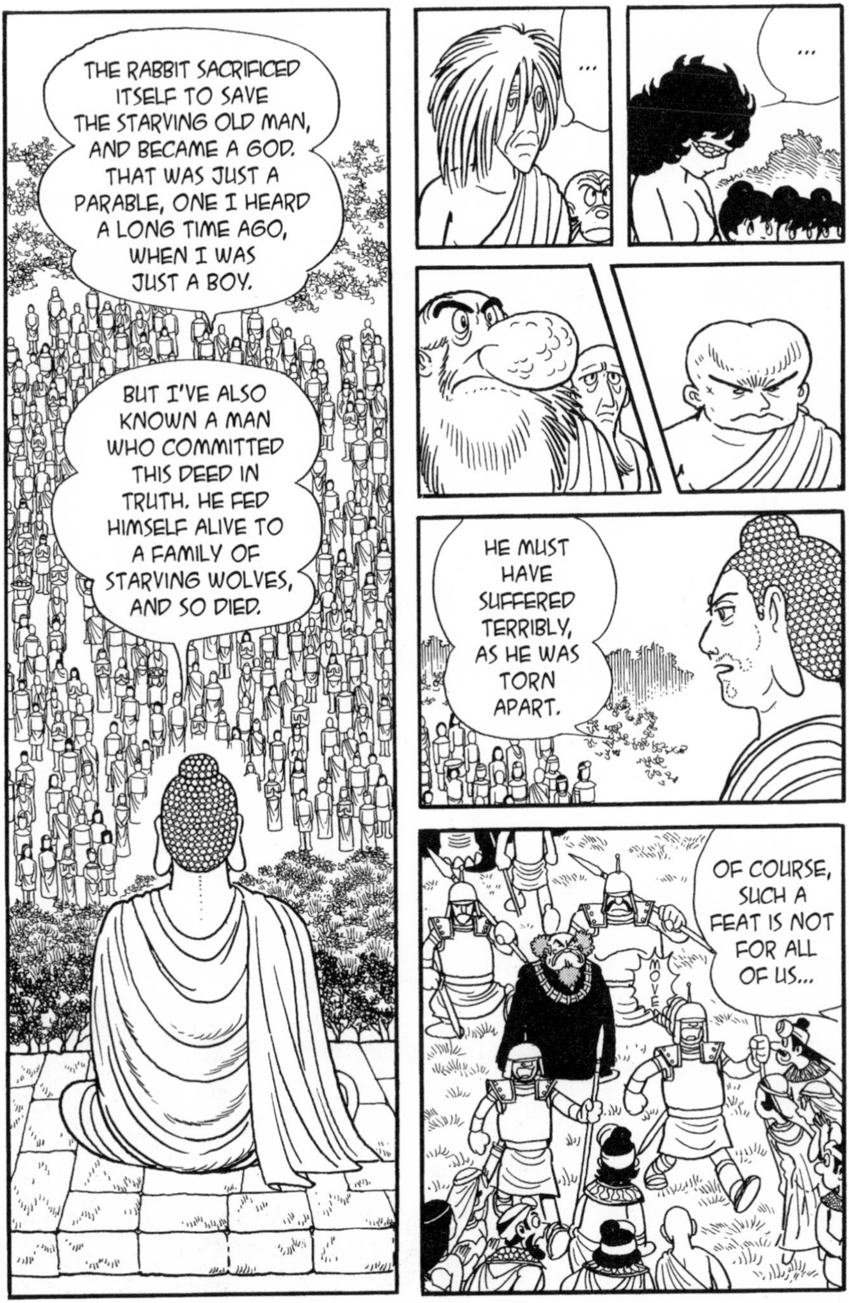
THE RABBIT SACRIFICED ITSELF TO SAVE THE STARVING OLD MAN, AND BECAME A GOD. THAT WAS JUST A PARABLE, ONE I HEARD A LONG TIME AGO, WHEN I WAS JUST A BOY.
BUT I'VE ALSO KNOWN A MAN WHO COMMITTED THIS DEED IN TRUTH. HE FED HIMSELF ALIVE TO A FAMILY OF STARVING WOLVES, AND SO DIED.
...
...
HE MUST HAVE SUFFERED TERRIBLY, AS HE WAS TORN APART.
MOVE
OF COURSE, SUCH A FEAT IS NOT FOR ALL OF US...

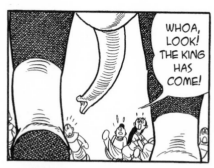

WHOA, LOOK! THE KING HAS COME!

BE SEATED, BE SEATED!

HIS MAJESTY HAS COME TO LISTEN TO BUDDHA'S SERMON!

RIGHT THIS WAY, MILORD. OVER HERE.

BUT EACH OF YOU CAN DO WHAT YOU CAN.

IF YOU ARE RICH, YOU CAN GIVE TO THOSE WHO SUFFER. IF YOU ARE STRONG, YOU CAN SUPPORT THOSE WHO SUFFER.

IF YOU ARE NEITHER RICH NOR STRONG, YOU CAN LISTEN TO THEM AND OFFER YOUR SYMPATHY, TELLING THEM YOU ARE SORRY.

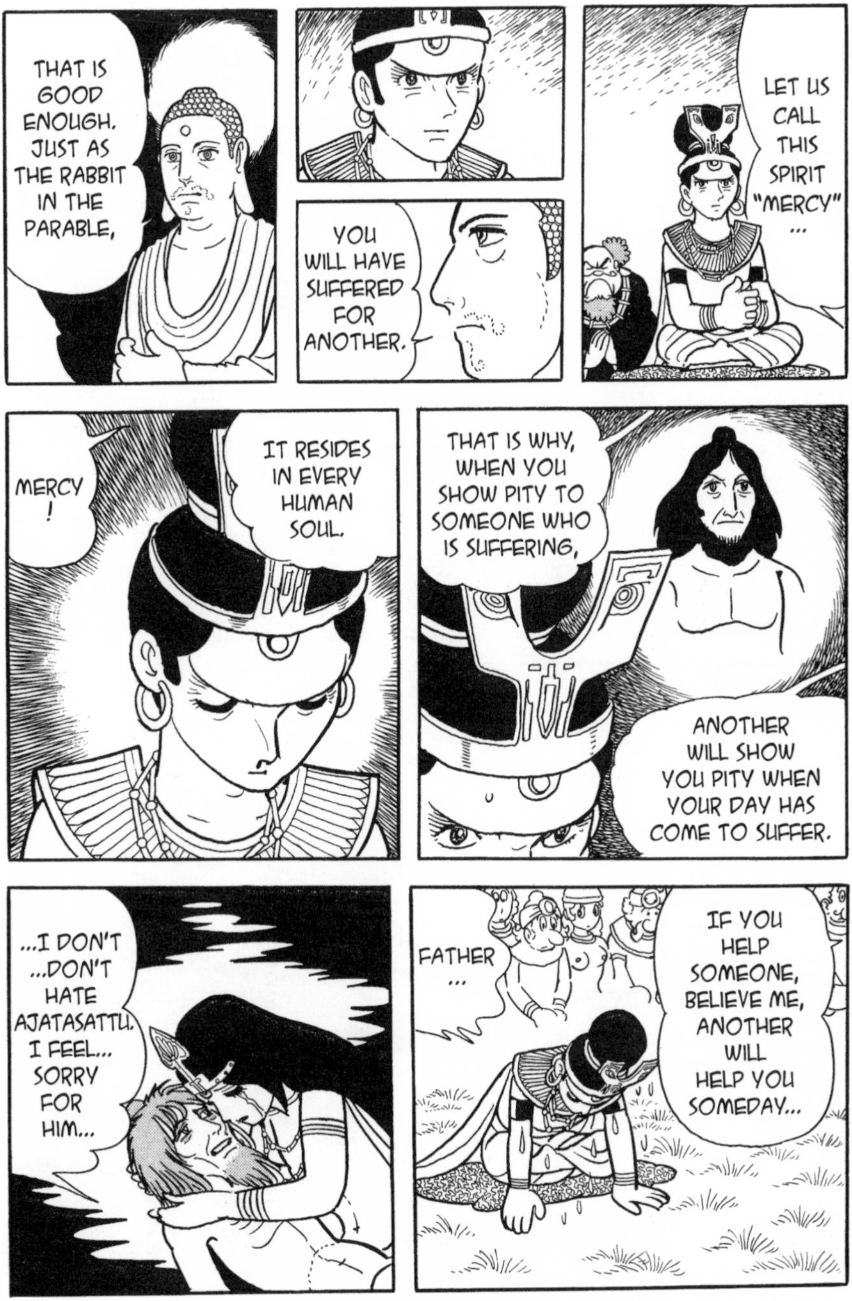
THAT IS GOOD ENOUGH. JUST AS THE RABBIT IN THE PARABLE,
YOU WILL HAVE SUFFERED FOR ANOTHER.
LET US CALL THIS SPIRIT "MERCY" ...
MERCY !
IT RESIDES IN EVERY HUMAN SOUL.
THAT IS WHY, WHEN YOU SHOW PITY TO SOMEONE WHO IS SUFFERING,
ANOTHER WILL SHOW YOU PITY WHEN YOUR DAY HAS COME TO SUFFER.
...I DON'T ...DON'T HATE AJATASATTU. I FEEL... SORRY FOR HIM...
FATHER ...
IF YOU HELP SOMEONE, BELIEVE ME, ANOTHER WILL HELP YOU SOMEDAY...

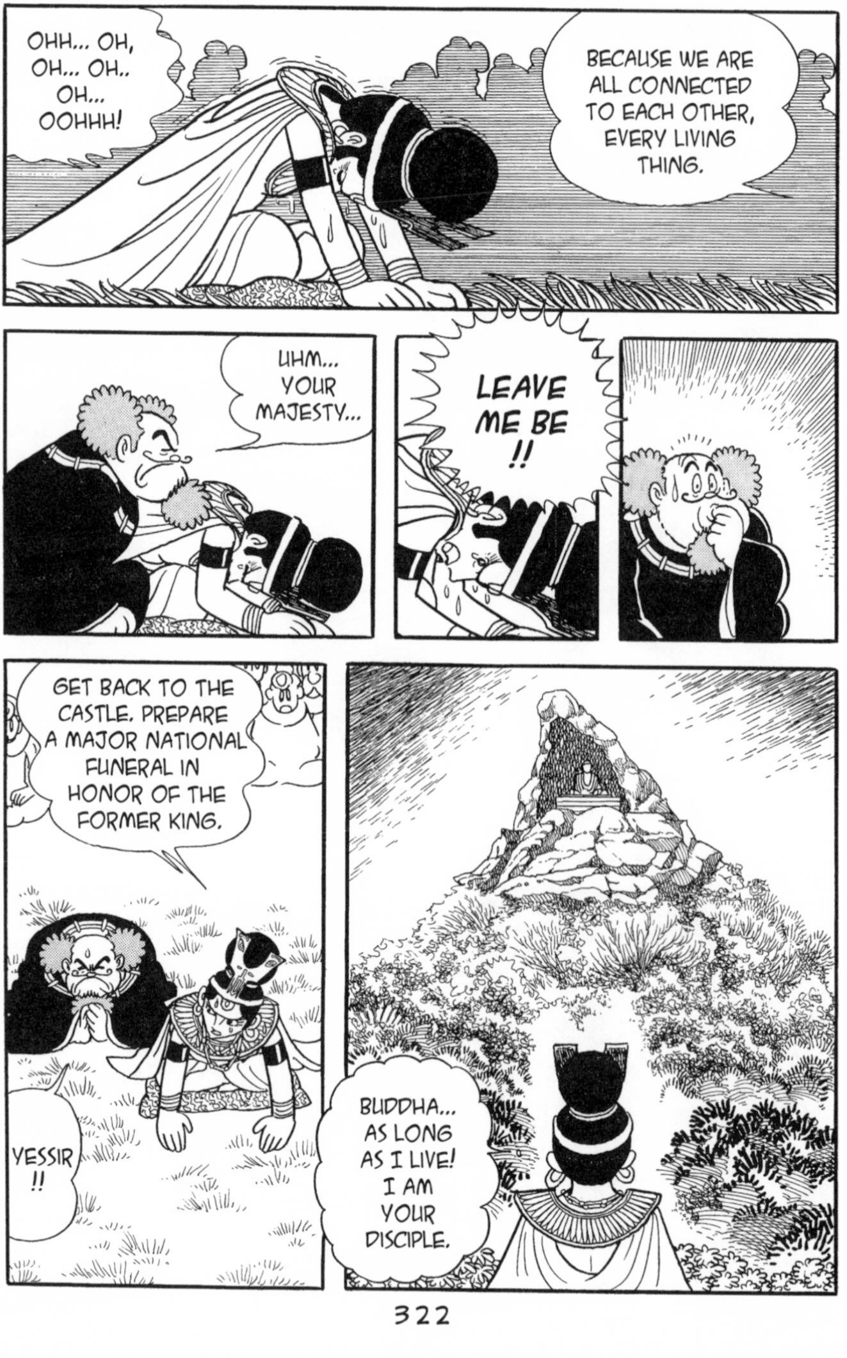
OHH... OH, OH... OH.. OH... OOHHH!
BECAUSE WE ARE ALL CONNECTED TO EACH OTHER, EVERY LIVING THING.
UHM... YOUR MAJESTY...
LEAVE ME BE !!
GET BACK TO THE CASTLE. PREPARE A MAJOR NATIONAL FUNERAL IN HONOR OF THE FORMER KING.
YESSIR !!
BUDDHA... AS LONG AS I LIVE! I AM YOUR DISCIPLE.

CHAPTER FOUR

The End of the Journey

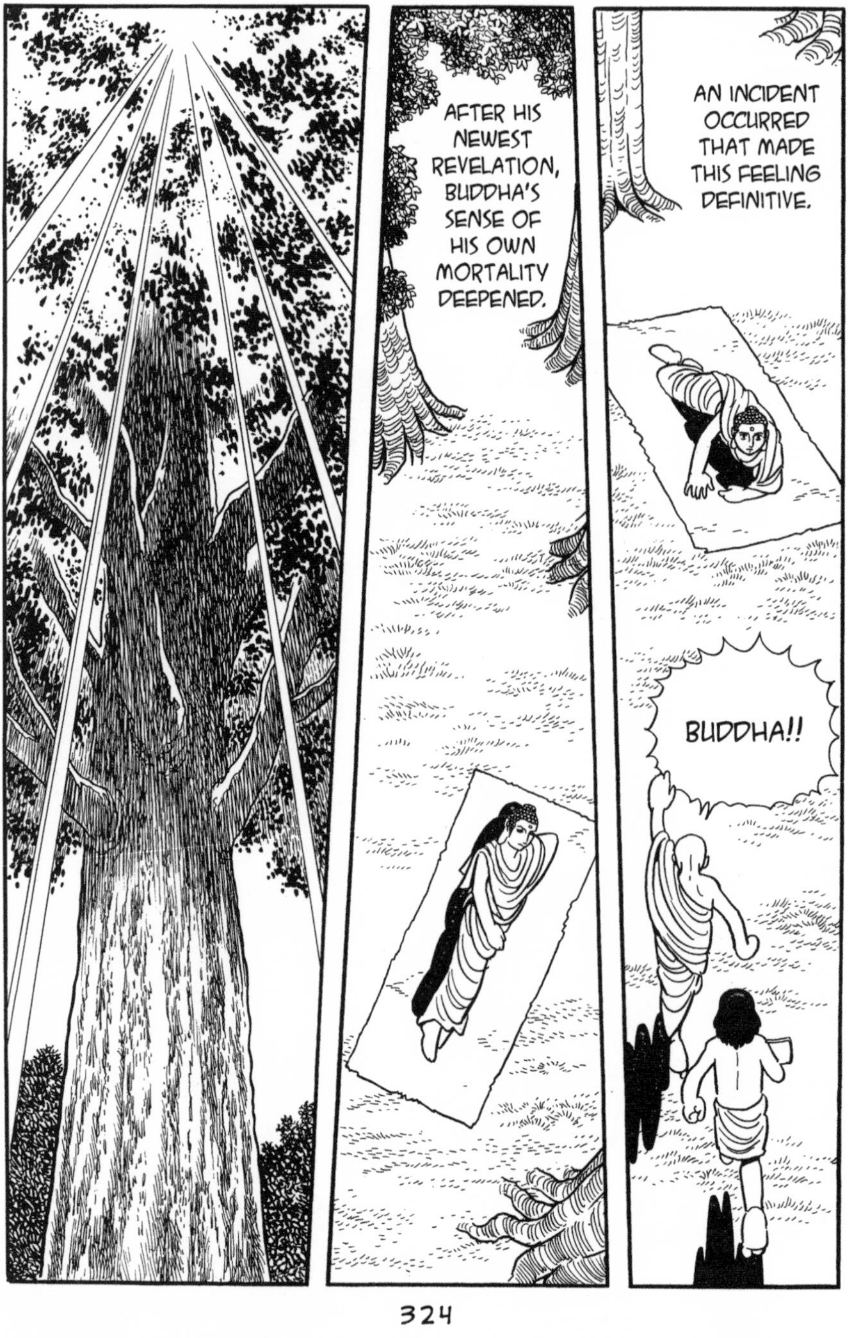
AFTER HIS NEWEST REVELATION, BUDDHA'S SENSE OF HIS OWN MORTALITY DEEPENED.
AN INCIDENT OCCURRED THAT MADE THIS FEELING DEFINITIVE.
BUDDHA!!

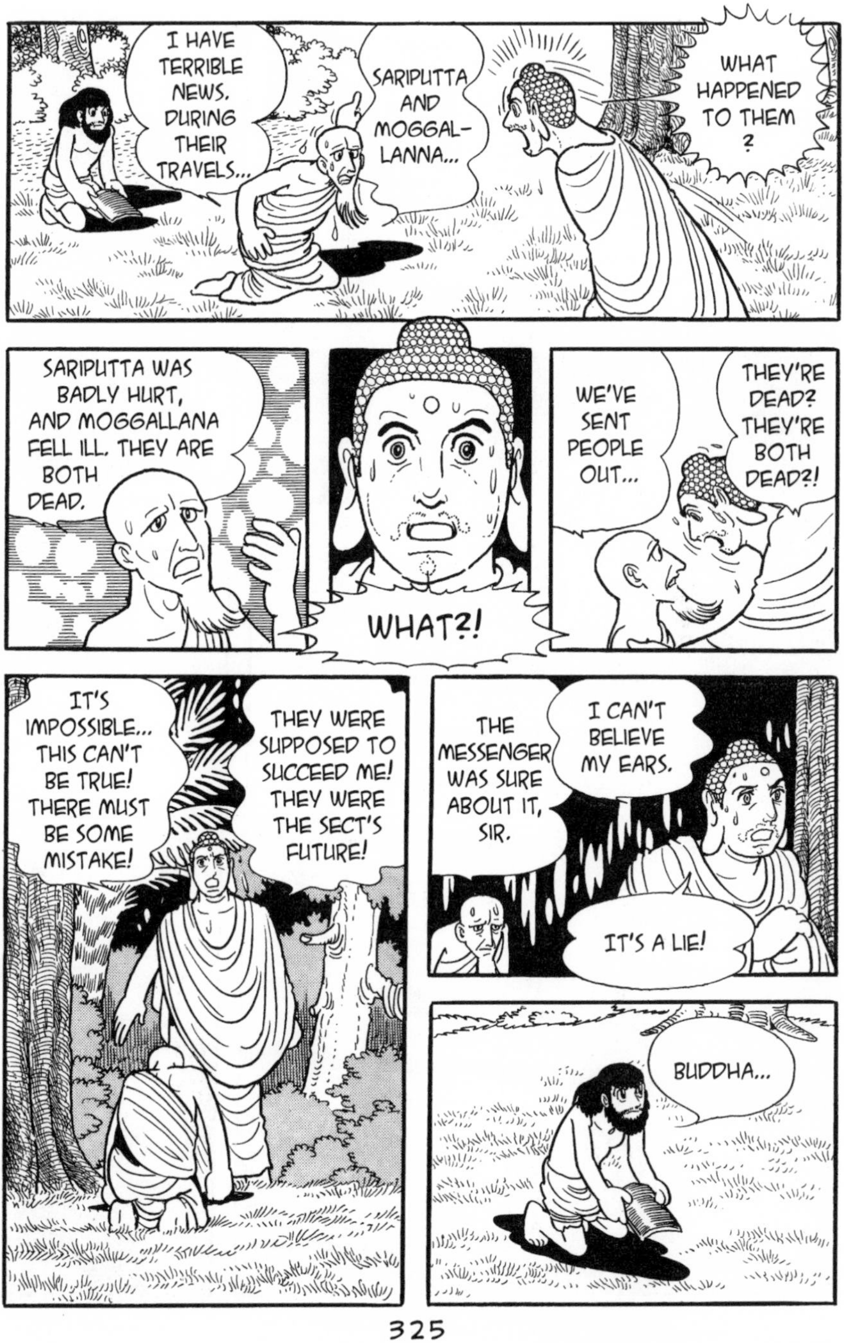

I HAVE TERRIBLE NEWS. DURING THEIR TRAVELS...
SARIPUTTA AND MOGGAL-LANNA...
WHAT HAPPENED TO THEM?
SARIPUTTA WAS BADLY HURT, AND MOGGALLANA FELL ILL. THEY ARE BOTH DEAD.
WHAT?!
WE'VE SENT PEOPLE OUT...
THEY'RE DEAD? THEY'RE BOTH DEAD?!
IT'S IMPOSSIBLE... THIS CAN'T BE TRUE! THERE MUST BE SOME MISTAKE!
THEY WERE SUPPOSED TO SUCCEED ME! THEY WERE THE SECT'S FUTURE!
THE MESSENGER WAS SURE ABOUT IT, SIR.
I CAN'T BELIEVE MY EARS.
IT'S A LIE!
BUDDHA...

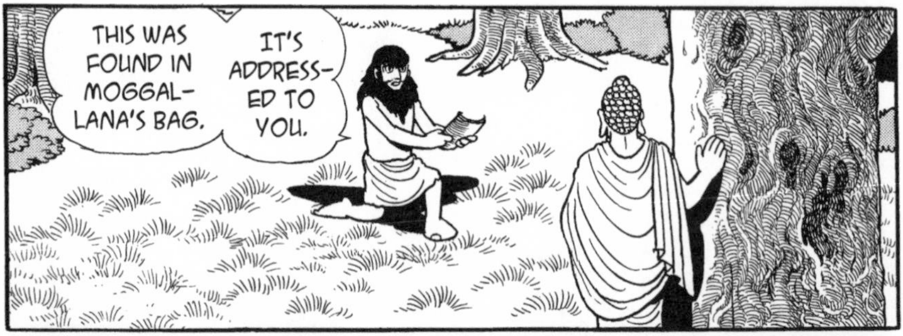
THIS WAS FOUND IN MOGGAL-LANA'S BAG.
IT'S ADDRESS-ED TO YOU.

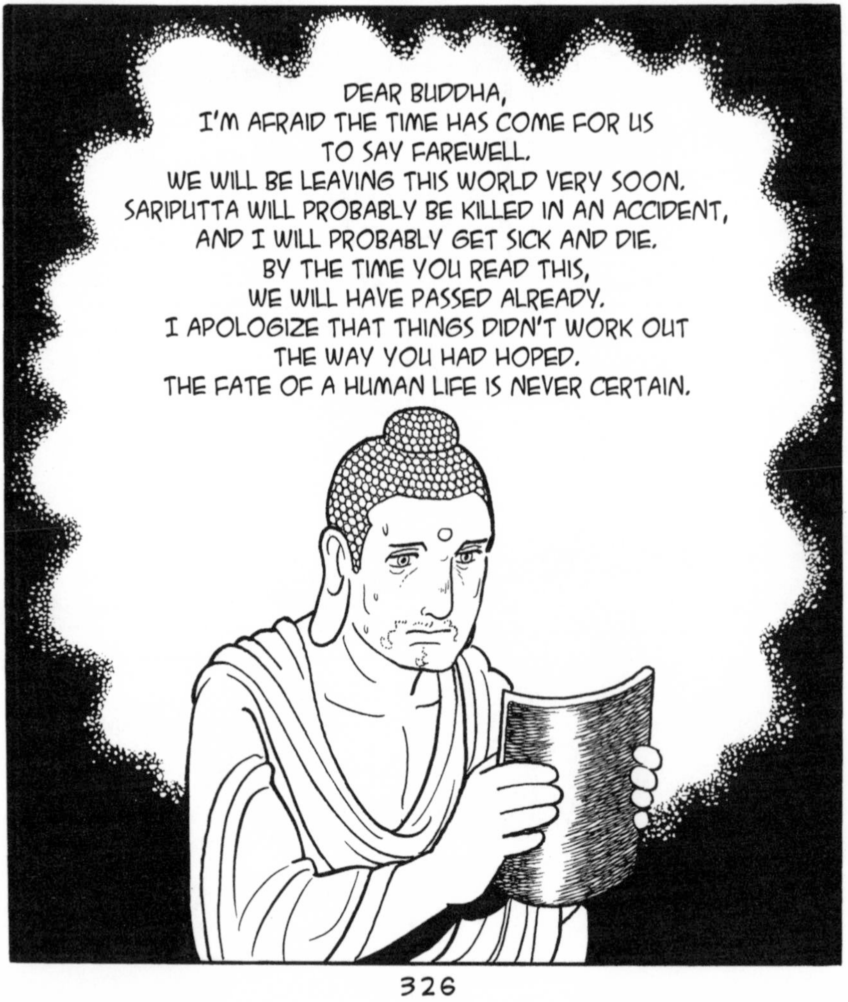
DEAR BUDDHA,
I'M AFRAID THE TIME HAS COME FOR US TO SAY FAREWELL.
WE WILL BE LEAVING THIS WORLD VERY SOON.
SARIPUTTA WILL PROBABLY BE KILLED IN AN ACCIDENT,
AND I WILL PROBABLY GET SICK AND DIE.
BY THE TIME YOU READ THIS,
WE WILL HAVE PASSED ALREADY.
I APOLOGIZE THAT THINGS DIDN'T WORK OUT
THE WAY YOU HAD HOPED.
THE FATE OF A HUMAN LIFE IS NEVER CERTAIN.

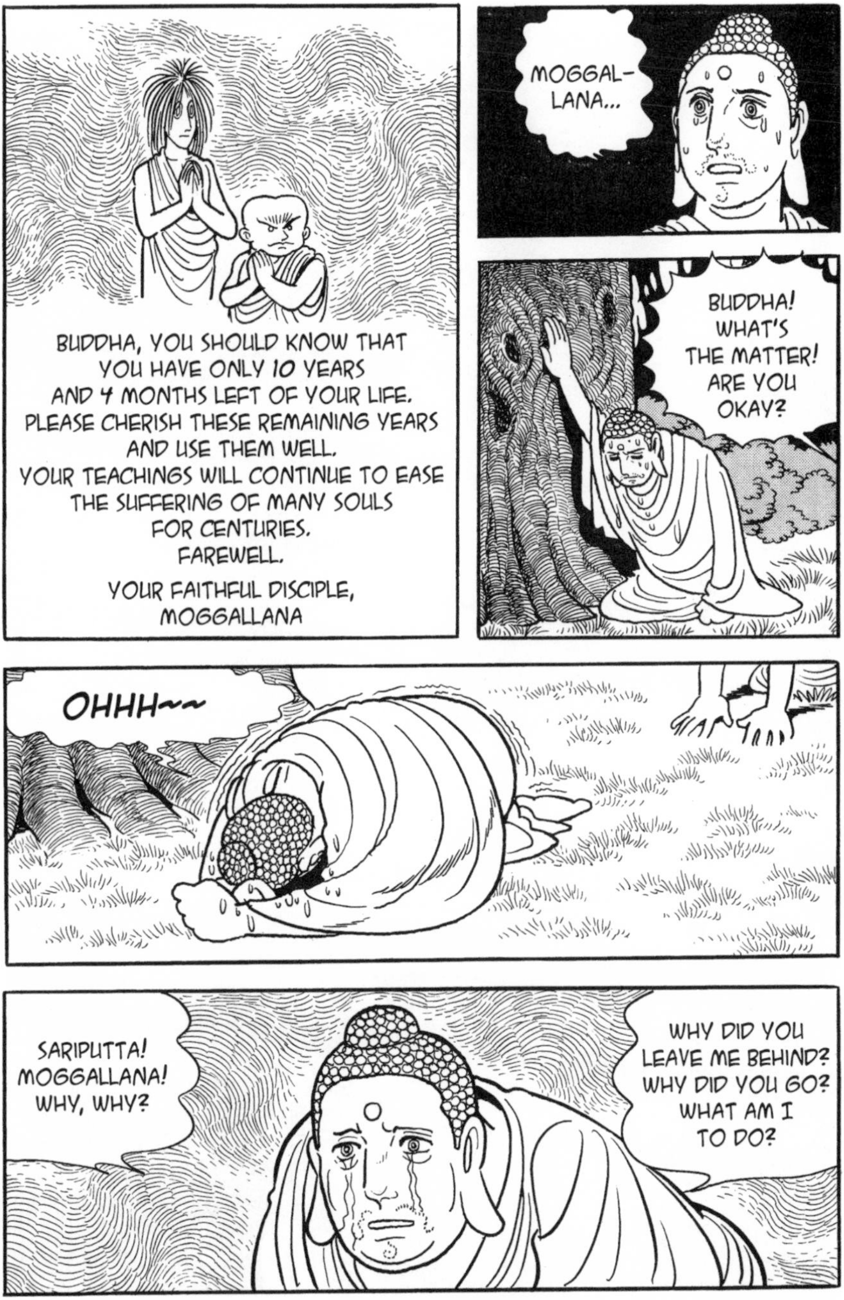
BUDDHA, YOU SHOULD KNOW THAT YOU HAVE ONLY 10 YEARS AND 4 MONTHS LEFT OF YOUR LIFE. PLEASE CHERISH THESE REMAINING YEARS AND USE THEM WELL. YOUR TEACHINGS WILL CONTINUE TO EASE THE SUFFERING OF MANY SOULS FOR CENTURIES. FAREWELL.
YOUR FAITHFUL DISCIPLE, MOGGALLANA
MOGGAL-LANA...
BUDDHA! WHAT'S THE MATTER! ARE YOU OKAY?
OHHH~~
SARIPUTTA! MOGGALLANA! WHY, WHY?
WHY DID YOU LEAVE ME BEHIND? WHY DID YOU GO? WHAT AM I TO DO?

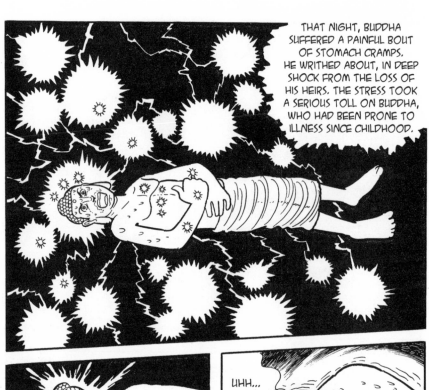

THAT NIGHT, BUDDHA SUFFERED A PAINFUL BOUT OF STOMACH CRAMPS. HE WRITHED ABOUT, IN DEEP SHOCK FROM THE LOSS OF HIS HEIRS. THE STRESS TOOK A SERIOUS TOLL ON BUDDHA, WHO HAD BEEN PRONE TO ILLNESS SINCE CHILDHOOD.

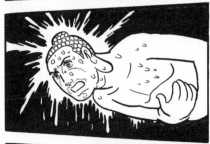

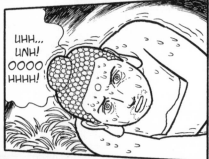

UHH... UNH! OOOO HHHH!

SIDDHARTHA! SIDDHARTHA!

WHO... WHO'S THERE? WHO'S CALLING MY NAME?

WHO ARE YOU...?

YOU'VE LIVED QUITE LONG ENOUGH, I SAY.

IS THAT YOU, MARA?

DIE!

YOU'RE DONE WITH THIS WORLD. DIE. PASS FROM THIS WORLD AND FIND ETERNAL PEACE.

I WON'T LISTEN TO YOUR WICKED ADVICE, MARA!

MY LIFE IS MINE TO LIVE!

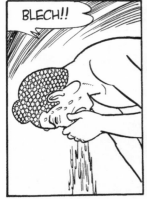

BLECH!!

"COUGH" BLAAAH! BLECH... GEH...BLECH!!

THE REST OF MY LIFE...

329

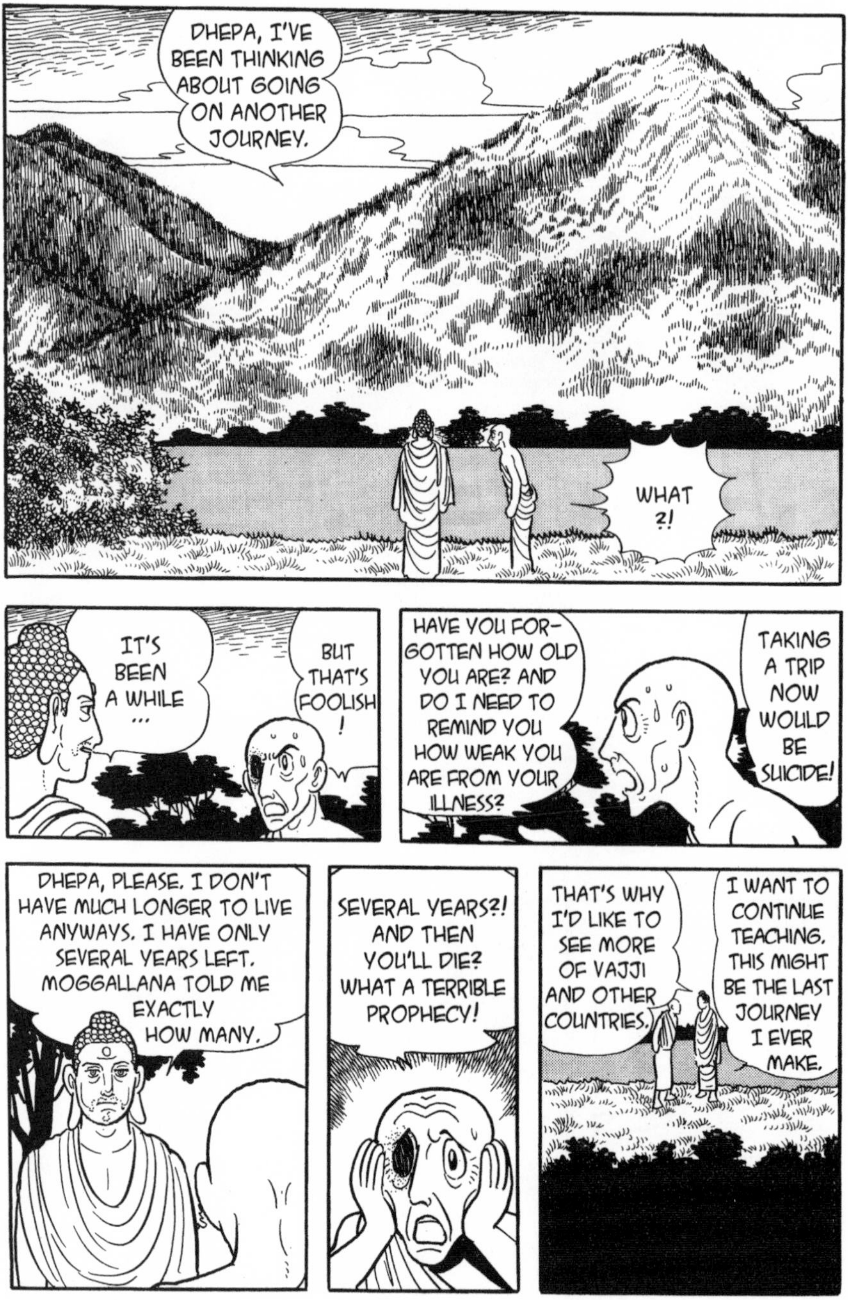
DHEPA, I'VE BEEN THINKING ABOUT GOING ON ANOTHER JOURNEY.
WHAT ?!
IT'S BEEN A WHILE ...
BUT THAT'S FOOLISH !
HAVE YOU FORGOTTEN HOW OLD YOU ARE? AND DO I NEED TO REMIND YOU HOW WEAK YOU ARE FROM YOUR ILLNESS?
TAKING A TRIP NOW WOULD BE SUICIDE!
DHEPA, PLEASE. I DON'T HAVE MUCH LONGER TO LIVE ANYWAYS. I HAVE ONLY SEVERAL YEARS LEFT. MOGGALLANA TOLD ME EXACTLY HOW MANY.
SEVERAL YEARS?! AND THEN YOU'LL DIE? WHAT A TERRIBLE PROPHECY!
THAT'S WHY I'D LIKE TO SEE MORE OF VAJJI AND OTHER COUNTRIES.
I WANT TO CONTINUE TEACHING. THIS MIGHT BE THE LAST JOURNEY I EVER MAKE.

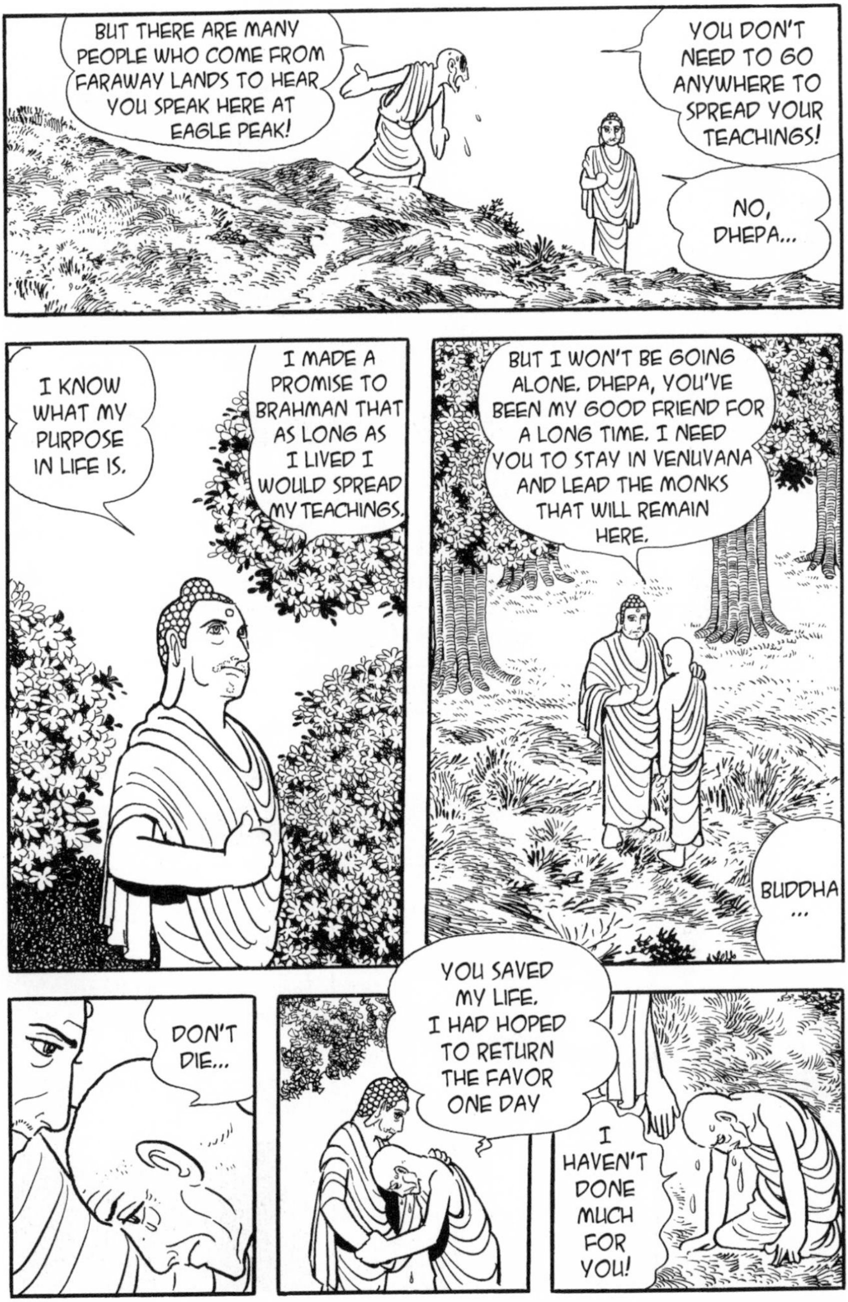
BUT THERE ARE MANY PEOPLE WHO COME FROM FARAWAY LANDS TO HEAR YOU SPEAK HERE AT EAGLE PEAK!
YOU DON'T NEED TO GO ANYWHERE TO SPREAD YOUR TEACHINGS!
NO, DHEPA...
I KNOW WHAT MY PURPOSE IN LIFE IS.
I MADE A PROMISE TO BRAHMAN THAT AS LONG AS I LIVED I WOULD SPREAD MY TEACHINGS.
BUT I WON'T BE GOING ALONE. DHEPA, YOU'VE BEEN MY GOOD FRIEND FOR A LONG TIME. I NEED YOU TO STAY IN VENUVANA AND LEAD THE MONKS THAT WILL REMAIN HERE.
BUDDHA ...
DON'T DIE...
YOU SAVED MY LIFE. I HAD HOPED TO RETURN THE FAVOR ONE DAY
I HAVEN'T DONE MUCH FOR YOU!

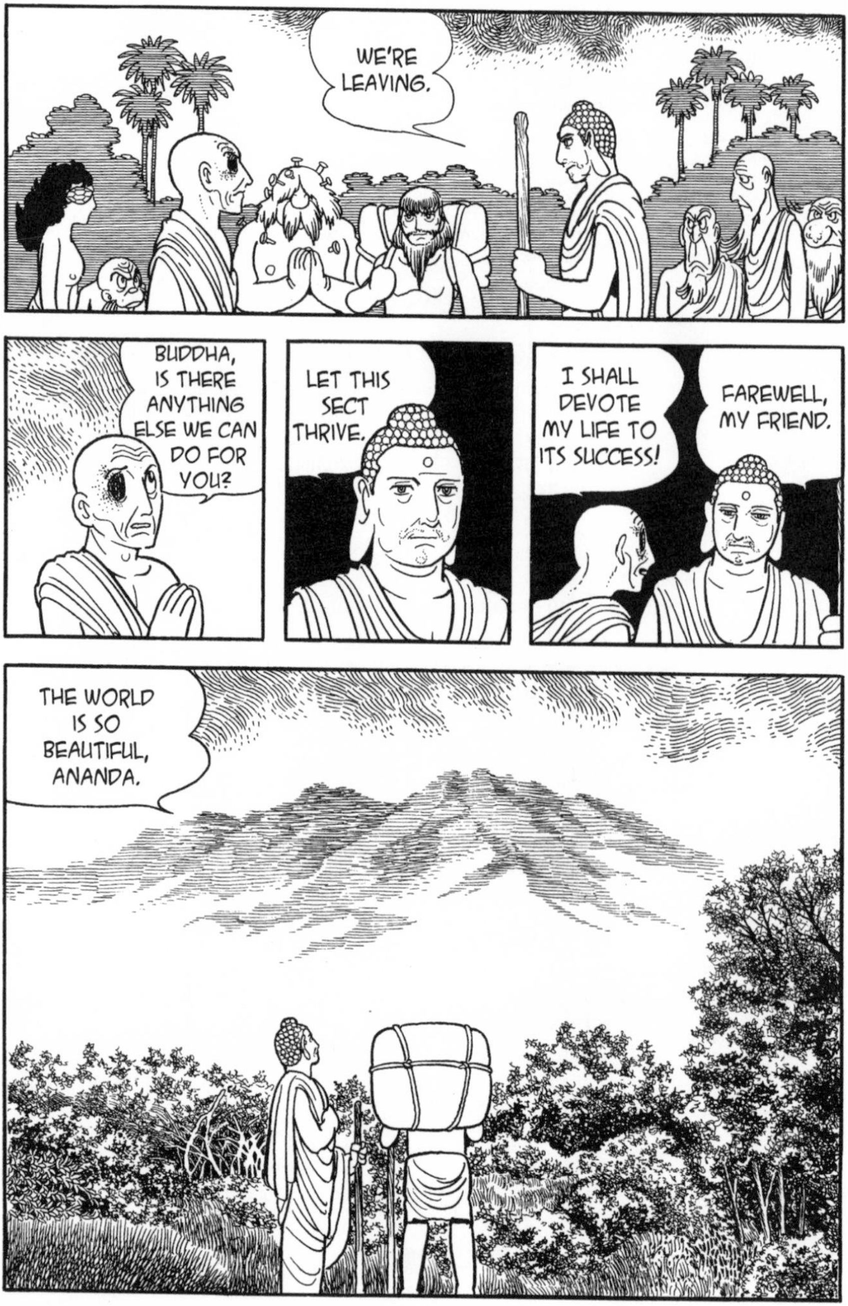
WE'RE LEAVING.
BUDDHA, IS THERE ANYTHING ELSE WE CAN DO FOR YOU?
LET THIS SECT THRIVE.
I SHALL DEVOTE MY LIFE TO ITS SUCCESS!
FAREWELL, MY FRIEND.
THE WORLD IS SO BEAUTIFUL, ANANDA.

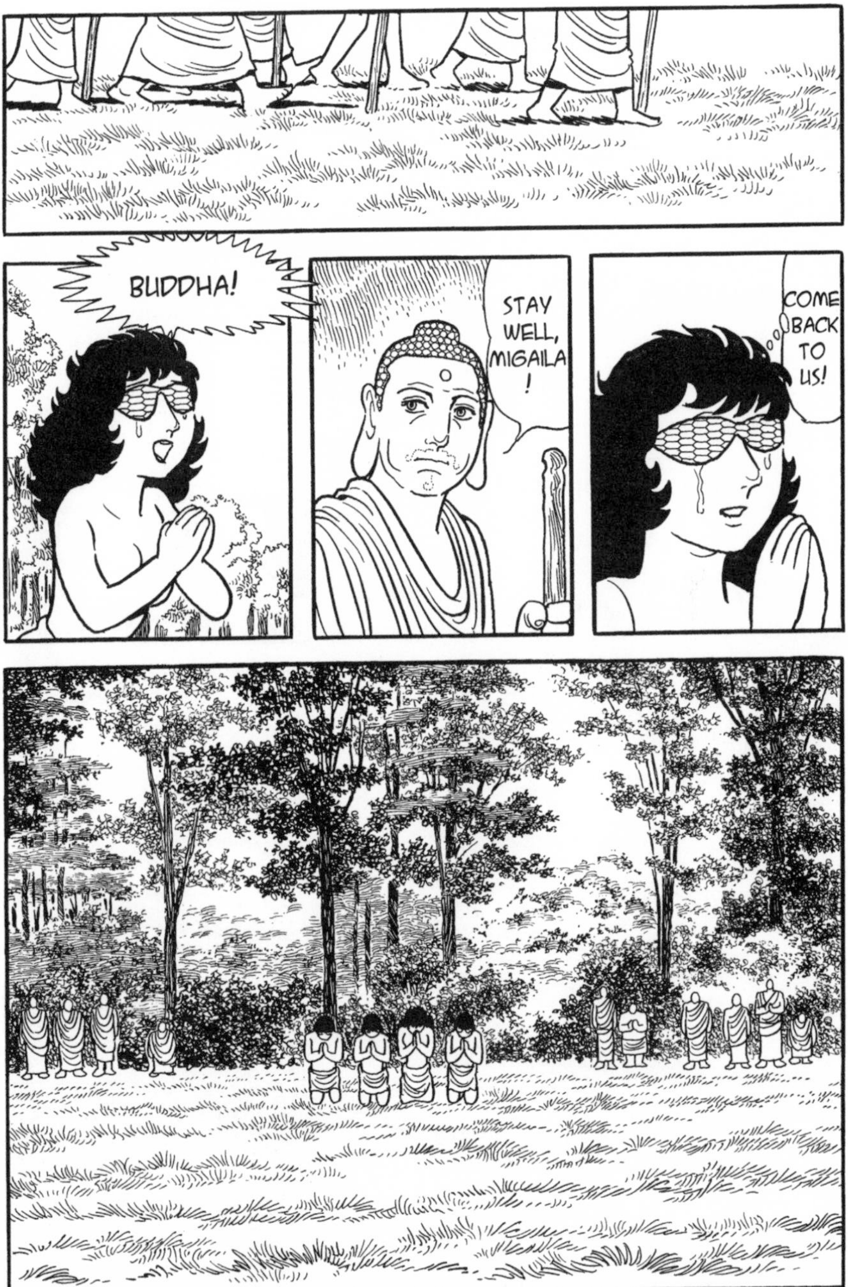
BUDDHA!
STAY WELL, MIGAILA!
COME BACK TO US!

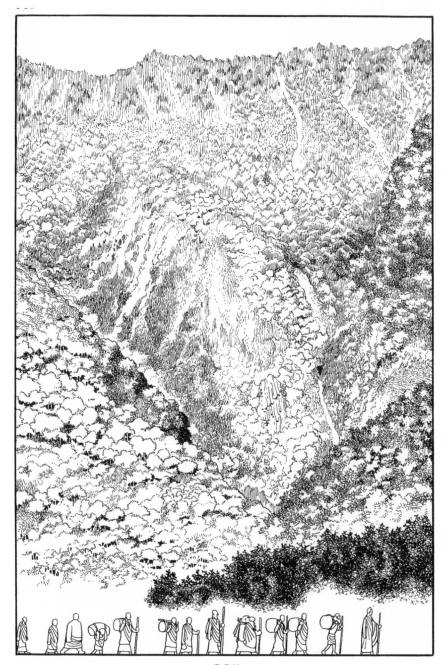

334

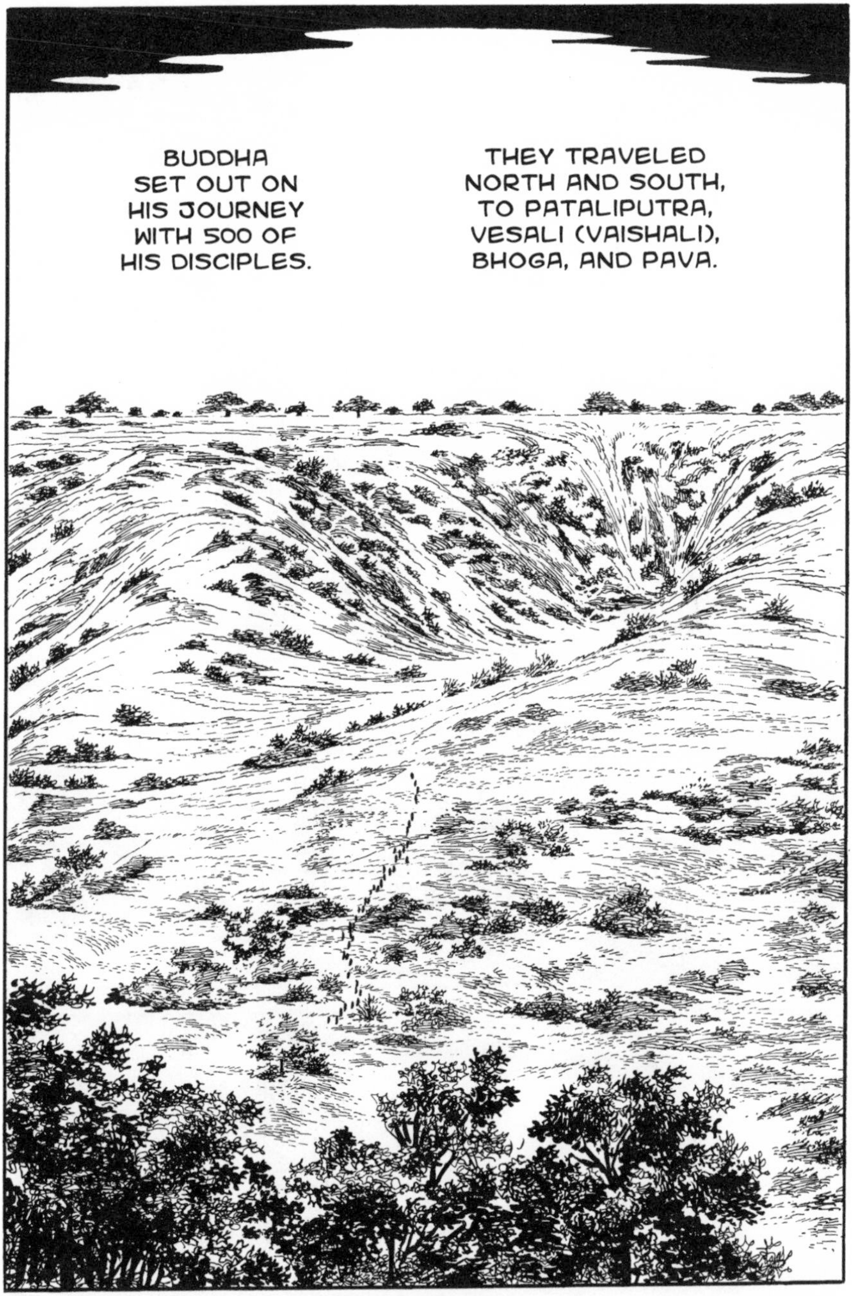
BUDDHA SET OUT ON HIS JOURNEY WITH 500 OF HIS DISCIPLES.
THEY TRAVELED NORTH AND SOUTH, TO PATALIPUTRA, VESALI (VAISHALI), BHOGA, AND PAVA.

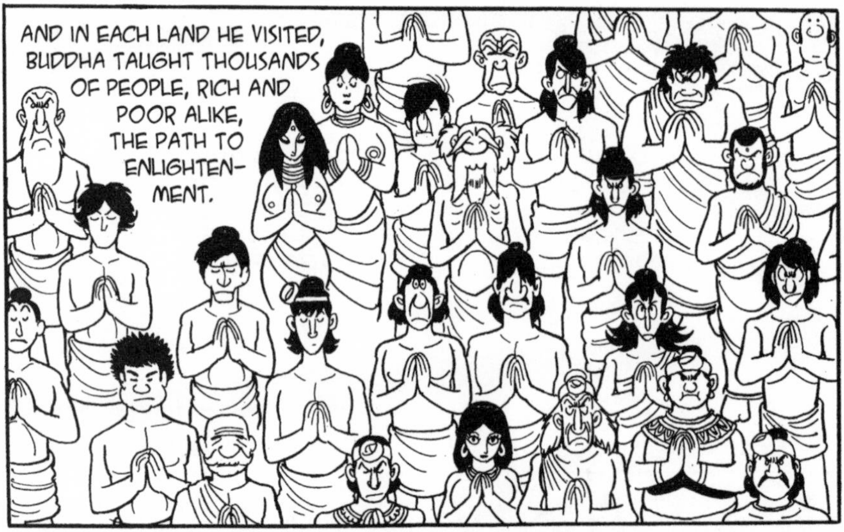
AND IN EACH LAND HE VISITED, BUDDHA TAUGHT THOUSANDS OF PEOPLE, RICH AND POOR ALIKE, THE PATH TO ENLIGHTEN-MENT.
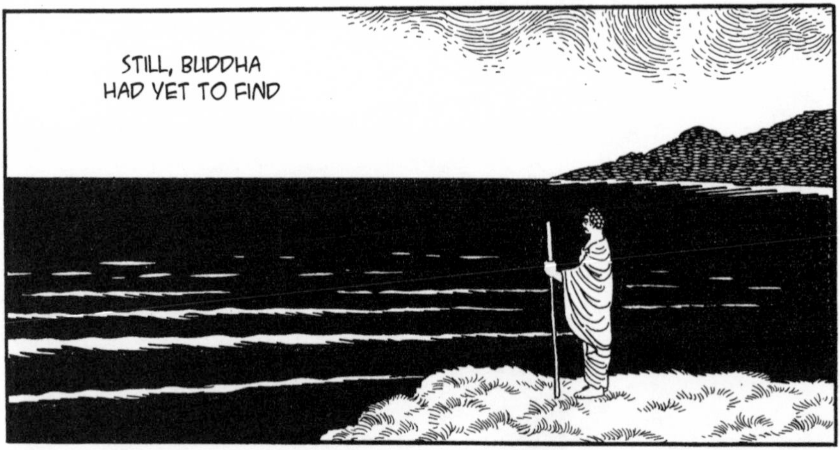
STILL, BUDDHA HAD YET TO FIND
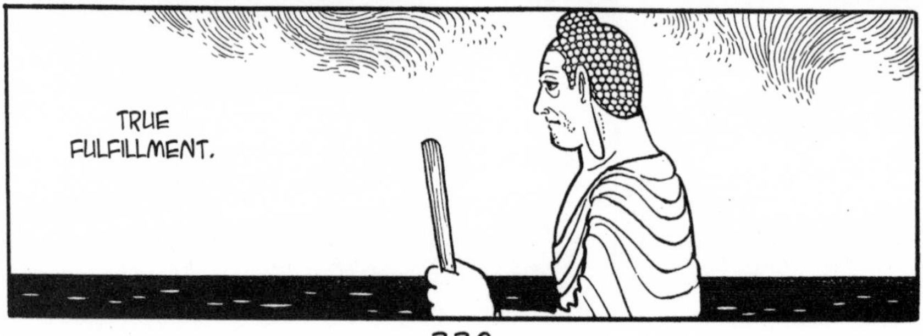
TRUE FULFILLMENT.

SOMETHING
IS MISSING.

WHAT ARE
LIVING
THINGS
?

WHAT
IS LIFE
?

WHY
DO WE
LIVE
?

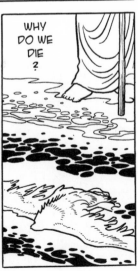

WHY
DO WE
DIE
?

337

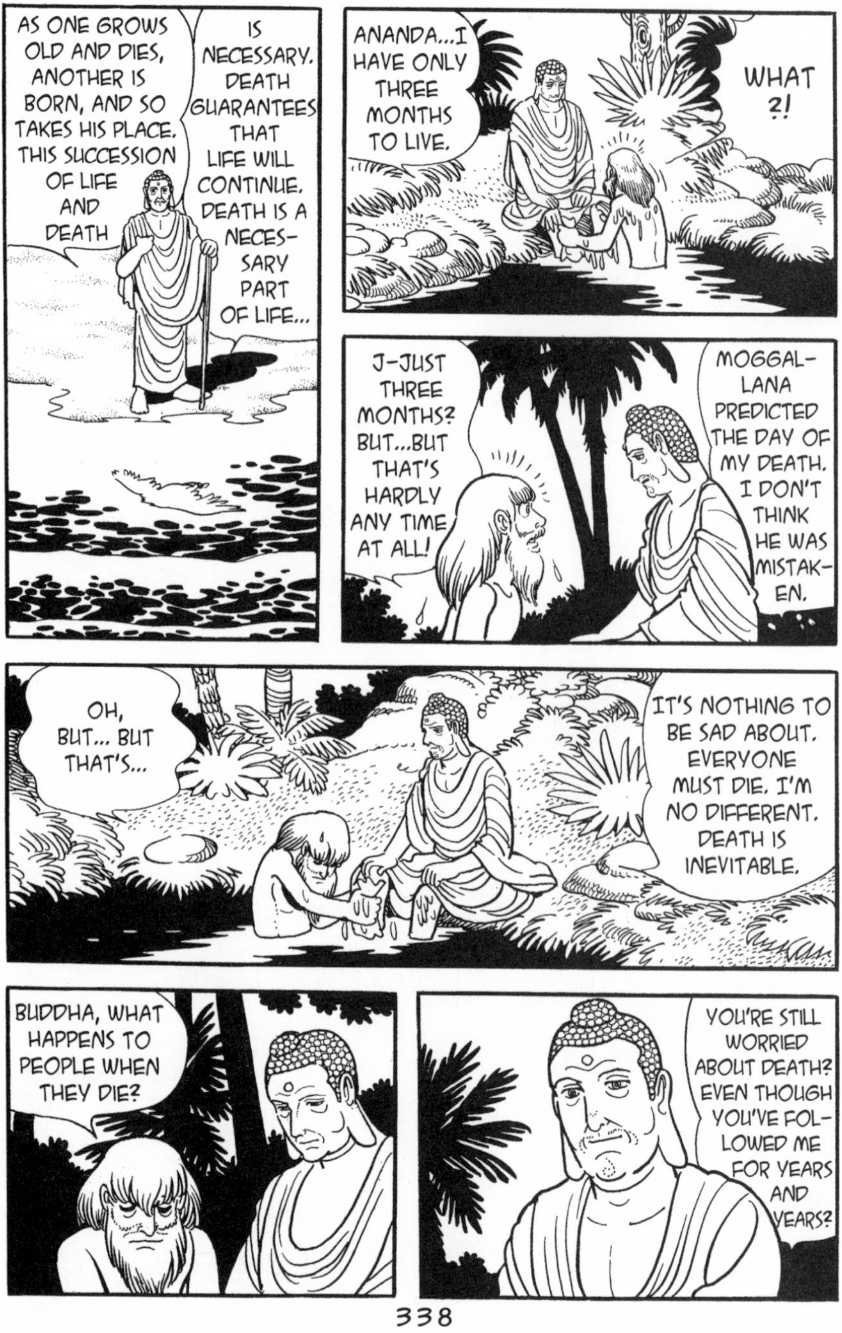
AS ONE GROWS OLD AND DIES, ANOTHER IS BORN, AND SO TAKES HIS PLACE. THIS SUCCESSION OF LIFE AND DEATH
IS NECESSARY. DEATH GUARANTEES THAT LIFE WILL CONTINUE. DEATH IS A NECES-SARY PART OF LIFE...
ANANDA...I HAVE ONLY THREE MONTHS TO LIVE.
WHAT ?!
J-JUST THREE MONTHS? BUT...BUT THAT'S HARDLY ANY TIME AT ALL!
MOGGAL-LANA PREDICTED THE DAY OF MY DEATH. I DON'T THINK HE WAS MISTAK-EN.
OH, BUT... BUT THAT'S...
IT'S NOTHING TO BE SAD ABOUT. EVERYONE MUST DIE. I'M NO DIFFERENT. DEATH IS INEVITABLE.
BUDDHA, WHAT HAPPENS TO PEOPLE WHEN THEY DIE?
YOU'RE STILL WORRIED ABOUT DEATH? EVEN THOUGH YOU'VE FOL-LOWED ME FOR YEARS AND YEARS?

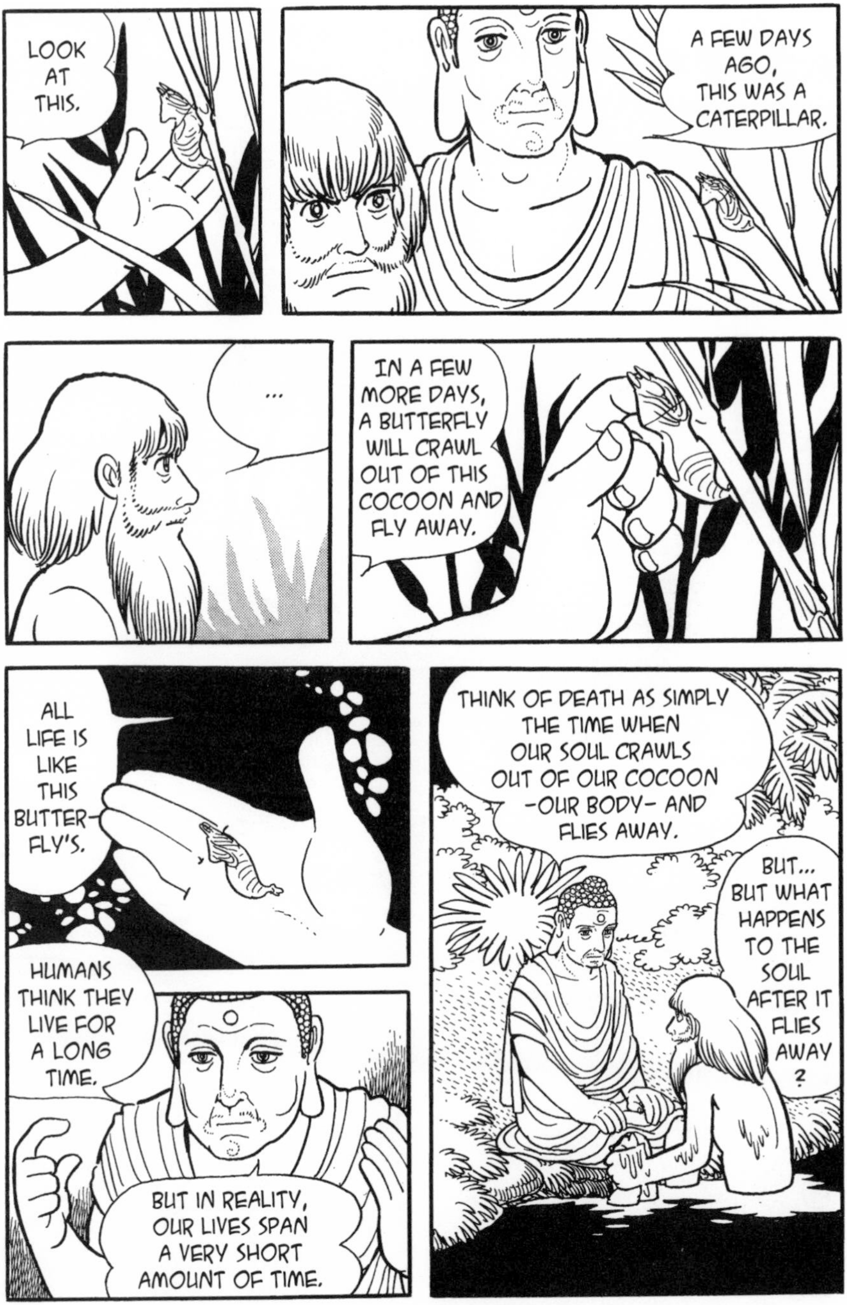
LOOK AT THIS.
A FEW DAYS AGO, THIS WAS A CATERPILLAR.
...
IN A FEW MORE DAYS, A BUTTERFLY WILL CRAWL OUT OF THIS COCOON AND FLY AWAY.
ALL LIFE IS LIKE THIS BUTTER-FLY'S.
HUMANS THINK THEY LIVE FOR A LONG TIME.
BUT IN REALITY, OUR LIVES SPAN A VERY SHORT AMOUNT OF TIME.
THINK OF DEATH AS SIMPLY THE TIME WHEN OUR SOUL CRAWLS OUT OF OUR COCOON -OUR BODY- AND FLIES AWAY.
BUT... BUT WHAT HAPPENS TO THE SOUL AFTER IT FLIES AWAY ?

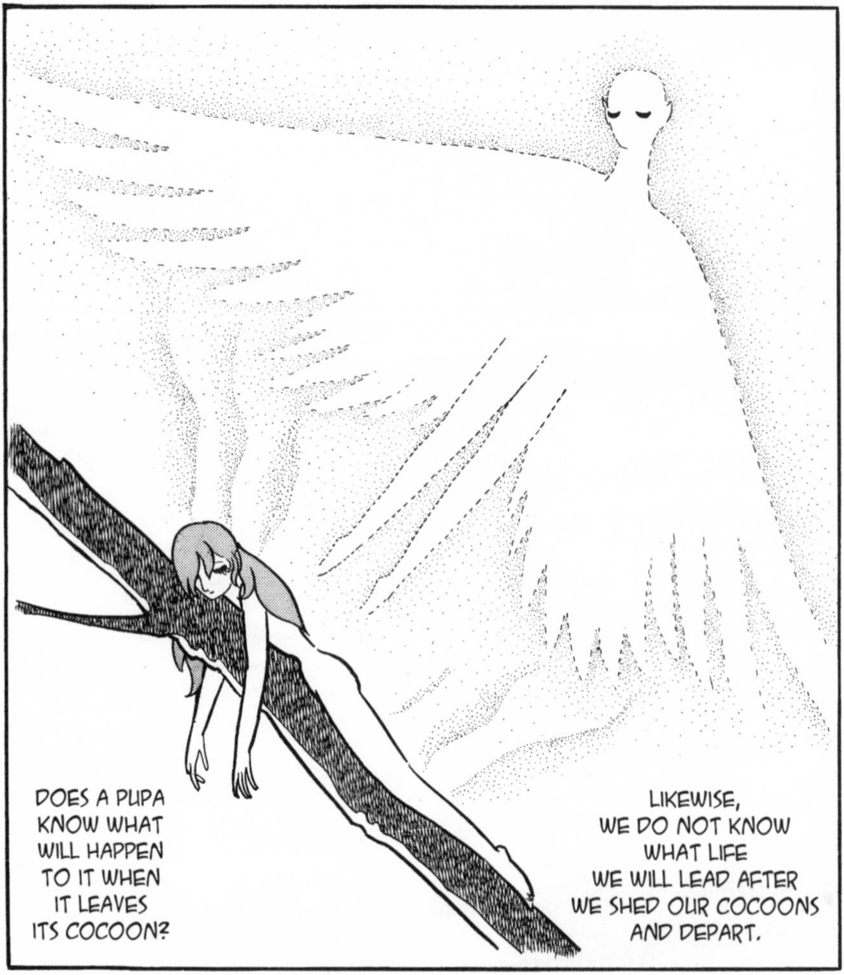
DOES A PUPA KNOW WHAT WILL HAPPEN TO IT WHEN IT LEAVES ITS COCOON?
LIKEWISE, WE DO NOT KNOW WHAT LIFE WE WILL LEAD AFTER WE SHED OUR COCOONS AND DEPART.

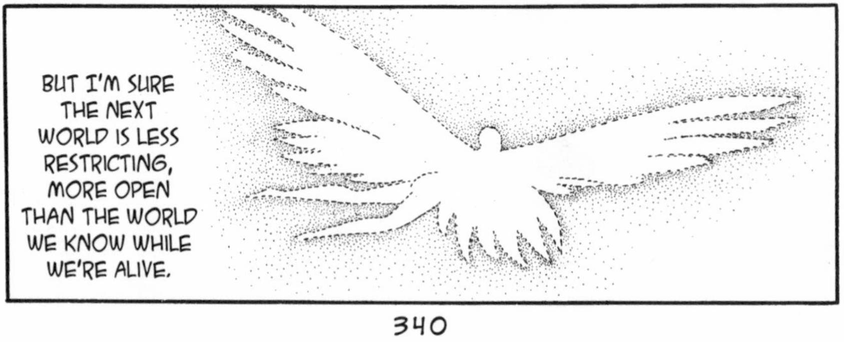
BUT I'M SURE THE NEXT WORLD IS LESS RESTRICTING, MORE OPEN THAN THE WORLD WE KNOW WHILE WE'RE ALIVE.

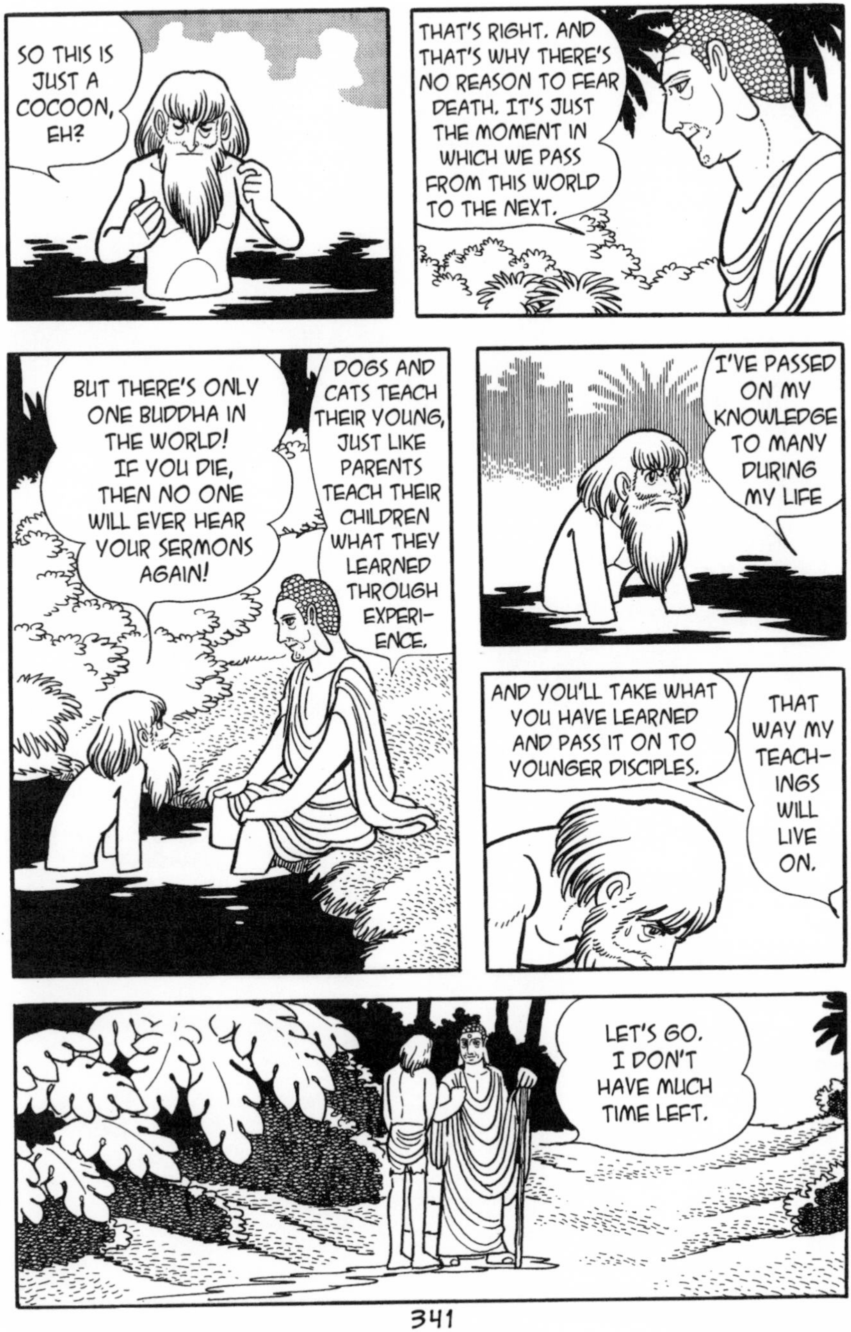
SO THIS IS JUST A COCOON, EH?
THAT'S RIGHT. AND THAT'S WHY THERE'S NO REASON TO FEAR DEATH. IT'S JUST THE MOMENT IN WHICH WE PASS FROM THIS WORLD TO THE NEXT.
BUT THERE'S ONLY ONE BUDDHA IN THE WORLD! IF YOU DIE, THEN NO ONE WILL EVER HEAR YOUR SERMONS AGAIN!
DOGS AND CATS TEACH THEIR YOUNG, JUST LIKE PARENTS TEACH THEIR CHILDREN WHAT THEY LEARNED THROUGH EXPERIENCE.
I'VE PASSED ON MY KNOWLEDGE TO MANY DURING MY LIFE
AND YOU'LL TAKE WHAT YOU HAVE LEARNED AND PASS IT ON TO YOUNGER DISCIPLES.
THAT WAY MY TEACHINGS WILL LIVE ON.
LET'S GO. I DON'T HAVE MUCH TIME LEFT.

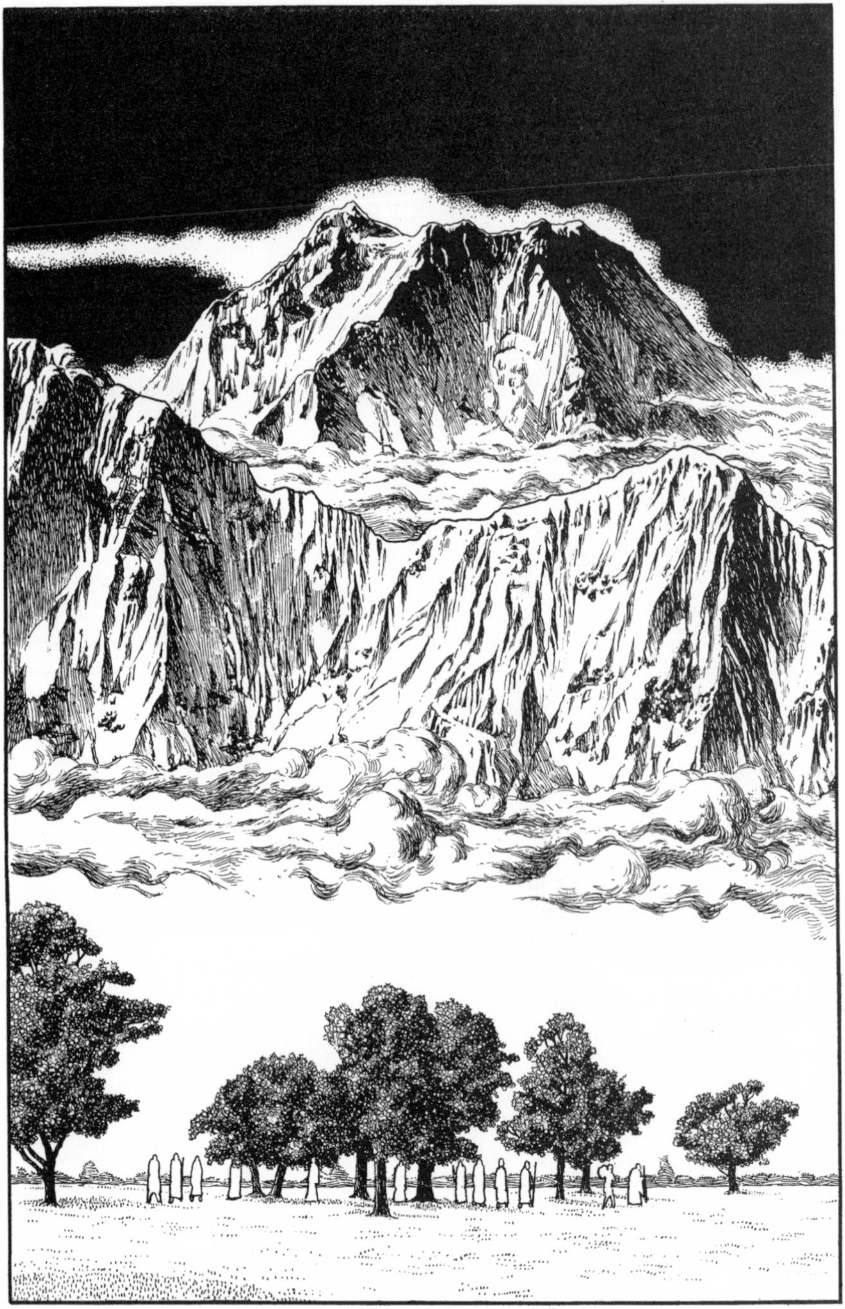

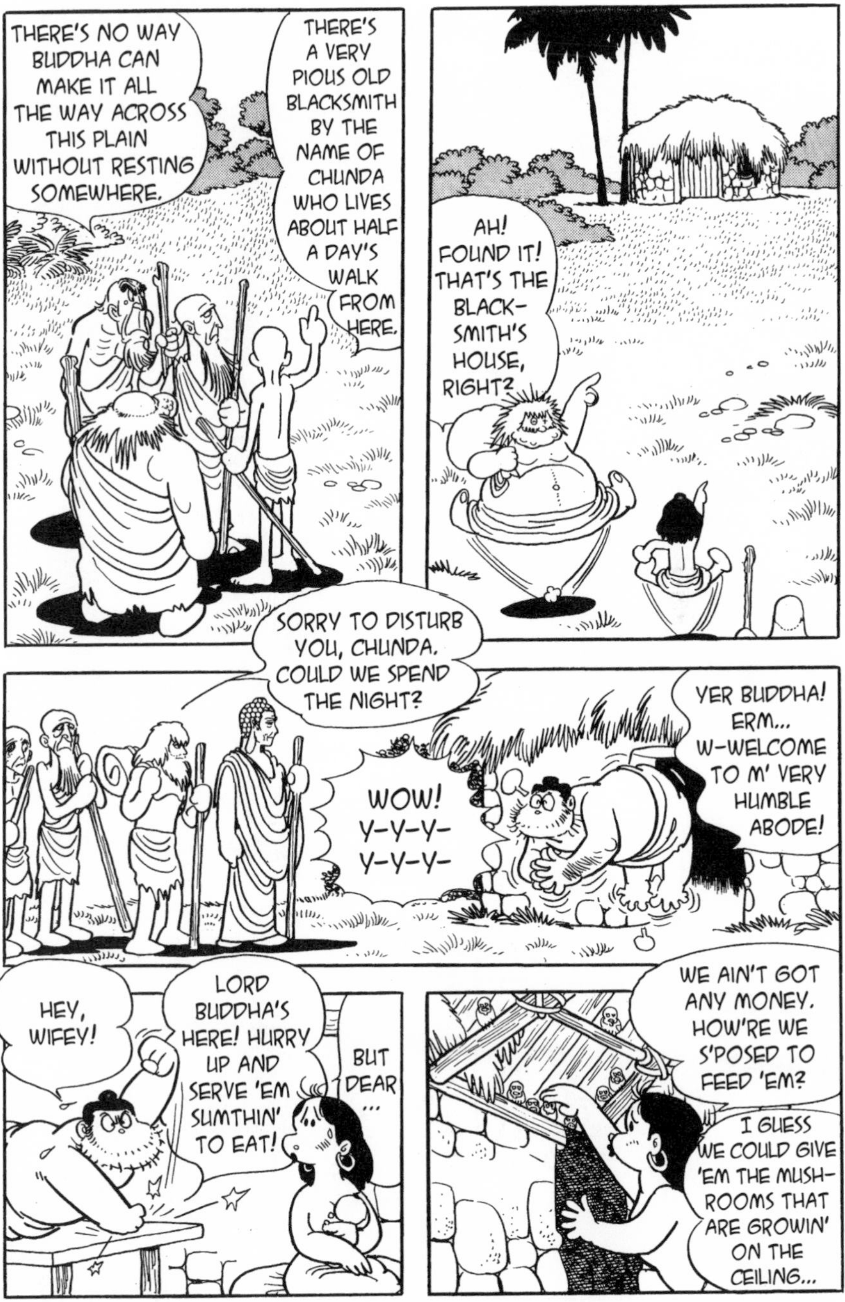
THERE'S NO WAY BUDDHA CAN MAKE IT ALL THE WAY ACROSS THIS PLAIN WITHOUT RESTING SOMEWHERE.
THERE'S A VERY PIOUS OLD BLACKSMITH BY THE NAME OF CHUNDA WHO LIVES ABOUT HALF A DAY'S WALK FROM HERE.
AH! FOUND IT! THAT'S THE BLACK-SMITH'S HOUSE, RIGHT?
SORRY TO DISTURB YOU, CHUNDA. COULD WE SPEND THE NIGHT?
WOW! Y-Y-Y- Y-Y-Y-
YER BUDDHA! ERM... W-WELCOME TO M' VERY HUMBLE ABODE!
HEY, WIFEY!
LORD BUDDHA'S HERE! HURRY UP AND SERVE 'EM SUMTHIN' TO EAT!
BUT DEAR ...
WE AIN'T GOT ANY MONEY. HOW'RE WE S'POSED TO FEED 'EM?
I GUESS WE COULD GIVE 'EM THE MUSH-ROOMS THAT ARE GROWIN' ON THE CEILING...

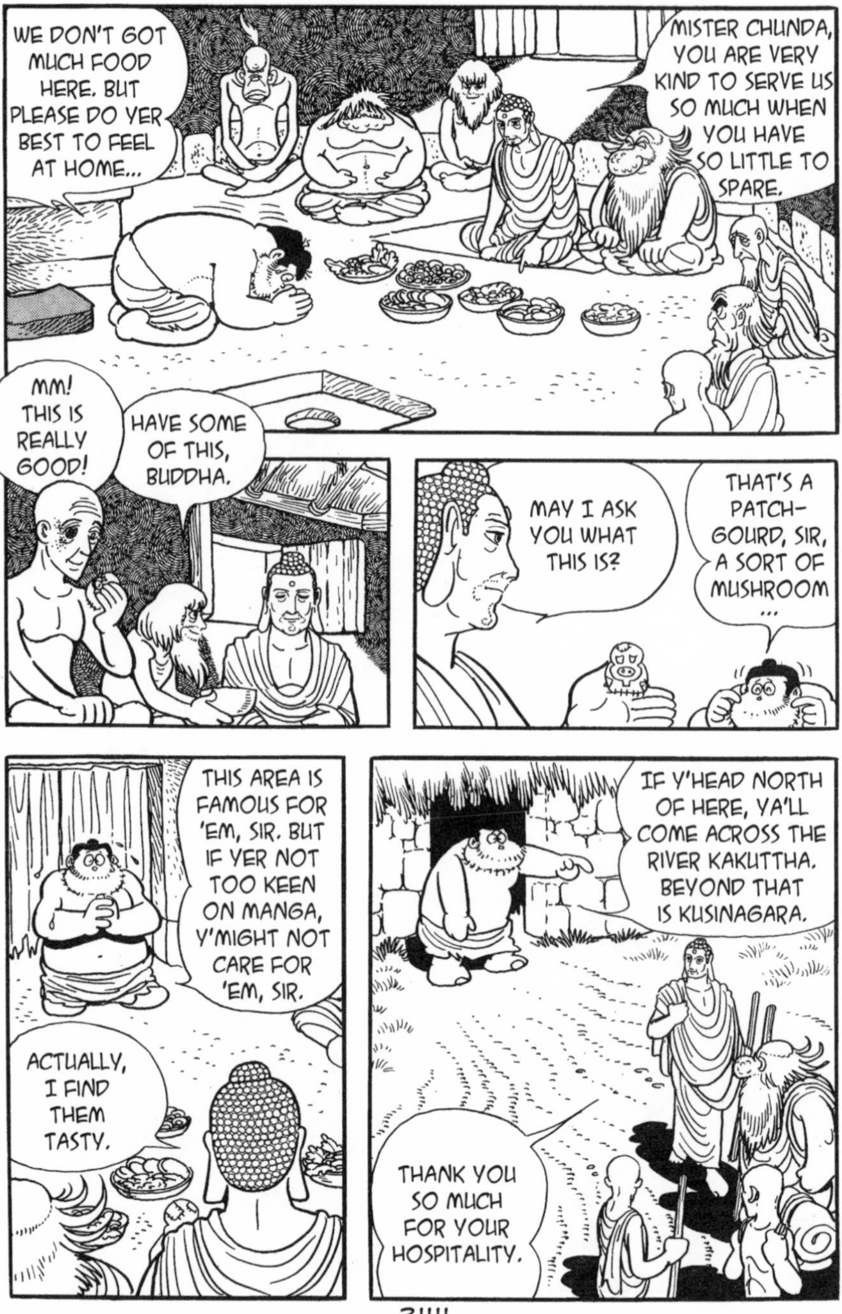
WE DON'T GOT MUCH FOOD HERE. BUT PLEASE DO YER BEST TO FEEL AT HOME...
MISTER CHUNDA, YOU ARE VERY KIND TO SERVE US SO MUCH WHEN YOU HAVE SO LITTLE TO SPARE.
MM! THIS IS REALLY GOOD!
HAVE SOME OF THIS, BUDDHA.
MAY I ASK YOU WHAT THIS IS?
THAT'S A PATCH-GOURD, SIR, A SORT OF MUSHROOM ...
THIS AREA IS FAMOUS FOR 'EM, SIR. BUT IF YER NOT TOO KEEN ON MANGA, Y'MIGHT NOT CARE FOR 'EM, SIR.
ACTUALLY, I FIND THEM TASTY.
IF Y'HEAD NORTH OF HERE, YA'LL COME ACROSS THE RIVER KAKUTTHA. BEYOND THAT IS KUSINAGARA.
THANK YOU SO MUCH FOR YOUR HOSPITALITY.

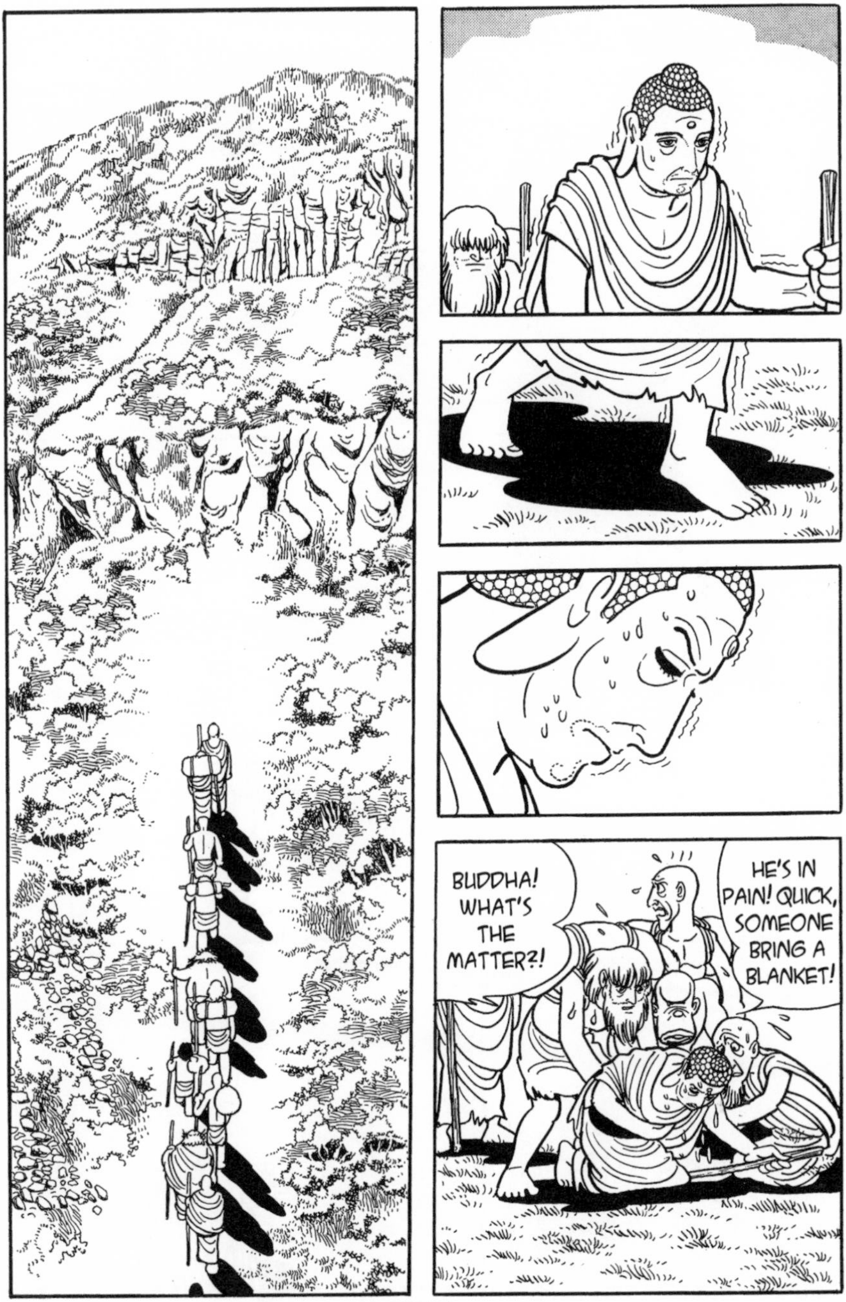
BUDDHA! WHAT'S THE MATTER?!
HE'S IN PAIN! QUICK, SOMEONE BRING A BLANKET!

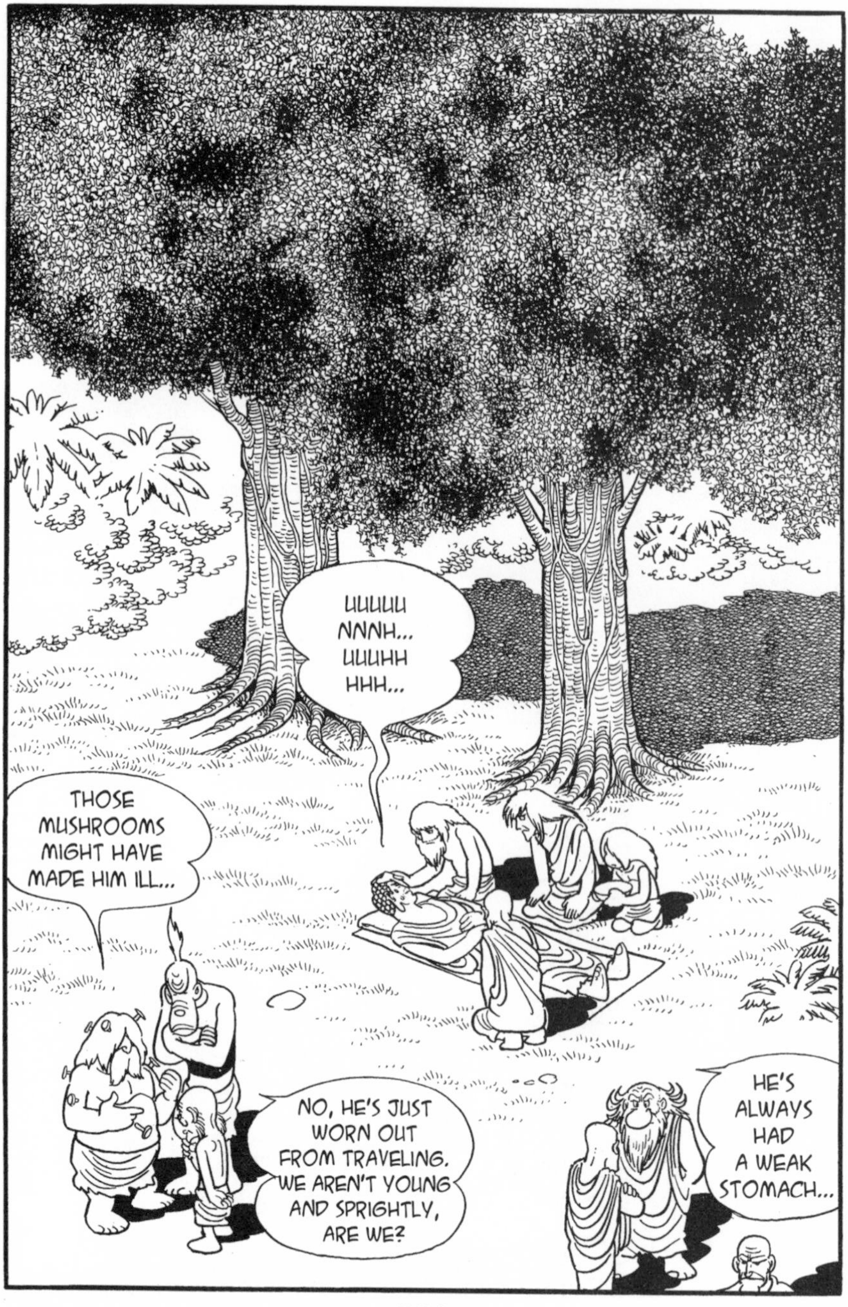
UUUUU NNNH... UUUHH HHH...
THOSE MUSHROOMS MIGHT HAVE MADE HIM ILL...
NO, HE'S JUST WORN OUT FROM TRAVELING. WE AREN'T YOUNG AND SPRIGHTLY, ARE WE?
HE'S ALWAYS HAD A WEAK STOMACH...

OOO OH!!

HE HAS TERRIBLE DIARRHEA! I'LL TAKE CARE OF IT. PLEASE BRING ME A LOT OF WATER!

WE WILL.

I'LL SEE WHAT I CAN DO ABOUT GETTING MORE CLOTHS.

UNNH! UUUU HHHH...

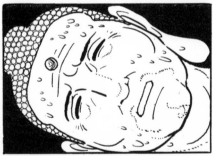

ANANDA... PLEASE LET ME LIE ON MY SIDE... WITH MY HEART ELEVATED...

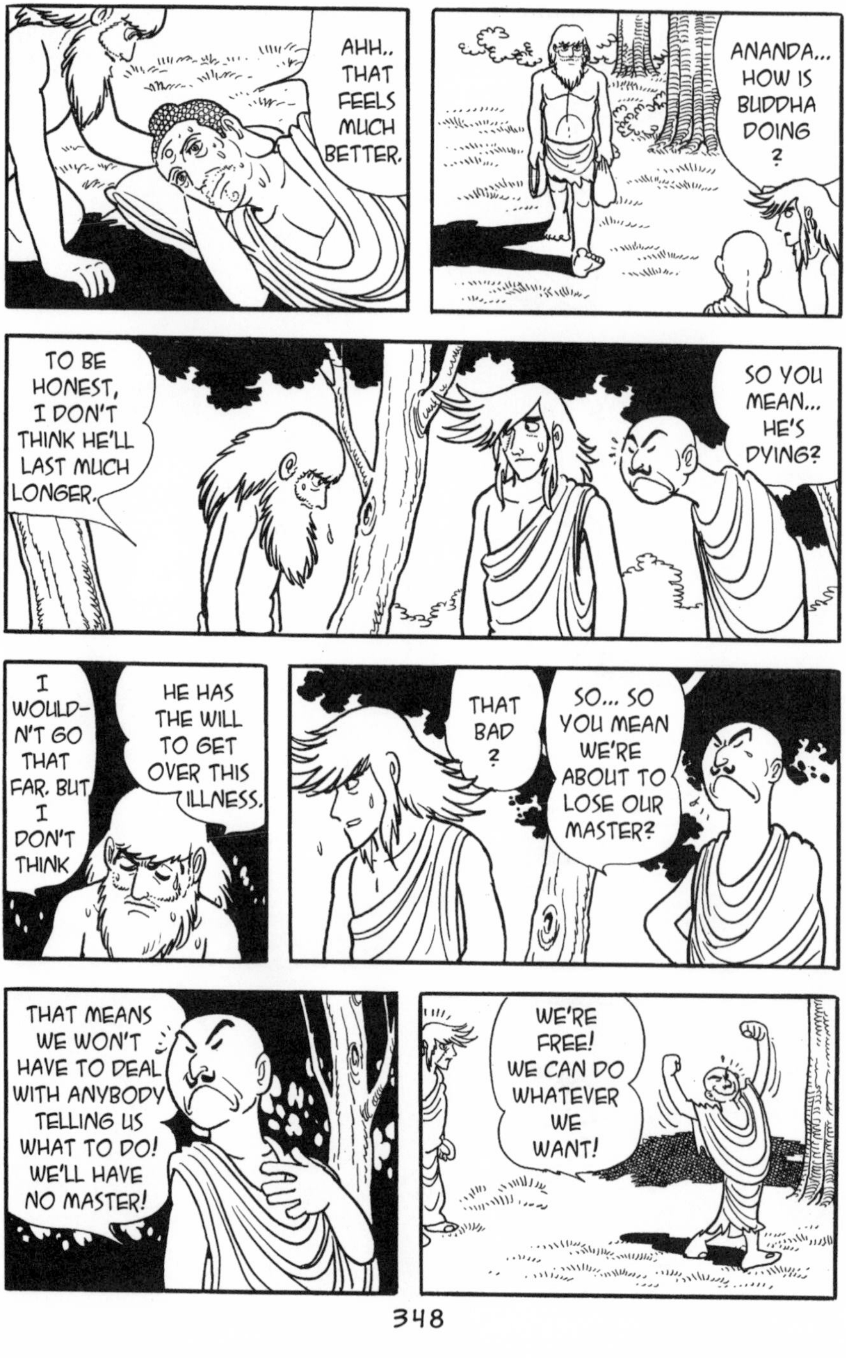
AHH.. THAT FEELS MUCH BETTER.
ANANDA... HOW IS BUDDHA DOING ?
TO BE HONEST, I DON'T THINK HE'LL LAST MUCH LONGER.
SO YOU MEAN... HE'S DYING?
I WOULDN'T GO THAT FAR. BUT I DON'T THINK
HE HAS THE WILL TO GET OVER THIS ILLNESS.
THAT BAD ?
SO... SO YOU MEAN WE'RE ABOUT TO LOSE OUR MASTER?
THAT MEANS WE WON'T HAVE TO DEAL WITH ANYBODY TELLING US WHAT TO DO! WE'LL HAVE NO MASTER!
WE'RE FREE! WE CAN DO WHATEVER WE WANT!

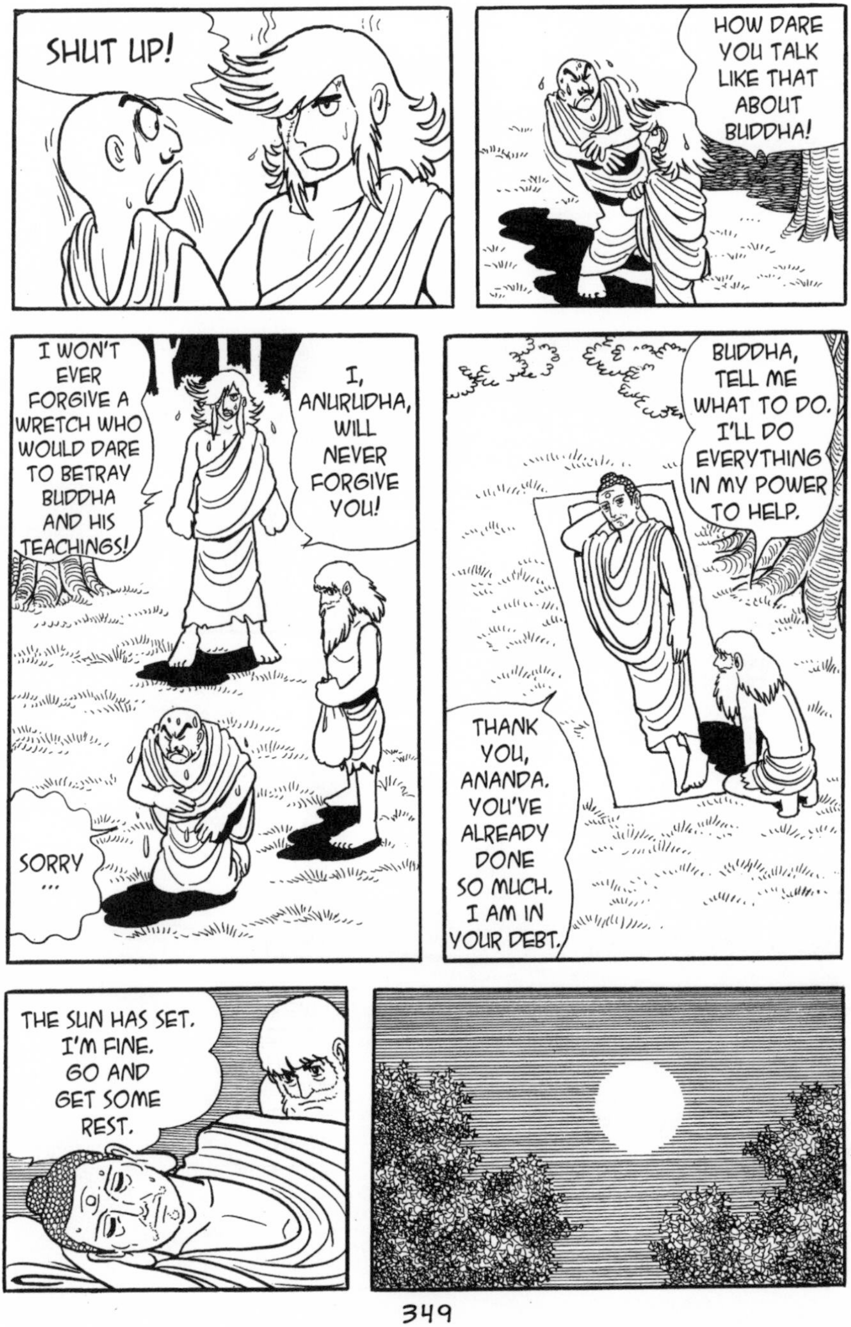
SHUT UP!
HOW DARE YOU TALK LIKE THAT ABOUT BUDDHA!
I WON'T EVER FORGIVE A WRETCH WHO WOULD DARE TO BETRAY BUDDHA AND HIS TEACHINGS!
I, ANURUDHA, WILL NEVER FORGIVE YOU!
SORRY ...
BUDDHA, TELL ME WHAT TO DO. I'LL DO EVERYTHING IN MY POWER TO HELP.
THANK YOU, ANANDA. YOU'VE ALREADY DONE SO MUCH. I AM IN YOUR DEBT.
THE SUN HAS SET. I'M FINE. GO AND GET SOME REST.

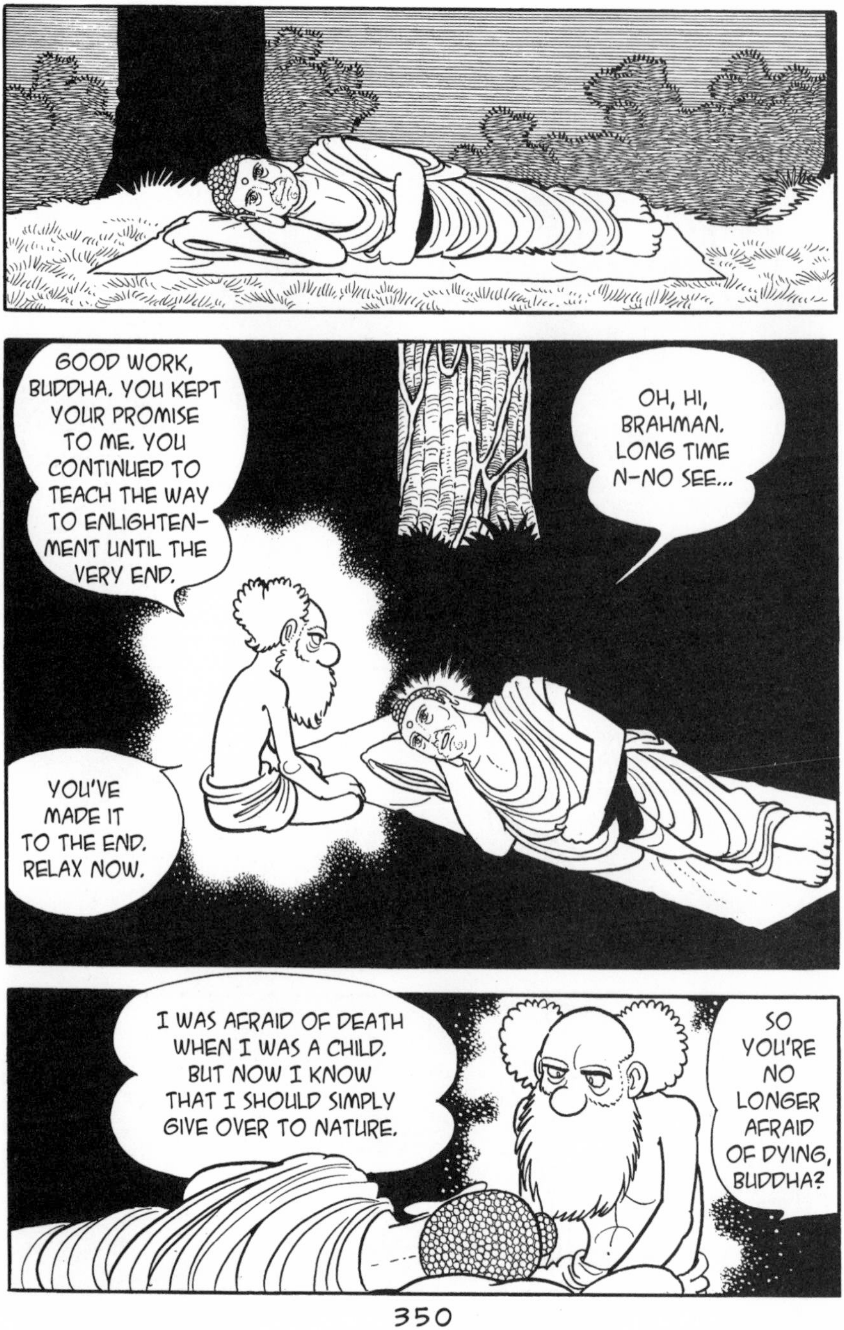
GOOD WORK, BUDDHA. YOU KEPT YOUR PROMISE TO ME. YOU CONTINUED TO TEACH THE WAY TO ENLIGHTENMENT UNTIL THE VERY END.
OH, HI, BRAHMAN. LONG TIME N-NO SEE...
YOU'VE MADE IT TO THE END. RELAX NOW.
I WAS AFRAID OF DEATH WHEN I WAS A CHILD. BUT NOW I KNOW THAT I SHOULD SIMPLY GIVE OVER TO NATURE.
SO YOU'RE NO LONGER AFRAID OF DYING, BUDDHA?

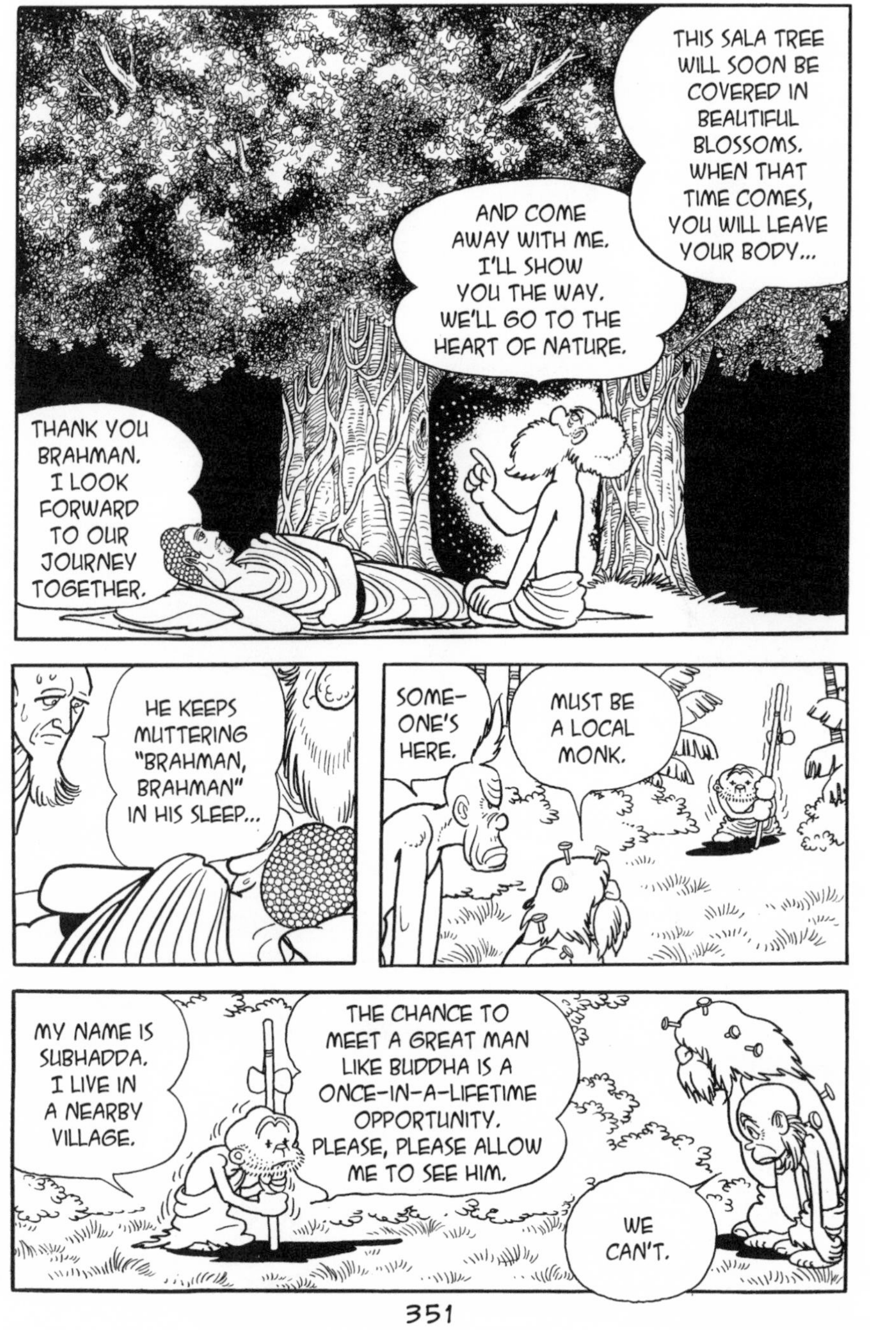
THIS SALA TREE WILL SOON BE COVERED IN BEAUTIFUL BLOSSOMS. WHEN THAT TIME COMES, YOU WILL LEAVE YOUR BODY...
AND COME AWAY WITH ME. I'LL SHOW YOU THE WAY. WE'LL GO TO THE HEART OF NATURE.
THANK YOU BRAHMAN. I LOOK FORWARD TO OUR JOURNEY TOGETHER.
HE KEEPS MUTTERING "BRAHMAN, BRAHMAN" IN HIS SLEEP...
SOME-ONE'S HERE.
MUST BE A LOCAL MONK.
MY NAME IS SUBHADDA. I LIVE IN A NEARBY VILLAGE.
THE CHANCE TO MEET A GREAT MAN LIKE BUDDHA IS A ONCE-IN-A-LIFETIME OPPORTUNITY. PLEASE, PLEASE ALLOW ME TO SEE HIM.
WE CAN'T.

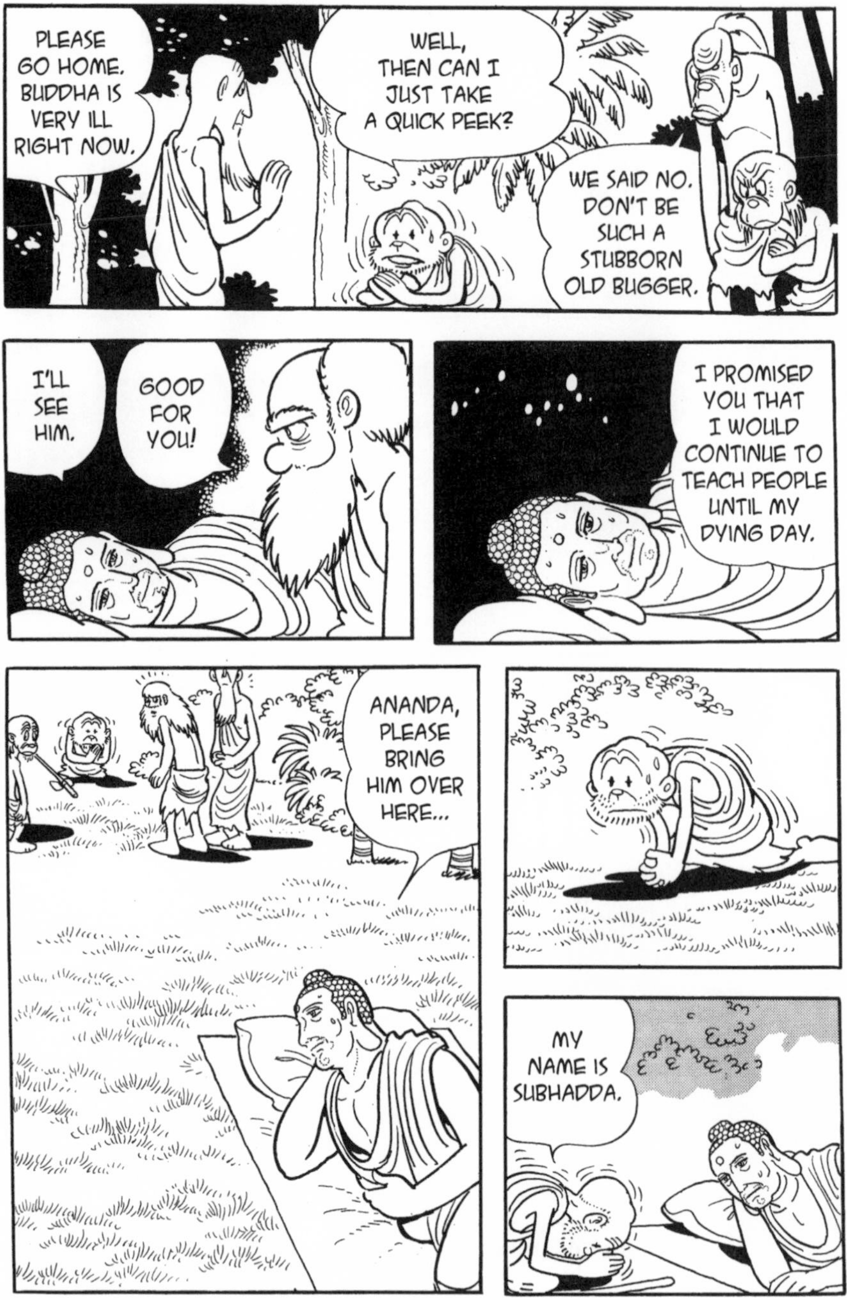
PLEASE GO HOME. BUDDHA IS VERY ILL RIGHT NOW.
WELL, THEN CAN I JUST TAKE A QUICK PEEK?
WE SAID NO. DON'T BE SUCH A STUBBORN OLD BUGGER.
I'LL SEE HIM.
GOOD FOR YOU!
I PROMISED YOU THAT I WOULD CONTINUE TO TEACH PEOPLE UNTIL MY DYING DAY.
ANANDA, PLEASE BRING HIM OVER HERE...
MY NAME IS SUBHADDA.

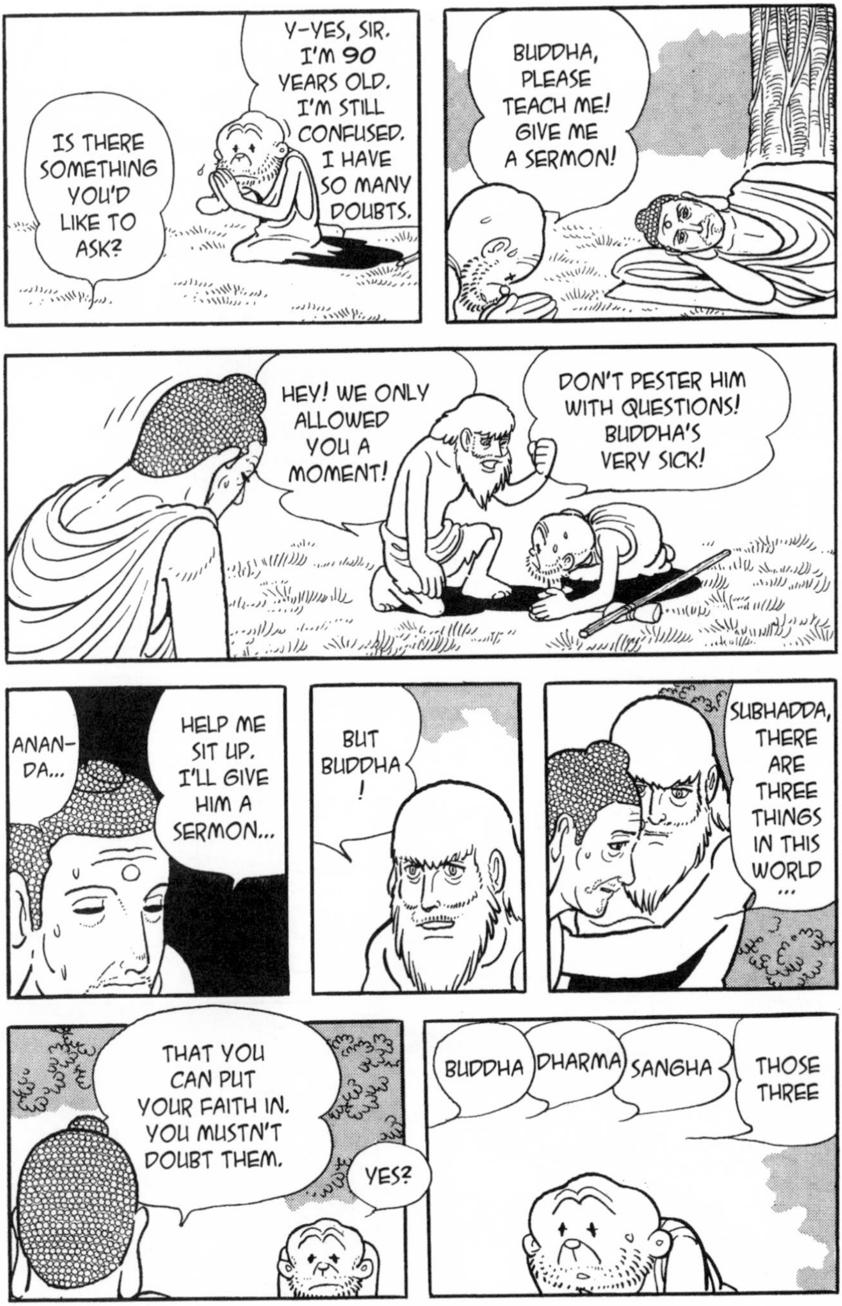
IS THERE SOMETHING YOU'D LIKE TO ASK?
Y-YES, SIR. I'M 90 YEARS OLD. I'M STILL CONFUSED. I HAVE SO MANY DOUBTS.
BUDDHA, PLEASE TEACH ME! GIVE ME A SERMON!
HEY! WE ONLY ALLOWED YOU A MOMENT!
DON'T PESTER HIM WITH QUESTIONS! BUDDHA'S VERY SICK!
ANAN-DA...
HELP ME SIT UP. I'LL GIVE HIM A SERMON...
BUT BUDDHA!
SUBHADDA, THERE ARE THREE THINGS IN THIS WORLD...
THAT YOU CAN PUT YOUR FAITH IN. YOU MUSTN'T DOUBT THEM.
YES?
BUDDHA
DHARMA
SANGHA
THOSE THREE

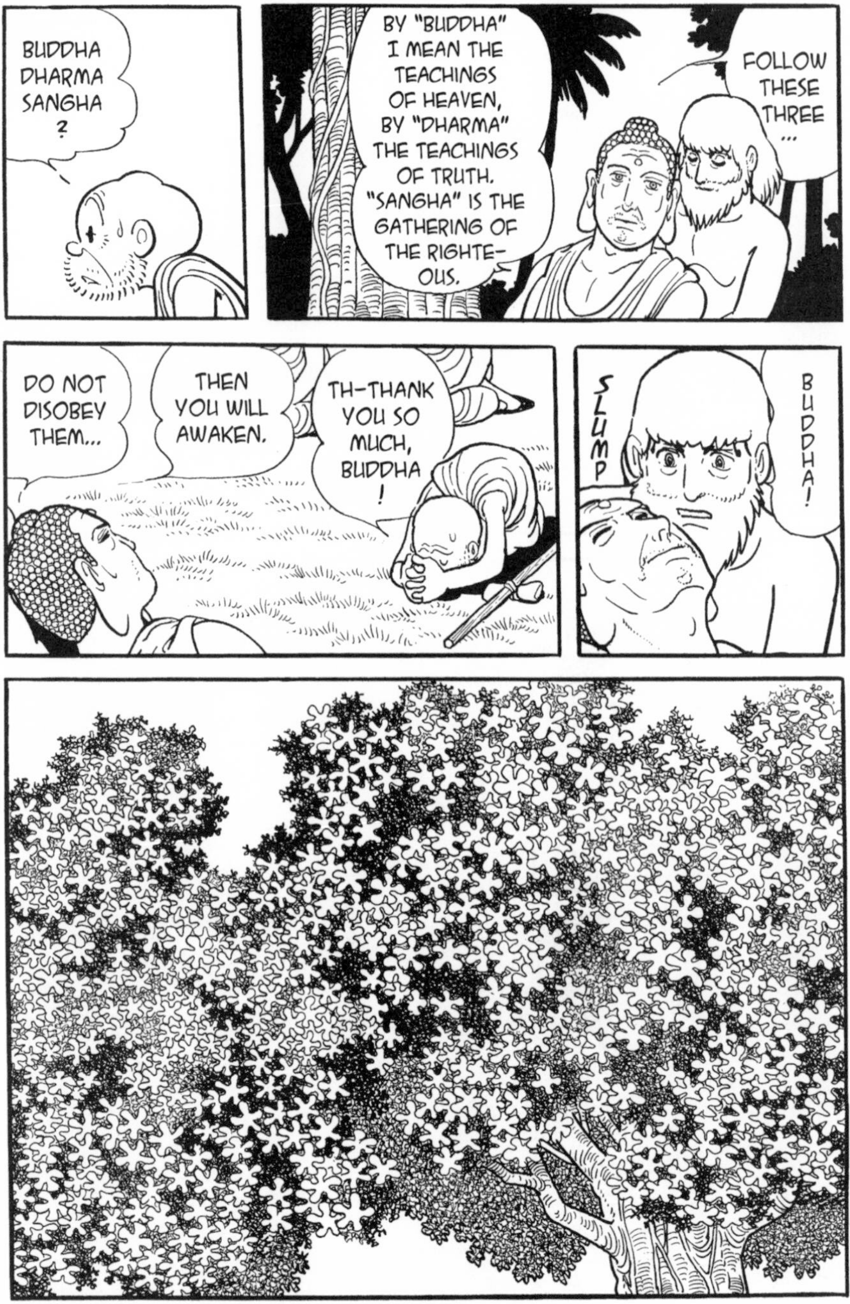
BUDDHA DHARMA SANGHA ?
BY "BUDDHA" I MEAN THE TEACHINGS OF HEAVEN, BY "DHARMA" THE TEACHINGS OF TRUTH. "SANGHA" IS THE GATHERING OF THE RIGHTE-OUS.
FOLLOW THESE THREE ...
DO NOT DISOBEY THEM...
THEN YOU WILL AWAKEN.
TH-THANK YOU SO MUCH, BUDDHA !
SLUMP
BUDDHA!

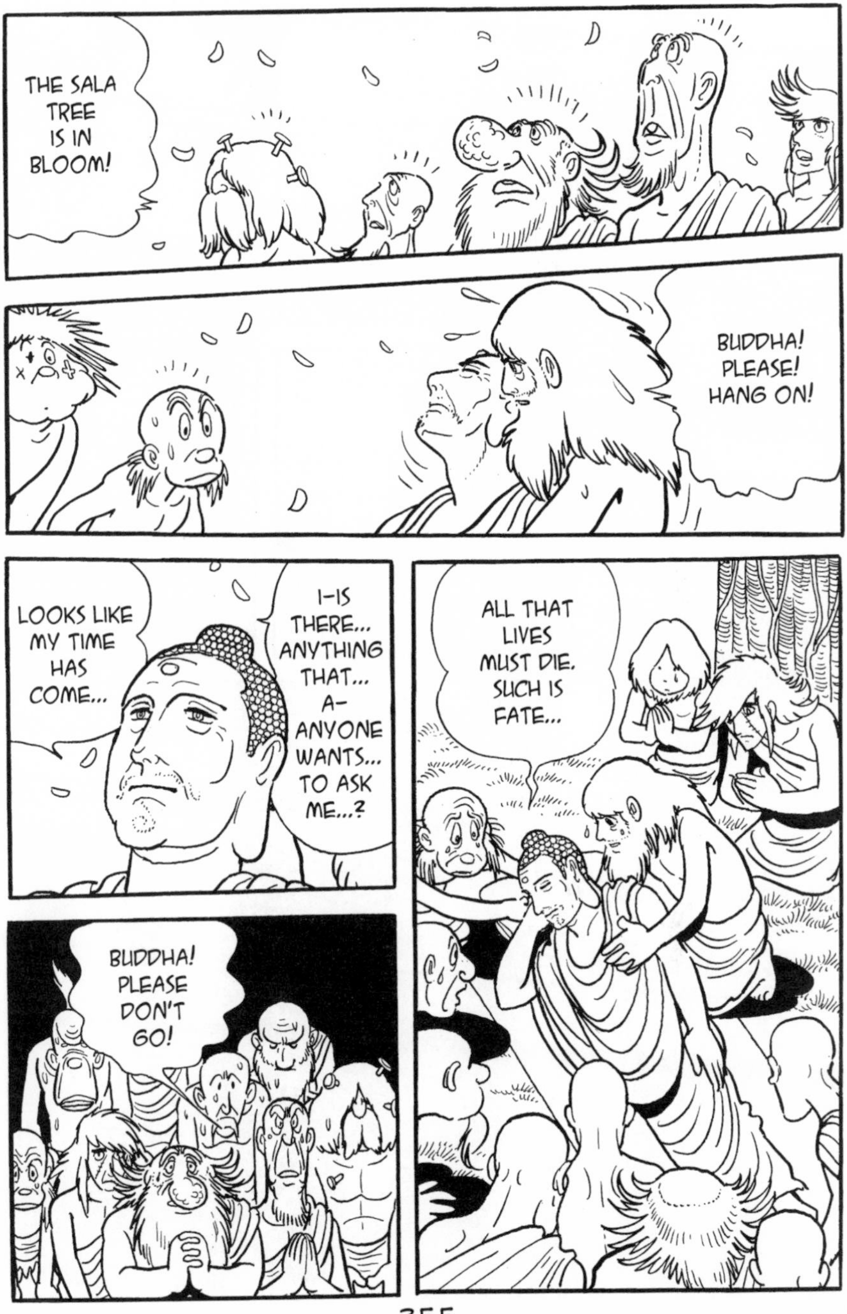
THE SALA TREE IS IN BLOOM!
BUDDHA! PLEASE! HANG ON!
LOOKS LIKE MY TIME HAS COME...
I-IS THERE... ANYTHING THAT... A-ANYONE WANTS... TO ASK ME...?
BUDDHA! PLEASE DON'T GO!
ALL THAT LIVES MUST DIE. SUCH IS FATE...

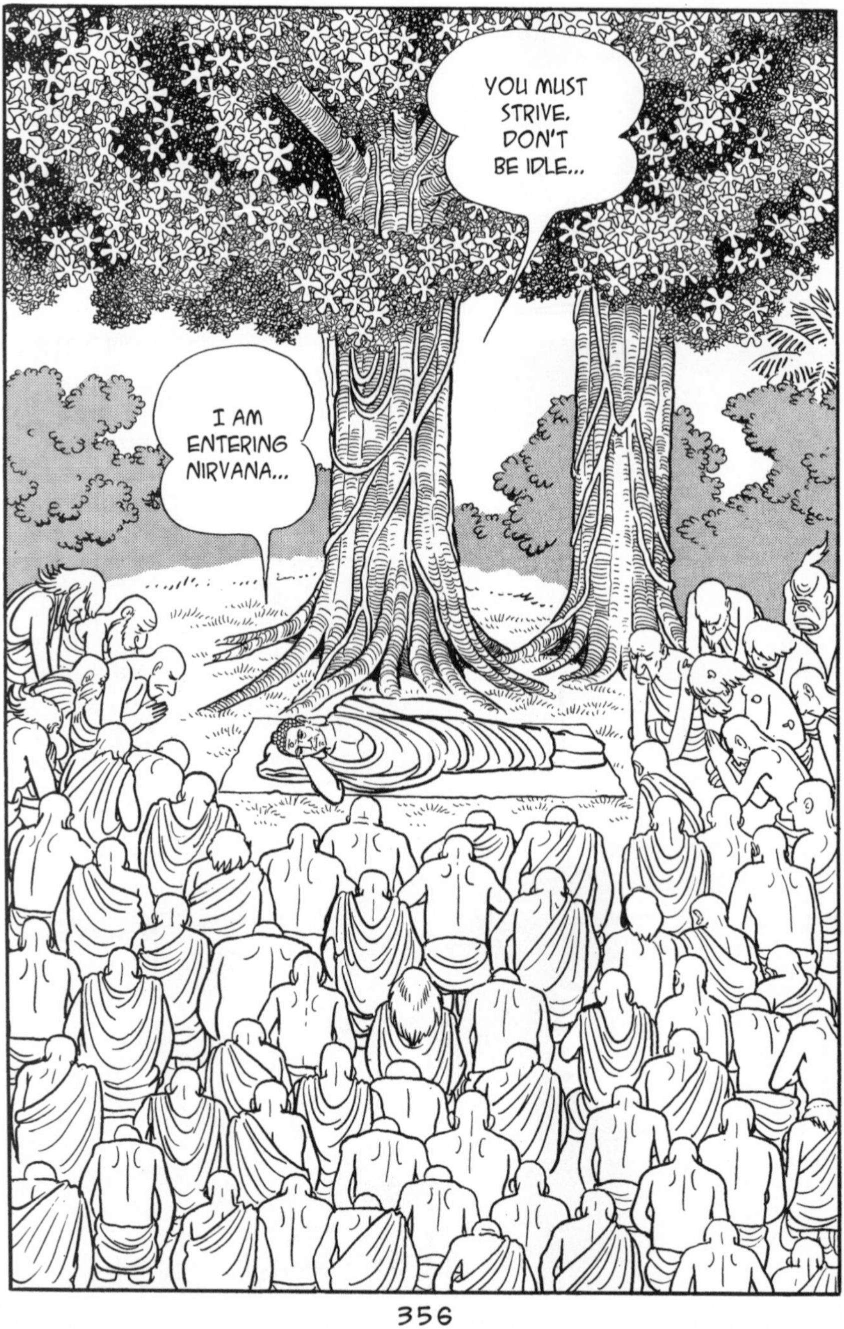
YOU MUST STRIVE. DON'T BE IDLE...
I AM ENTERING NIRVANA...

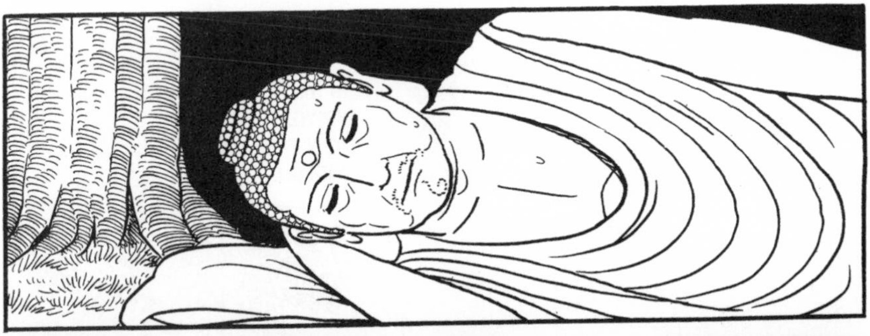

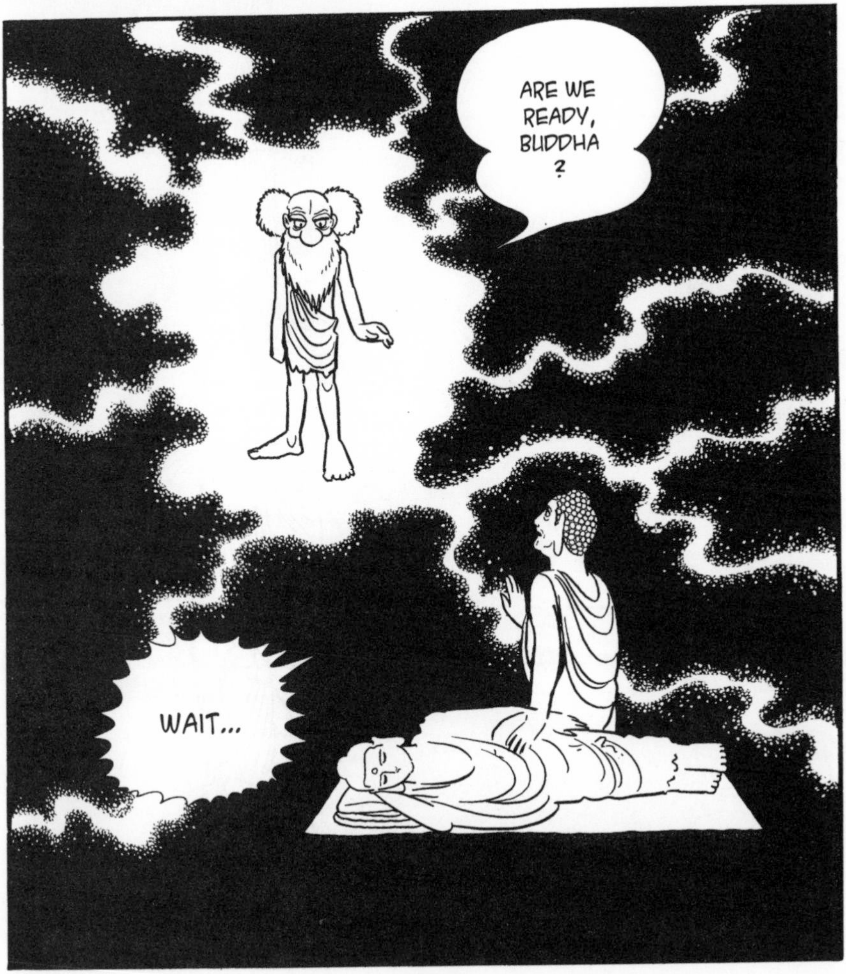
ARE WE READY, BUDDHA ?
WAIT...

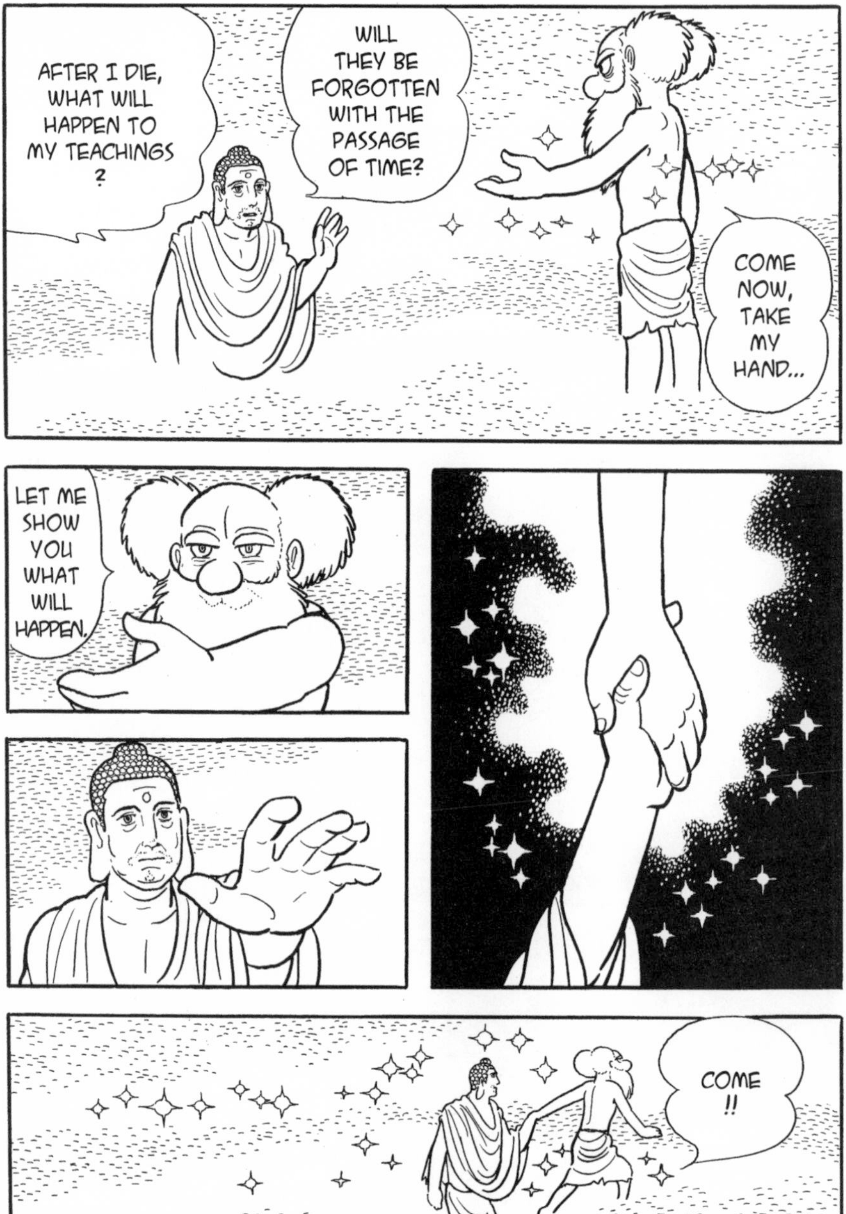
AFTER I DIE, WHAT WILL HAPPEN TO MY TEACHINGS ?
WILL THEY BE FORGOTTEN WITH THE PASSAGE OF TIME?
COME NOW, TAKE MY HAND...
LET ME SHOW YOU WHAT WILL HAPPEN.
COME !!

AND SO
BUDDHA
PASSED AWAY.

THOSE DISCIPLES
WHO WERE BY
HIS SIDE STARTED TO WEEP.
SOME WRITHED IN GRIEF,
WHILE OTHERS
STRETCHED THEIR ARMS
TOWARDS HEAVEN,
LAMENTING HIS PASSING.

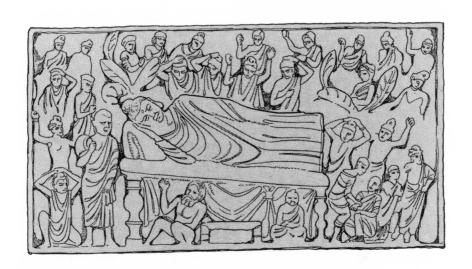

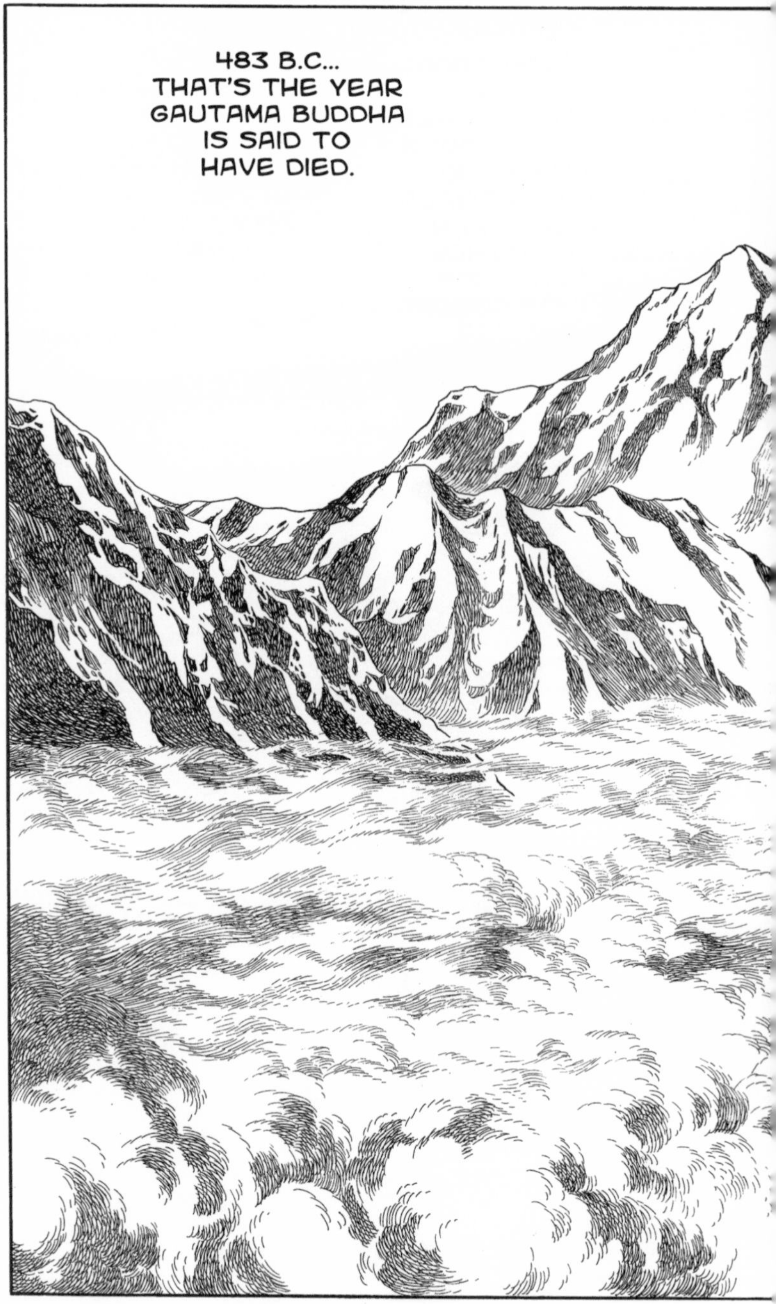
483 B.C... THAT'S THE YEAR GAUTAMA BUDDHA IS SAID TO HAVE DIED.

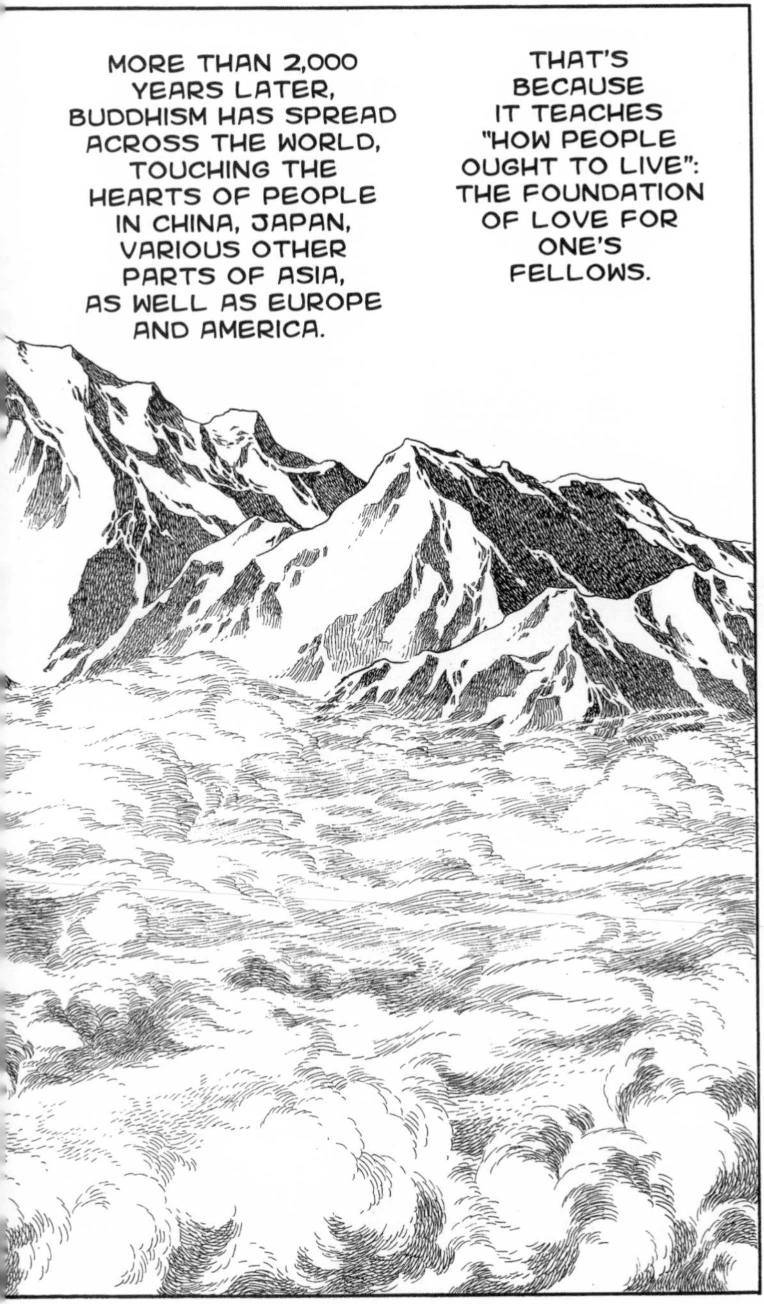
MORE THAN 2,000 YEARS LATER, BUDDHISM HAS SPREAD ACROSS THE WORLD, TOUCHING THE HEARTS OF PEOPLE IN CHINA, JAPAN, VARIOUS OTHER PARTS OF ASIA, AS WELL AS EUROPE AND AMERICA.
THAT'S BECAUSE IT TEACHES "HOW PEOPLE OUGHT TO LIVE": THE FOUNDATION OF LOVE FOR ONE'S FELLOWS.

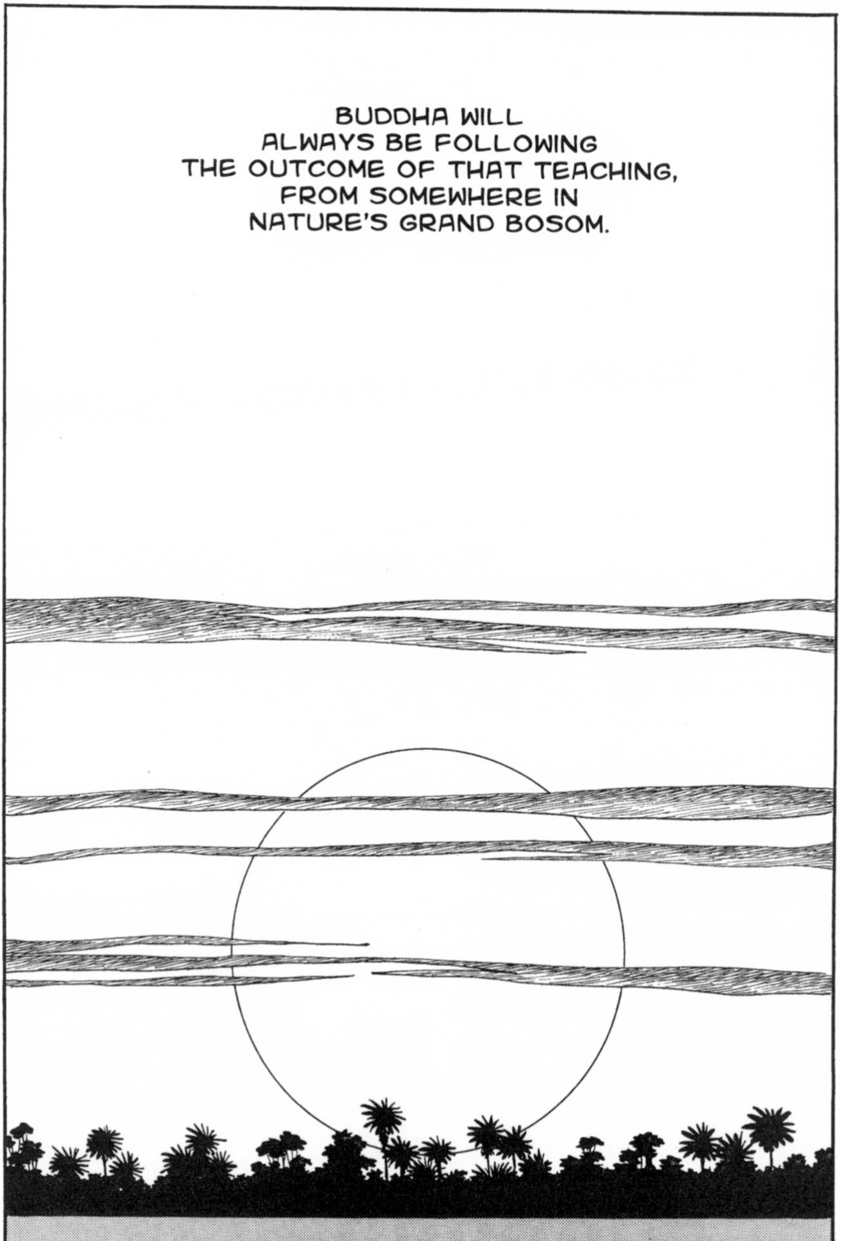
BUDDHA WILL ALWAYS BE FOLLOWING THE OUTCOME OF THAT TEACHING, FROM SOMEWHERE IN NATURE'S GRAND BOSOM.

THE END

Osamu Tezuka (1928-89) is the godfather of Japanese manga comics. He originally intended to become a doctor and earned an M.D. before turning to what was then a medium for children. His many early masterpieces include the series known in the U.S. as *Astro Boy*. With his sweeping vision, deftly intertwined plots, feel for the workings of power, and indefatigable commitment to human dignity, Tezuka elevated manga to an art form. The later Tezuka, who authored *Buddha*, often had in mind the mature readership that manga gained in the sixties and that has only grown ever since. The Kurosawa of Japanese pop culture, Osamu Tezuka is a twentieth-century classic.

Whether you like Japanese stuff

READ

For those unfamiliar with contemporary Japanese fiction, here is a quick overview of some of the most absorbing writing in Japan today – all available in translation from Vertical!

Gangster noir
Ashes by Kenzo Kitakata

"*Ashes* depicts yakuza life with a unique understanding and edge-of-your-seat reality."
–*Midwest Book Review*

New Age mystery
Outlet by Randy Taguchi

"Her sexual encounters may have a healing power...and the novel's dark twists and turns should keep readers hooked until the surprising climax."
–*Publishers Weekly*

For upcoming titles, visit

or just like good books,

DIFFERENT
READ

**V
E
R
T
I
C
A
L.**

Comedy of manners
Twinkle Twinkle **by Kaori Ekuni**
"This book is simple. This book is a pearl. This book
is like water, clear and loose and natural and fluid."
–BUST magazine

Ghost story
Strangers **by Taichi Yamada**
"An eerie ghost story written with hypnotic clarity.
He is among the best Japanese writers I have read."
–Bret Easton Ellis, author of American Psycho

Fantasy epic
The Guin Saga **by Kaoru Kurimoto**
"Readers should be cautioned that once you start
this journey, it will be nearly impossible to leave it
unfinished." *–SFRevu*

"A rousing tale of intrepid heroes, horrid villains and wicked supernatural creatures. A fast read."
—*Publishers Weekly*

"Enormously entertaining" —*Orlando Sentinel*

"A swashbuckling fantasy...action is always center stage...intense...dreamlike."
—*Seattle Times*

"Japan's answer to *The Lord of the Rings*"
—*The Globe and Mail*

THE GUIN SAGA

KAORU KURIMOTO

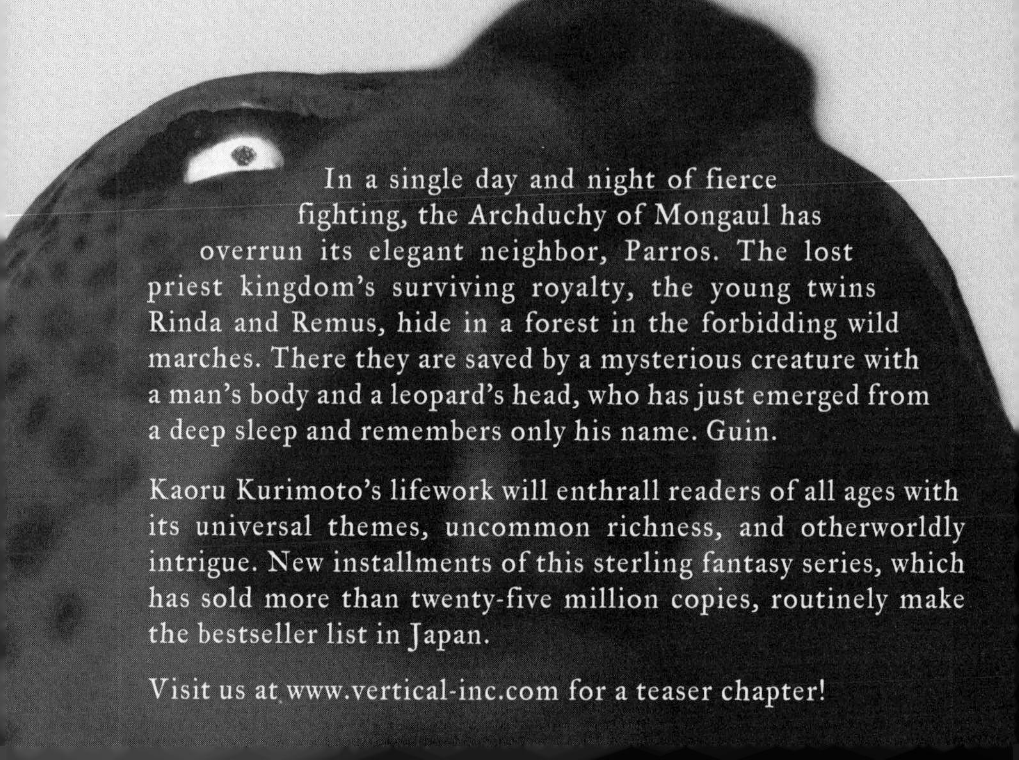

In a single day and night of fierce fighting, the Archduchy of Mongaul has overrun its elegant neighbor, Parros. The lost priest kingdom's surviving royalty, the young twins Rinda and Remus, hide in a forest in the forbidding wild marches. There they are saved by a mysterious creature with a man's body and a leopard's head, who has just emerged from a deep sleep and remembers only his name. Guin.

Kaoru Kurimoto's lifework will enthrall readers of all ages with its universal themes, uncommon richness, and otherworldly intrigue. New installments of this sterling fantasy series, which has sold more than twenty-five million copies, routinely make the bestseller list in Japan.

Visit us at www.vertical-inc.com for a teaser chapter!